MW00581297

Security Law and Methods

SECURITY LAW AND METHODS

James F. Pastor, Ph.D., J.D.
Assistant Professor
Calumet College of St. Joseph

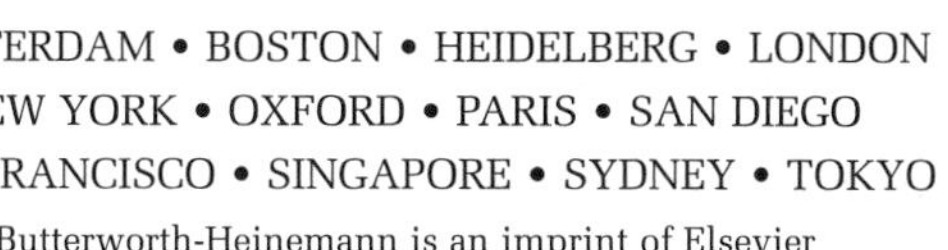
AMSTERDAM • BOSTON • HEIDELBERG • LONDON
NEW YORK • OXFORD • PARIS • SAN DIEGO
SAN FRANCISCO • SINGAPORE • SYDNEY • TOKYO
Butterworth-Heinemann is an imprint of Elsevier

Acquisitions Editor: Pamela Chester
Assistant Editor: Kelly Weaver
Marketing Manager: Christian Nolin
Project Manager: Jeff Freeland
Cover Designer: Alisa Andreola
Compositor: CEPHA Imaging Private Limited
Cover Printer: Phoenix Color Corp.
Text Printer/Binder: The Maple-Vail Book Manufacturing Group

Butterworth–Heinemann is an imprint of Elsevier
30 Corporate Drive, Suite 400, Burlington, MA 01803, USA
Linacre House, Jordan Hill, Oxford OX2 8DP, UK

Library of Congress Cataloging-in-Publication Data
Pastor, James F., 1957–
Security law and methods / James F. Pastor
p. cm.
Includes bibliographical references and index.
ISBN-13: 978-0-7506-7994-7 (alk. paper)
ISBN-10: 0-7506-7994-8 (alk. paper)
1. Private security services--law and legislation--United States. 2. Premises liability--United States. 3. Facility management--Law and legislation--United States. 4. Data protection--Law and legislation--United States. 5. Offenses against the person--United States. 6. Terrorism--Prevention--United States. I. Title.

KF5399.5.P7P37 2007
344. 7305'23--dc22

2006048393

British Library Cataloguing-in-Publication Data
A catalogue record for this book is available from the British Library.

ISBN 13: 978-0-7506-7994-7
ISBN 10: 0-7506-7994-8

For information on all Butterworth–Heinemann publications visit our Web site at www.books.elsevier.com

Printed in the United States of America
06 07 08 09 10 11 10 9 8 7 6 5 4 3 2 1

To the Great God, may your protection, justice, and mercy be upon your people.

Contents

Preface

This book represents a growing area of the law—both in its sophistication as a legal discipline and of its importance to this society. The sophistication relates to the diverse and wide ranging legal disciplines which form around the notion of security. The term security can apply to a wide ranging set of issues, from crime to terrorism, and other forms of less violent—but nonetheless inappropriate—behavior, such as theft and sexual harassment. In this way, the theme of this book focuses on crime and misconduct. This theme is coupled with certain suggested security methods designed to negate, or at least diminish, its consequence.

In post 9/11 America, the issue of security has taken on new implications. While crime has plagued American society for generations, there is a new, much more deadly threat associated with terrorism. This is not to imply that "normal" crime does not matter. Indeed, crime in any form can be debilitating to society—and deadly to unfortunate victims. This book is an attempt to understand both the legal exposures related to crime, and the security methods designed to prevent crime. In this way, this book breaks new ground. It is designed to explain crime prevention methods in light of legal and security principles. To my knowledge, the combination of these principles—at least in terms of this overall substance—is unprecedented.

This book is built around a collection of cases and laws from different state and federal jurisdictions. The cases were researched from various on-line data bases. I selected cases based on the following criteria. First, I sought new cases. Since this discipline is still rather new and necessarily dynamic, selecting recent cases will better illustrate the current principles and parameters of the law. Sometimes, however, more established cases have obtained a good deal of precedent and historical value. In order to account for such, I selected a few older but key cases. These older cases are useful because the decisions are particularly well written, and because they provide a comprehensive analysis of the particular area of the law.

Second, I also sought cases that were factually interesting, sometimes even controversial. For example, there is a growing body of cases surrounding security issues after 9/11. These cases are instructive, in that the delicate balance between security and liberty (i.e., rights or conveniences) is being flushed out—often within private environments or by private parties. Unlike the myriad number of cases involving this balance within policing, these cases are now being addressed within leases, contracts, and large semi-private forums, such as shopping malls and "trophy buildings" like the Empire State Building. Indeed, the litigation related to the first World Trade Center bombings are likely to be cited and analyzed for years to come.

Finally, while most of the cases involve private parties, there is some focus on private-public policing, and on governmental employees. In this sense, security law is broader than security versus police. Indeed, the line is increasingly being blurred. Hence, the book is broader than private security because private security is now a broader topic. Particularly since 9/11, private security is not just confined to the property lines of the business. Now it is part of the public safety apparatus. Security personnel are intimately involved in the protection of critical infrastructure, mass private property (also considered semi-public environments such as shopping malls, concert and sport facilities), and even within public streets, parks and business districts. One of the strengths of this book is that these factors are currently taking shape. Hopefully it will provide insightful and useful guidance as we go forward under an uncertain legal and security environment.

Once the cases were selected, I liberally edited the court decision in order to craft the language around certain objectives. First, I omitted most of citations from the case. Most citations were deemed inappropriate due to the nature and purpose of the book (see below discussion). Second, most of the procedural aspects of the case were omitted. Since this book is geared toward security studies by law/graduate students and professionals, the use of excessive citations and procedural language does little to further the study of security law. Such procedural niceties are only useful for attorneys crafting research, or litigation tactics and strategies. They are not useful in the body of security law. For those attorneys and law students who use this book, they have ample opportunity to study civil procedure in other legal books and disciplines.

Instead, I sought to present the key factual and legal principles related to security law. This is the key benefit of this book. These cases, if critically examined, are instructive at the factual and principal level. Since no two cases are factually alike, the presentation of factual scenarios coupled with sound legal reasoning will enable the reader to understand the exposure he or she may face as a security practitioner. For attorneys, these cases will provide the framework for a niche "public safety" practice, as a personal injury litigator, or as a counsel for a large corporation. In any event, the cases focus on substance, not procedure.

The third editing objective was to commence with a brief overview of the case and the decision. In this way, the reader will know from the outset what the case is about and who won. Hopefully, this will help to focus the reader, particularly those who are unfamiliar with case law. The intention is to get a quick understanding in order to fully understand the reasoning of the decision.

Fourth, the cases were organized around certain subjects. Subjects include defamation, invasion of privacy, negligence, and the like. Sometimes there will be overlap in these areas. For example, a case listed under defamation may involve several other legal theories, such as wrongful discharge, battery, and intentional infliction of emotional distress. When this occurs, I tried to classify the case into the dominant subject. Admittedly, this was not a perfect exercise. For those cases that seem to be better served in another subject, you can attribute this error to my editing process—and to the diverse nature of security law. Hopefully it will be attributed more to the latter than the former.

Following the presentation of the cases, I provide a brief case comment. Sometimes the comment will emphasize principles derived from the case. Other times, I will focus on specific facts that turned the decision. The case may also be contrasted with another case, to illustrate differences in how the case was approached, or the decision of the court. In addition to these techniques, discussion questions are presented at the end of the section in order to facilitate classroom discourse and individual analysis. Using these techniques, the goal is to get the reader to think critically about the case—and the relevant principles and facts contained in these cases.

In each section or chapter, I introduce the elements of the particular cause of action. Since each legal theory has particular elements, I highlight these prior to presenting the case. At appropriate points, certain suggested security methods which relate to the particular cause of action are presented. In this way, the reader should have a grasp of the legal theory, its elements and principles, and of the security methods designed to reduce the likelihood of its occurrence—or at least to limit the liability exposure if it does occur.

Part One provides an overview of Premises Liability and Negligence. Chapter 1 serves as an introduction to the key cause of action in security law: negligence. In this chapter the elements are presented in some detail. In addition, the notion of premises liability, which is based on negligence, is analyzed from historical to contemporary times. Included in this analysis, a chart listing premises liability standards in each state is presented. The benefit of this chart is to provide a handy resource for research and comparative analysis. Chapter 2 presents various Negligent Employment based causes of action, such as Negligent Hiring, Negligent Supervision and Training, and Negligent Entrustment. Chapter 3 presents Investigative Cases and Methods.

Part Two provides an overview of Intentional Torts and Claims. Chapter 4 presents Torts of Physical Nature. These causes of action range from assault and battery, false arrest/false imprisonment and malicious prosecution, and trespass. Chapter 5 focuses on Torts of Personal Nature, such as defamation and invasion of privacy. Chapter 6 delves into Workplace

Violence, with an explanation of its definitions, risk factors, implications and illustrative cases. Chapter 7 presents Sexual Harassment, with definitions, principles, defenses, and illustrative cases.

Part Three shifts to Agency and Contract based claims. Cases in this section include Agency and Related Theories (Chapter 8), and Contract actions involving insurance coverage, security services contracts, and leases (Chapter 9).

Part Four takes a comprehensive analysis of the issues related to Legal Authority and Liability. This section includes constitutional and statutory claims relating to the use of force, arrest powers, and distinctions between private and public policing. In this section, Chapter 10 presents cases dealing with Off-Duty Police, and Chapter 11 presents Special Police/Private Security cases.

Part Five addresses Terrorism & Future Issues. In this section, the issues and implications of terrorism coupled with relevant definitions are presented. Chapter 12 discusses Terrorism Cases, including current and significant case law. Chapter 13 presents relevant Terrorism Statutes and Indicators designed to detect and prevent terrorist acts. Finally, Chapter 14, Conclusions, serves to address future issues relating to security and public safety.

Finally, from a personal note, putting this book together has been a goal for many years. Since my law school days, I have been intrigued by this subject, and the desire to contribute to the public safety of this country. This coalesced for me in the mid-1990s when I taught Legal and Ethical Principles in Security Management for Webster University. At the time, Webster University and ASIS International (formerly American Society for Industrial Security) formed a joint undertaking to develop one of the first, if not the first, graduate degree in security management. I was fortunate to have been an instructor almost from the onset of the program.

The Webster University class was taught as a case study, using Private Security Law (David A. Maxwell) and Private Security and the Law (Charles P. Nemeth). Both of these authors were pioneers in this subject. They helped to frame my thoughts, deepen my understanding, and inspire me to build my own case book. Indeed, as the years passed, the cases within these books became dated. Looking around for other case books, one was struck by the lack of comprehensive work in this important subject. Comparing the large number of books on criminal law, I was amazed that so few focused on security law. Given the lack of published case books in this area, I admit to doubting whether the subject was too obscure or diverse to be considered a legal discipline. Then 9/11 occurred.

The day prior to this fateful day, I defended my doctoral dissertation entitled: The Functional and Constitutional Implications of Private Security Patrols on Public Streets. At that time, this topic was something only university professors would care about. It was probably too esoteric for the marketplace. In a similar vein, one may ask whether a security law case book is also too esoteric? Based on the events since 9/11, including the wars in Afghanistan and Iraq, the anthrax attacks, the bombings in Bali, Spain, London, the daily terrorist acts in Iraq, the sustained rioting in France, the "cartoon" riots in numerous countries, the growing violence of criminal gangs, the continued impact of workplace violence, the Iranian nuclear threat, the question of the existence—or threat—of WMD, and from many similar concerns, my conclusion is a resounding no!

Notwithstanding the impact of these events, I am convinced this subject—security law—is too important to ignore. It is comprehensive and growing in significance. Someday, it will be regarded as a legal discipline. In the meantime, to those readers who struggle through these cases, you are the next generation of security and legal practitioners who will carry on this important subject. Hopefully, with this collective analysis and efforts, we can make this country a safer place to live and work. At the same time, our clients and employees may also benefit from a reciprocal reduction in liability concerns and exposures. If this book achieves even a small measure of success, it is this goal it should be measured by.

James F. Pastor, Ph.D., J.D.
Lemont, Illinois
April 10, 2006

Acknowledgments

There are numerous individuals who have contributed to this book, sometimes in ways that they may not even be aware of. While I cannot name and thank each person individually, please know that you have made a difference in my life.

Of special note are certain people who directly made this book come to life. Dr. Richard Ward, Dean and Director of Criminal Justice at Sam Houston State University, has been a mentor for years. From my days as a police officer, you exposed me to the desire to grow academically and intellectually, and to understand the gravity of terrorism in relation to public safety. Your insight and work product was and is an inspiration. Joseph N. DuCanto, Esq., also deserves special mention, as he provided a critical opportunity by serving as the general counsel of his security services firm. I learned a lot about the business of security, and the legal exposures of such through the years I served your firm.

In addition, I want to thank my friends and colleagues at Calumet College of St. Joseph. Of note are President Dennis Rittenmeyer, Ph.D.; Vice President of Academic Affairs, Michele Dvorak, Ed.D.; Graduate Director David Plebanski, Ph.D.; Law Enforcement Management Director Michael J. McCafferty, J.D.; Assistant Professor Dean Angelo, Ed.D.; Professor Emeritus K. James McCaleb, Ph.D.; Dean of Students, James Adducci, J.D.; Public Safety Institute Executive Director Geoff Anderson; Associate Directors John Tsolakos and Dr. Gary Jones; Supervisor Nick Zivanovic; Coordinator of Graduate Student Services Mary Severa; and Director of Public Relations Rada Indjich.

This same regard is for my doctoral dissertation committee for their help in framing this work—which hopefully builds on the foundation established in the dissertation. Drs. Wayne Kerstetter, Jess Maghan, Melissa Marschall, Evan McKenzie, and particularly the committee chairman, Richard Johnson, your insights and direction are most appreciated. Your efforts and insights will never be diminished or forgotten.

To my friends and colleagues in the security and policing industries, I wish you safety and God speed as you work to protect your clients, communities, and ultimately, this country. While I do not "know" most of your identities, I do know your work. For those I do know as individuals, there are simply too many people to name. Either way my respect and regard go out to you. Indeed, your work often goes unnoticed and unappreciated. In some measure, this book is dedicated to your work. My regards also extends to those at the International Association of Professional Security Consultants (IAPSC), ASIS International, and the Illinois Association of Chiefs of Police (IACP). In addition, special regards to Daniel S. McDevitt and Thomas Elward, who I had the pleasure to work with at SecureLaw Ltd. Your work product and knowledge was and is both professional and insightful.

My regards to those at Butterworth-Heinemann, especially Mark Listewnik, Jeff Freeland, Kelly Weaver, and Pam Chester, and to other editors and support personnel, your help and work is most appreciated. In particular, my thanks and regards to Ellen Persio for your editing. You have greatly improved this document.

Finally and most importantly, to my wife, Rose Ann, my mother and family; thanks again for helping me through another book. It seems that they do not get any easier. The help, encouragement, and support of my loving wife make this book both possible and more worthwhile. My thanks and love is with you all.

Part One

Premises Liability and Negligence

This book aims to demonstrate how crime and misconduct relate to liability exposure and security methods. Part I is designed to provide the reader with a thorough understanding of the tort of negligence, including certain negligence-related claims. Since numerous security and crime related claims are based on negligence, it is important to provide an underlying analysis of the causes of action in this field of study. In addition, since investigative cases and techniques and security and risk management methods are critical to the litigation process, these will also be highlighted.

1

Introduction

It may be helpful to provide some context for this book by beginning with a brief summary of the discipline of security law and a description of the historical, theoretical, and situational factors that have led to our current circumstances in security and policing.

SECURITY LAW AS A DISCIPLINE

The concept of security law requires an understanding of many diverse legal disciplines. These disciplines range from negligent and intentional torts to contract and insurance provisions, agency and vicarious liability theories, and constitutional and criminal laws. Despite their obvious diversity, these disciplines are linked in this context by the impact of crime and misconduct. Hence, this legal analysis should be supplemented with "security sense" and experience.

As with any discipline or endeavor, experience in private security law is critical. In my hundreds of contract negotiations involving security matters, I have often been struck by the attorneys' unfamiliarity with security issues and with the security industry in general. This should not surprise anyone. Indeed, attorneys, like most other professionals, typically develop a niche or an area of practice that focuses on a particular legal discipline. For example, family law attorneys focus on divorce, support, child custody, and like matters. Similarly, personal injury attorneys litigate negligent and intentional torts. In this sense, I advocate thinking about security law as a discipline.

As recently as three decades ago, there was little interest in the notion of elder law. Those who practiced family law were relegated to the category of "divorce lawyers." Similarly, the discipline of environmental law had not yet been conceived. Since then, new legal disciplines have emerged to serve the changing needs of the marketplace and of society. Currently attorneys practice in niches devoted to the aging population, to changing family norms, and to the protection of the environment.

In post 9/11 America, the emphasis on security has been heightened. While some people continue to question the extent of the threat facing this country, those who study terrorism and security know that the threat remains real. Indeed, the threat of violence, particularly from terrorism, violent gangs, and lone psychopaths, is likely to persist. Violence is as old as human nature. I see no end to violence as long as human nature exists.

As with any trend, those who are closer to the issue see the picture with more clarity. In addressing this area of the law, I have been blessed with a rather unique set of skills and experiences. As a young police officer in the early to mid-1980s, I attended law school with the intention of focusing on public safety and security. While I did not fully realize the importance of this legal training at that time, it enabled me to be a better police officer. As a tactical police officer in the gang crime unit, I patrolled the South Side of Chicago on "missions" designed to actively seek out crimes committed by gang members. I arrested hundreds of gang members, mostly for crimes involving drugs, illegal gun possession, and violence.

My law school experience helped me understand the legal limits of my role as a police officer. It helped me grasp the legal principles surrounding search and seizure, the nuances of warrant requirements, and other police procedures. In this sense, being a good police officer requires knowledge of the law. The better a police officer understands the law, the more effectively he or she can perform the job.

The same holds true for the security professional. In many ways, the issues confronting security personnel are actually much more complicated than those facing the average police officer. Unlike the typical police officer, the security professional must be equipped to *prevent* as well as temper the consequences of occurrences such as workplace violence, sexual harassment, internal theft, and threats from criminals and even terrorists. Simply put, to deal appropriately with the many diverse and complex legal issues within this field, the security professional needs to possess expertise that extends beyond the rather narrow confines of criminal law.

This maze of legal issues is further complicated by the unfortunate, but inevitable, lack of consistency created by differing state laws. Unlike criminal law, which involved numerous U.S. Supreme Court decisions, the subject areas within security law are largely based on state court decisions. Because so few U.S. Supreme Court decisions relate to security law, security professionals, and their legal advisors, tend to focus much more on state laws within their particular environment. The many variations in security laws among different states present a real challenge to corporations with properties and service provisions in different states. This situation also complicates the task of developing a comprehensive book on security law.

By now some readers may be asking: Why should I care about court decisions—made by judges and juries—who have little understanding of security methods and principles? The short answer is liability. Liability often drives the implementation of security methods. Stated another way, the exposure of potential liability—often in damage awards reaching six, seven, or even eight figures—has motivated many corporations; either private, public, or municipal, to worry about security. Of course, some organizations continue to insist that it "won't happen here." Nonetheless, many unfortunate businesses and property owners find themselves on the wrong end of a lawsuit, faced with substantial potential exposure or actual liability. Hence, court decisions have provided substantial incentive for organizations to face the impact of crime and misconduct. The old adage of "pay me now or pay me later" has been a powerful motivator to take the threat of crime and misconduct seriously.

Let me clarify a key point. I do not advance or subscribe to the notion that security methods are directly related to liability exposure. To do so would equate life with money. This is not my intention. My point is that the legal system has shaped security methods and even, to a large degree, the security industry. This is so in a number of ways. Since the consequences of security breaches vary, or are not directly quantifiable prior to the incident, the typical property or business decision maker may believe that little or no security is sufficient. When no crime is committed, the decision proves correct. This mind-set gives rise to the inevitable questions: Why spend money on security? Why inconvenience your employees, tenants, or customers with security protocols that seem unnecessary? Coupled with the natural human tendency to believe that bad things happen only to others, this attitude leads many to assume, often incorrectly, that their environment or workplace is safe.

Now add hefty and highly publicized court decisions to the mix. At this point, many people will sit up and take notice. While some may still cling to a false sense of security, reasonable and prudent decision makers now see the implications much more clearly. The implications, of course, are more than just money damages. Loss of reputation, goodwill, business continuity, and of course, the lives and property of those affected by a workplace crime are also involved. The need to prevent such losses is a strong incentive to pay attention to security. With these implications in mind, I will provide an overview of the historical and theoretical underpinnings of this book.

HISTORICAL PERSPECTIVES

Centuries of history related to security and policing can be summarized in one overriding human theme: survival. The security of the individual, the family, the community, and even the nation-state are all tied to this basic need. As an indicator of its importance, Maslow classifies security as a second-tier need in his hierarchy of needs, just above food, clothing, and shelter.[1] Given the importance of security, it is understandable that humans have developed various mechanisms designed to foster this goal.

While this summary represents only a cursory view of the historical complexities of security, the issues raised in this overview are intended to provide a pointed and appropriate framework for private security law.

For centuries, people in the community have acted as the security force within the community. Indeed, the "job" of security was not even a job. It was the duty of all able-bodied men to protect their homes and their community.[2] There were no police to call. Instead, the people acted in self-defense or in defense of their community. Through much of history, security was seen as the province of the people. This viewpoint was so entrenched that it even served as one of the guiding principles of the founder of Britain's first professional police force, Sir Robert Peel, who asserted: *The people are the police, the police are the people.*[3]

Before the formation of public police, self-help and self-protection were considered the foundations of law enforcement and public order.[4] Throughout much of recorded history, kings were primarily concerned with conducting warfare and protecting their land from invaders. This changed when the legal system or the justice process came to be regarded as a cash cow.[5] The subsequent expansion of the internal justice process was justified by the concept of the king's peace. The term *king's peace* equated to law and order.

As the power of the king evolved, many offenses that were previously regarded as intentional torts (wrongs subject to civil action) were deemed crimes against the king's peace.[6] Reynolds observes this key fact: "Whereas the spoils of tort law belonged to the victims, the spoils of criminal law went to the king."[7] Based on this principle, acts previously considered torts such as arson, robbery, and murder could be declared crimes. The incentive to expand the king's peace was clear. If people could be declared criminals, their property could be confiscated by the king.[8] Such declarations allowed the king to collect property or revenue from the "criminal." Likewise, the criminal could be punished (or even executed) for deeds against the king, his sovereignty, and his people.[9]

The change from a tort-centered to a crime-centered system directly affected those who were to be compensated. Traditionally, the injured person (or his or her family) was to be financially compensated by the person who caused the injury. Many victims favored treating offenses as civil torts, because this provided them with a way to collect financial compensation.[10] The typical compensation involved some financial or property transfer to the victim or the family of the victim from the person who caused the injury. However, once the act was declared a crime, the financial benefit through fines, confiscation of property, and the like was transferred to the king.

It is important to note, however, that this increasing expansion of the criminal law was not without justification. Those who favored increasing sovereignty of the king believed it would reduce the incidence of retribution by private citizens, as well as provide for legitimate sanctions by government.[11] Government sanctions against criminals were deemed legitimate because they removed the need for the victim (or his or her family) to retaliate against the offender.

Traditional codes of family honor could lead to bloody feuds that persisted for generations. By assuming the right to avenge harm on behalf of all the people, the state (or king) also assumed the obligation to ensure swift, sure justice, as well as to protect the rights and safety of the public. This type of system promised not only to limit the scope of retributive violence, but also to transfer the costs of seeking justice to the state, while assuring victims that they could rely on state's vast powers to redress their grievances.

The desire to limit the use of power or coercion to the government rested on sound reasoning. Naturally, there was a desire to reduce the amount of violence. Many believed that responding to violent acts based on the "eye for an eye" code of justice served only to perpetuate violence. Notwithstanding the potential for deterrence, or even the justification of retribution, the notion that government should be the arbitrator of violence had compelling logic. According to this way of thinking, putting the government in charge of retribution would help limit the use of violence by private citizens. As a consequence, government was increasingly saddled with the burden of controlling crime and capturing and punishing criminals.

Notwithstanding this gradual transfer of authority to government (or to the throne), the burden of law and order rested on the citizenry for a large part of recorded history. In early times, crime control of the town or community was provided by people through the use of the "hue and cry."[12] A hue and cry was a call to order. It was designed to alert the community that a criminal act had occurred or was occurring. Upon this call to order, able-bodied men responded to lend assistance, or to pursue the criminal. This ancient crime protection system is remarkably similar to the "observe and report" function of private security, absent the pursuit and capture of the criminal. The theory behind observe and report is that the security officer should act as a deterrent to crime. When a crime is observed, the task of the security officer is to gather information about the criminal (or the crime), and then immediately report such to the public police—in effect, serving as the "eyes and ears" of the police.[13]

Over time, however, the custom of hue and cry gave way to a more defined system of crime prevention. This system, known as "watch and ward," entailed more formalized crime prevention methods. It was headed by shire reeves appointed by the king.[14] The shire reeves, in turn, appointed constables to deal with various legal matters. Both the shire reeve (later shortened to sheriff) and the constable were the forerunners of modern sworn law enforcement officers.[15] This system furthered the legitimacy of public officers in crime prevention and control, with the appointment of individuals who reported directly to the king.

Early American colonies adopted this watch-and-ward system. Partly due to the deficiencies inherent in this system, however, some towns supplemented this method with night watches conducted by citizens appointed by the local government.[16] Unfortunately, these unpaid, ill-trained, and ill-equipped constables often failed to control crime. As a result, businessmen hired their own security to protect themselves and their business or property.[17] These early security providers, however, did not protect the general population. Most people had to fend for themselves. Towns and villages were largely unprotected, except by those who lived there.

Based on these circumstances, some criminologists and historians believe that the emergence of municipal police forces were a direct result of the growing levels of civil disorder within society.[18] Indeed, Miller emphasized that in 1834, known as the "year of riots," legislators in New York decried the need for order. This outcry for order translated into more "security" forces. It became increasingly clear that the established system of crime prevention was not working. In this sense, the riots acted as a trigger, helping to bring about the institution of municipal police departments.

The emergence of public police, as with any societal initiative, was not without its problems and detractors. Many people argued that a full-time police force was too expensive. Certainly, the traditional methods were less costly because the major portion of these protective services was provided by unpaid volunteers.[19] Another economic objection was based on the argument that the newly created public police agencies were unable—or unwilling—to provide for the security needs of the commercial sector.[20] To support this assertion, critics of public policing could point to the situation in America's "Wild West." The western territories had few government-employed police officers. This lack of police officers was especially problematic for newly developing mobile commercial enterprises, such as the railroad industry. Labor unrest, especially in the steel, coal, and railroad industries, further drove the demand for security.[21] Not surprisingly, this growing need for security significantly drained resources from already overextended municipal police departments.[22] In order to serve this growing market, Allan Pinkerton formed the first contracted private security firm in America.[23] This occurred in 1850, at a time when many municipal police departments were in their infancy. Thus, paid security forces were developing even while the growth of public police departments was still in its early stages.

Other criticism of early policing pointed to the dangers of a government monopoly on policing,[24] fearing that it could lead to the development of excessive police power.[25] To these people, the cop on the beat represented an "ominous intrusion upon civil liberty."[26] To others, the concern for security overrode the integrity of constitutional provisions. Thus, the tension between the desire for security and the desire to maintain constitutional protections became critical in the debate over this policing initiative. Likewise, the difficulty of balancing public safety with individual rights continues to fuel controversy over current security initiatives—whether public or private.

As public policing began to take hold, certain legal decisions carved out the specific duties of the government in regard to the safety and security of its citizens. As noted earlier, the historical roots of policing stemmed from the notion that citizens were obligated to maintain law and order. This notion was consistent with the ideals of the framers of the U.S. Constitution. They assumed that law-abiding people would be largely responsible for their own safety.[27] As a result, the framers of the Constitution did not define any specific governmental obligation to protect citizens from crime. The U.S. Supreme Court upheld the principle that government does not have a specific duty to protect individuals in the famous case entitled *South v. Maryland* (1856). In its decision, the Court refused to create this duty based on the belief that it would "impose a crushing economic burden on government." Instead, the Court held that government had a general duty to enforce laws, but not to protect any particular person. Significantly, the *South v. Maryland* Court held that:[28]

> There is no constitutional right to be protected by the state against being murdered by criminals.... The constitution is a charter of negative liberties, it tells the state to let people alone, it does not require the federal government or the state to provide services, even so elementary a service as maintaining law and order.[29]

This decision provided the intellectual principle that the government is not responsible for the safety of its citizens—as it related to criminal activity. Accordingly, citizens are expected to secure their own safety from criminals, independent of the protection from government. This basic principle has not changed. Absent the duty from a third party, usually imposed on a corporation or a property owner, the burden is on each individual to provide for his or her own safety and security.[30]

This brief historical perspective illustrates the impact of crime on civilized society. In days of old, security was the province of the people. In contemporary times, "the people" typically pay others for protection. Citizens pay taxes for municipal policing. Clients pay contracted fees to security firms. Both of these methods of maintaining public safety and providing security services are accepted as contemporary norms. However, as will be more fully articulated later, there is a growing trend for citizens to pay security firms for protection within the public realm. This creates a sort of *back to the future* circumstance, where "the people" are taking more responsibility for their own security.

The payment of monies for private security services raises an important question: Is it appropriate for clients, who are citizens of a governmental entity, to pay a private firm for security, or even public safety services? My answer is yes. To answer this question for yourself, you might begin by asking yourself these questions: Is it wrong to pay for personal protection? If public police cannot or will not provide for your personal protection, is it inappropriate to pay a security firm to do so? Viewed from this perspective, affirming the individual's right of self-defense seems the only reasonable approach.

Because the job of private security professionals involves the imminent threat of violence, their effectiveness almost inevitably depends on their ability to use appropriate tactics, including the use of force. Regardless of the situation that prompts the use of force or the mere imposition of verbal commands, the use of coercive measures is subject to monitoring by the legal system, either through judicial and legislative pronouncements. Thus, those who are in the business of security have a responsibility to stay informed about the legal limits of their power and authority. As the role of security providers in society continues to expand, the need to understand private security law becomes increasingly important. This book attempts to address that need.

CRIME, CRIMINOLOGY, AND SECURITY LAW

Security personnel seek to prevent crime by attempting to predict reasonably foreseeable crime and develop precautions against it.[31] Whether a crime is foreseeable and whether it can be prevented is often based on an understanding of the environment and of the offender.

A substantial body of law has grown around the notion of the environmental aspects of crime. Many researchers believe that an area often undergoes a transition from relatively few crimes toward a high incidence of crime or a heightened fear of crime, caused in part, by lack of order.[32] For example, order maintenance theories contend that crime problems initially arise from relatively harmless activities, such as drinking on the street, graffiti on buildings, and youths loitering on street corners. If these activities go unchecked, the level of fear and incivility in the area begins to rise and more serious crimes, such as gang fights or even drive-by shootings, may take place. The underlying theory is that the presence of disorder tends to reduce the social controls previously present in the area. This results, at least in theory, in the increased incidence of crime, particularly serious crime. Increased crime, in turn, contributes to the further deterioration of the physical environment and economic well-being of the community.

The development of order maintenance theories can be traced to a line of thinking that developed over time. These theories focused on conditions in cities, particularly in the slums. In these areas of the city, conditions included "physical deterioration, high density, economic insecurity, poor housing, family disintegration, transience, conflicting social norms, and an absence of constructive positive agencies."[33] Over time, researchers began to focus less attention on socioeconomic factors, and more on the physical characteristics of the community, or on the environment. The focus on the physical characteristics of the space where crime occurred resulted in a substantial body of scientific research, including that of Cohen and Felson. They argued that the completion of a crime requires the convergence in time and space of an offender, a suitable target, and the "absence of guardians capable of preventing the violation."[34] The guardians include police, security, citizens, and "place managers" who are either formally or informally responsible for a particular property or location.[35]

This focus on environmental factors is seen in a number of studies. For example, Gibbs and Erickson found that the daily population flow in large cities "reduces the effectiveness of surveillance activities by increasing the number of strangers that are routinely present in the city, thereby decreasing the extent to which their activities would be regarded with suspicion."[36] The implication was that the more crowded an area became, the less likely it was for strangers to be noticed. Thus, with less natural surveillance from community residents, more crime might develop. Consequently, Reppetto concluded that the social cohesion and informal surveillance declines with the large number of people living in a given area.[37]

Similarly, Lewis and Maxfield focused their research on specific physical conditions within the environment. They sought to assess how the environment affected the level of crime and the fear of crime. Their research design took into account such factors as abandoned buildings, teen loitering, vandalism, and drug use. They believed these factors draw little attention from the police partially because the public police have limited resources to effectively deal with these problems.[38] The researchers noted that such problems, nonetheless, are important indicators of criminality within any community.

These problems are considered indicators of the "level of incivility" in an area and are thought to contribute to a sense of danger and decay. The presence of danger and decay, in turn, increases the perceived risk of victimization.[39] In this sense, the presence of incivility may lead to crime, or it may simply cause an area to *seem* dangerous. Indeed, while some incivilities are not even criminal, they are disconcerting nonetheless. For example, groups of teens walking through a neighborhood may be legal but still raise fears within the community. As such, these studies concluded that policymakers should focus on "neighborhood level" approaches to reducing crime and fear.

This research was supported and further validated by subsequent studies. Covington and Taylor conducted research into what they termed the "incivilities model." They argue that people perceive "cues" to the underlying level of disorder in their immediate environment. When people sense negative cues in their environment, they feel more vulnerable and fearful.[40] In essence, they become more aware that they may be at risk of being criminally victimized. Consequently, cues representing incivility may serve as an early warning or an indicator that the environment may be ripe for serious crimes.

What are these cues, or the signs of crime? According to Covington and Taylor, there are several indicators or cues. They fall into two distinct categories: social and physical. Social cues include public drinking, drug use, loitering, and disturbances such as fighting and arguing. These activities may be deemed disturbing to some people, and dangerous to others. Physical cues include litter, graffiti, abandoned buildings and vacant lots, and deteriorating homes and businesses.[41] While these conditions may not be inherently dangerous, they create the impression that the neighborhood is declining. This impression, in turn, may foster an attitude that the people in the neighborhood do not care about their homes or their community. As a consequence, those intending to commit crime may view the perceived lack of care as an invitation for criminal activity.

Subsequent research by Fisher and Nasar further validated this logic. They studied the effects of "micro-level" cues. Micro-level clues involve a specific place or location. The authors found that such cues relate to fear in three specific criteria:[42]

- Prospect—openness of view to see clearly what awaits you.
- Escape—ease of departure if you were confronted by an offender.
- Concealment—extent of hiding places for an offender

Based on an analysis of these criteria, the authors concluded that areas that lack open views and avenues of escape for potential victims while offering criminals effective hiding places are ripe for crime. When faced with these conditions, individuals tend to feel a greater exposure to risk, lose their sense of control over their immediate environment, and are more aware of the seriousness or the consequences of attack.[43] This conclusion further advanced the concept of "situational crime prevention." This approach advocates the examination of the actual criminal event or incident. When doing so, it is considered key to assess how the "intersection" of potential offenders connected with the opportunity to commit crime. This level of analysis focuses on how to prevent this "intersection" from occurring. According to this way of thinking, reducing the criminal's opportunity to commit crime should enable individuals to avoid crime. Consequently, the commission of a particular crime could be prevented through specific measures designed to reduce the offender's ability (or even propensity) to commit crimes at a specific location.[44]

The conclusions from these studies have been echoed by a number of other authors, including Kelling, who asserts that citizens regularly report their biggest safety concerns to be activities such as "panhandling, obstreperous youths taking over parks and street corners, public drinking, prostitution, and other disorderly behavior."[45] All of these factors have been identified as precursors to more serious crime. Moreover, the failure to correct these behaviors is often perceived by potential offenders as a sign of indifference—which may lead to more serious crime and urban decay.[46] According to this thinking, the most effective way to reduce crime is to address both the physical and social conditions which foster criminal behavior and to prevent such conditions from festering into more serious levels of incivility and decay.

The logic behind and conclusions derived from these studies have been embraced by both public police and private security. The key component of these studies, in both the public and private sectors, is order maintenance. Order maintenance techniques are designed to improve physical conditions within a specific geographic area. This can be accomplished in a number of ways, including the rehabilitation of physical structures, the removal or demolition of seriously decayed buildings, and the improvement of land or existing buildings by cleaning and painting. Other environmental improvements, such as planting flowers, trees or shrubs, and various other methods to enhance the "look and feel" of an area are also recommended.[47] These physical improvements are then coupled with efforts to reduce or eliminate certain anti-social behaviors. The reduction or the elimination of problematic social behaviors is at the core of an order maintenance approach to crime prevention. The objective is to address these behaviors before more serious crimes occur.

Viewed from this broad environmental perspective, the topic of security becomes wide ranging. It can encompass services as seemingly diverse as trash collection and private police patrols that are in fact linked by the common goal of improving conditions within a neighborhood. Given the important role of the environment in the development of crime, the need to control physical conditions and public activities within a particular environment is paramount. The advent of terrorism will only magnify this environmental focus. In today's world, many formerly unremarkable occurrences can seem ominous. An unattended package left on a street corner might turn out to be a lethal bomb. The illegally parked vehicle in your neighborhood could be a tragedy in the making. In this new reality, the importance of an orderly and clean environment cannot be understated. Of course, these perceived or potential threats are difficult to remedy. Nonetheless, this growing emphasis on the environment has been echoed by Kaplan, who views the environment as *the* security issue of the early twenty-first century.[48]

In public policing, these order maintenance techniques are encompassed in the concept of "community policing."[49] The core of community policing is for policing efforts to extend beyond the traditional goal of crime fighting. It is to focus on fear reduction through order maintenance techniques.[50] In this way, crime and fear reduction through order maintenance are in accordance with the environmental theories articulated above.

This focus on prevention has traditionally dominated the decisions of security industry officials.[51] Indeed, the similarity of private security techniques and community policing techniques can be narrowed to one core goal: both are intended to utilize proactive crime prevention that is accountable to the customer or the citizen.[52] Private security's traditional "client focused" emphasis on preventing crime—not merely making arrests after a crime has occurred, directly relates to this approach. With community policing seeking to achieve this same goal, the functions of police and security have or will inevitably move closer together. Of course, private security is particularly well suited to serve in a crime prevention or order maintenance role. This has been its role for generations. At least partly because of its focus on the property and financial interests of their clients, private security has long since replaced public police in the protection of business facilities, assets, employees, and customers.[53] This is because private security personnel provided what the public police could not accomplish. Specifically, the industry provided services for specific clients, focusing on the protection of certain assets, both physical and human, as their primary and even exclusive purpose.

The increase in tort causes of action, known as either premises liability or negligent security, has fueled explosive growth in the security industry, and in the business of personal injury attorneys.[54] These lawsuits stem from negligence based legal theories, which question whether the business or property owner knew or should have known that a criminal would come along and commit a crime within the property. Hence, the crime victim could sue the business or property owner (and indirectly its insurance company) for the actions of the criminal. The logic of this cause of action rests on the theory that the owner contributed to the crime, or at least, allowed the crime to occur by failing to take remedial action. According to this logic, the property or business owner, who did not commit the crime, is nonetheless guilty of negligence by allowing the conditions conducive to crime to occur or to fester. Thus, the failure to cure the conditions served to "invite" the criminal act.

These causes of action are based on two contemporary developments. First, the impact of crime has created substantial damage—in human and economic terms. Faced with these financial and human tragedies, courts began to develop the logic and reasoning to support these lawsuits. Second, these lawsuits were intellectually justified by the previously described body of knowledge relating to crime. This thinking was further supported by the Restatement of Torts 2nd, Section 344, which provides the crime victim (plaintiff) must prove both of the following conditions:[55]

1. Owner knew (or should have known) the premise was not secure.
2. Negligent features of premises allowed the crime to occur.

Scientific studies relating to the relationship between crime and the environment are compelling. As noted previously, numerous studies have provided a wealth of evidence that criminals do not act arbitrarily and randomly. Indeed, despite the public's abhorrence of criminal conduct, criminals tend to view the decision to commit a crime as a rational choice. The offender may weigh the risk of being caught versus the benefit from the crime. If the potential gain outweighs the risk, then it is more likely the crime will occur. Based on this logic, it seems reasonable to infer that crimes tend to occur in locations that minimize the criminal's risk of being caught while maximizing his or her advantage. Indeed, criminological research has demonstrated that certain factors may lead to crime.

These factors include: disorderly conditions, diminished lighting, high prospect for escape, increased ability to conceal the crime, and various other factors related to the criminal decision process.[56] Such factors may even invite crime. For example, Gordon and Brill argue that poor lighting not only fails to prevent crime, but acts as a "crime magnet."[57] For these reasons, it was not a great leap for courts to begin to accept the counterintuitive notion that the property or business owner should pay for the actions of the criminal.

A significant consequence of this thinking was to extend legal exposures to a new class of defendants: property and business owners. This exposure, in turn, became a motivator for many owners to institute security measures within and around their property or business location. In this sense, potential liability served as both a carrot and a stick. The carrot was the advantage that promised to accrue to property or business owners who established a safe and secure place in which to do business, and to live or work in. Certainly, maintaining a safe and secure environment could not hurt the reputation of the business, or the viability of the property. Conversely, the stick was substantial potential liability, with large jury awards, that could occur in the event of a crime on their property. In addition, media exposure stemming from such incidents could create a reputational and public relations nightmare for the owner of the business or property where the crime occurred. Clearly these factors provided substantial negative motivation to secure the premises from criminals.

This carrot and stick approach led to the growing use of private security personnel and methodologies. This boded well for the security industry. Business and property owners started to think and worry about security. They became more proactive in their approach to a safe and secure environment. For security firms, the need for increased vigilance created a larger and larger market of potential clients. It brought security further and further into the realm of the average citizen. Security personnel began to be routinely used at businesses and large corporations, now often focusing on the *protection of employees and clients*, instead of simply preventing them from stealing. In this sense, security became more mainstream. It is part of the hospital you visited, part of your workplace, and part of the apartment building you live in. Consequently, the security industry moved into the lives of average people. No longer was it just the public police who serviced the people; now there was another service provider, this one operating out of the private realm. Now private security was "the people." This closeness to mainstream society also increased the scope of the services provided by private security.

As premises liability and negligent security lawsuits developed, the liability of business and property owners extended farther and farther beyond the "protected facility." The seemingly ever-expanding perimeter was the result of court decisions. It was not uncommon for incidents in parking lots to create liability exposure. Indeed, liability exposure may even be claimed to apply to attacks that occur *beyond the perimeters of the property or business.*[58] In fact, lawsuits have succeeded in cases of criminal attacks that occurred down the street from the property or business held liable. As liability exposure expanded, so did the security perimeter and methodologies. Consequently, it is now common for security patrols and hardware for properties and businesses to extend into the streets and other public areas, in the quest to prevent crime and to provide a safe and secure environment.

Conversely, public police have a much more difficult task incorporating crime prevention into their organizational structure as a result of the broader societal mission to universally enforce laws throughout society, as well as to preserve democratic and constitutional ideals. Considering that the already overburdened public police are also faced with economic and operational constraints, it is not unreasonable to conclude that the role of private security will continue to increase. This relationship between crime and security has been pointedly summarized by Thompson. In addition to the criminological theories summarized previously, he outlines the increased incidence of security liability to the following factors:[59]

- Increased crime
- Growth of private security
- Greater public awareness of litigation
- Greater number of attorneys
- Increased publicity about criminal incidents

CONTEMPORARY CIRCUMSTANCES

The relative size and scope of policing and security are well known in industry circles. Much of this data is derived from the groundbreaking Hallcrest studies. These studies reveal that in 1981, the security industry spent approximately $21.7 billion, compared to the $13.8 billion spent on public policing. In 1991, these expenditures rose to $52 billion for private security, compared to only $30 billion for public policing.[60] By the year 2000, private security spent approximately $104 billion, while public policing spent only $44 billion.[61] This ratio of expenditures reveals that about 70 percent of all money invested in crime prevention and law enforcement is spent on private security. Furthermore, statistics reveal that the annual growth rate for private security is about double the growth rate of public policing.[62] Through the year 2004, private security grew at a rate of 8 percent per annum.[63] Most of this growth was prior to September 11, 2001. These figures illustrate that private security is one of the fastest growing industries in the country.[64]

Following the terrorist attacks of September 11, 2001, some security firms predicted revenue growth in the range of 10 to 12 percent per year.[65] One verifiable example of this growth is the increased presence of private security officers in New York City since 9/11. In September 2001, there were 104,000 security officers in New York City. By October 2003, the number of security officers there had risen to 127,006.[66] This level of growth is not atypical of the expansion of the security industry in other parts of the country.

The number of security employees in relation to police further emphasizes the growing predominance of the security industry in the crime reduction arena. Consider some historical trends. From 1964 to 1991, employment in private firms increased by an astonishing 750 percent, with the number of firms providing security and investigative services increasing by 543 percent.[67] Public policing agencies also grew their number of full-time sworn police personnel to about 700,000. The number of police personnel, however, pales by comparison of recent security industry estimates of 2 million people employed by security firms.[68] In some urban areas, such as El Paso, Texas, the number of private police is estimated to exceed that of public police by a ratio of 6 to 1.[69]

The growth of private security is reflected in recent financial and hiring data from two huge international firms that dominate the security industry. Securitas, a Swedish based firm, had revenues of $5.8 billion with a net income of $115.2 million in 2001.[70] It employs 220,000 people worldwide, with 98,000 in the United States. Since 9/11, they have hired more than 10,000 additional guards to serve U.S. accounts. Similarly, the Danish firm Group 4 Securicor had revenues of $2.81 billion dollars, with a net income of $3.7 million dollars in 2001. This firm employs 400,000 full- and part-time personnel worldwide, with 53,000 in the U.S., of which about 3 to 5 percent are directly attributable to 9/11.[71] By any account, these are impressive numbers, both in terms of revenue and employee growth. Overall, the data suggest that the private security is so disproportionately large compared to that of public policing, some observers argue that private security is now *the primary protective resource* in the nation.[72] Based on expected additional terrorist incidents, these numbers will likely grow—possibly substantially.

Likewise, the ratio of public police officers to reported crimes has undergone a dramatic change. In the 1960s, there were about 3.3 public police officers for every violent crime reported. In 1993, there were 3.47 violent crimes reported for every public police officer.[73] While crime levels have decreased since then, these statistics illustrate that each public police officer in contemporary America must deal with 11.45 times as many violent crimes as police from previous eras. Walinsky notes that if this country were to return to the 1960s ratio of police to violent crimes, about 5 million new public police officers would have to be hired by local governments.[74] This has not occurred and will not occur. Instead, the security industry has stepped in to serve this growing market need.

Justice Department data reveal that despite the decreasing ratio of the number of police to that of violent crimes, the economic costs of public policing increased from $441 million in 1968 to about $10 billion in 1994.

This represents a 2,100 percent increase in the cost of public policing, while the number of violent crimes exploded 560 percent from 1960 to 1992.[75] Thus, as crime rates increased, the tax monies used to "combat" crime also dramatically increased. While more recent Justice Department data reveals that crime has decreased from 1994 to 2004, one obvious question begs to be answered: Would spending additional money on public policing, in fact, reduce crime? Based on this short historical and statistical overview, the answer appears to be no. The most obvious conclusion to be drawn from these statistics is this: Over the last generation, the relationship between the amount of crime and the amount of money spent on public policing has changed radically.

As dramatic as these statistics may seem, numerous authors assert that the security industry should not be assessed on data alone. Indeed, the sheer and undeniable growth of the industry can be viewed by its involvement in businesses, homes, and communities throughout the country.[76] This involvement stems from such diverse services as alarm systems, security guard services, and investigative and consulting services. Indeed, the impact of the security industry may even be more substantial than what this data suggests. For example, one observer noted, "We are witnessing a fundamental shift in the area of public safety. It's not a loss of confidence in the police, but a desire to have more police."[77] Indeed, there are appropriate comparisons being made of the security industry in relation to the advent of public policing in the mid-1850s. In light of the historical summary, this comparison of private security to the advent of public police seems right on the mark.

Numerous authors have argued that there is a need for more police, or at least more protective services.[78] Other authors have a more critical view. They doubt the capability of the public police to provide an appropriate level of protection.[79] In either case, private policing may be seen as the "wave of the future."[80] Similarly, another author observed, "People want protection, and what they cannot get from the police, they will get from private security companies."[81] This statement has particular significance in light of the current increased terrorist threat. The authors of the *National Policy Summit* suggest a connection between this threat and the conflicting roles facing modern police departments. In their analysis, police are finding that in addition to the crime-fighting duties, they now have significant homeland security duties.[82]

The impact of crime on average people suggested by a 2004 survey conducted by the Society of Human Resource Managers (SHRM) is worth considering. The researchers asked, "Do you feel safe at work?" The majority of respondents answered no. Indeed, for almost every demographic and industry category, safety at work ranked at the top or near the top in terms of employee priorities. Specifically, safety was the number one issue for women, and tied for first with benefits for older employees. Overall, "feeling safe at work" was ranked "very important" by 62 percent of the respondents, up from about 36 percent two years previously.[83]

Business leaders also need to assess the current threat environment and consider security countermeasures. A Booz-Allen Hamilton study conducted in 2002 surveyed seventy-two CEOs from firms with more than $1 billion in annual revenues. This study revealed their post-9/11 security concerns. This survey found that 80 percent of respondents believed that security is more important now than it was prior to 9/11, with 67 percent actually incurring or anticipating substantial new security costs.[84] In addition, expenditures for security-related personnel and hardware were tracked and summarized in another study (see Table I-1).[85] The data in this table reveal an increase in the use of various security methods as well as a reduction of security expenditures by some firms. This trend in the data seems to suggest that despite the threat posed by crime and terrorism, some organizations still remain content to believe that "it won't happen here."

Other more recent studies conducted after the London train bombings and Hurricane Katrina reveal that "there is an increased focus on domestic safety and security."[86] One study revealed that 56 percent of companies have revised their disaster preparedness plans, while 44 percent have not. Again, the statistics suggest that while some people will seek to prepare for or prevent a disaster, others prefer to merely to hope for the best.[87] As previously asserted, this mind-set will always exist in some measure—despite the liability exposure and security threats facing society.

Considering the impact of liability exposure upon business, the incentive to provide security is substantial. In 2004, the U.S. Chamber of Commerce reported that small businesses incurred more $88 billion annually in litigation expenses.[88] An employment law firm's annual survey in 2003 reported that 57 percent of companies had an employee file a lawsuit against the company, up 8 percent from 2002.[89] The EEOC itself collected more than $420 million dollars from employers who had violated discrimination laws. Of course, regardless of whether a lawsuit has any legal merit, litigation has both direct and indirect costs to the employer.

Table I-1 Security Budgets and Expenditure

Expenditure Area	% Increased	% Stayed the Same	% Decreased
Internal Security Personnel	32%	52%	11%
Internal Security Operations	40%	50%	7%
Security Consulting	23%	43%	27%
Contract Guards	32%	37%	22%
Personnel Screening	34%	49%	12%
Access Control	55%	31%	8%

Note: Percentages shown as presented by study. Percentages not rounded, remainder is unknown/undecided.

These costs may include attorneys' fees, lost productivity, decreased employee morale, increased turnover, and poor public relations. Clearly, it is important to provide a secure workplace environment, since crime prevention and misconduct reduction have wide-ranging implications.

NEGLIGENCE ELEMENTS AND PRINCIPLES

In order to assess the liability exposure related to crime and misconduct, one must consider the tort of negligence. Negligence can be defined as the failure or omission to do something that a reasonable and prudent person would do, or doing something a reasonable and prudent person would not do. Negligence causes of action have four elements: duty, breach of duty, causation, and damages. As was explained previously, government has no constitutionally defined duty to prevent crime. Crime has traditionally been considered a superseding cause that broke the causation connection in a negligence-based claim. This superseding cause in a negligence action is illustrated in Figure I-1.

Duty

Duty is the standard of care that a reasonable and prudent person is required to maintain. This standard is objective. Unfortunately, it is difficult to definitively determine an objective standard. It is based on what a reasonable and prudent person would do or not do.[90] The logic is that the imposition of a duty often affects an individual's behavior, since people tend to conform to the duty in order to avoid potential liability.[91] In the context of crime, the imposition of a duty is designed to keep people safe from crime. This does not require preventing the crime from occurring. Sometimes crime cannot reasonably be prevented. In a perfect world, no crime would occur. Of course, this world is far from perfect. It is clear all crime cannot be prevented, even if the property and business owner tried to prevent it. Indeed, courts do not require perfection. What is typically required is the institution of reasonable security methods in order to diminish the probability that crime will occur. In achieving this standard, security

Figure I-1 Crime as a superseding cause in negligence.

methods can stem from a brighter light bulb to Fort Knox—and anywhere in between. How then does a reasonable and prudent person assess what security methods would be sufficient? The answer is the proverbial million dollar question. Indeed, in security litigation, it is often a multi-million dollar proposition.

Fortunately, there are principles that can be used to assess the appropriate level of duty. Broadly speaking, duty can be defined by particularized relationships and by the concept foreseeability.[92] Courts typically consider duty of care as being based on three broad factors: the circumstances, the terms of the contract (if any), and the expectations of the "special relationship" between the parties (if any). Before considering these factors, some additional explanation is necessary.

First, the notion of a special relationship imposes a duty on the business or property owner. Such relationships include that of common carriers, such as trains and buses, to their passengers. The relationship between hotels and their guests is another example. Implicit in these relationships is a circumstance in which the safety and security of the subordinate party (the passenger and the guest) are in the hands of the business owner and proprietor. In the logic of this relationship, the superior party (owner and proprietor) has an increased or enhanced duty to protect those who depend on that party for their safety and security. Since the existence of a special relationship is often posed in security litigation, these issues will be developed throughout this book.

The second aspect of duty relates to the terms and conditions of the contract, if one exists. This assessment is typically straightforward. Generally, what is articulated in the contract is what is required by the respective parties. In this way, the duty is based on the language of the contract, or the agreement of the parties. These issues will be more fully developed in Chapter 9.

The third aspect of duty is the most difficult to assess because it is based on the circumstances surrounding the incident. With this assessment, the operative facts often dictate whether a duty exists, or the extent of the duty imposed. In this thinking, a general principle is relevant to the assessment. As danger increases, the actor (owner or proprietor) is required to exercise caution commensurate with the risk. For example, if the risk of crime is particularly great, then the required security measures to prevent crime may increase. The appropriate relationship between the risk of danger and the commensurate duty, however, is tricky to definitively define. Indeed, doing so can be construed as both an art and a science. This is what makes the analysis contained in this book pertinent and relevant. Performing a reasonable and prudent analysis to determine the appropriate security precautions for addressing a particular level of risk requires an understanding of both legal principles and security methods.

The typical approach to such an analysis is based on foreseeability.[93] The concept of foreseeability can include what the actor (owner or proprietor) actually knew, as well as what that actor reasonably should have known.

Thus the actor may be required to anticipate the risk of harmful acts of third persons. This thinking mirrors the description of a landowner's duty of care in the Restatement (Second) of Torts, which provides that reasonable care must be exercised to discover what harmful acts are being committed or are likely to be committed, give an adequate warning, or otherwise protect the visitors against the harmful acts.[94] In this sense, foreseeability may be determined in terms of past experience and future probabilities. It is based on whether the likelihood of conduct by third parties will endanger the safety of those within the particular environment. This assessment takes into account a number of factors, including the following:

1. Crime rates and prior similar crimes
2. Lack of customary security measures (by business in area or by particular location)
3. Statutory violations (repair or maintain building)
4. Nature of the business
5. Area or neighborhood where the business is located
6. Standard of security methods in the particular industry
7. Hours of business operation for the business
8. Specific complaints about crime, misconduct or suspicious behavior at the location
9. Expert advise from police or security consultants
10. Relationship between owner's conduct or action and the injury incurred
11. Extent of injury incurred by the victim (plaintiff)
12. Moral blame attached to the conduct or inaction of the business proprietor
13. Public policy considerations related to preventing harm, including the magnitude and consequence of burden of preventing such harm
14. Availability and cost of insurance for the risk involved

Obviously, these factors are detailed and fact specific. They are also complex to assess and difficult to predict. This list demonstrates the diverse factors that courts may use to assess foreseeability. However, it is important to distinguish factors from tests. Factors are facts or situational assessments. Tests are legal standards. Typically, tests will often focus on certain specific factors, as being more important to the particular test. For example, in a prior similar incidents test, the lack of any previous crime would defeat the claim. Conversely, in the totality of the circumstances test, the court would consider all factors, not just previous crimes. Consequently, the particular test used by the court is a, or even *the*, critical determination of liability.

There are various tests that courts use to determine foreseeability. Specific tests include: (1) the specific harm test, (2) the prior similar incidents test, (3) the totality of the circumstances test, (4) the balancing test, (5) the known aggressor/imminent danger test, (6) the actual or constructive knowledge test, (7) the special relationship/special circumstances test, and (8) blending of various tests. While these tests have some overlap, their basic characteristics can be described.

Under the specific harm test, a landowner owes no duty unless the owner knew or should have known that the specific harm was occurring or was about to occur. As this is a very restrictive standard, most courts are unwilling to hold that a criminal act is foreseeable only in these situations.

Under the prior similar incidents test, a landowner may owe a duty of reasonable care if evidence of prior similar incidents of crime on or near the landowner's property shows that the crime in question was foreseeable.[95] Although courts differ in the application of this rule, all agree that the important factors to consider are the number of prior incidents, their proximity in time and location to the present crime, and the similarity of the crimes.[96] Courts differ in terms of how proximate and similar the prior crimes are required to be as compared to the current crime. Courts can apply more liberal or more conservative standards for this test. For example, in a gun assault case, one court held that although there were 57 crimes reported over a five-year period, only six involved a physical touching. In this conservative jurisdiction, the assault with a gun was deemed unforeseeable. Conversely, in a liberal jurisdiction, two prior burglaries of apartments were sufficient to make a rape in an apartment foreseeable. Notwithstanding this difference, this test typically depends on the location, nature, and extent of those previous criminal activities and their similarity, proximity or other relationship to the crime in question.

While this approach establishes a relatively clear line when landowner liability will attach, some courts have rejected this test for public policy reasons. The typical public policy criticism is that the first victim in all instances is not entitled to recover. As such, if there were no prior similar incidents, landowners have no incentive to implement even nominal security measures. Hence, some argue this test incorrectly focuses on the specific crime and not the general risk of foreseeable harm. Indeed, one can make the logical argument that the lack of prior similar incidents relieves a defendant of all liability. This is so, even when the criminal act was, in fact, foreseeable due to generalized crime within the community. However, advocates of this standard argue that merchants should be responsible only for the dangerous conditions they created. In this sense, prior similar incidents would act as "constructive notice," which protects the interests of the customer, while giving the property or business owner a fair opportunity to take steps to shield them from liability.[97]

Under the totality of the circumstances test, a court considers all of the circumstances surrounding an event to determine whether a criminal act was foreseeable. This may include the nature, condition, and location of the property and the larger community, as well as prior similar incidents in and around the property in question.[98] Courts that employ this test may do so out of dissatisfaction with the limitations of other tests, such as the prior similar incidents test. The thinking behind this test is that all relevant factors associated with the crime should be taken into account. The wide scope of this test is favored by those who seek to prevent crime—and by those who advocate liability for those who fail to prevent crime.

A frequently cited limitation of this test is that it tends to make foreseeability too broad and unpredictable, effectively requiring that landowners anticipate crime. Indeed, the numerous factors cited above are difficult to assess and predict. Sharp argues that foreseeability alone does not create a duty. Rather, the ability to have foreseen and *prevented* the harm is the key determinative of responsibility inherent in this duty.[99] Nonetheless, this test is very popular with courts as it gives a wide-ranging analysis to all relevant factors related to the incident. Hence, this test is useful because it can incorporate all relevant factors. However, it is difficult to apply for the same reason.

Under the balancing test, courts balance "the degree of foreseeability of harm against the burden of the duty to be imposed."[100] In other words, as the foreseeability and degree of potential harm increase, so does the duty to prevent it. However, the burden of preventing foreseeable crime must also be considered. For example, in high-crime areas, the burden of preventing crime may become too onerous as to drive away all commerce. Hence, this test seeks to balance the foreseeability of crime against the burden of preventing crime. In this assessment, the burden is considered in various ways, including the cost of security measures, the economic impact of a "hardened" business environment, and the feasibility of security measures to actually prevent crime. Because this is a difficult "balancing act," this test still relies heavily on prior similar incidents in order to ensure that an undue burden is not placed on business or landowners.

Under the known aggressor/imminent danger test, courts assess whether the owner or proprietor had reason to know that a particular assailant is aggressive, belligerent, or prone to violence against customers or patrons. This is a very factually specific test, where knowledge of the particular offender's actual violent propensities is critical to imposing liability. If this knowledge is not shown, then liability for the crime will not attach.

In a similar test, the actual or constructive knowledge test, the owner or proprietor must have knowledge, either actual or constructive, of the threat posed by an offender or of the crime that was likely to occur. As with known aggressor/imminent danger test, this is a very restrictive test. It requires a high level of knowledge and specificity of the offender or of the crime. One distinction between this test and the known aggressor/imminent danger test, is that actual or constructive knowledge test provides for a longer temporal assessment. In order for liability to attach, the former focuses more on the time frame between the knowledge and the crime. The latter allows for liability with less emphasis on time considerations, with more emphasis on what the business or property owner knew—or should have known—about the potential for crime to occur. While this is not a definitive distinction between the two tests, it is a way to frame the logic of both.

As mentioned earlier, the special relationship/special circumstances test focuses on the relationship of the parties, such as hotel-guest, carrier-passenger, and the like. This test, however, also looks at the circumstances surrounding this relationship. In this way, the status of the parties (special relationship) is coupled with relevant factors (special circumstances) in the assessment of liability.

As shown by the short descriptions of these different tests, there is substantial variance in how liability assessments are made. The fact that different states use different tests further complicates the task of assessment. Consequently, the following table was developed as a reference to facilitate the process.[101] Before using this table, a few caveats are in order.

First, the table lists tests applied in each state. While this information appears straightforward, the fact that some states have developed standards that are difficult to characterize in any definitive manner creates some ambiguity. For example, some states will use a defined test, such as prior similar incidents, but will differ in its application. In this way, a particular state may use a more liberal view versus others that may use a more conservative approach. Hence, even when the test is defined, the application of the test may vary based on a liberal or conservative bend or mind-set of the court.

Second, the chart lists tests that are sometimes adaptations from several different tests that are often also difficult to characterize in any defined way. For example, when one compares the actual or constructive test to the aggressor/imminent danger test, the distinctions are fine or slight. In the former, the test seems to combine knowledge of the offender and of a particular crime, while the latter focuses much more directly toward the particular offender who may commit a particular violent crime. This assessment also takes into account the temporal factor discussed previously. In fact, the distinctions between these tests may be so fine as to be legally and factually meaningless. Notwithstanding this assertion, the test articulated by the court is the one listed in the chart.

A third issue related to this caveat is that sometimes a particular state will not articulate a particular test or it will change from one test to another. Since legal standards are very fact specific, courts may tend to frame the legal analysis around the facts of a particular case. Hence, sometimes there is a "chicken and an egg" scenario. Stated another way, it is difficult to assess which is paramount, the legal standard or the facts. The interrelationship between the two sometimes makes it hard to distinguish which has first priority.

Given these complicating factors, the reader should review Table I-2 with some caution. Despite these caveats, this table nevertheless remains a valuable tool. Indeed, the value of this table is that it attempts to define a difficult, often fluid, area of the law. To the best of my knowledge, no other author has developed a table of this type. Hopefully, the attempt to place clear distinctions between the varying state laws into an easily reviewable table can be a useful tool for those who need to get a sense of the law in a particular state, or of the broader concept of security law. While it may appear that the caveats mentioned above "swallow" the table, the reality is that the chart reflects the difficulty in assessing security law generally. That is, security standards, just like legal standards, are very fact specific. Sometimes facts are difficult to neatly categorize. As a result, security and legal standards are also hard to categorize. This is one of the reasons why books such as this one are useful and necessary. Stated another way, the value of the table (and this book) are that they shed light on difficult and fluid subject matter.

The table includes three general categories: the state, the legal test, and the legal authority. When using the table for litigation or security

Table I-2 Security/Legal Test by State

State	Legal Test	Legal Authority
Alabama	Actual or Constructive Knowledge	*Whataburger, Inc., v. Rockwell,* 706 So. 2d 1220 (1997) *Broadus v. Chevron,* 677 So. 2d 199 (1996) *Baptist Memorial Hospital v. Gosa,* 686 So. 2d 1147 (1996) *E.H. v. Overlook Mountain Lodge,* 638 So. 2d 781 (1994)
Alaska	Known Aggressor/ Imminent Danger	*Hedrick v. Fraternal Order of Fishermen,* 103 F. Supp. 582 (1952)
Arizona	Totality of the Circumstances	*Gipson v. Kasey,* 129 P. 3d 957 (2006) *McFarlin v. Hall,* 619 P. 2d 729 (1980)
Arkansas	Known Aggressor/ Imminent Danger	*Boren v. Worthen National Bank,* 921 S.W. 2d 934 (1996)
California	Prior Similar Incidents	*Wiener v. Southcoast Child Care,* 88 P. 3d 517 (2004) *Mata v. Mata, 105 Cal. App.* 4th 1121 (2003) *Delgado v. Trax Bar & Grill,* 75 P. 3d 29 (2003)

Table I-2 Security/Legal Test by State—cont'd

State	Legal Test	Legal Authority
Colorado	Totality of the Circumstances	*Keller v. Koca*, 111 P. 3d 445 (2005) *Taco Bell v. Lannon*, 744 P. 2d 43 (1987)
Connecticut	Totality of the Circumstances	*Monk v. Temple George Associates*, 869 A. 2d 179 (2005) *Stewart v. Federated Dept. Stores*, 662 A. 2d 753 (1995) *Antrum v. Church's Fried Chicken*, 499 A. 2d 807 (1985)
Delaware	Totality of the Circumstances	*Koutoufaris v. Dick*, 604 A. 2d 390 (1992) *Hughes v. Jardel*, 523 A. 2d 518 (1987)
District of Columbia	Totality of the Circumstances	*Bailey v. District of Columbia*, 668 A. 2d 817 (1995) *Doe v. Dominion Bank*, 963 F. 2d 1552 (1992) *District of Columbia v. Doe*, 524 A. 2d 30 (1987) *Kline v. 1500 Massachusetts Ave. Apts.*, 439 F. 2d 477 (1970)
Florida	Actual or Constructive Knowledge	*T.W. v. Regal Trace Ltd.*, 908 So. 2d 499 (2005) *Menendez v. The Palms West Condo Assoc.*, 736 So. 2d 58 (1999)
Georgia	Totality of the Circumstances	*Agnes Scott College, Inc. v. Clark*, 616 S.E. 2d 468 (2005) *Sturbridge Partners v. Walker*, 482 S.E. 2d 339 (1997) *Wiggly Southern v. Snowden*, 464 S.E. 2d 220 (1995)
Hawaii	Totality of the Circumstances w/Special Relationship	*Doe Parents No. 1 v. State Depart., of Educ.*, 58 P. 3d 545 (2002) *Maguire v. Hilton Hotels*, 899 P. 2d 393 (1995) *Doe v. Grosvenor Properties*, 829 P. 2d 512 (1992)
Idaho	Totality of the Circumstances	*Sharp v. W.H. Moore*, 796 P. 2d 506 (1990)
Illinois	Special Relationship/ Special Circumstances	*Salazar v. Crown Enterprises, Inc.*, 767 N.E. 2d 366 (2002) *Hills v. Bridgeview Little League*, 745 N.E. 2d 1166 (2000)

Continued

Table I-2 Security/Legal Test by State—cont'd

State	Legal Test	Legal Authority
Indiana	Totality of the Circumstances	*Zambrana v. Armenta,* 819 N.E. 2d 881 (2004) *Delta Tau Delta v. Johnson,* 712 N.E. 2d 968 (1999)
Iowa	Totality of the Circumstances	*Alexander v. Medical Associates Clinic,* 646 N.W. 2d 74 (2002) *Tenney v. Atlantic Associates,* 594 N.W. 2d 11 (1999)
Kansas	Totality of the Circumstances	*Gardin v. Emporia Hotels, Inc.,* 61 P. 3d 732 (2003) *Seibert v. Vic Regnier Builders,* 856 P. 2d 1332 (1993)
Kentucky	Known Aggressor/ Imminent Danger	*Waldon v. Paducah Housing Authority,* 854 S.W. 2d 777 (1991) *Heathcoate v. Bisig,* 474 S.W. 2d 102 (1971)
Louisiana	Balancing Test: Foreseeability w/Burden	*Thompson v. Winn-Dixie,* 812 So. 2d 829 (2002) *Posecai v. Wal-Mart,* 752 So. 2d 762 (1999)
Maine	Totality of the Circumstances	*Stanton v. Univ. of Maine,* 773 A. 2d 1045 (2001) *Schlutz v. Gould Academy,* 332 A. 2d 368 (1975)
Maryland	Status or Special Relationship	*Hailman v. M.J.J. Production,* 2 F. 3d 1149 (1993) *Tucker v. KFC National Management,* 689 F. Supp. 560 (1988)
Massachusetts	Totality of the Circumstances	*Luisi v. Foodmaster Supermarkets,* 739 N.E. 2d 702 (2000) *Whittaker v. Saraceno,* 635 N.E. 2d 1185 (1994) *Flood v. Southland Corp.,* 616 N.E. 2d 1068 (1993)
Michigan	Special Relationship/ Special Circumstances	*Stanley v. Town Square Co-Op,* 512 N.W. 2d 51 (1993) *Harkins v. Northwest Activity Center,* 453 N.W. 2d 677 (1990) *Williams v. Cunningham Drug Stores,* 418 N.W. 2d 381 (1988)

Table I-2 Security/Legal Test by State—cont'd

State	Legal Test	Legal Authority
Minnesota	Special Relationship/ Special Circumstances	*Errico v. Southland Corp.*, 509 N.W. 2d 585 (1993) *Anders v. Trester*, 562 N.W. 2d 45 (1997) *Erickson v. Curtis Investment*, 447 N.W. 2d 165 (1989)
Mississippi	Actual or Constructive Knowledge	*Gatewood v. Sampson*, 812 So. 2d 212 (2002)
Missouri	Split Authority between: special relationship/ special circumstances and prior similar incidents	*L.A.C. ex rel. D.C. v. Ward Parkway Shopping Center*, 75 S.W. 3d 247 (2002) *Hudson v. Riverport Performance Arts*, 37 S.W. 3d 261 (2000) *Richardson v. QuikTrip Corp.*, 81 S.W. 3d 54 (2002)
Montana	Prior Similar Incidents	*Peschke v. Carroll College*, 929 P. 2d 874 (1996)
Nebraska	Totality of the Circumstances	*Doe v. Gunny's Ltd.*, 593 N.W. 2d 284 (1999)
Nevada	Totality of the Circumstances	*Doud v. Las Vegas Hilton Corp.*, 864 P. 2d 796 (1993) *Early v. N.L.V. Casino Corp.*, 678 P. 2d 683 (1984)
New Hampshire	Blended four standards: Special Relationship Special Circumstances Overriding Foreseeability Assumed Duty	*Walls v. Oxford Management*, 633 A. 2d 103 (1993)
New Jersey	Totality of the Circumstances	*Saltsman v. Corazo*, 721 A. 2d 1000 (1998) *Morris v. Krauszer's Food Stores, Inc.*, 693 A. 2d 510 (1997) *Clohesy v. Food Circus Supermarkets*, 694 A. 2d 1017 (1997)
New Mexico	Prior Similar Incidents	*Wilson v. Wal-Mart*, 117 F. 3d 1429 (1997)
New York	Prior Similar Incidents/ Actual or Constructive Knowledge	*Po W. Yuen v. 267 Canal Street Corp.*, 802 N.Y.S. 2d 306 (2005)

Continued

Table I-2 Security/Legal Test by State—cont'd

State	Legal Test	Legal Authority
New York (cont'd)		*Moskal v. Fleet Bank,* 694 N.Y.S. 2d 555 (1999) *Jacqueline S. v. City of New York,* 598 N.Y.S. 2d 160 (1993)
North Carolina	Balance between: Totality of the Circumstances and Prior Similar Incidents	*Vera v. Five Crow Promotions, Inc.,* 503 S.E. 2d 692 (1998) *Purvis v. Bryson's Jewelers,* 443 S.E. 2d 768 (1994)
North Dakota	Balance between: Totality of the Circumstances and Prior Similar Incidents	*Zueger v. Carlson,* 542 N.W. 2d 92 (1996)
Ohio	Totality of the Circumstances	*Krause v. Spartan Stores, Inc.,* 815 N.E. 2d 696 (2004) *Collins v. Down River Specialties,* 715 N.E. 2d 189 (1998) *Hickman v. Warehouse Beer Systems,* 620 N.E. 2d 949 (1993)
Oregon	Known Aggressor/ Imminent Danger	*Allstate Ins., v. Tenant Screening Services,* 914 P. 2d 16 (1996)
Pennsylvania	Actual or Constructive Knowledge	*Rabutino v. Freedom State Realty Co., Inc.,* 809 A. 2d 933 (2002) *Rosa v. 1220 Uncle's Inc.,* 2001 WL 1113016 (2001)
Rhode Island	Totality of the Circumstances	*Volpe v. Gallagher,* 821 A. 2d 699 (2003)
South Carolina	Totality of the Circumstances	*Jeffords v. Lesesne,* 541 S.E. 2d 847 (2000) *Callen v. Cale Yarborough Enterprises,* 442 S.E. 2d 216 (1994)
South Dakota	Special Relationship/ Special Circumstances	*Smith ex rel. Ross v. Lagow Construction & Developing,* 642 N.W. 2d 187 (2002)
Tennessee	Balancing Test: Foreseeability w/Burden	*Patterson Khoury v. Wilson World Hotel-Cherry Road, Inc.,* 139 S.W. 3d 281 (2003) *McClung v. Delta Square Ltd.,* 937 S.W. 2d 891 (1996)

Table I-2 Security/Legal Test by State—cont'd

State	Legal Test	Legal Authority
Texas	Prior Similar Incidents	*Western Investments, Inc. v. Maria Urena,* 162 S.W. 3d 547 (2005) *Timberwalk Apartments v. Cain,* 972 S.W. 2d 749 (1998) *Nixon v. MR Property Management,* 690 S.W. 2d 546 (1985)
Utah	Known Aggressor/ Imminent Danger	*Steffensen v. Smith's Management Corp.,* 862 P. 2d 1342 (1993)
Vermont	None	
Virginia	Blends: Special Relationship/ Special Circumstances w/Known Aggressor/ Imminent Danger	*Yuzefousky v. St. John's Wood Apartments,* 540 S.E. 2d 134 (2001) *Gupton v. Quicke,* 442 S.E. 2d 658 (1994)
Washington	Special Relationship/ Special Circumstances	*Kim v. Budget Rent A Car Systems,* 15 P. 3d 1283 (2001) *Nivens v. 7-11 Hoagy's Corner,* 943 P. 2d 286 (1997)
West Virginia	Special Relationship/ Special Circumstances	*Doe v. Wal-Mart Stores, Inc.,* 479 S.E. 2d 610 (1996) *Miller v. Whitworth,* 455 S.E. 2d 821 (1995)
Wisconsin	Totality of the Circumstances	*Peters v. Holiday Inns,* 278 N.W. 2d 208 (1979)
Wyoming	Balancing Test: Foreseeability w/Burden	*Krier v. Safeway Stores 46, Inc.,* 943 P.2d 405 (1997)

purposes, please check the case authority and research the law of the state to assess its current legal standard.

Breach of Duty

Breach of duty is characterized by a failure to act or by conduct that falls short of the applicable standard of care. In essence, the actor failed to do what a reasonable and prudent person would do in the circumstance. Alternatively, the actor did something that a reasonable and prudent person would not do in the circumstance.

For example, consider the hypothetical case of a security officer assigned to guard a movie theater. If a fire started in the theater, the security officer would be required to take some affirmative act, such as calling 911, notifying supervisory personnel, or escorting patrons from the facility. If the security officer failed to carry out any such act, this omission would likely be deemed a breach of duty by a court. Alternatively, if the security officer yelled "fire" in the crowded theater and then ran out of the facility, this conduct would also likely be deemed a breach of duty by a court. In either case, there is an affirmative duty to act in a reasonable and prudent manner under the circumstances. The failure to do so may result in the breach of the duty of care.

Generally, in the context of security personnel, the standard of care is based on how a reasonable officer confronted with a similar situation would act. Absent some affirmative misconduct by a security officer, the failure to prevent a criminal act is usually not considered a breach of duty. The key issue is whether the security officer promptly reported the incident, and took other appropriate measures to secure people and property in and around the crime scene. In the context of property or landowners, the standard of care is the duty described in the discussion and in Table I-2. If this duty is not adhered to, it is deemed breached.

Causation

The legal term for causation is proximate cause. This element imposes rational limits on liability based on some cogent connection between the conduct and the harm suffered. Generally, the closer the connection between the conduct and the harm (damage), the most likely the conduct will be deemed the proximate cause of the harm. This connection is assessed in terms of time, space or distance, sequence of events, and the like. A typical assessment of causation is through the substantial factor test. In this test, the question is whether the defendant's conduct (or omission) was a substantial factor of the incident causing (or contributing) the injury or the harm. For example, if a crime would have occurred despite any reasonable security precautions, then the causation element was not satisfied.[102] The question of causation in security cases typically involves two key issues:

1. Whether certain security measures would have likely dissuaded the offender from committing the crime
2. Even if the offender would not have been deterred, whether certain security measures would have enabled security or police officers to interdict the offender

Damages

The damage element stems from the breach and is connected by causation to the harm or injury. In the elements of negligence, the harm or the injury is called damage(s). There are many types of damages and many ways to calculate damages. Types of damage claims include:

1. Compensatory (general) damages entail the non-tangible impact, including:
   a. Mental anguish
   b. Emotional distress
   c. Pain and suffering
   d. Loss of enjoyment
2. Special (economic) damages entail the tangible impact, including:
   a. Medical expenses
   b. Lost earnings
   c. Lost earning capacity (future earnings)
   d. Rehabilitative expenses
   e. Future medical expenses
3. Exemplary (additional) damages entail supplementary penalties, including:
   a. Punitive (for punishment and deterrence)
   b. Treble (three times)
4. Wrongful death relates to the damages created by the death of the person

While there is no set calculation of damages, my experience is that the following formula is typical in a negligent tort claim. Typically the economic damage amount can be calculated to a rather precise figure. Remember this aspect of damages is the most tangible. This figure will be the total of each subsection of this category. For example, consider these damage amounts:

1.	Medical expenses:	$50,000
2.	Lost earnings:	$10,000
3.	Lost future earning capacity:	None
4.	Rehabilitative expenses:	$10,000
5.	Future medical expenses:	$10,000
	Total economic damages:	$80,000

Using this figure as a baseline, the formula requires this amount be multiplied to represent the general (non-economic) damages. This calculation is as follows:

$80,000 (economic damages) × 3 or 5 or 7 (general damages) = Total demand or total value of claim.

Here the intangible aspect is the appropriate multiple to be used in this equation. If the multiple is three (3), then the equation is: $80,000 × 3 = $240,000. If the multiple is five (5), then the equation is: $80,000 × 5 = $400,000. If the multiple is seven (7), then the equation is: $80,000 × 7 = $560,000. The numbers would change depending upon the multiple used in the formula. In this way, the higher the multiple, the higher the recovery. In my experience, it is unusual to obtain a multiple in double digits. While this does occur, it is not very frequent. The key to the amount of the multiple depends on a number of factors, including the negotiation or litigation skills of the attorneys, the sympathy generated by the plaintiff (or lack thereof), the ease of demonstrating liability (or stated in the opposite way—the difficulty in proving liability), the forum where the case was filed, the existence and amount of insurance coverage, and the other factors which are relevant to the particular case.

Finally, if punitive or treble damages are relevant, these would be applied as a separate category. For example, treble damages are three times the total damages. Treble damages are damage provisions derived from specific statutes. They are designed as incentives to increase the likelihood that the statute would not be violated. In essence, treble damage clauses triple the value of the claim. This can be a real motivation in potential litigation.

Punitive damages are designed to punish the bad conduct of the defendant, and act as an example to deter others from similar bad conduct. Two key U.S. Supreme Court cases govern the standard of punitive damages.[103] These cases provide that punitive damages should be framed within three "guideposts." These are the degree of reprehensibility, the ratio between compensatory and punitive damages, and of awards in similar cases. These guideposts were summarized by Stamatis and Muhtaris.[104] As to the degree of reprehensibility, it is generally considered the most important indicator. This indicator has great significance in security law claims, as it looks at the defendant's conduct in light of the following:[105]

1. Whether the defendant caused physical as opposed to only economic pain
2. Whether the defendant showed indifference to or reckless disregard for health or safety of others
3. Whether the defendant was involved in repeated acts or omissions
4. Whether the injury or harm was caused by an intentional act, not simply an accident

As to the other two indicators, the ratio between compensatory and punitive damages is deemed the least important factor.[106] Indeed, the case of *State Farm Auto Insurance Co. v. Campbell, 538 U.S. 408 (2003)* stands for the proposition that there is no "bright line" mandate between these types of damages. In this way, the court held that there is no one standard, no "one size fits all formula." Consequently, the range of damages that could be applied is based on the facts and circumstances of the case.

Whatever the "correct" amount is deemed to be, the key in this regard is to understand the formula used to assess the "value" of these cases. Of course, value does not just equate with money. The damage done to crime victims often is not corrected by money. What is the value of losing a loved one? Can a woman who was brutally raped be adequately compensated?

What about the victim of an armed robbery who has to return to work—the scene of the crime—to continue to serve his clients? Can these people be "fixed" by money? Many, if not most, would answer no. Unfortunately, the legal system can do little more for these victims other than to award money damages. Money is intended to make the victim whole. As inadequate as this may be, this is the best that the system can achieve. Of course, the better answer is to prevent the crime from occurring. Hopefully this book will help serve to achieve this goal, even in some small measure.

When considering how to limit crimes by third parties, or at least limit the liability exposure from such, there are three basic approaches: pre-incident assessments, post-incident investigations, and legal defenses and theories. Each approach is distinct. Each approach, however, is interrelated to the others. For example, if there was no pre-incident assessment, then this will affect the post-incident investigation, which in turn relates to the legal defenses and theories tied to the case. Each of these approaches will be presented independently, but keep in mind that they are interrelated. This will become more obvious when the legal defenses and theories are presented.

PRE-INCIDENT ASSESSMENTS

Specific security assessment techniques have been advocated for many decades. In the past few decades, however, the amount of attention paid to this issue has significantly increased. Thompson, for example, has proposed various measures for avoiding liability. These include the following:[107]

1. Develop pre-employment screening procedures.
2. Maintain security personnel training standards and document training sessions.
3. Become familiar with the neighborhood and crime data of the surrounding community.
4. Maintain close working relationships with local police officials.
5. Emphasize that security officers must remain active and visible at all times.
6. Develop comprehensive security plans.
7. Maintain extensive record keeping and documentation of complaints and crimes within the facility.
8. Document every step in the security process.

These factors have been cited in numerous security surveys and risk assessments. While these can be complicated endeavors, some general factors common to security surveys and risk assessments will be outlined. For starters, while there are some distinctions between a security survey and a risk assessment, this analysis will characterize these as being similar tools. Probably the most defined distinction between these tools is that risk assessments tend to be more comprehensive, both in terms of its scope and its sophistication.

In general, the desire to manage risk is a baseline goal. Risk management can be defined as a "systematic, analytical process to determine the likelihood that a threat will harm physical assets or individuals and then to identify actions to reduce risk and mitigate the consequences of an attack."[108] The first aspect of the assessment regards the sources of threats, which can be either internal or external.[109] Sources of threats can be generally categorized as human errors, system failures, natural disasters, and malicious or violent acts. This last threat is the source of the security exposures addressed in this book.

It is important to assess the assets within the organization that are subject to these threats. A typical analysis would categorize assets to include the following broad areas:

1. People
2. Money or other liquid capital
3. Information
4. Equipment
5. Finished/unfinished goods
6. Processes
7. Buildings/facilities
8. Intangible assets such as intellectual property

Once these assets are identified and categorized, the next step is to specify risk events and vulnerabilities. This assessment is designed to identify the types of incidents which could occur at a site based on a number of factors, including previous incidents at the site, incidents at similarly situated sites, incidents common to the particular industry or geographic location, and recent developments or trends.[110] In this way, vulnerability assessments identify weaknesses that may be exploited by specific threats, and then suggest options that address those weaknesses.[111] These risk events and vulnerabilities are subdivided into three categories: crimes, non-criminal events, and consequential events. For the purposes of this book, the most relevant category relates to crime. In order to assess the vulnerability to crime events, there are numerous data sources that may be relevant, including the following:[112]

- Local police crime statistics and service calls
- Uniform Crime Reports (UCR) complied and published by the FBI
- Internal security incidents and crime reports
- Demographic data such as economic conditions, population density and transience, and unemployment rates
- Prior criminal and civil complaints brought against the enterprise
- Data and information from professional associations related to industry specific problems or trends in criminal activity

- Other environmental factors such as climate, site availability, and the presence of "crime magnets"

Once these factors are assessed, the next step is to assess the probability and criticality of the threats in relation to the particular assets. Probability is defined as "the chance, or in some cases, the mathematical certainty that a given event will occur, the ratio of the number of outcomes in an exhaustive set of equally likely outcomes that produce a given event to the total number of possible outcomes."[113] In essence, probability is based on the likelihood that the threat would occur. This is classified from high probability (expect occurrence), to moderate (circumstances conducive to possible occurrence) to low (unlikely occurrence). Criticality is defined as "the impact of a loss event, typically calculated as the net cost of that event."[114] Essentially, criticality means the value of the asset and the extent of the impact of such on the organization. Criticality is subdivided into three categories:

- Devastating—catastrophic
- Moderate—survivable
- Insignificant—inconsequential

If the asset is deemed so critical that its loss would be devastating or catastrophic to the organization, then even if the probability of the threat is low, the organization may desire to focus a certain amount of security resources and personnel to keep the threat from being realized. Conversely, if the threat probability is low, and the asset criticality is insignificant, there is very little reason why an organization would devote security resources and personnel in an attempt to prevent its occurrence. This is because even if the incident did occur, it would have only an insignificant or inconsequential impact. Hence, why care about threats that do not matter?

Of course, any threat that results in harm to an employee, customer, or any individual cannot be deemed as insignificant or inconsequential. Even the lowest-paid employee, who may be readily replaced by the pool of prospective employees, is a critical asset in terms of security liability. Indeed, the costs of not protecting the employee may be substantial. These include not only tort-based damages, but also public relations and reputational damages, adverse employee morale, and disruption of operations.[115] Consequently, all people on the premises—whether employees, customers, vendors, agents, and possibly even trespassers—must be considered a critical factor in this analysis.

While it is impossible to protect all people at all times, the typical legal standard is to provide reasonable and prudent security methods based on the circumstances. Generally, the level of security methods should be commensurate with the level of risk. The greater the risk of harm, the more security methods deemed necessary. In security parlance, when security methods are implemented, it is termed "mitigation of risk."[116]

A more specific threat assessment tool is known as a Predatory Prevention Matrix. This matrix has four components: Policy, Control, Risk, and Phases of Attack.[117]

1. Policy: In regard to this component, the key is to assess all company policies in light of security or the specific incident or crime that occurred. Here the focus is on how security methods are advanced and implemented. The objectives of each policy should be communicated to all employees, as to obtain their "buy in."
2. Control: Once the policies are articulated and implemented, the key here is to show the interaction between the policy and control mechanisms. Stated another way, the goal is to show that the policy was developed and revised. This is shown through the documentation and assessment measures, which include the following:
    a. Documentation that explains the nature of the security problem or exposure
    b. Measures used to track the problem, such as reports, surveys, audits, and liaison with policing agencies
    c. An assessment of how this information is actually used, and a plan for updating the policies and procedures in light of the assessment measures mentioned above
3. Risk: With this component, it is important to show that the policies and documentation were used to determine risk and to attempt to reduce criminal opportunities. In this way, the key is to demonstrate that preventive methods were used to assess and reduce risks, including crime. In order to do this, it is important to use the logic from criminological theories summarized earlier. Specifically, there are three elements of risk:
    a. Criminal intent
    b. Criminal capacity
    c. Opportunity (this is the only controllable factor):
    The opportunity element of risk is typically broken down further into either random or nonrandom opportunity. In order to reduce liability, the defendant should show the crime was random. Conversely, if the crime was not random, a premeditated opportunity by the offender is implied. If the crime was premeditated (nonrandom), one may infer that the offender took advance notice of the security weaknesses of the environment, and committed the crime at the location because of that weakness.
4. Phases of Attack: An assessment of this helps to determine if the crime was random or premeditated (non-random). There are three phases to an attack:
    a. Invitation: This is defined as any situation that prompts a criminal to initiate the crime. Any number of factors, such

as poor lighting, broken window(s), lack of security hardware or controls, and even an open door may constitute an invitation.

b. Confrontation: This is anything that makes the invitation less attractive. The logic for considering this factor is based on the fact that if the criminal does not face sufficient confrontation, then the opportunity will not be reduced or removed. Without some level or type of confrontation, it then becomes probable that crime will occur. Here a confrontation can be something as simple as a light turning on (or being on), a security officer (or other "guardian") turning the corner, or even a locked door.

c. Time: This phase entails a time sequence. If there is sufficient time for security to intervene, then crime was not spontaneous or random. Generally, if all three phases of the attack occur within a few seconds, then it follows that there was insufficient time to prevent the event, making the crime unpreventable and probably spontaneous or random.

In assessing the viability of this matrix in terms of its ability to affect crime decision making, it is important to ask certain questions: Are security policies and methods in place at the property or business? If they are in place, are they fully implemented and assessed? Is there documentation to support the adherence to these policies and methods, along with their continued viability? These questions go to critical principles. For example, simply having a security policy or a security method may not be an effective defense. It must also have been fully implemented and communicated. In addition, the mere existence of security personnel is not an effective defense. Instead, the key is whether the security officers were properly trained and continuously informed, with their feedback considered. These factors must be supported with ongoing documentation.

Most security surveys and risk assessments entail extensive use of checklists. In order to get more sense of the scope of these tools, the following items are typically assessed. Keep in mind that these items are also often assessed in post-incident assessments, because this information is critical in determining whether a property or business owner contributed to a reasonably safe environment.

One key factor in conducting a security survey or risk assessment is to think of the protected property in terms of its threats and corresponding risks to assets within the environment. In order to protect assets from known threats, it is necessary to implement controls to counter the threats. These controls typically are subdivided into three general categories: personnel management, technology and information security, and physical security. Each of these categories has its own set of applicable controls. However, as with other aspects of security, these controls must be integrated into a cohesive mixture of policies, personnel, and technology. This integration is often pictured as "layers" of security. These layers are designed to provide protection for diverse assets against different threats.

When assessing physical security, the goal is to provide layers of security. These layers can be pictured as circles that extend progressively inward from the perimeter of the property. Indeed, as the threats become more lethal, the desire may be to expand the perimeter even beyond the property line. As will be articulated in subsequent chapters of this book, one of the ways that the outer perimeter is being expanded is to employ security personnel and security technologies in the public way. Suffice to state at this point, the more the perimeter is expanded with security controls, the greater the ability to control threats to the protected facility. Hence, think of the perimeter in terms of the classical historical example, where the thick and high walls of the castle were encircled by a mote filled with water and even predatory fish. While this perimeter does little to prevent crime from those who belong within the environment, such as employees, clients, customers, and vendors, it does provide the initial layer of protection for the environment. Consequently, it is often critical to expand the perimeter as far beyond the protected facility as possible, and to control access within this perimeter to only allow people who have a legitimate purpose for entrance.

This perimeter of the property represents the first layer or the large concentric circle. As one moves inward from the perimeter, there should be various security methods used to control access to protected assets. These security methods include security personnel and personnel policies. These aspects will be addressed in other chapters. As to the physical security methods, the following should be inspected. In this inspection, the condition and functionality of each aspect must be thoroughly documented.[118]

1. Fencing—includes barbed wire or decorative fences
2. Doors/locks have a wide variety of designs and application, including:
    a. Combination locks
    b. Dead bolts and chains
    c. Electronic door contacts
    d. Panic bars
    e. Card access
    f. Peepholes
    g. Revolving door/man trap devices
3. Windows—protective and privacy designs include:
    a. Glass break detectors
    b. Shades/curtains/blinds
    c. Bars
    d. Shatter resistant coverings
    e. Bullet/bomb-resistant glass

4. Cameras and video surveillance systems—including recording procedures and capabilities
5. Lighting—including standards for different areas, such as parking lots and common areas
6. Motion detectors—including infrared, heat-detecting types
7. Metal detectors—including handheld and walk-through models
8. Explosive detectors—including dogs and various technologies
9. Communication devices—including the following:
   a. Phones (cell, hardwire, satellite, walkie-talkie)
   b. Emergency call-boxes and intercoms
   c. Burglary and holdup alarms
   d. Door buzzers
   e. Pendent devices
   f. Central station or control center
10. Access control devices and methods—this entails a climate of watchfulness, including:
    a. Guard/reception desk
    b. Exterior door controls (piggybacking)
    c. Positioning of furniture, aisles, displays, etc.
    d. Resistance barriers
    e. Height/depth of counters
    f. Number of access points
    g. Signage (trespassing and other notices)
    h. Shrubbery types and placement
    i. Natural barriers designed into landscape
    j. Jersey barriers and other structural barriers
    k. Visitor/patient/client/ escort policies and procedures
    l. Identification and badging policies and technologies
11. Assess the adequacy of security personnel, including:
    a. Number of guards on staff and on duty during typical shift
    b. Background of security personnel and extent of background check
    c. Age and physical condition of the security personnel
    d. Wage levels of security personnel by rank
    e. Nature and scope of training and related documentation
    f. Area patrolled plus the frequency of patrols and the functions involved
    g. Equipment used and carried by security personnel
    h. Uniform type and condition

POST-INCIDENT ASSESSMENTS

In the event of a crime or other misconduct within the protected facility, it is critical that proactive assessments be part of the response plan.

Particularly if the crime is of a violent nature, there is often much confusion and disruption associated with the incident. This can create stress for the organization's employees, customers, and decision makers. Indeed, the involvement of police, media, and prosecutors is likely to exasperate an already stressful situation. Thus, confusion will typically rule the day. As a result, it is critical that decision makers take an active role in the response. While it is obviously necessary to tend to the needs of the people affected, it is equally vital to consider the effect of the incident on business continuity, organizational morale, and public relations, to name a few key concerns. Unfortunately, even while these issues are being addressed, the liability exposure related to the incident must also be considered.

The extent and scope of the response will depend on the situation at hand. When this response is being considered, it is useful to think in terms of what a jury would see at a trial. Some readers may see this as a rather clinical or even callous view of a response plan, particularly when the incident involves injuries or deaths. However, from my perspective, the sooner one places the matter into a civil liability context, the more professional and appropriate the response is likely to be. This assertion requires further elaboration.

Suppose that a robbery at the business results in the murder of an employee. As tragic as this event is to the employee's family, friends, and coworkers, it also represents substantial potential for liability exposure. The sooner the event is viewed as a liability, the more likely that rational thinking will prevail over emotion. Granted, it is necessary to accept and endure some measure of emotion and grieving. Emotion is indeed necessary and appropriate for the grieving process. This being said, corporate decision makers must relatively quickly begin to assess the crime from the perspective of a trial.

In this scenario, of course, it is critical that the business work closely with police during the initial and investigative stages of the crime. It is suggested that corporate security personnel, or even security consultants, participate at some level with the police investigation. While the level of cooperation often depends upon the seriousness of the crime and the skill levels of the parties and agencies involved, some basic principles may help guide the response plan.

The first principle is to treat all parties affected by the event with dignity. Obviously, this entails sympathy and care for the injured or the family of those who died. This empathy should be sincere and manifested in personal, humane, and financial ways. It is important to include coworkers, customers, and others who may have been affected by the crime. Showing empathy enhances the sense of dignity for all involved. Empathy can be shown in any number of ways from personal visits to providing food and flowers; giving employees time off from work; paying for medical, rehabilitation, or burial costs; and by genuinely respecting and caring for the needs of those affected. This level of concern should be shown regardless of whether litigation is anticipated or even if it is threatened. In other words, do the right thing not because it may help avoid litigation, but rather simply because it is the right thing to do.

Indeed, even if the incident results in litigation, demonstrating empathy and respect to all those affected is likely to have a positive impact on the jury. The jury will know that the company cared about those affected by the crime. It is not a far stretch to connect this post-incident approach with the attitude taken by the company prior to the crime. In this sense, if you care about people after the crime, a jury will be more willing to accept that you cared about the well being of people prior to the crime. This has a positive effect on both the liability assessment and on the damage phase of the trial.

The second principle is to attend to the dignity of those involved without getting enmeshed in the cause(s) or the blame for the crime. This is particularly relevant to the victim and the family of the victim. It is inevitable that during the trauma and grieving related to the crime, emotions will turn to assign blame for the crime. Company representatives must not get involved in discussions about who was to blame, what "caused" the crime, or how it could or should have been prevented. It is critical to stay away from these issues. However, if some response is impossible to avoid, then the blame for the crime should be placed on the perpetrator of the crime. If this is deemed appropriate, it should be firmly asserted and then dropped. Do not dwell on this issue. Instead, focus the conversation and attention to the needs of the victim, and the well-being of those affected. It is unwise to dwell on the "blame game." It can be problematic to both the potential for and the implications of future litigation. Consequently, the best practice is to focus on human needs, not human emotions.

The third principle is that the response should mirror the methods and theories of the potential lawsuit. Indeed, whether or not a lawsuit is anticipated, the best practice is to prepare for one as soon as professionally possible. This assertion holds true for the company where the harm occurred as well as for the injured party. Whether the party involved is the potential defendant or the potential plaintiff, I recommend engaging a security expert to investigate and systematize the relevant facts of the incident as soon as possible. This assertion is almost the exact opposite of what is typical. More often than not, both sides typically wait until the last possible moment to engage an expert. Often, the reason for the delay is financial, since both sides do not want to spend money until they have to. The natural human tendency to hope that litigation will not be necessary is often involved. Unfortunately, both justifications are illogical and are generally unrealistic.

The failure to engage an expert immediately after the incident almost inevitably results in a tactical and strategic failure. From a tactical perspective, a prompt and professional response strongly demonstrates that the event is being taken seriously. Ironically, when a party fails to engage professional resources to deal with the situation, this lack of response sends the worst possible message. The other party will read this message either as "you do not care how this occurred" or "you are not willing to prevent this from happening again." Conversely, the party that responds promptly and professionally, sends a message that speaks from a position of strength: If a lawsuit is filed, the defendant or the plaintiff (depending upon who is initiating the response) will have a decided advantage. This advantage is based on the evidence and analysis that will be in place to defend or prosecute the case.

From a strategic perspective, the collection and analysis of the facts and circumstances immediately following the incident is critical for evidentiary purposes. For example, the more time that passes after the incident, the less value photographs, interviews, and site inspections will be. Indeed, a direct counter to these untimely investigative techniques will inevitably be made. Even if the police use and document these same investigative techniques, the expert will be required to defend his or her opinions when based on such evidentiary material. Of course, experts are often forced to base their opinions on these secondary sources, such as police investigative material. From the perspective of the expert, and of "best evidence" practice as articulated in civil procedure, it is certainly advantageous for experts to base opinions on their own work product and on firsthand observations.[119] Consequently, the engagement of the expert immediately following the incident will facilitate the timely collection and documentation of facts and circumstances as they existed at the time of the incident in question, or shortly thereafter.

With these principles articulated, there are numerous investigative or consultative methods that can be addressed. Depending upon the specific facts and circumstances, some of the items that follow may be irrelevant, while others may need to be delved into more extensively. In any case, these items are listed to provide more specific guidance beyond the underlying principles. Included in these techniques are the physical security measures itemized above in the pre-incident assessments. These techniques coupled with the following items should be considered:[120]

1. Conduct title searches of the property (vehicle, real, and personal) involved in the incident. These title searches should also include inquiries into prior ownership and recent transactions, prior criminal incidents, security measures previously used, and any other information related to the property.
2. Collect and analyze police reports and crime information. This entails the following:
    a. Police case, arrest, investigative supplementary reports
    b. Crime scene sketches and photos
    c. Dispatch logs and 911 tapes
    d. Copies of witness statements
    e. Crime data for the location and surrounding area
    f. Police case, arrest, investigative and supplementary reports for prior crimes at this location and similar crimes in the surrounding area
    g. Uniform Crime Reports (UCR) for crime data in area
    h. Crime reporting and trend analysis through CAP Index or a similar firm

   i. Policies and procedures of the company, particularly those relating to security
   j. Security incident reports or documents related to prior crimes or complaints of misconduct or security concerns
   k. Any other relevant information and data related to the incident
3. Collect newspaper articles related to the incident (headlines or news reports can be excellent and powerful exhibits for a jury)
4. Obtain census data on relevant factors including the following:
   a. Unemployment rates
   b. Poverty levels
   c. Property values, businesses, and locations in the area
   d. Demographic makeup of the community
5. Obtain industry/trade journals and periodicals that contain the following:
   a. Crime prevention articles
   b. Past articles on crimes similar to the incident in question
   c. Industry standards for security and crime issues
6. If security personnel were employed at the location, consider evidence of their security practices and standards, such as the following:
   a. Hiring policies and practices (including background checks and employment criteria)
   b. Training policies and standards (including any related documentation)
   c. Personnel file of security officers and supervisors present at the scene
   d. Company policies and procedures relating to the administration and operation of the firm (contract security) or of the security department (proprietary security)
   e. Post orders and other site-specific security methods (including any related documentation)
   f. Time and attendance policies and related documentation
   g. Crime and incident reporting policies and procedures (including any related documentation)
   h. Contract and related legal documents (if contract security firm)
   i. Bargaining unit agreement and related documents (if unionized employees)
7. Assess whether any building or health code violations or deficiencies are present at the location or have previously been filed at this location
8. Obtain blueprints, surveys, and/or aerial photos of the location
9. Conduct site surveillance, record and note the following:
   a. Type and method of security measures used
   b. Hours and methods of security posts and patrols

   c. Number and appearance of security personnel
   d. Relative visibility of security personnel and measures in light of the traffic patterns and frequency of visitors, customers, and employees
   e. Presence of loitering teens, suspected gang members, or drug transactions
   f. Presence of disorderly conditions such as noisy individuals, loud music, reckless or excessive vehicle use and operations
10. Conduct site inspection, record and note the following:
   a. Initial walk-through to gain perspective
   b. Photo and/or video record the property and crime scene
   c. Consider blind spots, hiding areas, and design features of the property
   d. Assess appearance of the property, including presence of graffiti; alcoholic beverage containers; containers and wrappers commonly used for illicit and illegal drugs; broken windows, trash, or other evidence of disorderly conditions
   e. Record the activity in adjacent and surrounding areas, including any commercial activity, any disorderly conditions, and the security measures and personnel used (if any)
   f. Create site plan and note all relevant features
11. Interview all relevant parties including the property managers and previous owners, reporting and investigating police officers, security officers and supervisor present at time, and any witnesses and the victim(s) (if possible), seeking the following information:
   a. The sequences and circumstances of the crime
   b. Prior criminal activity
   c. Prior security-related complaints
   d. Prior security-related incidents
   e. Knowledge of any previous lawsuits
   f. Information of any changes in security methods or personnel (prior to crime)
   g. Information of any changes in security methods or personnel (subsequent to crime)
   h. Information relating to former owners, tenants, or businesses at location
   i. Any concerns about security or personal observations prior to the crime
12. Interview offender(s) if possible, asking the following questions:
   a. Did you act alone or with others (who were the others)?
   b. What factors influenced your decision to commit the crime (victim perceived as easy mark, ease of escape, remote or isolated location, site lines, lack of security, or lighting, etc.)?
   c. Were you loitering on the premises before crime (how long, who present, where, etc.)?

d. Had you visited the location previously (day, week, month—frequency)?
e. Did you notice any security measures, such as cameras, guards, cash handling, access controls, etc?
f. How long did it take to commit the crime, how long did you think about committing the crime?
g. What is the frequency of crime in the area?
h. Have you committed any previous crimes at that location?
i. Have you committed any similar crime at another location?
j. Is there any other relevant information that would shed light on the incident and the decision to commit the crime at this location?

In summary, the desire is to obtain as much information about the location, the circumstances surrounding the crime and the criminal decision, including any information of previous crimes in and around the location. As this information is collected, documented, and analyzed, consider criminological theories, threat and risk assessment methods, security measures, and relevant legal theories and elements as the cause of action (or possible cause of action). The goal is to understand everything possible about why the offender decided to commit the crime and the sequence of its commission, what features and history of the environment may have contributed to the crime, how security measures may have contributed to or prevented the crime, where the offender and security measures were located, and similar questions. The engagement of these questions, through documents, information, and analysis, is the goal of this process.

LEGAL DEFENSES AND THEORIES

This section will complete the analysis related to premises liability or negligent security. As articulated above, the assessment of these claims requires a pre- and post-incident analysis that considers the facts of the case in light of the legal standards used by the relevant state court to determine liability. While there is no perfectly objective way to accomplish this challenging task, the more one can articulate relevant facts to applicable legal tests, the better the chance of a successful litigation. Indeed, the better you understand the legal standards of your state, the more suitable your security methods should be. This interrelationship between the facts, the law, and security methods manifests itself throughout this book. The effective application of these principles and this interrelationship in real life circumstances requires a delicate balance between the art and the science of security law.

In this assessment, the difficult question is how to assess the applicable legal standard in relation to the crime versus the duty of care imposed upon property owners to protect those who are affected by the crime. In legal terms, this is often decided based on the concept of foreseeability. Most people would agree that this is both an objective and subjective consideration. The objective aspect is to use one's life experiences to determine what a reasonable person would do in any given circumstance. The subjective aspect is the particular bias or "worldview" each person possesses. While the legal system seeks to limit, if not negate, subjective considerations in favor of an objective standard, it is virtually impossible to completely eliminate the bias contained in all people. Indeed, the system tacitly acknowledges the implications of subjective considerations when it allows jury consultants to help litigation attorneys select a jury. Of course, these consultants attempt to populate the jury based on personal characteristics favorable to the particular litigant (either plaintiff or defendant). Further, procedural techniques such as venue and forum can be used to steer the trial toward a particular demographic (e.g., socioeconomic, racial, cultural, etc.) that reflects characteristics of one of the parties to the lawsuit. Finally, jury selection techniques such as pre-emptory challenges and jury questionnaires are also designed to screen juries with actual or potential biases from the trial. In any event, the key here is to understand that the legal system seeks to facilitate objective standards, but it cannot completely eliminate subjective considerations.

This issue of objective versus subjective often becomes relevant in security-related claims, particularly in the application of the legal standard and of legal defenses. In terms of foreseeability, which is a critical component of duty, there are many in urban America who deem crime as a natural result of human interaction. These people often see and hear of crime, particularly in new reports, on a daily basis. To those with this worldview, crime is foreseeable because it is around them every day. In terms of foreseeability, this cuts both ways. Those who see almost all crime as "foreseeable" generally view the use of security methods to counter crime from one of two extreme perspectives. Either they regard security methods as useless (since crime is inevitable) or their demand for them is limitless (in a desperate attempt to control crime). The "proper" amount of security, of course, is somewhere between none and Fort Knox. This determination is at least partly dependent on one's worldview.

Conversely, there are still people in this country who are "shocked" when a crime occurs on their block or in their work site. These people tend to live their lives with the subjective notion that crime does not happen here. Indeed, crime is something that will "not happen to me." To these people, crime is the plight of others, typically the downtrodden, the poor, and the lower classes. While it is statistically true that crime, particularly violent and predatory crime, occurs in poor communities at a higher rate than other socioeconomic areas, the threat of crime is not limited to poor areas. Indeed, some criminals target more affluent communities and businesses because the assets are greater and are more commonplace. Consequently, the relationship between worldview and the legal standard of foreseeability must be considered.

This relationship is minimized in civil litigation because the issue of foreseeability is often a legal question for the court. This means the judge may be asked, through either a motion to dismiss or a motion for summary judgment, to assess this question as a matter of law. Hence, each of the legal standards articulated in this chapter can be initially decided by the trial judge. In practice, the trial judge is to assess the facts derived from the lawsuit (such as deposition testimony, affidavits, and documentary evidence) along with the assertions in the complaint in making this determination. This question is most typically determined in the summary judgment stage of the litigation. The standard for summary judgment is whether "any genuine issues of material fact exist."[121] The court is to rule as a matter of law to determine whether the plaintiff has presented enough evidence to allow the case to go to the jury. This is designed to filter out cases that are not supported by the requisite amount or scope of facts compared to the legal standard in the state. In legal parlance, this is known as "surviving summary judgment." The key assessment in premises liability or negligent security cases is whether the legal standard of duty—usually through foreseeability—has been demonstrated by the plaintiff. Indeed, it is the plaintiff's burden to show this.

In theory, the judge makes this determination without personal bias, and in accord with the legal standards established in the state. However, there are dilemmas that arise when one compares theory with practice.

First, as evidenced by the legal standards presented earlier, the application of legal standards is somewhat fluid and artful. It is fluid because courts are still crafting standards to reflect the "public policy" of the state. In this way, the legal standard operates as a baseline for courts to determine when and how business and property owners are liable for the crimes of others. This determination encompasses a myriad of potential factors. Indeed, what constitutes "sound" public policy is a rather nebulous combination of politics, economics, education, urban planning, and a host of other disciplines. In this sense, the worldview and biases of the decision makers are inevitably attached to this policy determination.

The legal standard for liability from crime may be lower in a liberal state. In this mind-set, public policy and legal decision makers would be more inclined to accept the notion that responsibility should be shifted to others who have the financial resources to care for others—particularly innocent victims of a crime. Conversely, in more conservative states, public policy considerations and the applicable legal standard may focus on the notion of personal responsibility and accountability. This may be extended to those victims of crimes, even if they may not have been able to prevent the crime by their own devices. From this point of view, those who have contributed to the occurrence of the crime, through their own negligence or improper decision making, are less apt to find "public policy" reasons to provide them with a legal benefit. Consequently, the appropriate application of legal standards based on public policy considerations is a very difficult assessment, replete with a complicated mixture of sophisticated disciplines and personal and judicial preferences. As will be demonstrated throughout this book, a similar combination of diverse and difficult assessments must be made on the "proper" application of security methods.

Second, the assessment of appropriate legal standards may be ambiguous because these cases are very fact-specific. As with any discipline that is fact-specific, the ability to discern definitive standards is complicated by the mix of facts involved in the assessment. Since facts do not always line up clearly, they are often hard to classify according to a legal standard. By way of example, consider the question of foreseeability. Aside from the different standards used by different states, typically the answer to this question requires the court to consider the number and types of prior crimes, the extent of crime in the larger community, the difficulty involved in preventing the particular crime, the nature of the business, the security methods typical in the particular industry, and numerous other factors. Getting an accurate assessment of all these factors, and then cleanly articulating them into an objective legal standard, is an intellectual challenge for courts and for the legal system.

Going beyond this challenge, another consideration in security cases relates to legal defenses. Legal defenses are factual assertions designed to limit or negate liability. In essence, they are affirmatively pled facts that go to the question of the existence or the amount of liability. In order to have a legal defense available, the defendant would have to plead the specific defense in its answer to the plaintiff's complaint. The timing of this assertion typically occurs at the filing of the answer, or later in an amended answer. While the procedural requirements of legal defenses are beyond the scope of this book, it is sufficient to understand that legal defenses must be affirmatively pled in order to be applicable. The most common defenses in security-related claims are contributory negligence and assumption of risk.

Contributory negligence is the failure of the plaintiff to exercise due care for his or her own safety. This defense is similar to the duty imposed on the defendant. In each instance, the actor is required to exercise the requisite care as a reasonable and prudent person under the circumstances. As we have seen earlier, the defendant has a duty to the plaintiff based on this standard. In the defense of contributory negligence, the plaintiff has a duty to exercise caution for his or her own safety, as any other reasonable and prudent person is required to do. In this sense, the plaintiff has a duty to protect him or herself. When the plaintiff fails to do so, the defense may be applicable.

In contributory negligence states, if the plaintiff is deemed more than 50 percent negligent, then he or she is barred from recovery. In making this assessment, the difficult question is how to assess the respective degrees of fault. For example, in a litigation resulting from a robbery in an isolated section of a public parking facility, the question of contributory negligence may manifest itself in various ways. In this assessment, the actions or inactions of the plaintiff may be relevant. Did the plaintiff pay attention to the circumstances as he or she approached the vehicle, or was the plaintiff blissfully ignorant of the approaching offender? Did the plaintiff have the vehicle keys ready to enter the vehicle, or was he or she fumbling through pockets and purse compartments for keys? Did the plaintiff ask for an escort from security personnel or parking attendants? Did the plaintiff park in an isolated section of the facility because that was the only spot available, or was it a decision based on the desire to keep the vehicle from being dented by others entering and existing their vehicles? These questions, and may others, illustrate that there is no "clean" way to differentiate, for example, whether the plaintiff may have been 40 percent or 60 percent negligent in any given fact pattern.

With this analysis, the degree of negligence assigned to the plaintiff is then deducted from the jury award. For example, if the jury finds liability totaling $100,000.00, with a finding of 30 percent contributory to the plaintiff, then the award will be reduced by this amount ($100,000 minus $30,000 [30 percent] equals $70,000). In this formula, the finding of contributory negligence of 30 percent acts as a setoff from the total damage award. Remember, if the plaintiff is more than 50 percent negligent (in contributory negligence), there is no setoff, because any degree of negligence beyond 50 percent would negate any recovery by the plaintiff. If, however, the defendant is deemed to be willful and wanton, the plaintiff's contributory negligence will not be considered, as willful and wanton conduct serves to bar evidence of plaintiff's negligence.

Closely related to contributory negligence is comparative negligence. Comparative negligence also proportions liability based on respective fault. Unlike contributory negligence, however, there is no cutoff for degrees of negligence beyond 50 percent. Here the damage award is divided based on the degree of fault assigned to the plaintiff. In this way, the plaintiff could be deemed 70 percent negligent and still recover based on this proportional formula ($100,000 recovery minus $70,000 [70 percent] equals $30,000 award).

Another legal defense is known as assumption of risk. In this defense, the court considers whether the plaintiff voluntarily consented to encounter a known risk. Generally, in order to assert an effective defense, three elements must be shown:[122]

1. Plaintiff knew of the particular hazard
2. Plaintiff appreciated the risk of harm
3. Plaintiff willingly encountered or accepted the risk

In assessing these elements, the burden is on the defendant, who affirmatively pleads the defense, to show that the plaintiff knew of the risk, appreciated the harm it posed, and willingly accepted the risk. As is typical, these are very fact-specific assertions. There are many circumstances in which this defense is relevant. For example, consider a security firm that engages with a client to protect a property located in a high crime area.

If an employee of the security firm is subsequently injured by an armed intruder, the owner of the property would likely assert an assumption of risk defense if the employee of the security firm sued on a premises liability claim. The logic of this defense is that the security officer knew of the hazard of crime in the area, appreciated the risk, and willingly accepted such by the very nature of the employment. In essence, being employed as security to guard against known threats is part and parcel of the job. If the defendant can show this defense, this acts as a complete bar to the cause of action. Of course, in this scenario, workers' compensation statutes may also bar the tort claim.

Going beyond consideration of these defenses, the final aspect of a security law case requires some assessment of the specific legal tests within the particular jurisdiction. For example, if the case occurred in a state with a totality of the circumstances test, then the plaintiff and the defendant are required to analyze the facts in a broad light. Since this test is designed to take into account all the factors associated with the incident, any and all factors deemed relevant should be assessed. Of course, in this analysis, the plaintiff would seek to emphasize each factor that would make the crime foreseeable and preventable, while the defendant would emphasize factors that appear to make the occurrence of the crime remote, unusual, and unpreventable.

Similarly, in a known aggressor and imminent danger test, the plaintiff would emphasize factors that demonstrate the offender posed a known danger, either by past incidents, verbal threats, criminal history, or even violent propensities. On the other hand, the defendant would seek to show that any threat posed by the offender was unknown, speculative, or unconnected to the crime. In this way, both the plaintiff and the defendant must be prepared to present the facts in accordance with their position. This is so regardless of what legal test is used.

Generally speaking, the plaintiff seeks facts to illustrate that the crime was foreseeable and preventable. The defendant, conversely, seeks facts to illustrate that the crime was not foreseeable and was not preventable. In each case, both parties must be prepared to fully investigate the facts surrounding the incident. Both parties must then articulate and present the facts in light of their respective interests. This, in essence, is the nature of the adversarial system. Depending upon the position one takes of this system, the approach can be viewed as either fortunate or unfortunate.

Regardless of your particular viewpoint, one feature that is not subject to much debate is that crime creates tragic and far-reaching implications in society. The "correct" way to remedy the impact of crime poses extraordinary legal and public policy questions.

There are reasonable people and arguments on both sides of the issue. Some people desire to provide crime victims with the benefits of a liberal system designed to transfer the costs and responsibility of crime prevention to property and business owners. In this way, the costs of increased security methods are then further transferred to customers, clients, and even to insurance carriers. With this mind-set, crime victims should be provided legal remedies. These remedies, in turn, provide the incentive for the property and business owners to institute appropriate security methods. These security methods, in turn, are designed to reduce crime in and around the property or the business. The costs of this increased crime prevention, in turn, are passed on to the customer and client of the property or business. The reduced incidence of crime from these security methods, in turn, results in lower insurance claims, due to the reduction in the number and seriousness of claims. The reduction costs of insurance claims, in turn, results in lower premiums to the property and business owner. In essence, those who share this perspective believe that markets forces will serve to reduce the incidence of crime, without adversely affecting the legal and economic system. This, they would argue, is good public policy!

Viewed from a more conservative perspective, the argument against making property and business owners liable for the crimes of others rests on the notion of accountability and individual responsibility. According to this argument, the criminal is the person responsible for the crime, not the property or business owner. By imposing liability against those not responsible for the crime, the legal system is creating a perverse result—making innocent parties responsible for the criminal acts of third parties. This, it is argued, provides a disincentive for people to take steps to protect themselves. In this way, the potential crime victim may not take his or her own security as seriously, since someone will be liable for the damages created by the criminal. Furthermore, the notion that someone should "step into the shoes" of the criminal and pay for the consequences of criminal conduct simply fosters a "welfare state" mentality, in which the victims of society constantly seek people to pay for their plight. Indeed, those who oppose premises liability and negligent security argue that even government has largely disavowed liability for failure to prevent crime. If government, with its resources and policing agencies, cannot prevent crime, why should property and business owners have to pay for the failure to prevent crime?

As evidenced by these contrasting arguments, there are compelling points to be made on both sides of the debate. Notwithstanding the merits of either argument, this book seeks to present the subject of security law in an even-handed, comprehensive manner. Given my background, I tend to be more aware of the need for security than others. Indeed, many in this society have not experienced the effects and implications of crime firsthand. Many, if not most, have not studied the issues surrounding crime and security. As such, I come at this subject with a worldview and bias toward security.

This worldview, however, has been tempered by years of study and thoughtful analysis. In developing my understanding of crime and security, I have tried to deal with the issues and implications involved in a dispassionate, almost clinical manner. My use of the word *dispassionate* here reflects my efforts to remain impartial about security issues rather than a lack of passion for the subject. In fact, I have a passionate interest in keeping people safe and secure. Nevertheless, the study of crime and security requires the ability to step away from the emotions prompted by the effects of crime on its victims and its implications for society. This clinical understanding of the issues and implications involved in security is the key to dealing with them effectively. This is not to say that the plight of the crime victims does not matter. Nothing could be further from the truth. It is to say, however, that decisions about crime and security should be made with reasoned, prudent analysis—with logic and facts—instead of emotion and fear. As will be made plain in this book, the threat of terrorism only further emphasizes the truth of this assertion. Indeed, terrorism is *designed* to promote fear and emotional responses. Hopefully, this book will enable the reader, and a future generation of leaders, to effectively deal with the notion of security and crime, including the implications of terrorism.

NOTES

1. Robbins, Stephen P. (2003). *Organizational Behavior* (10th ed.). Upper Saddle River, NJ: Prentice Hall; and Clifford, Mary (2004). *Identifying and Exploring Security Essentials*, Upper Saddle River, NJ: Prentice Hall.
2. Pastor, James F. (2003). *The Privatization of Police in America: An Analysis and Case Study*. Jefferson, NC: McFarland and Company.
3. Oliver, Willard M. (2004). *Community-Oriented Policing: A Systematic Approach to Policing* (3rd ed.). Upper Saddle River, NJ: Prentice Hall.
4. Pastor op cit. at 33. Also see Nemeth, Charles P. (1989). *Private Security and the Law.* Cincinnati, OH: Anderson Publishing Company; and Shearing, Clifford D., and Phillip C. Stenning (1983). Private Security: Implications for Social Control. *Social Problems* 30 (5).
5. Pastor op cit. at 34. Also see Reynolds, Morgan O. (1994). Using the Private Sector to Deter Crime. *National Center for Policy Analysis,* March; and Benson, Bruce L. (1990). *The Enterprise of Law: Justice Without State.* San Francisco, CA: Pacific Research Institute for Public Policy.
6. Pastor op cit. at 34. Also see Johnston, Les (1992). *The Rebirth of Private Policing*. London: Routledge.
7. Reynolds op cit. at 2.
8. Johnston op cit. at 2.
9. Pastor op cit. at 34.
10. Ibid at 34.
11. Pastor op cit. at 34–35; Nemeth op cit. at 2; and Benson op cit. at 12.
12. Pastor op cit. at 35; and Nemeth op cit. at 2.
13. Pastor op cit. at 35.
14. Pastor op cit. at 35; and Nemeth op cit. at 3.
15. Pastor op cit. at 35; and Nemeth op cit. at 3.
16. Pastor op cit. at 36; and Reynolds op cit. at 3.
17. Pastor op cit. at 36; Nemeth op cit. at 3; and Benson op cit. at 74. Also see Warner, Sam Bass (1968). *The Private City.* Philadelphia: University of Pennsylvania Press.

18. Warner op cit. at 78; and Pastor op cit. at 36. Also see Spitzer, Steven and Andrew T. Scull (1977). Privatization and Capitalist Development: The Case for Private Police. *Social Problems* 25 (1): pp. 18–28; and Miller, Wilbur R. (1977). *Cops and Bobbies: Police Authority in New York and London, 1830–1870*. Chicago: University of Chicago Press.
19. Warner op cit. at 80; and Pastor op cit. at 36.
20. Pastor op cit. at 38; and Nemeth op cit. at 6–7.
21. Nemeth op cit at 6–7; and Pastor op cit. at 38.
22. Pastor op cit. at 38; and Spitzer and Scull op cit. at 21.
23. Spitzer and Scull op cit. at 45; and Pastor op cit. at 38.
24. Pastor op cit. at 36; Johnston op cit. at 24; and Miller op cit. at 3.
25. Miller op cit. at 3.
26. Miller op cit. at 3; and Pastor op cit. at 36.
27. Reynolds op cit. at 1; and Pastor op cit. at 68.
28. Reynolds op cit. at 1 and Pastor op cit. at 68.
29. Reynolds op cit. at 1 and Pastor op cit. at 68.
30. Pastor op cit. at 69.
31. Gordon, Corey and William Brill (1996). The Expanding Role of Crime Prevention Through Environmental Design in Premises Liability. *National Institute of Justice,* April.
32. See Covington, Jeanette and Ralph B. Taylor (1991). Fear of Crime in Urban Residential Neighborhoods: Implication of Between and Within Neighborhood Sources for Current Models. *The Sociological Quarterly* 32 (2): pp. 231–249; Lewis, Dan A. and Michael G. Maxfield (1980). Fear in the Neighborhoods: An Investigation of the Impact of Crime. *Journal of Research in Crime and Delinquency,* July, pp. 160–189; and Kelling, George (1995). Reduce Serious Crime by Restoring Order. *The American Enterprise,* May/June.
33. McLennan, Barbara N., ed. (1970). *Crime in Urban Society.* London: Cambridge University Press.
34. Cohen, Lawrence E., and Marcus Felson (1979). Social Change and Crime Rate Trends. *American Sociological Review* 44: pp. 588–607.
35. Felson, Marcus (2002). *Crime and Everyday Life*. Thousand Oaks, CA: Sage Publications.
36. Gibbs, Jack P. and Maynart L. Erickson (1976). Crime Rates of American Cities in an Ecological Context. *American Journal of Sociology* 82: pp. 605–620.
37. Jackson, Pamela Irving (1984). Opportunity and Crime: A Function of City Size. *Sociology and Social Research* 68 (2): pp. 173–193.
38. Lewis and Maxfield op cit. at 187; and Pastor op cit. at 54.
39. Lewis and Maxfield op cit. at 162; and Pastor op cit. at 54.
40. Covington and Taylor op cit. at 232; and Pastor op cit. at 55.
41. Pastor op cit. at 55.
42. Fisher, Bonnie and Jack L. Nasar (1995). Fear Spots in Relation to Micro-level Physical Cues: Exploring the Overlooked. *Journal of Research in Crime and Delinquency* 32 (2): pp. 214–239.
43. Fisher and Nasar op cit. at 234–235; and Pastor op cit. at 56.
44. Pastor op cit. at 56.
45. Kelling op cit. at 36; and Pastor op cit. at 56.
46. Pastor op cit. at 56.
47. Pastor op cit. at 57. Also see Bazyler, Michael J. (1979). The Duty to Provide Adequate Protection: Landowners' Liability for Failure to Protect Patrons from Criminal Attack. *Arizona Law Review* (21): pp. 727–737.

48. Kaplan, Robert (1994). The Coming Anarchy. *The Atlantic Monthly,* February.
49. Pastor op cit. at 57; and Kelling op cit. at 25. Also see Moore, Mark H., and Robert C. Trojanowicz (1988). Perspectives on Policing: Corporate Strategies for Policing. *National Institute of Justice,* Office of Justice Programs, November; and Palango, Paul (1998). On the Mean Streets: As the Police Cut Back, Private Cops Are Moving In. *MacLeans,* 111 (2), January 12; Robinson, Matthew (1997). Why the Good News on Crime. *Investor's Business Daily,* April 30; Seamon, Thomas M. (1995). Private Forces for Public Good. *Security Management,* September; Kolpacki, Thomas A. (1994). Neighborhood Watch: Public/Private Liaison. *Security Management,* November; Spencer, Suzy (1997). Private Security. Onpatrol.com/cs.pivsec.html; Cox, Steven M. (1990). Policing into the 21st Century. *Police Studies* 13 (4): pp. 168–177.
50. Pastor op cit. at 58.
51. Pastor op cit. at 58. Also see Chanken, Marcia and Jan Chaiken (1987). Public Policing—Privately Provided. *National Institute of Justice,* Office of Justice Programs, June; and Cunningham, William C., John J. Strauchs, and Clifford W. Van Meter (1991). Private Security: Patterns and Trends. *National Institute of Justice,* Office of Justice Programs, August.
52. Kolpacki op cit. at 47; and Pastor op cit. at 58.
53. Pastor op cit. at 58.
54. Ibid at 58–59.
55. Bazyler op cit. at 736–737.
56. Bazyler op cit. at 733. Also see Davey, Caroline L., Andrew B. Wootton, Rachel Cooper, and Mike Press (2005). Design Against Crime: Extending the Reach of Crime Prevention Through Environmental Design. *Security Journal* 18 (2): pp. 3951; and McKay, Tom (2004). How Are Behavior, Crime and Design Related? *Security Management,* May.
57. Gordon and Brill op cit. at 5.
58. See for example, *McClung v. Wal-Mart,* 270 F. 3d 1007 (6th Cir. 2001).
59. Thompson, Michael (1986). Cutting Your Security Risk. *Security Management,* September.
60. Cunningham et al. op cit. at 1–2; and Pastor op cit. at 42.
61. Cunningham et al. op cit. at 2; and Pastor op cit. at 42.
62. Cunningham et al. op cit. at 2; and Pastor op cit. at 42.
63. Bailin, Paul (2000). Gazing into Security's Future. *Security Management,* November.
64. Clifford op cit. at 304; and Pastor op cit. at 42. Also see Zielinski, Mike (1999). Armed and Dangerous: Private Police on the March. *Covert Action Quarterly.* Caq.com/caq/caq54p.police.html.
65. Perez, Evan (2002). Demand for Security Still Promises Profit. *The Wall Street Journal,* April 9.
66. National Policy Summit: Building Private Security/Public Policing Partnerships to Prevent and Respond to Terrorism and Public Disorder, *Community Oriented Policing Services,* U.S. Department of Justice, 2004.
67. Benson, Bruce (1997). Privatization in Criminal Justice. *National Institute of Justice,* Office of Justice Programs.
68. Zielinski op cit. at 1; and Pastor op cit. at 42.
69. DuCanto, Joseph N. (1999). Establishment of Police and Private Security Liaison. Manuscript presented at the 45th annual seminar of the American Society of Industrial Security, Las Vegas, NV, September 27–30.
70. Perez op cit. at 4; Pastor op cit. at 42–43, and www.securitasgroup.com.

71. Ibid, and www.g4s.com.
72. Bailin op cit. at 12; Cunningham et al. op cit. at 1; and Pastor op cit. at 44.
73. Walinsky, Adam (1993). The Crisis of Public Order. *The Atlantic Monthly,* July.
74. Walinsky op cit. at 40; and Pastor op cit. at 43.
75. Walinsky op cit. at 40; and Pastor op cit. at 43.
76. Pastor op cit. at 44; and Zielinski op cit. at 1. Also see Carlson, Tucker (1995). Safety Inc.: Private Cops Are There When You Need Them. *Policy Review* 73, Summer; and Goldberg, Ceil (1994). New Roles for Private Patrols. *Security Management,* December.
77. Tolchin, Martin (1985). Private Guards Get New Role in Public Law Enforcement. *The New York Times,* November 29.
78. Walinsky op cit. at 44; and Cunningham et al, op cit. at 2. Also see West, Marty L. (1993). Get a Piece of the Privatization Pie. *Security Management,* March; and Dilulio, John J. (1995). Ten Facts About Crime. *National Institute of Justice,* Office of Justice Programs, January 16.
79. Benson, Bruce L. (1990). *The Enterprise of Law: Justice Without State.* San Francisco, CA: Pacific Research Institute for Public Policy.
80. Goldberg op cit. at 12; and Pastor op cit. at 44.
81. Kolpacki op cit. at 47; and Pastor op cit. at 44.
82. National Policy Summit: Building Private Security/Public Policing Partnerships to Prevent and Respond to Terrorism and Public Disorder, *Community Oriented Policing Services,* U.S. Department of Justice, 2004.
83. Schramm, Jennifer (2004). Feeling Safe. *HR Magazine,* May.
84. Taken from Booz-Allen Hamilton website on September 16, 2002 at www.boozallen.com.
85. *Security Management* (2002) October.
86. Lockwood, Nancy R. (2005). Crisis Management in Today's Business Environment: HR's Strategic Role. *SHRM Research Quarterly* (4).
87. Ibid at 2.
88. Maseda, Mike (2005). How to Ensure You're Not Courting Workplace Litigation. *San Antonio Business Journal,* May 30.
89. Ibid.
90. Kaufman, Uri (1990). When Crime Pays: Business Landlords' Duty to Protect Customers from Criminal Acts Committed on the Premises. *South Texas Law Review* 31 (89).
91. Bazyler op cit. at 734.
92. Sharp, Rex A. (1987). Paying for the Crimes of Others? Landowner Liability for Crimes on the Premises. *South Texas Law Review* 29 (11).
93. Bazyler op cit. at 751.
94. See for example, *Ali Sameer v. Tahir Butt,* 343 Ill. App. 3d 78, 796 N.E. 2d 1063 (2003).
95. Gordon and Brill op cit. at 4–5.
96. Sharp op cit. at 65–66; and Kaufman op cit. at 96.
97. Kaufman op cit. at 114.
98. Sharp op cit. at 65; and Kaufman op cit. at 96–96.
99. Sharp op cit. at 44.
100. See for example, *Posecai v. Wal-Mart,* 752 So. 2d 762 (1999).
101. This chart adapted from Young, Eric G. (2005). Cause of Action Against Tavern Owners, Restaurants, and Similar Businesses for Injuries Caused to

Patrons by the Criminal Acts of Others. *WestLaw:* Causes of Action Second Series, 26 Causes of Action 2d 1; and from independent research conducted by this author.

102. See for example, *Toscano-Lopez v. McDonalds,* 193 Cal. App. 3d 495 (1987).
103. *State Farm Auto Insurance Co. v. Campbell,* 538 U.S. 408 (2003); and *BMW of North America v. Gore, 517 U.S. 559 (1996).*
104. Stamatis, Peter S. and Alexander T. Muhtaris (2005). Maximizing Punitive Damages. *Illinois Bar Journal* 93, March.
105. Ibid at 21.
106. Ibid at 21.
107. Thompson op cit. at 47.
108. Homeland Security: Challenges and Strategies in Addressing Short and Long Term National Needs (2001). *General Accounting Office,* from testimony of Comptroller General David M. Walker, before the Committee on the Budget, U.S. House of Representatives.
109. Ahrens, Sean A. and Marieta B. Oglesby (2006). Levers Against Liability. *Security Management*, February.
110. ASIS International, General Security Risk Assessment (2003).
111. Homeland Security: Challenges and Strategies in Addressing Short and Long Term National Needs at 8.
112. Ibid at 12; and International Association of Professional Security Consultants (IAPSC) Forensic Methodology, Best Practices #2, June 2000.
113. Ibid at 5.
114. Ibid at 4; and Homeland Security: Challenges and Strategies in Addressing Short and Long Term National Needs at 7–8.
115. Kaufman op cit. at 118.
116. ASIS International, General Security Risk Assessment at 14.
117. Lombardi, John H. (2001). Not Guilty by Reason of Security. *Security Management*, May.
118. The items in this list were derived from various sources, including Leo, Thomas W. (1994). Site Security. *Security Concepts*, September; Yeager, Robert (1986). *The Failure to Provide Security Handbook*, Columbia, MD: Hanrow Press; Residential Security Survey (5/1975), Chicago Police Department, CPD-52.184; and International Association of Professional Security Consultants (IAPSC) Forensic Methodology, Best Practices #2, June 2000.
119. See for example, Federal Rules of Civil Procedure, Rule 703, 28 U.S.C.A.
120. Everett, Peter S. (1998). Direct Examination of Security Experts. *Trial*, March; Talley, Larry (2000). Using Experts in Premises Cases. *Trial,* April; and International Association of Professional Security Consultants (IAPSC) Forensic Methodology, Best Practices #2, June 2000.
121. See for example, *Nickelson v. Mall of America Company*, 593 N.W. 2d 723 (1999).
122. See for example, *Clarke v. Broadway Motor Trucks,* 372 F. Supp. 1342 (1990).

2

Negligent Employment Claims

NEGLIGENT HIRING

Cause of Action and Elements

Negligent hiring is a cause of action relating to the failure of an employer to properly screen an employee, who subsequently commits a crime or an act of misconduct while on the job. Generally, the employer has a duty to exercise ordinary care in hiring individuals who, because of the nature of the employment, could present a threat of harm or injury to a third party.[1] The appropriate level of care required of the employer is commensurate with the type of position for which the employee is hired. For example, if the employee conducts service calls in customers' homes or workplaces, then the potential of harm is greater than an employee who conducts internal sales calls. In this sense, it is more important to screen the employee who does service calls, as compared to the internal sales position. The elements of negligent hiring generally constitute the following:[2]

1. Employer knew or should have known that the employee had a particular unfitness for the position so as to create a danger of harm to third persons;

2. The particular unfitness was known or should have been known at the time of the employee's hiring or retention; and
3. This particular unfitness proximately caused the plaintiff's injury.

The key to this cause of action usually goes to the level of background investigation conducted by the employer. In this sense, the key question is whether a reasonable background investigation would discover a particular unfitness, such as a criminal record, a mental health commitment, or even a poor evaluation from a former employer. If so, then the court is likely to find that the employer should have known of the particular unfitness. It stands to reason, therefore, the failure to conduct any background inquiry is not an effective defense. Indeed, it is often deemed as a breach

of duty. Assuming the court would find that the unfitness should have been discovered, then the only remaining element is whether the unfitness proximately caused the injury or harm. If this causal connection is shown, then the liability for the crime or act of misconduct falls on the employer. This may be so regardless of whether the crime or act was performed in the scope of the employee's duties or to further the employer's goals. However, one other possible defense is available to the employer. Liability for the harm or injury must have been reasonably foreseeable to the employer. In any event, generally, background checks or investigations may include the following:

- Criminal convictions
- Credit checks
- Motor vehicle checks
- Verification of application information
- Personal references
- Contact persons acquainted with the applicant/employee
- Civil/bankruptcy court record searches

CASES

The following cases are actual court decisions. Certain aspects of the opinion that are not relevant to this book were edited out. The integrity of the court's decision, however, has been maintained.

356 Ill. app. 3d 642, 826 N.E.2d 1030

Appellate Court of Illinois, First District, Third Division

AISHA BROWNE, PLAINTIFF-APPELLANT v. SCR MEDICAL TRANSPORTATION SERVICES, INC., A CORPORATION, DEFENDANT-APPELLEE.

March 30, 2005

Background

Passenger brought action against medical transport company, seeking to hold company liable for driver's alleged sexual assault of passenger. The Circuit Court, Cook County, granted company's Motion for Summary Judgment. Passenger appealed.

Holdings

The appellate court held that:

1. Company did not know and could not have known of its driver's criminal history and, thus, could not be held liable in negligence to passenger; and
2. Alleged incident between medical transport company driver and passenger in which driver exposed himself and attempted to kiss passenger did not put company on notice that driver posed a danger to its passengers and did not render company liable to another passenger who allegedly was sexually assaulted by driver.

Affirmed

The contract between SCR and the CTA provided that SCR would perform certain specialized transportation services for people with disabilities and the CTA would agree to provide a subsidy to SCR for each person transported "in accordance with the terms and conditions set forth herein." The contract limited service to "those people with disabilities who are properly certified and are enrolled in the Special Services Program." According to

SCR president, Pamela Rakestraw, since SCR's inception in 1986, it has provided para-transit services to disabled persons only pursuant to written contracts.

SCR's services have never been available to the general public. Pursuant to SCR's contract with the CTA, SCR was to provide services only to disabled persons certified under the Americans with Disabilities Act of 1990, 42 U.S.C. Section 1201, and who placed a reservation with SCR for a specific trip or arranged for a prescheduled subscription service. SCR would then subject each trip request to a screening process whereby an SCR employee would check the requesting rider's computer file before scheduling a trip to determine if the passenger was eligible not only for para-transit services but also for the specific ride requested. SCR could and did refuse requests for trips from disabled persons who were either not properly certified by the CTA, who were not enrolled in the CTA's Special Services Program, or who were not eligible for the specific ride requested.

Robert Britton was hired in 1994 by a company known as Labor Leasing to become a driver for SCR. On January 5, 1995, Britton became an employee of SCR when the service agreement between Labor Leasing and SCR terminated. Pursuant to SCR's contract with the CTA, any driver in the Special Services Program must be pre-certified by the CTA. Prior to certification, SCR had to show that it applied for a criminal background check on the driver. SCR submitted Britton's name to the Illinois State Police for a background check, but did not submit his fingerprints. Pamela Rakestraw stated in her deposition that she was unaware of any law that required SCR to submit Britton's fingerprints with his background check. The background check indicated Britton had no prior convictions. Specifically, the letter stated: "Based upon the information contained in your request, no conviction information was identified. This response is not a guarantee that conviction information on this individual does not exist under other personal identities. It is common for criminals to use false names and dates of birth which will not be identified by a non-fingerprint request for conviction information.

Britton's record from the City of Chicago, Department of Police, which was made part of the record on appeal, indicates that Britton had a long criminal history of arrests, but no prior convictions before the July 1995 assault of Browne. The report also indicates that Britton used the alias "Robert Vaughn."

At Britton's discovery deposition, Britton stated he never told SCR that he had previously used the name Robert Vaughn. He further stated he had no prior convictions before he was hired by SCR or before the alleged assault of Browne. Nancy Isaac, the CTA's general manager for paratransit operations, stated in her deposition that after the CTA received the results of Britton's background check, he was certified by the CTA. She also stated that prior arrests would not warrant decertification by the CTA, but prior convictions would.

Several months prior to the incident involving Browne, one of SCR's customers, Esperanza Banda, accused an SCR driver of exposing himself to her and attempting to kiss her. Britton was suspected because he was the driver of the vehicle that was transporting Banda at the time of the alleged incident. Britton denied the allegations and Banda was unable to identify Britton in a lineup. Both Pamela and Stanley Rakestraw went to Banda's treatment center from where she had been picked up and spoke with one of Banda's therapists. The therapist indicated that Banda had a boyfriend at the center, which was not looked upon with favor and Banda tried to hide this from her mother. The therapist suggested that Banda might have thought she would get into trouble because she had been seen kissing her boyfriend, so she fabricated a story that Britton tried to kiss her. Stanley Rakestraw also stated in his deposition that when he informed SCR's other drivers about Banda's allegations, they indicated that they would sometimes have to pull over and separate Banda and another individual because they were 'making out' in the vehicle.

Negligent Hiring

Browne contends the circuit court erred in granting SCR's motion for summary judgment because a question of fact existed as to whether Browne established a cause of action against SCR for the negligent hiring of Britton. Browne argues that SCR should have learned of Britton's criminal history before he was hired because SCR was required to submit Britton's fingerprints to the Illinois State Police pursuant to section 28b of the Metropolitan Transit Authority Act. Browne further argues that the incident with Esperanza Banda should also have put SCR on notice that Britton posed a danger to its customers.

In a cause of action for negligent hiring, the plaintiff must plead and prove (1) that the employer knew or should have known that the employee had a particular unfitness for the position so as to create a danger of harm to third persons; (2) that such particular unfitness was known or should have been known at the time of the employee's hiring or retention; and (3) that this particular unfitness proximately caused the plaintiff's injury.

Here, the record indicates that SCR did not know or could not have known about Britton's "criminal history." SCR submitted Britton's name to the Illinois State Police to ascertain whether Britton had any prior convictions, not prior arrests. In response to SCR's request, the letter stated that "no conviction information was identified." Although the letter indicated there was no "guarantee" that conviction information did not exist because "criminals" can use false names that would not be identified by a non-fingerprint request, the record indicates Britton had no prior convictions when he was hired. Britton's "rap sheet" indicates he had been arrested numerous times for various offenses, which included rape; however, none of these arrests resulted in convictions. Even if SCR had complied with section 28b and submitted Britton's fingerprints, SCR still would not have learned of Britton's prior arrests. Therefore, we cannot conclude that SCR knew or should have known of Britton's criminal history.

Further, the incident involving Esperanza Banda would not have put SCR on notice that Britton posed a danger to its passengers. Although Banda reported that a driver had exposed himself to her, she was unable to identify Britton as the driver. Also, when the Rakestraws spoke with Banda's therapists about the incident, the therapists indicated that Banda could have fabricated the story. Under these circumstances, we find the circuit court did not err in granting summary judgment.

Accordingly, we affirm the judgment of the circuit court.

CASE COMMENT

The court found against the plaintiff largely on the difference between a criminal conviction and an arrest. Once an individual is convicted of a crime it becomes public record. An arrest, however, is not deemed part of the public record. In this case, the offender was arrested a number of times, including rape. However, he was not convicted. Further, the prior incident in which he attempted to kiss a female customer was not adequate notice to the employer because the girl could not identify the offender. Consequently, the court found the employer did not know nor should it have known of the employee criminal inclination which could result in the harm done to the plaintiff (victim).

386 F.3d 623

United States Court of Appeals, Fourth Circuit

KRISTIN D. BLAIR, PLAINTIFF-APPELLANT v. DEFENDER SERVICES, INCORPORATED, DEFENDANT-APPELLEE.

Oct. 25, 2004

Background

College student sued janitorial staffing company in state court for injuries sustained as a result of a violent attack upon her by an employee of the staffing company on college campus, alleging claims for negligent hiring, retention and supervision, and for respondeat superior liability. The staffing company removed to the United States District Court for the Western District of Virginia, which granted staffing company's motion for summary judgment, and student appealed.

Holdings

The court of appeals held that:

1. Staffing company could not be liable under the theory of respondeat superior, but
2. Genuine issues of material fact precluded summary judgment for staffing company on student's claims for negligent hiring and negligent retention.

Affirmed in part, reversed in part, and remanded

On the morning of March 26, 2001, at approximately 11:30 a.m., Kristin D. Blair, a 19-year-old college freshman at Virginia Polytechnic Institute and State University, entered the digital-art classroom in Henderson Hall on the Virginia Tech campus to work on a project prior to the commencement of a 2:00 p.m. class session. When Blair arrived, other students were completing a class in the room. By 12:30 p.m., all but a few of these students had departed. Around that time, a man wearing blue jeans and a gray T-shirt with a colorful logo entered the room and soon departed. A few minutes later, that same man returned and asked Blair, who was now alone in the classroom, when the next class started.

At approximately 12:45 p.m., Blair left the classroom and observed the same man standing in the middle of the hallway, with a large gray bucket beside him. After walking to the end of the hallway, Blair entered a unisex bathroom. When she opened the restroom door to leave, the same man was standing in the doorway. Suddenly, this individual grabbed Blair by her neck and pushed her back into the bathroom. While straddling Blair and using both hands to strangle her, the attacker pushed her to the floor. Blair lost consciousness during the attack. She awoke on the bathroom floor, with her face swollen to the extent that she only could see out of one eye. Blair then left the bathroom and began screaming for help. A member of the Virginia Tech administrative staff approached her and asked, "who did this?" Blair pointed to the same man whom she had seen earlier and who was standing in the hallway.

The man identified by Blair was James Lee Harris, an employee of Defendant, which, pursuant to a contract, provided janitorial staffing services on Virginia Tech's campus. Eleven months prior to his attack on Blair, a protective order had been issued against Harris in the Giles County Juvenile and Domestic Relations Court. This protective order resulted from a criminal complaint having been filed by a woman who had been physically assaulted by Harris at a restaurant.

Harris previously had worked for Defendant during a brief period from November 1998 until January 1999. At that time, Defendant required Harris to complete an application that included a question concerning any criminal charges, to which Harris answered that he had no prior criminal convictions. Pursuant to a contract with Virginia Tech, Defendant assigned Harris to perform custodial work at Virginia Tech under Virginia Tech's supervision. That contract required Defendant to perform criminal background checks on all Defendant personnel assigned to the Virginia Tech campus. A criminal background check of Harris was not completed by Defendant during this two-month period.

In January of 1999, Harris quit his employment with Defendant, and became employed directly by Virginia Tech for approximately one year. Harris returned to the employment of Defendant for a brief two weeks in October of 2000. Once again Harris, completed another application and indicated no criminal convictions. Defendant did not conduct a criminal background check with respect to Harris during this second brief period of employment.

On February 5, 2001, Defendant once again hired Harris. Unlike Harris' prior employment with Defendant, he was not required to complete any application on this third occasion. As with the previous occasions, Defendant did not conduct a criminal background check on Harris prior to his employment. Defendant's representatives did, however, contact some of the personal references provided by Harris. While Harris did not have a record of any criminal convictions, he was subject to the aforementioned court protective order in neighboring Giles County.

At all times, the contract between Defendant and Virginia Tech specifically required Defendant to perform criminal background checks on all personnel assigned to Virginia Tech property. Expert testimony offered in opposition to Defendant's Motion for Summary Judgment presented the view that Defendant's pre-employment screening of Harris was inadequate. Specifically, there was evidence that Defendant would have discovered that Harris was the subject of a protective order and criminal complaint in the neighboring county if a background investigation had been conducted as required.

A. The Respondeat Superior Claim

The Supreme Court of Virginia in the cases of *Gina Chin & Assocs. v. First Union Bank* and *Majorana v. Crown Cent. Petroleum Corp.* addressed the elements of a claim against an employer for the wrongful acts of an employee based on the doctrine of respondeat superior. In *Gina Chin,* the court noted that "almost from its first consideration by the courts of this Commonwealth ... the determination of the issue [of] whether the employee's wrongful act was within the scope of his employment under the facts of a particular case has proved vexatious."

In *Majorana,* the court explained that: "When the plaintiff presents evidence sufficient to show the existence of an employer-employee relationship, she has established a *prima facie* case triggering a presumption of liability ... the burden of production then shifts to the employer, who may rebut that presumption by proving that the employee had departed from the scope of the employment relationship at the time the injurious act was committed."

Even viewing the facts in the light most favorable to Blair on this issue, we find that the district court correctly concluded that Harris's actions had nothing to do with his performance of janitorial services. The district judge thoroughly reviewed applicable Virginia law in reaching this conclusion.

It is well established that the simple fact that an employee is at a particular location at a specific time as a result of his employment is not sufficient to impose respondeat superior liability on the employer. However, as the district court noted, Virginia courts have not "automatically" placed intentional torts outside the scope of employment for purposes of vicarious liability. The district judge correctly noted that the test set forth in the *Gina Chin* case is whether "the service itself, in which the tortious act was done, was within the ordinary course of the employer's business."

In *Kensington Associates v. West* the court reversed a jury verdict in favor of a plaintiff-construction worker, and entered final judgment in favor of the employer of an individual who had engaged in "horseplay" in shooting the plaintiff. The court noted that this horseplay was not done to further the employer's interest. In *Abernathy,* the court reversed a jury verdict and held "as a matter of law" that a delivery man was not acting within the scope of his employment when he participated in a scuffle over who had caused a traffic accident.

The present case falls within the ambit of these Virginia cases. Harris's assault on Blair is clearly distinguishable from situations where the employee's wrongful conduct was related to the nature of the employment. In the *Gina Chin* case, a bank teller embezzled money, while in the *Majorana* case, a gas station employee sexually harassed a customer during payment by the customer. When Harris embarked on independent acts to attack Blair, he clearly acted outside the scope of his employment. We hold that this act was so great a deviation from Defendant's business that the district court correctly granted Defendant's Motion for Summary Judgment on the respondeat superior liability claim as a matter of law.

B. The Negligent Hiring and Negligent Retention Claims

In *Big Stone,* the court recognized a duty of a company to exercise "reasonable care" in a hiring decision, and a distinction between the hiring and the retention of an employee. Subsequently, the Supreme Court of Virginia explicitly recognized the independent torts of negligent hiring in *Davis v. Merrill.*

In *J. v. Victory Tabernacle Baptist Church* the mother of a 10-year-old girl brought suit against a church and its pastor as a result of the rape and sexual assault of the girl by an employee of the church. It was alleged that when the church hired this employee it "knew, or should have known, that [the employee] had recently been convicted of aggravated sexual assault on a young girl, that he was on probation for the offense, and that a condition of his probation was that he not be involved with children.

The court held that the plaintiff had asserted a claim of negligent hiring, distinct from a claim for respondeat superior liability. The court discussed at length its earlier opinion in *Davis v. Merrill, supra,* noting that when the wrongdoing employee in that case "was interviewed ... no one made inquiry concerning his past record, habits, or general fitness," and further commented to the effect that "had [the employer] investigated, it probably would not have offered the assailant the job."

In the instant case, the district court found that "no reasonable trier of fact" could find that Defendant knew or should have known of Harris's criminal problems in the neighboring county some eleven months earlier. We respectfully disagree. There is a genuine issue of material fact with respect to whether Defendant should have known of Harris's violent conduct, as the undisputed facts are that Defendant never conducted any type of criminal background check on Harris prior to employing him. While Defendant can certainly argue that such a background check would not have resulted in the discovery of the protective order issued in April 2000, and a jury could certainly so find there is expert testimony proffered by Blair that a background check would have indicated the existence of a protective order resulting from a criminal complaint.

The trial court and Defendant placed great reliance on the Virginia Supreme Court's opinion in *Southeast Apts. Mgmt., Inc. v. Jackman.* In that case, a tenant was molested by a maintenance person of the apartment building after his entry into her apartment. The tenant claimed that the owner of the apartment building breached its duty "to exercise reasonable care in the hiring of its employee ... or ... in the retention of the employee." The court noted its earlier opinions in *Victory Tabernacle, supra,* and *Davis v. Merrill, supra,* in establishing the tort of negligent hiring. In providing further edification of this tort, the court cited the following summary provided by a Minnesota state court:

> Liability is predicated on the negligence of an employer in placing a person with known propensities, or propensities which should have been discovered by reasonable investigation, in an employment position in which, because of the circumstances of the employment, it should have been foreseeable that the hired individual posed a threat of injury to others.

In applying the above principles to the facts before it, the court in *Southeast Apts.* held that the evidence was "insufficient to make out a prima facie case of negligent hiring or negligent retention." The facts presented in *Southeast Apts.* were that the owner had "received a detailed application containing information about [the employee's] personal background, work experience, and behavioral history." In responding to the application inquiry, the employee denied any engagement in "34 types of criminal behavior, except traffic violations." Furthermore, he denied any criminal convictions "in the past seven years." In addition to the thorough steps taken by the employer, the evidence in *Southeast Apts.* indicated that the wrongdoing employee had two previous bad-check charges totaling $10.29. Importantly, there were no criminal convictions or protective orders involving violent acts perpetrated on women.

The facts in the instant case are clearly distinguishable from those found in *Southeast Apts.,* and are much closer to the facts addressed by the Supreme Court of Virginia in *Victory Tabernacle.* In the present case, Defendant failed to conduct a background check of Harris on three different occasions. It is undisputed that Defendant was contractually obligated to Virginia Tech to conduct a background check of employees such as Harris. Furthermore, the instant record includes the statement of Virginia Tech's Director of Housekeeping, who indicated that he would not have allowed Harris to perform janitorial services at Virginia Tech had he known of Harris's propensity for violence.

With respect to Blair's claim of negligent hiring, we find that there is a genuine issue of material fact concerning whether Harris's violent propensities should have been discovered by Defendant prior to Harris's being placed into an employment situation in which he posed a threat to Virginia Tech students. Similarly, in addressing Blair's claim of negligent retention, we find that there is a genuine issue of material fact regarding whether Defendant, having originally employed Harris, should have known or discovered Harris's dangerous propensities as a result of the protective order issued eleven months earlier. Quite simply, based on the facts of the instant case, these are questions to be resolved by the jury as the finder of fact.

For the foregoing reasons, we affirm the district court's granting of summary judgment on the respondeat superior claim, but vacate the district court's order granting summary judgment on Blair's claims of negligent hiring and negligent retention, and remand this case for further proceedings consistent with this opinion.

AFFIRMED IN PART, REVERSED IN PART, AND REMANDED.

CASE COMMENT

This case provides an excellent analysis of the elements of negligent hiring, and serves to counter *Browne* as the court focused heavily on the failure to conduct any background investigation. In *Browne,* there was a background check, but it did not disclose arrests. In *Blair,* there was no background check conducted even though a contract provision required it. Consequently, the failure to even attempt to check the background of employees resulted in possible liability to the employer.

DISCUSSION QUESTIONS

As an employer, should you exclude applicants with criminal convictions from employment? Should the possibility or the evidence of rehabilitation be considered? If so, what is your liability exposure if you hire an individual with a conviction, who appears to be rehabilitated, but subsequently commits a crime against one of your customers? How should you reconcile the competing interests of keeping criminals out of your workplace, while allowing people a second (or another) chance?

NEGLIGENT SUPERVISION, TRAINING, AND RETENTION

Cause of Action and Elements

These causes of action are separate but are often asserted as alternative theories in civil complaints. These theories are typically combined because the failure to adequately train is often a reflection of, or the result of, the failure to adequately supervise.

Negligent supervision stems from the duty of an employer to exercise due or reasonable care in supervising its employees.[3] As in negligent hiring, the level of supervision should be commensurate with the degree of potential harm derived from the employee. To use the earlier example, a service worker who drives to customers homes and workplaces should be supervised to a greater degree than compared to the inside sales representative. This level of supervision goes not only to operational and performance standards, but also to the personal circumstances of the employee. Stated another way, supervision is not just for work performance and purposes. It should also include monitoring of the employee's sobriety, attitude, appearance, and emotional state.

If a plaintiff can show that the failure to supervise was causally connected (proximate cause) to the injury or harm, then the employer would be liable for such. Similarly, if the employer failed to adequately supervise the employee to the point that appropriate corrective measures were not implemented, the plaintiff may also assert a negligent retention cause of action. Since supervision is closely related to correction and discipline, these theories are often asserted in combination. In a negligent supervision or retention claim, the court will look to the level of direct supervision exerted over the employee, the corrective measures applied, and the extent of discipline imposed. In order to correct or discipline, the court will look to the following factors:

1. Counseling and reprimands
2. Re-assignment
3. Re-training
4. Rehabilitation
5. Closer supervision or controls
6. Levels of progressive discipline
7. Discharge

Negligent training operates under similar logic. The level or standards of training must be reasonable, and commensurate to accomplish the work task.[4] Here again, training is not just for operational and performance purposes. It should also relate to how the training (or lack thereof) may potentially endanger or injure third parties.

Key areas of training standards relating to security personnel and criminal conduct include:

- Legal powers and limitations
- General duties and specific post orders
- Report writing
- Use of emergency and security devices
- Emergency procedures
- Weapons training standards
- Vehicle training standards
- Use of force, arrest, and search and seizure

321 F. supp.2d 358

United States District Court, D. Connecticut

MELISSA BURFORD, PLAINTIFF v. MCDONALD'S CORPORATION, CARL FIELD, TIMOTHY MICHAUD, AND RONALD FEDOR, DEFENDANTS.

June 2, 2004

Background

Restaurant employee sued employer, supervisor, store manager, and district manager, alleging sexual harassment and retaliation in violation of Title VII, and asserting negligent supervision claim under Connecticut law. Defendants moved for summary judgment.

Holdings

The district court held that:

1. Employee established prima facie case of sexual harassment;
2. Store manager was not liable for negligent supervision; and
3. District manager was not liable for negligent supervision.

Motion granted in part and denied in part

The relevant background is as follows: Plaintiff worked at the McDonald's in Groton, Connecticut, from November 20, 2000, until she was transferred to the Waterford, Connecticut, location on July 21, 2001. Defendant Field was acting supervisor of the Groton location between April 2, 2001, and June 11, 2001. Plaintiff alleges that Field sexually harassed her on numerous occasions, mostly in May and June, including, among other allegations, repeated incidents of sexual comments and physical contact. Plaintiff also asserts that as a result of complaining about the harassment, she did not receive a promotion she had been promised. Plaintiff complained to the McDonald's service center and met with an investigator on July 18, 2001. She was transferred out of the Groton location on July 21, 2001.

A. Title VII—Hostile Work Environment

Plaintiff has asserted that she was subjected to a hostile work environment in violation of the prohibition on discrimination on the basis of sex in the workplace set forth in Title VII of the Civil Rights Act of 1964. 42 U.S.C. § 2000e "To prevail on a hostile work environment claim, a plaintiff must demonstrate: (1) that [the] workplace was permeated with discriminatory intimidation that was sufficiently severe or pervasive to alter the conditions of [the] work environment, and (2) that a specific basis exists for imputing the conduct that created the hostile environment to the employer." The Supreme Court has ruled that a work environment must be both subjectively and objectively hostile and abusive in order to establish a hostile environment claim. "The conduct alleged must be severe and pervasive enough to create an environment that would reasonably be perceived, and is perceived, as hostile or abusive."

"A plaintiff alleging a hostile work environment "must demonstrate either that a single incident was extraordinarily severe, or that a series of incidents were 'sufficiently continuous and concerted' to have altered the conditions of her working environment." To decide whether the threshold has been reached, courts examine the case-specific circumstances in their totality and evaluate the severity, frequency, and degree of the abuse. Relevant factors include the frequency of the discriminatory conduct; its severity; whether it is physically threatening or humiliating, or a mere offensive utterance; and whether it unreasonably interferes with an employee's work performance."

The Second Circuit has recently cautioned the district courts considering hostile environment claims. The Second Circuit explained that "while the standard for establishing a hostile work environment is high, we have repeatedly cautioned against setting the bar too high, noting that while a mild, isolated incident does not make a work environment hostile, the test is whether the harassment is of such quality or quantity that a reasonable employee would find the conditions of her employment altered for the worse. The environment need not be unendurable or intolerable. Nor must the victim's psychological well-being be damaged. In short, the fact that the law requires harassment to be severe or pervasive before it can be actionable does not mean that employers are free from liability in all but the most egregious cases." With this admonition in mind, the court concludes that plaintiff has presented sufficient evidence to allow a trier of fact to conclude that she subjectively experienced the environment as hostile. She testified at her deposition that the sexual harassment she claims to have been subjected to made it difficult for her to work at the store, that she wanted to leave work, and that the experience made her physically ill. Therefore, Plaintiff has provided sufficient evidence at this stage of the proceeding to satisfy the subjective prong of the hostile work environment test.

McDonald's principal claim on its motion for summary judgment is that plaintiff has not satisfied the objective portion of the test—that is, that even taking her allegations as true, they do not rise to the level of a hostile work environment as the Supreme Court and the Second Circuit have defined it. In her deposition and pleadings, plaintiff has alleged a long series of harassing acts by Field, including comments he made about plaintiff's anatomy, insinuating comments about proposed sexual activity between plaintiff and Field, unwanted physical contact by Field, and attempts by Field to look down plaintiff's shirt. Plaintiff testified that Field's sexual comments occurred almost every day that they were in the store together. Insofar as all disputed issues of fact must be viewed in the light most favorable to plaintiff, the court accepts all these allegations as true and concludes that the harassment alleged by plaintiff, if believed, could be sufficient to allow a jury to conclude that she was subjected to a hostile work environment as defined by the Supreme Court and the Second Circuit. That is, the court concludes that plaintiff has alleged, and provided evidence of, harassment "of such quality or quantity that a reasonable employee would find the conditions of her employment altered for the worse."

McDonald's argues that the sexual harassment plaintiff claims she was subjected to "does not rise to the level of severity and frequency sufficient to alter the terms and conditions of Burford's employment" and it cites a series of cases from the Second Circuit and the District of Connecticut that granted motions for summary judgment dismissing hostile environment claims. However, a number of the cited cases allege conduct that was less pervasive or severe than that claimed here. Additionally, the recent cautions by the Second Circuit about "setting the bar too high" further suggest to this court that, though plaintiff's claims in this case are perhaps close to the bar, the behavior alleged is severe and pervasive enough to allow her to present those claims to a jury.

Plaintiff thus advances to the second stage of the hostile environment analysis, at which she must demonstrate that "a specific basis exists for imputing the conduct that created the hostile environment to the employer." Following Supreme Court precedent, the Second Circuit has held that "in contrast to allegations of harassment by co-workers or customers, employers are presumptively liable for all acts of harassment perpetrated by an employee's supervisor." In this case, Field was plaintiff's acting supervisor during the period in which she claims to have been harassed. As a consequence, McDonald's is presumptively liable for the harassment. Nevertheless, "the employer will avoid liability if it can plead and prove, as an affirmative defense, that (1) the employer exercised reasonable care to prevent and promptly correct any sexual harassment by such a supervisor, and (2) the employee unreasonably failed to avail herself of any corrective or preventative opportunities provided by the employer or to avoid harm otherwise." McDonald's asserts that it did exercise reasonable care and that plaintiff unreasonably failed to avail herself of corrective or preventative opportunities provided by the employer.

The court believes that plaintiff has raised a material issue of fact as to the application of the affirmative defenses in this case. First, the affirmative defense is only available to McDonald's if plaintiff suffered no tangible employment action. Here, plaintiff claims she was denied a promotion she had been promised because of her complaints about the alleged harassment. If her allegations are true, the affirmative defense would not be available to McDonald's. Second, assuming the affirmative defense were available, plaintiff has asserted facts which, if believed, would demonstrate that her actions in availing herself of corrective or preventative opportunities were reasonable. For example, she has asserted that she complained about Field's harassing conduct to a number of employees at the store, including the supervisor, and that she called McDonald's help line five times before she received a response. Again, if true, the jury could conclude that her actions constituted a reasonable attempt to take advantage of McDonald's corrective or preventative opportunities, thereby negating its affirmative defense. Because there are genuine issues of material fact on McDonald's affirmative defense, summary judgment on that defense is inappropriate.

B. Negligent Supervision Claims Against Defendants Fedor and Michaud

Plaintiff has also sued defendant Fedor, the district manager in charge of the Groton location, and defendant Michaud, the Store Manager of the Groton location, for negligent supervision of Field. To prove a claim of negligent supervision under Connecticut law, "a plaintiff must plead and prove that he suffered an injury due to the defendant's failure to supervise an employee whom the defendant had a duty to supervise. A defendant does not owe a duty of care to protect a plaintiff from another employee's tortious acts unless the defendant knew or reasonably should have known of the employee's propensity to engage in that type of tortious conduct." Defendants move for summary judgment on the basis that plaintiff has not offered any evidence that Fedor or Michaud had any reason to believe that Field would commit the acts of which he is accused and that Michaud had no supervisory authority over Field as they occupied parallel positions.

Plaintiff has not submitted evidence to support a negligent supervision claim against Michaud. It is undisputed that Michaud was on sabbatical from April 2001 through June 11, 2001, the period of the alleged harassment. Michaud could hardly be faulted for failing to supervise Field while Michaud was on sabbatical. Insofar as Michaud had no duty to supervise Field while on sabbatical, there can be no claim for negligent supervision. Additionally, Plaintiff specifically testified that when Michaud returned to the store, she told him about the harassment and Field's harassing behavior immediately stopped. Because there are no genuine issues of material fact regarding plaintiff's negligent supervision claim against defendant Michaud and the undisputed facts will not support such a claim as a matter of law, the court grants Defendant Michaud summary judgment on plaintiff's negligent supervision claim.

With regard to Fedor, plaintiff testified at her deposition that she told him about the harassment sometime after Memorial Day, 2001, and that he told her to give it time because Michaud was coming back shortly and that everything would be fine once Michaud returned from sabbatical. According to plaintiff, Fedor also told her that he would tell Field to leave plaintiff alone. Based upon plaintiff's own testimony, the court concludes that plaintiff cannot sustain a negligent supervision claim against defendant Fedor. The evidence presented indicates that Fedor was on notice of Field's propensity to engage in the tortious conduct only from the time of plaintiff's complaint to him sometime after Memorial Day. Plaintiff has not specified a single harassing incident that occurred after that date, nor has she presented evidence that Fedor failed to tell Field to leave her alone, as Fedor had promised. Plaintiff has thus failed to "plead and prove that [she] suffered an injury due to the defendant's failure to supervise an employee whom the defendant had a duty to supervise." Because there are no genuine issues of material fact regarding plaintiff's negligent supervision claim against defendant Fedor and the undisputed facts will not support such a claim as a matter of law, the court grants defendant Fedor summary judgment on plaintiff's negligent supervision claim.

CASE COMMENT

While the court found that a hostile workplace existed, there was no evidence that the supervisors knew of such nor did they fail to act once the allegations became known. Interestingly, one of the supervisors was on sabbatical, thereby could not have been aware of the hostile workplace. Once the other supervisor learned of the complaint, the hostile workplace immediately ceased, thereby inferring that the supervisor properly corrected the offending behavior. Consequently, the plaintiff could not show that either of the supervisors was guilty of negligent supervision.

141 Idaho 524, 112 P.3d 812

Supreme Court of Idaho

JANE ROE, JOHN ROE AND JANE DOE, PLAINTIFFS-APPELLANTS v. ALBERTSON'S, INC., TIM REPP, INDIVIDUALLY AND IN HIS CAPACITY AS A MANAGER OF ALBERTSON'S INC., ET AL, DEFENDANTS-RESPONDENTS.

May 4, 2005

Background

Minor employee and her parents brought action against supervisor and employer, asserting several tort claims arising out of alleged sexual relationship between employee and supervisor. The District Court, Fourth Judicial District, Ada County, granted employer's Motion for Summary Judgment. Employee and parents appealed.

Holdings

The supreme court held that:

1. If an injury is cognizable under the workers' compensation law, then any common-law remedy is barred, but if the injury is not cognizable under workmen's compensation, then the employee is left to a remedy under the common law;
2. Alleged sexual intercourse between employee and supervisor did not constitute an "accident" under Workers' Compensation Act, and thus employee's allegedly ruptured hymen did not amount to an "injury" that was compensable under the Act, and employee's tort claims were not subject to Act's exclusive-remedy provision.

Reversed and remanded

Both Doe and Repp began working for Albertson's Store No. 161 in July 1999. Doe, a minor, worked as a courtesy clerk (grocery bagger). Repp, who was 38 years old, was employed as an assistant front end manager. Front end managers supervise courtesy clerks.

Beginning in September 1999, Repp started to show favoritism to Doe. He would invite Doe into areas prohibited to courtesy clerks, walk Doe to her car, allow Doe extended breaks, and allow her to act as a cashier, although company policy required that cashiers be 18 years old. In November 1999, Repp made sexual advances to Doe. During November the two kissed, fondled each other, and engaged in oral sex while on duty at Albertson's. The two attempted to have sexual intercourse while at the store, but, because it was too physically painful for Doe, they stopped. By November some employees knew, while others simply questioned the relationship.

On December 4, 1999, store Director Jim Johnson began an investigation. He spoke separately to Doe and Repp. Both Doe and Repp denied the relationship. Johnson suspended Repp pending further investigation. After the investigation, Johnson concluded Repp and Doe had not been involved in a sexual relationship. Nevertheless, as a result of Repp's inappropriate behavior with Doe, on December 9, 1999, Albertson's suspended Repp for six days, demoted him to the position of checker, and transferred him to a different Albertson's store.

After his transfer, Repp continued to communicate with Doe. With Albertson's continuing the investigation, he instructed Doe to deny everything. On or about December 17, Repp asked Doe to meet him at the Albertson's where he worked. She did so, and the two then left Albertson's premises driving to Hillside Park where they engaged in sexual intercourse.

Doe's mother discovered information that caused her to believe Doe and Repp were having a romantic relationship. Doe's mother notified Albertson's on January 25, 2000. Two days later, Albertson's re-interviewed Repp. This time Repp admitted he and Doe were involved in a romantic relationship. Albertson's terminated Repp's employment. Subsequently, Repp pleaded guilty to the crime of statutory rape and was sentenced on October 19, 2000. Repp served one year in jail and one year on work release, and is serving ten years probation.

On May 11, 2001, Doe and her parents filed a complaint against Repp and Albertson's. Albertson's denied responsibility, asserting several defenses including that the Idaho's Workers' Compensation Law precluded recovery. Albertson's moved for summary judgment. The district court originally denied summary judgment. The court found Doe's alleged injury, a broken hymen, met the definition of injury provided by I.C. Section 72-102(17)(c). Furthermore, the alleged injury qualified as an "accident" as the term is defined in [the statute]. The district court also presumed the injury arose out of and in the course of employment. The district court then analyzed whether the exception provided in I.C. Section 72-209(3) applied to circumvent the worker's compensation law. The district court determined that when viewing the facts in a light most favorable to Doe, there was enough evidence presented to deny summary judgment because there was an issue whether or not Albertson's impliedly authorized Repp's behavior. The district court then granted summary judgment in Albertson's favor, finding the [statutory] exceptions were inapplicable and that the workers' compensation law precluded the suit against Albertson's.

Analysis

Appellants argue the district court erred in holding that the workers' compensation law barred the appellants' complaint. Appellants contend this is in error because Doe's injuries were not compensable under workers' compensation and therefore the tort action may be maintained in district court against Albertson's. Albertson's disagrees and argues that the only remedy available to an employee is via the workers' compensation law. Albertson's asserts that the declaration of police power section and the exclusive remedy provision of the workers' compensation law specifically abolished all claims against the employer.

In looking at the intent behind I.C. Sections 72-201 and 72-211 we have said, "the legislature removed from the sphere of civil actions, all suits against an employer for damages on account of personal injury or death of an employee, where such injury or death rises out of and in the course of the employment...." In 1969, this court reaffirmed the holding in *Gifford,* recognizing that the "rule of law may in some cases deprive persons of remedy for damages which they had prior to the passage of the Workmen's Compensation Law...."

When interpreting these statutes we must conclude, as we have in the past, that if an injury is cognizable under the worker's compensation law then any common law remedy is barred, but if the injury is not cognizable under workmen's compensation, then the employee is left to a remedy under the common law.

Doe and her parents argue that Doe did not suffer an injury as defined by the workers' compensation law. They contend Doe did not suffer "violence to the physical structure of the body." They assert Does injuries are psychological and therefore, not compensable under workers' compensation. The district court concluded Doe suffered an injury, a broken hymen, caused by an accident.

Idaho Code Section 72-102(17)(a) defines injury as "a personal injury caused by an accident arising out of and in the course of any employment covered by the workers' compensation law." Injury is "construed to include only an injury caused by an accident, which results in violence to the physical structure of the body."

Even if we were to assume Does alleged broken hymen constitutes a physical injury, we find it difficult to classify Repps and Does actions as an accident. Her ruptured hymen was not "an unexpected, undesigned, and unlooked for mishap, or untoward event." It was something that typically occurs when a virgin engages in sexual intercourse.

Although a seventeen-year-old such as Jane Doe is incapable, under the laws, of giving consent to sexual intercourse, such inability to legally consent to the act does not mean that either the act of sexual intercourse or the physical consequences of such sexual intercourse (a ruptured hymen) were "an unexpected, undesigned, and unlooked for mishap, or untoward event." Since there was no accident as defined by I.C. Section 72-102(17)(b), Jane Doe did not suffer a personal injury and her claims are not pre-empted by the Workers' Compensation Law. The district court erred in determining that Doe's injuries were compensable under workers' compensation, thereby barring her claim in district court.

The "exclusive remedy" provision of the workers' compensation law is not a bar to Doe's and her parents' claims against Albertson's. The district court's order granting Summary Judgment is reversed.

CASE COMMENT

This case illustrates the competing interests inherent in a state workers' compensation statute versus common law negligence. The workers' compensation statute is designed as exclusive compensation for workplace injuries. Negligence claims, such as negligent supervision, are designed to compensate the employee for wrongs committed within the context of employment. Here the employer attempts to use the workers' compensation statute as a bar to the common law claim. The court properly declined to do so. It is rather audacious to argue that the injury to the plaintiff was the result of an "accident" which the statute requires. The court properly negated this argument. It found that the conduct of the supervisor was not the result of an accident, and that the injuries were of an emotional and personal nature.

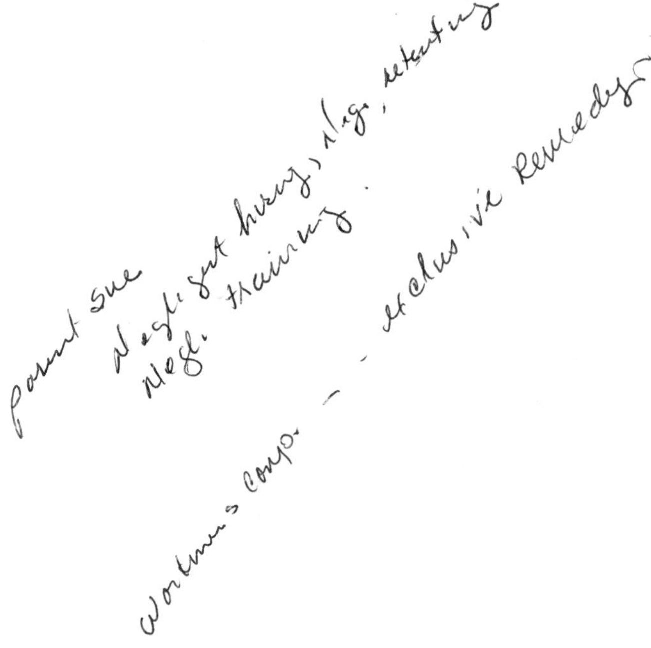

852 So. 2d 5

Supreme Court of Mississippi

HEATHER GAMBLE, A MINOR, BY AND THROUGH HER MOTHER AND ADULT NEXT FRIEND, REBECCA GAMBLE v. DOLLAR GENERAL CORPORATION, A TENNESSEE CORPORATION, AND SHERI THORNTON.

Aug. 7, 2003

Background

Patron filed complaint against store and store's employee, alleging assault, negligence, and other claims resulting from employee allegedly accusing patron of shoplifting and grabbing patron by patron's panties, and patron filed amended claim against store alleging fraud regarding concealment of existence of liability insurance. After jury verdict in favor of patron on original complaint, the Circuit Court, Lamar County, dismissed the amended claim. Parties appealed.

Holdings

The supreme court held that:

1. Issue of whether store was negligent in failing to provide to employee training regarding shoplifting policy was for jury; and
2. Issue of whether store's failure to train employee evinced wanton and reckless disregard for store patron's rights was for jury.

Affirmed in part; reversed and rendered in part

On March 19, 1999, at about noon, Gamble, a 19-year-old college student, stopped by the Dollar General store in Purvis, Mississippi, to purchase a shirt to wear to work. She stated that she needed a new shirt because she had soiled her shirt with oil pastels while in art class at Pearl River Community College. Gamble did not find anything at the Dollar General and proceeded to the Family Dollar store to look for a shirt. Upon leaving the Dollar General store, Gamble observed that a Dollar General employee had rushed up behind her car to write something down, as if she were writing down her license tag number.

After Gamble arrived at the Family Dollar store, she noticed that the same individual who wrote down her tag number had followed her to the Family Dollar store and parked directly behind her, blocking her vehicle. At this point, Gamble asked the "angry-looking" individual, Thornton, why she was following her and why she had taken down her tag number. Thornton approached Gamble and asked her what she had in her pants. Gamble thought she may have had an outline from class in her back pocket, so she reached in her back pocket but had nothing. Thornton then grabbed at Gamble's panties from the back of her pants and tugged on them. At this point, it became obvious to Gamble that Thornton was accusing her of shoplifting. The two exchanged a few words, and Thornton left, satisfied that Gamble had not shoplifted.

Gamble went to the police station to report the incident. The police officers told Gamble that they would investigate the incident and speak with Thornton. The officers testified that Gamble was extremely upset and crying because of the incident. Testimony from Gamble's parents and a friend of Gamble's was also presented to the jury. Gamble testified that she felt like she had been assaulted and humiliated by Thornton. She stated that no one from Dollar General had ever apologized to her for the incident. She testified that the incident has upset her emotionally, has affected her grades, has caused her to suffer from insomnia about four nights a week and has caused her embarrassment.

Discussion

Dollar General argues that the jury should not have been allowed to hear Gamble's claim of negligent training. Dollar General had a written shoplifting policy that stated that no employee should leave a store to go after a suspected shoplifter and no employee should ever touch a shoplifter. Dollar General argues that this policy was provided to Thornton and that she read and understood the policy. Gamble asserted at trial that merely providing the policy to Thornton, without actually providing any training, was sufficient evidence to establish a claim of negligent training.

Gamble has simply misstated her issue with regard to her claim for negligent training. Instead of claiming that Dollar General's training was inadequate or negligent, Gamble's claim is better understood as an allegation that Dollar General provided no training. Stated as an issue of no training, the jury could infer Dollar General's negligence without the need of expert testimony on proper or adequate training. The jury could properly find that Dollar General was negligent in failing to provide training to Thornton.

There was also testimony that Thornton, a regional manager, was required to go to other stores to train employees in dealing with shoplifting. However, other than receiving a booklet, there was no evidence that showed that Thornton had received any training. Based on Dollar General's failure to show any training provided to Thornton, other than handing her a manual, it was proper to allow the jury to consider the issue of negligence for Dollar General's failure to train its employee.

The punitive damage context indicates a claimant must prove by "clear and convincing evidence that the defendant against whom punitive damages are sought acted with *actual malice, gross negligence which evidences a willful, wanton or reckless disregard for the safety of others, or committed actual fraud* (emphasis added)." The trial court, when faced with the issue of punitive damages, looks at the totality of the circumstances to determine if a reasonable, hypothetical trier of fact could find either malice or gross neglect/reckless disregard. The facts must be highly unusual as punitive damages are only awarded in extreme cases. There must be ruthless disregard for the rights of others, so as to take the case out of the ordinary rule.

Although we found that Dollar General failed to provide additional training to its employees, we acknowledge that it did provide Thornton a manual. Dollar General had a written shoplifting policy that stated that no employee should leave a store to go after a suspected shoplifter and no employee should ever touch a shoplifter. Of significant importance, the record reflects that Thornton had received the manual, yet ignored the policy. Thornton followed Gamble out of the store, wrote down her tag number, then confronted and touched her. Thornton testified that the store policy was "in black and white, and I should have known it and should have followed it, and just didn't. I mean, the policy is there in black and white for all the employees at Dollar General." Once Gamble left the store, Thornton should have considered the incident to be concluded. Thornton admitted to not following store policy. However, she, in effect, ignored the policy and followed Gamble from the store on her own initiative. It is inconceivable that under the facts of this case, Dollar General was assessed punitive damages. These acts were done by Thornton alone, violating the store policy.

No proof was offered to the jury that demonstrated Dollar General had any knowledge of prior incidents committed by this employee. Clearly, punitive damages against Dollar General should not have been allowed. Thornton was reprimanded for this mistake by Dollar General. More importantly, Dollar General had not received any other prior complaints or incidents regarding Thornton's alleged propensity for committing such acts as complained about here. Indeed, if such notice of prior complaints existed and Dollar General did not have a policy regarding shoplifting violations, then, and only then, would a punitive damages instruction have been warranted. The facts of this case do not warrant a punitive damage assessment. While Dollar General may have been negligent in its training, its actions do no rise to the level of actual malice or gross negligence. Accordingly, this court reverses and renders the $100,000 punitive damages assessed against Dollar General.

All of Dollar General's issues on cross-appeal are without merit with the exception of punitive damages. Therefore, Gamble's award of $100,000 in punitive damages against Dollar General is reversed. In all other respects, the trial court's judgment is affirmed.

CASE COMMENT

This case illustrates the significance of training in order to prepare employees to adhere to corporate policies. Here the court focused on the fact that the employee was simply "handed" the policy, without any training and preparation related to such. However, notice the decision on punitive damages. If the employer failed to codify a policy, then the punitive damage claim may have been affirmed by the appeals court. Instead, since the employer had a policy, it was not reckless to the point of being liable for punitive damages. Therefore, the key is to codify appropriate policies and procedures, and train the employees on the requirements of such. This case clearly illustrates that both the policy and the training are necessary elements to limit or negate liability exposure.

111 P.3d 445

Supreme Court of Colorado

DONALD KELLER, INDIVIDUALLY AND D/B/A CONTINENTAL CLEANERS, PETITIONER v. TUGBA KOCA, A MINOR CHILD, BY AND THROUGH HER LEGAL GUARDIAN, PAULA ALPAR, RESPONDENT.

April 18, 2005

Background

Victim, who was sexually assaulted by employee, brought action against employer for negligent supervision and premises liability. Following a bench trial, the District Court, Boulder County, entered judgment for victim. Employer appealed. The court of appeals affirmed, and the supreme court granted employer's petition for certiorari.

Holding

The supreme court held that employer did not owe duty to victim, since harm to her was not foreseeable risk. Judgment of the court of appeals reversed and matter remanded with directions to that court.

Donald Keller, defendant below and petitioner before this court, owned and operated a dry cleaning business in Boulder, Colorado. Keller hired Firat Uzan, a male employee, in 1990 and then promoted him to the position of General Manager in the spring of 1995. As General Manager, Uzan had keys to the premises and was responsible for operating the dry cleaning business, which included opening and closing the store, in Keller's absence and at his direction. However, Uzan did not have the authorization to bring third parties to the business during non-working hours.

On a Sunday morning in the spring of 1997, Uzan brought a 12-year-old girl, the plaintiff Tugba Koca, to the business. Testimony revealed that Uzan was a family acquaintance and had asked Koca's parents if she could go with him to the dry cleaners and help with opening the doors of the business so that the carpets could be professionally cleaned. While there, Uzan brought Koca into the back office where he locked the door and sexually assaulted her.

Uzan was subsequently convicted of sexual assault of a child and sentenced to the Department of Corrections. The plaintiff then filed this civil action against Keller claiming that Keller, as the employer and owner of the dry cleaning business where the assault occurred, was negligent in his supervision of Uzan. The complaint alleged that Keller knew that Uzan had sexually harassed young women at the cleaners and that despite knowing that "his employee was a sexual predator," Keller continued to allow Uzan to work alone and unsupervised with his own access to the premises.

The trial court, acting as the finder of fact, found that Keller was negligent in his supervision of Uzan and awarded damages. The court cited testimony from three former women employees who told Keller that Uzan had sexually harassed and fondled them during business hours prior to the incident identified by the plaintiff. The young women related several instances where, during business hours, Uzan asked them to perform sexual acts as well as touched their breasts and buttocks. All three quit their positions and told Keller of the episodes. Additionally, one of the employee's mothers called Keller warning of civil liability. The three women also complained to police about Uzan's conduct but the police did not initiate charges against him. When Keller confronted Uzan about these complaints, Uzan denied any sexual misconduct and Keller did not pursue the matter any further.

Keller appealed the trial court's finding of liability and the court of appeals affirmed. The court reasoned that Keller had knowledge of the previous assaults and that "there was a risk that Uzan would sexually assault a young woman or girl on the premises if left unsupervised." Thus, it held that Keller had a duty to take reasonable steps to prevent Uzan from working alone and unsupervised and the breach of this duty resulted in the harm to the plaintiff.

Analysis

The issue that we address is the extent to which an employer owes a duty of care to prevent harm caused by an employee. We begin by setting forth the legal principles that guide us in determining whether an employer is liable in tort for the negligent supervision of his employee.

Courts consider a number of factors to determine whether a duty exists, including: the risk involved, the foreseeability of the injury weighed against the social utility of the actor's conduct, the magnitude of the burden of guarding against injury or harm, and the consequences of placing the burden on the actor. "No one factor is controlling, and the question of whether a duty should be imposed in a particular case is essentially one of fairness under contemporary standards—whether reasonable persons would recognize a duty and agree that it exists."

To establish liability, the plaintiff must prove that the employer has a duty to prevent an unreasonable risk of harm to third persons to whom the employer knows or should have known that the employee would cause harm. An employer "who knows or should have known that an employee's conduct would subject third parties to an unreasonable risk of harm may be directly liable to third parties for harm proximately caused by his conduct."

While the tort of negligent supervision applies to instances where the employee is acting outside his scope of employment, it does not extend to *all* acts undertaken by an employee that are actionable in tort. In cases of negligent supervision "liability of the employer is predicated on the employer's antecedent ability to recognize a potential employee's 'attribute[s] of character or prior conduct' which would create an undue risk of harm to those with whom the employee came in contact in executing his employment responsibilities." "Liability results under the rule stated in this Section, not because of the relation of the parties, but because the employer antecedently had reason to believe that an undue risk of harm would exist because of the employment." "The master as such is under no peculiar duty to control the conduct of his servant while he is outside of the master's premises, unless the servant is at the time using a chattel entrusted to him as servant."

Thus, where a plaintiff asserts a claim for negligent supervision, the question of whether the employer owes a duty of care to the injured third party boils down to issues of knowledge and causation—whether the employee's acts are "so connected with the employment in time and place" such that the employer knows that harm may result from the employee's conduct and that the employer is given the opportunity to control such conduct. This court stated: "Thus a master may be bound to control acts of his servants that they do entirely on their own account but that are closely enough connected with the employment in time and space to give the master a special opportunity to control the servant's conduct."

In *Fletcher v. Baltimore & P.R. Co.*, the United States Supreme Court recognized instances where an employer may be liable in tort for permitting employees to engage in acts that may give rise to a claim for negligence. There, the court held that the railroad company owed a duty of care to passersby when it allowed its employees to throw large pieces of wood from the train on their way home from a day's work. The court recognized that throwing large pieces of wood from the train created a risk that people lawfully on the adjacent street would be harmed by one of those pieces of wood. Thus, a nexus existed between the employer's knowledge of the employees' activities and the risk of harm when a person was hit by one of those pieces of wood sufficient to allow a jury to determine whether the defendant negligently supervised its employees.

Similarly, this court in recognizing a claim for negligent supervision acknowledged a connection between the employer's knowledge of the employee's propensity to act in a particular manner and the employer's duty to take reasonable steps to prevent the employee from acting in such a manner. The plaintiff in *Destefano* sued the Diocese of Colorado Springs for the negligent supervision of a priest who in the course of providing marriage counseling engaged in sexual relations with the plaintiff, Destefano. Destefano alleged that the diocese knew or should have known that the priest had engaged in sexual relations with other women "similarly situated" to the plaintiff and that the diocese failed to take any action to limit his contact with potential clients. Thus, it was the connection between the very risk of harm that the diocese either knew or should have known would occur and the actual harm, sexual relations with a parishioner seeking counseling, which sustained Destefano's claim for relief.

In both of these cases, the duty imposed on the defendant was to take reasonable steps to prevent the foreseeable harm of a known risk—the person harmed was one who would likely be harmed by the known risk posed by the employee. The custom of permitting employees of the railroad company to throw wood from the train created a risk that they would damage property or harm someone near the tracks. Allowing the priest to continue to counsel clients created a risk that he would become sexually involved with those clients. In both cases, the very harm that the risk implied did indeed occur.

The plaintiff did not present any evidence at trial that Keller knew or should have known that Uzan would bring a 12-year-old girl, with no connection to the dry cleaners, to Keller's place of business when it was closed and then sexually assault her there. However, there was substantial evidence that Keller knew of Uzan's proclivities to engage in lewd and sexual behavior with the female employees on the premises during business hours. Three young women employees testified that they had quit after Uzan groped and fondled them. He also sexually propositioned these young women and made other sexually explicit statements. Testimony also established that Keller did not take any corrective action against Uzan except to confront him about the truth of the allegations after an employee's mother warned of potential litigation. This proof supports a finding that Keller knew that Uzan's continued employment created a risk that young women working at the dry cleaners and potential customers would be subject to sexual contact and lewd behavior during business hours and Keller therefore had a duty to take reasonable steps to prevent *that* harm from occurring.

While Keller may have had a duty to take reasonable steps to protect women employees and customers from the known risk of harm that Uzan posed to these women during working hours, this known risk does not extend to the sexual assault suffered by Koca. She was neither an employee nor a customer. No evidence links Uzan to a sexual assault of a young girl at the business when it was closed and when he was supposed to be working alone. There was no evidence indicating that Keller knew or should have known that Uzan would bring a 12-year-old girl, the daughter of a friend, to his place of business during off-hours and sexually assault her there. Nor was there any evidence that it was reasonably foreseeable that an employee who created a sexually hostile work environment would then abuse his access to the premises and take a young girl with no connection to the business to that place of employment for the purposes of committing a sexual assault.

This case arguably presents a close question of whether the employer's knowledge creates a duty to take reasonable steps to prevent a particular harm from occurring. But, in order for a duty of care to exist, there must be a connection between the employer's knowledge of the employee's dangerous propensities and the harm caused. This connection is crucial to decide whether an employer owes a duty of care.

Although Uzan posed a known risk of harm that he would subject women working at the cleaners and customers to lewd behavior and sexual contact, the necessary link to connect the employer's knowledge of the risk posed by the employee and the harm that occurred does not exist. There is no evidence that Keller knew or should have known that Uzan's proclivities created a risk of harm to a 12-year-old girl, with no connection to the business, who was then brought to the employer's place of business, in violation of the employer's rules, while the business was closed to the public, to sexually assault her. Therefore, we hold that Keller did not owe a duty of care to Koca under these circumstances.

Koca asserts that we should apply a more sweeping approach in determining whether the risk posed by Uzan imposed upon Keller a duty to prevent harm to her by essentially arguing that he owed a duty of care to all women and girls who came on the premises irrespective of whether Keller could anticipate their presence. This plaintiff has undoubtedly suffered great harm from the assault in this case. However, we do not embrace a theory of negligent supervision that would be an open invitation to sue an employer for the intentional torts of an employee founded upon a generalized knowledge of that employee's prior conduct. This court stated: "We emphasize that an employer is not an insurer for violent acts committed by an employee against a third person."

Conclusion

For the reasons stated, we reverse the decision of the court of appeals and remand this case to that court to consider the plaintiff's alternate theory of premises liability. Chief Justice MULLARKEY, dissenting.

I respectfully dissent from the majority's opinion holding that Donald Keller, the owner of Continental Cleaners, owed no duty of care to Tugba Koca when she was sexually assaulted on the premises by Keller's employee, Firat Uzan, who managed the store. I would affirm the decision of the court of appeals.

The majority takes an unreasonably narrow view of Keller's duty of care that is contrary to the law and to the facts. The trial court found that "Keller had notice of Uzan's propensity for illegal behavior related to minors as well as a propensity for sexual harassment and assault on young women." In making this finding, the court relied on what it described as the "consistent and credible" testimony of three young women that they had been sexually harassed and sexually assaulted by Uzan when they were employed at the cleaners, and by a complaint from a female customer. All three former employees, as well as the mother of one of them, complained directly to Keller. The three also reported Uzan's actions to the police.

The trial court found that "Mr. Uzan's assault of Ms. Koca was remarkably similar to the assaults reported by the three former employees." According to the trial court, the most serious allegations by the employees concerned conduct by Uzan that occurred "in the back room of the Cleaners with the door closed." As the majority notes, Uzan assaulted Koca in the back room with the door locked.

The majority states only that "there was substantial evidence that Keller knew of Uzan's proclivity to engage in lewd and sexual behavior with female employees on the premises during business hours." In my view, the majority misrepresents the evidence, especially the severity of the attacks on the three employees. The evidence, as found by the trial court, is that Keller knew or should have known that Uzan sexually harassed and sexually assaulted young female employees in the same manner and in the same place where he subsequently sexually harassed and sexually assaulted Koca.

The majority, however, concludes that "there is no evidence that Keller knew or should have known that Uzan's proclivities created a risk of harm to a 12-year-old girl, with no connection to the business, who was then brought to the employer's place of business, in violation of the employer's rules, while the business was closed to the public, to sexually assault her." I question the majority's reliance on work rules because the trial court did not make any findings that Keller had work rules or that Uzan violated them. More importantly, the law imposes liability on Keller because Koca was attacked on the business premises by Keller's manager Uzan. No additional business connection is required. The Restatement Second of Agency Section 213 (1958), provides that liability for negligent supervision is appropriate if an employer is negligent either in employing improper persons in work involving risk to others *or* in failing to prevent tortious conduct from occurring on the work premises. The standard is written in the disjunctive and when, as here, the tort occurs on the premises, the victim need not have any additional connection to the business.

The majority states as fact that "Uzan was not authorized to bring third parties to the business during non-working hours." However, there is no factual finding to that effect. Not only is the majority's reference to work rules unsupported by trial court findings but it also conflicts with the trial court's description of work place practices at Keller's business.

This was a small, poorly-run "mom and pop" business, not a large corporation with personnel policies that were enforced by management. With Uzan as manager, inappropriate as well as illegal conduct was tolerated and facilitated. Whatever rules Keller may have had, they were not enforced.

The fact that the assault did not occur during working hours is irrelevant in this case because Keller allowed Uzan to be on the premises, without supervision, whenever he wished. There is no dispute that the assault on Koca occurred on a Sunday morning in the back room of the cleaners. Uzan's ostensible reason for being at the store was to admit a worker to clean the store's carpets. Surely, the majority would not contend that because the store was not open for business, Keller would have had no liability if Uzan had attacked the carpet cleaner as he attacked Koca.

In my opinion, Keller owed a duty of care to Koca. Keller's duty was not limited to business hours or to those who were customers or employees because he gave Uzan unrestricted access to the premises and he knew that Uzan repeatedly sexually assaulted young women on the premises.

For these reasons, I respectfully dissent.

CASE COMMENT

This case presents an excellent example of the pointed arguments from the perspectives of both the business and the victim. The majority decision found that there was insufficient knowledge by the business owner that the manager would commit the sexual assault of a young girl outside of business hours. The court discussed this question in light of the incident being foreseeable. This standard goes to the question of whether the employer knew or should have known of the propensities of the employee in relation to the harm or injury incurred. While it is true that the employer had knowledge of prior—and similar—bad conduct of the manager, the court was unwilling to connect this knowledge to the facts of this case. The fact that the sexual assault did not occur during business hours, and it did not involve a subordinate employee (as did the other incidents), made the incident "unforeseeable" in the judgment of the majority. The dissent, however, makes a compelling case that the prior behavior of the manager makes the sexual assault of the girl foreseeable. It is a close call. The "right" opinion in these cases usually reflects your experiences, biases, and worldview. This is a good example why these cases are hard to predict and prevent.

DISCUSSION QUESTIONS

How would you have ruled in the above case and why? Base your opinion both on the facts of the case and of the relevant legal standards. In negligent supervision and training cases, what are the employer's best defenses, and what issues and facts should the plaintiff seek to present?

NEGLIGENT ENTRUSTMENT

Cause of Action and Elements

The tort claim of negligent entrustment usually stems from an individual being injured from the inappropriate use of an instrumentality (such as a vehicle, mace and other chemical sprays, handcuffs and batons, and handguns or other weapons such as tazers). Clearly, this cause of action is similar to the logic of negligent training, where inappropriate training or the failure to train may result in liability to the employer. The elements of a negligent entrustment claims are generally threefold:[5]

1. The making available to another a chattel which the supplier
2. Knows or should have known the user is likely to use in a manner involving risk of physical harm to others
3. The supplier should expect to be endangered by its use.

Considering these elements, the "supplier" is typically the employer. When the chattel or instrumentality is such that it is known to involve risk of harm to others, then the employer may be liable for the damages related to the harm. The key ways to reduce liability in these instances is to provide appropriate levels of training, codify policies and procedures related to their use, and to monitor the employees' behavior and of their use of the particular instrumentality.

60 F. Supp. 2d 496

United States District Court, D. Maryland

RONALD W. MCGUINESS v. BRINK'S INCORPORATED.

Aug. 20, 1999

Background

In action against armored car service to recover for injuries suffered in shooting involving firearm issued by service, Brink's moved to dismiss.

Holding

The district court held that service's issuance of firearm to employee was not proximate cause of plaintiff's injuries.

Motion granted

Brink's is in the business of transporting, protecting and storing the coin, currency, negotiable instruments, and other valuables of its customers. On or about December 16, 1994, Brink's and one of its employees, Norma Jean Brashear, applied for and submitted an application for a handgun permit to the Maryland State Police department indicating that Brashear was in line to be promoted to a driver and/or messenger. Such a position would require Brashear to pick up and deliver valuables, necessitating the carrying of a firearm. The Maryland Police approved the handgun permit for Brashear on or about February 15, 1995. The license permitted Brashear to carry her firearm between her residence and the Brink's office while actively engaged as an armored car guard and/or driver and while on duty as a Brink's employee.

On August 25, 1995, Raymond Ratliff shot and injured the plaintiff, Ronald McGuiness. The assailant shot McGuiness with the firearm owned by Brink's and issued by Brink's to Brashear. The plaintiff alleges that the weapon used by Ratliff in the shooting was provided to Ratliff with the full permission of Brashear. At the time of the shooting, Ratliff and Brashear, who were cohabitating, were allegedly driving around in an attempt to make a drug deal. Allegedly, Ratliff used the gun to warn McGuiness, who was approaching their vehicle, to stay away. When he did not, Ratliff shot him.

McGuiness was shot in his left shoulder, which resulted in paralysis on his left side due to the bullet lodged in his spinal column. McGuiness is suing for past and future lost wages, mental anguish, pain and suffering, and future miscellaneous losses. McGuiness seeks $5,000,000.00 for each count in his complaint.

Count I—Negligence

Under Maryland law, there is no special duty to protect another from criminal acts by a third person, in the absence of a statute or a special relationship.

McGuiness argues that Brink's had a duty to safely control a dangerous instrumentality affirmatively placed in the public sector as a condition of employment of Brashear, thereby creating a dangerous agency. It is the plaintiff's position that when a dangerous instrumentality such as a firearm is involved, the duty owed is a duty to the public at large and that there need be no special relationship as argued by the defendant.

The Maryland Court of Appeals has recently rejected such a high standard for firearms. In *Valentine,* the defendant was a gun retailer who had two guns stolen from the store. An unknown assailant used one of the stolen guns and killed the plaintiff's wife. The court ruled that "although the inherent nature of guns suggests that their use may likely result in serious personal injury or death to another," this does not create a duty to third persons. To find such a duty, the court held, would effectively be "regulating the merchant. This type of regulation is the realm of the legislature and is not appropriate as judicial enactment."

Hence, the question is whether there should be more liability for issuing a handgun to a properly permitted employee than displaying weapons for sale to the public as in *Valentine.* It is arguable that Brink's would have a duty where a shop owner would not. A shop owner sells firearms to any person meeting the state permit requirements. Brink's supplies firearms to its employees to be used to further Brink's interest as an employer. When uniformed Brink's employees carry their weapons, they are representing Brink's. A company should have more control over its employees than over its customers. Hence, a company is more accountable for the actions of its employees than for the actions of its customers. Nonetheless, it is unnecessary to determine what duty Brink's had to third parties. The factual scenario at issue precludes a finding of liability due to lack of proximate cause.

Brink's argues that two actions supersede any liability of Brink's. First, Brashear illegally lent her weapon to Ratliff and second, Ratliff criminally shot the plaintiff. Brink's argues that there is no liability where the intervening act is neither invited by or is an ordinary response to the original act. For example, using a car to run someone down is not what one normally does with a car. However, while shooting someone may not be what everyone with a firearm does, is it arguably the intended usage of the instrumentality.

In *Hartford Insurance Co. v. Manor Inn of Bethesda* the Maryland Court of Appeals held that unforeseeable criminal acts break the chain of causation, relieving the original negligent actor of liability. In *Hartford,* the defendant's employee left a van unattended with the doors unlocked and the keys in the ignition. The van was stolen and negligently driven into the injured party's car. The court found the defendant could have anticipated and prevented the theft of the car. The *Hartford* court assumed that this was negligent, but found that the negligent driving was not foreseeable, and was hence a superseding cause of injury relieving the employer of liability. "Liability may not be imposed if for example the negligence of one person is merely passive and potential, while the negligence of another is the moving and effective cause of the injury...."

In the instant case, there are two independent causes of the injury: (1) the illegal loan of the weapon and (2) Ratliff's subsequent criminal use of it to shoot the plaintiff. Brashear affirmatively took action by criminally lending her firearm to the assailant. Ratliff then criminally shot the victim. The court finds this scenario unforeseeable and far too attenuated to hold Brink's liable. As discussed, *supra,* Maryland law holds that unforeseeable criminal acts supersede liability. While it may be that Brink's is subject to a higher standard of liability for a firearm than for an automobile, it is not so high as to hold Brink's liable where there are two unforeseeable criminal actions. The actions of Brink's are not the proximate cause of Ratliff's injury and hence, Brink's is not liable for negligence as a matter of law.

Count II—Negligent Entrustment

The tort of negligent entrustment was first recognized by the Maryland Court of Appeals. Maryland has adopted the Restatement (Second) of Torts Section 390 (1965) as its standard for negligent entrustment. Section 390 states:

> One who supplies directly or through a third person a chattel for the use of another whom the supplier knows or has reason to know to be likely because of his youth, inexperience, or otherwise, to use it in a manner involving unreasonable risk of physical harm to himself and others whom the supplier should expect to share in or be endangered by its use, is subject to liability for physical harm resulting to them.

McGuiness alleges that there was a negligent entrustment of a firearm from Brink's to Brashear and that the issuance of the firearm to Brashear enhanced the likelihood and/or risk that a third person would use the firearm to harm the public at large and/or the plaintiff in particular. Brink's argues this theory seeks to expand the negligent entrustment doctrine to include a vicarious liability component that the doctrine does not contemplate. Brink's argues that the risk of harm encompassed by the doctrine is harm caused by the one to whom the gun was supplied—the entrustee.

The Maryland Court of Special Appeals "recently clarified the elements of negligent entrustment in *Wright v. Neale* as:

1. The making available to another a chattel which the supplier
2. Knows or should have known the user is likely to use in a manner involving risk of physical harm to others
3. The supplier should expect to be endangered by its use."

"The principal feature of this tort is the knowledge of the supplier concerning the likelihood of the person to whom he entrusts the chattel to use it in a dangerous manner."

"The cause of action for negligent entrustment is based on the requisite knowledge of the supplier of the chattel. If the supplier knows or should know of the entrustee's propensities to use the chattel in an improper or dangerous manner, the entrustor owes a duty to foreseeable parties to withhold the chattel from the entrustee."

McGuiness alleges that Brink's had reason to know that Brashear, due to "reckless and unstable propensities," was liable to use the firearm in a manner involving unreasonable risk of physical harm to others. "The entrustor may be charged not only with what he or she actually knew, but with what he or she should have known." If the circumstances suggest that further inquiry is appropriate and the entrustor fails to make a reasonable investigation, the entrustor may be liable. The question is whether the plaintiff has alleged any facts, which if assumed to be true, would indicate that Brink's knew or should have known that Brashear was in any way incompetent.

The plaintiff avers that at the time Brink's hired Brashear until after the time when McGuiness was shot, Brashear used crack cocaine on a daily basis. Brashear allegedly was a daily abuser of alcohol and frequently used marijuana during that time period. At no time during Brashear's employment with Brink's did Brink's subject her to a drug screening test. Furthermore, Brashear allegedly used a cellular telephone issued by Brink's to send and receive calls related to cocaine and marijuana sales. This allegedly took place in the four months preceding the shooting. These calls were apparently frequently late at night.

> One who supplies a chattel for the use of another who knows its exact character and condition is not entitled to assume that the other will use it safely if the supplier knows or has reason to know that such other is likely to use it dangerously, as where the other belongs to a class which is notoriously incompetent to use the chattel safely, or lacks the training and experience necessary for such use, or the supplier knows that the other has on other occasions so acted that the supplier should realize that the chattel is likely to be dangerously used, or that the other, though otherwise capable of using the chattel safely, has a propensity or fixed purpose to misuse it. See Restatement (Second) of Torts § 390.

Certainly, a drug addict/dealer may have a fixed purpose for a firearm. In the context of supplying an automobile to an incompetent driver, the court of appeals in stated: "The doctrine requires scienter and has been applied in cases involving automobiles where the owner knew or should have known that the use of the entrusted car by the entrustee would likely involve unreasonable risk." The important wording to note is "in cases involving automobiles." Certainly, public policy may dictate another standard for entrustment of firearms.

Brink's argues that it cannot be held liable for negligent entrustment because it was Ratliff and not Brashear, the entrustee, who caused the injury. The classic example in the Restatement (Second) of Torts Section 390 is where A permits B, an inexperienced driver, to use his car. B invites C, who knows of his inexperience, to drive with him. While driving, B crashed into D, harming both B and C. In this example neither B nor C may recover against A, but A is subject to liability to D. Hence, if Brashear herself had shot the victim, Brink's could be liable for negligent entrustment if McGuiness were able to prove that it was negligent to entrust Brashear with the gun. However, in this case, A gave the gun to B who then in turn gave it to C who shot D. If such a scenario transpired in the automobile case, it seems that A would not be liable because it is too far attenuated.

In *Curley,* the court of appeals did recognize that the entrustor is only responsible for the subsequent negligent acts of the entrustee if a reasonable man could have foreseen the negligent acts. Similarly, in *Kahlenberg,* the court again asserted that the liability of the entrustor is based "upon the negligent entrustment when it operates as a concurrent cause with the negligence of the entrustee." The language in these two cases suggests that the entrustee, of legal necessity, must be negligent for the cause of action of negligent entrustment to arise. "Whether the exceptions stated in Comment c to the Restatement or any other exception will be applied in Maryland will have to be decided in another case on another day." However, there may be something different about the nature of a firearm, which would lead to another conclusion. Nonetheless, as above, there is no proximate cause. If Brashear had done the shooting, then this matter may have gone to the jury. However, because she did not, the count must be dismissed.

Count III—Negligent Hiring/Retention

Maryland has recognized that an employer has an obligation to the public to use due care in selecting and retaining only competent and careful employees. To maintain a cause of action for negligent hiring/retention under Maryland law, the plaintiff must establish: (1) that Brashear was an employee of Brink's; (2) that Brashear was incompetent; (3) Brink's actual or constructive knowledge of that incompetence; (4) Brashear's act or omission caused the plaintiff's injury and (5) that Brink's negligence in hiring or retaining Brashear was the proximate cause of the plaintiff's injury.

The complaint states that Brink's knew or should have known she was reckless, negligent and/or otherwise incompetent and that she was potentially dangerous because she habitually failed at the end of her work shift to return the handgun issued to her by Brink's. The plaintiff argues that Brink's negligently retained Brashear because had Brink's performed drug screening, the tests allegedly would have revealed that Brashear had a chronic substance abuse problem for at least the four months prior to the shooting.

As with the first two counts, the issue of causation persists. The fourth element of negligent hiring or retention requires that the employee's action be the cause of the plaintiff's injury. Brashear gave her firearm to Ratliff. It was Ratliff's criminal act which caused Ratliff's injury, not Brashear's action. The fifth element requires that Brink's proximately caused McGuiness' injury. As previously discussed, no action of Brink's proximately caused the plaintiff's injury. Accordingly, Count III, Negligent Hiring/Retention, must be dismissed.

Order

Accordingly, these complaints are dismissed with prejudice. Based on the foregoing analysis, the defendant's Motion to Dismiss is hereby granted.

CASE COMMENT

The court in this case provides an excellent analysis of the relevant legal standards and of somewhat unusual facts. Here the court found that Brink's was not liable for negligent entrustment and was not liable for the other related negligent claims. The key to this decision was the fact that the Brink's employee, Brashear, did not actually commit the shooting. Instead, Brashear gave her gun to a friend, who ended up shooting the plaintiff. The court held that Brink's could not have reasonably foreseen Brashear doing so, thereby negating the proximate cause between the act and the injury. It is interesting that the court found against Brink's even though the plaintiff argued that Brashear was a drug abuser. In my opinion, if the plaintiff could have factually substantiated this allegation, the court would have been much more inclined to find against Brink's. The logic of this assertion, of course, is that drug abusers should not be issued firearms. Issuing firearms to drug addicts could reasonably result in the injury complained of in this case, as almost any fact pattern is conceivable in light of the volatile mixture of drugs and guns. From the plaintiff's perspective, the failure to provide any evidence to this allegation was fatal to the case.

895 So. 2d 1114

District Court of Appeal of Florida, Fourth District

K. M., A MINOR, BY AND THROUGH HER PARENT AND NEXT FRIEND, D. M., AND D. M., INDIVIDUALLY, APPELLANTS, PUBLIX SUPER MARKETS, INC., A FLORIDA CORPORATION, APPELLEE.

Jan. 26, 2005

Background

Employee's child, who allegedly was sexually abused by co-employee when co-employee was baby-sitting child in co-employee's home, brought action against employer, whose manager knew that co-employee was baby-sitting child and that co-employee was on parole from a previous conviction for attempted sexual battery on a minor under 12. The Circuit Court for the Seventeenth Judicial Circuit, Broward County, dismissed action, and child appealed.

Holding

The district court of appeal held that employer did not have a duty to warn employee about co-employee's criminal background, given that the warning pertained to the employees' personal relationship outside of work.

Affirmed

When K. M. was 7 years old, her mother was employed at a Publix supermarket in Broward County. She worked in the business office with store manager David Moses. Moses scheduled the mother to work in the early mornings and late afternoons. This schedule required the mother to make child care arrangements for K. M. The mother arranged for another Publix employee, Robert Woodlard, to baby-sit. Woodlard and the mother had become friends through their Publix jobs and Woodlard agreed to care for K. M. at his home. This arrangement enabled the mother to work the required hours.

Moses was aware that Woodlard was taking care of K. M. In addition, because he had been contacted by the Department of Corrections, Moses also knew that Woodlard was on parole from a previous conviction for attempted sexual battery on a minor under 12. According to the amended complaint, based on that information, Moses knew or should have known that Woodlard was unfit to provide child care, but failed to warn the mother of that danger. Unaware of Woodlard's criminal background, the mother entrusted K. M. to him over a three-month period. During that time, Woodlard sexually abused K. M. on at least two occasions.

K. M. contends that this case falls under Section 302B of the Restatement (Second) of Torts (1964), which provides, in pertinent part, that an "omission may be negligent if the actor realizes or should realize that it involves an unreasonable risk of harm to another through the conduct of ... a third person which is intended to cause harm, even though such conduct is criminal."

However, the Section 302B negligence standard applies only if the actor is under a duty to avoid the unreasonable risk. "The duties of one who omits to act are ... in general confined to situations where there is a special relation between the actor and the other which gives rise to the duty." Restatement (Second) of Torts Section 302.

The general rule is that a party has no legal duty to "prevent the misconduct of third persons." As the court noted "Florida courts have long been loathe imposing liability based on a defendant's failure to control the conduct of a third party."

Florida recognizes the special relationship exception to the general rule of non-liability for third-party misconduct. The existence of a special relationship gives rise to a duty to control the conduct of third persons so as to prevent them from harming others. Florida has adopted the "special relationship" test set forth in the Restatement (Second) of Torts, Section 315, which states:

In *Daly v. Denny's Inc.* we wrote that: "the duty to protect strangers against the tortious conduct of another can arise if, at the time of the injury, the defendant is in actual or constructive control of":

1. the instrumentality,
2. the premises on which the tort was committed, or
3. the tortfeasor.

Here, the injury did not occur on Publix's premises, did not involve an instrumentality such as a car, and Publix did not have the right to control Woodlard when he was away from work on his own time. There is no duty so to control the conduct of a third person as to prevent him from causing physical harm to another unless, under Section 315 General Principle:

(a) A special relation exists between the actor and the third person which imposes a duty upon the actor to control the third person's conduct, or

(b) A special relation exists between the actor and the other which gives to the other a right to protection.

Comment c to Section 315 provides: the relations between the actor and a third person which require the actor to control the third person's conduct are stated in Sections 316 to 319. The relations between the actor and the other which require the actor to control the conduct of third persons for the protection of the other are stated in Sections 314A and 320.

Sections 316 and 318 of the Restatement relate to the duty of a parent to control the conduct of a child and the duty of a possessor of land or chattels to control the conduct of a licensee, respectively, and neither are applicable here. Nor does K. M. fall under Sections 314A or 320, since she was not in the custody of Publix at any time and they did not have a common carrier-passenger, innkeeper-guest, or possessor of land-invitee relationship.

Section 317 involves the duty of a master to control the conduct of a servant. As formulated by the Restatement, that duty is limited to acts committed by employees (1) with the employer's chattels or (2) upon the premises of the employer or premises upon which the servant is privileged to enter only as the employer's servant. This section does not affect K. M.'s case because the criminal attacks occurred off Publix's premises and did not involve its property. Although there was an employment relationship between Publix and the mother, that relationship did not place a duty upon Publix with regard to its employees' extracurricular relationship. The mother's personal situation–that she needed child care in order to work—did not create a duty where one would not otherwise exist. To address one of K. M.'s arguments, the occurrence of the assault off-premises takes this case out of Section 317, and precludes an action against Publix for negligent retention.

Finally, Section 319 of the Restatement imposes a duty of care upon one "who takes charge of a third person whom he knows or should know to be likely to cause bodily harm to others if not controlled." Here, Publix did not "take charge" of Woodlard to the extent necessary to fall within this section. In *Schmidt v. HTG, Inc.* the Kansas Supreme Court reviewed the law on Section 319 and concluded that a state parole officer did not take charge or exercise control over a parolee within the meaning of Section 319 so as to gives rise to a duty to control the conduct of a third party to prevent harm to others. As a civilian employer, Publix exerted far less control over Woodlard than a parole officer, so Section 319 is inapplicable here.

When this court has recognized a duty to take precautions against the criminal acts of third parties, it has required the existence of a "special relationship." In *Nova Southeastern,* a university assigned an adult student to an off-campus internship site that the university knew was located in a high crime area. The adult student filed suit after she was criminally assaulted in the parking lot of that site. Both this court and the supreme court found that the adult student–university relationship was a special relationship that imposed a duty on the school to act reasonably in providing educational services and programs.

K. M. relies upon *Shurben v. Dollar Rent-A-Car,* however, that case demonstrated a special relationship between the plaintiff and the defendant that does not exist in this case. The *Shurben* plaintiff was an out-of-town tourist. The complaint alleged that "(1) at the time of [plaintiff's] trip in early 1992 rental cars bore a license plate designation which knowledgeable criminals knew identified the car as a rental; (2) at that time there had been repeated instances of criminal activity directed at tourists in rental cars in certain areas of Miami and that Dollar was aware of those instances; and (3) Dollar knew that [the plaintiff] was an arriving British tourist without specific information as to the existence of the special license plate designation or the crimes directed at tourists."

The trial court entered dismissal after finding that those allegations did not give rise to a legal duty. The third district reversed, holding that a legal duty did exist under Section 302B, particularly in light of defendant's "superior knowledge."

Shurben did not specifically mention the special relationship doctrine. However, we explained in *Family Services* that *Shurben* "demonstrated that Florida courts have been especially sensitive in finding the requisite special relationship to exist." The special relationship in *Shurben* was the customer-rental agency relationship.

The special relationship test is a limitation on the scope of one's liability for the intentional acts of third parties. The Restatement and Florida law set parameters on employers' liability for the acts of their employees. As the second district has explained, once liability began to be imposed on employers for acts of their employees outside the scope of employment, the courts were faced with the necessity of finding some rational basis for limiting the boundaries of that liability; otherwise, an employer would be an absolute guarantor and strictly liable for any acts committed by his employee against any person under any circumstances. Such unrestricted liability would be an intolerable and unfair burden on employers.

To expand employers' liability in this area would have "broad ramifications," requiring employers to monitor their employee relationships apart from work, in areas such as commuting and socializing (holding that employer who fired inebriated employee and ordered him off the work site did not owe a duty to users of public highways who might later be injured by the employee).

Without any special relationship, this case falls under the general rule of "Section 314 of the Restatement (Second) of Torts (1964), which provides that the fact that a person realizes or should realize that action on his part is necessary for another's aid or protection does not of itself impose a duty to take such action." In the absence of specific threats, courts in other states have not imposed a duty to warn third parties of the criminal backgrounds of persons released from custody (providing that family members of paroled sex offender had no duty to warn girlfriend of their family member's prior criminal history, such that girlfriend could not bring suit for boyfriend's sexual assault of her minor child; court held that no duty placed on a county for failing to warn parents of neighborhood children of juvenile offender released on temporary leave to his mother's custody, even where county knew of offender's "dangerous and violent propensities regarding young children"; holding that private citizen who had child sex offender as a guest in his home after the offender's release from prison did not have a duty to warn neighborhood parents and the local police about the offender's presence).

The facts of this case did not impose a duty on Publix with respect to its employee's away-from-work childcare decisions. An employer does not owe a duty to persons who are injured by its employees while the employees are off duty, not then acting for the employer's benefit, not on the employer's premises, and not using the employer's equipment.

Affirmed

CASE COMMENT

The "entrustment" in this case was a baby with a convicted child molester. Based on the language of the decision, it is clear that the court did not desire to expand the notion of entrustment to this fact pattern unless some "special relationship" existed. The court provides an excellent analysis of relevant cases and principles articulated in the Restatement of Torts in coming to the conclusion that the employer was not liable because the plaintiff failed to show the existence of a "special relationship." As tragic as this case is, the court properly analyzed the facts and the law.

DISCUSSION QUESTIONS

In light of the liability exposures inherent in having private security personnel being armed with firearms and using patrol vehicles, is it a good business practice to do so? Give arguments for and against this question. Further, in light of the threat of terrorism, does the potential for catastrophic incidents outweigh the potential for liability exposure? What are the appropriate legal and public policy responses to this situation?

NOTES

1. See *Daisley v. Riggs Bank, N.A.*, 372 F. Supp. 2d 61 (2005); and *Browne v. SCR Medical Transportation Services, Inc.*, 826 N.E. 2d 1030 (2005).
2. See *Browne v. SCR Medical Transportation Services*, 826 N.E. 2d 1030 (2005).
3. See *Patino v. Complete Tire, Inc.*, 158 S.W. 3d 655 (2005); *Bolduc v. U.S.*, 402 F. 3d 50 (2005); and *Estevez-Yalcin v. The Children's Village*, 331 F. Supp. 2d 170 (2004); and *Keller v. Koca*, 111 P. 3d 445 (2005).
4. See *Jama v. U.S. I.N.S.*, 334 F. Supp. 2d 662 (2004); *Longshore v. Saber Security Services, Inc.*, 619 S.E. 2d 5 (2005); and *Arnold v. Janssen Pharmaceutica, Inc.*, 215 F. Supp. 2d 951 (2002).
5. See *Wright v. Neale*, 555 A. 2d 518 (1989); and *Daly v. Denny's Inc.*, 694 So. 2d 775 (1997).

3

Investigative Cases and Methods

NEGLIGENT INVESTIGATIONS

Cause of Action and Elements

This chapter is a composite of various causes of action relating to the investigation of workplace allegations and criminal acts. Usually these claims result from the treatment of the individual who is under suspicion for some type of wrongdoing. Allegations relating to improper interrogations, improper investigative techniques, and improper detainment procedures are typically raised by the plaintiff.

An interview is often differentiated from an interrogation. An interview usually relates to a general questioning of an individual who is not a suspect or a target of an investigation. An interview can be defined as a "relatively formal conversation conducted for the purpose of obtaining information."[1] By contrast, an interrogation usually entails a more accusatory, or at least, a more targeted attempt to elicit information from an individual who is suspected of committing a particular crime. Interrogations can be defined as a "systematic questioning of a person suspected of involvement in a crime for the purpose of obtaining a confession."[2] Typically this entails questioning initiated by state actors (usually police or other law enforcement officials) after a person has been deprived of freedom of movement in any significant way. Implicit in this definition of interrogation is the requirement that the individual be in some form of custody. This requirement does not apply to general on-the-scene, nonaccusatorial questioning. It also does not apply to spontaneous, volunteered statements. While each interrogation involves its own particular facts, typically the goals are as follows:[3]

- To learn the truth about the crime and how it occurred
- To obtain an admission of guilt from the suspect

- To obtain all relevant facts to determine the method of operation and the circumstances of the crime
- To gather information that enables investigators to arrive at logical conclusions
- To provide information for use by prosecutors in possible court action

Generally, an interrogation will take place during the course of an investigation. In essence, the purpose of an investigation is to simply "reconstruct the past." More specific goals are to determine if a crime has been committed; to discover all relevant facts; to collect evidence related to the crime; to recover any property taken in the crime; and to identify, locate, and apprehend the perpetrator.[4] Often the investigation also entails the prosecution of the offender and a determination of the motive and means (modus operandi) of the crime.[5]

CASES

81 Ark. App. 441, 105 S.W.3d 369

Court of Appeals of Arkansas, Division II

GENE ADDINGTON v. WAL-MART STORES, INC.

April 23, 2003

Background

Former employee brought action against former employer for outrage, false-light invasion of privacy, intrusion invasion of privacy, defamation, and negligence after employee was terminated for stealing items from employer. The Circuit Court, Benton County, granted employer's motion for summary judgment. Former employee appealed.

Holdings

The court of appeals held that:

1. Conduct of employer in conducting an investigation of employer for alleged stealing was not so extreme and outrageous as to be beyond all possible bounds of decency to establish tort of outrage;
2. Employer representative's written and oral statements made during employer's investigation of employee for stealing were not made with actual malice to sustain a cause of action for invasion of privacy; and
3. Genuine issue of material fact existed as to whether employee's consent to search his property was freely and voluntarily given.

Affirmed in part; reversed and remanded in part

Gene Addington is the former maintenance supervisor of Wal-Mart's home office maintenance facility in Bentonville. In August of 1998, he was terminated when it was discovered that he was in possession of property that belonged to Wal-Mart. He later filed suit against Wal-Mart, alleging that in conducting the investigation that led to his termination,

Wal-Mart committed the above-mentioned tortious conduct. To place his allegations in context, it is necessary to recite a history of the investigation and surrounding events.

On August 13, 1998, two Wal-Mart loss-prevention officers, Jim Elder and Keith Womack, began surveillance of Bob Kitterman, an employee of Wal-Mart's home office maintenance department. The surveillance led to the discovery that Kitterman and his son-in-law were in possession of tools and other property allegedly stolen from Wal-Mart. On August 17, another maintenance facility employee, David Clark, was interviewed with regard to stolen property. A subsequent search of Clark's home resulted in the seizure of approximately 400 items that Wal-Mart contended were stolen from its facility. Thereafter, on August 20, 1998, Elder and Womack, along with personnel officer Melinda Hass, interviewed the other employees of the maintenance department. During the interviews, employee Hays Buenning admitted to being in possession of Wal-Mart property that he did not own. A search of Buenning's home by Elder and Womack revealed several items allegedly belonging to Wal-Mart. Buenning was suspended, and he spoke with Addington on the phone that night, telling Addington that his (Buenning's) house had been "ransacked."

The next day, August 21, 1998, Womack conducted an interview with Addington. He asked Addington if he had any property that belonged to Wal-Mart. Addington admitted that he had some light poles in his yard that had been given to him by his supervisor Bob Murphy and a VCR and monitor that he had gotten from David Clark, though he was not sure if they belonged to Wal-Mart. According to Addington, Womack asked if they might go to Addington's home to view the light poles.

Addington agreed, and Elder and Womack followed him in a separate car. While they were en route, Elder called for a Benton County deputy to meet the men at Addington's house, telling the dispatcher that stolen property from Wal-Mart was located there. When the deputy arrived, Elder asked Addington to sign a consent form to allow a search of his home. Addington refused until he could speak with his wife, who was inside the home. After speaking with Mrs. Addington, who became very upset, Addington again communicated his refusal to sign the consent form, and he went back inside the house. The men stayed on the premises, however, and Addington observed Elder walking toward his shop building.

Addington returned to the front porch and reiterated that he would not sign the consent. According to Addington, Womack said, "Well, we'll just call the IRS and let them do the math." During this same time frame, Elder said to Addington, "Gene, I can get a search warrant. I've already talked to someone." Also, according to Mrs. Addington, Womack stated at some point that "we don't need the media involved in this" or "we don't need to get the media up here." Addington went back inside, called attorney Paul Davidson, and told him that he was afraid that, if he did not consent to the search, his job would be in jeopardy. Davidson told him that, while he did not have to consent to the search, Wal-Mart could probably obtain a warrant and that, if he was convinced that refusal to consent would result in his termination, he should allow the search. At that point, Addington went back outside and signed the consent form. The time span between the parties' arrival at the Addington property and the signing of the consent form was approximately thirty minutes. During this time, the deputy never spoke with Addington; he sat in his car in the driveway.

After Addington signed the consent form, Elder conducted a search of Addington's shop with the deputy alongside him. Elder questioned Addington about where he had obtained various items. Addington explained where he had purchased the items and, once a satisfactory explanation was given, Elder mentioned it no further. However, Addington admitted that, in addition to the light poles, monitor, and VCR, he had some toilets and water heaters that he had removed from a Wal-Mart facility. Additionally, he had a security camera, which he had purchased from a Wal-Mart vendor for $5.00, in violation of company policy. Elder confiscated the monitor and VCR and asked Addington to disconnect the camera and bring it with him to the office on Monday. Addington was suspended on the spot and later terminated. In all, five employees were fired as the result of this investigation. Wal-Mart's handling of the investigation has led to several lawsuits being filed by the men accused.

The supreme court has formulated four factors necessary to establish the tort of outrage: (1) the actor intended to inflict emotional distress or knew or should have known that emotional distress was the likely result of his conduct; (2) the conduct was extreme and outrageous, was beyond all possible bounds of decency, and was utterly intolerable in a civilized community; (3) the actions of the defendant were the cause of the plaintiff's distress; and (4) the emotional distress sustained by the plaintiff was so severe that no reasonable person could be expected to endure it.

Despite judicial recognition of this tort, the courts have addressed it in a cautious manner and have stated that recognition of it is not intended to open the doors of the courts to every slight insult or indignity one must endure in life. In particular, the courts have taken a narrow view of claims that arise out of the discharge of an employee. The reason is that an employer must be given considerable latitude in dealing with employees, and at the same time, an employee will frequently feel considerable insult when discharged.

The type of conduct that meets the standard for outrage must be determined on a case-by-case basis. We require clear-cut proof to establish the elements in outrage cases. Merely describing the conduct as outrageous does not make it so. Clear-cut proof, however, does not mean proof greater than a preponderance of the evidence.

The trial court ruled that the facts presented by Addington were not so outrageous or extreme as to go beyond all possible bounds of decency and further, that Addington's symptoms did not constitute emotional distress so severe that no reasonable person should be expected to endure it. We agree with the trial court.

On the first of the eight factors alleged by Addington to support his claim, Addington has misrepresented his own deposition testimony. He testified that, when Elder, Womack, and Hass met with the maintenance employees on August 20, Elder "went through some of these techniques as how they do it and what they do, and a reference was made to people sitting in trees observing other people to watch them and all that." Addington acknowledged that Elder did not say anyone was sitting in trees watching Addington. Further, Addington said that nothing at the August 20 meeting made him mad or was considered by him to be inappropriate. On the second factor, Addington attempts to base his outrage claim on the fact that Wal-Mart labeled a coworker a liar and a thief. Addington cites no authority, and we have found none for the proposition that insulting a third person may give rise to outrage. On factor number three, Wal-Mart's use of the police for intimidation purposes is not well borne out here. Although a deputy was present when the consent to search was being offered to Addington, the deputy sat in Addington's driveway while the controversy over the consent was going on. Addington stated that the only conversation he had with the deputy was when he eventually signed the consent form "to get rid of them." Addington also stated that the deputy "never stepped foot on my grass or on my sidewalk." Further, when the search took place, the deputy did not go into Addington's home, although he did go into his shop.

On the fourth factor—the mention of the IRS—there is no question that a threat to notify the Internal Revenue Service is an intimidating technique, but we do not think it constitutes outrage. The reference to the IRS was vague in nature, and there was no evidence that Addington was particularly susceptible to a mention of the IRS. The "comments about stolen property" that Addington mentions in factor number five references Elder's description of the security camera as stolen and Elder's question to Addington, during the search of the shop, "where is the pallet of tools?" Accusations of theft, however, do not constitute outrage. As for Wal-Mart's failure to investigate whether Addington had permission to take the light poles home, as alleged in factor number six, Wal-Mart did conduct an investigation, although it may have been incomplete. Wal-Mart asked Addington's supervisor if he had given Addington permission to take the poles, and the supervisor said "absolutely not." It later developed that an employee said that she had overheard the supervisor giving Addington permission to take the poles. While this might constitute a lack of thoroughness by Wal-Mart, it is not the type of conduct that goes beyond all bounds of decency.

Regarding Elder and Womack's failure to leave when Addington declined to sign the consent form, undeniably they were putting pressure on him by their continued presence. However, they never tried to enter his home or use physical violence. Finally, on factor number eight, we fail to see how the threat of obtaining a search warrant is outrageous conduct when Addington had already acknowledged that he had property belonging to Wal-Mart in his home and his attorney had likewise told him that Wal-Mart could probably get a warrant.

Whether each of the above factors is taken individually or they are considered as a whole, we do not believe Wal-Mart's conduct rose to the level of that required for outrage. Although Wal-Mart's conduct was aggressive and intimidating, it did not go beyond all bounds of decency, especially when we consider some of the conduct that employers in other cases have committed and not been held liable. In light of our holding that Wal-Mart's conduct did not transcend the bounds of decency, we need not address whether Addington sustained emotional distress so severe that no reasonable person could be expected to endure it.

We turn now to Addington's cause of action for intrusion invasion of privacy. Intrusion is the invasion by a defendant upon the plaintiff's solitude or seclusion. Arkansas courts have seldom adjudicated intrusion claims. The tort consists of three parts: (1) an intrusion; (2) that is highly offensive; (3) into some matter in which a person has a legitimate expectation of privacy. A legitimate expectation of privacy is the touchstone of the tort of intrusion.

Wal-Mart argues here, as it did in *Lee* that there was not an intrusion because there was a consent to the search. Addington argues that a fact question remains as to whether his consent was freely and voluntarily given. We agree.

Though the validity of consent in a civil case does not involve a defendant's motion to suppress evidence seized in a criminal case, the standard for determining valid consent in the criminal context is helpful. Consent must be given freely and voluntarily to be valid. It must be shown that there was no duress or coercion, actual or implied. The voluntary nature of consent must be judged in light of the totality of the circumstances. In a civil case, the issue of whether consent was valid is a question of fact that must be decided by the trier of fact.

In *Lee*, the supreme court upheld the jury's verdict for David Clark on this count in a situation involving similar circumstances. As in that case, there are several particulars here that create a fact question on the issue of whether Addington's consent was voluntarily given: the threat of the IRS (a factor in *Lee*); the fact that Addington declined to consent three times, yet Elder and the officer remained on the premises (which is more indicative of coercion than in *Lee*, where there was one request to consent made at the premises); Addington's fear that he would lose his job if he did not consent (a factor in *Lee*); mention of the media, as testified to by Mrs. Addington (when she was aware that in Clark's case, media coverage had been substantial); and the fact that Addington agreed to go to his home in the first place only to allow Womack to look at the light poles (similar to the situation in *Lee*).

One factor that distinguishes this case from *Lee* is that, before signing the consent, Addington took the opportunity to consult with counsel. However, while Addington's consultation with an attorney before signing the consent form is certainly a factor to be considered in determining the voluntariness of his actions, we do not deem it conclusive. By that point, Addington had already refused to consent three times and had been subjected to the other coercive actions. The totality of the circumstances, in particular the fact that Addington declined to consent three times before succumbing, leads us to conclude that a fact question remains as to whether his consent was voluntarily given.

Finally, we address Addington's argument that summary judgment was inappropriate on his negligence claim. Addington's complaint alleged that Wal-Mart negligently failed to investigate whether Addington possessed stolen property and negligently supervised its employee, Jim Elder. The trial court ruled that there was no basis for the negligent investigation claim and that Addington failed to submit evidence that Wal-Mart knew or should have known of some prior conduct by Elder that would have put it on notice that Elder was a danger to other persons.

In his brief, Addington relies on Elder coming out to Addington's property under the guise of looking only at the light poles as evidence of a negligent investigation. While this fact may be relevant to Addington's other claims, we fail to see how it constitutes negligence. In any event, we cannot conceive how Wal-Mart could be liable for negligently determining that Addington possessed stolen property when it is undisputed that he did possess Wal-Mart property without authorization. Addington simply makes no convincing argument on this point.

The trial court's grant of summary judgment is reversed and remanded on the intrusion invasion-of-privacy count and affirmed on all other counts.

Affirmed in part; reversed and remanded in part.

CASE COMMENT

This case illustrates that investigative techniques used by Wal-Mart security were not so unreasonable as to be actionable in the tort of outrage. However, the invasion of privacy claim relating to the search of the plaintiff's home may have exposed Wal-Mart to liability. Notice that regardless of the fact that the plaintiff signed a "consent form," the court still questioned whether consent was free of duress and coercion. This is so due to the factual basis surrounding the execution of the form. The court noted that the plaintiff refused to sign the form on three occasions, and "had been subjected to the other coercive actions." These factors led the court to conclude that the execution of the consent form may have been coerced. This was in spite of the fact that the plaintiff consulted with an attorney before doing so!

243 F. Supp. 2d 1313

United States District Court, M.D. Florida, Orlando Division

MARANDA STIRES, PLAINTIFF v. CARNIVAL CORPORATION D/B/A CARNIVAL CRUISE LINES, DEFENDANT.

Nov. 7, 2002

Background

Passenger brought diversity action against cruise line for various causes of action.

Holdings

On motion by cruise line to dismiss, the district court held that:

1. Allegations of passenger were sufficient to state claim that cruise line was negligent in screening, hiring, investigating, retaining, and supervising head waiter and its other employees, and that such negligence was proximate cause of her claimed damages;
2. Allegations of passenger were sufficient to state claim that cruise line was vicariously liable for intentional torts of its employees, including intentional infliction of emotional distress;
3. Passenger properly pled her fraud and misrepresentation claim against cruise line with sufficient particularity.

Motion granted in part and denied in part

In response to an advertisement in her home state of Ohio, plaintiff, Maranda Stires, along with her grandmother, mother, and cousin, planned a cruise with defendant Carnival Corporation d/b/a Carnival Cruise Lines on the M/S *Tropicale.* Stires and her family boarded the *Tropicale* on September 23, 2000, in Florida.

Soon after boarding the ship, one of the ship's headwaiters, Ruben Sanchez, began making sexual overtures towards Stires. On September 28, 2000, at approximately 12:20 a.m., Stires left the casino on the eighth floor of the *Tropicale* to search for her cousin in the dining room. Sanchez, while allegedly acting in concert with other employees, took Stires to the floor on which the crew's quarters were located and proceeded to sexually assault her. Later that same night, Sanchez recommenced the sexual assault. However, this time, Sanchez did not stop at assaulting Stires, but proceeded to commit sexual battery on Stires. During the course of the sexual assault and battery, Sanchez repeatedly referred to Stires as a *"puta,"* the Spanish word for whore. After the sexual battery, Stires returned to her cabin, where she collapsed.

After washing her face and hands, Stires located her mother and told her of the battery. Stires and her mother asked Carnival's employees if Stires could make a report to the captain of the *Tropicale.* The employees declined the request. Instead, the employees directed Stires to the ship's nurse and doctor, who performed a physical examination on Stires. The examination revealed signs of the sexual battery. During the course of the examination, the doctor remarked "Ruben and the other waiters, oh yes, we on the ship know all about them." Stires inquired if that meant that Carnival knew of Sanchez's sexual propensity. The doctor replied, "You have to understand that I'm paid by Carnival."

Following the examination, Stires asked if she could shower. She was not permitted to do so. As a result, Stires was forced to remain in the soiled condition for 48 hours after the battery. The staff did, however, promise that upon docking, they would ensure that Stires would be taken to a local hospital. Carnival did not keep this promise.

Subsequently, Stires requested all documents and information in Carnival's possession concerning the sexual battery. Carnival produced no documents and told Stires that Sanchez was a Colombian national with no ties to the United States. Carnival further stated that there had been no previous problems and that Carnival would ensure that Sanchez was deported from the United States. Purportedly, Carnival made these false representations in order to induce Stires' reliance thereon.

A. Negligent Investigation, Hiring, Retention, Supervision, and Management

Carnival asserts that Stires has failed to aver facts sufficient to show a breach of duty to exercise reasonable care in hiring. Carnival's assertion is misplaced. In order to state a cause of action for the tort of negligent hiring or retention recognized in Florida, a plaintiff must allege facts showing that the employer was put on notice of the harmful propensities of the employee. The principal difference between negligent hiring and negligent retention is the time at which the employer is charged with knowledge of the employee's unfitness. Negligent hiring occurs when, prior to the time the employee is actually hired, the employer knew or should have known of the employee's unfitness, and the issue of liability primarily focuses upon the adequacy of the employer's pre-employment investigation into the employee's background.

Stires alleges that Carnival was negligent in screening, hiring, investigating, retaining, and supervising Sanchez and its other employees and that such negligence was the proximate cause of her damages. Furthermore, in the factual allegations of her complaint, Stires asserts that Carnival and its employees (the medical staff) were aware of Sanchez's propensities. Dismissal for failure to state a claim is inappropriate unless it appears that the plaintiff can prove no set of facts in support of her claim which would entitle her to relief. Hence, dismissal is inappropriate.

B. Intentional Infliction of Emotional Distress—Respondeat Superior

"To prove intentional infliction of emotional distress under Florida law, (a) plaintiff must prove: (1) deliberate or reckless infliction of mental suffering; (2) by outrageous conduct; (3) which conduct must have caused the suffering; and (4) the suffering must have been severe." The Restatement (Second) further provides:

Extreme and outrageous conduct ... It has not been enough that the defendant has acted with an intent which is tortious or even criminal, or that he has intended to inflict emotional distress, or even that his conduct has been characterized by "malice," or a degree of aggravation which would entitle the plaintiff to punitive damages for another tort. Liability has been found only where the conduct has been so outrageous in character, and so extreme in degree, as to go beyond all possible bounds of decency, and to be regarded as atrocious, and utterly intolerable in a civilized community. Generally, the case is one in which the recitation of the facts to an average member of the community would arouse his resentment against the actor, and lead him to exclaim, "Outrageous!" It is not enough that the defendant intended to inflict emotional distress, that the defendant's intent was tortious or criminal, or that the conduct was motivated by malice. Furthermore, under Florida law, whether a person's conduct is sufficiently outrageous or intolerable as to form the basis for a claim of intentional infliction of emotional distress is a matter of law for the court, not a question of fact.

As discussed in *Doe,* Carnival is vicariously liable for the intentional torts of its employees, including the intentional infliction of emotional distress. Although the basis of this claim is the same as the negligence claims, at this stage of the proceedings, it cannot be said that Stires can prove no set of facts that would entitle her to relief. Therefore, this count should not be dismissed.

C. Fraud and Misrepresentation

The elements for actionable fraud are (1) a false statement concerning a material fact; (2) knowledge by the person making the statement that the representation is false; (3) an intention that the representation induces another's reliance; and (4) consequent injury by the other party acting in reliance on the representation.

A reading of the amended complaint reveals that Stires has properly pled her fraud and misrepresentation claim with sufficient particularity. Stires alleges specific misrepresentations of Carnival both written and oral, knowledge on the part of Carnival that the statements were false when the misrepresentations were made, where the misrepresentations occurred, that the statements were made to induce Stires to rely on them, and Stires' detrimental reliance on the statements. Accordingly, dismissal is not proper.

For the foregoing reasons, defendant's Motion to Dismiss is **GRANTED in part** and **DENIED in part.**

CASE COMMENT

This case involves an attempt by the employer to "cover up" an alleged crime or at least a failure to treat the plaintiff's allegation seriously. The company's actions are especially egregious given the nature of the crime of rape. It seems apparent that the court viewed the response by the employer lacking, both in terms of the failure to adequately investigate the crime, and in its false statements made in response to this action. This is a classic example of how not to respond. Simply stated, employers must take allegations seriously. This is particularly relevant of serious allegations, which must be taken seriously, and investigated rigorously.

297 A.D. 2d 205, 746 N.Y.S. 2d 141

Supreme Court, Appellate Division, First Department, New York

EDDIE BROWN III, PLAINTIFF-RESPONDENT v. SEARS ROEBUCK AND CO., DEFENDANT-APPELLANT.

Aug. 1, 2002

Background

Former employee filed suit against his former employer for false arrest, false imprisonment, malicious prosecution, wrongful termination, negligent investigation and intentional infliction of emotional distress. The Supreme Court, Bronx County, granted former employer's motion for summary judgment in part, and dismissed claims for false arrest, false imprisonment, and negligence investigation. Former employer appealed.

Holdings

The supreme court, appellate division, held that:

1. Former employer did not initiate criminal proceeding against former employee;
2. Probable cause existed for former employee's arrest on suspicion of unlawful use of customer's credit card, and
3. Criminal proceeding against former employee on suspicion of misuse of customer's credit card was not terminated in his favor.

Reversed

Plaintiff was formerly employed as a sales associate in the computer department of defendant Sears' store on Fordham Road in the Bronx. On September 18, 1996, plaintiff entered a transaction into a cash register for the sale of an Apple computer, charging it to the account number of a Sears credit card holder named Gwendolyn Taylor.

Plaintiff's employee number appears on Sears' computer detail display of the receipt and he readily admits that he is the person who conducted the sale. Plaintiff claims he received a telephone order from a woman who identified herself as Gwendolyn Taylor. The computer receipt includes a notation that reads "Gwen Taylor/Freeman will [be] picking it [*sic*] up the Apple computer." Plaintiff denies having made this notation. In November 1996, Gwendolyn Taylor complained to Sears that she had not purchased the computer and had not authorized anyone else to purchase a computer using her credit card.

Around the same time, David Sankar, the Loss Prevention Manager at Sears, was investigating the conduct of another Sears employee, Al Freeman, a coworker of plaintiff's in the computer department, regarding merchandise returned without original receipts and the unauthorized use of a credit card belonging to another Sears customer. After Sankar reviewed the relevant documentation with his supervisors, Sears determined to have the matter reviewed by the police.

Sankar met with Detective Stangenburg and provided him with documentation concerning Freeman. During the meeting, Stangenburg inquired about an employee number on one of the receipts, and when advised it was plaintiff's, Stangenburg said he would need to speak to plaintiff and requested further information concerning the Gwendolyn Taylor transaction, including a statement from Ms. Taylor. According to Stangenburg, Sankar also told him that plaintiff and Freeman were "working together," and that he (Sankar) had seen plaintiff pick up the computer. Sankar denies making these two statements. Stangenburg then turned over the documentation provided by Sankar to Detective Lauler.

On March 9, 1997, Stangenburg came to the Sears store and arrested Al Freeman, charging him with multiple counts of larceny, possession of stolen property, and unlawful use of a credit card in a complaint signed by Sankar. Freeman pled guilty to the charges, none of which concerned the Gwendolyn Taylor transaction.

On March 11, 1997, Detective Lauler and another officer went to Sears to speak with plaintiff. Plaintiff agreed to accompany the officers to the precinct, where they interviewed him. According to plaintiff's hearing testimony, he initially denied knowing a customer "Ms. Taylor," after which Lauler told him he was under arrest. Then, after hearing Ms. Taylor's full name, he "remembered some things" and told Lauler that he had taken a telephone order from Gwendolyn Taylor and "security was investigating the situation." Lauler's notes of the interview reveal that plaintiff stated that he took a telephone order from Ms. Taylor and that he intended to deliver the computer via shuttle service. Plaintiff was then arrested by Lauler.

On March 12, 1997, Sankar signed a criminal complaint charging plaintiff with the crimes of grand larceny in the fourth degree and two counts of criminal possession of stolen property in the fourth degree. The factual allegations of the complaint alleged, *inter alia*, that plaintiff, a Sears cashier, typed in the credit card number of Gwendolyn Taylor to purchase an Apple computer for $2,865.36 and that according to Ms. Taylor, she did not purchase said computer nor authorize anyone to use her credit card number to make such purchase. Ultimately, however, the charges against plaintiff were dismissed at the request of the Bronx District Attorney's Office.

Plaintiff commenced the instant action against Sears and the City of New York. After depositions, the City's Motion for Summary Judgment was granted. The court found that probable cause for plaintiff's arrest existed as a matter of law based on the information contained in the criminal complaint, which plaintiff never disputed, as well as the additional suspicion arising from the notation on the receipt that someone named Freeman would pick up the Apple computer and the coincidence that plaintiff's coworker named Al Freeman had recently been arrested for the fraudulent use of a Sears credit card.

On appeal, Sears argues that the IAS court should have dismissed the malicious prosecution claim against it based on the prior judicial finding, affirmed by this Court, that probable cause existed for plaintiff's arrest. Sears further contends that plaintiff has failed to make a sufficient showing as to the other required elements of a malicious prosecution cause of action. We agree that plaintiff's cause of action for malicious prosecution fails as a matter of law.

The record likewise establishes the existence of probable cause to arrest plaintiff. Probable cause consists of such facts and circumstances as would lead a reasonably prudent person in a similar situation to believe plaintiff guilty. Where there is no real dispute as to the facts or the proper inferences to be drawn from such facts, the issue of probable cause is a question of law to be decided by the court. At the time of plaintiff's arrest, the uncontradicted evidence showed that plaintiff's employee number appeared on the receipt for the Taylor transaction; plaintiff admitted that he entered Taylor's credit card number to effect the transaction; Taylor signed a statement saying that she did not purchase the computer and did not authorize anyone else to make the purchase or use her credit card; the sales receipt stated that "Gwen Taylor/Freeman" would pick up the computer; and Al Freeman, a coworker of plaintiff, had recently been arrested for fraudulent use of a credit card. This evidence easily satisfies the probable cause standard.

Nor does plaintiff's allegation of falsified evidence by Sankar vitiate the finding of probable cause. Existence of conflicting evidence during investigation does not negate finding of probable cause, although relevant to the issue of guilt beyond a reasonable doubt at trial. As [the criminal court] found, probable cause existed for plaintiff's arrest without any reference to the alleged statements made by Sankar, rendering them mere surplusage. Moreover, as indicated, since there is no evidence in the record that this evidence contributed in any way to plaintiff's arrest, it cannot undermine the probable cause finding. The existence of probable cause bars plaintiff's claims for malicious prosecution as a matter of law.

We further conclude that the criminal proceeding against plaintiff was not terminated in his favor. "A plaintiff in a malicious prosecution action must show, as a threshold matter, that the criminal proceeding was finally terminated." A disposition of a criminal action "which does not terminate it but permits it to be renewed" cannot serve as the basis for malicious prosecution action.

Here, the case was dismissed at the request of the Bronx District Attorney's office, although the record is silent as to the reason. Thus, it is unclear whether the dismissal was based on the merits, facial insufficiency of the accusatory instrument, in the interests of justice or for some other reason. Accordingly, since the record discloses only that the District Attorney voluntarily discontinued the prosecution without any determination on the merits, and there is no evidence that the prosecution formally abandoned charges against the accused, plaintiff has failed to raise an issue of fact as to termination of the proceeding in his favor.

Although the IAS court failed to rule on plaintiff's cause of action for intentional infliction of emotional distress in its summary judgment decision, this claim should also have been dismissed. Plaintiff's allegation that Sankar gave false information to the police, even if true, did not describe conduct "so outrageous in character, and so extreme in degree, as to go beyond all possible bounds of decency, and to be regarded as atrocious, and utterly intolerable in a civilized community." Nor can plaintiff establish the element of a causal connection between Sears' conduct and his alleged injury since, as indicated, there is no evidence that Sankar's alleged false statements played any role in the determination to arrest plaintiff.

CASE COMMENT

This case connects an inadequate investigation allegation with the existence (or lack thereof) of probable cause and the merits of the arrest and prosecution. In this case, the plaintiff argued that the investigation was tainted by false statements and evidence, which were improperly used against him to "justify" the arrest and prosecution. If false evidence was in fact used to establish probable cause, then it would naturally negate the validity of the arrest and subsequent prosecution. Since the criminal charges against the plaintiff were dismissed by the prosecutor's office, the plaintiff argued that Sears was guilty of malicious prosecution.

While the elements of a malicious prosecution claim will be articulated in Chapter 4, it is sufficient to note, as did the court, that the plaintiff must show that the criminal proceeding was terminated in his favor. In this case, the court emphasized that the record was unclear as to why the case was dismissed. In so stating, the court concluded that the plaintiff failed to show this necessary element of a malicious prosecution claim. Further, the court held that there was ample evidence to support probable cause, thereby inferring that the investigation conducted by security and the police was sufficient to warrant probable cause to arrest the plaintiff.

636 N.W.2d 74

Supreme Court of Iowa

STEVEN JOHN THEISEN, APPELLANT v. COVENANT MEDICAL CENTER, INC., APPELLEE.

Nov. 15, 2001

Background

Former employee brought action against employer for negligent investigation and wrongful discharge, among other claims, alleging employer's request for voice print analysis violated prohibition against compelled polygraph examination. The District Court, Black Hawk County, granted summary judgment for employer, and employee appealed.

Holdings

The supreme court held that:

1. Voice identification procedure requested by employer violated neither statute prohibiting employers from requiring employees to submit to polygraph examination, as a condition of employment, nor public policy; and
2. Employer had no duty to conduct a reasonable investigation in favor of at-will employee.

Affirmed

On the evening of May 22, 1995, someone left an obscene message on the voice mail of Bobbie Hartwig, a nurse at Covenant Medical Center in Waterloo. Hartwig discovered the message when she arrived at work the next morning. She contacted her supervisor, Nancy Schuler, about the call. Schuler, who is also the head of the Quality Services department, advised Hartwig that nothing further needed to be done unless Hartwig received additional calls or messages. Hartwig also called Steve Theisen, Covenant's security manager, to report the call. Theisen never returned her call.

Although Hartwig had not immediately mentioned it to Schuler or Theisen, upon hearing the first words of the obscene message she recognized the voice as Steve Theisen's. In her words, she "just knew the minute [she] heard his voice that it was him." She thought the whole thing must be a joke but was troubled by the idea that it might be more than that. Hartwig replayed the message for her husband, Gary. Based on his own interaction with Theisen in the small town where they lived, he also believed the voice was Theisen's. Several days later, Bobbie Hartwig played the message for Schuler, who was also Theisen's supervisor. Schuler also identified the voice as Theisen's. Both Gary Hartwig and Schuler identified the voice as Theisen's before Bobbie Hartwig revealed her own belief.

Schuler and Ray Fusco, Covenant's vice president for employee resources, began a sexual harassment investigation. The investigation included making a tape of the obscene call and submitting it for voice print analysis or spectrography along with comparison voicemail messages known to have been left by Theisen. Covenant's voice analyst, Mindy Wilson, ultimately concluded that she could not arrive at a "solid" identification because the obscene message was too brief to provide a good comparison with the known samples of Theisen's voice. But she concluded Theisen could not be eliminated as a suspect and recommended that he furnish an exemplar of the obscene message for analysis.

Approximately one month after the initial incident, Theisen met with Schuler and Fusco. Theisen was told about the phone call and that four persons had identified the voice as his. After listening to the message, Theisen denied he was the speaker. Schuler and Fusco then asked Theisen to submit to voiceprint analysis. Theisen said he would have to think about it. Schuler and Fusco then suspended Theisen for two weeks to allow him to consider his decision. After the meeting, Theisen returned to his office to retrieve personal items before security officer Roger Shook escorted him out of the building.

Theisen consulted with an attorney and thereafter refused to submit an exemplar of his voice for analysis. His counsel advised Covenant by letter that Theisen's refusal rested on their belief that Iowa Code Section 730.4 "strictly prohibited" such testing. Covenant responded by firing Theisen.

Theisen then initiated a review of his termination in accordance with the "Fair Treatment" provisions of Covenant's employee handbook. Several meetings took place between Theisen, his employee representative, Schuler, and Fusco. Repeated requests that Theisen submit to voice analysis were rejected. He ultimately submitted an exemplar to his own expert, however. The expert reported "no similarities" between the voice sample submitted by Covenant and the voice sample furnished by Theisen. Thereafter, Theisen submitted his report to a nine-member employee committee who, after interviewing all the pertinent players, unanimously recommended Theisen's reinstatement.

Covenant's president, Raymond Burfeind, ultimately reviewed the actions of his staff, along with all the material collected during the Fair Treatment process. Based on his review, Burfeind upheld the termination.

He advised Theisen by letter that his decision was based on Theisen's refusal to comply "with reasonable requests which could have determined with more certainty the facts that were present."

In its summary judgment decision, the court acknowledged that voiceprint analysis "may be used as evidence to help prove a person lied," but concluded that this did not make the procedure a prohibited polygraph examination governed by Section 730.4. Because Covenant's request for voiceprint analysis did not violate Section 730.4, the court ruled Covenant's decision to fire Theisen breached no public policy preventing termination of his at-will employment status.

The court likewise rejected Theisen's negligent investigation claim, noting that such a cause of action has not been recognized in this context and likely would not be inasmuch as an at-will employee could be terminated with no investigation at all. This appeal by Theisen followed.

Voice print analysis and Iowa Code Section 730.4. Theisen argued in the district court, and urges on appeal, that Iowa Code Section 730.4 prohibited Covenant from requesting that he submit to voiceprint analysis as a condition of keeping his job. Because Covenant's conduct violated public policy, Theisen contends, the fact that he was an employee-at-will presents no obstacle to the prosecution of his claim. Thus, before turning to the statute, we review briefly the employment-at-will doctrine.

Employment-at-will. The doctrine of employment-at-will, well established in Iowa law, permits an employer or employee who is not under contract to terminate employment at any time for any lawful reason. This court has recognized only two exceptions to the doctrine. First, an employee handbook that specifically limits termination of employment except under certain conditions or for cause may create a contract of employment. Second, we have held that an employer may not terminate an employee for a reason that violates public policy. To defeat the presumption of at-will employment, such policy must be well recognized and defined, generally by state constitution or statute.

Theisen contends, and for purposes of summary judgment we find, that Covenant fired him because he refused to submit to voice print analysis. Covenant's request, Theisen argues, violated the public policy expressed in Iowa Code Section 730.4. Thus, his argument continues, Covenant could not lawfully discharge him for failure to comply. To determine whether the district court correctly rejected these contentions, we turn to the statute at issue.

Iowa Code Section 730.4. The statute upon which Theisen relies provides, in pertinent part, as follows: an employer shall not as a condition of employment, promotion, or change in status of employment, or as an express or implied condition of a benefit or privilege of employment, knowingly do any of the following: (a) Request or require that an employee or applicant for employment take or submit to a polygraph examination, (b) Administer, cause to be administered, threaten to administer, or attempt to administer a polygraph examination to an employee or applicant for employment.

Of particular significance to this case, a polygraph examination is defined by statute as any procedure which involves the use of instrumentation or a mechanical or electrical device to enable or assist the detection of deception, the verification of truthfulness, or the rendering of a diagnostic opinion regarding either of these, and includes a lie detector or similar test.

The district court, focusing on the common meaning of polygraph as an instrument used to determine truthfulness by measuring physiological reactions to responses to questions, determined that voiceprint analysis does not "assist in the detection of deception" in the way a lie detector does. Theisen contends the court erred because it disregarded the definition of "polygraph examination" supplied by Section 730.4(1). He argues that when the statute was amended in 1988 to define a polygraph examination as a procedure, rather than a specific device or machine, the legislature significantly broadened the types of activities prohibited. *Compare* Iowa Code Section 730.4(1) (1985) (defining "polygraph" as "any mechanical or electrical instrument or device" used to determine truthfulness), *with* Iowa Code Section 730.4(1) (1989) (defining "polygraph *examination*" to include "any *procedure*" involving the use of instrumentation or mechanical device to *"assist* the detection of deception" or verification of truthfulness, including "a lie detector or similar test" (emphasis added). In other words, instead of merely prohibiting the use of a specific machine to detect truthfulness, Theisen claims the legislature intended by its 1988 amendment to outlaw all *procedures* used by employers to measure veracity. This would include, he argues, the voiceprint analysis requested by Covenant.

Even if Theisen is correct about the legislature's intent to broaden the reach of Section 730.4, we are not convinced that the statute prohibits what Covenant sought from Theisen here. Covenant asked Theisen to submit to voiceprint analysis, a procedure which compares a known voice sample with an unknown sample as a way of identifying the unknown voice. The procedure is a method of identification. It is perhaps not as exact as fingerprinting or DNA analysis, but it is a method of identification nonetheless. And while the procedure may remotely aid the detection of deception or verification of truthfulness, as Covenant concedes, that is not its function or purpose. Truthfulness comes into the picture only when the subject denies making the unknown statement. The truth or veracity of the denial cannot be measured by voice print analysis. It remains an *identification* tool, no matter what the subject's response.

Contrary to Theisen's assertions, the language of Section 730.4 gives no indication that the legislature intended to prohibit the use of methods or devices designed to counter an employee's denial of wrongdoing. The statute clearly places limits on the testing or analysis to which an employer can be subjected, but it does not prohibit an employer from using *identification* techniques such as comparison of photographs, fingerprints, or voiceprints. Legislative intent is revealed by what a statute says, not what it could or should have said. An identification technique does not become a polygraph examination, prohibited by statute, simply because an employee adamantly denies certain behavior and the truthfulness of the denial becomes an issue.

To summarize, we think the plain language of Section 730.4 pertains to devices, such as polygraphs, that purport to measure the truth or veracity of an employee's statement. The statute does not, by its terms, prohibit lawful tests or procedures used by an employer in the identification of employees suspected of workplace crime. Nor has Theisen advanced a cogent argument explaining how an employer's use of voiceprint analysis violates any other well-defined public policy.

Application of law to undisputed facts. Because the voice identification procedure requested by Covenant violated neither law nor public policy, Covenant's decision to terminate Theisen for failing to cooperate in the investigation was not wrongful. Theisen was an at-will employee. The district court correctly ruled that his claims for wrongful and retaliatory discharge fail as a matter of law.

Negligent investigation. Theisen next claims that Covenant owed him a duty of care to conduct a reasonable, non-negligent investigation prior to firing him. Although it is not entirely clear on what grounds his claim rests, Theisen appears to first analogize his claim to a cause of action for negligent hiring, retention and supervision. In the alternative he claims that when Covenant undertook its sexual harassment investigation, it assumed a duty to Theisen to conduct that investigation in a reasonable manner.

Covenant counters that Theisen's claim of negligent investigation poses "a full, frontal attack" on the Iowa law of employment at-will. It analogizes Theisen's claim to the claim of negligent discharge rejected by this court. If an employer cannot be found liable to an at-will employee for negligent discharge, Covenant argues, that same employer should not be liable for any steps taken prior to the discharge. Covenant also argues that if the court recognizes a cause of action for negligent investigation in favor of at-will employees, it will turn every employer's termination decision into a jury question of reasonableness, thus completely swallowing the employment-at-will doctrine.

As with Theisen's first claim, our analysis is grounded in the basic nature of at-will employment: an employer can terminate an employee for any reason or no reason at all, so long as the reason does not violate public policy. We have already discussed the public-policy exception first recognized in *Springer.*" The other exception arises when an employee handbook or policy manual creates a unilateral employment contract. In *Huegerich*, an at-will employee fired for violating IBP's look-alike drug policy asked this court to create a new exception to at-will employment—negligent discharge.

The plaintiff in *Huegerich* alleged, and the district court found, that IBP negligently administered its drug policy by failing to provide an orientation program or advising that an employee could be terminated if caught in possession of look-alike drugs. This court, noting the myriad of other states that had rejected such a negligent discharge claim, likewise rejected Huegerich's argument. Our decision rested on the belief that imposing "a duty of care upon an employer when discharging an employee ... would radically alter" the doctrine of employment-at-will.

Theisen resists Covenant's analogy to *Huegerich*, insisting that a claim of negligent investigation is more akin to the claims of negligent hiring and supervision recognized by this court in *Godar*. The plaintiff in *Godar*, who had been abused throughout his youth by a school district employee, sued the school district, alleging negligence in hiring, supervision, and retention. Although we concluded that *Godar* raised insufficient facts to generate a jury question of negligence, we recognized the viability of such a cause of action based on the "principle that a person conducting an activity through employees is subject to liability for harm resulting from conduct in the employment of improper persons involving risk of harm to others."

Theisen theorizes that claims of negligent hiring, supervision and retention provide the basis for a negligent investigation claim because hiring, supervision, and retention are all based on an employer's investigation of an employee and his or her conduct or the lack of any such investigation. He specifically challenges the actions leading up to his own termination, including the fact that the investigation was initiated by Nancy Schuler, a supervisor with whom Theisen had a contentious relationship.

The weakness in Theisen's theory is that it still rests on a decision to terminate him, which Covenant could do for any lawful reason or for no reason at all. Employment at-will, by definition, does not require an employer's decision to be logical or rational. Theisen's claim of negligent investigation goes to the heart of the employer's decision-making process. To allow such a claim would not only contravene this court's denial of a negligent discharge claim in *Huegerich*, but it would also create an exception swallowing the rule of at-will employment (holding that because an employer could fire an employee for any reason or no reason "it was equally at liberty to discharge [the employee] for a reason based on incorrect information, even if that information was carelessly gathered"; rejecting wrongful discharge claim based on negligent investigation of criminal matter as public policy exception to doctrine of at-will employment).

In the alternative, Theisen asserts that even if Covenant was not compelled to undertake an investigation prior to firing him, once it did so it had a duty to conduct the investigation with reasonable care. Covenant counters that its duty to investigate the obscene voice mail message was a duty running in Hartwig's favor as the victim of possible sexual harassment. Following through on that obligation, Covenant urges, does not mean it assumed a duty to Theisen, an at-will employee who was the suspected perpetrator.

Theisen rests his claim of duty on the Restatement (Second) of Torts Section 323. Under that restatement section: one who undertakes, gratuitously or for consideration, to render services to another which he should recognize as necessary for the protection of the other's person or things, is subject to liability to the other for physical harm resulting from his failure to exercise reasonable care to perform his undertaking, if: (a) his failure to exercise such care increases the risk of such harm, or (b) the harm is suffered because of the other's reliance upon the undertaking.

Theisen's reliance on Section 323 is misplaced. Covenant undertook its investigation to pursue allegations of sexual harassment, a duty which it owed to Bobbie Hartwig, not Theisen. And although an assumed duty recognized by Section 323 may also run in favor of a third person, under that section a party who undertakes to perform a service to another which is essential for the protection of a third person is only liable to the third person for *physical* harm. Even if Covenant should have recognized the need to protect Theisen, Theisen did not suffer any physical harm. Thus none of the Restatement sections on which Theisen relies establishes a duty on Covenant's part to conduct a reasonable investigation in his favor.

Finally, we reject Theisen's contention that our decision in *Schoff v. Combined Insurance Co.* recognized an employee's cause of action against an employer for negligent supervision and retention of another employee. He asserts that, by analogy, an employee should be permitted to maintain an action against an employer for negligent investigation. But, as already discussed, an employer has no duty to conduct a reasonable investigation in favor of an at-will employee. In the absence of a duty of care, *Schoff* does not support Theisen.

In summary, the district court correctly dismissed Theisen's negligent investigation claim. We therefore affirm the court's summary judgment for Covenant in its entirety.

CASE COMMENT

This case presents an excellent illustration of several competing interests revolving around workplace misconduct. First, the plaintiff asserts that the voice exemplar violated a state statute that prohibits forcing an individual to take a lie detector test. This question turned on the definition of "polygraph examination" as compared to a subsequent statute that seemed to broaden the definition to include any related "procedure." The plaintiff asserted the voice exemplar constituted a "procedure" as defined by the legislator. The court disagreed. It held that the voice exemplar is best characterized as an "identification" tool, not as a lie detection technique. As such, the court held it was used in relation to the investigation to identify the offending party, not necessarily to detect deception of the plaintiff.

Second, and more important to this section, the court directly addressed plaintiff's negligent investigation claim. In doing so, the court emphasized that as an at-will employee, the employer has no duty to build evidence through an investigation in order to terminate the employee. An at-will employee can be terminated for any reason, absent a contract provision in the handbook or in violation of an accepted public policy protection. Since the court found the voice exemplar did not violate the state statute, there was no public policy violation. In addition, the plaintiff could not point to any handbook provision that purported to give him contractual rights.

Notwithstanding these conclusions, the court further concluded that the employer had no duty to conduct an investigation to support the termination of the plaintiff. Thus, any argument by the plaintiff related to his "negligent investigation" claim is unwarranted. This is so because no investigation was necessary. Further, while the employer had a duty to the *victim* to conduct an investigation based on her sexual harassment claim, this duty to the victim does not give the at-will employee (plaintiff) the right to a full and comprehensive investigation which would factually "justify" the decision to terminate him. Consequently, the court noted that the plaintiff's desire to require an investigation that would substantiate the decision to terminate would "radically alter" the at-will doctrine. In this sense, the court asserted that the at-will doctrine allows employers great discretion relative to employment decisions. If the duty of an investigation were required to support employment decisions, then the at-will doctrine would be left without any actual meaning.

This case, therefore, illustrates the delicate balance between diligently investigating misconduct claims, such as sexual harassment, which are designed to assess the merits of the allegation and to protect the interests of the victim. On the other hand, the court would not require that the investigation be used to justify the employment decision against an at-will employee. Hence, it is important to distinguish the purpose of the investigation. An investigation should be done for the interests of the victim and the larger workplace. It should not be conducted, however, to justify the discipline of an at-will employee. While there are exceptions to this general principle, such as when the investigation may or will result in criminal charges (as in *Brown v. Sears,* supra), the merits of the investigation should not be designed to "prove" that the particular employee committed the misconduct or crime. It is important to remember that if the case is not criminally prosecuted, there generally is no duty to the at-will employee that the investigation is full and complete.

This being said, however, the employee can assert certain attacks, such as discrimination based on race, sex, age, disability, and the like. In these instances, the completeness and diligence of the investigative process is subject to court scrutiny, at least as far as it supports the discrimination allegations made by the plaintiff. Consequently, this is a difficult balance. On one hand, an employer should conduct complete and thorough investigations—when an investigation is deemed necessary. On the other hand, an investigation of an at-will employee is not necessarily obligated to "justify" an employment action, such as the termination of his or her job. Employers are well advised to consult attorneys familiar with these issues in order to frame and articulate the extent and purpose of any workplace investigation. Hopefully, these cases coupled with the discussion below will be useful in assessing the best practice. Suffice it to say, however, that these decisions must be based on particular facts and circumstances. The correct decision should be based on a case by case approach, guided by legal acumen and sound judgment.

884 A.2d 255

Superior Court of Pennsylvania

ROSARIO ANGELOPOULOS, AN INDIVIDUAL, APPELLEE v. LAZARUS PA, INC., RICH'S DEPARTMENT STORES INC., AND FEDERATED DEPARTMENT STORES INC., APPELLANTS.

Nov. 4, 2005

Background

Customer, who was handcuffed by store's employee after eating two pieces of chocolate in store, brought action against store. Following a jury trial, the Court of Common Pleas, Allegheny County, Civil Division, granted customer's motion for new trial. Store appealed.

Holdings

The superior court held that the jury's finding that store's detention of customer was done in reasonable manner, for reasonable time, and for proper purpose was against the weight of the evidence, and punitive damages may be warranted.

Affirmed

While shopping at a Lazarus Department Store, Angelopoulos approached an irresistible display of Godiva chocolate. According to Angelopoulos, one box of chocolates did not have a lid, and the interior cellophane wrapper covering the chocolate was slashed on both sides of the box. At trial, Angelopoulos described the display as follows:

> It was just a treat to look at it, so I go to look at it and I touch it and I move my eyes to the side and I see the small box with the plastic—like something had a slide—slashed it, kind of curled up, like it was saying, Please help yourself. Thinking that the open box was a free sample, Angelopoulos thought, I said, Oh, my God. If anything, it was my cholesterol that came to me. Should [I] have one? And I said, Well, one

> won't hurt me. That was my feeling. And I took the box and I took one. Unable to resist temptation, Angelopoulos succumbed to the call of the chocolate, ate a piece, and then returned to the display several minutes later and consumed a second piece. Thinking that the chocolates were a free sample, Angelopoulos did not pay for either morsel of chocolate.

Several minutes later, Michael Demicco, a loss prevention associate for Lazarus, followed by Janet Lesure, a trainee for loss prevention, approached Angelopoulos. Demicco requested that Angelopoulos follow him to the loss prevention office located in the Lazarus store. Angelopoulos complied. Demicco and Ms. Lesure searched Angelopoulos's purse and bags, and Ms. Lesure performed a search of her body. Angelopoulos was then handcuffed to a table affixed to the floor. Her identification documentation and her Lazarus credit card were taken from her purse.

Demicco presented Angelopoulos with a statement of admission. He completed her name and address and the dollar amount of the merchandise allegedly taken by Angelopoulos. Only the signature line was blank. Angelopoulos objected to the admission form and asked to see the store manager. Llewellyn, a store supervisor, entered the room and agreed to find the store manager. He returned, accompanied by Patty Connelly, a store manager. Angelopoulos asked to have the handcuffs removed and Ms. Connelly indicated that she did not have the power to have the handcuffs removed and that it was the policy of the loss prevention group to handcuff everyone suspected of shoplifting.

After repeated refusals to sign the admission form, Angelopoulos ultimately did agree to sign the form provided that Demicco wrote on the form, "Took 2 pieces of chocolate out of box and ate it without purchase. Foil was cracked." She was then released from the handcuffs. Demicco then told Angelopoulos that Lazarus must take her photograph, to which she objected. She then scratched out her signature from the admission form. Throughout the detention process, Angelopoulos was kept handcuffed continuously for a period of approximately 50 to 55 minutes. Lazarus filed no charges against Angelopoulos as a result of the incident.

Angelopoulos subsequently filed a complaint against Lazarus. The jury found Lazarus not liable. The trial court granted Angelopoulos' Motion for a new trial. The trial court reaches this conclusion based upon a confluence of factors, all of which were in play on the day in question: the handcuffing of Angelopoulos; the refusal to release Angelopoulos from the handcuffs once she objected; the use of the handcuffs and detention to accomplish a purpose beyond one of the six reasons enumerated in the Retail Theft Act; the duration of the detention; the presentation of the admission form; and the refusal of Lazarus to release Angelopoulos when she stated that she would not sign the admission form, even though there was no longer any reason to continue to detain her for one of the enumerated purposes under the Act. Thereafter, Lazarus filed the instant timely appeal.

The Retail Theft Act provides, in relevant part, as follows: A peace officer, merchant or merchant's employee or an agent under contract with a merchant, who has probable cause to believe that retail theft has occurred or is occurring on or about a store or other retail mercantile establishment and who has probable cause to believe that a specific person has committed or is committing the retail theft may detain the suspect in a reasonable manner for a reasonable time on or off the premises for all or any of the following purposes: to require the suspect to identify himself, to verify such identification, to determine whether such suspect has in his possession unpurchased merchandise taken from the mercantile establishment and, if so, to recover such merchandise, to inform a peace officer, or to institute criminal proceedings against the suspect. Such detention shall not impose civil or criminal liability upon the peace officer, merchant, employee, or agent so detaining. Thus, the Act authorized Lazarus to detain Angelopoulos, without civil liability, for the purpose of (a) identifying Angelopoulos, (b) verifying her identity, (c) determining whether she had unpurchased merchandise in her possession, (d) recovering unpurchased merchandise from Angelopoulos' possession, (e) informing a peace officer, and (f) instituting criminal proceedings.

In this case, the trial court determined that Lazarus's detention of Angelopoulos violated the Act, as Lazarus held Angelopoulos beyond the time necessary to conduct the purposes authorized by the Act. The trial court explained its determination as follows:

> [T]he use of handcuffs is not a *per se* violation of the Retail Theft Act so long as the handcuffs are used to accomplish one or more of the enumerated justifications of a detention. It is apparent that Lazarus handcuffed Angelopoulos initially for legitimate purposes. However, once they were able to identify Angelopoulos (they had her identification documentation and her Lazarus charge card), and confirm by searching her that she did not possess any unpurchased merchandise (she was only observed eating two pieces of chocolate), there was no longer any reason to detain her, and unquestionably no reason to keep her handcuffed. Fifty to fifty-five minutes appears to be an unusually long period of time under the circumstances for a few ministerial acts. Lazarus had no intention of informing a peace officer at that time nor did they intend to detain her for the purpose of instituting criminal proceedings at that time. There no longer existed any statutorily permitted reasons to continue her detention. At that point, Angelopoulos should have been released from her handcuffs as she had repeatedly requested. Once they refused to release her, as testified to by Demicco, the handcuffing went beyond the bounds of the principal reasons behind the Act, and beyond the bounds of decency. To continue to keep her handcuffed, while presenting to her for her signature what is essentially a confession form, is clearly unjustified.

The trial court's determination is supported by the overwhelming evidence of record. At trial, Demicco, Lazarus's loss prevention specialist, testified that he observed Angelopoulos on a video security monitor. Over a span of about four minutes, Demicco saw Angelopoulos eat two pieces of Godiva chocolate from an opened box on a store display. As a result, Demicco approached Angelopoulos and asked her to follow him to an "apprehension room."

The testimony at trial reveals that Demicco escorted Angelopoulos to the apprehension room at 3:45 p.m. Once Demicco and Angelopoulos arrived in the apprehension room, a female security guard performed a pat-down search of Angelopoulos, after which she was handcuffed to a table in the room. Also upon entering the room, someone from the loss prevention department searched Angelopoulos's bags to make certain no other unpurchased goods were present in the bags. Demicco asked for and received Angelopoulos's identification. At that point in time, Angelopoulos asked to be released from the handcuffs.

Rather than releasing Angelopoulos from the handcuffs, Demicco showed Angelopoulos an "admission form," and explained to her that once he wrote down her general information, "it was up to her if she wanted to admit to it, then she would sign it. If not, then she would be released." Demicco further testified that he would not release Angelopoulos from the handcuffs "until I got down her general information and *explained [the form] to her*."

Demicco acknowledged that Angelopoulos, at first, did not want to sign the form. When Demicco refused to release Angelopoulos from the handcuffs, Angelopoulos asked to see a store manager. Demicco first brought Llewellyn, the manager of loss prevention for Lazarus's South Hills Village store, to speak with Angelopoulos. When Llewellyn refused to release Angelopoulos from the handcuffs, she again asked to speak with a store manager. At that time, Patty Connelly, the executive vice-president of the store, arrived to speak with Angelopoulos. Connelly declined to interfere.

At trial, Llewellyn admitted that Angelopoulos asked to be released from the handcuffs as soon as he entered the room. Llewellyn further admitted that prior to his encounter with Angelopoulos, he had checked out Angelopoulos' credit history at the store. Thus, the record is clear that at the very latest, Lazarus possessed the information necessary to identify Angelopoulos, and to verify her identity, at the beginning of the encounter between Llewellyn and Angelopoulos.

Demicco testified that if a person refused to sign the "admission form," they would be released from the handcuffs and be "free to go." Thus, the record is also clear that Lazarus did not intend to detain Angelopoulos for the purpose of calling a peace officer or initiating criminal proceedings, but for the purpose of presenting an admission form and gaining the suspected shoplifter's signature on that form.

Based upon the foregoing, we discern no abuse of discretion by the trial court. At the *very latest*, Lazarus's authority to detain Angelopoulos ended prior to the time Llewellyn entered the apprehension room.

The only purpose for further detaining Angelopoulos was to secure her signature on an admission form. We agree with the trial court's conclusion that Lazarus's continued detention of Angelopoulos, in handcuffs, exceeded all bounds of decency and we express our outrage at such a procedure. Such coercive tactics are not authorized by the Retail Theft Act. Accordingly, we affirm the trial court's grant of a new trial based upon Angelopoulos' challenge to the weight of the evidence.

Lazarus next claims that the trial court erred in submitting the issue of punitive damages to the jury. According to Lazarus, there was no evidence that Lazarus "acted with malice, ill-will, or in reckless disregard of Angelopoulos' rights." We disagree.

"Punitive damages are awarded to punish a defendant for certain outrageous acts and to deter [it] or others from engaging in similar conduct." In general, the assessment of punitive damages is proper whenever a party's actions are of such an outrageous nature as to demonstrate intentional, willful, wanton or reckless conduct resulting from either an evil motive or because of a reckless indifference to the rights of others. It is the role of the trial court to determine, in its discretion, whether the plaintiff has presented sufficient evidence from which a jury could reasonably conclude that the defendant acted outrageously.

As set forth above, the evidence of record supported the trial court's conclusion that Lazarus detained Angelopoulos in violation of the Retail Theft Act for an unreasonable period of time, in an unreasonable manner, and for a nefarious purpose. At the very least, Lazarus's conduct exhibited a reckless indifference to the rights of Angelopoulos. Accordingly, we discern no error by the trial court in submitting the issue of punitive damages to the jury. Thus, Lazarus is not entitled to relief on this claim.

For the foregoing reasons, we affirm the Order of the trial court awarding a new trial to Angelopoulos. Order affirmed.

CASE COMMENT

This case represents a classic example of overzealous security personnel and methods. In this case, the court noted that the security personnel initially had probable cause to detain and investigate the theft of chocolates—as evidence by the video surveillance. Once the plaintiff was confronted, identified, and searched for further evidence of theft, any additional detainment, especially by the use of handcuffs, was improper. The continued detainment was not only violative of the Retail Theft Act, it also exposed the store to punitive damages due to the overzealous actions of the security personnel. In addition, the fact that the supervisor and the vice president did not intercede to resolve this manner, the exposure to the store is elevated due to apparent corporate acquiesce to this excessive conduct.

Investigative Methods

Legal Guidelines

While it is beyond the scope of this casebook to provide a list of comprehensive and exhaustive guidelines, some useful principles may help the reader understand and prepare for interrogations and investigations. While all cases are fact-driven, certain guidelines can be articulated. In order to more fully appreciate the assessments needed to achieve this balance, the following legal guidelines may be helpful (for additional information please refer to the citations and to your legal counsel for further guidance).

As explained in the above case, the at-will doctrine essentially provides that an employee can be discharged at any time, with or without cause. Obviously, this provides the employee with little job security or protection. It also provides a great deal of discretion related to employment actions by the employer. As noted by the *Theisen* court, there are certain generally accepted exceptions to this doctrine. They typically entail the following:

1. Legislative prohibitions which provide restrictions on employment decisions that are based on certain individual characteristics, such as race, age, sex, religion, disability, family and health reasons, and the like. Typically, these causes of action stem from employment actions that are motivated by discriminatory purposes.
2. Contractual prohibitions which typically relate to union contracts or contracts between the individual and the employer. In most union contracts, the employer must show "just cause" before an employee can be subject to an adverse employment action. In essence, just cause is defined as "cause outside of legal cause, which must be based on reasonable grounds, and there must be a fair and honest cause or reason, regulated by good faith."6 In order to show this standard, certain factors are considered. If any question is answered "no" then it is typically deemed just cause did not exist. The factors include the following:
   a. Was employee forewarned that offense could result in sanction?
   b. Was employer's position regarding the employee's conduct reasonable?
   c. Did the employer investigate before acting?
   d. Was the investigation fair?
   e. Was there substantial evidence to support the charges against the employee?
   f. Were the employer's actions non-discriminatory?
   g. Was the degree of discipline reasonably related to the nature of the offense and the employee's past record?
3. Handbook provisions also can affect the at-will doctrine. As noted in the above discussion, these provisions can bind

the employer to sanction the employee only in a manner that is consistent with the language of the handbook. In this sense, employers must be careful not to use language that would appear to establish a contract between the parties. It is advised that handbooks should include a conspicuous disclaimer that affirmatively states:

a. No contract between the parties exists.
b. Limits the validity of any oral statements to the contrary.
c. Re-affirm at-will status of employees.

In assessing handbook language, it is advisable to avoid or qualify language such as "permanent employment" and "job security." These phrases entail some expectation that the employment provides more than an "at-will" status.

4. Public policy exceptions also may affect the at-will status. The often common exceptions are job protections afforded to "whistleblowers" who disclose information related to criminal activity within the company. In addition, a widely accepted exception is retaliation against an employee who previously filed a worker's compensation claim. In both instances, the public policy exception is designed to protect employees from retaliation. In the former instance, it protects employees who report criminal activity (whistleblowers), and in the latter, it protects employees who exercise their right to claim workplace injuries (worker's compensation).

Interrogations

Interrogations should be obtained freely and voluntarily, with no force, pressures, duress and/or coercion applied in an attempt to gain the confession or to elicit information.[7] When the person being interviewed is considered a suspect to a crime, absent some extenuating circumstances, the police must first advise the suspect of their Miranda rights prior to engaging any questioning. The purpose of Miranda is to dispel the compulsion inherent in custodial surroundings and interrogations. The elements of a Miranda warning consist of:[8]

1. Right to remain silence
2. Advisement that any information elicited can be used in court against him/her
3. Right to an attorney
4. If the suspect cannot afford an attorney, one will be provided free of charge.

These Miranda rights are only applicable if "state action" is involved. This is so because the Fifth Amendment protection against self-incrimination is only applicable when government agents or actors are conducting the interrogation. However, as will be presented in Part IV, the distinction between state and private action is not always clear. As a rule of thumb, if the interrogation (or any prior or subsequent investigation involved police officers or other government law enforcement officials), then it may be wise to administer Miranda warnings. While it is difficult to make any blanket assertion, since all cases have different factual basis, it is particularly important to do so if criminal prosecution of the suspect is intended or even likely.

The logic of this assertion goes to three premises. First, if the suspect subsequently contends that any confession was obtained under duress or coercion, a signed statement where the suspect waives Miranda can be powerful evidence that statement was indeed voluntary. While this is not "definitive" evidence, it is certainly useful. Another evidentiary technique is to record the statement by audio or video means. Second, in the event that the court deems that the Fifth Amendment is applicable—by finding state actor(s) was involved—the failure to obtain a waiver of Miranda may preclude any statement from being admitted in the criminal trial. Third, the administration of Miranda warnings is also a clear and powerful indicator that the interrogation was done in a professional and reasonable manner. Again, while this is not definitive proof that the interrogation was not coerced or made under duress, it is nonetheless, an excellent indicator of professionalism and reasonableness. Consequently, for these reasons, I generally recommend that private security personnel issue Miranda warning under the same circumstances as when police officers are required to do so.

Some may disagree with this general proposition.[9] While it makes sense not to administer Miranda warnings when the law would not require such, the reasons for doing so, as articulated above, should be considered in situations when criminal prosecution is intended or even possible.

The circumstances surrounding an interrogation must be assessed in light of their objective reasonableness. In making this assessment, courts often look to the location, setting, and techniques used in the interrogation (or the interview). Some guidance may be useful.

Setting

The room where the interrogation takes place can be critical.[10] It should allow for privacy, but not so remote as to be isolated from the workforce. An isolated interrogation room may expose the employer to allegations that the interrogation was coerced, or conducted in a surreptitious manner. In this sense, balance the dignity and privacy of the accused against the perception that the interrogation was conducted in a secret and secluded place. In the latter sense, this gives the perception the employer had something to hide, as opposed to simply providing the employee his/her privacy. Remember in these circumstances, perception often becomes reality.

The placement of furniture and office equipment should also be considered. If possible, the door should be closed, or cracked open. It should not be locked. The individual being interrogated (or interviewed) should be seated in a chair near the door, without any furniture or other items obstructing an easy exit from the room. In addition, a telephone should be within reach of this individual at all times. Further, any item which could be construed as intimidating or coercive should be removed from the room or not be in plain view of this individual. For example, while it is generally neutral to have the personnel files of the employee in view, it may be inappropriate to expose the contents of the file. This is especially true if the file contained sentimental or incriminating photos, medical information, and the like—unless these items are directly tied to the allegations being investigated. Similarly, other office items such as letter openers, which may be construed as weapons should be removed from the room or hidden in desk drawers. Weapons or instrumentalities of police or security personnel (such as handcuffs, chemical sprays, etc.) should also either be removed prior to coming into the interrogation room, concealed under clothing, or placed in locked drawers. In sum, any item which can be used as a weapon or used for intimidation or coercion (either real or potentially) should be appropriately dealt with.

Conduct of Interrogation

One of the first things that should be accomplished is that the purpose of the interrogation (or interview) must be clearly articulated. It is also important to state that the results will be confidential, as only employees who have a "need to know" will be informed of such. If appropriate, the individual should be informed that the results may be used in court, in other aspects of this investigation, or in any larger investigation. It is important to note that the role of the interviewer is to gather facts. The company policy relative to the investigation should be clearly stated. For example, in sexual harassment investigations, the policy of the company, with its affirmation not to tolerate harassment, should be made clear. The questions posed should be related and relevant to the allegations that are the subject of the investigation. Any questioning that appears to be "fishing" for facts, or that is overtly accusatorial, is generally unwise and even illegal.

It is highly recommended that all conversations should be recorded, preferably video, but at least by audio means. The recording should be made known on the record, with the individual being questioned acknowledging his or her consent to the recording. The time of the commencement should be noted, as should any breaks that are offered and/or requested. The time the questioning re-commences after a break should also be noted on the record. Of course, the interrogation should not involve any coercive tactics, including loud and argumentative questioning, the threat or manifestation of physical pain or abuse, and the like.

In the event that the individual has a union representative or legal counsel, there are certain guidelines that are relevant. First, the representative or counsel has no right to direct the individual not to answer any question. Typically, most union contracts and company policies require the employee to cooperate with any internal investigation. This includes answering all questions posed during an interrogation—unless it is irrelevant to the allegations. Even then, it is advisable to answer the question under an appropriate objection. This is particularly true for law enforcement and security officers and others who are contractually required to cooperate with an investigation. In addition, the representative or counsel cannot answer the question for the individual. Indeed, it is axiomatic that the individual must answer the question, not their representative or counsel. Nor can the representative or counsel interfere with the interview. While occasional objections for the record may be appropriate, any conduct that would reasonably be construed as interference or harassment by the representative or counsel should not be allowed. Finally, the interrogation should not be unreasonably delayed waiting for the representative or counsel. Generally, reasonableness is determined by the seriousness of the offense, and the potential that negative consequences would result from the delay.

Content of the Statement

In the event that the questioning results in a confession, the individual should acknowledge each and every element of the crime or act of misconduct. This requires some factual elaboration of the events which lead up to the incident, the incident itself, and any relevant circumstances subsequent to the incident. Even if the individual provides this information orally on the video or audio tape, it is useful to have this statement codified in written form, so the individual can sign the statement. The language in the statement should reflect the words and phases of the individual. Attempts to "clean up" the grammatical and jargon used in the statement should be done sparingly. In addition to this factual recitation, the signed statement should have language that waives Miranda, and asserts that the statement is given voluntarily and without coercion or duress.

The statement should seek to codify the key descriptive questions: Who? What? When? How? Where? and Why? While all cases are unique, some basic factors should be addressed, including:

1. Physical contact and verbal conduct of the incident
2. Context and sequences of the contact and conduct
3. Names of witnesses, or potential witnesses
4. Reaction to the occurrence by victim, offender and witnesses
5. Responses by the offender
6. Dates and times of all reports, both verbal and written reports

7. Dates and methods of individuals who were aware of the incident
8. What victim desires as the result of the investigation
9. Awareness of company policies and procedures related to the allegations
10. Awareness of the implications for violating company policies and procedures
11. Description of prior training (and timing) relating to company policies and procedures

Investigative Issues

An effective investigative plan should include the elements of the crime, the amount of resources needed, budgetary constraints, legal theories and defenses, and a defined purpose and scope of the investigation. In addition, consideration must be given to the availability and reliability of any and all witnesses, the sufficiency of evidence, and any implications of the investigation, including liability exposures and negative publicity. These issues, and others, require a great deal of judgment and expertise, both from the perspective of the law and of investigative techniques.

Investigative Process

It is typical that the personnel files of the complainant, witnesses, and the accused be reviewed at the initial stage of the investigation. The information contained in these files generally cannot be used in the legal proceeding—unless they support the specific allegation. The personnel file may be useful, however, to assess a number of potentially relevant factors, including:

1. Job performance reviews
2. Prior disciplinary history
3. Prior civil litigation, including harassment claims
4. Prior criminal convictions
5. Prior domestic abuse claims (if relevant)
6. Departmental staffing and production reports
7. Any other relevant information

Attorney Work Product Doctrine

This doctrine may provide an exception to discovery requirements in matters that are subject to subsequent litigation. While this doctrine varies from state to state, there are certain general principles that may be helpful. In general, the work product doctrine relates to the information and decision making used by the attorney in providing legal advice to clients.[11] Generally, the privilege attaches when the litigation is pending or reasonably foreseen. In workplace misconduct cases, it can be argued that any case that results in some employment action, from a suspension to discharge, is likely to result in litigation. Indeed, even in cases that do not result in any employment action, such as sexual harassment cases where the alleged offending individual is not sanctioned, either appropriately or inappropriately, the employer is still susceptible to litigation if the victim believes the allegations were not handled correctly.

In any event, the privilege should be established before any investigation takes place. This should be codified in a memorandum from the corporate counsel to the investigator. The memorandum should articulate the basis for the privilege and the information flow directly from the investigator to the attorney. In addition, the memorandum should articulate that any and all information derived from the investigation is strictly confidential, subject to only those corporate officials with a "need to know" basis. If the investigator is also an attorney, this may enhance the applicability of the work product doctrine, as the communication flows directly from attorney to attorney. However, the fact that an attorney does the investigation may not be determinative. Some courts will give credence to an attorney investigator only to the extent that the investigation is of the type that would require legal expertise.[12]

NOTES

1. See Lyman, Michael D. (2005). *Criminal Investigation: The Art and the Science* (4th ed.). Upper Saddle River, NJ: Prentice Hall.
2. Lyman op cit. at 183. Also see Osterburg, James W., and Richard H. Ward (2000). *Criminal Investigation: A Method for Reconstructing the Past* (3rd edition). Cincinnati, OH: Anderson Publishing Company; and Black's Law Dictionary (1979) (5th ed.). St. Paul, MN: West Publishing.
3. Lyman op cit. at 188.
4. Osterburg and Ward op cit. at 5–10.
5. Ibid at 150.
6. Black's Law Dictionary (5th ed.) (1979). St. Paul MN: West Publishing Company.
7. Lyman op cit. at 182–183.
8. *Miranda v. Arizona*, 384 U.S. 436 (1966); and Inbau, Fred E., Bernard J. Farber, and David W. Arnold (1996). *Protective Security Law* (2nd ed.). Burlington, MA: Butterworth-Heinemann.
9. For example, Inbau et al. assert that "security officers, as well as regular police officers, should avoid administering Miranda warning when not legally required to do so." See Inbau op cit. at 75.
10. For discussion on the setting of an interrogation, see Inbau et al. op cit. at 75–79; Lyman op cit. at 194–208; and Osterburg and Ward op cit. at 333–344.
11. See Black's Law Dictionary.
12. For examples of Attorney Work Product cases with an internal investigation component, see *Sonnino v. University of Kansas Hospital Authority,* 221 F.R.D. 661 (D. Kansas, 2004); *Navigant Consulting Inc., v. Wilkinson,* 220 F.R.D. 467 (N.D. Texas, 2004); *261 Coastline Terminals of Connecticut Inc. v. U.S. Steel Corporation,* 221 F.R.D. 14 (D. Conn., 2003); and *In Re Theragenics Corporation Securities Litigation,* 205 F.R.D. 631 (N.D. Georgia, 2002).

Part Two

Intentional Torts and Claims

This section will present various intentional torts and claims, and outline typical causes of action found in security litigation.

ASSAULT AND BATTERY: CAUSE OF ACTION AND ELEMENTS

An assault occurs where a person (1) acts intending to cause a harmful or offensive contact with the person of the other or a third person, or an imminent apprehension of such contact, and (2) the other is thereby put in such imminent apprehension of receiving a battery.[1] Battery goes one step beyond assault in that a harmful contact actually occurs.[2]

FALSE ARREST, FALSE IMPRISONMENT, AND MALICIOUS PROSECUTION: CAUSE OF ACTION AND ELEMENTS

The above causes of action were combined in this section based on the commonality of their elements. In many instances, these causes of action are pled in one lawsuit. This is because the facts resulting in the lawsuit often stem from an allegation of false arrest, which leads to a false imprisonment, which leads to a malicious prosecution claim. Hence, the theories often build on each other. One cause of action can sequentially lead to another. Of course, any one theory can be pled without the others. This can and does occur. Depending upon the facts and circumstances, this may be the appropriate legal decision.

False arrest can be defined as a forceful and unlawful restraint of the liberty of another without proper legal authority.[3] In thinking about this definition, it is important to consider a few important, but often misunderstood, caveats. First, an arrest can occur without physical restraint. Indeed, the definition of an arrest is "to deprive a person of his liberty by legal authority."[4] In this way, an arrest can be accomplished when the "arrestee" reasonably believes that his or her freedom of movement is restrained. Second, an arrest can occur without a formal declaration of such. Hence, it is not necessary to say, "You're under arrest." Indeed, an arrest can even be accomplished without words. An arrest can occur simply by physical movements or constraint of movements. Third, the plaintiff need not prove that the defendant actually ordered or directed the arrest. Instead, the plaintiff must simply show that the defendant encouraged, promoted, or instigated the arrest. For example, if a police officer is called to a facility by security personnel, who then provide information that results in the police officer arresting an individual, the security personnel may be deemed to have encouraged or instigated the arrest—even though the arrest was actually made by the police.

False imprisonment entails a restraint of movement, but not necessarily actual physical holding, confinement, or detention. Again, there are a lot of misconceptions of this cause of action. These include the following. First, as with false arrest, false imprisonment may arise out of acts, gestures, words, or similar means, which induce a reasonable apprehension that force or constraint will be used. Second, the subjective state of mind of the plaintiff is irrelevant. In this sense, the key is the actions or words of the defendant which furnish a basis for a reasonable apprehension of present confinement. In order to assess whether "confinement" actually, or objectively, occurs, certain factors are relevant (see "Investigative Methods" at the end of Chapter 3 for additional explanation):

1. Manner of detention
2. Place of detention
3. Length of detention
4. Treatment during detention, such as phone calls, bathroom, or other breaks, swearing, etc.

Once a prima facie case of false imprisonment is established, the defendant can then assert a showing of probable cause as a defense to the claim. Probable cause must be based upon the existence of facts or credible information that would induce a person of ordinary caution to believe the accused person to be guilty of the crime for which he is charged.[5] In making the assessment as to the existence of probable cause, it is necessary to make the inquiry from the perspective of the person making the arrest.

The determination of probable cause is mixed question of law and fact. When the facts are not in dispute, the question of probable cause is for the court (judge) to decide. However, the determination of probable cause does not end the inquiry. Indeed, factors that occur after probable cause is established, such as the length and manner of the detention, could be actionable despite the legality of the initial confinement.

Malicious prosecution deals with the liability of persons who initiate prosecution for purposes other than for enforcing the criminal law or bringing an offender to justice. Typically this cause of action stems from allegations of hostility, spite, hatred, or ill will toward the accused, or to obtain a private advantage from the accused (such as forcing the payment of money or to improperly obtain property). Elements of the cause of action include the following:[6]

1. Commencement of a prosecution against the plaintiff
2. Legal causation of the prosecution by the defendant
3. Termination of the case in favor of the plaintiff
4. Absence of probable cause for such proceeding
5. Presence of malice (ill will, reckless disregard of rights)
6. Damages suffered by the plaintiff (the arrestee/initial defendant)

TREPASS: CAUSE OF ACTION AND ELEMENTS

Trespass entails entering, remaining or passing onto another's land or property without permission, consent, lawful authority or right.[7] Typically, this requires some assessment of whether there was permission or consent to be upon the property. While this is often straightforward, the key is to establish who owes the property, and whether the person upon the property had a legal right to be there. The right to be there is based on a factual analysis of permission, consent, and legal authority. Since this issue is often fairly simple, cases with a trespassing component coupled with a different twist were selected for review and critique.

DEFAMATION: CAUSE OF ACTION AND ELEMENTS

Defamation is holding an individual up to ridicule, scorn, or contempt that tends to injure a person's reputation, lessen the esteem or respect in which that person is held, or excite unpleasant or derogatory opinions or feelings against the person. The law of defamation embraces the "twin torts" of libel (written) and slander (verbal). The key is the publication of statements that "tend to injure an individual's reputation and good name."[8] The typical issues and elements in a defamation action are as follows:[9]

1. Unprivileged publication of false statements.
2. Publication (communication) to a third party is required.
3. Communication is privileged when it is made on a proper occasion, from a proper motive, in a proper manner, and based upon reasonable cause.
4. Communication must be on a "need to know" basis.
5. Truth is a complete defense to a defamation action.

It is important to consider several underlying principles related to these issues and elements. The first key consideration is to understand that publication requires communication to a third party by verbal, written, or electronic means, or even by physical acts. In this way, a key element of any defamation claim is proof of publication by the defendant to someone other than the subject of the allegedly defamatory statement. In essence, the defamed party has not suffered injury until someone other than himself learns of the defamation.

However, some communication is protected because it is considered privileged. For example, an employer may be entitled to qualified immunity for statements made to an employee to protect the employer's interest, and this privilege extends to situations in which the employee feels compelled to repeat such statements.[10] In assessing this privilege, courts will look at the circumstances, the purpose, and manner of this communication. This privilege is typically limited to communications on a "need to know" basis. This means that the communication was published only to those individuals who should be told, under reasonable circumstances and for a proper business or legal purpose.

In order for the privilege to apply, a defendant must prove four things: (1) the statement was made in good faith, (2) the defendant had an interest to uphold, (3) the scope of the statement was limited to the identified interest, and (4) the statement was published on a proper occasion, in a proper manner, and to proper parties only. The privilege may be lost, however, if the speaker acts with actual malice, or exceeds or abuses the privilege through, for example, excessive publication or through publication to persons other than those who have a legitimate interest in the subject of the statements.

The communication of potentially defamatory information is often raised when an employer is asked to provide a reference for a former employee. In general, there is no legal duty to warn a prospective employer of a former employee's negative behavior. In circumstances where the former employee was terminated for illegal or improper behavior, the employer is faced with a dilemma: communicate the reference accurately and face a possible defamation lawsuit, or provide accurate, but neutral and guarded information that does not reflect the actual reason why the employee is no longer employed by the company. While I cannot provide definitive guidance—since the cases tend to be fact specific—the best practice is to communicate only actual confirmed behavior, rather than rumors or inexpert assumptions of the cause(s) of the behavior. In this way, it is important to ensure that the information conveyed is truthful, backed by substantial evidence and presented in an appropriate way.

It is also important to note that truth is a complete defense to a defamation action. This means if the communicated statement is true, then the individual who communicates it cannot be liable for the publication. This does not mean, however, that a lawsuit will not be filed—and legal costs will be expended to defend the claim. Obviously, this is not a perfect solution.

Finally, an even more difficult circumstance occurs when the person making the statement can reasonably foresee that the person defamed will be compelled to repeat the defamatory statement to a third party.

This typically occurs when the former employee is questioned by a prospective employer as to the reasons why he/she was terminated. In these circumstances, the theories of compelled self-publication and qualified immunity intersect. In this sense, the question becomes whether the privilege that attaches to an employer's statements concerning the reasons for the termination applies when the terminated employee repeats those statements to others. According to some courts, it would make little sense to deny the privilege when the same communication is being conveyed by a different mode of publication. Indeed, in the employment context, the qualified privilege is the only effective means of preventing every termination decision from automatically becoming a case of defamation. As the Minnesota Supreme Court observed:

> It is in the public interest that information regarding an employee's discharge be readily available to the discharged employee and to prospective employers, and we are concerned that, unless a significant privilege is recognized by the courts, employers will decline to inform employees of reasons for discharges.[11]

Based on this reasoning, it may be wise to assert a qualified privilege for statements made concerning the reasons for an employee's discharge, regardless of whether the employer or employee publishes the statement. Without such a privilege, employers would be stymied in their ability to effectively deal with personnel matters. Employers would be left with the choice of giving no reason for terminating employment or hoping an employee will not reveal the reason for discharge to a prospective employer.[12] Obviously this would make little sense.

INVASION OF PRIVACY: CAUSE OF ACTION AND ELEMENTS

Invasion of privacy is a general term used to describe the right of individuals to withhold themselves or their property from public scrutiny. The essence of the theory is the right to be left alone. The key assessment is whether the individual had a reasonable expectation of privacy. This is determined by an objective standard—would a reasonable person believe that his or her privacy is protected? If the answer is in the affirmative, then an expectation of privacy exists. If not, then no privacy right exists.

The operation of privacy rights can be found in the workplace in various ways and in various levels. First, it is now accepted practice to have caveats related to privacy in corporate e-mail and website accounts. These caveats typically give the employer the right to monitor employee usage, thereby diminishing or negating any expectation of privacy related to the use of corporate e-mail, intranet, and websites. In addition, many, if not most, companies use cameras for various forms of surveillance, including the activities of its employees. Courts have upheld unconcealed video cameras.

Also, some companies provide for the ability to monitor the phone lines used by employees in the regular course of business.

Second, most companies have issued various caveats related to physical searches and seizures of property found or contained within the corporate facility. These caveats can be found in company handbooks, bargaining unit agreements, facility access signage, and the like. In essence, these caveats typically provide that the employer reserves the right to inspect packages and property brought into, found at, or contained within the facility. This often expands to the right to search the person of an individual entering the facility, and to seize any contraband found during said search. The logic of these searches and seizures is that the individual "consents" to such by their entry into the facility—or even by their status as an employee of the company. While there are many nuances of consent, as discussed above, the key is whether the individual had a reasonable expectation of privacy. The cases presented below will illustrate some of the issues involved in this assessment.

One of the most common causes of action related to invasion of privacy is known as outrageous conduct, which can be defined as the intentional and wrongful invasion of one's right to privacy which results in harm. There are four elements of this claim:[13]

1. Intrusion is one that is highly offensive or objectionable to the reasonable person, with the interference of intrusion being substantial.
2. Intrusive conduct goes beyond the limits of social toleration.
3. Outrage can cause mental suffering, shame, or humiliation to a person of ordinary sensibilities.
4. Assess the particular relationship of the parties, and the actual or apparent authority of one party over the other.

In addition to outrageous conduct, there are four other causes of action that relate to invasion of privacy. These can be summarized as follows:

1. Appropriation of another's name or likeness for the benefit or advantage of the intruder.
2. Intrusion upon the seclusion or solitude of another by invading his or her home or by eavesdropping.
3. The public disclosure of private facts of another without consent, permission, or legal authority.
4. Publicity that places another in a false light.

NOTES

1. See *Thomas v. City of Seattle,* 395 F. Supp. 2d 992 (2005); and *Woods v. Miamisburg City Schools,* 254 F. Supp. 2d 868 (2003).
2. See *Croft v. Grand Casino,* 910 So. 2d 66 (2005).

3. See Black's Law Dictionary op cit.
4. Ibid.
5. Osterburg, James W. and Richard H. Ward (2000). *Criminal Investigation: A Method for Reconstructing the Past* (3rd ed.).
6. See *McNeely v. The Home Depot, Inc.,* 621 S.E. 2d 473 (2005).
7. See Black's Law Dictionary (1977) 5th ed. St. Paul, MN: West Publishing Company.
8. See *Hagberg v. California Federal Bank, FSB,* 81 P. 3d 244 (2004).
9. See *Vargas v. The Beer Garden et al.,* 791 N.Y.S. 2d 521 (2005).
10. See, for example, *Popko v. Continental Casualty Co.,* 823 N.E. 2d 184 (2005), which involved internal (within the company) comments related to the employee's performance review.
11. See *Theisen v. Covenant Medical Center,* 636 N.W. 2d 74 (2001).
12. Ibid.
13. See *Kline v. Security Guards, Inc.,* 386 F. 3d 246 (2004).

4

Torts of Physical Nature

A. ASSAULT AND BATTERY

04 C 7930

United States District Court, N.D. Illinois, Eastern Division

MUHAMMAD ASAD ALI, M.D., PLAINTIFF v. WAL-MART STORES, INC., DEFENDANT.

Sept. 21, 2005

Background

This case comes before the court pursuant to plaintiff Muhammad Asad Ali, M.D. suit against defendant Wal-Mart Stores, Inc. in a three count complaint alleging state law claims of false arrest and battery by reason of race. Wal-Mart has moved for summary judgment on the last claim only.

Holding

For the following reasons, the court grants the Motion for Summary Judgment.

Ali and his mother, Kahkushan Arshad, are originally from Pakistan. On November 19, 2003, they were shopping together at a Sam's Club in Evanston and decided to purchase some Brita water filters. According to

Ali, he noticed an opened box of Brita filters sitting on a shelf, picked it up, placed it in his shopping cart, and continued shopping. When Ali reached the checkout stand, the cashier noticed that the box was opened and sealed it with a piece of tape. Ali paid for the items in his shopping cart and headed towards the exit.

Ali and his mother left the building and were quickly stopped by a Wal-Mart security guard, John Paul Arellano, who asked Ali if he had forgotten to pay for any of the items in his shopping cart. When Ali answered no, Arellano grabbed him by the arm and led him to an office inside the store. Arellano accused Ali of trying to steal a Brita filter by placing a seventh filter in a box of six. There was indeed a seventh filter in the box, but Ali denied stealing the filter and insisted that it was already in the box when he removed it from the shelf. Nevertheless, Arellano called that police and completed a "Loss Prevention Apprehension Report." In the report, which includes a space for a description of the suspect, Arellano noted (incorrectly) that Ali was Indian. The police arrived, handcuffed Ali, escorted him out of the store, and drove him to the police station. He remained there for four to five hours until his brother and mother picked him up. A Cook County judge eventually acquitted Ali of theft after a bench trial in state criminal court.

Ali claims that the experience caused him a great deal of anxiety. Because he is in the United States on a visa based on his profession, he was worried that he would be deported and that his mother and sister would have no one to support them financially. He claims that he did not receive any counseling for his anxiety because he was concerned that if he did, other doctors would find out what happened.

Battery by Reason of Race

Illinois provides a civil remedy for any victim of a hate crime. A hate crime occurs when, among other things, an individual commits a battery by reason of the actual or perceived race of another. Ali claims that a jury reasonably could find that Arellano committed a battery against him by reason of his race when Arellano grabbed Ali by the arm and led him back to the store. Ali claims that because his mother was wearing traditional Pakistani dress at the time of the incident and because of the notation in the apprehension report that he was "Indian," a jury reasonably could find that the battery was racially motivated.

Ali cites *Johnson* in support of his argument. In *Johnson*, the defendants were criminally convicted of burning a cross in the African American plaintiffs' yard and throwing a brick through their window. The plaintiffs then sued the defendants in a civil suit for the same offense. The court held that, because of the criminal conviction, summary judgment for the plaintiffs was proper. *Johnson* does not control this case. Arelleno was not convicted of a hate crime, and Ali's evidence is nothing like what is inherent in burning a cross.

Another case, which was not cited by the parties, addresses the type of evidence needed to prove that a defendant committed a crime by reason of race. In *Davis*, the court examined whether the evidence was sufficient to uphold the defendant's conviction for a hate crime. Though the court recognized the issue was a close one, it held that the defendant's statement "F ... you nigger," was enough for a jury reasonably to conclude that race motivated the defendant's attack. Here, there was no such racial utterance or derogatory comment. The only reference that Arellano made to Ali's race was in a standard report Arellano completed after Ali was stopped. The reference identified Ali as Indian, was not derogatory in any way, and is not evidence of racial animus. Ali also points to the fact that Arshad was wearing traditional Pakistani clothing and that Wal-Mart security guards pay attention to clothing during their surveillance. These facts only suggest that Arellano noticed what Ms. Arshad was wearing, not that Arellano's detention of Ali was motivated by race. Under the circumstances, no jury reasonably could find that Arellano committed a battery against Ali because of race.

Conclusion

For the foregoing reasons, the court grants defendant's Motion for Summary Judgment.

CASE COMMENT

In this case, the court found insufficient evidence that that defendant security guard committed a battery by reason of race. In coming to this conclusion, the court inferred that the requisite mental state did not exist. In essence, based on the facts presented, the plaintiff failed to show that a battery occurred.

791 N.Y.S.2d 521

Supreme Court, Appellate Division, First Department, New York

MANUEL VARGAS, PLAINTIFF-APPELLANT v. THE BEER GARDEN, INC., ET AL., DEFENDANTS-RESPONDENTS, "JOHN DOE" ETC., ET AL., DEFENDANTS. THE BEER GARDEN, INC., ET AL., THIRD-PARTY–PLAINTIFFS-RESPONDENTS v. GSS SECURITY SERVICE, INC., THIRD-PARTY–DEFENDANT-RESPONDENT, CHARLES R. GARELICK, ET AL., THIRD-PARTY DEFENDANTS.

Feb. 17, 2005

Background

Alleged victim of assault by security guard brought personal injury action against nightclub, and nightclub brought third-party action against security company and security guard. The Supreme Court, New York County, dismissed complaint at the close of evidence. Alleged victim appealed.

Holding

The supreme court, appellate division, held that nightclub did not exercise sufficient control over security guards on its premises to render nightclub their special employer.

Affirmed

Under no reasonable view of the evidence could a jury find that the nightclub exercised sufficient control over the security guards on its premises to render it their special employer. It does not avail plaintiff that the nightclub decided the number of guards needed on a particular night and where on its premises the guards should be posted at any given time, and also required that the guards not carry weapons and never fight back with patrons or people on the street and thereby could be said to have given them instructions relating to the manner in which they performed their work.

The same instructions were also given to the guards by their general employer, third-party defendant security company, an independent contractor in the business of providing security guards to the hotel and entertainment industry, which retained exclusive control over the guards' hiring and firing, wages, work hours and work assignments.

We have considered plaintiff's other arguments and find them unavailing.

CASE COMMENT

Here the court found for the nightclub because they had little control over the operations of the security guard firm. Hence, the alleged assault committed by a security officer was not attributable to the nightclub. If an assault actually occurred, the security firm could still be liable.

B. FALSE ARREST, FALSE IMPRISONMENT, AND MALICIOUS PROSECUTION

621 S.E.2d 473

Court of Appeals of Georgia

McNEELY v. THE HOME DEPOT, INC., ET AL.

Aug. 30, 2005

Background

Security guard responsible for retrieving cash deposits brought malicious prosecution action against store and store employee. The trial court granted summary judgment in favor of store and store employee. Guard appealed.

Holding

The court of appeals held that sufficient probable cause existed to suspect guard was involved in scheme to steal money, and thus, guard did not have claim for malicious prosecution.

Affirmed

According to the record, the Home Depot store had a vault room that was connected to a transfer room by a two-sided transfer safe. Under Home Depot's store policy, employees assigned to the vault room would count deposits before putting the money in a marked bag and placing the bag in the transfer safe. The deposits were logged in, and the log sheet was also put in the transfer safe. When a Brink's employee arrived, he would enter the transfer room, for which only he and select Home Depot managers had keys. He would open the two-sided transfer safe from inside the transfer room and compare the deposits in the safe to those listed on the log sheet. The Brink's employee would then verify that the deposits in the safe matched those on the log sheet, and he would sign the log sheet to indicate that he had picked up the deposits.

On September 22, 1997, McNeely was responsible for retrieving the deposits from a Home Depot store. Upon opening the safe, McNeely noted that one bag that was listed on the log was not actually in the safe. The vault employee searched the vault room for the deposit, but was unable to find it. McNeely ultimately left without signing for the missing deposit, and when he returned to Brinks, both he and his truck were searched for the missing bag.

After McNeely left Home Depot, Jim Trask, the loss prevention supervisor, entered the transfer room where McNeely had been. After searching the room, Trask found the missing deposit bag hidden underneath a stack of empty deposit bags. Trask then created a "dummy" deposit bag, which he hid under the deposit bags. When the next Brink's employee, Tim Cody, arrived, he retrieved the dummy bag and left the store with it. This incident was captured on videotape.

The police were summoned, and a detective reviewed the videotape. According to Trask, the detective told him that there was sufficient information to obtain a warrant. Thus, Trask swore out a warrant against both McNeely and Cody. Cody apparently confessed to stealing the money, but did not implicate McNeely. Nonetheless, McNeely was arrested and spent several days in jail. McNeely testified that he was taken into a courtroom to have the charges against him read aloud, but when asked whether he wanted the charges read, he declined because he already knew the charges against him. Eventually, the charges against McNeely were dismissed due to insufficient evidence.

McNeely filed suit against Home Depot and Trask, alleging that the defendants prosecuted him "without probable cause and with malice." The defendants moved for summary judgment, and the trial court granted the motion. Specifically, the trial court found that McNeely had not presented "evidence of an inquiry before a committing court," which is required to sustain a malicious prosecution claim. This appeal ensued.

In order to prevail on a claim for malicious prosecution, a plaintiff must show the following: "(1) a criminal prosecution; (2) instigated without probable cause; (3) with malice; (4) pursuant to a valid warrant, accusation, or summons; (5) that terminated in the plaintiff's favor; and (6) caused the plaintiff damage." For purposes of such claim, the prosecution must be "carried on," which requires "an inquiry before a committing court." If a person is merely arrested pursuant to a warrant, a claim for malicious prosecution will not lie.

Here, the trial court found that McNeely presented no evidence that he was taken before a committing court. However, there was evidence via McNeely's deposition testimony that he was brought before a judge, which raises an inference that he was taken before a committing court. Regardless of whether this was sufficient evidence of prosecution, we nonetheless find summary judgment appropriate because probable cause existed for Home Depot and Trask to suspect McNeely.

The focus in a probable cause inquiry is "whether the facts *as they appeared at the time of instituting the prosecution* were such as to lead a person of ordinary caution to entertain a belief that the accused was guilty of the offense charged." In other words, the question is, not whether plaintiff was guilty, but whether defendants had *reasonable cause to so believe*—whether the circumstances were such as to create in the mind of defendants a *reasonable belief* that there was probable cause for the arrest and prosecution. Probable cause is defined to be the existence of such facts and circumstances as would excite the *belief* in a reasonable mind, that the person charged was guilty of the crime for which he was arrested and prosecuted.

The record shows that the missing deposit was supposed to be in the transfer safe when McNeely arrived. The bag ultimately was discovered hidden in the transfer room—a room last occupied by McNeely. When the next Brink's employee arrived, he retrieved what he believed to be the deposit bag from its hiding place. Under these circumstances, a reasonable person of ordinary caution would be justified in suspecting that McNeely was involved in a scheme to steal money from Home Depot and that he had hidden the bag in the transfer room. Given the existence of probable cause, the trial court properly granted summary judgment in favor of the defendants. Although the existence of probable cause was not the basis for the court's ruling, a judgment right for any reason will be affirmed.

Judgment affirmed.

CASE COMMENT

The court assessed the facts of the arrest in light of the elements of a malicious prosecution claim. In this case, the presence of probable cause to arrest was fatal to the plaintiff's claim. Specifically, the court found that the deposit bag was hidden in a room last occupied by the plaintiff, and as such, his arrest was reasonable under the factual circumstances.

910 So. 2d 66

Court of Appeals of Mississippi

MELVIN CROFT, APPELLANT v. GRAND CASINO TUNICA, INC., CHRISTOPHER SMITH AND JOHN DOES 1–5, APPELLEES.

Jan. 11, 2005

Background

Employee, who was discharged from casino and arrested after criminal charges were brought against him by casino over the taking of a $100 token, filed suit against casino and its security investigator, claiming malicious prosecution, false arrest, abuse of process, civil conspiracy, menace, assault and battery, and intentional infliction of emotional distress. The Circuit Court, Tunica County, entered summary judgment for casino and its investigator, and employee appealed.

Holdings

The court of appeals held that:

1. Casino had "probable cause" to initiate criminal charges against employee over employee's taking of a $100 token, and since casino had probable cause, employee could not prevail on his malicious prosecution claim; and
2. Since casino had probable cause to file criminal charges against its employee, casino's act of having employee arrested did not constitute false arrest.

Affirmed

Croft worked for Grand Casino Tunica, Inc., for seven months as a member of a hard count team. It was his duty as a member of the hard count team to service the slot machines by removing the coin buckets from the machines, replacing them with empty bins and placing the bins on a cart and taking the coin buckets to the hard count room for counting. Then the same process would be used to collect paper money from another part of the machine. Coins that are placed into a slot machine by patrons fall through the machine into the bucket while paper money goes into a bill validator located on the machine's door. He worked usually with a team of eight and there were four security guards with the team to clear patrons away from the machines as they were counted and to observe the counting team members. The team members dress in jumpsuits without pockets in order to prevent theft by team members during a count.

On April 12, 2001, Croft reported for his shift at 4 a.m. and was given his assignment as part of the team and performed one count. On the second count at about 5 a.m. Croft's team was performing a bill validator drop count. A fellow team member, James McKinley, opened the slot machine door on a $100 slot machine and a $100 token fell into the tray. McKinley continued opening slot machines. When Croft came by to scan the machine, he saw the $100 token in the machine's tray. Instead of collecting the $100 token for the count or alerting the security guard who was standing nearby, Croft did nothing to advise casino personnel about the token. Croft contends that he thought the coin belonged to no one. He then walked over to a patron and told him that there was a coin in one of the machines. The patron retrieved the $100 token and cashed it in. After Croft finished the hard count, he sought out the patron to make sure he had understood that the $100 token was in the bin of a machine. The patron thanked Croft for the information and shook Croft's hand. In the handshake the patron passed a $20 bill to Croft. Croft then gave the $20 bill to coworker McKinley.

At the time this incident was occurring, casino security surveillance team members became suspicious. Senior Internal Auditor Jana Daniels, who was on the casino floor observing the hard count, saw Croft approach a patron and whisper something to him. She observed the patron walk to the $100 slot machine and look in the tray and return to Croft and talk to him again and then return to the area of $100 slot machines and take a token from the tray and put it in his pocket. At that point Daniels called surveillance who reviewed the tape and confirmed the specifics of Croft's appropriation of the $100 token.

About two hours after the incident Croft was told by his supervisor that he and coworker McKinley needed to go with security and they were escorted by two security guards to the office of casino security investigator Chris Smith. McKinley told the investigators that when the door of the machine was opened the $100 token fell out and he told Croft about the coin. McKinley said Croft told him he was going to get it and McKinley advised him that he couldn't have the coin on him. McKinley said Croft then asked him if he could get a guest to get the token, cash it in and give him the money. McKinley gave investigator Smith a $20 bill which was folded up in a square shape, which he said was given to him by Croft.

Croft was questioned by Smith and remained in his office for about 30 minutes. He said that during that the entire investigation while he was at the casino he was never touched by Smith or the security guards. Croft gave a statement of his versions of the events, which did not differ from what has been set out above.

After interviewing the witnesses and looking at the surveillance tape, Smith believed that the elements of embezzlement had been met and called the Tunica County Sheriff's Department. Davis signed an affidavit against Croft alleging petit larceny. A deputy came to the casino, placed Croft in handcuffs and escorted him out of the casino and to jail. Croft's employment was terminated and coworker McKinley was suspended.The petit larceny charge was later dismissed in the justice court, after which Croft initiated this litigation. Additional facts will be related during the discussion of the issues.

The Malicious Prosecution Claim

The elements of the tort of malicious prosecution are: (1) the institution of a proceeding; (2) by or at the insistence of the defendant; (3) the termination of such proceedings in the plaintiff's favor; (4) malice in instituting the proceedings; (5) want of probable cause for the proceeding and (6) the suffering of injury or damage as a result of the prosecution. All six of these elements must be proven by a preponderance of the evidence. The tort is defeated if any one of the elements is not proven.

Our supreme court has said that malicious prosecution suits are not favored but must be "managed with great caution." "Their tendency is to discourage prosecution of crime as they expose the prosecutor to civil suits, and the love of justice may not always be strong enough to induce individuals to commence prosecution when if they fail, they may be subjected to the expenses of litigation even though they are found not liable for damages."

Croft argues in his brief that he did not remove the token from the slot machine or assist anyone in taking the token. However, this is in direct opposition to how he testified in his deposition. In the deposition he testified that after he saw the $100 token in the slot machine tray he didn't report it to management even though an auditor was standing nearby, nor did he retrieve the coin and place it with the funds to be taken to the hard count. Instead he determined to appropriate the money for himself. He told a patron where the token was and according to surveillance tapes he gave him directions to it twice. The patron cashed in the token and then gave Croft a $20 bill folded so as not to be detected in a handshake.

While Croft has arguably met the first three and sixth elements of a claim for malicious prosecution, he has failed to meet claims four and five. He has failed to show that there was malice on the part of the defendants in signing the petit larceny affidavit against him and has failed to show that the defendants lacked probable cause in signing the charges against him.

Malice in the law of malicious prosecution does not refer to mean or evil intent but rather connotes a prosecution instituted primarily for a purpose other than that of bringing an offender to justice. In *Nassar*, the court said that in order to determine malice the court must look to the defendant's state of mind, not his attitude.

Croft argues that there were several facts from which a jury could conclude that the defendants acted with malice in bringing criminal charges against him. Viewing the evidence in the light most favorable to Croft we find there are no disputed facts which show any malicious action on the part of the defendants. Instead from Croft's own testimony the lack of malice can be shown. He admitted to not reporting the token to management, admitted to alerting a patron to the fact that there was a $100 token in the tray and admitted that he accepted a $20 kickback which he called a tip from the fortunate patron.

Croft states in his brief that at no time did he remove the coin from the tray of the machine. While this may be technically true, what is more important is that he caused the token to be taken from the tray by telling a patron of its location. But for his telling the patron the token would have remained in the custody of the casino. Croft also argues in support of malice that he refused the $20 from the patron. The record shows just the opposite:

Q. Did [the customer] say anything to you the second time?
A. Yes. He thanked me.
Q. Do you recall exactly what he said?
A. Just thanks.
Q. Did you shake his hand? Did he give you a $20 bill in the handshake?
A. Yes.

Croft's actions aroused casino security and an investigation of theft began pursuant to established casino policies. The senior auditor on the casino floor saw the suspicious behavior and alerted surveillance who reviewed the tape and confirmed that the token had been taken through the efforts of Croft and the patron. Security Investigator Smith interviewed Croft's coworker McKinley who confirmed that Croft had told the patron about the token and had received $20 in return. In fact, McKinley said Croft gave the money to him. Croft was interviewed and admitted to telling the patron about the location of the token and accepting $20 in exchange for the information. Determining that he had evidence of wrongdoing, Smith made out an affidavit against Croft, who was arrested by Tunica County authorities.

We find no rush to judgment by the casino to have Croft arrested and find that he was only arrested after a thorough investigation was conducted which included a chance for him to give his side of the story. Nor does the evidence show that Croft was singled out for punishment for any reason other than for what he did on the day of the token theft. Croft has offered no evidence that the defendants acted with any motive other than as law-abiding citizens attempting to see that a law violator was brought to justice.

The second reason summary judgment is appropriate is that Croft's claim of malicious prosecution must fail because the defendants had probable case to initiate the criminal affidavit against Croft.

Probable cause in a malicious prosecution action requires the concurrence of an honest belief in the guilt of the person who is accused and reasonable grounds for such belief. Unfounded suspicion and conjecture are not proper bases for finding probable cause.

The existence of probable cause, which involves only the conduct of a reasonable man under the circumstances, usually is taken out of the hands of the jury, and held to be a matter for decision by the court. That is to say, the court will determine whether upon the appearances presented to the defendant, a reasonable person would have instituted the proceeding. The probable cause is determined from the facts apparent to the reasonable person at the time the prosecution is initiated. The tort of malicious prosecution must fail where the party has probable cause to institute an action.

Following an investigation which included reviewing videotape and interviewing witnesses, the casino security investigator concluded that an embezzlement had occurred. The investigation was not begun as an effort to single out Croft for prosecution, but was begun because security personnel detected his suspicious actions involving the taking of a $100 token. The affidavit which Smith signed against Croft was for petit larceny of the $100 token. The petit larceny statute in effect at the time stated that the crime of petit larceny occurs when "any person shall feloniously take, steal and carry away any personal property of another under the value of Two Hundred Fifty Dollars ($250.00), he shall be guilty of petit larceny and upon conviction, shall be punished by imprisonment in the county jail not exceeding one (1) year or by fine of not exceeding One Thousand Dollars ($1,000.00), or both." Thus, the elements of the crime are the feloniously taking, stealing and carrying away of any personal property of another with a value under $250.

We find that there was more than sufficient evidence of probable cause for Smith to initiate criminal charges against Croft. First, it is undisputed that the coin was the property of the casino. It was a $100 token that the casino used in its $100 slot machines. The fact that it fell out into the tray and was not in the bin does not take away the casino's ownership of the token. Croft knew when he saw the token fall into the tray that it wasn't "finder's keepers," that it was casino property just like the hundreds of other tokens he had collected in his job as a hard count team member. But instead of reporting the coin to the nearby auditor or the nearby security or to management, he determined to take it for his own use through the use of an intermediary, the fortunate casino customer whom he alerted about the token. The $100 token was carried away by the customer and cashed in and thus the casino had taken from it an item with a value of less than $250. Croft's actions did not go unrewarded as he received a $20 kickback from the customer.

Under these facts we find that Smith on behalf of the casino possessed sufficient probable cause at the time the affidavit was filed charging Croft with petit larceny and thus Croft's action for malicious prosecution must fail. This issue is without merit.

False Arrest Claim

False arrest is an intentional tort which occurs when one causes another to be arrested falsely, unlawfully, maliciously and without probable cause. If there is probable cause for the charges made, then the plaintiff's arrest is supported by probable cause, and a claim for false arrest must fail.

Once again the key to resolving this issue is to examine whether the defendants had probable cause to bring the charges against Croft. As discussed above, we find that there was abundant probable cause for Croft's arrest. The arrest followed an internal investigation by the casino which consisted of personal interviews of the principals and eyewitnesses and a review of casino surveillance tape. All of this evidence including the statement of Croft himself showed that he had participated in taking a $100 token from the casino. Having found sufficient probable cause we find this issue without merit.

THE JUDGMENT OF THE CIRCUIT COURT OF TUNICA COUNTY IS AFFIRMED.

CASE COMMENT

Here again, the court properly analyzed the facts in relation to the elements of malicious prosecution and false arrest. Both claims were defeated because the court found probable cause to affect the arrest of the plaintiff. The standard for probable cause is whether the arrest was "objectively reasonable" at the time of the arrest.

355 Ark. 138, 133 S.W.3d 393

Supreme Court of Arkansas

MICHAEL PATRICK SUNDEEN v. KROGER AND JERRY HART.

Dec. 4, 2003

Background

Patron brought action for malicious prosecution against store and its security guard after patron was arrested by security guard, who was off-duty police officer, for obstructing governmental operations and for attempting to influence governmental operations. The Circuit Court, Pulaski County, granted store's summary judgment motion, and patron appealed. The court of appeals affirmed, and patron appealed.

Holding

The supreme court held that patron's conviction in the district court were conclusive proof of existence of probable cause for store to initiate criminal proceedings, and without the lack of probable cause, patron was unable to establish the elements necessary to maintain a malicious prosecution action.

Affirmed

On December 21, 1999, Sundeen was shopping at the Kroger store on Asher Avenue in Little Rock. While there, Sundeen asked store employee, Angela Bryant where he could find marshmallows. Bryant, who was talking to a co-worker, said that she thought they were on aisle 16 or 17. At that point, Bryant claimed that Sundeen made a rude comment to her, and, in return, Sundeen responded that Bryant was rude to him. Sundeen went to the customer service desk to complain about Bryant. At the same time, Bryant went to security guard Jerry Hart to complain about Sundeen. Hart, an off-duty Little Rock police officer, approached Sundeen as he stood in line at the customer service desk and said that he needed to talk to him. Sundeen told Hart that he did not have anything to say to him. Hart said that Sundeen then became loud and belligerent, so Hart took him by the arm and escorted him upstairs to the security office.

According to Hart, Sundeen persisted in being loud and rude, which led Hart to arrest Sundeen for obstructing governmental operations. Sundeen responded, saying that he was going to contact his lawyer and the store manager and "have Hart's job." Hart then told him he was also under arrest for attempting to influence governmental operations. The charges were tried in Little Rock District Court, and Sundeen was found guilty of both charges. Sundeen appealed to Pulaski County Circuit Court, but prior to trial, the prosecutor nolle prossed the charges.

The primary issue in this appeal, then, is whether the circuit court, hearing the motion for summary judgment in the malicious prosecution case, was entitled to look at Sundeen's prior district court convictions in order to determine whether there was probable cause for the criminal proceedings. In the context of a malicious prosecution action, the existence of probable cause is to be determined by the facts and circumstances surrounding the commencement and continuation of the legal proceedings. Probable cause for prosecution must be based upon the existence of facts or credible information that would induce a person of ordinary caution to believe the accused person to be guilty of the crime for which he is charged.

Here, Sundeen argues that because the charges against him were previously nolle prossed in circuit court, there is no evidence of a criminal conviction in the lower district court. While it is true that the entry of a *nolle prosequi* is a sufficiently favorable termination of a proceeding in favor of the accused, it is not, standing alone, evidence that probable cause was lacking (acquittal does not necessarily show a want of probable cause in the prosecution).

Arkansas cases have consistently held that a judgment of conviction by a court of competent jurisdiction is conclusive evidence of the existence of probable cause, even though the judgment is later reversed. In *Alexander*, appellant Alexander was convicted of "wrongful disposition of title-retained property" in municipal court, but upon appeal to circuit court, the charge was dismissed. Alexander subsequently brought a malicious prosecution lawsuit against her accusers, but the trial court directed a verdict in favor of the defendant, Laman. This court affirmed, writing as follows:

> Upon this proof the court was right in instructing a verdict for the defendant. It was incumbent on the plaintiff to show, as an essential element of her cause of action, that the defendant acted without probable cause in having her arrested. That element of [Alexander's] case is necessarily lacking, for it is settled that a judgment of conviction by a court of competent jurisdiction is conclusive evidence of the existence of probable cause, even though the judgment is later reversed. Since the municipal court's judgment, in the absence of fraud in its procurement, was *conclusive* evidence of the existence of probable cause, [Alexander] was not entitled to retry an issue already determined. The Restatement

> (Second) of Torts Section 667(1) (1977) is in accord; it provides that "[t]he conviction of the accused by a magistrate or trial court, although reversed by an appellate tribunal, conclusively establishes the existence of probable cause, unless the conviction was obtained by fraud, perjury or other corrupt means."

The fact that the prosecution chose to nolle prosse the charges against him, however, is of no import, and does not, under this court's case law, affect the prior determination of probable cause. In, this court emphasized that in making a probable cause determination in the context of a malicious prosecution suit, the court "concentrates on the *facts before the action commenced* (emphasis added)." Probable cause is determined by the facts and circumstances surrounding the *commencement* of the legal action.

Therefore, the question in this case is whether Jerry Hart had probable cause to arrest Sundeen for interference with governmental operations and attempting to influence a governmental official. Here, Sundeen's own affidavit supports a finding of probable cause; he averred that, when asked by Hart, Sundeen did not step out of line at the Kroger store. Sundeen also admitted that he told Hart he wanted to find out who Hart's supervisor was so Sundeen could "have" his job.

In sum, we conclude that there is no need to overrule our prior case law, as Sundeen suggests. The circuit court hearing Sundeen's malicious prosecution case was correct to grant Kroger's motion for summary judgment, because Sundeen's district court conviction, even if later reversed, was conclusive proof of the existence of probable cause for Kroger to initiate criminal proceedings. Without the lack of probable cause, Sundeen was unable to establish the elements necessary to a malicious prosecution action, and summary judgment was entirely correct.

With respect to Sundeen's malice argument, malice can be inferred from lack of probable cause. Malice has been defined as "any improper or sinister motive for instituting the suit." However, when probable cause exists and there is no strong evidence of malice, a charge of malicious prosecution cannot succeed. Here, there was probable cause for the initiation of proceedings against Sundeen; on appeal, however, he fails to point to any particular facts or evidence he introduced in the trial court that would support his contention that there was a genuine issue of material fact to be resolved regarding malice.

Simply put, Sundeen offered no proof whatsoever of any coercive actions or efforts to extort anything from him; therefore, we affirm the trial court's decision to grant Kroger's Motion for Summary Judgment.

Affirmed

CASE COMMENT

This case also turns on the existence of probable cause. Since the court found probable cause to arrest, the decision to nolle prosequi the charges against him were not determinative. In this sense, the court emphasized that the key factor is whether there was probable cause to affect the arrest. The fact that the charges were not pursued by the local prosecutor, was of no legal merit. Consequently, these cases illustrate the importance of conducting a thorough, professional investigation prior to the institution of criminal proceedings. With this, the facts can be discerned to determine if probable cause exists

332 F. Supp. 2d 1367

United States District Court, D. Oregon

APRILL CAMPBELL, PLAINTIFF v. SAFEWAY, INC., A DELAWARE CORPORATION, DEFENDANT.

Aug. 25, 2004

Background

Former employee brought action against her former employer, alleging state law claims for false imprisonment. Employer moved for summary judgment.

Holdings

The district court held that:

1. Genuine issue of material fact existed as to whether store personnel confined employee during interview held in store office on suspicion that she stole money from cash register, precluding summary judgment on false imprisonment claim; and
2. Genuine issue of material fact existed as to whether "merchant exception" to tort liability for false imprisonment was applicable.

Plaintiff worked at the Springfield, Oregon Safeway store from September 1999 until March 2001. On February 22, 2001, plaintiff worked the night shift as a cashier and person in charge, or "PIC." While Campbell was the last cashier to leave the store that night, other cashiers aside from plaintiff worked at her registers.

The next morning, the store's morning-shift bookkeeper discovered that some money was missing since Paula Frazer, the evening-shift bookkeeper, had last audited the registers the night before. As a result, the bookkeepers and Amanda Carter, the store manager, initiated an investigation. Defendant claims the documents Frazer reviewed showed about $800 was missing; plaintiff, in contrast, argues the documents do not show that $800 was missing.

During the investigation, store personnel discovered that three $20 bills, which had been placed under the pan in plaintiff's register the night before, were missing. Plaintiff's register's tape showed the three bills had not been paid out to customers. Carter also personally reviewed all the transactions from the night before and concluded the three bills had not been paid out to customers. Plaintiff, therefore, became a suspect.

Almost two weeks later, on March 5, 2001, Carter called plaintiff into her office so store security personnel could interview her. Plaintiff did not know why she was called into the office until after Carter closed the office door behind them. Dave Curtis, a Safeway security guard, conducted the interview. During the interview, the parties were arranged thusly: security guard Curtis sat behind the desk facing two chairs. Plaintiff sat in one of the chairs while Carter sat in the other chair, which was situated behind plaintiffs chair and near the door. When plaintiff realized Curtis believed she had stolen from the store, she turned longingly to look at the door. At which point, Carter shuffled her chair directly in front of the door, blocking the office's only exit.

In response to Curtis's initial questions regarding whether plaintiff had acted in such a way as to affect adversely Safeway's assets, plaintiff insisted she did not know what Curtis was talking about or what he wanted to hear. When it became abundantly clear Curtis was accusing plaintiff of theft, she repeatedly denied the allegation. While plaintiff concedes Curtis never yelled at her, she describes Curtis's tone as harsh and aggressive. Indeed, at one point, in response to plaintiff's denials of wrongdoing, Curtis warned her if she did not lose her "cocky attitude," he was "going to take her outside and kick her ass." Curtis further suggested to plaintiff that if she denied knowing anything she would go to jail, because he is not one "to waste time." He also explained to plaintiff, at least twice, that when an employee accused of theft asks to "see proof" that employee is "automatically taken to jail." As further warning, Curtis told plaintiff he had never been sued, so she should not "even consider" suing him.

Exasperated, plaintiff finally asked Curtis, "What do you want me to say?" Curtis responded that if she would sign a confession she would not be taken to jail, everything would be handled internally, and she would be able to get home to see her children. Plaintiff, therefore, agreed to sign a confession, which Curtis dictated to her. Curtis asked plaintiff how much the confession should state she took; plaintiff responded, "I don't know, $20, let's say $20, I just want to go home." Curtis told plaintiff "to get real" and ultimately settled on a much higher figure; the confession, in pertinent part, stated: "For the last 12 months I have taken $800 from registers, I knew this was wrong and it will never happen again. I am a single mom and sometimes get strapped for payday." Plaintiff signed the dictated confession and a promissory note agreeing to pay the store $800, even though plaintiff testified she had no idea where Curtis came up with the $800 figure. Carter, in fact, testified she had "no idea" how the $800 figure was derived. As part of the confession, plaintiff also agreed to pay $150 in so-called investigation costs.

Despite the confession, plaintiff denies she ever took any money from the store. According to plaintiff, she only signed the confession because she was afraid that she would go to jail and that "this man [she] did not know was going to kick [her] ass." She also feared she would not be home when her children returned from school unless she agreed to sign the confession. At that time, plaintiff had two children, ages eight and eleven, one of whom, Cori, was in a "special needs" program at school. As part of the special-needs program, plaintiff had to be home to greet the school bus, because the bus driver would not allow Cori to disembark without plaintiff's assistance.

Curtis testified he knew plaintiff was a single mother. Indeed, at some point during the interview, in the context of discussing possible jail time, Curtis asked plaintiff, "don't [your children] need to come home from school soon?" Plaintiff testified the interview lasted a total of about three and a half hours, while defendant says it lasted no more than two and a half hours. The parties agree that plaintiff never expressly asked to use the phone, leave the office, or see a union representative.

Defendant fired plaintiff on or about March 6, 2001. Plaintiff was able to secure a new job within a week of defendant's terminating her. Plaintiff, however, alleges she experienced serious emotional distress after the incident involving Curtis. She alleges she could not sleep for the first couple days after the incident. After those couple days, plaintiff says she began sleeping more than usual and stopped eating, causing her to lose weight. She further alleges she did not change clothes for at least a week after the incident.

False Imprisonment Claim

To state a claim for false imprisonment, a plaintiff must show the defendant caused an unlawful confinement of plaintiff. The threshold element of confinement may be satisfied by establishing that the defendant did at least one of four things: (1) put up actual or apparent physical barriers to prevent plaintiff's exit, (2) used physical force to prevent exit, (3) used threats of force to prevent exit, or (4) asserted legal authority to prevent exit. As long as one of these four methods of showing confinement is met, the confinement "need not be for more than a brief time."

Of course, the confinement must have been unprivileged to support a claim. Confinement is privileged when it qualifies for protection under the statutory "merchant exception." The contours of the exception are as follows:

> Notwithstanding any other provision of law, a peace officer, merchant or merchant's employee who has probable cause for believing that a person has committed theft of property of a store or other mercantile establishment may detain and interrogate the person in regard thereto in a reasonable manner and for a reasonable time.

Under Oregon's merchant exception, then, the existence of probable cause does not inherently shield the merchant from tort liability; the confinement also must have been consummated in a "reasonable manner and for a reasonable time." Whether the confinement was reasonable in manner and time is an issue for the jury unless the court determines that, even"accepting the evidence most favorable to plaintiff, the detention was reasonable."

Defendant Safeway argues that plaintiff's false imprisonment claim fails, as a matter of law, for two reasons: (1) there was no confinement, and (2) any confinement is protected by the merchant exception.

1. Confinement

Construing the record in plaintiff's favor, as the court must, defendant's conduct caused confinement. There was no confinement initially because plaintiff voluntarily accompanied Carter to the office. Nor did closing the office door give rise to confinement. Confinement, however, arose during the course of the interview, as discussed below.

First, the record shows that defendant established a physical barrier to prevent exit. After plaintiff turned to look at the office's closed door and only exit, Carter moved her chair so as to block the exit, evidencing an intent to ensure plaintiff did not try to leave. Based on this conduct, plaintiff testified she felt she could not leave the office. These facts are sufficient to create a jury issue as to whether defendant erected a physical barrier to keep plaintiff from leaving the office. For instance, unlike the case at bar, the security guard in *Roberts* unequivocally told the suspected employee she was "free to leave at any time." And at one point, in response to a specific question whether she wanted to end the interview, plaintiff responded she did not wish to end it.

Moreover, aside from Carter's using her chair as a physical barrier, evidence of Curtis's verbal threats gives rise to material issues of fact regarding confinement. As stated, Curtis threatened to take plaintiff out back and "kick [her] ass." Curtis also repeatedly indicated plaintiff would be taken immediately to jail if she did not confess. Defendant correctly observes that a threat of force constitutes confinement only when the threat was "such as to create a reasonable apprehension that force will be used for the purpose of effectuating the present confinement." That is, it is only when threats "are relative to a present threatened confinement that they can be said presently to deprive one of liberty." Thus a "mere threat to prosecute in the future" is not sufficient to constitute a confinement.

Drawing all inferences in plaintiff's favor, Curtis threatened plaintiff with physical force "for the purpose of effectuating" the confinement. Curtis made the threat in response to plaintiff's "cocky attitude," which, reading the record in plaintiff's favor, amounted to nothing more than repeated denials of wrongdoing. It is therefore reasonable to infer that Curtis threatened plaintiff in an effort to compel her to stay put and confess to the alleged theft. In addition, plaintiff's evidence shows Curtis made clear that if plaintiff did not confess, proof or no proof, she would immediately be taken to jail and thus would not get home in time to meet her children. On that point, it is notable that in *Roberts* the court made the following observation:

> In, there was direct testimony that plaintiff was told that if she left the office they would take her to jail and that she could go only if she confessed. The threat was geared to her present confinement and was properly held to constitute false imprisonment. Although Curtis did not expressly tell plaintiff she would go to jail if she left the office, drawing inferences in plaintiff's favor, Curtis wanted plaintiff to understand she would physically be taken to jail unless she admitted to wrongdoing. (Including such things as "[Curtis] kept implying, now, remember, you don't want to go to jail. You need to get home to your children.... He said I will take you to jail if you don't sign the confession.")

In sum, Curtis did not make future threats, in the face of which plaintiff could have freely walked away without confessing, but instead threatened force and jail time with "the purpose of effectuating [a] present confinement."

2. Merchant Exception

The merchant exception does not save defendant from a trial. Even assuming defendant had probable cause to believe initially that plaintiff had taken some money, material fact issues exist regarding whether the confinement and interrogation were conducted in a "reasonable manner and for a reasonable time."

Taken together, the facts (read in plaintiff's favor) could cause a jury to conclude defendant acted unreasonably. Although defendant found $60.00 missing from plaintiff's particular register, the record does not indisputably support Curtis's attempt to require plaintiff to pay the store $800.00. Both plaintiff and her boss, Ms. Carter, testified they did not know how that amount was derived. Even assuming the store had lost $800.00, on this record, the court cannot say conclusively it was reasonable for defendant to seek reimbursement of the full amount from plaintiff.

Perhaps most troubling, Curtis used plaintiff's vulnerable position as a single mother to persuade her to sign the confession admitting she stole the $800. Curtis knew plaintiff was a single mother and had to be home to meet her children. Curtis effectively created an unreasonable choice, which did nothing to enhance the reliability of any confession: either confess in writing to stealing an amount of money plaintiff repeatedly denied taking or else fail to get home to meet her minor children who needed her.

Moreover, Curtis essentially gave plaintiff no opportunity to respond or demand proof, repeatedly threatening her with immediate jail time if she even asked about proof. Curtis also preempted any questions plaintiff may have had about his tactics by warning her no one had ever sued him and not to "even think about it." In addition, accepting plaintiff's best estimate, the confinement lasted more than three hours, thus making it more likely plaintiff would backtrack on her consistent denials and finally agree to confess, despite Curtis's clear message he did not need any proof to send plaintiff to jail. In addition to threatening jail time, Curtis's frustration with plaintiff's denials caused him to threaten her with physical violence.

In sum, even accepting defendant's argument it had probable cause initially to confine plaintiff, a jury could find it acted unreasonably "in detaining her with the bullying tactics and threats detailed by her, in an attempt to prove her guilt, or to make her confess that she intended" to steal from the store. Bearing in mind the issue of reasonableness generally is one for the jury, the court finds material issues of fact precluding summary judgment on plaintiff's false imprisonment claim.

Conclusion

For the foregoing reasons, the court DENIES defendant Safeway's Motion for Summary Judgment. The court finds there are simply too many fact issues to hold that plaintiff, as a matter of law, cannot prove her claims. IT IS SO ORDERED.

CASE COMMENT

The court powerfully articulated the facts in this case, which clearly illustrate the liability of Safeway. Here again, the security personnel acted improperly in their zealous attempt to solve the theft. While it is certainly prudent and proper to diligently investigate crimes within the store, the manner in which this case was handled was beyond the bounds of professionalism. Even assuming that the plaintiff was guilty of the theft, the interrogation left the store exposed to liability well beyond the value of the missing money which triggered the theft. Consequently—and ironically—without proper investigative and interrogation methods, the store can be liable for many times the value of the theft being investigated.

87 Cal. App. 4th 1320, 105 Cal. Rptr. 2d 320

Court of Appeal, Second District, Division 4, California

GORDON ECKER, PLAINTIFF AND APPELLANT v. RAGING WATERS GROUP, INC., DEFENDANT AND RESPONDENT.

March 23, 2001

Background

Amusement park visitor, who was detained by park security and was subsequently acquitted on charge of annoying or molesting a child under 18, sued park for malicious prosecution, false imprisonment and related tort claims. The Superior Court, Los Angeles County, granted nonsuit to park on all claims. Visitor appealed.

Holdings

The court of appeal held that:

1. Videotape of adolescent boys that security officer seized from visitor's video camera was admissible, even if action of seizing and viewing videotape without visitor's knowledge or consent was unreasonable;
2. Park had probable cause to procure visitor's arrest, thus defeating malicious prosecution claim; and
3. Disputed factual issue existed as to whether park's security personnel acted reasonably under all the circumstances in their detention of visitor, precluding a judgment of nonsuit on visitor's remaining tort claims pursuant to a defense provided in penal code.

Reversed and remanded

This appeal arises out of the following series of events. Gordon Ecker went to Raging Waters amusement park. Several adolescent boys complained to park security that Ecker was following and videotaping them. Security observed Ecker and confirmed he was surreptitiously videotaping juveniles. After uniformed security personnel approached Ecker, he went with them to their office. While he was there, a Raging Waters security officer, without Ecker's knowledge or consent, took the videotape from his camera and viewed it. The videotape consisted exclusively of shots of the bodies of adolescent boys. Raging Waters security contacted law enforcement. Los Angeles County Deputy Sheriffs arrived and took Ecker into custody for the misdemeanor offense of annoying or molesting a child under the age of 18. Ecker had been detained for three hours by Raging Waters security without being told of the nature of the complaint or being questioned about his actions. The District Attorney filed a misdemeanor charge against Ecker. A jury returned a verdict of "not guilty." The evidence established the following events.

Ecker held a season pass to Raging Waters. Prior to the day in question, he had visited the park several times in 1998. On June 13, 1998, he went to the park by himself. He brought and used a video camera as he had in the past. Raging Waters has no policy against videotaping in the park.

Four adolescent brothers were visiting the park together. On several occasions, they saw Ecker with a video camera. The boys never saw Ecker, who was alone, go on any of the rides but instead "always [saw him] at the end of the rides." One of the boys, Jeremy G., testified: "It looked like he [Ecker] was videotaping, but he never had the camera up at his side. He always had it down at his side. When someone would be going down [a ride], he would have his camera hang with him and moved his body and followed them with the camera...." This seemed "really weird" to the boys so they would go to a different ride if they saw Ecker. Because the boys had seen Ecker "a couple of times before doing the same thing" and it "really bother[ed]" them, they went to the park security.

They spoke to park security "for about 15, 20 minutes." They told security all of the foregoing, including the fact that during that day Ecker had filmed them "maybe an hour, hour and a half." They explained that Ecker's filming "bothered so bad because we had to keep going different ways, and we felt like we had to move away. We felt like we wanted to beat him up, but we didn't. That's how bad it bothered us. This guy is really doing something wrong to us."

When asked how they knew Ecker was filming them, "[o]ne of the elder boys indicated that he had sent his younger brother to the top of the waterslides, and observed [Ecker's] actions.... [T]he actions of his brother sliding down the slide and the actions of [Ecker] coincided. As his younger brother slid down the waterslide, [Ecker] pointed his camera directly at his younger brother, and remained pointed at the younger brother as the brother exited the bottom of the slides. As the younger brother walked past [Ecker], exiting the waterslide, [Ecker] continued to point his camera at the younger brother...." The boys had dubbed Ecker "the Stalker" because they had previously seen him film others in the park. Manuel Iniguez, the security guard who first interviewed them, opined that "[t]he boys appeared quite disturbed and upset by [Ecker's] actions."

Clayton Stelter, Raging Waters' security supervisor, was informed of the above and went to look for Ecker. Stelter observed Ecker with his "video camera underneath his arm. And it appeared that he was walking along and would either follow certain juveniles or would, as they pass, turn and pan with the camera and follow them with the camera." He also saw him "rest[ing] the camera on [an] arm rail [of rope bridges], videotaping the kids coming across the ropes...." These observations took "10 to 20 minutes" after which Stelter concluded they "had a valid complaint" but "didn't know really legally what [they] had...." Stelter and two other guards approached Ecker, identified themselves as security officers, told him they "had a complaint, and ... asked if he could help [them] resolve it." They neither touched him nor took his video camera. According to Stelter, Ecker agreed to go to the security office, although Ecker's declaration, which will be set forth later, averred he felt he had no choice. Stelter testified that if Ecker had not agreed to accompany them, they would have let him go because they "are not allowed to detain anyone...." Stelter conceded he and the other guards did not discuss the option of giving Ecker a warning rather than asking him to come with them; that he did not ask Ecker to stop filming because he "wasn't sure that we had anything in reference to any criminal matter or any—if the kids had a valid complaint at all"; and that there was no particular reason they could not have attempted to resolve the complaint on the spot as opposed to in the security office. It was stipulated that security had no information that Ecker had spoken with or touched any minor that day.

At the security office, Ecker was told to leave his belongings, including the video camera, in the lobby and to have a seat in the office. Ecker complied. At some later point, Stelter, without Ecker's knowledge or permission, took the videotape from the camera, left the office, and viewed a portion of it in another office. The portion he saw "was focusing on chubby male juveniles from the neck down." Stelter did not question Ecker about what he had seen on the videotape.

The Raging Waters security manual explains that the "primary concern" of its Security Department is "prevention and reaction to incidents that are undesirable to our guests...." Security enforces park rules and regulations but "actual enforcement of laws" is the responsibility of law enforcement, "with Raging Waters Security personnel assisting as needed." The manual defines various crimes. Disturbing the peace includes "creating a disturbance that offends others." The manual authorizes immediate detainment of a suspect in the case of serious felonies and "where the immediate detainment of the suspect is necessary to secure the safety of the park guests and surrounding community." The manual also provides: "Some of the minor crimes and rule infractions can be handled by counseling and following one of the disposition [release] options." Stelter testified he did not follow the latter option with Ecker because "the conduct involved juveniles and to protect.... Raging Waters and ourselves personally [the security guards], if we did have a felony that was committed in our presence and we didn't do anything to assist the victims or anything like that, then we would be held liable...."

Because the security personnel were unsure which, if any, crime Ecker had committed, they called the Los Angeles County Sheriff's Department. While they were waiting for the deputies to arrive, Ecker asked "how long is this going to take...." Stelter told him they "were working on it. If he could hang on for a second for us, we were trying to figure out or take care of the problem...." The deputy sheriffs took Ecker into custody for the misdemeanor offense of annoying or molesting a child under the age of 18. Thereafter, the District Attorney elected to prosecute him for that crime. The jury returned a "not guilty" verdict.

Subsequently, in the civil action, the trial court granted nonsuit on the malicious prosecution action, finding probable cause existed as a matter of law. It also granted nonsuit on Ecker's three other causes of action, finding that the defense provided by [citation omitted] applied as a matter of law. This appeal by Ecker follows.

"Unjustifiable criminal litigation, causing damage to reputation and the expense of defending proceedings, gives rise to the tort of malicious prosecution, which consists of initiating or procuring the arrest and prosecution of another under lawful process, but from malicious motives and without probable cause. One who procures a third person to institute a malicious prosecution is liable, just as if he instituted it himself. The test is whether the defendant was actively instrumental in causing the prosecution."

Ecker sued for malicious prosecution based upon the claim that Raging Waters, without probable cause, and with malice, caused a criminal prosecution to be initiated against him which terminated in his favor through a "not guilty" verdict. In the trial court, the *only issue* litigated and decided in regard to this tort was whether Raging Waters had acted with probable cause. We therefore confine our discussion to that element.

In *Sheldon*, our Supreme Court clarified that "the probable cause element calls on the trial court to make an objective determination of the 'reasonableness' of the defendant's conduct, i.e., to determine whether, on the basis of the facts known to the defendant, the institution of the prior action was legally tenable. The resolution of that question of law calls for the application of an *objective* standard to the facts on which the defendant acted. Because the malicious prosecution tort is intended to protect an individual's interest 'in freedom from unjustifiable and unreasonable litigation', if the trial court determines that the prior action was objectively reasonable, the plaintiff [e.g., Ecker] has failed to meet the threshold requirement of demonstrating an absence of probable cause and the defendant [e.g., Raging Waters] is entitled to prevail." When the facts known by the defendant are not in dispute, "the probable cause issue is properly determined by the trial court under an objective standard...."

In this case, the facts regarding the existence of probable cause fall into three categories: (1) the complaints made by the boys to Raging Waters security; (2) security's subsequent observations of Ecker; and (3) the videotape. None of these facts was disputed. Ecker's argument to the contrary is unavailing. He does not point to any evidence which contradicts these facts, but merely argues Raging Waters security did not conduct a sufficient investigation or that Raging Waters security could have handled the matter differently than it did. That argument misses the mark. Whether the malicious prosecution defendant conducted a sufficient or adequate investigation is legally irrelevant to the probable cause determination. Instead, Ecker's argument addresses a separate issue: whether Raging Waters' actions were reasonable under all of the circumstances, an issue we will analyze later when we discuss the applicability of.

Because the state of Raging Waters' factual knowledge was undisputed, it was for the court to decide whether such facts constituted probable cause. That undisputed evidence established the following. Several adolescent boys complained that Ecker, whom they never saw use any of the park rides, had been following and videotaping them in a surreptitious manner. On prior visits to the park, the boys had seen Ecker film others and consequently referred to him as "the Stalker." To confirm their suspicions, one of the older boys watched Ecker as his younger brother used one of the waterslides. He saw Ecker point his camera in the direction of his younger brother as he slid down the slide, exited the slide, and walked away. In explaining these events to security, the boys were visibly upset and disturbed. After Stelter was informed of the foregoing, he watched Ecker for 15 to 20 minutes. His observations confirmed the complaints: Ecker, while holding his camera at his side, was actually videotaping juveniles. Stelter and two other guards approached and asked Ecker to come to the security office. Later, Stelter viewed the videotape and saw it consisted solely of shots of the bodies of adolescent boys. At that point, law enforcement was called. Based upon all of these circumstances, it was objectively reasonable to suspect that Ecker's actions of following male juveniles and videotaping their bodies in a secretive manner—actions which clearly disturbed and upset the boys who had complained—were criminal.

Ecker's argument to the contrary is not persuasive. He places great reliance on Stelter's testimony that he (Stelter) was not sure which park rule had been violated or which law, if any, Ecker had broken. That fact does not have the legal significance attached to it by Ecker.

The proper inquiry in resolving the question of probable cause is to determine whether the prior action was *objectively* reasonable. If the trial court determines that it was, "the malicious prosecution plaintiff has failed to meet the threshold requirement of demonstrating an absence of probable cause, and the defendant is entitled to prevail."

By a parity of reasoning, the fact Stelter (and other Raging Waters personnel) were uncertain of the precise crime Ecker may have committed is irrelevant to the determination of probable cause. The issue is whether it was objectively reasonable to suspect Ecker had committed a crime. It was. Determination of the crime(s) to be charged is authority properly vested in a prosecuting agency, not a private amusement park such as Raging Waters.

In sum, based upon the undisputed facts, the trial court properly determined it was objectively reasonable to suspect Ecker had committed a crime, thereby establishing probable cause. This negated an essential element of Ecker's claim for malicious prosecution: lack of probable cause. The trial court therefore correctly granted nonsuit on the malicious prosecution claim.

As stated earlier, in addition to suing for malicious prosecution, Ecker also sued Raging Waters for false imprisonment, and related claims. The trial court granted nonsuit on those claims, finding the defense applied as a matter of law. As set forth in our earlier discussion, the first element of probable cause was established as a matter of law. Because lawful amusement park rules necessarily include obedience to the proscriptions found in the Penal Code, the security personnel had, as a matter of law, probable cause to believe Ecker was "not following lawful amusement park rules."

It is in regard to the second element—park personnel acted reasonably under all of the circumstances—the trial court erred in granting nonsuit. Raging Waters was not entitled to a finding as a matter of law that its security personnel acted reasonably under all of the circumstances. For one thing, Ecker's uncontradicted declaration established he was held for at least three hours in a physically uncomfortable surrounding in which he was never asked one question about his actions. For another thing, Stelter conceded that without Ecker's permission or knowledge, he took the videotape from the camera and viewed it. In addition, when security first approached Ecker, they did not explain the complaint to him and did not seek an explanation from him for his actions. Ecker's declaration disputed Stelter's claim he agreed to go to the security office; Ecker asserted that when approached by the three uniformed security officers, "it was clear ... [he] was required to go ... and ... was not free to leave." Although Raging Waters security had the options of simply asking Ecker either to stop videotaping or to leave the park, they pursued neither one. In sum, whether Raging Waters security personnel acted reasonably under all of the circumstances is a disputed factual issue which should not have been resolved by granting nonsuit to Raging Waters. We express no opinion as to how the issue should be ultimately decided but simply find nonsuit was an improper vehicle by which to resolve it.

The judgment is reversed and the matter is remanded to the trial court for further proceedings consistent with this opinion.

CASE COMMENT

In this case, again, the security personnel initially had probable cause to detain and to arrest the plaintiff. However, the extent of the detention and the scope of the search may have been unreasonable. While the court left this question open, the conduct of the security personnel now requires a trial to determine its reasonableness. Conducting a trial on this issue is an expense that could have been avoided. Consequently, the conduct of security personnel will be assessed in its entirety—from the initial "stop" to the outcome of the arrest (if applicable). At each stage of the encounter, professionalism must prevail.

DISCUSSION QUESTIONS

How is probable cause assessed, objectively or subjectively? If you are deemed to have probable cause to arrest, what further requirements are necessary to avoid possible liability exposure? How does probable cause relate to investigations and interrogations in light of the decisions in the above cases?

C. TRESPASS

68 So. 2d 164

Court of Appeal of Louisiana, Fourth Circuit

MARVIN LEBOVITZ v. SHERATON OPERATING CORPORATION D/B/A SHERATON NEW ORLEANS HOTELS, ET AL.

Feb. 11, 2004

Background

Plaintiff, who was arrested for trespassing at hotel, brought action against hotel alleging false arrest and slander. The Civil District Court, Orleans Parish, denied hotel's Motion for Summary Judgment, and hotel petitioned for supervisory writ.

Holding

The court of appeal held that fact issues precluded summary judgment for hotel.

Writ denied

The plaintiff entered the Sheraton Hotel on Super Bowl Sunday, February 3, 2002, allegedly to get a shoeshine. The hotel was under the impression he was scalping tickets to the game. The hotel avers a security guard asked him to leave and that he refused. The plaintiff claims he agreed to leave but not until he could speak with a manager. He alleges he was dragged into the street with his pants legs still rolled up. The guard called NOPD, and the plaintiff was arrested and charged with trespassing. The plaintiff filed suit, essentially alleging false arrest, but specifically alleging that the hotel made false statements causing the arrest, failed to determine his purpose in the hotel, acted rashly and arbitrarily, and slandered him. The hotel filed a motion for summary judgment on the basis that Louisiana's trespass laws allow the hotel to ask anyone to leave. The trial court denied the motion, and the hotel seeks this court's supervisory jurisdiction.

Discussion

Here, there are obvious facts in dispute about whether the hotel threw the plaintiff out on the street after he asked to see a manager, whether he refused to leave, and what statements the guard made to NOPD. The trespassing statute does not shield the hotel from potential civil liability. Even if the statute gives the hotel authority to ask persons to leave, it does not give it the authority to make false statements to the police leading to persons' arrests. We deny the writ application since the trial court did not err.

CASE COMMENT

Here the issue was not whether the person was a ticket scalper or merely someone seeking a shoe shine. Instead, the case turned on the treatment of the individual, and whether the security personnel made false statements to the police to justify the arrest. Notwithstanding the statute allowing for authority to dismiss trespassers from the hotel, the appeals court denied the hotel's summary judgment motion, as there remains a factual question as to the conduct of the security personnel.

861 A.2d 1135

Supreme Court of Vermont

KAREN KEEGAN v. LEMIEUX SECURITY SERVICES, INC., AND BARR & BARR, INC.

Sept. 28, 2004

Background

College security officer who was injured after entering a construction site to allegedly ensure the safety of a trespasser brought negligence action against contractor and security service hired by contractor to guard the construction site. The Chittenden Superior Court granted defendants' Motion for Summary Judgment. Officer appealed.

Holding

The supreme court held that defendants owed no greater duty to officer than they owed to trespasser, and thus officer failed to show that defendants breached a duty owed to her, precluding recovery on negligence claim.

Affirmed

In the fall of 2000, Middlebury College contracted with Barr to serve as a general contractor on a dormitory construction project in the middle of the campus. Barr, not the College's security personnel, was responsible for safety within the site. The College was concerned with keeping students away from construction site hazards and, as a result, Barr had a continuous six-foot chain-link fence installed to secure the majority of the project. An unrelated excavation and paving project made it impossible to erect the security fence around a portion of the site, so Barr employed free-standing chain-link panels, saw-horse barriers, and caution tape to prevent entry to that area. In spite of these barriers, unauthorized people on occasion used the construction site as a short cut across campus. In response, Barr hired Lemieux to patrol the site on weekend evenings in the hope of further discouraging trespassers.

On the night of November 19, 2000, Keegan was conducting a routine patrol of College buildings when she saw four men dismantling the construction site barriers. When she called out to them, they fled and eventually entered the construction site at a different point by going over the chain-link fence. Allegedly to secure the safety of the trespassers, she radioed her supervisor and followed the four intruders into the construction site. Keegan testified at her deposition that she knew the construction site was dangerous, slippery, and littered with construction debris.

Shortly after entering the site, Keegan saw another officer approaching her, chasing a young man later identified as Nicholas Atwood. Keegan reached out to grab Atwood, but she slipped on the "wet ground ... [and] construction material," injuring her knee, arm, and back. Atwood continued through the construction site and climbed over an intact portion of the six-foot chain-link fence. Keegan's colleagues followed Atwood over the fence, caught him, and tackled him onto the ground. The officers then took Atwood to the campus security office, identified him as a non-student, gave him a trespass notice, and advised him that he could not come back on campus. Keegan's injury required lateral release surgery, which left her with a permanent impairment to her knee.

Keegan collected workers' compensation for her injury and later filed suit against Barr and Lemieux. She claimed that, but for Barr's negligent failure to provide sufficient fencing around the site and Lemieux's negligent failure to adequately patrol the site, she would not have needed to enter the construction site to secure the safety of the trespassers and would not have been injured. Defendants filed motions for summary judgment on three separate grounds. First, they argued that they owed no duty to maintain better fencing or greater security to protect Keegan from an injury she obtained while attempting to rescue trespassers on the site. Second, Barr and Lemieux insisted that Keegan's claim was barred by the firefighter's rule. Finally, they argued that Keegan could not show that their conduct was the proximate cause of her injury.

The superior court granted Barr and Lemieux's summary judgment motion, reasoning that when Keegan entered the construction site to rescue a trespasser, Barr and Lemieux's duty to Keegan was no greater than the duty owed to the trespasser. The court held that since an owner or occupier of land must refrain only from subjecting a trespasser to willful and wanton misconduct, Keegan failed "as a matter of law to show ... breach of a duty owed her." Relying on (citation deleted) the court rejected Keegan's argument that an owner or occupier of land owes a duty to a rescuer independent of its duty to the person being rescued. On appeal, Keegan argues that the trial court misconstrued the law when it held that Barr and Lemieux did not owe her a duty of care independent from that owed to the trespasser she was allegedly rescuing. As explained below, we agree with the trial court.

Taking Keegan's allegations as true, as we must, it is evident that Barr and Lemieux are entitled to judgment as a matter of law. To prove a negligence claim, Keegan must show that defendants owed her a duty, that they breached the duty, that she suffered actual injury, and that defendants' breach proximately caused her injury. Thus, the "governing issue" here is "whether the law imposed upon [defendants] a duty of care"—a determination the trial court must make as a matter of law.

State courts that have considered this issue have "rejected the concept of an independent duty to a rescuer without an underlying tortious act to the person actually placed in peril." The duty owed to Keegan as a rescuer therefore derives from the underlying duty, if any, owed to the person she was allegedly rescuing when she was injured. In Vermont, a landowner or occupier generally owes no duty of care to a trespasser, except to avoid willful or wanton misconduct. Therefore, if the rescuee is a trespasser, the landowner owes no duty to the rescuee or the rescuer, other than to avoid willful or wanton misconduct.

Although she does not clearly articulate the elements of her negligence claim, Keegan's argument rests on the notion that Barr and Lemieux owed her a duty to maintain a sufficient fence and to adequately patrol the site to prevent intentional trespassing. This novel theory of liability runs counter to the rule explained above that a landowner or occupier can be held liable for a rescuer's injury only to the extent it owed, and breached a duty to, the rescuee. Neither Barr nor Lemieux owed a duty to Atwood as a trespasser, beyond avoiding willful or wanton misconduct. Thus, defendants owed no greater duty to Keegan as a rescuer.

Keegan next relies on *Cameron*, arguing that defendants owed her a direct duty as an invitee, not a vicarious duty transmitted through the trespasser. She argues that this follows because she had to enter the site to pursue the trespassers as a result of defendants' negligence. In *Cameron*, we held a landowner liable to a police officer who fell when a step on the landowner's stairway broke. Because the landowner was aware that, as a routine part of his beat, the officer walked up the stairs to check the locks on the building, we held that the landowner had "a reasonable opportunity to make the premises safe or to warn plaintiff." In so holding, we observed that the officer did not use the stairs "in an emergency in the discharge of his police duties" or "to make an arrest or chase a thief or burglar."

By contrast, Keegan does not seek to hold defendants liable by claiming she sustained an injury due to a defect on the property that defendants should have fixed or warned her about. Rather, she claims that defendants failed to prevent the intentional trespass that resulted in her presence at the construction site in the first place. Thus, our holding in *Cameron* does not support Keegan's claim. Therefore, because Keegan failed as a matter of law to show an essential element of her negligence claim—the breach of a duty owed to her—the trial court correctly rejected it.

Finally, because we find no basis on which Keegan can recover on her negligence claim, we see no reason to explore the firefighter's rule advanced by Barr and Lemieux.

Affirmed

CASE COMMENT

Here the security officer's claim failed largely due to the fact that the property owner only has a duty to avoid willful or wanton misconduct. Since the plaintiff could not show this, the property owner was not liable for her injuries. Using this same logic, since the plaintiff could not show that the property owner breached its duty, there was no liability to the plaintiff.

DISCUSSION QUESTIONS

In a trespass action, does the property owner have the right to treat the trespasser in any manner deemed appropriate? What is the applicable standard of care required of the property owner? What are the likely public policy reasons for this standard?

5

Torts of a Personal Nature

A. DEFAMATION

443 Mass. 52, 819 N.E. 2d 550

Supreme Judicial Court of Massachusetts, Suffolk

MICHAEL PHELAN v. MAY DEPARTMENT STORES COMPANY, ET AL.

Decided Dec. 16, 2004

Background

Former employee, who had been escorted around workplace by a security guard during his former employer's investigation into alleged accounting irregularities, brought action against former employer and superiors, alleging false imprisonment and defamation. After jury found in favor of former employee on both claims, the Superior Court Department, Suffolk County, allowed former employer's Motion for Judgment Notwithstanding the verdict on the defamation claim. Former employee appealed. The appeals court reversed and remanded with instructions.

Holding

The supreme judicial court held that former employee's belief that his co-workers viewed him in a defamatory light was insufficient to establish defamatory publication.

Judgment of the superior court affirmed.

This case arises from a July 10, 1998, investigation by Filene's, a division of the May Department Stores Company, into allegations that Michael Phelan was attempting to hide significant accounting discrepancies from his superiors. Phelan brought an action against May, Michael Geraghty (Filene's chief financial officer), and Donald Lane (Filene's controller) (collectively, the defendants), alleging that their conduct during the investigation had constituted false imprisonment and defamation. A jury found in favor of Phelan on both claims and awarded him damages of $1,500 for false imprisonment and $75,000 for defamation. With respect to Phelan's defamation claim, the defendants moved for judgment notwithstanding the verdict (judgment n.o.v.), contending that Phelan had produced insufficient evidence on which a jury reasonably could have found either (1) the conduct alleged had defamatory significance to those witnessing it; or (2) the defendants had lost their conditional privilege to publish arguably defamatory material about Phelan. The superior court allowed the motion for judgment n.o.v., doubting that Phelan had set forth sufficient evidence of publication and concluding that he had failed to overcome the defendants' conditional privilege.

Based on the testimony at trial, the jury could have found the following facts. Phelan was employed as assistant director of accounts payable for Filene's where, among other tasks, he was responsible for managing "vendor violations" and the related budget. Vendor violations occurred when vendors failed to comply with Filene's shipping or purchase order requirements, and Filene's imposed a charge on them to cover the additional costs. To challenge an imposed charge, a vendor would submit to Filene's a "vendor violations package," addressing why the charge was unjustified and requesting a refund. This package would be processed by Phelan's department, and if it was determined that the charge had been improperly assessed, the vendor would receive a repayment.

In 1997, Geraghty directed Phelan to pay "prior year invoices" (PYIs) from the vendor violations budget, notwithstanding the fact that severe fiscal problems had arisen in the past from this practice. Phelan and his direct supervisor, Catherine Rooney, warned Geraghty and Lane that this practice was ill advised, in that it hindered their ability to make timely repayments to deserving vendors and to meet budgetary goals. Nonetheless, Phelan was not instructed to stop this practice.

During this time, unbeknownst to Phelan, a backlog of vendor violations packages had begun to accumulate in the hands of Phelan's subordinate, Geoffrey Meade, who was in charge of evaluating these packages. In early July 1998, Meade finally told Phelan about the backlog, indicating that the amount due to vendors was approximately $200,000. Phelan and Rooney promptly notified their supervisor, Michael Basler, who was Filene's assistant controller. As it turned out, the problem was significantly greater than Phelan had been led to believe; Meade reported to Basler that the backlogs and unpaid PYIs totaled $491,995. Meade attempted to shred his backlog of vendor violations packages, but the documents were ultimately retrieved.

At this juncture, Geraghty, Lane, and Basler decided to conduct an investigation and audit of the vendor violations program. On the morning of July 10, 1998, Lane interviewed Phelan as to alleged accounting irregularities and then directed him to Basler's office. Lane instructed a Filene's security officer, Johnny Guante, to guard Phelan, purportedly so that Phelan would not "influence" or "intimidate" his subordinates, who were being questioned as part of the investigation. Phelan was not permitted to use the telephone. Throughout the day, Guante relocated Phelan to various available offices and conference rooms, escorted him to the restroom, and accompanied him to the cafeteria. Coworkers did not speak with Phelan as he was moving about the building with Guante. Although Guante did not wear a badge or other insignia that identified him as a security guard, and did not carry a weapon or handcuffs, he did wear dark trousers, a shirt, a tie, and a blazer that Filene's had issued to him and that was similar to the clothing worn by other security guards in the store. Phelan felt embarrassed and humiliated because of his observation that, everywhere they went, coworkers were staring at him while he was in the company of security personnel. At the end of the day, Phelan was returned to Basler's office, was informed that he was being suspended, and was escorted out of the building by another Filene's executive. Phelan's employment with Filene's subsequently was terminated.

To prevail on his defamation claim, Phelan had to establish that the defendants published a false statement about him to a third party that either caused him economic loss or was of the type that is actionable without proof of economic loss. A false statement that "would tend to hold the plaintiff up to scorn, hatred, ridicule, or contempt, in the minds of any considerable and respectable segment in the community," would be considered defamatory, and the imputation of a crime is defamatory per se, requiring no proof of special damages. The element of publication is satisfied where the defamatory communication is transmitted to even one person other than the plaintiff.

The defendants contend that they were properly entitled to judgment n.o.v. on Phelan's defamation claim because their conduct did not convey a clear and unambiguous false statement about Phelan and, in the absence of evidence that an observer interpreted the defendants' conduct as conveying such a meaning, Phelan has failed to establish defamatory publication. We agree.

A threshold issue in a defamation action, whether a communication is reasonably susceptible of a defamatory meaning, is a question of law for the court (court decides whether communication is capable of particular meaning and whether such meaning is defamatory). However, "where the communication is susceptible of both a defamatory and non-defamatory meaning, a question of fact exists for the jury" (jury decides "whether a communication, capable of a defamatory meaning, was so understood by its recipient").

When assessing the import of physical acts, which are at issue here, rather than written or spoken words, this objective test is equally applicable. Although not explicitly recognized in prior Massachusetts case law, we conclude that defamatory publication *may* result from the physical actions of a defendant, in the absence of written or spoken communication. "The word *communication* is used to denote the fact that one person has brought an idea to the perception of another." The meaning of communication, "whether by written or spoken words or otherwise," is that which recipient understands it to convey. Defamation requires "a communication, defined as conduct that brings an idea to the perception of others." "An individual's actions, separate from any written or spoken statements, may be sufficient grounds for a jury to find a cause of action [for defamation]."

Even viewing the evidence in the light most favorable to Phelan, as we must, the defendants' conduct was ambiguous and open to various interpretations. The actions of Guante in escorting Phelan about the office on July 10, and in relocating him to various conference rooms, did not have a specific, obvious meaning and did not necessarily convey that Phelan had engaged in criminal wrongdoing. There was no chasing, grabbing, restraining, or searching such as would have conveyed a clear and commonly understood meaning. From the mere fact that he was being accompanied by a security guard, observers could have thought, for example, that the defendants were sequestering Phelan so that he could not communicate with others, or so that he could provide confidential assistance with their investigation. Where Guante's communication, through physical action, was ambiguous, it was for the jury to decide whether such communication was understood by Phelan's coworkers as having a defamatory meaning.

Phelan had the burden of proving that a reasonable third person observing Guante's conduct would have understood it to be defamatory.

Phelan presented no such evidence to satisfy his burden of proof. He testified that he was embarrassed and humiliated by the defendants because other employees stared at him in the company of Guante. However, Phelan's own belief that others viewed him in a defamatory light, without more, was insufficient to establish defamatory publication. In other words, Phelan was not competent to testify as to his coworkers' interpretation of Guante's actions and whether, as a result of what they saw, they viewed Phelan with scorn, hatred, ridicule, or contempt. Publication to Phelan cannot be substituted for publication to a third party. To satisfy his burden of proof, Phelan needed to present testimony from at least one coworker who observed Guante's actions and interpreted such actions as defamatory. Where purported slander made by expressions and gestures, and not solely by words, it was necessary to inquire of witnesses what they understood defendant to mean both as to person intended and charge made against him. Because he failed to do so, we conclude that he did not establish the essential elements of defamation.

In light of our conclusion, we need not consider whether the defendants' conduct was protected by an employer's conditional privilege to publish defamatory material where the publication is reasonably necessary to the protection or furtherance of a legitimate business interest.

The judgment notwithstanding the verdict is affirmed.

CASE COMMENT

This case illustrates the issues surrounding publication by a "physical act." Here the physical act was being escorted by security personnel. The plaintiff asserted that this act exposed him to ridicule, scorn, and contempt. He tried to make this assertion because coworkers were "staring" at him as he was being escorted by security. The court found this insufficient evidence of defamation. This cause of action failed because the plaintiff did not obtain testimony from his coworkers to make the connection between the physical act and the defamatory ridicule. In order to make this connection, the coworkers would need to testify that the act caused them to think in certain ways about the plaintiff (i.e., in ridicule, scorn, or contempt). Because the physical act could be viewed in a neutral or even positive light, the actual perception of the coworkers who witnessed the escort was required to complete the elements of defamation.

272 Ga. App. 469, 612 S.E. 2d 617

Court of Appeals of Georgia

McCLESKY v. THE HOME DEPOT, INC., ET AL.

March 25, 2005

Background

Former employee brought action against former employer and company that provided report to former employer purportedly showing that former employee had falsified employment application, alleging claims for negligence, defamation, libel, and slander. The court, DeKalb County, granted company summary judgment. Former employee appealed.

Holdings

The court of appeals held that:

1. Criminal background check of former employee, which stated that former employee "may or may not have" been convicted of a felony within the past five years while using an alias, fell within intra-corporate exception to publication rule, and
2. Assistant manager's disclosure to employee that former employee was terminated after giving false information on his employment application and because he had committed a felony-child molestation was privileged.

Affirmed

McClesky applied for employment with Home Depot in August 1999. In his employment application, McClesky indicated that he had *not* been convicted of a felony or misdemeanor within the past five years. Home Depot hired McClesky. As part of the hiring process, McClesky signed a consent form, permitting Home Depot and its agent to perform a background check. This consent form provided, in pertinent part, that McClesky "released Home Depot and/or its agents and any person or entity, which provides information pursuant to this authorization, from any and all liabilities, claims or lawsuits in regard to the information obtained from any and all of the above referenced sources used." In October 2000, Home Deport requested that Vericon conduct a criminal background search on McClesky.

A third party actually conducted the investigation. After receiving the report, Vericon faxed the results of the investigation to Home Depot on November 13, 2000. The report suggested that McClesky had used the name Edward James Sims, Jr., as an alias and that Sims had been convicted for several crimes in 1998.

On November 16, 2000, Home Depot terminated McClesky for falsifying his employment application. According to McClesky, he never used Edward James Sims as an alias and did not commit the crimes referred to in the report.

McClesky contends that the trial court erred in granting summary judgment to defendants on his claims for libel and slander, asserting that the release did not bar these claims because defendants were grossly negligent and acted with malice. The following are pertinent to the resolution of these contentions: McClesky was terminated at a meeting attended by Ricky Jordan, the manager at the store where McClesky worked, William Gonzalez, an assistant manager in the lumber area where McClesky worked, and Carla Brown, a Home Depot loss prevention supervisor. Jordan, as the store manager, had the responsibility for terminating employees at that Home Depot store and organized the meeting.

During the meeting, Jordan informed McClesky that he was being terminated for falsifying his employment application when he stated he had not been convicted of a felony in the past five years. McClesky denied that he had been convicted of a felony during that time, although he admitted being on probation for a crime committed outside the five-year period. Brown then listed the crimes on the background report that Sims was reported to have committed within the last five years. McClesky denied having committed those crimes, and said the report was in error. McClesky was nevertheless terminated and given separation paperwork showing that he was being terminated for falsification of company records. McClesky testified in his deposition that he was escorted from the meeting and the premises by a man wearing a Home Depot shirt who was also in attendance at the meeting. According to McClesky, that man did not work at the Home Depot store where he worked. Although Gonzalez recalled that another person was in the meeting, he testified in his deposition that he did not know this person, and could not recall if he took part in any of the discussions with McClesky. Gonzalez subsequently filed an affidavit stating that although it was still his testimony that he did not know the other person who attended the meeting, he could identify the person as working in the Home Depot loss prevention department. Gonzalez also averred that it was not unusual to have personnel from that department attend termination meetings when there were issues concerning employee falsification or security.

After the meeting, Jordan, Gonzalez and Brown stayed behind to discuss the meeting and Brown told the other two that they should respond to inquiries from other store employees about McClesky's termination by saying that he was "no longer with us and leave it at that."

Based on these facts, the trial court found that summary judgment for defendants was appropriate because the evidence showed there had been no publication. We agree.

Publication is indispensable to recover for slander. Generally, publication is accomplished by communication of the slander to anyone other than the person slandered. Over the years, however, an exception to the broad definition of publication has evolved: when the communication is intra-corporate, or between members of unincorporated groups or associations, and is heard by one who, because of his/her duty or authority has reason to receive information, there is no publication of the allegedly slanderous material, and without publication, there is no cause of action for slander.

Thus, the relevant question is whether, because of their duty or authority, the persons attending the termination meeting had reason to receive the information disseminated during that meeting. It is clear that Jordan, Gonzalez and Brown had such authority, and McClesky does not contend otherwise. McClesky, however, focuses on the presence of the other Home Depot employee who has never been identified by name. However, that person was identified as a Home Depot loss prevention supervisor and evidence was presented that personnel from that department attend termination meetings when issues relating to employee falsification or security are of concern, such as was the situation here. And McClesky's own testimony establishes that this person was there for security reasons since he escorted McClesky off the premises once the meeting ended and McClesky had been terminated. The fact that, as McClesky repeatedly points out, this person did not work at the Home Depot store where McClesky worked does nothing to advance McClesky's argument that the person did not have the requisite authority to receive the information. Brown was also a loss prevention supervisor who did not work in the store where McClesky was employed, and yet her authority to attend the meeting is not disputed. The trial court did not err in granting summary judgment on this basis.

McClesky also contends summary judgment to the defendants was precluded because the facts show that Jordan and Gonzalez told Home Depot employee Jonathon Erhorn that McClesky was terminated for giving false information on his employment application and that he had committed a felony—child molestation. The record shows that Erhorn was a friend of McClesky's and they worked in the lumber department together. Although Erhorn testified in his deposition that he "never really considered [him]self as a supervisor" and that he "was just a lumber associate that was curious and asked a question" he also testified that he acted as the "lead lumber person" or "backup supervisor" and was "second in charge behind [the lumber department supervisor] Greg Simon." The record also shows that Erhorn was told about the circumstances surrounding McClesky's termination only after he questioned Gonzalez about McClesky's absence.

According to Erhorn, he initially questioned Gonzalez because McClesky was scheduled to come in at a critical time. Gonzalez at first told Erhorn simply that McClesky had been terminated and that he could not tell him why. Erhorn let it drop at that time, but then called Gonzalez later in the day because "I really wanted to know why he left ... why he was fired. He was a hard worker, and I don't see how he could have got fired." At that time Gonzalez instructed Erhorn to come to the conference room, and both Jordan and Gonzalez were there when he arrived. Jordan told Erhorn that "whatever was said in that room [had to] stay in that room," and Gonzalez told Erhorn that McClesky was fired because he had been convicted of a felony—child molestation. Erhorn testified in his deposition that he felt like Jordan was trying to act as a mediator during the meeting and that "Jordan didn't want me to leave Home Depot just because whenever [McClesky] leaves is going to put more work on [me] and Greg Simon." Erhorn also testified that he talked to McClesky several weeks later and that McClesky "told [him] the exact thing that [Gonzalez] told [him] ... that he was fired from Home Depot because he had a prior conviction of child molestation."

Pretermitting whether summary judgment was proper because the statements were unpublished, we agree that summary judgment was proper for the additional reason stated by the trial court.

OCGA Section 51-5-7 provides that statements made in the good faith performance of a public or private duty are privileged, unless, as provided in OCGA Section 51-5-9, "the privilege is used merely as a cloak for venting private malice." "To make the defense of privilege complete, in an action for slander, or libel, good faith, an interest to be upheld, a statement properly limited in its scope, a proper occasion, and publication to proper persons must all appear."

We find the analysis in *Jones* to be controlling here. In *Jones*, the plaintiffs were terminated for the stated reason that they had sold drugs on the employer's premises. Another employee who was friends with plaintiffs questioned a security guard about the termination, and, according to the employee, the guard told him that plaintiffs had been fired for selling narcotics on the premises. Plaintiffs, however, denied that they had ever sold drugs, and contended that they were fired in retaliation for their union organizing activities.

In concluding that the statement, even if made, was privileged, this court first noted that "statements made in response to inquires as to another person are deemed privileged when the inquirer is one naturally interested in his welfare." The Court then went on to note that a qualified privilege also exists in those cases involving an employer's disclosure of the reasons concerning an employee discharge to fellow employees "where the disclosure is limited to those employees who have a need to know by virtue of the nature of their duties (such as supervisors, management officials, ... etc.) and those employees who are otherwise directly affected... by the discharged employee's termination...."

In *Jones*, we considered the following facts to be pertinent: the employee who made the inquiry was more than "a 'fellow general employee,' for not only did he work directly with the appellants on a day-to-day basis, he was a close personal friend as well.... It is also undisputed that [the] alleged disclosure to [the coworker] came in direct response to [the coworker's] inquiry and outside the presence of other persons." Clearly, the same circumstances exist here. Erhorn and McClesky were friends and worked closely together. Erhorn initiated the inquiry concerning why McClesky was not at work, and persisted in knowing why McClesky was fired. Erhorn had good reason to question his absence since Erhorn's ability to get his work done was directly affected. Erhorn was taken into a private room and told of the circumstances of the termination, and specifically instructed that what was said was to remain confidential. Under these facts, we have little hesitancy in concluding that "the alleged disclosure must ... be considered privileged as a matter of law, and it follows that the trial court did not err in granting the [defendants'] Motion for Summary Judgment."

Judgment affirmed.

CASE COMMENT

This case illustrates two aspects of a defamation action. First, the plaintiff contends that certain individuals who participated in the termination meeting had no reason for being there. In this way, individuals who did not have a "need to know" were exposed to the reasons for his termination. Second, the plaintiff contends that the company communicated information about the reason for his termination to another co-worker. The court rejected both contentions. As to the first, the court found that the fact an individual who was not assigned to the particular store was present in the termination meeting was to no avail. As to the second contention, the court found that the communication was privileged due to the purpose and manner in which the information was conveyed.

372 F. Supp. 2d 702

United States District Court, E.D. New York

ANA ASTO, PLAINTIFF v. JOHN MIRANDONA, ET AL. DEFENDANTS.

March 29, 2005

Background

Contract security officer brought action alleging that employee of federal agency defamed her.

Holdings

The district court held that:

1. Federal employee made alleged statements within scope of his employment; and
2. Officer did not show that employee acted out of personal motives or malice.

Motion granted

This action arises out of a defamation suit brought by Ana Asto against John Mirandona and other unnamed defendants in New York State Supreme Court based on events occurring at John F. Kennedy International Airport on January 28–29, 2002.

Mirandona is the Port Director at JFK for the United States Customs and Border Protection division of the Department of Homeland Security, formerly the Immigration and Naturalization Service. As Port Director, Mirandona is responsible for the inspection and admission of all foreign passengers traveling through JFK. In January 2002, Mirandona supervised approximately 500 INS employees and contract security officers from Wackenhut Correction Facility who worked in the Federal Inspection Service area at JFK. At the time of the events giving rise to this suit, plaintiff was a Wackenhut employee stationed in the FIS in the Secondary Inspections area. Plaintiff was usually partnered with fellow Wackenhut employee Thomas Kavanaugh on her duties.

In response to complaints from detained aliens at JFK that personal items had been stolen from their luggage during their inspections, the Office of the Inspector General within the U.S. Department of Justice ("OIG") conducted an undercover operation on January 28, 2002. Due to the fact that the complainants were detained while plaintiff and Kavanaugh were on duty, and because plaintiff was specifically named by one of the complainants, the OIG conducted its undercover operation while plaintiff and Kavanaugh were working. During the operation, in which an undercover agent posed as a detainee, Kavanaugh was observed entering the baggage room and opening the agent's luggage. Ultraviolet dye that had been on the money planted in the agent's luggage was also found on Kavanaugh's hands. Plaintiff was not observed engaging in any improper behavior, though there is some dispute as to whether she lied to the OIG agent about Kavanaugh's whereabouts in order to keep him from getting into trouble.

At some point in January 2002, Mirandona learned that plaintiff was the target of an OIG investigation into the complaints about items having been stolen from detainees' luggage. On January 29, 2002, after arriving at JFK, Mirandona was shown the video surveillance of Kavanaugh taking money from the agent's bag and then returning it to the bag. Mirandona instructed Kavanaugh and plaintiff to leave the FIS area, at which point the following exchange took place:

Mirandona to Kavanaugh: "I don't want you here. I don't want [plaintiff] here either."

Kavanaugh to Mirandona: "Let [plaintiff] work in the house. [Plaintiff] did not have nothing [*sic*] to do with this."

Mirandona to Kavanaugh: "That's not up to me. That's up to Regis."

Mirandona to Pilliggi: "Take [Kavanaugh's] ID and take [plaintiff's] too. Escort them out."

Pilliggi to Mirandona: "I already took [Kavanaugh's]." Kavanaugh: "OK."

Plaintiff to Pilliggi: "This is very injustice [*sic*], sir, I didn't do anything."

Kavanaugh to Pilliggi: "I know when John calms down he will realize that [plaintiff] had nothing to do with this."

In a letter dated January 29, 2002, the United States Customs Service Director for the JFK port of entry, Susan Mitchell, revoked plaintiff's access to the FIS, stating: the U.S. Customs Service may revoke access to the Customs Security Area (i.e., Federal Inspection Sites) from airport employees if the employee is convicted of a felony or if the continuation of privileges is deemed to "endanger the revenue or security of the area." A recent investigation revealed information about you which triggers the use of the above provision. As a result, your access to the Customs Security Area is hereby revoked. Specifically, on January 29, 2002, while working at Terminal 4 you were observed, while under surveillance, pilfering items from the baggage of an individual under the custody of the Immigration and Naturalization Service.

Pursuant to (citation deleted), your access to U.S. Customs Security areas is permanently revoked. Plaintiff appealed the decision of the USCS, and in a March 5, 2002, letter Mitchell granted the appeal and reinstated plaintiff's access to the Customs Security Area at JFK, noting that her access had previously been revoked "pursuant to derogatory information received from the Department of Justice, Office of the Inspector General concerning her involvement in an investigation conducted by them." On April 16, 2002, plaintiff's employer, Wackenhut Correctional Center, sent her a letter stating "due to an investigation, which is still ongoing, we have been instructed as per the Immigration and Naturalization Service to remove you from the INS contract effective April 25, 2002."

Discussion

New York law holds that an employee's tortious acts fall within the scope of his employment if "done while the servant was doing his master's work, no matter how irregularly, or with what disregard of instructions." The following factors have been weighed by courts in making such a determination: (1) whether the time, place and occasion for the act was connected to the employment; (2) the history of the employer-employee relationship in actual practice; (3) whether the act is one commonly done by such an employee; (4) the extent to which the act departs from normal methods of performance; and (5) whether the act was one that the employer could reasonably have anticipated.

Applying the preceding principles to the facts of this case, the evidence in the record leaves little doubt that if Mirandona made the allegedly defamatory statements complained of by plaintiff, he did so in the scope of his employment. While plaintiff alleged in her complaint that Mirandona accused her of "pilfering" items from the luggage of detainees on the morning of January 29, 2002, in the context of the conversation among herself, Mirandona, Kavanaugh, and Assistant Port Director Pilleggi, she later admitted in her deposition testimony that Mirandona made no such statement on that occasion. Plaintiff did testify that Mirandona said (1) he wanted her and Kavanaugh both gone, (2) that plaintiff and Kavanaugh had been working together for a long time, and (3) that he did not want to hear anything from plaintiff. Such statements, if made, were made by Mirandona while he was performing his duties as Port Director in supervising contract employees like plaintiff. This conversation took place immediately after Mirandona had seen the videotape of Kavanaugh going through the undercover agent's luggage and handling the money planted there and indicates Mirandona's determination that, based on the results of the undercover operation, plaintiff and Kavanaugh should no longer be given access to the secured inspection area, a determination that was within Mirandona's authority to make.

Plaintiff, reluctant to abandon the "pilfering" allegation entirely, also argues in her brief that Mirandona must have, at some point, told Mitchell or told someone who told Mitchell that plaintiff had been observed "pilfering" items from detainee's luggage because that was what Mitchell accused her of in the letter and only Mirandona could have been the source of that allegedly defamatory information. Notwithstanding the dubious logic of this argument, plaintiff testified in her deposition that, apart from what Mirandona said to her in the course of the conversation discussed above, he made no other allegedly defamatory comments. However, even if Mirandona did tell Mitchell or someone who relayed the information to Mitchell that plaintiff had "pilfered" objects from the detainees' baggage, any such statement would still have been within the scope of Mirandona's employment, as it would have been related to the undercover investigation of an employee under Mirandona's supervision and would have been relevant to Mirandona's determination as to whether plaintiff should continue to have access to the secured area. Furthermore, it is certainly foreseeable that Mirandona, in responding to the problem created by the stolen items, would have to make statements concerning his perception of the likely culpability of the suspects under investigation.

Even if the statements reflected an incorrect assessment of plaintiff's involvement, that would not place the statements outside the scope of his employment, as under New York law an employee's actions need only be generally foreseeable to the employer to fall within the scope of employment.

Plaintiff argues that Mirandona's statements were outside the scope of his employment because they were made with personal animus: "We submit that, upon information and belief, on or about January 28, 2002, defendant John Mirandona spoke maliciously of the plaintiff when he communicated to the Area Director of the USCS Susan Mitchell, or some third party that the plaintiff was observed pilfering the items of personal property of a detainee." New York law holds that a defendant "does not act within the scope of his employment when he engages in tortious conduct for personal reasons separate and distinct from the interests of his employer."

Plaintiff's evidence that Mirandona possessed some personal motive causing him to maliciously defame plaintiff is her wholly conclusory argument that Mirandona's "demeanor" during the course of the January 29, 2002, conversation at the airport "is emblematic of someone acting with malice." Plaintiff argues that the alleged exchange, in which Mirandona both said that plaintiff was implicated in the thefts because she had worked with Kavanaugh for a long time and refused to listen to her protestations of innocence, "demonstrates that despite being advised by the OIG criminal investigators that the plaintiff was not observed attempting to pilfer any luggage, defendant Mirandona still wanted her FBI access revoked regardless of the exculpatory evidence."

However, not only do the referenced statements and actions by Mirandona fail to demonstrate any personal motivation on his part, plaintiff's own deposition testimony serves once again to negate any inference that could possibly be raised. Plaintiff testified that she had no personal contact with Mirandona except for a brief greeting at Christmas, that she never reported to Mirandona, and that she had no reason to believe that any of the statements made by Mirandona in the conversation referenced above were motivated by personal reasons. Thus, there is simply nothing in the record to indicate that Mirandona acted out of personal motives or malice in making any statements about plaintiff.

As a final note, it is interesting that before plaintiff decided to challenge the Government's certification, she appeared to readily admit that Mirandona was acting within the scope of his employment: "On or about January 29, 2002, at John F. Kennedy International Airport, defendant JOHN MIRANDONA, **acting in his position as Assistant Area Port Director**, did speak of the plaintiff the following false and defamatory words...." Thus, it is unclear that plaintiff was even entitled to discovery on this issue in the first place. She is certainly not entitled to more.

As the record clearly indicates that any allegedly defamatory statements made by Mirandona were made within the scope of his employment with a federal agency, the certification by the United States Attorney must be upheld, and the United States is properly substituted as the party defendant.

Conclusion

Because defendant Mirandona was acting within the scope of his employment at the time he allegedly uttered defamatory remarks about plaintiff, the Government's certification is upheld, the United States is hereby substituted as defendant, and the claims against Mirandona are dismissed.
SO ORDERED.

CASE COMMENT

The plaintiff asserted a supervisor made defamatory statements, suing him in his individual capacity, rather than as an employee of the federal government. The lawsuit was framed this way because a federal statute bars defamation actions against the U.S. government. The court found that the allegedly defamatory statements were communicated in the scope and course of his employment. Further, because the plaintiff failed to show that the communication was not done with malice or for any personal reason, the communication was not actionable against the individual supervisor.

B. INVASION OF PRIVACY

374 Md. 665, 824 A. 2d 107

Court of Appeals of Maryland

RITE AID CORPORATION, ET AL., v. DEXTER HAGLEY, ET AL.

May 13, 2003

Background

Father who had taken film, containing pictures of himself and his son in bathtub, to store for developing brought breach of privacy and related claims against store and its manager who, believing that pictures were child pornography, had contacted police, thereby causing father to be transported to police station for questioning. The Circuit Court, Baltimore City, entered summary judgment for store and its manager, and father appealed. The court of special appeals ruled that certain claims were appropriately resolved on summary judgment, and remanded case. Store and manager filed petition for writ of certiorari, and the father filed cross-petition.

Holding

The court of appeals held that the availability of other alternatives, and the possibility, even probability, that the situation might have, or should have, been handled more effectively and sensitively, while perhaps suggesting negligence, did not equate to bad faith or a lack of good faith in connection with determining whether store and its manager, as reporters of child abuse, were entitled to statutory immunity from suit.

Affirmed in part; reversed in part; and remanded with directions.

Dexter Hagley and his former wife, Lystra Martin, are the parents of Kerwyn Hagley (collectively, "respondents"). On March 23, 1999, Mr. Hagley took an undeveloped roll of film to the Rite Aid store in the Alameda Shopping Center in Baltimore City for processing, as he had done on "many" previous occasions. Opting to have the film printed by the store's one-hour developing and printing process, he completed the required form and left the film with the store manager, Robert Rosiak, one of the petitioners, who developed the film. Sixteen photographs were printed from the roll of film. Four of them depicted Mr. Hagley and a young boy, later determined to be his then 8-year old son, in a bathtub.

The court of special appeals described these four photographs, in its unreported opinion, as follows:

"Mr. Hagley was wearing shorts; Kerwyn was naked. The first of those photographs show Mr. Hagley sitting in the tub of soapy water, with Kerwyn sitting on his lap. Mr. Hagley's left arm was around the upper part of the boy's body, with his left hand on Kerwyn's right shoulder. Kerwyn's left hand was in his lap, and his father's right hand was on or over the boy's left hand. Both were laughing. The second photograph shows Mr. Hagley sitting in the tub, with his left hand hidden behind Kerwyn's thigh. The boy was standing with his back to the camera, looking over his shoulder toward the camera. Both were laughing. The third photograph shows Mr. Hagley sitting in the tub, looking up at Kerwyn, who was standing facing the camera. The fourth photograph shows Mr. Hagley and Kerwyn sitting in the tub, at the tap end, looking toward the camera."

Mr. Rosiak was troubled by the photographs of Mr. Hagley and the child because, in at least one of the photographs, Mr. Hagley's hand appeared to be "cupping" the child's genitals. Finding them ambiguous, he was not certain how to interpret them.

When Mr. Hagley returned to the store to pick up the processed film (i.e., photographs and negatives), Mr. Rosiak refused to give him the photographs. Mr. Hagley asked why, and Mr. Rosiak answered: "I'm seeing some things in those pictures, and I don't think I can give them to you." Despite Mr. Hagley's request that he do so, Mr. Rosiak refused to show Mr. Hagley the photographs or explain their objectionable content. When pressed further for an explanation, he stated "I'm seeing signs of child pornography, pedophile [*sic*] and improper touching of a minor." That comment, Mr. Hagley alleges, was made loudly and in the presence of other Rite Aid customers. Mr. Hagley advised Mr. Rosiak that the child depicted in the photographs was his 8-year-old son, Kerwyn, and that the photographs were taken by the child's mother, Ms. Martin. Mr. Hagley subsequently brought Ms. Martin to the store to verify that statement.

Apparently unsatisfied with Mr. Hagley's explanation and still unsure of how to resolve the matter, Mr. Rosiak requested that Mr. Hagley return to the store at 1:00 p.m., at which time a supervisor would have an answer. He then consulted Rite Aid headquarters, and was instructed to report the matter to law enforcement and turn the photographs over to them. Mr. Rosiak complied with that instruction by contacting the Baltimore City Police. Upon returning to the store a few minutes before the appointed hour, Mr. Hagley observed Mr. Rosiak having a conversation with a group of people. As described by the intermediate appellate court:

> When Mr. Hagley returned to the store several minutes before 1:00 p.m., he observed Mr. Rosiak *showing the photographs* [emphasis added] to three other people and discussing the pictures with them. Mr. Hagley recognized those three people: one was an employee of Rite Aid, whom he knew only as "Chris" (assistant manager Carrissa Esposito); the second

> was a mall security guard he knew as Mr. Byrd; and the third was another mall security guard whose name he did not know. Mr. Rosiak was asking their opinion of the photographs, but each of them declined to venture an opinion. When Mr. Rosiak and the others saw Mr. Hagley, who was about twelve feet away, the conversation stopped.

Shortly after the group that Mr. Rosiak had been talking to dispersed and there had been a brief conversation between Mr. Hagley and Mr. Rosiak, three uniformed Baltimore City police officers arrived at the Rite Aid store. They were met by Mr. Rosiak who escorted two of the officers into his office. Mr. Hagley remained in the store with the third officer. After meeting with Mr. Rosiak and examining the photographs, the officers questioned Mr. Hagley briefly. Being, like Mr. Rosiak, uncertain as to whether the photographs depicted child abuse, the officers called a detective with the child abuse unit of the criminal investigation division to examine some "questionable photographs of a young child."

The detective came to the Rite Aid Store. After reviewing the photographs and questioning a few people, he determined that the child in the photographs was Mr. Hagley's son, but that the photographs were "questionable." Believing, therefore, that further inquiry was warranted, he thus took possession of the photographs, later, submitting them to the evidence control unit, and caused Kerwyn to be taken into the custody of Child Protective Services in order to be interviewed at the Baltimore Child Abuse Center. In addition, the detective sought the opinion of the Baltimore City State's Attorney Office as to whether the content of the photographs warranted the filing of criminal charges.

Mr. Hagley was transported to the police station for questioning by one of the police officers. According to the detective, he was never placed under arrest and, in fact, was free to leave at any time. According to Mr. Hagley, although he was told by the police officers that he could leave, subject to later being picked up at home and taken to the police station, the detective told him that he had to come downtown to answer questions at the police station. He indicated further that he was not told he was free to leave the police station until approximately 7:00 p.m., when, after questioning and investigation, the State's Attorney's Office had determined that no criminal charges were warranted. Thereafter, Mr. Hagley, was driven back to the Alameda Shopping Center to retrieve his car.

To address and combat the problem of child abuse and neglect, the Maryland General Assembly, by mandated the reporting of suspected child abuse or neglect to the appropriate authorities and "giving immunity to any individual who reports, in good faith, a suspected incident of abuse or neglect." The policy underlying the reporting requirement imposed, and the immunity given, "is to protect children who have been the subject of abuse or neglect" (stating that the purpose of the reporting requirements is "to redress previous abuse and to prevent future incidence thereof"). Thus, imposes a duty on health practitioners, police officers, educators or human service workers, to report suspected child abuse or neglect encountered in their professional capacity to the local department, appropriate law enforcement agency or the appropriate institution head.

The legislature understood that the purpose of mandating reporting of child abuse and neglect would be undermined if a person making a good faith report, that later proved to be false, were to be subjected to civil liability. Consistent with what every state in the nation was doing, the legislature intended to encourage the good faith reporting of suspected child abuse to authorities without the fear of civil and criminal liability for reports later determined to be unfounded. Consequently, at the same time that it mandated reporting, the General Assembly granted statutory immunity from civil and criminal liability to "any person *who in good faith* makes or participates in making a report of abuse or neglect or participates in an investigation or a resulting judicial proceeding (emphasis added)."

The term *abuse* is defined in the statute to include "sexual abuse of a child, whether physical injuries are sustained or not." The photographing of a nude child for one's own benefit or advantage can constitute sexual abuse under Maryland law (which defined *sexual child abuse* as "any act that involves sexual molestation or exploitation of a child by a parent or other person who has permanent or temporary care or custody or responsibility for supervision of a child"). The court of special appeals held:

> To be convicted of exploitation and, therefore, child abuse, threats, coercion, or subsequent use of the fruits of the acts are not necessary. The State need only prove, beyond a reasonable doubt, that the parent or person having temporary or permanent custody of a child took advantage of or unjustly or improperly used the child for his or her own benefit.

Although critically important to its application in a given factual situation, the statutes do not define *good faith*. Under well-settled rules of statutory construction, however, its meaning can be discerned. The term should be given its plain and ordinary meaning. Using that rule as a guide, the court of special appeals has interpreted the "good faith" requirement of. It reasoned:

> "Good-faith" is an intangible and abstract quality that encompasses, among other things, an honest belief, the absence of malice and the absence of design to defraud or to seek an unconscionable advantage. To further illuminate the definition of "good-faith," we have found it most instructive to compare the definition of "bad-faith." "Bad-faith" is the opposite of "good-faith"; it is not simply bad judgment or negligence, but implies a dishonest purpose or some moral obliquity and a conscious doing of wrong. Though an indefinite term, "bad-faith" differs from the negative idea of negligence in that it contemplates a state of mind affirmatively operating with a furtive design. Thus, we would infer that the definition of "good-faith" means with an honest intention.

We agree. Under that definition, to be entitled to the statutory immunity, a person must act with an honest intention (i.e., in good faith), not simply negligently, in making or participating in the making of a report of abuse or neglect or when participating in an investigation or resulting judicial proceeding.

Analysis

The trial court resolved all inferences from the record against the petitioners, as the moving party, and concluded that there was no genuine dispute of material fact, warranting trial. The court of special appeals agreed with respect to the counts other than the defamation count and the breach or invasion of privacy counts.

The respondents do not agree. They submit that they have offered evidence to rebut the petitioners' claim of good faith reporting. In an attempt to ascribe, and justify, a sinister motive to Mr. Rosiak's actions in reporting the contents of the photographs, the respondents have fashioned a number of general allegations, hypothetical scenarios and alternative courses of action that Mr. Rosiak could, and they contend, should, have taken before reporting suspected child abuse based on the photographs. None of these allegations address directly the state of mind of Mr. Rosiak with respect to the content of the photographs. The respondents do not attempt to allege that Mr. Rosiak knew, or had reason to know, that the photographs did not depict child abuse and made a report of suspected child abuse in spite of that knowledge. Nor do they contend that Mr. Rosiak misstated or mischaracterized what he saw on the photographs, either to the police or to anyone else, or that he made untruthful or reckless remarks with regard to their content.

The respondents note, instead, that Mr. Rosiak did not strictly abide by a Rite Aid internal-company memorandum which outlined the procedure for dealing with sexually explicit photographs. In addition, the respondents complain that Mr. Rosiak did not discuss the matter with Mr. Hagley in private, before deciding what to do, although he did discuss the photographs privately with the police officers. The respondents also characterize as evidence of bad faith, Mr. Rosiak's exclusion of Mr. Hagley from the private discussion he had with the police. The respondents contend that if Mr. Rosiak were truly interested in protecting a possible victim of child abuse, he would not have left Mr. Hagley, the potential abuser, alone in the store while making the report to the police, where Mr. Hagley was free to "possibly escape the scene." And the fact that Mr. Rosiak, although viewing it as odd, did not inform the police that Mr. Hagley had brought the child's mother to the store to resolve the misunderstanding is further indication, they argue, of his lack of good faith. Finally, the respondents argue that Mr. Rosiak's bad faith can be inferred because he set Mr. Hagley up to be arrested by instructing him to return to the store at 1:00 p.m. and having the police arrive virtually simultaneously. Collectively, these acts, the respondents maintain, could lead a reasonable juror to infer that Mr. Rosiak was not interested in disclosing all sides of the story to the police or that he harbored an ill motive toward Mr. Hagley, and, consequently, was not acting in good faith.

We, however, are at a loss to discern how any of these facts, whether considered singly or collectively, could lead to an inference that Mr. Rosiak lacked good faith in reporting suspected child abuse. As the court of special appeals pointed out:

> Those assertions do not ... give rise to any reasonable inference that Rosiak did not honestly believe that the photographs were suggestive of child pornography or child abuse. He did not know Hagley; there was no suggestion of any fact that might even suggest a motive, other than a belief that the photographs depicted a form of child abuse, for Rosiak to call the police. Rosiak's conduct toward Hagley after he saw the photographs might suggest feeling of anger, disgust, or perhaps revulsion, but such emotions can only be explained as reactions to what Rosiak believed that the photographs depicted.

What the respondents' general allegations do indicate is that there were other alternatives available to Mr. Rosiak for handling the situation and that, perhaps, it could have, and probably, should have been handled better. But the availability of other alternatives, and the possibility, even probability, that the situation might have, or should have, been handled more effectively and sensitively, while perhaps suggesting negligence, does not equate to bad faith or a lack of good faith. And, as we have seen, negligence is not sufficient to negate good faith. What steps Mr. Rosiak could have taken is not determinative; what actions Mr. Rosiak did, in fact, take is the determinative question.

Whether Mr. Rosiak strictly followed the Rite Aid policy in dealing with the photographs cannot rebut his claim of good faith in reporting his suspicion that the photographs depicted child abuse. Mr. Rosiak certainly could have timed his call to the police differently; however, that he did not does nothing to establish that he did not act in good faith in making the report of suspected child abuse.

Furthermore, Mr. Rosiak's discussion of the photographs with the police officers in a private office casts no light whatsoever on his motive in reporting what he believed to be suspected child abuse. The fact that Mr. Rosiak maintained a private office in the store is only relevant to show that he had an alternative forum for discussing the matter with Mr. Hagley and, thus, could have avoided the allegedly defamatory speech. The maintenance of a private office is not relevant, however, to show that Mr. Rosiak did not act in good faith or whether the allegedly defamatory speech is immune from suit under the statutes. Moreover, although Mr. Rosiak may have thought it was odd for Mr. Hagley to return with the child's mother to explain the photographs, his failure to disclose that fact to the police, again, is not suggestive of a lack of good faith. Mr. Rosiak was certainly under no duty to convey the suspected child abusers' explanation of the photographs to the authorities. The immunity statutes do not require a reporter of suspected child abuse to verify every detail of the suspected conduct or perfectly recount all that he or she is told in order to be found to have acted in good faith when making the report. The statutes simply require that the reporter make a report in good faith. Thereafter, law enforcement or the appropriate department of social services personnel are charged with investigating the facts surrounding that report.

For the respondents to oppose the summary judgment motion successfully, they must have made a showing, supported by particular facts sufficient to allow a fact finder to conclude that Mr. Rosiak lacked good faith in making the report of suspected child abuse. They might have done so by producing specific facts showing that Mr. Rosiak knew, or had reason to know, that the photographs did not depict a form of child abuse and, in total disregard of that knowledge, filed a report anyway. What the respondents have produced are general allegations, that simply show that all of Mr. Rosiak's actions in making the report can be second-guessed. Legitimizing this sort of Monday-morning quarterbacking would render the immunity conferred by the statute essentially useless.

Notwithstanding its application to the different counts alleged, all of the conduct by Mr. Rosiak in this case was, as the petitioners point out, closely related both in terms of time and subject matter. Thus, what Mr. Rosiak did and the conversations he had with Mr. Hagley all occurred within the space of a few hours, in the Rite Aid store and was concerned with the course of action he should pursue as a result of the contents of some photographs he had developed for Mr. Hagley. What Mr. Rosiak said to Mr. Hagley about what he saw in the photographs had no independent relevance; it was only because of the decision Mr. Rosiak was required to make with respect to reporting suspected child abuse, that the explanation was made. That it was made in the presence of others does not change this basic fact. Neither can the conferring with others concerning the decision to be made separate that fact from the basic issue, whether what Mr. Rosiak observed in the photographs was suspected child abuse, which Mr. Rosiak was legally required to report.

We agree with the petitioners that the Court of Special Appeals has interpreted the child abuse reporting statutes too narrowly. First, the statutes cover more than making a report. They recognize that individuals, other than the reporter, may play a role in the making of the report, although they may not themselves make it. In addition, the statutes cover investigations and resulting judicial proceedings. As the appeals court interprets those statutes, a reporter, admittedly acting in good faith in making a report of suspected child abuse, may nevertheless be held liable civilly if, during the course of deciding whether to make a report, he or she mentions the nature of the concern he or she has and happens to do so, perhaps negligently, in the presence of someone other than a police officer, or seeks the advice of someone other than a police officer to assist in the decision making. Thus, the appellate court does not seem to take into account the breadth of the statutes or give effect to any of the conduct warranting immunity, except reporting. Such an interpretation and result, fly in the face of the purpose of the statutes and undermine the statutes' effectiveness; reports of suspected child abuse, in the case of ambiguous conduct, as in this case, either will not be filed or, if they are, they will be filed without the careful consideration allegations based on ambiguous conduct deserve to, and should, receive.

We hold that the court of special appeals erred in reversing the judgment of the trial court with respect to the counts alleging invasion of privacy and defamation.

CASE COMMENT

This case illustrates the difficult balance of a reporting statute that requires the disclosure to law enforcement authorities of possible child abuse against the privacy rights of the person who is suspected of child abuse. These reporting statutes are designed to protect children from sexual and physical abuse. However, these mandated disclosure statutes may result in violating the privacy of individuals in the quest to keep children safe. The court in this case gave great discretion to the reporter in order to maintain the incentive to report. In this way, if the reporter did not have a sufficient level of immunity from prosecution by the alleged child abuser, then why would any reasonable person report the suspected abuse? The court held that the immunity was rather broad, and protected the reporter from liability, even considering the questionable way he communicated the allegations of child abuse.

326 Mont. 93, 107 P. 3d 471

Supreme Court of Montana

JACK BARR, PLAINTIFF AND APPELLANT v. GREAT FALLS INTERNATIONAL AIRPORT AUTHORITY, CITY OF GREAT FALLS, DEPARTMENT OF POLICE AND STATE OF MONTANA DEPARTMENT OF JUSTICE, DEFENDANTS AND RESPONDENTS.

Decided Feb. 22, 2005

Background

Former airport security officer brought action against airport, city police department, and state department of justice, alleging violation of his right to privacy and related claims arising from his termination from employment prior to expiration of six-month probationary period, allegedly due to another security officer obtaining information regarding former officer's prior arrest. The District Court, Cascade County, granted summary judgment to defendants. Former officer appealed.

Holdings

The supreme court held that officer had no subjective or actual expectation of privacy in his initial arrest record from another state, such as would implicate provision of state constitution protecting his right to privacy; and also could not establish any other cause of action related to the disclosure of his arrest record.

Affirmed

In the fall of 1998, Barr applied for a part-time security officer position with the airport. During his interview for the position, Barr consented to a criminal background check.

The airport participates in the Criminal Justice Information Network (CJIN), but must submit any criminal background request through an agency with computer terminal access to the CJIN database, which is a computer controlled telecommunications network that interfaces with computerized databases maintained by various law enforcement agencies throughout the nation. The National Crime Information Center (NCIC) is a computerized information system which links local, state, and federal criminal justice agencies for the purpose of exchanging information, including criminal history repositories of the states and FBI. GFPD is a terminal agency with access to the CJIN system; it has the capability to perform criminal background checks.

On September 14, 1998, Bruce Sanford, an airport security officer, contacted GFPD and requested a criminal background check on Barr for the preceding ten years. The background check did not reveal any arrests. Barr was hired as a part-time probationary security officer for the airport on October 2, 1998.

On November 7, 1998, John Vanni, an airport security officer contacted GFPD employee Gina Vincent and, without permission from the airport, requested a criminal background check on Barr. The result of this request revealed Barr had been arrested in Alaska in 1968 for criminal nonsupport. Vanni reported this arrest to Cynthia Schultz, the airport manager, who told Vanni it was not his concern.

Barr was terminated from his employment at the airport on March 18, 1999, prior to the expiration of the six-month probationary period. Barr filed this lawsuit alleging numerous causes of action. All three defendants filed motions for summary judgment. Their motions were granted on July 2, 2003. Barr now appeals from the district court's grant of these motions.

Discussion

Barr argues the unauthorized disclosure of criminal justice information by the State, and its use and dissemination by Vanni, was a violation of his right to privacy under Article II, Section 10 of the Montana Constitution as well as a violation of the Montana Criminal Justice Information Act of 1979 (MCJIA). He also claims such was a violation of the 1974 National Crime Prevention Policy Compact (the Privacy Act), codified at 5 U.S.C. Section 552(a) and Section 44-5-601, MCA, et seq. Barr, in essence, claims the defendants failed to meet state and federal constitutional and statutory standards imposed for the protection of his privacy.

The defendants argue Barr's 1968 Alaska arrest was not confidential criminal justice information; rather, it was public information that anyone could access. They assert that Barr's right to privacy was not violated by any dissemination of this information. The State claims that, contrary to Barr's assertions, the civil remedy provisions of the Privacy Act do not provide a private cause of action against a state agency.

The Montana Legislature has defined confidential criminal justice information as: criminal investigative information, criminal intelligence information, fingerprints and photographs, criminal justice information or records made confidential by law, and any other criminal justice information not clearly defined as public criminal justice information. Pursuant to (citation deleted), public criminal justice information includes Barr's initial arrest record at issue. Thus, under MCJIA, Barr's Alaska arrest was clearly public information.

Aside from the MCJIA, this court has adopted a two-part test to determine whether Barr has a constitutionally protected privacy interest in this information: (1) whether the person involved had a subjective or actual expectation of privacy, and (2) whether society is willing to recognize that expectation as reasonable.

In this instance, Barr had no subjective or actual expectation of privacy in his initial arrest record; it constitutes public information that anyone could access. He admitted in his deposition that his arrest record was public information. Although it may be difficult to access the arrest record, it is still public information. Thus, the district court did not err when it concluded Barr's 1968 Alaska arrest was public information and that there was no breach of the MCJIA.

Under the particular circumstances of this case, where Barr knew that the record of his long past arrest was public information and he also consented to a criminal background check, he had no actual or subjective expectation of privacy. Further, in this case, Barr was a security officer entrusted with helping to ensure the safety of the traveling public, and the record in question is specifically designated as public information by statute. Thus, under these facts, we conclude the public is not willing to recognize Barr's claimed expectation of privacy as reasonable.

As the State points out, the civil remedy provision of the federally enacted Privacy Act only applies to actions against a federal agency (holding the Privacy Act applies only to federal agencies and that state agencies are immune from liability under the Act). There are no federal agencies named as defendants in this lawsuit. Accordingly, the district court was correct when it granted the defendants' motions for summary judgment and held Barr's claim under the Privacy Act of 1974, 5 U.S.C. Section 552(a), failed as a matter of law.

Barr also asserts the airport's conduct, in not hiring him as a permanent employee, violated his civil rights under 42 U.S.C. Section 1983, and resulted in a conspiracy denying him immunities and privileges under the law, contrary to 42 U.S.C. Section 1985(3). In regard to this civil rights claim, the airport argues that municipalities are not liable, for the constitutional torts of their employees under the theory of respondeat superior.

GFPD makes a similar argument, stating that in order for a municipality to be liable under these statutes there must be a policy or custom of the government entity itself which inflicts the injury complained of by the plaintiff. GFPD argues Barr cannot show this.

The State argues Barr's claims under 42 U.S.C. Sections 1983 and 1985(3) fail as a matter of law because the Department of Justice is not a "person" within the meaning of Section 1983 and Section 1985(3) and therefore this statute has no applicability.

Barr's claimed civil rights violations stem from an invasion of his privacy, which we have already determined did not occur. Thus, he cannot establish a Section 1983 violation of his right to privacy.

Likewise, Barr did not offer proof of a policy or custom utilized by the defendants which resulted in a violation of his civil rights.

Under *Monell v. Dept. of Soc. Services*, municipalities such as the airport and GFPD cannot be held liable unless action pursuant to official municipal policy of some nature caused the constitutional tort. Barr offered no proof of a custom or policy of refusing to hire probationary employees who complained that their privacy rights had been violated. Accordingly, Barr has no valid claim under 42 U.S.C. Sections 1983 and 1985(3) against any of the defendants. The district court did not err when it granted the defendants' motions for summary judgment and held Barr's civil rights claims failed as a matter of law.

Barr also argues the defendants violated NCIC regulations by improperly disseminating criminal history record information and that this constitutes negligence *per se* under Montana law. The defendants argue that Barr cannot establish negligence per se because he failed to prove a predicate statutory violation as required by Montana law.

The doctrine of negligence per se, or negligence as a matter of law, provides that the violation of a statute renders one negligent under the law. To establish negligence *per se*, a plaintiff must prove that (1) the defendant violated the particular statute; (2) the statute was enacted to protect a specific class of persons; (3) the plaintiff is a member of that class; (4) the plaintiff's injury is of the sort the statute was enacted to prevent; and (5) the statute was intended to regulate members of defendant's class.

We have already determined that there was no violation of law pertaining to confidential criminal justice information. As Vanni was an Airport security officer, authorized to request the information provided, there was no violation of NCIC regulations. Thus, there is no predicate statutory violation on which to base a negligence *per se* claim. Accordingly, summary judgment in favor of the defendants was proper on Barr's negligence per se claim.

Since we have determined Barr's 1968 Alaska arrest was public information, and its dissemination was not improper, there was no duty owed to prohibit dissemination of the fact Barr had been arrested in 1968. Thus, the district court did not err in granting the defendants' Motions for Summary Judgment on this issue.

The judgment of the district court is affirmed.

CASE COMMENT

This case also illustrates the balance between a statute providing for disclosure of arrest information against the improper disclosure of private information. Since the court held that the plaintiff's arrest information was deemed "public information," he could not sustain an invasion of privacy claim. In addition, the plaintiff failed to show that the disclosure of the information violated his rights under the civil rights statute and that it constituted negligence per se.

347 F.3d 655

United States Court of Appeals, Seventh Circuit

JOHN DOE AND OTHER MEMBERS OF THE FOOTBALL TEAM AT ILLINOIS STATE UNIVERSITY, ET AL., PLAINTIFFS-APPELLANTS v. GTE CORPORATION AND GENUITY INC., DEFENDANTS-APPELLEES.

Decided Oct. 21, 2003

Background

College athletes brought action against Internet service provider (ISP) under Electronic Communications Privacy Act (ECPA). The United States District Court for the Northern District of Illinois dismissed action. Athletes appealed.

Holding

The court of appeals held that ISP was not liable to athletes for customer's use of service to display images of athletes who were unknowingly recorded unclothed while in locker room setting.

Affirmed

Someone secreted video cameras in the locker rooms, bathrooms, and showers of several sports teams. Tapes showing undressed players were compiled, given titles such as "Voyeur Time" and "Between the Lockers," and sold by entities calling themselves "Franco Productions," "Rodco," "Hidvidco—Atlas Video Release," and other names designed to conceal the persons actually responsible. All of this happened without the knowledge or consent of the people depicted. This suit, filed by football players at Illinois State University, wrestlers at Northwestern University, and varsity athletes from several other universities, named as defendants not only the persons and organizations that offered the tapes for sale (to which we refer collectively as "Franco"), plus college officials who had failed to detect the cameras (or prevent their installation), but also three corporations that provided Internet access and web hosting services to the sellers. The sellers either defaulted or were dismissed when they could not be located or served. The college officials prevailed on grounds of qualified immunity. The only remaining defendants are the informational intermediaries—large corporations, two thirds of them solvent. The solvent defendants are

GTE Corp. and Genuity Inc. (formerly known as GTE Internetworking), both of which are subsidiaries of Verizon Communications. The district court dismissed all claims against them in reliance on 47 U.S.C. Section 230(c).

After the judgment became final with the resolution or dismissal of all claims against all other defendants—the defaulting defendants were ordered to pay more than $500 million, though there is little prospect of collection—plaintiffs filed this appeal in order to continue their pursuit of the deep pockets.

According to the complaint, GTE provided web hosting services to sites such as "youngstuds.com" at which the hidden-camera videos were offered for sale. GTE did not create or distribute the tapes, which were sold by phone and through the mail as well as over the Internet. Although the complaint is not specific about just what GTE did, we may assume that GTE provided the usual package of services that enables someone to publish a website over the Internet. This package has three principal components: (1) static IP (Internet protocol) addresses through which the websites may be reached (a web host sometimes registers a domain name that corresponds to the IP address); (2) a high-speed physical connection through which communications pass between the Internet's transmission lines and the websites; and (3) storage space on a server (a computer and hard disk that are always on) so that the content of the websites can be accessed reliably.

Advertisements about, and nude images from, the videos thus passed over GTE's network between Franco and its customers, and the data constituting the website were stored on GTE's servers. Franco rather than GTE determined the contents of the site, though the complaint raises the possibility that GTE's staff gave Franco technical or artistic assistance in the creation and maintenance of its website. Sales occurred directly between Franco and customers; communications may have been encrypted (most commercial transactions over the Internet are); and GTE did not earn revenues from sales of the tapes. Franco signed contracts with GTE promising not to use the website to conduct illegal activities, infringe the rights of others, or distribute obscenity (a promise Franco broke). GTE thus had a contractual right to inspect each site and cut off any customer engaged in improper activity. We must assume that GTE did not exercise this right. Some domain administrators and other personnel maintaining GTE's servers and communications network may have realized the character of Franco's wares, but if so they did not alert anyone within GTE who had the authority to withdraw services. Managers were passive, and the complaint alleges that GTE has a policy of not censoring any hosted website (that is, that GTE does not enforce the contractual commitments that Franco and other customers make).

The district court's order dismissing the complaint rests on 47 U.S.C. Section 230(c), a part of the Communications Decency Act of 1996. This subsection provides:

(c) **Protection for "Good Samaritan" blocking and screening of offensive material.**

(1) **Treatment of publisher or speaker.** No provider or user of an interactive computer service shall be treated as the publisher or speaker of any information provided by another information content provider.

(2) **Civil liability.** No provider or user of an interactive computer service shall be held liable on account of—(A) any action voluntarily taken in good faith to restrict access to or availability of material that the provider or user considers to be obscene, lewd, lascivious, filthy, excessively violent, harassing, or otherwise objectionable, whether or not such material is constitutionally protected; or (B) any action taken to enable or make available to information content providers or others the technical means to restrict access to material described in paragraph (1).

These provisions preempt contrary state law. "No cause of action may be brought and no liability may be imposed under any State or local law that is inconsistent with this section." 47 U.S.C. Section 230(e)(3). But "nothing in this section shall be construed to limit the application of the Electronic Communications Privacy Act of 1986 or any of the amendments made by such Act, or any similar State law." 47 U.S.C. Section 230(e)(4). We therefore start with the question whether plaintiffs have a claim under the Electronic Communications Privacy Act.

Plaintiffs rely on 18 U.S.C. Sections 2511 and 2520, two provisions of that statute. Under Section 2511(1), "any person who—(a) intentionally intercepts, endeavors to intercept, or procures any other person to intercept or endeavor to intercept, any wire, oral, or electronic communication; (b) intentionally uses, endeavors to use, or procures any other person to use or endeavor to use any electronic, mechanical, or other device to intercept any oral communication" faces civil liability. Section 2520(a) creates a damages remedy in favor of a person "whose wire, oral, or electronic communication is intercepted, disclosed, or intentionally used in violation of this chapter." Franco and confederates intercepted and disclosed oral communications (the tapes have audio as well as video tracks) and thus are liable under Section 2511 and Section 2520. But what could be the source of liability for a web host?

GTE did not intercept or disclose any communication; and though one could say that its network was a "device" to do so, plaintiffs do not make such an argument (which would be equally applicable to a phone company whose lines were used to spread gossip). Instead plaintiffs say that GTE is liable for aiding and abetting Franco. Yet nothing in the statute condemns assistants, as opposed to those who directly perpetrate the act. Normally federal courts refrain from creating secondary liability that is not specified by statute. Although a statute's structure may show that secondary liability has been established implicitly, it is hard to read Section 2511 in that way. Subsection 2511(1)(c) creates liability for those who willfully disseminate the contents of unlawfully intercepted information. A statute that is this precise about who, other than the primary interceptor, can be liable, should not be read to create a penumbra of additional but unspecified liability.

What is more, GTE's activity does not satisfy the ordinary understanding of culpable assistance to a wrongdoer, which requires a desire to promote the wrongful venture's success. A web host, like a delivery service or phone company, is an intermediary and normally is indifferent to the content of what it transmits. Even entities that know the information's content do not become liable for the sponsor's deeds. Does a newspaper that carries an advertisement for "escort services" or "massage parlors" aid and abet the crime of prostitution, if it turns out that some (or many) of the advertisers make money from that activity? How about Verizon, which furnishes pagers and cell phones to drug dealers and thus facilitates their business? GTE does not want to encourage the surreptitious interception of oral communications, nor did it profit from the sale of the tapes. It *does* profit from the sale of server space and bandwidth, but these are lawful commodities whose uses overwhelmingly are socially productive. That web-hosting services likewise may be used to carry out illegal activities does not justify condemning their provision whenever a given customer turns out to be crooked. Franco did not demand a quantity or type of service that is specialized to unlawful activities, nor do plaintiffs allege that the bandwidth or other services required were themselves tip-offs so that GTE, like the seller of sugar to a bootlegger, must have known that the customer had no legitimate use for the service. Just as the telephone company is not liable as an aider and abettor for tapes or narcotics sold by phone, and the postal service is not liable for tapes sold (and delivered) by mail, so a web host cannot be classified as an aider and abettor of criminal activities conducted through access to the Internet. Congress is free to oblige web hosts to withhold services from criminals (to the extent legally required screening for content may be consistent with the first amendment), but neither Section 2511(a) nor Section 2520 can be understood as such a statute.

Section 230(c)(2) tackles this problem not with a sword but with a safety net. A web host that *does* filter out offensive material is not liable to the censored customer. Removing the risk of civil liability may induce web hosts and other informational intermediaries to take more care to protect the privacy and sensibilities of third parties. The district court held that subsection (c)(1), though phrased as a definition rather than as an immunity, also blocks civil liability when web hosts and other Internet service providers (ISPs) *refrain* from filtering or censoring the information on their sites. Franco provided the offensive material; GTE is not a "publisher or speaker" as Section 230(c)(1) uses those terms; therefore, the district court held, GTE cannot be liable under any state-law theory to the persons harmed by Franco's material. This approach has the support of four circuits. No appellate decision is to the contrary.

If this reading is sound, then Section 230(c) as a whole makes ISPs indifferent to the content of information they host or transmit: whether they do or do not take precautions, there is no liability under either state or federal law. As precautions are costly, not only in direct outlay but also in lost revenue from the filtered customers, ISPs may be expected to take the do-nothing option and enjoy immunity under Section 230(c)(1). Yet Section 230(c)—which is, recall, part of the "Communications Decency Act"—bears the title "Protection for 'Good Samaritan' blocking and screening of offensive material," hardly an apt description if its principal effect is to induce ISPs to do nothing about the distribution of indecent and offensive materials via their services. Why should a law designed to eliminate ISPs' liability to the creators of offensive material end up defeating claims by the victims of tortious or criminal conduct?

True, a statute's caption must yield to its text when the two conflict, but *whether* there is a conflict is the question on the table. Why not read Section 230(c)(1) as a definitional clause rather than as an immunity from liability, and thus harmonize the text with the caption? On this reading, an entity would remain a "provider or user"—and thus be eligible for the immunity under Section 230(c)(2)—as long as the information came from someone else; but it would become a "publisher or speaker" and lose the benefit of Section 230(c)(2) if it created the objectionable information. The difference between this reading and the district court's is that Section 230(c)(2) never requires ISPs to filter offensive content, and thus Section 230(e)(3) would not preempt state laws or common-law doctrines that induce or require ISPs to protect the interests of third parties, such as the spied-on plaintiffs, for such laws would not be "inconsistent with" this understanding of Section 230(c)(1). There is yet another possibility: perhaps Section 230(c)(1) forecloses any liability that depends on deeming the ISP a "publisher"—defamation law would be a good example of such liability—while permitting the states to regulate ISPs in their capacity as intermediaries.

We need not decide which understanding of Section 230(c) is superior, because the difference matters only when some rule of state law *does* require ISPs to protect third parties who may be injured by material posted on their services. Plaintiffs do not contend that GTE "published" the tapes and pictures for purposes of defamation and related theories of liability. Thus plaintiffs do not attempt to use theories such as the holding of *Braun v. Soldier of Fortune*, that a magazine publisher must use care to protect third parties from harm caused by the sale of products or services advertised within its pages, and we need not decide whether such theories (if recognized by state law and applied to ISPs) would survive Section 230(c). Instead, they say, GTE is liable for "negligent entrustment of a chattel," a tort that the Restatement (Second) of Torts Section 318 encapsulates thus:

> If the actor permits a third person to use ... chattels in his possession otherwise than as a servant, he is, if present, under a duty to exercise reasonable care so to control the conduct of the third person as to prevent him from intentionally harming others ... if the actor (a) knows or has reason to know that he has the ability to control the third person, and (b) knows or should know of the necessity and opportunity for exercising such control.

The idea is that if A entrusts his car to B, knowing that B is not competent to drive, then A (if present) must exercise reasonable care to protect pedestrians and other drivers. Plaintiffs want us to treat GTE's servers, routers, and optical-fiber lines as chattels negligently "entrusted" to Franco and used to injure others. But GTE did not entrust its computers, network, or any other hardware to Franco; it furnished a service, not a chattel.

Plaintiffs do not cite any case in any jurisdiction holding that a service provider must take reasonable care to prevent injury to third parties. Consider the postal service or Federal Express, which sell transportation services that could be used to carry harmful articles. As far as we can discover, no court has held such a carrier liable for failure to detect and remove harmful items from shipments. That likely is why plaintiffs have not sued any delivery service for transporting the tapes from Franco to the buyers. Similarly, telephone companies are free to sell phone lines to entities such as Franco, without endeavoring to find out what use the customers make of the service. Again plaintiffs have not sued any phone company.

Yet an ISP, like a phone company, sells a communications service; it enabled Franco to post a website and conduct whatever business Franco chose. That GTE supplied some inputs (server space, bandwidth, and technical assistance) into Franco's business does not distinguish it from the lessor of Franco's office space or the shipper of the tapes to its customers. Landlord, phone company, delivery service, and web host all *could* learn, at some cost, what Franco was doing with the services and who was potentially injured as a result; but state law does not require these providers to learn, or to act as Good Samaritans if they do. The common law rarely requires people to protect strangers, or for that matter acquaintances or employees. States have enacted statutes to change that norm in some respects; Dram Shop laws are good examples. Plaintiffs do not identify anything along those lines concerning web hosts.

Certainly "negligent entrustment of a chattel" is not a plausible description of a requirement that service providers investigate their customers' activities and protect strangers from harm. Nor does the doctrine of contributory infringement offer a helpful analogy. A person may be liable as a contributory infringer if the product or service it sells has no (or only slight) legal use, but GTE's web hosting services are put to lawful use by the great majority of its customers. (This is why ISPs are not liable as contributory infringers for serving persons who may use the bandwidth to download or distribute copyrighted music—and indeed enjoy safe harbors under the Digital Millennium Communications Act, discussed in *Aimster*, unless the ISP has actual notice that a given customer is a repeat infringer.) For the same reason, plaintiffs' invocation of nuisance law gets them nowhere; the ability to misuse a service that provides substantial benefits to the great majority of its customers does not turn that service into a "public nuisance."

Maybe plaintiffs would have a better argument that, by its contracts with Franco, GTE assumed a duty to protect them. No third party–beneficiary argument has been advanced in this court, however, so we need not decide how it would fare. None of the arguments that plaintiffs now make shows that any of the states where their colleges and universities were located requires suppliers of web hosting services to investigate their clients' activities and cut off those who are selling hurtful materials, so the district court's judgment is AFFIRMED.

CASE COMMENT

This case provides an excellent analysis of the issues and legal principles related to the dissemination of nude images over the Internet. In this case, the images are taken by concealed cameras in the showers and locker rooms of collegiate athletes. The athletes sought to hold the Internet service provider (ISP) liable for invasion of privacy. The court dismissed the case against the ISP, holding in essence, that the ISP did not conduct the invasion of privacy, nor did even publish the photos. Instead, the ISP merely transmitted the images via the Internet. Significantly, the ISP did not have liability unless it can be shown that it had actual knowledge of the obscene or offensive materials being transmitted.

DISCUSSION QUESTIONS

What aspects of your private life are available in the public realm? Are the integration and dissemination of public records on the Internet, such as court records, financial and property records, and even webcams affecting your expectation of privacy? Given the vast amounts of offensive and private information available on the Internet, should ISPs be required to act with more diligence relative to the dissemination of information? If not, why not?

6

Workplace Violence Cases and Methods

CAUSE OF ACTION AND STATISTICS

Unlike the other theories and causes of actions discussed in this book, workplace violence is actually better characterized as an environmental or location-based crime. Indeed, workplace violence is not, in itself, a statutory crime. If an individual commits a violent act in the workplace, that individual would be charged with whatever crime or crimes that violent act constitutes according to state or federal statutes. For example, if an individual strikes his of her supervisor, that individual could be charged with battery. Thus, workplace violence can consist of battery, assault, rape, and even homicide—depending on the facts of the incident.

Definitions

In an attempt to accurately conceptualize workplace violence, authors have offered definitions to identify the main tenets of the act. For example, workplace violence has been defined as a "complex reaction by an individual functioning under a set of conditions influenced by community and cultural factors."[1] In applying this definition, it is necessary to analyze the person, particularly in light of the work setting and social environment. A more strict definition was offered by Rob Kroft, who asserted that it consists of "violent acts, including physical assaults, threats of assault directed toward persons at work or on duty."[2]

As evidenced by the above definitions, there are many perspectives relating to workplace violence. These include Societal/Psychological Factors and Risk Factors. The former deal directly with causal factors, while the latter deal with situational factors.

Societal and Psychological Factors

These factors tend to view workplace violence from the perspective of the motivation of the offender. This assessment considers the triggers that lead one to commit workplace violence. These factors are not presented as "causes" in the sense a social scientist might use the term. Instead, they are better described as motivating factors that *may* lead an individual to act out violently. In this light, the assertion by Grossman is instructive:[3] "Nobody just snaps. You'll see behavior that builds up. Then there's a triggering event; a reprimand, a layoff, or a demotion that causes somebody to put into place their plan to act violently."

Such "triggering" factors typically include the following:[4]

1. Economic issues (such as poor economy, loss of job, and personal financial distress or bankruptcy)
2. Loss of self-worth (from identification with employment)
3. Increased stress levels (on and off the job)
4. Availability of firearms
5. Resentment toward employer, supervisors, or coworkers
6. Personality conflicts at work
7. Personal issues unrelated to work (such as divorce, alienation of lover, death of family member or loved one, illness or disability, etc.)

These factors are typically manifested in a certain profile and can serve as warning signs that reveal the propensity for violence. Acts of physical violence are often preceded by verbal threats. Sometimes the danger posed by these threats is obvious. At other times, the threats may be passed off as meaningless. In any case, it is important to pay attention to these indicators. The typical profile of someone likely to commit workplace violence is a man, between 25 and 40 years of age, who exhibits an inability to handle stress, tends to engage in manipulative behavior, and often complains about various job issues. This type of person tends to hold grudges, disrespects supervisors, and is prone to verbal or physical outbursts.[5]

Risk Factors

These factors tend to be more situational than motivational. They typically involve job characteristics such as the following:[6]

1. Contact with the public
2. Exchange of money
3. Delivery of passengers, goods, or services
4. Working with unstable or volatile persons in health care, social service, or police or security professions

5. Solitary or close working conditions
6. Late-night or early-morning shifts
7. Location in high crime areas
8. Guarding valuable property or possessions
9. Working in community-based settings

These situational factors were further evaluated by specific occupations. For example, a study of the 1,071 workplace homicides committed in 1994, the breakdown of victims revealed that 179 were supervisors or proprietors in retail stores, 105 were cashiers, 86 were taxi drivers, 49 were managers of restaurants or hotels, 70 were police officers or detectives, and 76 were security personnel.[7]

Statistical Analysis and Implications

The impact of workplace violence is personally, financially, and organizationally devastating. Studies and statistics have demonstrated this assertion. Some as far back as the early 1990s began to reveal the impact of workplace violence. For example, in 1993 the National Institute of Occupational Safety and Health revealed that the leading cause of death in the workplace for women was from violent acts. In addition, the same study asserted that workplace violence was the second leading cause of overall occupational death, exceeded only by motor vehicle-related deaths. Further, the study revealed about one million people are assaulted per year.[8]

Victimization surveys demonstrate the personal impact of workplace violence. Estimates revealed about 1,751,100 days are lost per year as a result of violence, from 160,000 annual injuries. This includes a breakdown of specific crimes that occur at work. About 8 percent of all rapes occur at work, 7 percent of all robberies, and 16 percent of all assaults.[9] Other more recent studies further elaborate the impact of workplace violence. For example, the cost of such violence to employees is about $55,000,000 annually in lost wages—which does not include sick and paid leave. In addition, the estimated annual cost of medical services was placed at $13.5 billion dollars.[10] The overall costs of workplace violence has been estimated to have grown from $4.2 billion annually in 1992 to $121 billion annually in 2002.[11]

The demographics and characteristics of workplace violence were further assessed by other studies. For example, a study of 125 workplace violence cases found that 97.5 percent of offenders were male, 81 percent used firearms, 23.8 percent committed suicide after the act, and 16.1 percent exhibited a history of mental problems or displayed warning signs before the act.[12]

Efforts to combat workplace violence have had some impact. Indeed, the annual number of deaths from workplace violence gradually declined each year starting from 1996 until 2000. Since then, the number of homicides has been generally increasing.[13]

Employers face numerous challenges in continued attempts to reduce the impact of workplace violence. Ironically, as will be illustrated in the cases below, certain laws, particularly the Americans with Disability Act (ADA) have complicated attempts to address potential violence. In addition, the Occupational Safety and Health Act (OSHA) mandates a workplace free from "recognized hazards that are causing or are likely to cause death or serious physical harm."[14] This provision is considered a "general duty" when the hazards involved:[15]

- Create a "significance risk" to employees in other than a "freakish" or utterly implausible concurrence of circumstances,
- Are known to the employer and are considered hazards in the employer's business or industry, and
- Are the type of hazards that the employer can reasonably be expected to prevent.

These are similar to the tort-based standards discussed previously. Obviously these legal standards present challenges to the employer, as does the prevention of workplace violence. The following cases help to illustrate these challenges.

CASES

136 F. 3d 1047

United States Court of Appeals, Fifth Circuit

DOUGLAS C. HAMILTON, PLAINTIFF-APPELLANT v. SOUTHWESTERN BELL TELEPHONE COMPANY, DEFENDANT-APPELLEE.

March 23, 1998

Background

Former employee sued former employer for discrimination under Americans with Disabilities Act (ADA) and for wrongful termination under Texas law. The United States District Court for the Northern District of Texas entered summary judgment for former employer. Former employee appealed.

Holdings

The court of appeals held that:

1. Employee failed to present evidence that his posttraumatic stress disorder (PTSD) was impairment that substantially limited major life activity, and thus he failed to make threshold showing of ADA-qualified disability;
2. Employee failed to show that employer regarded or treated him as having impairment; and
3. Even assuming employee was disabled, he was not terminated because of his disability, but because he violated employer's policy on workplace violence.

Affirmed

About four months before he was fired, Hamilton rescued a drowning woman. For a time following the rescue, he experienced a variety of mental disturbances and suffered "extreme fatigue" that limited his ability to perform manual tasks, such as mowing his lawn. He told his supervisor, Dennis Dorsey, that his pastor thought these problems were posttraumatic stress disorder ("PTSD") symptoms.

A month later, Hamilton verbally abused and struck a coworker on the job. Dorsey referred Hamilton to BELL's Employee Assistance Program

("EAP"), where a social worker concluded Hamilton was suffering from agitated depression and some posttraumatic symptoms. The social worker referred him to a private counselor. He was also evaluated by a psychiatrist, Babette Farkas. Both the social worker and Farkas reported PTSD. During this counseling and evaluation period, BELL received from members of Hamilton's department an anonymous letter that accused him of being a "disgusting, dangerous and abusive man and manager."

Hamilton, believing that his job pressures exacerbated his PTSD, sought to reduce the stress he experienced in his position in BELL's revenue management department. He expressed concern about participating in Project X, a project that discontinued service, without the usual 10-day notice, to minority customers whose accounts were delinquent. He resisted participating in the project because he believed that if he participated he could be personally charged with committing a third degree felony. Although he claimed to have drafted memoranda protesting Project X, no copies of the correspondence exist.

After he was fired, Hamilton sued BELL. The district court granted summary judgment on Hamilton's ADA claim, finding no genuine fact issue as to whether his medical condition substantially limited any major life activities such that his PTSD could be considered an impairment under the ADA. It also determined that Hamilton failed to adduce any evidence showing BELL fired him solely because of his disability. Hamilton now appeals.

To make out a prima facie case of discrimination under the ADA Hamilton must show that (a) he has a disability; (b) he is a qualified individual for the job in question; and (c) an adverse employment decision was made because of his disability. *See* 42 U.S.C. Section 12112(a). The threshold issue in a plaintiff's prima facie case is a showing that he suffers from a disability protected by the ADA. That statute confers a special meaning to the term "disability":

(A) a physical or mental impairment that substantially limits one or more of the major life activities of such individual;
(B) a record of such an impairment; or
(C) being regarded as having such an impairment.

The statute requires an impairment that substantially limits one or more of the major life activities. Whether an impairment is substantially limiting is determined in light of (1) the nature and severity of the impairment, (2) its duration or expected duration, and (3) its permanent or expected permanent or long-term impact. The EEOC regulations adopt the same definition of major life activities used in the Rehabilitation Act. "Major life activities means functions such as caring for oneself, performing manual tasks, walking, seeing, hearing, speaking, breathing, learning, and working."

To substantially limit means:

(i) Unable to perform a major life activity that the average person in the general population can perform; or

(ii) Significantly restricted as to the condition, manner or duration under which an individual can perform a particular major life activity as compared to the condition, manner or duration under which the average person in the general population can perform the same major life activity.

To determine if Hamilton has presented facts that indicate his PTSD is an ADA disability, we first examine whether his PTSD is an impairment that substantially limits any major life function other than working. Only if there is no evidence of impairment to the other major life functions is an impairment to working considered.

The EAP counselor found that Hamilton presented some symptoms of PTSD and Farkas, his treating psychiatrist, diagnosed PTSD. Hamilton claims his PTSD caused him to overeat to the point of being nauseous and having to go to bed, thus impairing his ability to care for himself. He attributes his thoughts of suicide and difficulty in concentration to the mental disorder. Additionally, Hamilton described episodes of fatigue that made it difficult for him to mow his lawn.

By his own admission, however, these impairments no longer exist and the major life functions described by the EEOC regulations have not been affected. We have noted that "the EEOC regulations provide that temporary, non-chronic impairments of short duration, with little or no permanent long-term impact, are usually not disabilities." Consequently, there was no evidence offered on which a jury could find that this impairment substantially limited a major life activity other than working.

We now examine the effect Hamilton's PTSD had on the major life activity of working. With regard to working:

Substantially limits means significantly restricted in the ability to perform either a class of jobs or a broad range of jobs in various classes as compared to the average person having comparable training, skills, and abilities. The inability to perform a single, particular job does not constitute a substantial limitation in the major life activity of working.

Hamilton presents no evidence that his disability prevents him from performing an entire class of jobs, or even a broad range of jobs. The symptoms he reported included crying when faced with stress, loss of temper, and an inability to deal with customer relation issues. By his own admission, however, Hamilton's performance level was "still ahead of his peers." He worked his regular hours until his termination except for the week he was given off to adjust to his medication. Although Dr. Farkas diagnosed Hamilton's condition as PTSD, she did not identify specific activities within his work environment that would be substantially limited by PTSD. Her prognosis was that Hamilton would be able to function normally without any medication. Interestingly, despite his claim that stress in his job exacerbated his PTSD and that the mental disorder made him unable to deal with customer relations, Hamilton ran his own software distribution business for almost a year after his discharge. He then became a senior consultant with another firm.

Hamilton retains the ability to compete successfully with similarly skilled individuals and no facts indicate that he is unable to perform a class of jobs nor a broad range of jobs. We agree with the district court that any work impairment Hamilton may have suffered was merely temporary; we have previously rejected attempts to transform temporary afflictions into qualifying disabilities. We hold that he has failed to present evidence to satisfy the threshold requirement of an ADA claim—that he has an impairment that substantially limits a major life activity.

Having no ADA recognized disability, Hamilton has thus failed to provide summary judgment evidence that he has a record of such an impairment that substantially limits a major life activity.

Also, there is no evidence presented that, although his PTSD did not rise to the level of an ADA disability, BELL treated Hamilton as having a substantially limiting impairment. In sum, we find that the record is without support for Hamilton's claim that the mental impairments imposed by his PTSD are severe enough or of sufficient duration to constitute a disability under the ADA.

Furthermore, even if Hamilton were disabled, the ADA requires that BELL's adverse employment action be taken because of his disability. Hamilton was not terminated because of his disability but rather because he violated BELL's policy on workplace violence.

Several weeks after the rescue, Hamilton, slamming an office door, angrily confronted a physically smaller female manager in front of witnesses after she returned to work from a shopping trip. In response to her appeal to not speak to her in such a tone, he slapped her hand down, yelling that she "get that f___ing finger out of my face." Additional profanity followed. He stormed from the office but then returned to continue his abusive harangue, yelling "You f___ing bitch!" BELL found this behavior to be an egregious violation of its policies, suspended Hamilton at the beginning of February and discharged him at the end of that month.

Although Hamilton argues that the incident was caused by his PTSD, we are persuaded that the ADA does not insulate emotional or violent outbursts blamed on an impairment. An employee who is fired because of outbursts at work directed at fellow employees has no ADA claim. BELL had instituted its policy against workplace violence, with provisions for suspension and dismissal for "extremely severe" offenses, before Hamilton's misconduct. As a BELL employee, Hamilton was held accountable for violating this policy. BELL cited this conduct as its reason for firing Hamilton; we do not regard this reason as pretextual merely because BELL failed to describe the misconduct as workplace violence until the Texas Employment Commission hearing.

The cause of Hamilton's discharge was not discrimination based on PTSD but was rather his failure to recognize the acceptable limits of behavior in a workplace environment. The nature of the incident, shown by the record, presents a clear case in which Hamilton was fired for his misconduct in the workplace. We adopt for an ADA claim the well-expressed reasoning applied in the context of a protected activity-retaliatory discharge claim: the rights afforded to the employee are a shield against employer retaliation, not a sword with which one may threaten or curse supervisors. Hamilton can not hide behind the ADA and avoid accountability for his actions.

For the reasons cited above, we affirm the grant of summary judgment.

CASE COMMENT

This case provides an excellent example of the impact of ADA requirements in relation to the threat of workplace violence. Here the employee acted in a belligerent and threatening manner. When his employer terminated the employment relationship, the plaintiff sought remedies based on the ADA. The court analyzed the definitional requirements of "disability." It concluded that the plaintiff did not show that he was "disabled" under the meaning of the act. Because he could not show the existence of a disability, he had no protection under the ADA. In addition, the court found sufficient evidence that he was terminated because of violations of the workplace violence policy.

Notwithstanding this conclusion by the court, this case illustrates the delicate balance faced by employers. On one hand, the ADA protects individuals who can demonstrate a disability from job actions. On the other hand, the employer must be cognizant of problematic employees who may pose a threat to other employees within the workplace, or to the interests of the employer. Certain mental disabilities, however, are often manifested by inappropriate or problematic behavior, such as exhibited by the plaintiff in this case. Consequently, employers must assess behavior in light of whether it is caused by a disability. If so, the next question is whether the employer can accommodate the disability without creating an undue hardship (or risk) within the workplace. This can be a difficult, factually intensive assessment. Other cases also demonstrate this delicate balance goes beyond ADA requirements to other constitutional and discrimination based claims.

334 Ill. App. 3d 926, 779 N.E. 2d 364

Appellate Court of Illinois, First District, Third Division

DARRYL N. VEAZEY, PLAINTIFF-APPELLANT v. LASALLE TELECOMMUNICATIONS, INC., DEFENDANT-APPELLEE.

Oct. 30, 2002

Background

Terminated employee brought action against employer alleging retaliatory discharge and related claims. Employer moved to dismiss. The Circuit Court, Cook County, granted employer's motion. Employee appealed.

Holding

The appellate court held that the employee failed to show any cause of action.

Affirmed

The plaintiff was employed by LaSalle from 1989 until October 25, 1996. In September 1996, the plaintiff's immediate superior, Ralph Newcomb, received a threatening message on his voicemail. Several individuals for whom the message was played believed that the voice on the message was that of the plaintiff. The matter was reported to the police. Approximately one month later, a female caller left a message on Newcomb's voicemail threatening Newcomb's wife.

On October 22, 1996, the plaintiff was summoned to LaSalle's regional office and questioned regarding the threatening messages. This meeting was attended by Mike Mason, LaSalle's Customer Fulfillment Manager, and Jack Burke, who was identified to the plaintiff as a "LaSalle troubleshooter." The plaintiff denied leaving any threatening messages on Newcomb's voicemail but was, nevertheless, ordered to read a transcript of the threatening message so that a recording of his voice could be made for comparison purposes. The plaintiff refused and was suspended from his job without pay.

The plaintiff next met with Mason and Burke on October 25, 1996, and was again ordered to provide a recording of his voice reading a transcript of the threatening message. When the plaintiff refused, his employment with LaSalle was terminated. The plaintiff filed a three-count complaint against LaSalle for various causes of action.

The tort of retaliatory discharge is an exception to the general rule that "at-will" employment is terminable at any time for any or no cause. In order to recover upon a claim of retaliatory discharge, a plaintiff must establish that he was discharged in retaliation for his activities and that the discharge violated a clear mandate of public policy. In this case, the plaintiff has pled both that he was discharged from his employment with LaSalle and that his discharge was as a consequence of his activities, namely, refusing to read a transcript of the threatening message left on Newcomb's voicemail. The question is whether the facts as alleged establish that the plaintiff's discharge was in violation of a clear mandate of public policy.

The plaintiff argues that the public policy violated by his discharge is the protection of the privilege against self-incrimination guaranteed by both the Fifth Amendment to the United States Constitution and article I, section 10 of the Illinois Constitution. LaSalle argues that a voice exemplar, such as that requested of the plaintiff, is not a testimonial statement and, as such, neither the Federal nor the state constitutional privilege against self-incrimination protects a person from being required to give one. LaSalle further asserts that the privilege against self-incrimination acts as a restraint upon the government only, not a limitation upon the activities of a private party.

As a preliminary matter, we will address the plaintiff's contention that his complaint does not allege that he was directed to give a voice exemplar. The term "exemplar" is defined as "one that serves as a model or example." Interpreted in their light most favorable to the plaintiff, the allegations of the complaint assert nothing more than the fact that the plaintiff was directed to "provide a tape recording of his voice reading the transcript of the message allegedly left" on Newcomb's voicemail so that LaSalle "could compare it to the threatening message left for Mr. Newcomb ... ostensibly for the purpose of determining whether or not ... [his] denial of involvement was truthful." The plaintiff asserts that, pursuant to voice recording standards adopted by the American Board of Recorded Evidence, a voice exemplar must be taken by trained professionals in a controlled setting in order to be valid for comparison purposes. We are not concerned with the question of whether the exemplar, if given, would have been valid. Rather, we need only consider whether the plaintiff alleged that LaSalle ordered him to give a voice exemplar for purposes of comparison. It is clear from the plaintiff's complaint that he alleged precisely that.

LaSalle is correct in its assertion that the constitutional privilege against self-incrimination restricts only government conduct. To establish violation of defendant's Fifth Amendment right against self-incrimination, plaintiff must demonstrate that plaintiff's conduct constituted state action and any interrogation subject to strictures of Fifth Amendment must be at hands of government actor. As LaSalle's conduct did not constitute state action, the trial court properly dismissed count I of the plaintiff's complaint, in which he alleged that he had been discharged in retaliation for invoking his constitutional right against self-incrimination.

Even if the constitutional protection against self-incrimination could be said to apply to LaSalle's conduct, the plaintiff failed to state a cause of action for retaliatory discharge. The United States Supreme Court has held that the privilege against self-incrimination guaranteed by the Fifth Amendment to the United States Constitution protects an accused only from being compelled to testify against himself or otherwise provide the state with evidence of a testimonial or communicative nature. However, the privilege offers no protection against one being compelled to speak for identification purposes. Simply put, compelled production of a voice exemplar for identification or comparison purposes does not violate the Fifth Amendment.

The fact that the plaintiff has cited his "rights against self incrimination as protected by the Illinois and United States Constitutions" as the public policy violated by his discharge does not of itself give rise to a claim for retaliatory discharge. "The test for determining if the complaint states a valid cause of action is whether the public policy clearly mandated by the cited provisions is violated by the plaintiff's discharge." Since being compelled to give a voice exemplar does not violate the privilege against self-incrimination guaranteed by the Fifth Amendment to the United States Constitution or article I, Section 10 of the Illinois Constitution, LaSalle's discharge of the plaintiff for refusing to give such an exemplar does not violate the public policy embodied in either constitutional provision. As a consequence, we find that count I fails to state a cause of action for retaliatory discharge and was, therefore, properly dismissed by the trial court.

To state a claim for civil conspiracy, a plaintiff must plead that two or more persons intentionally combined for the agreed purpose of accomplishing by concerted action either an unlawful purpose or a lawful purpose by unlawful means. However, the basis of a claim of civil conspiracy that may result in tort liability is not the mere combination of two or more persons, but the wrongful act alleged to have been done pursuant to the agreement.

Liberally construed, the plaintiff's civil conspiracy claim alleges that he was discharged both because he refused to give a voice exemplar and because of his race. As discussed above, however, the plaintiff's discharge for failing to give a voice exemplar cannot support a claim for retaliatory discharge and does not, therefore, constitute any wrongful act which can support a claim of civil conspiracy. We are left then with the issue of whether the plaintiff's allegation that LaSalle conspired to, and did, terminate his employment "because he was Black" can support a common law action for civil conspiracy.

The Illinois Human Rights Act (Act) is a comprehensive scheme of remedies and administrative procedures for redress of civil rights violations. Section 2-102(A) of the Act provides that it is a civil rights violation for any employer to discharge an employee on the basis of discrimination." The Act defines "unlawful discrimination" as discrim... against a person because of, inter alia, his race, color or national origin.

There can be no disputing the fact that the plaintiff's assertion that LaSalle, his employer, conspired to, and did, terminate his employment "because he was Black" alleges a civil rights violation within the meaning of the Act. As a consequence, no basis independent of the Act exists for imposing liability upon LaSalle predicated upon this charge, and the circuit court lacked jurisdiction to consider the claim.

Based on the foregoing analysis, the judgment of the circuit court granting LaSalle's motion to dismiss the plaintiff's complaint and each of the three counts pled therein is affirmed.

CASE COMMENT

In this case, the plaintiff was suspected of leaving a threatening message to his supervisor. When he was asked to submit a voice exemplar in order to compare the voice on the message with his voice, he refused. He was subsequently terminated. Plaintiff argues that the termination violated his constitutional rights and that his employment was wrongfully terminated. The court found no constitutional protection because his employer was not a state actor. The termination was not wrongful because there was no public policy violation. In this analysis, the court properly focused on the plaintiff's behavior and found that his allegations were insufficient to state a cause of action.

116 Wash. App. 127

Court of Appeals of Washington

DONALD ROEBER, APPELLANT v. DOWTY AEROSPACE YAKIMA, A WASHINGTON CORPORATION, RESPONDENT AND CROSS-APPELLANT.

March 11, 2003

Background

Discharged employee filed suit against his former employer, alleging that he was unlawfully terminated as a result of a sensory, mental, or physical disability, as a result of migraine headaches and a depressive disorder. The Superior Court, Yakima County, entered summary judgment for employer. Employee appealed, and employer cross-appealed.

Holding

The court of appeals held that evidence was insufficient to present prima facie case of disability discrimination.

Affirmed

Dowty is a Washington corporation that manufactures component parts for commercial and government aircraft. Mr. Roeber began working for Dowty in August 1980. At the time he was terminated in 1998, he held the position of manufacturing engineering programming specialist. Throughout his employment he received regular promotions and salary increases. His annual reviews indicated that he was a competent, valued employee who generally worked well with others. On the other hand, he often needed improvement in attendance and punctuality, and it was noted that, on occasion, he came across "too strong." According to Mr. Roeber, his work was stressful and the stress increased from 1997 on, when colleagues quit and the additional workload was placed on the remaining employees. He felt compelled to work over 50 hours per week to meet the company deadlines.

On Saturday, May 16, 1998, Mr. Roeber came to the office to assist with a project that was having problems. He attempted to enter through the "tool crib," an enclosed area with a locked steel mesh door. Because he saw no one there to let him in, he kicked the door a few times. Bruce Garner, the tool crib attendant, arrived and walked past Mr. Roeber to the tool crib window, where he talked to his son, James Garner. Feeling ignored, Mr. Roeber said something like, "Hey, Bruce, why don't you let me in so I can take care of this problem and go home." Bruce Garner opened the door but reportedly said, "You kick this door again, and I'm going to kick your ass."

As Mr. Roeber stepped through the door, Bruce Garner slapped him on the face "hard enough to cause a stinging sensation." Mr. Roeber was "instantly infuriated" and called the police to report an assault. As Mr. Roeber tried to leave the tool crib, Bruce Garner approached him. James Garner stepped between the two men and placed his hand on Mr. Roeber's chest. In response, Mr. Roeber stated something like, "Don't get in the middle of this or I'll have to take your head off to get you out of the way." Mr. Roeber later told his supervisor and the investigating police officer that he was so mad he could have killed Bruce Garner. He acknowledged stating, "If I had a gun, I would've killed him." However, he claimed the statement was merely a figure of speech.

Other witnesses presented a different scenario. According to Bruce and James Garner, Mr. Roeber arrived at the tool crib angry, kicked the door, and yelled while Bruce Garner was assisting his son with a tool. Bruce Garner reportedly thought Mr. Roeber was kidding. Playing along, he mock-threatened to box Mr. Roeber's face if he did not calm down, and tapped him on the cheek. At this point, the Garners claim, Mr. Roeber became extremely angry and James Garner stepped between the two men. James Garner asserts Mr. Roeber told him to "get out of the way or I'll rip your head off." Mr. Roeber's supervisor, who arrived soon after, reports that Mr. Roeber was very angry and stated, "if I had a gun I'd kill him right now." The investigating officer later stated he felt that Mr. Roeber was capable of carrying out his threat and warned against possible retaliation.

Mr. Roeber was suspended pending an investigation of the incident. Management asked him to submit a written statement of his version of the events. He complied with a letter dated May 26, 1998. In this letter he admitted stating "I was so mad I could have killed him," and "I'll have to take your head off to get you out of the way." However, he denied making a direct threat on anyone's life. He explained that the medication for his depression had not been working during the last couple of weeks and it scared him that he got so mad so quickly. However, he asserted that "this story has evolved way beyond the reality of what actually happened." He also wrote, I believe that calling the police as a response to any aggravating circumstance is a sensible course of action. I was not "extremely upset" until *after* Bruce slapped me and I needed an arbitrator to intervene. I still believe that, given the circumstances, it was the right thing to do.

On May 27, 1998, Mr. Roeber met with Human Resources Director Cheryl Dale, Vice-President of Operations Don Johnston, and Manufacturing Engineer Manager Mike Stanley. Although he stated he was surprised and concerned about how quickly his temper flared, Mr. Roeber asserted he handled the situation correctly. He was also surprised that his threats had been taken seriously. On May 29, Ms. Dale sent Mr. Roeber a termination letter. In it she explained that the company considered it unacceptable for an employee to intimidate or fight with a coworker. She further stated that Mr. Roeber's threats of violence had to be taken seriously due to the company's responsibility to provide a safe workplace.

In November 1998, Mr. Roeber filed a charge of discrimination with the Equal Employment Opportunity Commission. He claimed he was discharged due to a mental condition impairing his anger control. The EEOC dismissed this charge, finding no violation of the statutes, but advised Mr. Roeber of his right to file a lawsuit in federal court. Thereafter, Mr. Roeber filed a complaint in the United States District Court—Eastern District. He claimed violations of the Americans with Disabilities Act, 42 U.S.C. Section 12101, and the Washington State law against discrimination. The district court granted Dowty's motion for summary judgment on the ADA claim and dismissed the state law claims without prejudice. The Ninth Circuit Court of Appeals affirmed.

According to Mr. Roeber, he first consulted with a mental health counselor in 1988, when he was going through a divorce. At that time, he took an antidepressant for about ten days. He again sought counseling for depression in September 1992, when he was under substantial stress at work and a coworker recommended treatment for his mood swings. Dowty's Human Resources Director at that time, Bette Taylor, recommended that Mr. Roeber see therapist Gary Hammer, who provided care to Dowty employees as part of an employee assistance program. Mr. Roeber participated in counseling with Mr. Hammer for dysthymia (a depressive disorder) sporadically from September 1992 through mid-February 1995. In mid-April 1994, Mr. Hammer referred Mr. Roeber to nurse-practitioner Terence Walker for antidepressants. Treatment notes by Mr. Walker indicate that the medication seemed to alleviate some of the effects of Mr. Roeber's depression, including his inability to sleep and interact with others.

By 1997, Mr. Roeber was reportedly feeling overwhelmed at work. He asked Mr. Walker to send a letter to Dowty regarding the job stress. The letter, sent to Ms. Taylor on February 7, 1997, stated that Mr. Roeber had done "quite well" on antidepressants, but that he was now feeling extremely overwhelmed by the hours and responsibilities at work. Mr. Walker further stated that Mr. Roeber reported he had talked to his supervisors on several occasions to try to remedy the problems, but that he had not gotten any response. In conclusion, Mr. Walker wrote, "I hope you will be able to assist Don in his efforts to maintain his employment under less stressful conditions." There is no indication in the record that Dowty responded to Mr. Walker's letter or otherwise acted on it.

Mr. Roeber believes that one of the reasons he suffers a depressive disorder is that he is subject to migraine headaches. Since about 1991, he has suffered nearly daily migraines, although they have been controlled by medication since 1994. He claims that he failed to report to work or left work on occasion due to the headaches.

Prima Facie Case of Disability Discrimination

An employer who discharges an employee for a discriminatory reason faces a disparate treatment claim, while an employer who fails to accommodate an employee's disability faces an accommodation claim. Mr. Roeber alleges both disparate treatment and accommodation violations.

Disparate Treatment

In a disparate treatment discrimination case, the employee bears the first burden of setting forth a prima facie case of unlawful discrimination. An employee alleging disability discrimination must establish that he or she (1) is in a protected class (disabled), (2) was discharged, (3) was doing satisfactory work, and (4) was replaced by someone not in the protected class. The employee must present specific and material facts to support each element of this prima facie case. If the employee fails to set forth a prima facie case of discrimination, the employer is entitled to prompt judgment as a matter of law.

Once the employee establishes a prima facie case, a rebuttable presumption of discrimination temporarily takes hold. At this point, the burden shifts to the employer to present sufficient evidence of a legitimate and nondiscriminatory reason for the discharge. If the employer fails to meet this burden of production, the employee is entitled to an order establishing liability as a matter of law. However, if the employer presents sufficient admissible evidence to raise a genuine issue of fact as to whether it discriminated against the employee, the presumption established by the prima facie case is rebutted. The employee must then provide evidence that the employer's stated reason for the discharge is in fact pretext.

Considering the above, Mr. Roeber's first task in establishing a prima facie case was to present evidence that he has a disability. Pursuant to the regulations adopted under the auspices of the Washington Human Rights Commission, a condition is a disability if it is (1) an abnormality, and (2) is a reason why the person having the condition was discharged.

Mr. Roeber established with treatment records that he suffers from migraine headaches and a depressive disorder. Arguably these conditions are abnormalities. However, as discussed below in terms of accommodation, Mr. Roeber does not show that these conditions substantially limited his ability to perform his job.

As for the other elements of a prima facie case of disability discrimination, he established that he was discharged and that he did consistently satisfactory work for Dowty. He failed to establish, however, that he was replaced by someone outside his protected class, or that his disability was a reason he was discharged. Although he claimed he trained a person just before he was discharged, he provides no evidence that the person he trained was hired to replace him or that the person was not disabled. Further, he presents no evidence that his medical condition was discussed in any performance reviews or in the investigation that led to his termination. On this record, he does not establish a prima facie case of disparate treatment discrimination.

Further, even if we assume Mr. Roeber carried his initial burden, Dowty presents compelling evidence of a nondiscriminatory explanation for firing him. Its employee handbook states that employees will be disciplined (up to and including suspension or discharge) for "fighting on Company premises, horse-play, or intimidation or coercion of fellow employees." Following the allegations of Mr. Roeber's threatening behavior on May 16, 1998, Dowty management suspended Mr. Roeber and conducted an investigation into the incident. The managers concluded, based on statements from witnesses, Mr. Roeber, and the investigating officer, that Mr. Roeber's actions constituted unacceptable threats of violence against fellow employees.

Mr. Roeber fails to rebut this explanation with probative evidence of pretext. He argues first that his request for accommodation was closely followed by his discharge, raising an inference of a causal relationship. But the only pertinent evidence of a request for accommodation is the 1997 letter from Mr. Roeber's nurse-practitioner, and discharge occurred over a year later after a favorable employment review. Mr. Roeber also contends other employees who demonstrated threatening behavior were treated more favorably. However, two of the three employees who reportedly behaved inappropriately merely yelled in anger or threw a paper tablet against the wall. Three years prior to Mr. Roeber's discharge, an employee was referred to anger management counseling after he threatened to throw a fellow employee's glasses against the wall. Around that time, another employee reportedly threatened to kill a coworker; however, that incident is not contained in the personnel records. Except for the latter case, none of these other incidents rise to the level of threats to kill or to do great violence, and are thus distinguishable from Mr. Roeber's acts. The only incident regarding a threat to kill occurred before the current management was hired, and even that incident did not involve a threat to use a firearm. All together, these incidents do not establish that Dowty had a standard response to threats of extreme violence, or that it deviated from the standard in dealing with Mr. Roeber.

Ultimately, it is not unlawful for an employer to discharge an at-will employee because the employee is perceived to have misbehaved. Mr. Roeber does not raise a reasonable inference of pretext. Consequently, Dowty was entitled to judgment on the claim of disparate treatment discrimination as a matter of law.

Accommodation

To establish a prima facie case of failure to reasonably accommodate a disability, Mr. Roeber must show that (1) he had a sensory, mental, or physical abnormality that substantially limited his ability to perform the job; (2) he was qualified to perform the job; (3) he gave Dowty notice of the abnormality and its substantial limitations; and (4) upon notice, Dowty failed to affirmatively adopt measures available to it and medically necessary to accommodate the abnormality. Mr. Roeber fails to present sufficient evidence that his abnormality substantially limited his ability to perform his job, that he gave Dowty notice of his abnormality's substantial limitations, or that Dowty failed to adopt measures that were medically necessary to accommodate the abnormality.

A. Limitation of Mr. Roeber's Ability to Perform His Job

Although Mr. Roeber's medical records indicate that he suffered from headaches and depression for several years, his employment reviews show consistent satisfactory work with only minor problems in attendance and promptness. His migraines were successfully treated with medication, and he expressed satisfaction with the effects of his antidepressants. Even so, he clearly felt overwhelmed by the stress of deadlines and the long hours expected from management. While this stress had the potential to exacerbate his migraines and depression, the record does not indicate that he was actually substantially limited in his ability to work in his position.

B. Notice of the Abnormality's Substantial Limitation

The 1997 letter from Mr. Walker—Mr. Roeber's nurse-practitioner and counselor—indicated that Mr. Roeber had been taking antidepressants since 1994 and had "done quite well" under medication. Mr. Walker then explained that Mr. Roeber had recently reported feeling overwhelmed and at his "wit's end" due to pressures at work, including his work hours. Mr. Roeber reported that he had tried to talk to his supervisors "to try to remedy the situation," but he felt like he was not getting any response. Mr. Walker concluded with the following statements, "I hope you will be able to assist Don in his efforts to maintain his employment under less stressful conditions. If I can provide you with any additional information, please don't hesitate to contact me."

Even assuming Mr. Roeber had complained to his supervisors as often as he indicated in his affidavit, the record does not show that Dowty was given notice that his migraines and depressive disorder were substantial limitations. The only letter from a medical practitioner indicated that Mr. Roeber's condition was successfully treated with medication. He was never hospitalized or otherwise substantially limited in his ability to perform his job. Although he claims he sometimes missed work or had to leave work due to his headache pain, he also admits his injections of migraine medication usually prevented the headaches from developing or soon brought relief. The record simply does not support his contention that he gave notice to Dowty that he was significantly limited in his ability to perform his job.

C. Medical Necessity to Accommodate

Mr. Roeber reports that he "told numerous Dowty management personnel," about his migraines and his depressive disorder over the years. He also told them he was taking medication to control these problems. He contends Dowty had a responsibility to take steps to accommodate his limitations. However, he fails to show that accommodation was medically necessary. Mr. Walker's letter did not express an opinion regarding the medical necessity of changing Mr. Roeber's duties. He merely reported what Mr. Roeber had told him about his stress level and asked management to work with Mr. Roeber "to maintain his employment under less stressful conditions." Washington law does not require an employer to provide a disabled employee with accommodations that are not medically necessary.

Before Mr. Roeber found successful medication for his migraines, the vice-president of manufacturing told him to take breaks whenever he needed to for the headaches. Additionally, the employee carries the burden of showing that a specific reasonable accommodation was available to the employer when the disability became known. Mr. Roeber contends he asked for a demotion or for an off-hours work shift, but he does not indicate whether positions consistent with those requests were available. He shows neither that he was qualified for a vacant position nor that Dowty failed to notify him of job opportunities that would accommodate his alleged disability.

Generally the question of an employer's reasonable accommodation for an employee's disability is one for the jury. However, when the employee fails to establish either that a specific reasonable accommodation was available or that accommodation was medically necessary, the burden of production never shifts to the employer to show that the proposed solution was not feasible. In such case, the employer is entitled to judgment as a matter of law. Mr. Roeber fails to establish on the record that specific vacant positions were available at the time he gave notice of his limitations, or that accommodation was medically necessary. Consequently, the trial court correctly adjudicated his accommodation claim as a matter of law.

Affirmed.

CASE COMMENT

This court provided an excellent analysis of the facts and the law. Of significance in this case is the behavior of the plaintiff. From both the disparate treatment and the accommodation theories, the court properly used the burden shifting analysis. The initial burden is with the plaintiff, where he must show sufficient facts to establish the prima facie case. Next, the burden shifts to the employer to present facts to demonstrate non-discriminatory reasons for the job action. Finally, the burden then shifts back to the plaintiff, who must show that the reasons proffered by the employer were a pretext, that the actual reason for the job action was discriminatory. Based on this factual and legal analysis, the court found for the employer, finding sufficient evidence that the job action was based on the threatening behavior of the plaintiff.

208 F. 3d 217

United States Court of Appeals, Eighth Circuit

CHARLES R. BLANTON, APPELLANT v. PRESTOLITE WIRE CORPORATION, APPELLEE

Decided Feb. 29, 2000

Background

Terminated employee brought suit against employer, alleging that his termination had been based on a disability, in violation of Americans with Disabilities Act (ADA), and Arkansas Civil Rights Act. The United States District Court for the Eastern District of Arkansas granted summary judgment to employer. Employee appealed.

Holding

The court of appeals held that employee had failed to show that he was disabled or was perceived as disabled or that proffered nondiscriminatory justification for termination was pretextual.

Affirmed

Blanton failed to come forward at the summary-judgment stage with sufficient evidence to make a triable case on his claim that he was disabled or was perceived by Prestolite as being disabled. In addition, Blanton failed to provide evidence to show that Prestolite's legitimate, nondiscriminatory reason for firing him—that Prestolite believed Blanton was a serious threat to its employees—was pretextual. The evidence shows that Blanton was fired after he (1) threatened to "take out" certain of his co-employees who had allegedly wronged him, (2) threatened to "blow away" the building housing Prestolite's workers' compensation carrier, (3) brandished a handgun and threatened suicide during an appointment with his workers' compensation doctor, and (4) admitted to threatening a co-employee in a workplace dispute.

In short, Blanton failed to present any evidence from which a reasonable trier of fact could find that Prestolite's termination of his employment was the product of unlawful discrimination. Blanton cannot avoid the consequences of his failure of proof by arguing that Prestolite somehow caused his alleged disability, and the district court did not err in its order denying Blanton's motion for reconsideration by finding that argument to be wholly without merit.

Essentially for the reasons stated in the district court's order granting summary judgment, the judgment of that court is AFFIRMED.

CASE COMMENT

Here again the court properly used the burden shifting approach, finding that the termination was based on the threatening behavior of the plaintiff. Further, the plaintiff failed to show any evidence to demonstrate his termination was based on discrimination. Consequently, the employer was not liable for the A.D.A. claim.

322 F. 3d 75

United States Court of Appeals, First Circuit

FRED J. CALEF, JR., PLAINTIFF, APPELLANT v. THE GILLETTE COMPANY, DEFENDANT, APPELLEE.

Decided March 11, 2003

Background

Employee who was terminated after behaving in threatening manner toward coworkers sued employer, alleging it violated Americans with Disabilities Act (ADA) by terminating his employment. Employee also brought pendent state law claim alleging his discharge was in violation of public policy. The United States District Court for the District of Massachusetts granted summary judgment for employer and dismissed both federal and state claims. Employee appealed.

Holdings

The court of appeals held that:

1. Employee was not actually disabled under ADA, absent proof his attention deficit hyperactivity disorder (ADHD) substantially limited claimed major life activities of learning or speaking;
2. Employee also was not a "qualified individual with a disability" under ADA;
3. There was no reasonable accommodation that would have enabled employee to perform the essential functions of his job; and
4. State law claim was without merit.

Affirmed

Calef worked as a Production Mechanic at Gillette from August 22, 1989, to December 13, 1996. In the early 1990s Calef had several incidents with co-employees which led his supervisors to make written reports. In 1990 he "had words" with a coworker. On April 4, 1991, Calef and a coworker each received a warning after an altercation in which Calef, in anger, had threatened the coworker with physical harm after being so threatened himself.

On March 10, 1992, Calef and another employee had to be physically separated by a supervisor after an incident in which the employees angrily exchanged insults and profanity and squirted oil on each other; Calef says the other employee squirted first. Six days later Calef was involved in another argument with a group leader. That night Calef got in a heated exchange with a different group leader and questioned the group leader's performance.

As a result of this series of confrontations with his supervisors and coworkers—on April 4, 1991, March 10, 1992, and March 16, 1992—Gillette gave Calef a written warning, which said Calef was being told that actions of this nature will not be tolerated and any such actions in the future could result in a final warning which could ultimately lead to his termination from the payroll.

On September 13, 1995, Calef was involved in another incident, which resulted in his being issued a Final Warning. On that day, Calef had a confrontation with Jeanette St. Aubin, a machine operator who worked with him on the second shift. It was Calef's responsibility to investigate and repair the machines that St. Aubin operated when she reported trouble with them, as she did that day. After her encounter with Calef, St. Aubin, crying and shaking, went to see supervisor Frank Sciarini in his office. She said Calef had harassed her about her inability to run machinery and that whenever she had difficulties with her machine, Calef got mad at her and told her to speak English. St. Aubin further reported that Calef had come to her machine, pointed his finger in her face, raised his hand, made a fist, and stated, "Stop calling me or I'll punch you in the face." Calef admits raising his voice toward St. Aubin and he admits that he threatened to hit her. At the time, St. Aubin was two weeks shy of her sixtieth birthday. Calef says St. Aubin poked him in the chest and scratched his hand. He then threatened to hit her but immediately apologized and said he did not mean it. Calef admitted he "displayed irrational behavior in the incident."

Calef's Final Warning, dated September 15, 1995, was issued "for a display of conduct that [was] detrimental to the interest of the Company." It explicitly warned Calef "that any single infraction of [Company] policy in the future will result in his termination from the payroll." Calef reviewed and signed the Final Warning without objection.

Pursuant to the written Final Warning, Gillette referred Calef to the Employee Assistance Program (EAP). In lieu of EAP counseling, he started therapy with Janis M. Soma in September 1995. They first met on September 19, 1995. Dr. Soma diagnosed Calef as having attention deficit hyperactivity disorder (ADHD). At her recommendation, Calef received counseling and obtained a prescription for Ritalin. Dr. Soma's notes indicate that Calef had conflicts with others both at work and outside of work. After the initial meeting with Dr. Soma, for example, Calef had an incident outside of work. Despite the counseling and medication, his problems with threatening others continued. Calef says he began taking Ritalin in the fall of 1995 and took it in 1996. At his deposition, Calef testified that Ritalin "really helped" the symptoms of his ADHD. Specifically he stated:

"It cleared my everyday function, I was doing things without thinking about them, about completing tasks, more focused, more—it was like walking out of a fog and clearing everything up. With ADD I have to analyze a lot of things, and it's the turmoil of weighing things and balancing things before I actually do something typically, and with Ritalin it was clearing of—very clear and—everything was very clear." His symptoms of ADHD disappeared or significantly diminished after he started taking Ritalin.

On the specific question of his ability to manage his anger, Calef testified that his ADHD did not cause him to become angry. Dr. Soma's testimony agrees. She added that people with ADHD deal with anger more impulsively. Further, in highly stressful situations, people with ADHD may not focus as well as others do.

In early 1996, Calef told a nurse in Gillette's Medical Department, Cynthia Ross, that he had ADHD. He also told Joan Pemberton, the head of the Medical Department. Both nurses say that Calef was adamant they not disclose to others the fact that he had ADHD and they did not disclose it. There is a dispute about whether Calef's supervisors ever learned from the nurses or from another source that Calef had ADHD. We will infer in Calef's favor that Gillette had such notice.

In March 1996, Dr. Soma gave Calef a medical certificate to support his request for leaves under the Family and Medical Leave Act (FMLA). Calef was given over 40 days of FMLA leave between May and December of that year. In this sense, Calef requested and was given a reasonable accommodation. There was, though, evidence that Sciarini, the supervisor, did not like Calef taking FMLA days off.

Calef says he had been assigned to work on updated versions of the machines that he had serviced earlier and he found the new setting stressful. On May 24, 1996, Dr. Soma addressed a note to the Gillette Medical Department saying she had advised Calef it would be in his best interests to reduce his stressors at work. In particular, she asked if there was a means to reverse his reassignment at work. The letter did not refer to either ADHD or a request for a reasonable accommodation. In Calef's favor we will infer that this letter was adequate to request a reasonable accommodation. Gillette declined to change his assignment. Calef did not pursue the matter.

On July 3, 1996, Calef checked into Pembroke Hospital for depression. On July 17, after returning from hospitalization, Calef received medical clearance from the Hospital to work at Gillette "without restrictions." At his request, Gillette permitted him to work half days from July 22, 1996, through August.

Clinical notes from Dr. Soma indicate that, on August 16, 1996, Calef reported "good progress at work and in family. Sleeping well, blood pressure down, no alcohol use, and no suicidal ideation." He continued to see Dr. Soma at times, and her November 19, 1996, note indicated Calef was taking Zoloft and felt it helped him with anger management. Indeed, from his return on July 22, 1996 to December 6, 1996, Calef worked without noticeable incident or infirmity.

The incident which led to the termination of Calef's employment occurred on Friday, December 6, 1996. The day before, as was customary, Gillette sought volunteers for Sunday shifts. Mechanics usually like that shift since they receive double pay. Due to scheduling needs, the company had to know by Friday who would work that Sunday. Calef's group leader, Steven Pennington (who was senior to Calef and junior to Sciarini), asked for volunteers to work that Sunday and understood Calef to have volunteered. Calef's version is that he tentatively agreed to work and said he would get back to Pennington.

On Friday, December 6, management decided to run a particular production machine, thinking there was a danger of not meeting production quotas. At approximately 5:55 p.m., shortly before a meal break was scheduled to begin, Sciarini informed Pennington that the "Good News Plus" production machines would have to be run during the meal break. Pennington had short notice to find operators and mechanics who could run the machines during the break. Pennington attempted to find Calef in order to request that he delay his meal break and stay on duty while the machines were being run. However, Pennington was unable to locate Calef, so he arranged for another mechanic, along with some machine operators, to oversee the operation of the Good News Plus machines during the break.

Calef was "disgusted" that his machines had been run during the meal break. When he returned from the break, he "went to Frank Sciarini's office and asked why [his] machines were being run." Pennington and Sciarini both state that Calef was upset and, despite being told why the machines had to be run during the break, Calef declared, "You know what you did to me."

Approximately two hours before the end of Calef's shift on that same Friday night, December 6, Calef approached Pennington and informed him that he would not work the shift on the following Sunday, December 8. Pennington had already scheduled Calef to work it. Calef says Pennington became angry and yelled at him that he had to work on Sunday. Calef then walked away from Pennington, who was asking for an explanation of why Calef would not work the Sunday shift. Calef says Pennington was angry and yelling at him, "That's it for you. We are going to get rid of you." Pennington says Calef angrily told him "you know what you did to me," which Pennington interpreted to be a reference to the decision to run the Good News Plus machines during Calef's meal break. Pennington continued to ask for an explanation, but Calef would not explain himself. Instead, he repeated, "You guys know what you did to me," and walked away. To Pennington, Calef seemed irrational and increasingly erratic. Because of Calef's actions, Pennington feared for his own safety.

The two men separated. Pennington left Calef and reported the incident to Sciarini, his supervisor. Pennington told Sciarini what had happened and reported that he was afraid of Calef, that Calef was acting erratically and that Pennington could not work with him. Sciarini's notes of the incident, which he drafted the following day, state: "On Fri. Dec. 6, 1996, at 9:30 p.m., Steve Pennington my Group Leader came to my office telling me that he cannot work with Fred Calef. I am afraid of him, he is acting crazy."

Sciarini asked Calef to report to him, which Calef did. The two then went to a nearby office, where Sciarini asked Calef for an explanation of what happened on the production floor and what he had said to Pennington. Sciarini says he asked Calef if he was still receiving counseling and taking medication and that Calef replied that, while he was still in counseling, the only medication he was taking was blood pressure pills. Calef says he was asked what drugs he was on and replied that he was taking only his blood pressure medication.

Calef says Sciarini was screaming at him, lunging over his desk at him, and telling him he was going to work on Sunday. Sciarini, for his part, observed that Calef was "barely coherent." When Sciarini tried to tell him that it was wrong to walk away from a group leader, Calef repeatedly interrupted him, raised his voice, and talked nonsensically. Calef was making statements such as "you never tell me anything," and was talking about how his wife was mad at him. Sciarini was very uncomfortable with Calef's behavior and he, too, began to fear for his safety. In his summary of the incident, Sciarini wrote that Calef's "behavior was out of control" at this point.

Sciarini believed that Calef's behavior might be explained by his being under the influence of illegal drugs. He requested Calef accompany him to the Medical Department, which Calef did. When Calef and Sciarini arrived, Ross, the nurse who was friendly with Calef, was on duty. Sciarini took Ross aside, explained what had happened, and requested a drug test. Calef repeatedly insisted that the problem was not with him, but with his supervisors—Sciarini and Pennington–and that they, not he, should be required to take drug tests. Calef admits this and that he was speaking loudly.

A few minutes later Kristin Flanagan, a registered nurse scheduled to work the shift after Ross, arrived for duty. Flanagan is a veteran of the U.S. Air Force and served on active duty in the Persian Gulf during the Persian Gulf War. Even so, Ross did not feel comfortable leaving Flanagan as the only nurse on duty while Calef was in his agitated state.

Ross called for a security guard to come to the medical department and Gillette security member Tom Lonergan came to the area. Flanagan called the Manager of Gillette's Health Services, Joan Pemberton, at her home, explained the situation, and requested Pemberton's approval for a drug test. Pemberton specifically recalls Flanagan saying that Calef scared her. Ross, who knew Calef, also feared for her safety at the time, and she was frightened by Calef's agitated and threatening manner. Calef appeared to her to be extremely irrational, belligerent, and sarcastic. Ross also said that Calef was extremely uncooperative, provocative, hostile, and threatening.

Sciarini, Ross, and Flanagan explained to Calef that, pursuant to company policy, he was required to take the drug test. Calef eventually agreed to do so, but only after altering his consent form to read: "Requested Group Leader Steve Pennington to take same test." Flanagan administered the test, which later proved to be negative for illegal drugs.

Sciarini informed Calef that, because of his behavior, he was not to report to work over the weekend, and that he was to call Pemberton after 6:00 a.m. on the following Monday. Pursuant to Gillette policy, the medical staff could not let Calef drive himself home after taking the drug test. Flanagan and Ross wrote a contemporaneous report of the incident, which reflects that: [Calef] was requested to call his wife or friend to drive him home per policy. Calef said "the package store is closing soon and all I want to do is drive home and stop at a bar for a drink." Calef eventually called his wife, who picked him up.

Also on Monday, Sciarini reported the events to manager Joseph Donovan. Donovan also received reports from Pemberton and the supervisors involved. Consistent with Gillette's regular business practice, Donovan then drafted an Employee Contact Report dated December 19, 1996. The report summarized the basis for his decision to terminate the plaintiff's employment, which was then reviewed and approved by his supervisor, Division Head John Farren. It is undisputed that Donovan made the decision to discharge Calef and that his stated reason for discharging the plaintiff is set forth in the Contact Report. That report refers to Calef's disciplinary history, and describes the December 6 incident. The report says Calef's employment was being terminated because his behavior on that night was unacceptable; that it included insubordination and lack of cooperation with his supervisors when he refused a scheduled shift; and that Calef engaged in irrational behavior.

Calef says that he was disoriented, unfocused, and indecisive during these events of December 6. He says he was not screaming but did speak up "a little more than calmly, with a slightly raised voice." He admits he offended the nurses and that he was "real upset" and angry. He attributes all of this to his ADHD. He says under stress his ADHD symptoms of loss of coherent speech and thinking increased. Calef's basic position on the December 6 incident is that his behavior was caused by ADHD and that the reactions the Gillette employees had to him were unreasonable and motivated by biases against people with disabilities.

After the incident he spoke to medical department personnel to apologize and asked them to speak to Donovan about his ADHD. A nurse later reported that she had done so, but Donovan's mind was made up. Calef also called Sciarini to apologize.

In his post-Gillette employment, Calef went to work as a mechanic with the Coca-Cola Company in a job he described as being similar to the one he had held at Gillette. He did not ever inform Coca-Cola that he had ADHD. Indeed, Calef held a series of positions (many of which did not work out for reasons other than ADHD) which required him to learn particular job skills. On one job evaluation Calef was said to be "willing to learn and capable of doing so." He has been employed at Sears since April 2001, has never asked for an accommodation because of his ADHD, and testified that he learned needed skills for the job through a three-week, on-the-job training program.

Taking all inferences in his favor, Calef has failed to meet his burden of creating a triable issue that he was disabled under the terms of the ADA. A disability is an "impairment that substantially limits one or more of the major life activities." 42 U.S.C. Section 12102(2). Calef has not shown such an impairment. Nor has he shown, as he must, that he was qualified to perform the essential functions of his job, either with or without reasonable accommodation.

A. Substantially Limited in a Major Life Activity

Calef's argument that he was substantially limited in a major life activity rests, at its core, on evidence from Dr. Soma, his treating psychologist. Dr. Soma's affidavit correctly recognized that the relevant disability determination turns not on the symptoms of untreated ADHD, but on Calef's ADHD when he received medication and counseling. As to that, she opined, "At the time I treated him [in the mid-1990s], Calef was still substantially limited in the major life activities of learning and speaking (the latter more severe under high stress) notwithstanding his use of Ritalin." Nonetheless, the Supreme Court has recently required more analysis than a doctor's conclusory opinion:

> It is insufficient for individuals attempting to prove disability status under this test to merely submit evidence of a medical diagnosis of an impairment. Instead, the ADA requires [that claimants offer] evidence that the extent of the limitation caused by their impairment in terms of their own experience is substantial.

Calef relies on the fact that he scored "significantly below average" in a test designed to measure his resistance to distraction as tasks become increasingly more complex; he scored "significantly below the mean" on a test designed to measure his memory of complex visual organization and planning; he scored below the 25th percentile when asked to recall "a spatial task involving complex visual organization and planning"; he scored in the 16th percentile in "awareness of visual detail in the environment and visual sequencing ability"; he scored in the 2nd percentile "on a psychomotor task involving the rapid copying of figures associated with numbers"; and he scored in the 9th percentile "on a subtest requiring the solving of oral arithmetic problems." These factors were taken into account in the conclusion that, overall, Calef's learning ability was in the average range. Further, a neurologist he consulted in 2000 reported that

Calef said that Ritalin was "very effective in terms of his ability to concentrate, read, etc." but that Calef had stopped taking it because he thought it made him depressed.

More importantly, his life experience shows no substantial limitation on learning as required by *Toyota*. Calef has a high school GED, has taken other courses, and has received on-the-job training where he learned new job skills. His history both before and after Gillette shows no limitation in his learning ability. These facts doom the claim.

Calef's other asserted substantial limitation, in his speaking, fares no better. Both the medical assessment evidence and the evidence of his life experience render this claim meritless. A medical assessment conducted at the behest of Calef's own physicians reported that Calef "is attentive in conversation.... Language is normal." Indeed, a comprehensive neurological assessment conducted by Peter Rosenberger, M.D., the Director of the Learning Disorders Unit at Massachusetts General Hospital, concluded that Calef's verbal abilities were within average range, including his verbal productivity, articulation, fluency, grammar and syntax, and vocabulary. Psychometric testing performed by Dr. Rosenberger's clinic further concluded:

> Statistical analysis indicates that [Calef's] verbal comprehension abilities fall within the average range *(53rd le Index Score = 101).... Vocabulary development and general fund of information fall at the mean (50th le).*

There is no medical evidence to contradict these conclusions. There was no evidence that Calef could not perform the variety of speaking tasks central to most people's lives, outside the workplace as well as within. His job required him to speak with customers, supervisors, and others, and he did so satisfactorily. None of his performance evaluations note any difficulty in speaking. Further, to the extent ADHD was an impairment, a court is required to take into account the plaintiff's "ability to compensate for the impairment." Here, Calef compensated through Ritalin and counseling. His own testimony was that in 1996 Ritalin helped control most of the effects of ADHD while he was working: "Most all of it. I can't think of any that it didn't." Nor is there any evidence of difficulty in speaking in Calef's everyday life.

At most, Calef's evidence was that, despite taking Ritalin, he still had some difficulty in concentrating at work and would blurt out or interrupt people in conversation. There is no evidence at all that he was substantially limited in speaking outside of work. This is not enough to show a speaking disability under the ADA.

In the end, Calef's argument devolves into a claim that ADHD makes it more difficult for him to respond to stressful situations, that when he becomes angry, he sometimes loses control and can neither speak nor think well, and that this constituted a substantial limitation on a major life activity.

It is clear, though, as Dr. Soma's affidavit indicates, that the ADHD does not cause him to become angry. The issue is how he handles his resulting stress during the episodes in which he becomes angry. This claim would not, under *Toyota*, qualify as a substantial limitation on a major life activity. Very few people find handling stress to be easy. Many people do not think well in stressful situations and find it harder to speak well. There was no evidence in this record that plaintiff could not perform some usual activity compared with the general population, or that he had a continuing inability to handle stress at all times, rather than only episodically. Under our case law, these shortcomings in the evidence are fatal.

On different facts, ADHD might disable an individual such that the ADA applies. Calef, however, has not made the individualized showing about his particular limitations that *Toyota* requires. Merely pointing to a diagnosis of ADHD is inadequate.

B. Qualified Individual

Even if Calef were arguably disabled, he is not otherwise a "qualified" employee because, with or without accommodation, he could not perform an essential function of the job. Plaintiff bears the burden of showing he is qualified.

An employer may base a decision that the employee cannot perform an essential function on an employee's actual limitations, even when those limitations result from a disability. The statute requires that consideration "be given to the employer's judgment as to what functions of a job are essential." 42 U.S.C. Section 12111(8). It is an essential function of a job that a production manager be able to handle stressful situations (here, requests for overtime work and routine disagreements) without making others in the workplace feel threatened for their own safety. This function is both job-related and consistent with business necessity.

Gillette has consistently disciplined employees who engage in such behavior and who are unable to handle this essential function. Before Calef knew he suffered from ADHD, Gillette applied those standards to him. In 1992 he was warned about his confrontations with coworkers. In 1995 he was warned his employment would be terminated the next time he threatened an employee. Gillette has also terminated the employment of others who display similar behavior.

Put simply, the ADA does not require that an employee whose unacceptable behavior threatens the safety of others be retained, even if the behavior stems from a mental disability. Such an employee is not qualified. That was the point of our decision in *EEOC v. Amego, Inc.* It is also the view of every other circuit case which has addressed a similar situation under the ADA or the Rehabilitation Act. "One who is unable to refrain from doing physical violence to the person of a supervisor, no matter how unfair he believes the supervision to be or how provocative its manner, is simply not otherwise qualified for employment." The ADA is not a license for insubordination in the workplace."

Even if reasonable accommodations were pertinent, there was no reasonable accommodation which would have enabled him to perform the essential functions of his job. His uncontrollable anger was episodic and unpredictable. As the district court held, "These short leaves [are] not going to alleviate the threatening and abusive behavior because the stress arises out of the job." Gillette had tried to accommodate Calef—it had given him time off and reduced his work schedule when requested. That did not prevent his behavior on December 6.

We ***affirm*** the entry of summary judgment for Gillette dismissing all claims. Costs are awarded to Gillette.

CASE COMMENT

This case illustrates the factually driven nature of ADA and workplace violence claims. The court in this case, analyzed the facts in a comprehensive manner. In doing so, the court found that the plaintiff was not disabled under the requirements of the act. Further, the plaintiff was not considered "qualified" under the act because the employer sought to accommodate him despite the fact that he was not disabled. Indeed, the attempts to accommodate the plaintiff did not prevent his threatening behavior from occurring. Consequently, the plaintiff's claim must fail.

366 F. 3d 496

United States Court of Appeals, Seventh Circuit

ANTHONY D. BUIE, PLAINTIFF-APPELLANT v. QUAD/GRAPHICS, INC., DEFENDANT-APPELLEE.

Decided April 27, 2004

Background

Former employee sued former employer for discrimination under Americans with Disabilities Act (ADA) and retaliation under Family and Medical Leave Act (FMLA). The United States District Court for the Eastern District of Wisconsin entered summary judgment in favor of former employer. Former employee appealed.

Holdings

The court of appeals held that:

1. District court did not abuse its discretion in refusing to consider summary judgment affidavit as evidence that co-employees offered incorrect version of altercation and that employee did not threaten another co-employee;
2. Alleged temporal proximity between employee's announcement that he had AIDS and his suspension and termination did not establish violation of ADA; and
3. Employer's proffered nondiscriminatory reasons for suspending and terminating employee were not pretextual.

Affirmed

From November 28, 1997, through December 1, 1999, Buie worked in the finishing department at Quad/Graphics, which produces printed materials. Buie's supervisors warned him about frequent absenteeism three times between March 1998 and September 9, 1999. When providing the latest warning to Buie, his supervisor, Scott Connell, wrote that "if Anthony continues to have attendance problems he may be termed [*sic*] from Quad Graphics." Buie was nonetheless absent without excuse and without notice again on September 24 and October 10, 1999.

On October 15, 1999, Buie called Connell on the telephone—after his shift had already begun—and told him that he was sick and would not work that day. Connell responded by saying that Buie's job was in jeopardy. Buie then said that he had AIDS and that his absenteeism was because of the syndrome. This was the first time Quad/Graphics knew of Buie's condition. After Connell learned that Buie had AIDS, he told Buie (either on October 15 or October 17; Buie's affidavit provides both dates) not to return to work.

On October 21, 1999, at the instruction of Steve Kirk, the finishing department manager, Buie met with Caroline Vrabel, Quad/Graphics' corporate employee services manager. Vrabel told Buie that he could apply for FMLA leave for some of the absences when he had called in sick. She further told him not to report to work until he had completed the FMLA application and his attendance issue was resolved. Buie complied with Vrabel's directions. Only after Buie returned to work, however, did Frank Arndorfer, vice president of finishing operations, decide that his leave would be considered a disciplinary suspension for excessive absenteeism. Buie was unaware of that designation when he first left work.

Buie met with Vrabel and Arndorfer on November 10, 1999. Vrabel told Buie that she had excused many of his absences and requested that short-term disability benefits be paid to him for those absences. But Vrabel also stated that she had calculated that he still had accumulated 14 absences during the preceding 11 months that could not be excused, including six no-call, no-show absences. On November 16, 1999, Buie met again with Vrabel and Arndorfer. Arndorfer presented him with a last chance agreement and offered him the choice between signing the agreement or being fired immediately. The agreement, which Buie signed, stated that Buie could be fired for any violation of the employee services manual or the agreement itself. Buie then returned to work, but the peace was short lived.

On November 29, 1999, Buie had a confrontation with a superior, Harold Bridges, while the two were working on a conveyor belt. According to Bridges (who is black), after he upbraided Buie for falling behind in his work, Buie treated Bridges to an outburst about how Buie would work on the conveyor belt when he pleased and how Bridges and other black employees did not know how to "get over on these white mother _____ s." Bridges admitted that he replied by saying that "niggas [*sic*] always want something for nothing" and stated that Buie reacted to this remark by pushing bundles of publications off of the conveyor belt and refusing Bridges' order to return to work.

Connell soon learned of, and investigated, the incident. Several employees confirmed Bridges' version of events. Connell also asked for Buie's side of the story. Buie denied telling Bridges that he would work when he pleased, pushing publications off of the conveyor belt, and making the racist statement that Bridges attributed to him. Buie further explained he would not return to work under Bridges because of Bridges' own use of a racial slur. After considering the evidence, Connell issued a written warning to Buie.

Buie, for his part, did not let matters rest there. He knew that one of the employees who had corroborated Bridges' account was Diane Grignon and, on December 1, 1999, he confronted her. As Grignon soon told Connell, Buie pointed his finger at her and said, at a range where Grignon could feel Buie's spittle on her face, "I'll get you, bitch." As Grignon recounted, when she asked him whether that was a threat, Buie replied that it was and asked where her witnesses were. The confrontation ended with Grignon pushing Buie's finger from her face as Connell approached.

Later that day, Connell learned that the house mother of the halfway house in which Grignon resided had received a call from a man identifying himself as "Anthony." The caller said that if "something happens to [Grignon] on the bus tonight, it's her own fault." At that point, Connell, Kirk, and Arndorfer decided to fire Buie, whom they discharged the next day (December 2) through a letter signed by Arndorfer. Grignon was disciplined for her part in the incident, but not fired.

Buie's work-related troubles did not end with his discharge. He later was found guilty in the State of Wisconsin Circuit Court of Waukesha County for disorderly conduct as a result of his confrontation with Grignon. The state court found that the prosecution met its burden of proof establishing that this defendant was profane and otherwise disorderly. I would point to him getting within six inches of Ms. Grignon, putting his finger in her face so close and speaking in such a way and so close that the spitile [*sic*] would go across to her and making threatening remarks. This is all under circumstances tending to cause or provoke an immediate disturbance of public order.

The ADA forbids certain employers from "discriminating against a qualified individual with a disability because of the disability of such individual in regard to job application procedures, the hiring, advancement, or discharge of employees, employee compensation, job training, and other terms, conditions, and privileges of employment." 42 U.S.C. Section 12112(a) (2000). It is undisputed that Quad/Graphics is an employer covered by the ADA and that Buie is an "individual with a disability" for purposes of the statute. To prove that he suffered disability discrimination under the ADA, Buie may proceed under the direct or indirect methods. There are two types of permissible evidence under the direct method: direct evidence and circumstantial evidence. The former "essentially requires an admission by the decision maker that his actions were based upon the prohibited animus." The latter is evidence that "allows a jury to infer intentional discrimination by the decision-maker."

Buie may also proceed under the indirect method, which first requires him to establish a prima facie case of discrimination. To do so, Buie must show that (1) he is disabled under the ADA; (2) he is qualified to perform the essential functions of his job with or without reasonable accommodation; and (3) he has suffered from an adverse employment decision because of the disability. Were Buie to put forth a prima facie case, the burden would then shift to Quad/Graphics to articulate a nondiscriminatory reason for each adverse employment action. If Quad/Graphics were to meet its burden, Buie would then have to prove by a preponderance of the evidence that Quad/Graphics' proffered reasons were a pretext for intentional discrimination.

A. ADA Discrimination

Buie's theory of discrimination under the ADA is that, although he was a qualified employee, Quad/Graphics suspended him without pay, imposed a last chance agreement on him, and then fired him, because of what it regarded as his disability, AIDS.

1. Direct Method

We turn first to the direct method. As to the theories that Quad/Graphics violated the ADA by first suspending him without pay, and then discharging him, because he had AIDS, Buie put forth no direct evidence in support of either proposition. He did, however, present circumstantial evidence, namely the short time period between his suspension and the decision to fire him (they occurred on October 15 or 17 and December 1, respectively) and his announcement on October 15 that he had AIDS. In Buie's view, the timing of these events was suspicious and would allow a jury to conclude that Quad/Graphics acted as it did because of Buie's disability.

Suspicious timing is a type of circumstantial evidence under the direct method. However, a "temporal sequence analysis is not a magical formula which results in a finding of a discriminatory cause." By itself, temporal proximity would not normally create an issue of material fact as to causation, although it could suffice where the adverse action followed on the heels of the employer's discovery of the employee's disability.

Here, temporal proximity is all that Buie relies on under the direct method, and it does not create an issue of fact. Even when the record is viewed in Buie's favor, the undisputed evidence shows that he was on the brink of discharge before anybody at Quad/Graphics knew that he had AIDS. Connell warned Buie on September 9, 1999, that, if he continued "to have attendance problems" he could be fired. On September 24, October 10, and October 15, Buie nonetheless chose to miss work without excuse and without warning. It was only then, when Buie had every reason to believe that he was on the edge of termination, that he told Connell that he had AIDS. Quad/Graphics had already experienced serious difficulties with Buie's continued problems with attendance.

Also, after his disciplinary suspension, he had his aggressive encounter with, and made a threat toward, Grignon. All of these troubles occurred after Connell had already warned him that his job was in jeopardy. It is also worth noting that, after Buie's AIDS announcement, Vrabel made a concerted effort to qualify Buie for pay under the FMLA for some of his absences where he had called in sick. And although Buie belatedly complains about a last chance agreement, it did give him another chance to perform satisfactorily despite his attitude and excessive absences. His response to that opportunity, in short order, was his confrontation with Grignon. (We put Buie's confrontation with Bridges aside because Quad/Graphics does not cite that incident as a reason for firing Buie.) Under these circumstances, we conclude that no reasonable jury could infer simply from the temporal proximity among Buie's announcement that he had AIDS (on October 15) and his subsequent suspension (on October 15 or 17) and the decision to fire him (on December 1) that Buie was suspended or fired because of his disability. An eleventh-hour declaration of disability does not insulate an unruly employee from the consequences of his misdeeds. We conclude that, under the direct method, Buie has not created an issue of material fact as to his ADA claim.

2. Indirect Method

The indirect method, as we discussed above, first requires Buie to establish a prima facie case, at which point Quad/Graphics must put forth a nondiscriminatory reason for its action, which then requires Buie to show by a preponderance of the evidence that Quad/Graphics' stated reason was a pretext for discrimination. The district court entered summary judgment for Quad/Graphics because Buie had not established prong two of the prima facie case and, in any event, Buie failed to rebut Quad/Graphics' nondiscriminatory reasons for suspending and then firing Buie. We affirm on the latter ground and need not reach the former.

Before the district court, Quad/Graphics justified the decision to impose a suspension on Buie on the ground that it was disciplinary action appropriate to his absenteeism. It explained the decision of Connell, Kirk, and Arndorfer to fire Buie on two grounds: that he was chronically absent without excuse or warning, and that he threatened Grignon. These reasons are nondiscriminatory, and thus, to avoid summary judgment, Buie had to put forth evidence that they were actually lies designed to camouflage that Quad/Graphics really acted against Buie because he had AIDS. The district court concluded that Buie had failed to produce such evidence.

On appeal, Buie maintains that he met his burden, pointing to evidence that several employees who did not have AIDS, out of the 11,000 or so employed by Quad/Graphics, had problems with attendance and threats but were not fired or suspended. Specifically, Buie claims that "since Sherita Rideout, Chris Studzinski, Bruce Iwanski, and Diane Grignon, all had attendance problems and they all engaged in violence or threats of violence in the workplace, it would have been reasonable for the District Court to infer that Quad/Graphics tolerated attendance problems in conjunction with violence and threats of violence in the workplace." According to Buie, a jury could infer from this disparity that Quad/Graphics' professed reasons for suspending and firing him actually were lies designed to conceal its real, invidious reasons for those actions.

The disparate treatment of similarly situated employees who were involved in misconduct of comparable seriousness, but did not have a similar disability, could establish pretext. As to Rideout, Studzinski, and Iwanski, however, Buie puts forth no evidence that they were disciplined by any of the same people who disciplined him, which means that the discipline that they may (or may not) have received sheds no light on the decisions to suspend or terminate Buie. Consider *Timms v. Frank*, where the court reasoned that "it is difficult to say that the difference was more likely than not the result of intentional discrimination when two different decision makers are involved."

That leaves the ostensible evidence of pretext arising from Quad/Graphics' treatment of Grignon's problems with attendance and threats. Grignon, like Buie, was supervised by Connell and may have been supervised by Kirk and Arndorfer as well. However, Buie does not show that Grignon was treated differently for comparable misconduct. As to absenteeism, Buie maintains that "Grignon was absent fourteen times between 7/21/99 and 4/26/2000 (nine months), and she was disciplined for it on April 26, 2000." If true, this assertion would tend to show that Grignon was treated similarly for similar misconduct (although Buie's lack of specificity as to how Grignon was disciplined creates some ambiguity). Like Buie, Grignon was disciplined, but not fired, after Quad/Graphics concluded that she accumulated fourteen absences. Later, of course, Buie was fired—but not before he committed an act of disorderly conduct at work. Buie brazenly argues that he and Grignon were treated disparately because she was not also fired after engaging in a violent episode. However, the inflammatory incident for which Buie argues that Quad/Graphics should have fired Grignon is the very one that, as the Circuit Court of Waukesha County found, Buie provoked by getting within six inches of Grignon, pointing in her face, and making threatening remarks. An employer's decision to punish the instigator of a violent, or nearly violent, episode more severely than it treats his victim is evidence of rationality, not pretext. Buie has not rebutted Quad/Graphics' nondiscriminatory reasons for first suspending and later discharging him.

We affirm summary judgment as to Buie's claim under the ADA because he fails to create an issue of material fact under either the direct or indirect methods.

B. FMLA Retaliation

As discussed above, Buie may prove FMLA retaliation under the direct or indirect methods. Unfortunately, his brief as to this claim is difficult to decipher.

We begin with the direct method. Buie presents no direct evidence in support of this claim. The only circumstantial evidence to which he points is suspicious timing. Buie contends, as best we can discern, that the proximity between his announcement that he had AIDS (and, implicitly, Quad/Graphics' realization that Buie would request FMLA leave) and Buie's suspension and firing would allow a jury to infer retaliation. His suspicious timing argument regarding FMLA retaliation fails for the same reason it failed to prove ADA discrimination: given Buie's myriad problems at work, a reasonable jury could not conclude from timing alone that Quad/Graphics suspended or fired Buie because of his announcement that he had AIDS and, implicitly, because he would thus be requesting benefits under the FMLA.

Regarding the indirect method, for the same reasons discussed above in relation to the ADA claim, Buie fails to rebut the nondiscriminatory justifications that Quad/Graphics offered for his suspension and discharge. We conclude that summary judgment was proper as to Buie's claim for FMLA retaliation.

Even in light of that [self-serving affidavit—discussion omitted] evidence, we conclude that the record would not allow a reasonable jury to return a verdict in Buie's favor either as to his claim for ADA discrimination or his claim for FMLA retaliation.

Affirmed

CASE COMMENT

In this case, the court focused on facts in light of the appropriate legal analysis. The court distinguished the types of proof proffered by the plaintiff. In this analysis, the court looked at both the direct and indirect methods. Viewed from both perspectives, the court found there was insufficient evidence to sustain the ADA discrimination or the FMLA retaliation claim. In this analysis, the factual basis of the plaintiff's behavior was weighed against the allegations of his claims, resulting in the dismissal of both claims.

830 So. 2d 621

Supreme Court of Mississippi

KAY L. NEWELL (RODERICK) v. SOUTHERN JITNEY JUNGLE COMPANY D/B/A SACK AND SAVE.

Oct. 31, 2002

Background

Employee brought negligence action against her employer after being shot at work by her estranged husband. The Circuit Court, Lamar County, dismissed case. Employee appealed.

Holding

The supreme court held that employee's injury was not caused by employer's negligence; and husband's acts were intervening, superseding cause.

Affirmed

On October 14, 1997, Kay L. Newell was at her place of employment, a grocery store, Sack and Save, which is owned and operated by Southern Jitney Jungle Stores of America. Newell's estranged husband, William Roderick, entered Sack and Save and shot Newell four times with a .44 caliber handgun.

Several times before the shooting incident, Roderick appeared at the Sack and Save stalking, harassing, and threatening Newell in front of managers and other employees. The day before the shooting Roderick caused a disturbance at Sack and Save. Newell's supervisor helped her file charges against Roderick.

After the shooting, Newell filed this action claiming Sack and Save was negligent in failing to furnish her with a safe place to work and in failing to provide security for her. The motion to dismiss by the employers was granted. Newell appealed.

Discussion

Newell's complaint claims Sack and Save owed her a duty to provide a safe place to work and a duty to provide her security. Although not an insurer of an invitee's safety, a premises owner owes a duty to exercise reasonable care to protect the invitee from reasonably foreseeable injuries at the hands of another. Newell's claim, as an invitee as this court characterizes her, is brought under the theory of premises liability where Sack and Save's duty is properly stated as one of reasonable care.

We have stated two ways a plaintiff can prove proximate causation in premises liability cases: (1) that the defendant had actual or constructive knowledge of the assailant's violent nature, or (2) actual or constructive knowledge an atmosphere of violence existed on the premises. Newell's complaint alleges facts which indicate that it is under this first option she is attempting to proceed. However, the complaint also states that Newell's employer assisted her during this unfortunate ordeal to the point of helping her file charges against her husband the day before the shooting occurred. At the time of the attack, Newell was in a separately enclosed office behind a door that her husband had to "force" his way through. This indicates the door was either locked, or there was warning in advance of her husband's presence provided by coworkers such that countermeasures were taken.

In this case, the Sack and Save did nothing wrong; to the contrary, it attempted to help and had placed Newell in a secure location under lock and key. Kay Newell did nothing wrong, either. However, Sack and Save is not and should not become the guarantor of its employees' safety at all times.

The better method of examining this issue is under the traditional concepts of intervening and superseding causes. For such intervening and superseding cause to extinguish the liability of the original actor, the cause must be unforeseeable. Furthermore, "negligence which merely furnishes the condition or occasion upon which injuries are received, but does not put in motion the agency by or through which the injuries are inflicted, is not the proximate cause thereof."

We hold that Sack and Save's actions did not impel the assault by Newell's husband. Clearly the intentional acts of Newell's estranged husband in entering the Sack and Save armed with a gun, forcing entry into Newell's office, and shooting her are acts by a third party which are sufficient to terminate any liability Sack and Save might otherwise have. If not, this court would impose a duty approaching strict liability on landowners of the type we specifically denounced in *Crain v. Cleveland Lodge 1532, Order of Moose, Inc.*, "we refuse to place upon a business a burden approaching strict liability for all injuries occurring on its premises as a result of criminal acts by third parties."

There is no allegation of any intentional act or acts by Sack and Save. The complaint alleges that Sack and Save, knowing of Newell's estranged husband's potential dangerousness, failed to take sufficient precautions to protect her. There are no allegations that Sack and Save willfully caused Newell's injury.

Conclusion

The liability of landowners must end somewhere. We find the complaint insufficient in its averments of duty, breach of duty, and foreseeability to withstand a motion to dismiss for failure to state a claim. The judgment of the circuit court is affirmed.

Affirmed

CASE COMMENT

This case takes a different twist as the plaintiff seeks a tort-based remedy as opposed to a statutory or constitutional claim. In this analysis, the court found no negligence on the part of the employer. Indeed, since the plaintiff did not even allege willful or intentional acts on the part of the employer, the court found no trouble in dismissing the lawsuit. Further, the court found the employer could not prevent the violence of the husband. The language of the court was instructive, making this rhetorical assertion: "liability of landowners must end somewhere." In this case, the landowner (or employer) did not have liability.

DISCUSSION QUESTIONS

What issues and implications must an employer assess when faced with problematic or threatening behavior of an employee? What counsel would you suggest relative to this question? Assuming an employee is "disabled" under the ADA, does this status mean that an employer cannot institute a job action against the disabled employee? If your answer is no, what are the applicable standards or principles that control this assessment? From a tort-based theory, when would an employer be liable for an act of workplace violence?

SECURITY METHODS

One of the key defenses available to employers relates to the policies and procedures used within the company. Indeed, a critical component in avoiding liability, or at least minimizing it, is through proper internal security methods based on sound and prudent policies. Some suggested policies and procedures are summarized below.

Policy Considerations

It is critical to establish a system of documenting violent or harassing incidents, to articulate specific preventive strategies for such, and to demonstrate the commitment of the employer to effectively deal with any such incidents that do occur. Many security experts recommend instituting a zero tolerance policy for dealing with violent or harassing incidents[16] to clearly convey that violence and harassment of any kind—including threats and intimidation—will not be tolerated.[17] In order to ensure its directives can be carried out, the policy should include certain subsections.

The policy should articulate early warning signs of potential violence. These include aggressive and hostile behavior, racial or cultural epithets, harassing or intimidating statements, stalking, and physical assaults or threats of such.[18] In addition to listing these factors, the policy should encourage employees to report their observations or concerns. Beyond this encouragement, it may be appropriate to require employees to cooperate with any workplace violence investigation. At the least, the policy should require any supervisory employee to immediately report any suspected or unusual behavior. An investigation should be conducted as soon as possible following said report. Finally, the policy should specify that all information obtained would be considered confidential, and that no retaliation against anyone who comes forward with information of suspected or potential workplace violence will be tolerated.[19]

Pre-employment Screening Methods

As many cases have illustrated, it is necessary to conduct some type of background screening. The extent and scope of such is usually dependent on the following factors:[20]

1. Nature of the work to be performed
2. Assess to sensitive information
3. Potential liability associated with the job
4. Level, frequency, and manner of contact with the public
5. Type of client or public whom contact is made

The answers to these questions should dictate the level of background screening required for a given job. Depending on this assessment, the background screen may involve checking criminal, civil, credit, traffic, and prior employment history and personal references, and the like. In the event that the background screen reveals a criminal conviction, the EEOC has held that it is illegal to exclude a person from employment unless a justified business necessity could be shown.[21] Factors used to assess business necessity and job relatedness include:[22]

1. Nature and gravity of the crime
2. How long ago the crime was committed
3. Nature of the business and the job sought

In addition, the EEOC has consistently held that a current illicit drug user is not disabled, and thus, is not protected under the act.[23] The logic of this provision should seem clear. The legal basis is that ADA protects the illness, not illegal conduct. A former drug addict would have an illness, and is protected by the ADA based on this status. However, once the individual "falls off the wagon," the current illegal conduct is not protected by the ADA.

Application/Interview Questions and Statements

For protection in the event of a lawsuit, every business should make sure a statement clearly notifying job applicants that background screens will be performed, and that this statement is conspicuously featured on the front on its application for employment. In addition to this notification, the application should also include a statement requesting the applicant to consent to the background screen and a certification that any false statements made on the application will result in a sanction, up to and including termination.

Before an employment interview, the interviewer should carefully review the application and supporting materials, noting in particular any gaps in employment. During the interview, the candidate should be asked to explain any such gaps and to rate his or her ability to perform specific tasks included in the job description. The goal is to evaluate how well the skills and aptitudes of the candidate match the job requirements. The candidate should also be asked to describe his or her perception of the job. In addition, the skills and aptitudes identified for the position should be compared to the candidate's previous employment. Again, the goal is to seek evidence of favorable characteristics, such as team orientation, positive self-worth, or multi-tasking ability. It is important to note that the EEOC has determined that personality traits such as poor judgment, quick temper, or irresponsible behavior are not deemed a disability unless they are deemed symptoms of a mental or psychological disorder.[24] Based on the cases reviewed in this book, it is clear that this must be based on objective, professional assessment (see below for further discussion).

Incident Documentation Issues

Obtaining and documenting incidents in a systematic manner is critical for both effective internal decision making and for justifying decisions in an external forum, such as a court proceeding. The reporting and documentation procedures should specify who is responsible for the reporting, when the reporting is required, the purpose the reporting is designed to achieve, where the reporting channels flow, and what information should be collected and disseminated. In essence, the goal is to promote an "open door" policy coupled with assurances of confidentiality to the reporter. In addition to these reporting requirements, the policy statement should stress that no reprisals or retaliation will result from any reported incident. Indeed, it may be appropriate to sanction employees who fail to report an incident.

In addition to these reporting requirements, it is important to train employees to recognize early warning signs of problematic behavior and indicators of criminal (or even terrorist) activity. Indicators of stress-related or problematic behaviors are many and varied. These include injuries (such as cuts and bruises) to the employee, increased tardiness or absenteeism, performance or personality changes (such as withdrawal or temper outbursts), frequent or emotional phone calls, frequent medical or doctor visits, increased accidents, changes in personal appearance, and the like.[25] The goal of these measures is to recognize and deal with early warning signs of stress, thereby establishing a calmer, more productive work environment that in turn helps diminish the threat of employee violence.

Psychological and Drug Testing Methods

The same logic as with background screening also holds true in regard to these types of tests. The goal, of course, is to screen out problematic employees, either before or after they are hired. There are a number of ways to achieve this goal. First, by asserting a clear and unequivocal policy statement against drug usage or harassing, intimidating, or violent behavior, many problematic employees will self-opt out of the selection process. In other words, prospective employees with a history of problematic behavior or a current drug problem may decide that the screening procedures and policy goals do not suit their personality and that the job may not be worth the potential scrutiny of procedures and policies. Such policy statements should include the following:

1. Commitment to violence/drug-free workplace
2. Company philosophy and culture that supports that commitment
3. Program methodology for implementing the company philosophy

In the event that psychological or other testing designed to assess whether an employee poses a "direct threat" pursuant to ADA guidelines, the employer should be careful to develop a factual, professional assessment. At the outset, the employer must first establish whether the employee is "disabled" under the ADA. If so, then the employer must assess whether the employee could be reasonably accommodated. Here the key is to first determine if the direct threat could be eliminated by accommodation.[26] In this assessment, the employer must show that an actual direct threat is present, not simply a speculative or remote threat. To make this showing, the direct threat must be significant. The standard is a high probability of substantial harm.[27] Of course, this assessment must be based on objective evidence, including security risk assessments, medical diagnostics, and/or psychological testing.[28] It naturally follows that the more facts and objective assessments used, the more likely that the resulting conclusion will be sustained by a court.

If it is concluded that a direct threat exists that cannot be effectively resolved by reasonable accommodation, then the employer could assert that the risk of harm to employees is too great and the hardship to employer too great to allow the problematic employee to maintain his or her job. If this conclusion is reached, the employer must be able to articulate the following factors:[29]

1. Duration of the risk
2. Nature and severity of the potential harm
3. Likelihood or probability that the harm will occur
4. Imminence of the harm

While it may be impossible to accurately predict each of these factors, the employer must provide reasonable, objective analysis to candidly assess them coupled with a conclusion consistent with this assessment. The question to be determined is whether the employee poses a "high probability of substantial harm." The validity of the answer rests on whether the employer considered the four factors listed above. The determination must not be based on speculation, or a remote risk of harm.[30]

Threat Assessment and Response Plan

In regard to a crisis management strategy, it is important to develop not only a set of procedures to be used if a violent incident occurs but also a plan for how such a crisis might be avoided in the first place. In order to think through these issues in a sequential and rationale manner, this process can be divided into three phases: pre-incident, incident, and post-incident.[31]

In the pre-incident phase, the goal is to articulate the workplace violence policy and train to the policy. In addition, it is necessary to fully evaluate the potential threat. This evaluation can involve a number of steps, including but not limited to the following: (a) assessing the employee's personal situation and personnel file (including criminal history, family situation, emotional state, and financial circumstances); (b) interviewing coworkers and supervisors about specific conduct and indicators; (c) considering whether to obtain an order of protection (if applicable); (d) determining whether to provide EAP support or mental and medical health tests and assessments; (e) and interviewing the problematic employee. These measures could be supplemented by assessments of the physical security within the workplace, including access controls, key controls, emergency exit procedures, emergency communication procedures (including who calls the police), security posts, and patrols and procedures. Consideration may also be given to moving targeted employees—if this is considered necessary for security purposes.[32] Finally, the floor plan should be evaluated from the perspective of security and the availability of weapons, including potential weapons such as kitchen knives and letter openers.

During the incident phase, if the problematic employee is to be terminated, additional measures should be implemented. It is advisable to include personnel from various disciplines in this planning, such as legal, HR, security, and operations personnel. A script designed for use in the termination should be developed. The employer should map out the planned sequence of events, and consider securing and transferring personal property, and recovery of company property such as keys, access cards, documents, and the like. In addition, it is often advisable to provide outplacement services and severance benefits to the terminated employee. The key is to preserve the dignity, while simultaneously maintaining control over that individual, to the point that he or she is prevented from injuring others or himself or herself.[33]

In the post-incident phase, there should be a debriefing session, the facility should be secured, data and intelligence methods for follow-up, including possible monitoring of the problematic employee, should be assessed, and ongoing security protocols and procedures revised in light of this data and information flow. Overall, the objective is to establish ongoing procedures for assessing the subsequent level of risk.

Finally, one useful way to assess the potential for workplace violence is through the HARM Model Continuum. HARM is an acronym for Harassment, Aggression, Rage, and Mayhem. The logic of the model is that workplace violence usually occurs along a continuum of gradual problematic behaviors culminating in the violent incident. This model was summarized by Rudewicz as follows:[34]

Harassment represents the first level of behavior on the violence continuum. The behavior at this stage is not criminal conduct. Instead, it is usually considered inappropriate conduct. This includes slamming doors, glaring at coworkers, telling false stories about coworkers, and the like.

In the aggression stage, the behavior becomes more hostile. Here the behavior is designed to cause harm or discomfort. It may be directed at an individual employee or at the company in general. Such behavior includes slamming a door in the face of an employee, spreading damaging rumors about the company or coworkers, damaging an employee's personal property, sabotaging the company's property or products, and the like.

In the rage stage, the behavior is manifested by intense conduct. This conduct often causes fear and results in physical and emotional harm, or substantial property damage to business or personal property. Such behavior includes physically pushing coworkers, supervisors, and customers and conveying threats and hate messages.

The mayhem stage is characterized by physical violence, including guns and other weapons. Obviously, the goal is to intercede before the incident occurs. In order to have a safe and secure workplace, the employer must be proactive in the assessment of threats. It is important to emphasize that the employer has a legitimate right to maintain order and to establish a "civil and decent workplace."[35] Achieving this goal requires determining the proper application of security methods through legally appropriate means and analysis.

NOTES

1. Johnson, Dennis J., Joseph A. Kinney, and John A. Kiehlbauch (1994). Breaking the Cycle of Violence. *Security Management,* at 26.
2. Kroft, Rob (1994). *Security Concepts.*
3. Grossman, Robert J. (2002). Bullet Proof Practices. *HR Magazine,* November.
4. Ibid.
5. Viollis, Paul and Doug Kane (2005). At Risk Terminations: Protecting Employees, Preventing Disaster, taken from www.rmmag.com on 5-26-2005.
6. Taken from www.cdc.gov/noish/violrisk.html, on 9-16-2002.
7. Ibid.
8. Taken from www.bls.gov, on 8-14-2002.
9. Bachman, Ronet (1994). Violence & Theft in the Workplace: National Crime Victimization Survey. *Office of Justice Programs,* Bureau of Justice Statistics, July.
10. Grossman op cit. at 37.
11. Viollis and Kane op cit. at 1.
12. Johnson, Joseph A., and Dennis J. Kelly (1993). Breaking Point: The Workplace Violence Epidemic and What to do About It. *National Safe Workplace Institute.*
13. See U.S. Department of Labor at www.bls.gov.
14. Taken from the Workplace Violence Fact Sheet complied by *The National Institute for the Prevention of Workplace Violence.*
15. Ibid.
16. See *The National Institute for the Prevention of Workplace Violence* op cit.; and Rudewicz, Frank E. (2004). The Road to Rage. *Security Management,* February.
17. Rudewicz op cit. at 46.
18. Ibid at 46.
19. Ibid at 49.
20. Nixon, William B. (2002). What You Don't Know Can Hurt You. *Security Management*, April.
21. Barber, James S. (1995). Workplace Violence: An Overview of Evolving Employer Liability. *Illinois Bar Journal*, Vol. 83, September.
22. Nixon op cit. at 96; and *Title VII and Section 1981: A Guide for Appointed Attorneys in the Northern District of Illinois,* op cit. at 14.
23. Nixon op cit. at 98; and *Title VII and Section 1981: A Guide for Appointed Attorneys in the Northern District of Illinois,* op cit. at 2.
24. Barber op cit. at 466.
25. Grossman op cit. at 42; and Rudewicz op cit. at 41.
26. Barber op cit. at 465.
27. *Title VII and Section 1981: A Guide for Appointed Attorneys in the Northern District of Illinois,* op cit. at 12.
28. See, for example, *Sullivan v. River Valley School District,* 197 N.E. 2d 804 (1999).

29. Karr, Karen (2005). Will Rage Turn to Rampage? *Security Management,* October, pp: 67–73.
30. Ibid at 68.
31. Grossman op cit. at 37–39.
32. See Chapter 1 for further discussion on specific Security Methods.
33. See Viollis and Kane op cit. at 2–3; and Grossman op cit. at 39 for further suggestions.
34. Rudewicz op cit. at 42.
35. Bloom, Howard M. and Margaret R. Bryant (2005). Labor Law's Changing Tides. *Security Management,* August.

7

Sexual Harassment

CAUSE OF ACTION AND ELEMENTS

The statutory basis for sexual harassment claims is from Title VII of the Civil Rights Act of 1964, specifically 42 U.S.C. Section 2000e-2(a)(1). This cause of action is administered through the Equal Employment Opportunity Commission (EEOC), which essentially acts as a "gatekeeper" by evaluating and investigating sexual harassment claims. In order to have jurisdiction to pursue a sexual harassment claim in federal court, the EEOC must first issue a "right to sue letter." Once submitted, the plaintiff has ninety (90) days to file the lawsuit in federal court. The failure to file within this time frame, or the failure to obtain a right to sue letter will prove fatal to the lawsuit.[1]

Definitions and Concepts

The EEOC defines sexual harassment as "unwelcome sexual advances, requests for sexual favors and other verbal or physical conduct of a sexual nature constitutes sexual harassment when submission to or rejection of his conduct explicitly or implicitly affects an individual's employment, unreasonably interferes with an individual's work performance or creates an intimidating, hostile, or offensive work environment."[2]

Hostile work environment sexual harassment claim under Title VII consists of five elements: (1) plaintiff belongs to protected group; (2) she was subjected to unwelcome sexual harassment; (3) harassment complained of was based on sex; (4) harassment affected term, condition, or privilege of her employment; and (5) employer knew or should have known of harassment and failed to take prompt remedial action.[3]

While this legislation does not explicitly articulate types of sexual harassment, courts have distinguished two specific examples: quid pro quo and hostile work environment.

Quid pro quo harassment typically occurs when a supervisor or someone in a position of authority requests sex, or a sexual relationship, in exchange for not firing or otherwise punishing the employee, or in exchange for favors, such as promotions, raises, re-assignment, or change in benefits. A hostile work environment is generally considered to result from the presence of demeaning or sexual photos, jokes, or threats. The terms quid pro quo and hostile work environment are helpful, perhaps, in making a rough demarcation between cases in which threats are carried out and those where they are not or are absent altogether.[4]

The effects of these types of harassment have been further distinguished, with court decisions providing useful guidance as to the nature of the claim. For example, in hostile work environment cases, courts have noted that the environment must be both objectively and subjectively offensive, one that a reasonable person would find hostile or abusive, and one that the victim in fact did perceive to be so.[5] This assessment is made by looking at all the circumstances, including the frequency of the discriminatory conduct; its severity; and whether it is physically threatening or humiliating, as opposed to a merely offensive. The key is whether it unreasonably interferes with an employee's work performance. Thus, Title VII does not prohibit simple teasing, offhand comments, and isolated incidents (unless extremely serious). These will not amount to discriminatory changes in the "terms and conditions of employment."[6]

Significantly, the *Faragher* decision established that an employer is subject to vicarious liability to a victimized employee for an actionable hostile environment created by a supervisor with immediate (or successively higher) authority over the employee. When no tangible employment action is taken, the employer may raise an affirmative defense to liability or damages, subject to proof by a preponderance of the evidence. No affirmative defense is available, however, when the supervisor's harassment culminates in a tangible employment action, such as discharge, demotion, or undesirable reassignment.[7] The *Burlington* decision further articulated the significance of this principle. It stated "tangible employment actions are the means by which the supervisor brings the official power of the enterprise to bear on subordinates." A tangible employment decision requires an official act of the enterprise. Stated another way, it requires a company action. The decision in most cases is documented in official company records, and may be subject to review by higher-level supervisors. In this sense, the supervisor often must obtain the imprimatur of the enterprise and use its internal processes.[8]

Principles and Inquiries

Certain principles derived from relevant court decisions can be useful in evaluating sexual harassment claims:[9] In such cases, the following issues should be considered:

1. If the harassment came from someone other than a supervisor, can the plaintiff show that the employer had specific knowledge and that the employer failed to take corrective action?
2. Regardless of the source of the harassment, did employer conduct a prompt, objective, and thorough investigation?
3. Did the alleged harassment unreasonably interfere with the employee's work performance?
4. Was the severity of the harassing behavior sufficient to be considered actionable?
5. How did the victim conduct himself or herself and what was the context of the harassment?
6. Has an adverse employment action occurred?
7. The size and the nature of the business involved may affect the amount of damages and even whether liability exists.
8. Sexual harassment can be actionable by people of the same sex.

Employer Defenses

From these questions and considerations, certain defenses available to the employer may be applicable, such as the following:[10]

1. An unwelcome advance is usually not considered pervasive behavior.
2. Employer took reasonable steps to prevent the harassment.
3. Employer took immediate remedial measures to correct the harassing behavior.
4. Employee did not take advantage of remedial measures.
5. Employee did not timely complain about the alleged harassment.
6. Employer conducted timely, thorough, and fair investigation.

Due to the fact that sexual harassment cases were summarized in both this chapter and in other chapters under different legal theories, this chapter will present only a few cases for review. For additional cases, please see the endnotes at the end of this chapter, or look to cases in other chapters.

CASES

36 Cal. 4th 446, 115 P. 3d 77

Supreme Court of California

EDNA MILLER ET AL., PLAINTIFFS AND APPELLANTS v. DEPARTMENT OF CORRECTIONS, ET AL., DEFENDANTS AND RESPONDENTS.

July 18, 2005

Background

Female employees of California Department of Corrections filed complaint against Department and its director, alleging claims of sex discrimination as articulated under the California Fair Employment and Housing Act (FEHA). The Superior Court, Sacramento County, granted summary judgment in favor of Department and director. Employees appealed. The court of appeal affirmed, and the supreme court granted review.

Holdings

The California Supreme Court held that triable issue of fact existed, precluding summary judgment, whether warden's favoritism to three other subordinate woman employees with whom he had sexual affairs constituted sexual harassment. Judgment of the court of appeal reversed and matter remanded.

For the reasons explained below, we conclude that, although an isolated instance of favoritism on the part of a supervisor toward a female employee with whom the supervisor is conducting a consensual sexual affair ordinarily would not constitute sexual harassment, when such sexual favoritism in a workplace is sufficiently widespread it may create an actionable hostile work environment in which the demeaning message is conveyed to female employees that they are viewed by management as "sexual playthings" or that the way required for women to get ahead in the workplace is by engaging in sexual conduct with their supervisors or the management.

Plaintiff Edna Miller began working for the Department as a correctional officer in 1983. In 1994, while she was employed at the Central California Women's Facility (CCWF), she heard from other employees of the Department that the chief deputy warden of the facility, Lewis Kuykendall, was having sexual affairs with his secretary, Kathy Bibb, and with another subordinate, associate warden Debbie Patrick. In her declaration, Miller stated that she often heard Kuykendall at work arguing with Patrick concerning his relationship with Bibb. Another Department employee at CCWF, Cagie Brown, told Miller that she, too, was having an affair with Kuykendall. Brown admitted in her deposition that her affair with Kuykendall began at CCWF in 1994.

In 1994, plaintiff Miller complained to Kuykendall's superior officer at the CCWF, Warden Tina Farmon, about what she considered the "inappropriate situation" created by Kuykendall's relationships with Bibb, Brown, and Patrick. Farmon informed Miller that she had addressed the issue.

In February 1995, the Department transferred plaintiff Miller to the Valley State Prison for Women (VSPW), where Kuykendall now served as warden. In May 1995, Miller served on an interview committee that evaluated Bibb's application for a promotion to the position of correctional counselor, a position that would entail a transfer to VSPW. When the interviewing panel did not select Bibb, Miller and other members of the panel were informed by an associate warden that Kuykendall wanted them to "make it happen." Miller declared: "This was ... the first of many incidents which caused me to lose faith in the system ... and to feel somewhat powerless because of Kuykendall and his sexual relations with subordinates." There was evidence Bibb had bragged to plaintiff Mackey of her power over the warden, and a departmental internal affairs investigation later concluded Kuykendall's personal relationship with Bibb rendered his involvement in her promotion unethical.

Bibb's promotion was awarded despite the opposition of Patrick, who by now *also* had been transferred to VSPW. Miller believed that, as a result of Patrick's sexual affair with Kuykendall, Patrick had been awarded the transfer to VSPW and enjoyed unusual privileges, such as reporting directly to Kuykendall rather than to her immediate superior. Miller confronted Brown, who now *also* was employed at VSPW, concerning Brown's affair with Kuykendall. Brown, admitting the affair, bragged about her power over Kuykendall and stated her intention to use this power to extract benefits from him. Another Department employee, Frances Gantong, confirmed that, prior to Brown's transfer to VSPW, Brown told Gantong that Kuykendall promised to secure Brown's transfer to VSPW and to aid in her promotion to the position of facility captain. Miller also claimed Brown received special assignments and work privileges from Kuykendall, and Kuykendall's secretary, Sandra Tripp, agreed with this assessment.

In July 1995, Brown and Miller competed for a promotion to a temporary post as facility captain at VSPW. Brown announced to Miller that Kuykendall would be forced to give her, Brown, the promotion or she would "take him down" with her knowledge of "every scar on his body." Kuykendall served on the interview panel, conduct that the departmental internal affairs investigation report later branded unethical because of his sexual relationship with Brown. Brown received the promotion, despite

Miller's higher rank, superior education, and greater experience. According to Miller's deposition, the officers involved in the selection process expressed surprise that Brown had been promoted, because they had recommended Miller for the higher position, and these officers and other employees commented to Miller that Brown's selection was unfair. According to plaintiff's estranged husband, William Miller, also a Department employee, many employees were upset by Brown's promotion. They attributed the promotion to the sexual affair between Kuykendall and Brown, believing Brown to be unqualified. Brown and Miller later competed for promotion to a permanent facility captain position, and Brown again secured the promotion.

Within a year and a half, Brown was promoted to the position of associate warden, a pace of promotion that was unusually rapid. Kuykendall again served on the interview panel. Miller's failure to be promoted to the position of facility captain made her ineligible to compete for higher-ranking positions, and Brown became her direct supervisor. According to Cooper, the internal affairs investigator, William Miller informed Cooper that other employees were outraged by the pace of Brown's promotions and "employees were saying things like, what do I have to do, 'F' my way to the top?"

Miller stated in her deposition that she was afraid of complaining, because of the adverse employment actions taken against two other female employees who had complained concerning the warden's affairs, Frances Gantong and Sandra Tripp. Department employees were aware of all three of Kuykendall's sexual affairs at CCWF and VSPW, according to the Department's internal affairs investigation and the declarations and deposition testimony of employees. The internal affairs report noted that, as to Bibb and Brown, "both relationships were viewed by staff as unethical from a business practice standpoint and one [*sic*] that created a hostile working environment." During his investigation, internal affairs investigator Cooper encountered several employees who believed that persons who had sexual affairs with Kuykendall received special employment benefits. In her deposition, Cagie Brown acknowledged that there were widespread rumors that sexual affairs between subordinates and their superior officers were "common practice in the Department of Corrections" and that there were rumors that employees, including Bibb, secured promotion in this way.

Kuykendall conceded he had danced with Bibb at work-related social gatherings and there was evidence he telephoned her at home hundreds of times from his workplace. Employees, including Mackey and Miller, witnessed Bibb and Kuykendall fondling each other on at least three occasions at work-related social gatherings occurring between 1991 and 1998 where employees of the institution were present. One Department employee, Phyllis Mellott, also complained that at such a gathering Kuykendall had put his arms around her and another employee and made unwelcome groping gestures. Kuykendall was present with Bibb in

1998 when she was arrested for driving under the influence of alcohol, a circumstance of which Miller and other employees were aware. Kuykendall failed to initiate an internal affairs investigation concerning the incident or report his own involvement. He also conceded he had heard complaints that Patrick received favorable treatment because of her relationship with him.

Plaintiffs presented evidence that the three women who were having sexual affairs with Kuykendall—Patrick, Bibb, and Brown—squabbled over him, sometimes in emotional scenes witnessed by other employees, including Miller.

Miller experienced additional difficulties when chief deputy warden Vicky Yamamoto arrived at VSPW and interfered with Miller's direct access to the warden. Miller initially believed the conflict between the two women was not gender based, but came to believe that Yamamoto's subsequent interference with Miller's authority occurred because Miller had refused dinner invitations that Yamamoto did not extend to male employees. Miller refused these invitations because she had heard that Yamamoto was a lesbian, and Miller assumed Yamamoto's interest in her was sexual. Rumors circulated among prison employees that Yamamoto and Brown were engaged in a relationship that was "more than platonic."

According to Miller, in 1997, during a peer review audit at another prison, Miller complained to Gerald Harris, a chief deputy warden at the facility who also served as a sexual harassment advisor for the Department, concerning Kuykendall's sexual relationship with Brown and Brown's close relationship with Yamamoto, adding that Yamamoto was disrupting the work of the institution and that Kuykendall had not disciplined Yamamoto. In her declaration, plaintiff Miller stated she informed Harris that "I felt I was working in a hostile environment based on the sexual relationship between Brown and Kuykendall and the close relationship between Brown and Yamamoto." Following her meeting with Harris, Miller complained to Kuykendall concerning Brown and Yamamoto's interference with her duties.

According to Miller, after her complaint to Kuykendall, Brown and Yamamoto made Miller's work life miserable and diminished her effectiveness by frequently countermanding her orders, undermining her authority, reducing her supervisorial responsibilities, imposing additional onerous duties on her, making unjustified criticisms of her work, and threatening her with reprisals when she complained to Kuykendall about their interference.

In September 1997, Miller telephoned Brown to confront Brown concerning her relationship with Kuykendall and to complain about the mistreatment she had suffered at the hands of Brown and Yamamoto. During this conversation, which Miller permitted Mackey and others to overhear, Brown acknowledged that Yamamoto was heaping unjustified abuse on Miller and that Kuykendall was aware of Yamamoto's mistreatment of Miller but would do nothing to rectify the situation. Miller subsequently informed Cooper, the internal affairs investigator that during this telephone conversation Miller had threatened to make a public announcement concerning the affair between Brown and Kuykendall.

The next day, Brown accused Miller of tape recording their telephone conversation. Brown entered Miller's office, ordered plaintiff Mackey (Miller's assistant) to leave, and then physically assaulted Miller, holding her captive for two hours. When Mackey went to Yamamoto to secure assistance for Miller, Yamamoto did not intervene. When Miller reported the affray to Kuykendall and threatened to report his relationship with Brown to higher authorities within the Department, Kuykendall responded that no one would believe her. Kuykendall told Miller to take time off from work and that upon her return she would not be required to report to Brown or Yamamoto. He subsequently awarded her a promotion. Kuykendall failed to investigate the assault after Miller complained to him. The internal affairs investigation concluded that Brown had committed assault and false imprisonment and that Kuykendall's failure to intervene or to discipline Brown constituted a violation of Department policy.

Brown and Yamamoto continued to interfere with Miller's work. Miller made further complaints to Kuykendall in 1998, eventually stating she planned to file a harassment complaint. Kuykendall explained there was nothing he could do about the harassment, because of his relationship with Brown and Brown's relationship with Yamamoto. He complained of Brown's untrustworthiness, stating he was "finished" with Brown and adding, "I should have chosen you." Miller understood these words to mean "he should have chosen me to have a relationship with," explaining, "I knew what he meant. He didn't say what, but he meant as a relationship. That's what I took it as." When Miller announced she intended to file a harassment complaint against Kuykendall for his failure to control Brown and Yamamoto, Kuykendall advised her not to do so, stating she would only cause an ugly scandal. Miller continued that thereafter, "[p]retty much the institution was exploding ... everybody was basically taking complaints to Mr. Kuykendall, and that's when [the Office of Internal Affairs] came into the institution."

Miller stated that she joined three other employees early in 1998 in complaining confidentially to Lewis Jones, Kuykendall's superior officer and the Department's regional administrator, concerning Yamamoto (and Kuykendall's failure to curtail Yamamoto's abuse of Miller), stating that the "institution was out of control." She recalled that Jones stated "he was dealing with Mr. Kuykendall on the disruption of the institution," but Miller did not observe any follow-up. She did not complain to Jones specifically about sexual harassment.

Later in 1998, regional administrator Jones recommended a departmental Office of Internal Affairs investigation, which, as noted above, began investigating misconduct on the part of Kuykendall, Yamamoto, and Brown. Miller was required to cooperate, and she informed investigating officer Cooper of Kuykendall's sexual affairs with Brown, Bibb, and

Patrick, and of the substance of Brown's statements to her. Despite Cooper's assurance of confidentiality, Miller soon found that Brown was aware of Miller's statements, and Brown began a campaign of ostracism against Miller. According to Miller's declaration and deposition testimony, Yamamoto also harassed Miller with unannounced inspections and interference with her orders; Kuykendall withdrew accommodations that previously had been accorded Miller because of a physical disability, and even the inmates appeared to believe that Miller had attempted to have Kuykendall's employment terminated. On one occasion, Brown angrily confronted Miller about her statements to the internal affairs investigator, would not allow Miller to terminate the conversation, and followed Miller home to continue the harangue. Upon Miller's complaint, a court order issued requiring Brown to stay away from Miller.

Miller suffered increasing stress and resigned from the Department on August 5, 1998. She filed a government tort claim with the Department in November 1998, followed by a complaint with the Department of Fair Employment and Housing in March 1999. She filed her complaint in superior court on June 15, 1999. As a result of the internal affairs investigation, Kuykendall retired, Yamamoto was transferred and demoted, and Brown resigned with disciplinary proceedings pending.

Plaintiff Frances Mackey joined the Department in 1975 as a clerk and received a number of promotions. She was transferred to VSPW in 1996 as a records manager, with the promise that she would continue to receive "inmate pay" (which apparently comprised certain enhanced salary benefits that emanate from handling inmates directly). At her interview for the new position, she announced her ambition to be promoted to a position as a correctional counselor. Kuykendall told her if she improved the VSPW records office, he would award her such a promotion.

Mackey was aware of Kuykendall's sexual affairs with Bibb and Brown. In July 1997, Mackey learned that Brown, then associate warden of VSPW, believed Mackey had complained to Kuykendall concerning the sexual affair he was having with Brown. Mackey's supplemental "inmate pay" was withdrawn. Brown also subjected Mackey to verbal abuse in the presence of coworkers. Mackey believed these actions constituted a warning not to disclose the affair between Kuykendall and Brown. Mackey was certain that Brown was promoted to the position of associate warden not because of merit, but because of her sexual affair with Kuykendall. Mackey claimed Brown demeaned her in the presence of other employees and impeded the execution of Mackey's duties in various respects, and stated: "This situation created hostility among the employees in [Mackey's] Department." As observed by the Court of Appeal, "[t]he environment around the office became increasingly hostile because of Kuykendall's inability to control Brown." Mackey "felt powerless to take any action about the situation." Mackey was persuaded not to jeopardize her career, having observed the termination of the employment of another woman who had complained about Kuykendall's "improper affair." In September

1997, Mackey overheard Brown's telephone call to Miller and the next day observed Brown's physical assault on Miller. Mackey attempted to intervene to assist Miller. Miller told Mackey the assault occurred after she informed Brown she planned to complain concerning Brown's relationship with Kuykendall and "how it was affecting her career." Brown continued to demean Mackey in the presence of other employees and to interfere with the execution of her duties.

According to Mackey, correctional employee Greg Mellott told Mackey that his wife, also a correctional employee, had heard arguments between Bibb and Brown concerning Kuykendall. In her declaration, Mackey stated that "Greg Mellott revealed to me that the sexual relationships Kuykendall was having with Bibb and Brown [were] creating an impossible environment for his wife to work in" and that his wife had filed a complaint "about the improper practices she experienced in her employment."

Mackey was assured that her statements to the internal affairs investigator would be kept confidential, but they were not. Kuykendall subsequently reduced her responsibilities and denied her access to the work experience she needed in order to be promoted to the position of correctional counselor. Mackey testified in her deposition that she believed she failed to receive a promotion to that position because she was not sexually involved with Kuykendall.

In addition, Brown repeatedly interrogated Mackey about her statements to the internal affairs investigator and attempted to contact Mackey outside of work. Stress led to health problems, and Mackey was unable to work between August 1998 and January 1999. Upon her return to work, Mackey was demoted and suffered further mistreatment and humiliation. A few months later she resigned, finding the conditions of employment intolerable. Mackey filed a government tort claim with the Department in February 1999 and filed a complaint with the Department of Fair Employment and Housing in March 1999. Mackey joined Miller in filing suit on June 15, 1999, alleging, among other claims, sexual discrimination and retaliation in violation of the FEHA.

Past California decisions have established that the prohibition against sexual harassment includes protection from a broad range of conduct, ranging from expressly or impliedly conditioning employment benefits on submission to or tolerance of unwelcome sexual advances, to the creation of a work environment that is hostile or abusive on the basis of sex. Such a hostile environment may be created even if the plaintiff never is subjected to sexual advances. In one case, for example, a cause of action based upon a hostile environment was stated when the plaintiff alleged she had been subjected to long-standing ridicule, insult, threats, and especially exacting work requirements by male coworkers who evidently resented a female employee's entry into a position in law enforcement.

We have agreed with the United States Supreme Court that, to prevail, an employee claiming harassment based upon a hostile work environment must demonstrate that the conduct complained of was severe enough or sufficiently pervasive to alter the conditions of employment and create a work environment that qualifies as hostile or abusive to employees because of their sex. The working environment must be evaluated in light of the totality of the circumstances:

> [W]hether an environment is "hostile" or "abusive" can be determined only by looking at all the circumstances.... These may include the frequency of the discriminatory conduct; its severity; whether it is physically threatening or humiliating, or a mere offensive utterance; and whether it unreasonably interferes with an employee's work performance.

The United States Supreme Court has warned that the evidence in a hostile environment sexual harassment case should not be viewed too narrowly:

> The objective severity of harassment should be judged from the perspective of a reasonable person in the plaintiff's position, considering "all the circumstances." That inquiry requires careful consideration of the social context in which particular behavior occurs and is experienced by its target.... The real social impact of workplace behavior often depends on a constellation of surrounding circumstances, expectations, and relationships which are not fully captured by a simple recitation of the words used or the physical acts performed. Common sense, and an appropriate sensibility to social context, will enable courts and juries to distinguish between simple teasing or roughhousing ... and conduct which a reasonable person in the plaintiff's position would find severely hostile or abusive.

Our courts frequently turn to federal authorities interpreting Title VII of the Civil Rights Act. Although the FEHA [state statute] explicitly prohibits sexual harassment of employees, while Title VII does not, the two enactments share the common goal of preventing discrimination in the workplace. Federal courts agree with guidelines established by the Equal Employment Opportunity Commission, the agency charged with administering Title VII, in viewing sexual harassment as constituting sexual discrimination in violation of Title VII. In language comparable to that found in FEHA regulations, federal regulatory guidelines define sexual harassment as including unwelcome sexual advances, requests for sexual favors, and other verbal or physical conduct of a sexual nature that has the "purpose or effect of unreasonably interfering with an individual's work performance or creating an intimidating, hostile, or offensive working environment."

A lengthy policy statement issued by the EEOC has examined the question of sexual favoritism, relying in part upon a number of federal court decisions that have considered the kind of harassment claim brought by plaintiffs, namely one based principally on the favoritism shown by supervisors to employees who are the supervisors' sexual partners. In its 1990 policy statement, the EEOC observed that, although isolated instances of sexual favoritism in the workplace do not violate Title VII, widespread sexual favoritism may create a hostile work environment in violation of Title VII by sending the demeaning message that managers view female employees as "sexual playthings" or that "the way for women to get ahead in the workplace is by engaging in sexual conduct." We believe the policy statement provides a useful guide in evaluating the issue before us.

The EEOC policy statement is entitled Policy Guidance on Employer Liability under Title VII for Sexual Favoritism. The policy statement begins with an explanation that "an *isolated* instance of favoritism toward a 'paramour' (or a spouse, or a friend) may be unfair, but it does not discriminate against women or men in violation of Title VII, since both are disadvantaged for reasons other than their genders. A female charging party who is denied an employment benefit because of such sexual favoritism would not have been treated more favorably had she been a man, nor, conversely, was she treated less favorably because she was a woman."

The EEOC also discusses sexual favoritism that is more than isolated and that is based upon consensual affairs:

> If favoritism based upon the granting of sexual favors is widespread in a workplace, both male and female colleagues who do not welcome this conduct can establish a hostile work environment in violation of Title VII regardless of whether any objectionable conduct is directed at them and regardless of whether those who were granted favorable treatment willingly bestowed the sexual favors. In these circumstances, a message is implicitly conveyed that the managers view women as "sexual playthings," thereby creating an atmosphere that is demeaning to women. Both men and women who find this offensive can establish a violation if the conduct is "sufficiently severe or pervasive" to alter the conditions of [their] employment and create an abusive working environment.

An analogy can be made to a situation in which supervisors in an office regularly make racial, ethnic or sexual jokes. Even if the targets of the humor "play along" and in no way display that they object, coworkers of any race, national origin or sex can claim that this conduct, which communicates a bias against protected class members, creates a hostile work environment for them.

In addition, according to the EEOC, "managers who engage in widespread sexual favoritism may also communicate a message that the way for women to get ahead in the workplace is by engaging in sexual conduct or that sexual solicitations are a prerequisite to their fair treatment. This can form the basis of an implicit 'quid pro quo' harassment claim for female employees, as well as a hostile environment claim for both women and men who find this offensive."

Following the guidance of the EEOC, and also employing standards adopted in our prior cases, we believe that an employee may establish an actionable claim of sexual harassment under the FEHA by demonstrating that widespread sexual favoritism was severe or pervasive enough to alter his or her working conditions and create a hostile work environment. Furthermore, applying this standard to the circumstances of the present case, we conclude that the evidence proffered by plaintiffs, viewed in its entirety, established a prima facie case of sexual harassment under a hostile-work-environment theory. As we shall explain, a trier of fact reasonably could find from the evidence in the record set forth below that a hostile work environment was created in the workplace in question.

Over a period of several years, Warden Kuykendall engaged concurrently in sexual affairs with three subordinate employees, Bibb, Patrick, and Brown. There was evidence these affairs began in 1991 and continued until 1998. The affairs occurred first while Kuykendall and the women worked at CCWF, then continued when these individuals all transferred to VSPW. Kuykendall served in a management capacity at both institutions and served as warden at VSPW. When Kuykendall transferred from CCWF to VSPW, there was evidence he caused his sexual partners to be transferred to the new institution to join him. There was evidence Kuykendall promised and granted unwarranted and unfair employment benefits to the three women. One of the unfair employment benefits granted to Brown evidently was the power to abuse other employees who complained concerning the affairs. When plaintiffs complained, they suffered retaliation (and they believed two other employees were similarly targeted). Kuykendall refused to intervene and himself retaliated by withdrawing previously granted accommodations for Miller's disability after she cooperated with the internal affairs investigation.

Further, there was evidence that advancement for women at VSPW was based upon sexual favors, not merit. For example, Kuykendall pressured Miller and other employees on the personnel selection committee to agree to transfer Bibb to VSPW and promote her to the position of correctional counselor, despite the conclusion of the committee that she was not eligible or qualified. Committee members were told to set aside their professional judgment because Kuykendall wanted them to "make it happen."

In addition, on two occasions Kuykendall promoted Brown to facility captain positions in preference to Miller, although Miller was more qualified. Brown enjoyed an unprecedented pace of promotion to the managerial position of associate warden, causing outraged employees to ask such questions as, "What do I have to do, 'F' my way to the top?" Even Brown acknowledged that affairs between supervisors and subordinates were common in the Department and were widely viewed as a method of advancement. Indeed, Brown made it known to Miller that the facility captain promotion belonged to her because of her intimate relationship with Kuykendall, announcing that if she were not awarded the promotion she would "take him [Kuykendall] down" because she "knew every scar on his body."

There also was evidence that Kuykendall promoted Bibb from clerical to correctional staff duties despite her lack of qualifications, and at the same time refused to permit Mackey to secure the on-the-job training that would have enabled her to make a similar advance. On the basis of her knowledge of Kuykendall's sexual affairs, Mackey believed the reason he denied her this opportunity was that she was not his sexual partner.

The evidence suggested Kuykendall viewed female employees as "sexual playthings" and that his ensuing conduct conveyed this demeaning message in a manner that had an effect on the work force as a whole. Various employees, including plaintiffs, observed Kuykendall and Bibb fondling one another on at least three occasions at work-related social gatherings. One employee reported that Kuykendall had placed his arm around her and another female employee during one such social event, adding that Kuykendall had engaged in unwelcome fondling of her as well. Bibb and Brown bragged to other employees, including plaintiffs, of their power to extort benefits from Kuykendall.

Jealous scenes between the sexual partners occurred in the presence of Miller and other employees. Several employees informed the internal affairs investigator that persons who were engaged in sexual affairs with Kuykendall received special benefits. When Miller last complained to Kuykendall, he told her that Brown was manipulative, adding he was "finished" with Brown and should have chosen Miller—a comment Miller reasonably took to mean that he should have chosen Miller for a sexual affair.

There was evidence Kuykendall's sexual favoritism not only blocked the way to merit-based advancement for plaintiffs, but also caused them to be subjected to harassment at the hands of Brown, whose behavior Kuykendall refused or failed to control even after it escalated to physical assault. This harassment, apparently retaliatory, included loss of work responsibilities, demeaning comments in the presence of other employees, loss of entitlement to a pay enhancement and to disability accommodation, and physical assault and false imprisonment. Kuykendall explained to Miller that, because of his intimate relationship with Brown, he would not protect plaintiffs. In this manner, his sexual favoritism was responsible for the continuation of an outrageous campaign of harassment against plaintiffs.

Considering all the circumstances "from the perspective of a reasonable person in the plaintiff's position" and noting that the present case is before us on appeal after a grant of summary judgment, we conclude that the foregoing evidence created at least a triable issue of fact on the question whether Kuykendall's conduct constituted sexual favoritism widespread enough to constitute a hostile work environment in which the "message [was] implicitly conveyed that the managers view women as sexual playthings" or that "the way for women to get ahead in the workplace is by engaging in sexual conduct" thereby "creating an atmosphere that is demeaning to women." In terms we previously have borrowed from the United States Supreme Court in measuring sexual harassment claims, there was evidence of "sufficiently severe or pervasive" conduct that "altered the conditions of [the victims'] employment" such that a jury reasonably could conclude that the conduct created a work environment that qualifies as hostile or abusive to employees because of their gender.

We believe it is clear under California law that a plaintiff may establish a hostile work environment without demonstrating the existence of coercive sexual conduct directed at the plaintiff or even conduct of a sexual nature. Finally, we believe that even those courts focusing on a "sexually charged environment" would be satisfied that a triable issue of fact was presented by the evidence in this case, in view of the bragging, squabbling, and fondling that occurred.

To the extent defendants' contention is that a reasonable person in plaintiffs' position would not have found the work environment to have been hostile toward women on the basis of widespread sexual favoritism, we conclude that the lower courts erred in precluding plaintiffs from presenting this issue to a jury. The internal affairs investigation within the Department confirmed that Kuykendall's sexual favoritism occurred and was broadly known and resented in the workplace, and that several employees—including Brown—concluded that engaging in sexual affairs was the way required to secure advancement. There was evidence from which a jury reasonably could conclude that the entire scheme of promotion at VSPW was affected by Kuykendall's favoritism.

Certainly, the presence of mere office gossip is insufficient to establish the existence of widespread sexual favoritism, but the evidence of such favoritism in the present case includes admissions by the participants concerning the nature of the relationships, boasting by the favored women, eyewitness accounts of incidents of public fondling, repeated promotion despite lack of qualifications, and Kuykendall's admission he could not control Brown because of his sexual relationship with her—a matter confirmed by the Department's internal affairs report. Indeed, it is ironic that, according to defendants, a jury should not be permitted to consider evidence of widespread sexual favoritism that the Department itself found convincing.

Finally, defendants warn that plaintiffs' position, if adopted, would inject the courts into relationships that are private and consensual and that occur within a major locus of individual social life for both men and women—the workplace. According to defendants, social policy favors rather than disfavors such relationships, and the issue of personal privacy should give courts pause before allowing claims such as those advanced by plaintiffs to proceed. Defendants urge it is safer to treat sexual favoritism as merely a matter of personal preference, and to recall that the FEHA is not intended to regulate sexual relationships in the workplace, nor to establish a civility code governing that venue.

We do not believe that defendants' concerns about regulating personal relationships are well founded, because it is not the relationship, but its effect on the workplace, that is relevant under the applicable legal standard. Thus, we have not discussed those interactions between Kuykendall and his sexual partners that were truly private. Moreover, the FEHA already clearly contemplates some intrusion into personal relationships. Specifically the FEHA recognizes that sexual harassment occurs when a sexual relationship between a supervisor and a subordinate is based upon an asserted quid pro quo.

For the foregoing reasons, the judgment of the court of appeal is reversed to the extent it is inconsistent with our opinion, and the matter is remanded to the court of appeal for further proceedings consistent with this opinion.

CASE COMMENT

In this factually specific case, the court found that the series of sexual liaisons between Kuykendall and his female subordinates were sufficient to state a claim of sexual harassment initiated by another female employee. While the plaintiff was not part of the sexual affairs within the workplace, she could sustain a claim of sexual harassment against her employer. In reaching this decision, the court placed great emphasis on the affect of the sexuality within the workplace. Specifically, the message it conveyed to female employees is that they are viewed by management as "sexual playthings" or that the way required for women to get ahead in the workplace is by engaging in sexual conduct with their supervisors or the management. This sexually charged environment was deemed to have a sufficient factual basis to send the case to the jury. Thus, in a rather novel case, the court held the plaintiff could sustain a sexual harassment claim when she was not a target of the harassment or a participant in the sexual relations.

417 F. Supp. 2d 85

United States District Court, D. Massachusetts

MARY NEWELL, PLAINTIFF v. CELADON SECURITY SERVICES, INC., KEITH GREEN, RODNEY BUTLER, AND ABEDEKADER KOUIDRI, DEFENDANTS.

Jan. 17, 2006

Background

Former security guard sued former employer under Title VII and Massachusetts antidiscrimination statute, alleging sexual harassment and retaliation. Former employer moved for summary judgment.

Holdings

The district court held that:

1. Alleged harasser was not supervisor under doctrine of apparent authority;
2. Employer was not liable for any sexual harassment committed by alleged harasser as coworker; and
3. Security guard's transfer to another site was not adverse employment action.

Motion allowed.

Celadon is in the business of providing security services to various clients, primarily by providing uniformed security officers at the client's facilities. Newell was employed by Celadon as a security guard from December 2000 until May 18, 2001. Her immediate supervisor was the defendant Rodney Butler, who gave her work assignments. However, he did not work with her at her specific assignments.

The defendant Abedekader Kouidri was another employee of Celadon who worked as a security officer. At no time did Kouidri have any supervisory authority with respect to any other employee of Celadon, including Newell. As detailed, however, Newell contends that she thought that he was a supervisor. Prior to the incident which forms the basis of the instant litigation, Celadon had never received any complaints about Kouidri from any other employee or client alleging sexual harassment or any other type of discriminatory conduct.

As of May 2001, Celadon had at least 150 security officers and provided security to over 30 separate facilities. The security officers were routinely transferred to different facilities. At the start of her employment with Celadon, Newell was given written "Employment Terms & Conditions" which expressly stated that "I also understand that I am not assigned to any one particular site and at the companies' [*sic*] discretion may be moved at any time." During her employment with Celadon, Newell worked at approximately a dozen locations. Celadon security officers were required to wear uniforms when they were on duty, while certain supervisors were required to wear suits. As security officers, Newell and Kouidri were required to wear uniforms during their shifts.

Celadon provides all new employees with written employment policies, which are included in a document entitled "Celadon Employment Terms & Conditions." This document includes Celadon's policies prohibiting discrimination.

Events of May 5, 2001

On May 5, 2001, Newell and Kouidri were working at One Kendall Square. Newell worked two shifts that day, and she describes the relevant event as follows.

During the second shift, I was asked by the older security guard on the site to accompany Kouidri on a tour of the building so that I would know what to do in case I had to work alone. During this tour, Kouidri brought me to the basement in a poorly lit area. Kouidri grabbed my breast. I pushed him away. He then pushed me against the wall and kissed me. Apparently, the rest of the shift was uneventful. Newell reported the incident to Celadon two days later, on May 7, 2001.

Newell does not dispute that Kouidri was not actually a supervisor. However, she contends that she believed he was a supervisor because he was in "street clothes," not in uniform, on May 5, 2001, as well as on the one previous occasion she had seen him, and because he had a walkie-talkie. According to Newell, Kouidri's street clothes were a sweater and pants, not a suit. Newell admits that she never asked whether Kouidri was her supervisor, and he never said that he was a supervisor. Newell does not contend that, on the day of the incident, Kouidri purported to exert any supervisory authority over her. On the one earlier occasion that she had seen him, Kouidri was walking around a construction site and she was located at a desk. When he passed her, Kouidri allegedly yelled at her and ordered her to return to her desk when she left her desk to get a soda. Additionally, he was very pushy. According to Newell, however, when Kouidri suggested that she change her location, she simply disregarded the suggestion.

Celadon's Response to Newell's Complaint

Newell completed her shift on May 5, 2001, and worked at the same facility on May 6, 2001 (Sunday) and May 7, 2001 (Monday). On May 7, 2001 she reported the incident to a supervisor Frank Doran, and her immediate supervisor Rodney Butler was also notified. At the time of the report, according to Celadon, Kouidri was on vacation, and he voluntarily resigned at the end of the vacation without responding to Celadon's request to discuss the incident. Celadon contends that it tried to discuss the incident with Newell, but that she failed to respond to various calls, which Newell denies.

It is undisputed that Newell was assigned to work at Marina Bay in Quincy, a first-class condominium complex, beginning on Tuesday, May 8, 2001, through Friday, May 11, 2001. Newell had worked there previously, on May 3, 2001, as well. It also is undisputed that her shift was 5:00 p.m. to midnight Tuesday through Thursday. Marina Bay was difficult to get to by public transportation, and impossible to get home from, and Newell did not have a car. Consequently, Rodney Butler arranged for another supervisor, Defendant Keith Green, to pick Plaintiff up at the end of the shift at Marina Bay to take her home to Dorchester. Mr. Green picked Newell up at approximately 11:30 p.m. Tuesday through Thursday, May 8 through 10, 2001, without incident, and drove her home. Celadon contends that, consistent with the Friday and Saturday night shifts at Marina Bay, Newell's shift on Friday, May 11, 2001, was to end at 1:00 a.m., not midnight. Newell contends that her shift was to end at midnight, that she waited for Mr. Green until 12:45 a.m. and that when he failed to pick her up she started to walk home. According to Newell, the phone at Marina Bay did not work. Although it was a residential complex, Newell apparently did not ask to use anyone's phone, but rather started to walk home from Quincy to Dorchester. The walk home was very frightening, and eventually Newell made her way to a nursing home where she called a friend and made arrangements to get home.

Newell claims that she does not know the reason for her transfer to another site following her complaint. Newell asserts, and Celadon disputes, that the transfer to Marina Bay was "disadvantageous to her" in that it was inaccessible by public transportation, Newell worked alone and had no operable phone, and there were no double shifts available for extra money. According to Newell, she was paid $8.50 per hour at Celadon, except for training, but she only received $6.50/hour at Marina Bay. However, Newell's payroll records establish that she was paid $8.50/hour at Marina Bay, too.

On Friday, May 18, 2001, Newell went to Celadon and resigned. She signed a Separation Form confirming that she had "no claims against Celadon or any of its employees." Nevertheless, Newell filed a complaint with the MCAD. The Commission was "unable to conclude that the information obtained establishes a violation of the [discrimination] statutes" and dismissed the complaint on September 16, 2003. Newell commenced the instant litigation on March 1, 2004.

Newell asserts that she was very traumatized by her experiences at Celadon, suffered a severe deterioration in her mental health condition and had to be hospitalized. Newell has suffered from a major mental illness since she was approximately 16 years old. As a result of the events at Celadon, Newell contends that she was unable to maintain regular employment for approximately one year. Additional facts will be provided below where appropriate.

Celadon's Liability for Sexual Harassment by Kouidri

Newell's claims are based on the alleged sexual harassment perpetrated against her by her coworker, Kouidri. Sexual harassment is unlawful under both federal and state law. Thus, Title VII of the Civil Rights Act of 1964 makes it "an unlawful employment practice for an employer ... to discriminate against any individual with respect to his compensation, terms, conditions, or privileges of employment, because of such individual's race, color, religion, sex, or national origin." 42 U.S.C. Section 2000e-2(a)(1).

The applicable standards for assessing an employer's liability for its employees' conduct depend upon whether the offending employee is a supervisor or simply a coworker. Where the offending employee is a supervisor, the federal and state laws differ. Under federal law, an employer is vicariously liable when a supervisor creates a hostile work environment, subject, however, to a possible affirmative defense, commonly known as the *Faragher/Ellerth* defense, based on the relevant Supreme Court cases. The *Faragher/Ellerth* defense, which is available in the absence of a tangible adverse job action, "consists of two elements which, if proven, permit the employer to avoid liability. First, the employer must show that it exercised reasonable care to prevent and correct promptly the harassment. Second, the employer must show that the employee unreasonably failed to take advantage of any preventive or corrective opportunities provided by the employer or to avoid harm otherwise." Under Massachusetts law, however, employers are "strictly liable for supervisory harassment" so the *Faragher/Ellerth* defense is not available.

When coworkers, rather than supervisors, are the perpetrators of sexual harassment, both Title VII and Mass. Gen. Laws ch. 151B, apply the same standard in assessing employer liability. In such circumstances, "an employer can only be liable if the harassment is causally connected to some negligence on the employer's part. Typically, [under federal law] this involves a showing that the employer knew or should have known about the harassment, yet failed to take prompt action to stop it. This court concludes that Kouidri cannot be deemed to be a supervisor, and, consequently, Celadon is not liable under a theory of strict liability. The record also fails to establish that Celadon is liable under the lesser standard applied to coworker harassment.

1. Kouidri's Status—Co-employee or Supervisor

"The key to determining supervisory status is the degree of authority possessed by the putative supervisor. Thus, courts must distinguish employees who are supervisors merely as a function of nomenclature from those who are entrusted with actual supervisory powers." The First Circuit, considering "both common law agency principles and the purposes of the anti-discrimination and anti-retaliation laws" has determined that "the essence of supervisory status is the authority to affect the terms and conditions of the victim's employment," with such authority consisting primarily "of the power to hire, fire, demote, promote, transfer, or discipline an employee." Without some modicum of this authority, a harasser cannot qualify as a supervisor for purposes of imputing vicarious liability to the employer in a Title VII case, but, rather, should be regarded as an ordinary coworker. The same standard is applicable under Massachusetts state law.

In the instant case, the record is clear that Celadon did not grant Kouidri any supervisory authority over any other employees, including Newell. Without belaboring the point, Kouidri had no authority to take any steps which would affect the terms or conditions of any co-employee's employment. Consequently, there is no strict liability on the basis that Kouidri was a supervisor as a matter of fact.

2. The Doctrine of Apparent Authority

An employee may be deemed to be a supervisor under the doctrine of apparent authority. Thus, as the Supreme Court recognized in *Ellerth*, the "scope of employment does not define the only basis for employer liability under agency principles. In limited circumstances, agency principles impose liability on employers even where employees commit torts outside the scope of employment. The principles are set forth in the much-cited Section 219(2) of the Restatement" of the Law, Second, Agency, which provides, in relevant part, that the "master" may be liable where: "the servant purported to act or to speak on behalf of the principal and there was reliance upon apparent authority, or he was aided in accomplishing the tort by the existence of the agency relation."

In the instant case, the factual record does not support Newell's conclusion that she believed that Kouidri was her supervisor, with the type of authority sufficient to impose liability on Celadon for his behavior. Even if the record was sufficient, such a belief would not be reasonable. Therefore, as a matter of law, the facts presented by Newell do not support a finding of apparent authority.

Kouidri Did Not Represent Himself As a Supervisor

The record is undisputed that Kouidri did not hold himself out as a supervisor. Newell testified that Kouidri had never indicated he was a supervisor.

Moreover, he did not wear a suit—the type of clothing commonly worn by supervisors at Celadon. As the above-quoted section of the Restatement makes clear, the servant must have "purported to act or to speak on behalf of the principal." Absent any recognition by Kouidri himself of his status as a "supervisor," Newell's mistaken belief as to his status is insufficient to establish liability on the part of Celadon.

Newell's Perceptions

As a factual matter, Newell's conclusory assertion that she believed Kouidri was a supervisor is insufficient to establish that he had the type of authority necessary to impose liability on the part of the employer. As detailed above, absent "some modicum" of authority to affect the terms and conditions of the victim's employment, such as "the power to hire, fire, demote, promote, transfer, or discipline an employee, ... a harasser cannot qualify as a supervisor for purposes of imputing vicarious liability to the employer ... but, rather, should be regarded as an ordinary coworker."

In the instant case, there is no evidence that Newell believed Kouidri could significantly influence the terms and conditions of her employment or that Kouidri attempted to do so. According to the plaintiff, her immediate supervisor, who gave her work assignments, was Rodney Butler. She describes Kouidri as "an employee of Celadon." On the date of the incident, another security guard asked Newell to accompany Kouidri on a tour. Thus, Kouidri did not direct Newell in any way in connection with taking the tour of the building, much less purport to exert supervisory authority over her in connection with taking the tour. Once in the basement, Kouidri allegedly exerted physical force against the plaintiff. There is no evidence that he tried to exhort her to submit to his authority or otherwise threaten to affect the terms or conditions of employment.

While Newell claims that she believed Kouidri was a supervisor, there is no evidence that she believed he had the power to control her employment with Celadon. Thus, the totality of the relevant facts proffered by the plaintiff is as follows:

I believed that Kouidri was a supervisor at Celadon. Kouidri wore street clothes instead of a security uniform like the security guards wore. I had seen Kouidri once before at the same site. Kouidri wore street clothes then as well. My experience at Celadon was that supervisors did not wear security uniforms.

Kouidri acted like a supervisor on the earlier occasion. At that time, when I left my desk to get a soda, Kouidri yelled at me and ordered me to return to my desk. He told me that I was supposed to sit there and stay there. He was very pushy. He acted like a supervisor. He also walked around with a walkie-talkie. I was never given a walkie-talkie by Celadon. At most, Kouidri was pushy—there is nothing in the record that distinguishes his conduct towards her from an annoyed coworker who felt his colleague was not attending to her responsibility.

Newell does not assert that she believed that Kouidri could hire, fire or promote her, alter her job assignments or otherwise affect the terms and conditions of her employment. Nor is there any evidence that she went on the tour with Kouidri because of her mistaken belief as to his status. In fact, Newell testified that on an earlier occasion when Kouidri made a suggestion as to where she should sit, she disregarded the suggestion. Obviously, she did not feel that Kouidri had the authority over her to even change the location of her seat, much less hire or fire her. The facts put forward by the plaintiff simply do not rise to the level of creating vicarious liability on the part of Celadon for the activities of an employee mistakenly believed to be a supervisor by a co-employee. Moreover, any mistaken belief by the employee would simply not be reasonable.

3. Celadon's Liability for Co-employee Harassment

As detailed above, under both federal and Massachusetts law, "an employer is liable for the sexual harassment perpetrated by an employee if it knew or should have known of the harassment, unless the employer can show it took appropriate steps to halt the harassment." The undisputed facts establish that Celadon had no prior complaints about Kouidri or any information that would have led the company to believe that he would act inappropriately toward Newell or any other person. Under such circumstances, Newell has failed to establish Celadon's liability for the wrongful conduct of its employee.

Moreover, to the extent that Celadon's response to the situation is relevant, it was "prompt and appropriate." The response "must be reasonably calculated to prevent further harassment under the particular facts and circumstances of the case at the time the allegations are made." Here, Newell and Kouidri were separated and did not work together again. Regardless whether there was a full investigation, Kouidri did not return to work and he was deemed not eligible for rehire. That was sufficient.

Newell's Claim of Retaliation

Newell contends that Celadon retaliated against her for complaining about Kouidri's behavior. Thus, she complains that she "was transferred by Celadon to a less advantageous assignment with lower pay. Celadon, despite its denial, failed to provide plaintiff with an operable telephone at the site. In addition, Celadon left plaintiff stranded at that remote site on her last date of work." Because Newell has failed to establish that she suffered an adverse job action or that the transfer was wrongfully motivated, summary judgment must be entered in favor of Celadon.

Retaliation for engaging in a protected activity such as complaining about sexual harassment is prohibited under both federal and state law. Thus, under Title VII:

It shall be an unlawful employment practice for an employer to discriminate against any of his employees ... because he has opposed any practice made an unlawful employment practice by this subchapter, or because he has made a charge, testified, assisted, or participated in any manner in an investigation, proceeding, or hearing under this subchapter.

1. Adverse Employment Action

"Prohibited retaliatory actions are those that constitute a change in working conditions that create a material disadvantage in the plaintiff's employment." Adverse employment actions include, but are not limited to, "demotions, disadvantageous transfers or assignments, refusals to promote, unwarranted negative job evaluations, and toleration of harassment by other employees." In each case, the action must have been motivated by a wrongful intent.

Here, Newell "has failed to offer facts indicating that [her] informal complaint caused any adverse actions." While she complains about Marina Bay being a less favorable locale, when she signed on as an employee of Celadon her conditions of employment specifically recognized the fact that she would be assigned to different locations. Newell had worked at Marina Bay before the incident, and it was a regular site for which Celadon provided security guards. To the extent that transportation home was a problem, Celadon provided her with transportation, and her contention that she was paid less at the Marina Bay site is simply not supported by the record. Moreover, even accepting as true Newell's claim that the phone did not work at Marina Bay, there is no evidence to support a conclusion that having an inoperable phone was intentional or that it was anything other than a short-term problem. It was clearly contrary to the best interest of Celadon to tolerate a situation where its personnel, who were hired to provide security, did not have access to backup help in case of an emergency.

In short, Newell has failed to establish that the transfer to Marina Bay was an adverse employment action. It is well established that "a transfer or reassignment that involves only minor changes in working conditions normally does not constitute an adverse employment action." "The evidence presented here showed—at most—that the transfer resulted in some minor, likely temporary, changes in [Newell's] working conditions." Since Newell failed to prove that Celadon "took any action against [her] at all which was substantial enough to count as the kind of material disadvantage that is a predicate for a finding of unlawful retaliation," her claim must fail. Her claims "amount to no more than subjective feelings of disappointment and disillusionment. [She] offered no objective evidence that [she] had been disadvantaged in respect to salary, grade, or other objective terms and conditions of employment."

Newell's claim must fail for the additional reason that she has failed to establish "a causal link between the tangible employment action and the alleged harassment and harasser." There is simply nothing in the record to support a conclusion that the transfer was in any way intended to punish Newell. Rather, serving at different locales was a regular part of her job and the Marina Bay location was regularly served by Celadon.

2. Retaliatory Hostile Environment

Newell's claim that Celadon failed to pick her up on Friday night after work does not alter this court's conclusion that the record is insufficient to establish retaliation. Reading the record in the light most favorable to Newell, the company agreed to and did provide transportation to her for several nights. On Friday night, her lift did not come. The company's explanation that there was a misunderstanding as to when Newell's shift ended is logical and has not been refuted by the plaintiff. There is nothing in the record from which a jury could logically infer that Celadon anticipated that Newell would walk home if her ride did not appear. As Marina Bay is a residential complex, not a deserted warehouse, there were other phones around, even if they were not convenient. To the extent that Newell claims that she was intentionally stranded, her conclusion is based solely on "improbable inferences, and unsupported speculation" which is insufficient to overcome a motion for summary judgment.

Even assuming Newell was intentionally stranded, the record does not support a conclusion that Newell was subjected to a retaliatory hostile work environment. An employer "will be liable for retaliation if it tolerates severe or pervasive harassment motivated by the plaintiff's protected conduct." Even assuming that Celadon intentionally failed to drive Newell home, this incident was not so "severe or pervasive that it alter[ed] the conditions of the plaintiff's employment." While there are circumstances where one incident may be so severe as to create a hostile work environment, this is not such a situation. This one event, for which Celadon has offered a logical explanation, is insufficient to establish wrongful conduct or intent on the part of the defendant.

This court does not doubt that Newell sincerely believes that Celadon acted for the purpose of causing her harm. However, her "subjective and intangible impressions" are insufficient to support a retaliation claim and cannot form the basis "for legal intervention in the often fraught and delicate domain of personnel relations."

Conclusion

The plaintiff has failed to establish that Celadon is liable for the wrongful conduct of its employee, Kouidri, and has failed to establish a claim of wrongful retaliation for her complaint about Kouidri. For all the reasons detailed herein, Celadon's Motion for Summary Judgment is ALLOWED.

CASE COMMENT

This case provides an excellent example of the distinction between of harassment by a supervisor and harassment by a coworker. Clearly, it is easier to exert liability against the employer if the harassment comes from a supervisor. The court assessed the legal standard for a "supervisor," noting that the individual must possess the power to hire, fire, demote, promote, transfer, or discipline an employee. The alleged harasser did not possess these powers. Indeed, the court held that based on the facts of this case, it would be unreasonable for the plaintiff to even perceive the alleged harasser had such powers. In addition, the court held that the transfer of the plaintiff was not an adverse employment action, and that the failure to give her a ride home was not retaliation for complaining of sexual harassment. Based on these reasons, the court affirmed summary judgment against the plaintiff.

DISCUSSION QUESTIONS

If a supervisor sexually harasses a subordinate, is the employer automatically liable? If not, what other factor(s) must the plaintiff show? Can an employer limit its exposure in a sexual harassment case in any way? If so, how? If a male subordinate gropes a female supervisor, can the employer be liable? Explain your answer in light of the relevant legal standards and principles.

NOTES

1. Fridkin, Michael K., and Cythina A. Wilson (2002). *Title VII and Section 1981: A Guide for Appointed Attorneys in the Northern District of Illinois,* provided by Chicago Lawyers' Committee for Civil Rights.
2. Rubin, Paula N. (1995). Civil Rights and Criminal Justice: A Primer on Sexual Harassment. *National Institute of Justice,* Office of Justice Programs, October.
3. See Civil Rights Act of 1964, Section 701 et seq., and 42 U.S.C.A. Section 2000e et seq.
4. *Burlington Industries, Inc. v. Kimberly B. Ellerth*, 524 U.S. 742 (1998).
5. *Beth Ann Faragher v. City of Boca Raton*, 524 U.S. 775 (1998).
6. Ibid.
7. Ibid.
8. See *Burlington Industries, Inc. v. Ellerth,* 524 U.S. 742 (1998).
9. See for example *Schwartz v. Bay Industries, Inc.,* 274 F. Supp. 1041 (2003); *Tutman v. WBBM-TV,* 209 F. 3d 1044 (2000); *Oncale v. Sundowner Offshore Services, Inc.,* 118 S. Ct. 998 (1998); and *Haugerud v. Amery School District,* 259 F. 3d 678 (2001) for application of these principles.
10. See above cases for these defenses plus two U.S. Supreme Court cases cited earlier.

Part Three

Agency and Contracts

AGENCY AND RESPONDEAT SUPERIOR

The common theme of these causes of action is that the "master," or employer, may be liable for the acts of the "servant," or employee. As will be discussed below, there are a number of factors that affect the liability exposure of these parties.

Agency is the relationship wherein one party (agent) is empowered to represent or act for another (principal) under the authority of the principal. According to the Restatement of Agency 2d, the definition of this relationship is as follows: "Agency is the fiduciary relation which results from the manifestation of consent by one person to another that the other shall act on his behalf and subject to his control, and consent by the other so to act."[1] The principal is the one for whom the action is to be taken, while the agent is the one who is to act on the principal's behalf.

Stated more formally, the master is a principal who employs an agent to perform service in his affairs and who controls or has the right to control the physical conduct of the other in the performance of the service. Conversely, the servant is an agent employed by a master to perform service in his affairs whose physical conduct in the performance of the service is controlled or is subject to the right of control by the master.[2] In essence, Agency is the delegation of some lawful business activity of the employer, with more or less discretionary power, to another. This delegation entails more than permission. It involves a request, instruction, or command to act on behalf of the principal (employer).

Key components of this relationship include the principal's right to select the agent, to discharge the agent, and to direct both the work and the manner in which the work is done. The basic elements of Agency are as follows:[3]

1. Manifestation by principal that the agent shall act in his or her behalf

2. Agent's acceptance of the undertaking
3. Understanding of the parties that the principal is in control of the undertaking

From the perspective of security, this agency relationship may expose either party to danger or dangerous conditions. Generally, a party owes no duty of care to protect another from the harmful or criminal acts of third persons. However, there are at least four exceptions to this rule: (1) when the parties are in a special relationship and the harm is foreseeable; (2) when an employee is in imminent danger and this is known to the employer; (3) when a principal fails to warn his agent of an unreasonable risk of harm involved in the agency; and (4) when any party voluntarily or contractually assumes a duty to protect another from the harmful acts of a third party.[4] If one of these exceptions is shown, then one of the parties, typically the principal, has a duty to care, or at least warn, the other party of the danger posed.

Respondeat superior is a related doctrine that literally means "let the master answer."[5] Typically, the master will have to answer for the acts of his servant. In essence, this doctrine would serve to shift liability for the actions of the servant to the master. This is because the servant was acting on behalf of the master. Logically this makes sense, because the master's liability stems from the servant acting in his behalf. Hence, the wrong or injury caused by the servant was imbued to the master because the servant acted on behalf of the master. In this sense, the doctrine applies only when the relation of master and servant existed at the time of the injury, and in respect to the transaction from which it arose. Stated another way, the doctrine is not applicable when the injury occurred while the servant was acting outside the legitimate scope of authority.[6]

The key question related to scope of authority (or employment), requires that the servant do something in furtherance of the duties he owes to his master, and that the master is, or could be, exercising some control, directly or indirectly, over the servant's activities.[7] In this way, the activities of the servant must be fairly and reasonably incident to the employment, or logically and naturally connected with the employment. Hence, not all actions of the servant are attributable to the master. Actions done for personal desires or motivations by the servant are not attributable to the master. Generally, this question is framed by whether the action(s) was done in the "course and scope of the employment." This is a legal phase which refers to the servant acting as an employee for the principal. The factors to assess the "course and scope of employment" are as follows:[8]

1. Time, place and purpose of the act
2. Authorization of the act by the employer
3. Common performance of the act by employees on behalf of the employer

4. Extent to which employee's interests were advanced by the act
5. Length of departure of the employee from company business for personal interest
6. Furnishing of the means and instrumentalities by the employer that inflicted the injury
7. The knowledge on the part of the employer that the employee would do the act or had done the act before
8. Whether act was motivated, at least in part, to serve the employer
9. Whether misconduct of the employee was engendered by events or conditions of employment, such as responsibilities, conditions of workplace, and events at work

Closely related to these theories is the concept of Vicarious Liability. This entails indirect legal responsibility of the employer for the employees under his or her direction or discretion.[9] In this way, the terms *employer* and *employee* do not necessarily imply an employment relationship. It most often occurs in contracted relationships, where one party acts as an independent contractor and the other acts as the general contractor—or the employing party.

The existence of an independent contractor relationship versus an employee-employer relationship typically goes the issue of control. The right to control and the amount of control exercised by the "employer" over the "employee" is the key. In this sense, the more control exercised, the more likely the liability for an injury will shift to the employer. Of course, in most contractual relationships, the paying party (employer) will specify the work to be done. Typically this entails the delivery of a good or service based on some agreed upon price and standard. However, if the paying party (employer) exercises too much control over the *means*, *instrumentalities and results* of the work, then the "independent contractor" will lose its independence, and become an "employee." If this occurs, then liability for an injury or harm will shift to the employer. Similarly, if there is evidence of joint control by both the employer and independent contractor, then liability may be jointly shared by both parties.

In assessing whether a contractor is "independent" or an "employee," the courts will look at several factors, including the following:[10]

1. Extent of control by employer over details of the work
2. Whether the independent contractor is engaged in a distinct business or occupation
3. Skill required in the particular business or occupation
4. Whether the employer supplies the instrumentalities, tools, and place of work
5. Length of time for which the person is employed
6. Method of payment, either by time or by the job
7. Whether work is part of the regular business of the employer

8. Whether the parties believed that a master-servant relationship was created
9. Whether the employer is a business

As an additional component of this analysis, some work is deemed to be so dangerous or personal that the employer cannot delegate liability to an independent contractor. This is sometimes called the peculiar risk doctrine.[11] It is particularly relevant in the security industry, where sometimes the work to be performed is so dangerous or so critical that the employer cannot simply shift liability by hiring an independent contractor. The classical example of non-delegable duties is where those who manufacture, transport, and use explosives are exposed to liability, regardless of any attempts to transfer such to another party.

In summary, as you read these cases, consider the relationship between the parties, and the nature and the scope of the work involved. In doing so, the explanation for the court decisions will be determined by the answer to this examination.

CONTRACTS

The definition of a contract is an "agreement between two or more persons which creates an obligation to do or not to do a particular thing. The essential components are: competent parties, subject matter, legal consideration, mutuality of agreement, and mutuality of obligation."[12] Each of these factors can be extremely complicated and factually specific. Indeed, voluminous analysis and commentaries have been devoted to contract law. This level of sophistication and detail is well beyond the scope of this book. For our purposes, the focus of this chapter will be limited to the key contractual provisions commonly found in security agreements and in security litigation.

Understanding of security agreements requires basic knowledge of contract law. The most fundamental components of a valid contract are the existence of three elements: offer, acceptance and consideration. The typical initial assessment is whether the parties have a valid agreement. The classic standard is having established a "meeting of the minds." Essentially, this means that the offer was tendered by one party, then understood and accepted by the other. The level of understanding, however, does not require precision as to the exact details of the agreement.

Contract language is to be understood by giving its terms their customary, ordinary, and accepted meaning.[13] An unambiguous contract provision can only be reasonably construed in one way. Conversely, an ambiguous contract provision could be capable of two or more reasonable, alternative meanings. If a term is ambiguous, extrinsic evidence may be introduced to show both the intent of the parties and any possible special trade usage of terms.[14] Extrinsic evidence is any facts, documents or verbal assertions that help to explain an ambiguous provision in the contract.

The element of consideration requires the transferring of some value pursuant to the agreement. Consideration does not have to be money or even property. It could entail anything that has some intrinsic or personal value, such as time, attention, and even affection.[15]

The cases in this section deal with legal issues related to security. There are a number of legal issues that are common in security contracts. These issues will be highlighted in the cases. Of course, the purpose of this section is not to serve as a treatise on the nuances of contract law, but rather to present and discuss the typical issues that relate to security. Given this overview, Chapter 9 is subdivided into specific types of contracts: Insurance, Security Services, and Landlord Tenant, with relevant issues discussed in each subsection.

A. Insurance Policies and Contracts

Insurance contracts have two underlying obligations: a duty to defend the lawsuit and a duty to indemnify a loss, harm, or an injury.

In assessing these contract obligations, the court initially inquires as to the boundaries of coverage. This assessment is based on the language in the insurance contract. Second, the court reviews the allegations made in the lawsuit. In this way, the duty to defend is generally determined by comparing the allegations in the complaint with the language of the insurance policy. If this is unclear, courts may look beyond the complaint to extrinsic facts to establish the existence or nonexistence of that duty.

The duty to defend an insured on a claim arises when any part of a claim against the insured is arguably within the policy's scope.[16] Because insurance policies are considered adhesion contracts, courts will typically construe ambiguous terms in the insured's favor. This is consistent with the logic of rules relating to contract construction. Since the insurer wrote the contract and the insured purchased the policy with the intention of buying insurance, any ambiguity of contract language will be construed against the insurance company. As such, courts will construe ambiguous contract provisions in favor of the insured—in favor of coverage. In addition, when a complaint (lawsuit) fails to allege facts that clearly bring the claim within coverage, the insurer generally must defend if the plaintiff shows a potentiality of coverage. Indeed, the insurer is obliged to defend the insured even if the allegations are groundless, false, or fraudulent, and even if the insurer knows that the allegations are untrue.[17] This standard may require the insurance company to defend the claim, even though the lawsuit may have little chance of success on its merits.

If the court deems that there is a duty to defend, then the next question is whether there is a duty to indemnify. This entails the duty of the insurance company to pay for the loss, harm, or injury sustained in the lawsuit. Here again, courts will look at the language of the insurance contract. If the liability asserted from the litigation was not excluded in the insurance contract, then the insurer must indemnify the insured. In the context of security, the typical exclusion(s) relate to "intentional acts" (such as assault and battery), terrorism, and "misconduct."

Generally, the purpose of the intentional act exclusion is to exclude insurance coverage for wanton and malicious acts by an insured or by third parties related to the business of the insured. Aside from the contract language, the typical public policy argument in favor of this exclusion is that bad acts—such as assault and battery—should not be insured away. In this sense, there are good reasons to not allow the insured's bad acts to be protected by an insurance company. If this was allowed, then why should the insured care about committing bad acts? Indeed, why provide an incentive through legal and financial protections for the bad acts of the insured? Is it not better public policy to make the insured responsible for his or her individual bad acts? By precluding insurance, at least the incentive for doing bad acts is removed.

B. Security Service Contracts

Security service contracts are assessed in the same manner as any other contract would be. There are particular aspects of security service contracts, however, that are subject to litigation and dispute. These provisions typically relate to the Limitation of Liability clause, and the Indemnification or Hold Harmless clauses.

A Limitation of Liability clause (also called Liquidated Damage clause) provides a dollar limit for liability stemming from the contract. For example, in security alarm contracts, the typical limitation is $500 to $1,000.00, or the cost of the equipment, or the value of six monthly payments for the services rendered. With this limitation, the intention is to have any potential liability connected to the actual value of the contract.

This limitation is particularly important for security service providers. As one can imagine, when a security firm fails to provide the services contemplated in the contract, the consequences of such can be both financially and personally substantial. For example, the failure to act properly can result in personal injury, including death. Similarly, the failure to act properly can result in property loss valued in millions of dollars. When compared to the value of the contract, it is not hard to comprehend that even one incident could be disastrous to the security firm.

Two arguments are typically countered in an attempt to defeat this clause. First, the consequence to the party who has paid for the security services should also be considered. It is likely that the incident had disastrous consequences to the buyer of the security services. One cannot argue against this assertion. Surely, in the face of injury or death, and substantial loss of property, the consequence to the buyer of the security services is great—and unfortunate. The best answer to this situation is that the security firm is not an insurer. Indeed, if the security firm is to be potentially liable for the consequences of the failure to act (or an improper act), then the firm is actually performing a dual role: as security provider and as an insurer of consequential damages. When one considers the relative value of the typical security service contract, this potential exposure far outweighs the monies derived from the service. Indeed, if security firms were expected to be both a security provider and a potential insurer, why would any reasonable business owner do this work? From a financial perspective, the answer is easy. No prudent business person would accept such potential exposure, given the typical value of these contracts and of the profit market in the industry.

This circumstance is best left to the insurance market place to resolve. Buyers of security service, whether business or residential property owners, typically have insurance coverage for their property. With security services instituted within their property, there is another layer of protection afforded to the owner. In this way, security services added to the insurance coverage provides another protective method to secure the people and assets contained on the property.

Further, most insurance carriers view security services as a means to limit their exposure. This is so because the contracted security services are typically designed to act as a deterrent to crime and misconduct, and/or act as an early warning reporter in the event of a criminal act, fire, or other disaster. Indeed, depending upon the nature of the property, some insurance companies *require* certain types of security services, such as fire and security alarms. Consequently, based on this thinking, the limitation of liability clause serves the interests of the security firm, with the insurance company protecting the financial interests of the property owner. With this same logic, the insurance carrier also benefits from the protective services provided by security firms. As such, it is a win-win-win scenario.

Second, buyers (or potential buyers) of security services argue that "why should I pay for these services, if you will not do what you are contracted to perform?" The answer to this well-founded assertion is that the security firm *intends* to perform the services. However, all businesses will make mistakes. Indeed, security services often require judgment, often in stressful or even crisis situations. In these circumstances, no one is immune from making improper decisions. Even careless or grossly negligent decisions are to be expected. Unfortunately, in the security industry, when these mistakes or improper judgments are made, they often result in disastrous consequences. Consequently, as articulated above, this exposure cannot be accepted by prudent security firms.

Finally, the logic of Indemnification or Hold Harmless clauses is similarly explained. From the perspective of the security firm, these clauses serve to limit their potential liability. Indeed, these clauses provide for the buyer of security services to pay for damages when the security firm is sued by third parties. In the typical application of this clause, when a third party, who is not a party to the contract, is injured or harmed because of the actions or inactions of the security provider, these clauses provide that the damages relating to such be paid by the buyer of the security services. As is often the case, the insurance carrier for the buyer actually is obligated to pay for the damages. As articulated above, this is appropriate based on the protections provided within the market, and on the profit margin associated with the security service provider.

C. Landlord-Tenant Leases and Contracts

The operative legal questions in this subsection concern the obligations of leases and franchise agreements. The key aspects of these agreements relate to the amount and level of control each party exerts in the operation of the facility. Questions often relate to the ability to implement security hardware and methods. In this sense, liability for failure to provide security provisions intersects with the ability to implement such provisions. In essence, the operative legal questions are these: who is liable for failure to provide security, and who has the legal authority pursuant to the lease to implement security provisions? These same questions are raised in franchise agreements. As the cases will illustrate, maintaining a balance between the determination of "appropriate" security controls with the legal authority (from the underlying lease or franchise agreement) to implement these controls presents a real challenge.

NOTES

1. Closen, Michael L. (1984). Agency, Employment, and Partnership Law: Contemporary Cases and Materials. St. Paul, MN: Mason Publishing Company.
2. Closen op cit. at 7.
3. *Knight v. City Streets, LLC,* 167 S.W. 3d 580 (2005).
4. See *MacDonald v. Hinton,* 836 N.E. 2d 893 (2005).
5. See Black's Law Dictionary, 5th ed. (1979). St. Paul, MN: West Publishing Company.
6. Closen op cit. at 40.
7. See *Little v. Omega Meats,* 615 S.E. 2d 45 (2005).
8. See *Adorno v. Correctional Services Corporation,* 312 F. Supp. 2d 505 (2004).
9. Clifford, Mary (2004). *Identifying and Exploring Security Essentials.* Upper Saddle River, NJ: Prentice Hall.
10. Closen op cit. at 244.
11. See *McKown v. Wal-Mart Stores, Inc.,* 38 P. 3d 1094 (2002).
12. See Black's Law Dictionary, 5th ed. (1979). St. Paul, MN: West Publishing Company.
13. See Restatement of Contracts 2d (1981). Section 202. St. Paul, MN: American Law Institute Publishers.

14. See *IMT Insurance Company v. Crestmoor Golf Club*, 702 N.W. 2d 492 (2005).
15. See Restatement of Contracts 2d (1981). Section 71. St. Paul, MN: American Law Institute Publishers.
16. See *Gruetzmacher v. Acuity Insurance Company*, 393 F. Supp. 2d 860 (2005).
17. See *L.A. Connection v. Penn-America Insurance Company*, 843 N.E. 2d 427 (2005).

8

Agency and Related Theories

CASES

172 S.W.3d 361

Supreme Court of Kentucky

TOMMIE LEE PATTERSON, APPELLANT v. THOMAS C. BLAIR, JR.; AND TOMMY BLAIR, INC., D/B/A COURTESY AUTOPLEX, APPELLEES.

Sept. 22, 2005

Background

Dealership's customer, who refused to return vehicle or to pay amount allegedly due on sales transaction, brought civil action for assault against dealership and dealership's employee, who fired pistol at vehicle's tires in effort to repossess vehicle while customer was operating vehicle. Following a jury trial, the McCracken Circuit Court entered judgment in favor of customer. Customer appealed, and dealership cross-appealed. The court of appeals reversed. The supreme court granted discretionary review.

Holdings

The supreme court held that:

1. In determining whether employee was acting within scope of employment, focus is on employee's motive for his conduct, not on foreseeability of employee's conduct; and
2. Employee was acting within scope of employment.

Decision of court of appeals reversed and remanded.

Tommie Lee Patterson brought suit against Thomas Blair, Jr., and Courtesy Autoplex. Patterson alleged several causes of action against Blair, Jr., and claimed that Courtesy was vicariously liable for the tortious acts of its employee, Blair, Jr. A jury awarded Patterson damages of $42,465.18 and found that Courtesy was vicariously liable for Blair, Jr.'s conduct. A divided panel of the court of appeals held that Blair, Jr., was not acting within the scope of his employment and therefore concluded that Courtesy could not be held liable under respondeat superior. Having determined that the jury correctly determined that Blair, Jr., was acting within the scope of employment when he assaulted Patterson, we reverse the court of appeals and reinstate the jury's verdict against Courtesy.

On September 28, 1995, Patterson entered into an agreement with Courtesy to trade his Camaro for a new 1995 GMC Jimmy. At the time of the trade, Patterson owed $12,402.82 on the Camaro. Despite this, he incorrectly informed Courtesy that he owed only $9,500.00 on the car. The transaction occurred at a time when the bank was closed and Courtesy could not verify the payoff amount on the loan. Courtesy allowed Patterson to take possession of the Jimmy, but did not transfer title. An agreement was also executed providing that Courtesy would credit Patterson if he had overstated his outstanding indebtedness on the Camaro and, likewise, that he would pay the difference if his figure understated that amount. When the bank opened the next day, Courtesy discovered the amount Patterson actually owed on the Camaro. When notified of this discrepancy, Patterson refused to pay the additional sum and refused to return the Jimmy. Courtesy subsequently tried unsuccessfully to repossess the truck on at least two occasions.

On October 4, 1995, after investigating where he could find Patterson, Blair, Jr., and another Courtesy employee encountered Patterson, who was driving the Jimmy, on a public road. At a stoplight, Blair, Jr., exited his car and knocked on the Jimmy's driver-side window, demanding that Patterson get out of the vehicle. When Patterson refused, Blair, Jr., drew a pistol he was carrying and fired two shots in the front tire and two shots in the rear tire of the Jimmy. Ultimately, the disabled truck was impounded and returned to Courtesy by the police.

Courtesy obtained a judgment against Patterson for the Jimmy's loss in value. Citizens Bank, which had financed the Camaro that had been traded-in, obtained a judgment against Patterson for the remaining sum owed on its loan. Blair, Jr., was criminally prosecuted and was convicted of wanton endangerment in the first degree, a felony. Patterson sued Blair, Jr., and Courtesy under several different tort theories.

Discussion

Stated generally, the doctrine of respondeat superior, also called vicarious liability, provides the legal rationale for holding a master responsible for a tort committed by his servant. The origins of the doctrine of respondeat superior run deep in the common law. As Blackstone explained: "As for those things which a servant may do on behalf of his master, they seem all to proceed upon this principle, that the master is answerable for the act of his servant if done by his command either expressly given or implied...." Not surprisingly, vicarious liability is a long-standing principle of Kentucky's tort law.

The Rationale

Over the years, commentators have offered various justifications in support of respondeat superior liability. For instance, Judge Posner explained that the principle has sometimes been thought of as an example of the law's sympathy to "deep-pocket" arguments. Simply put, because employees often lack sufficient assets to pay tort judgments, respondeat superior is necessary to allow victims to reach into employers' deep pockets for compensation. Ultimately, however, this is an unsatisfactory, or at least incomplete, explanation, especially since the principle of respondeat superior evolved during a period in which the common law was not noted for its sympathy toward accident victims. Moreover, there are now limits on the employer's liability. The employer is strictly liable only for damages resulting from the tortious acts of his employees. A victim injured by an employee who is exercising due care and who has not acted intentionally has no claim against the employer. And the employer is only liable for acts of his employee committed in the scope of the employment.

Thus, it is clear that the justification for the rule has to be more than just forcing the employer to compensate victims because he can afford to do so. Various judges and commentators have recognized this inadequacy and have offered myriad alternate, or at least supplemental, and more robust rationales for the rule. One of these supplemental rationales for respondeat superior liability can be found in the field of economics.

The economic explanation for respondeat superior focuses first on the complete helplessness of the accident victim to avoid incorrect employment decisions by exercising care or by altering his activity. This in itself would be an insufficient reason for imposing strict liability if the employer could always, or at least most of the time, prevent negligence by his employees simply by exercising care in his selection and supervision of them. But employees will sometimes be careless even if they are carefully screened and supervised, if only because their lack of ready assets reduces their financial incentives to take care. And there are a number of activity measures (as distinct from care measures) that an employer can take to reduce accident behavior by his employees, including delegating more work to independent contractors and giving employees simpler tasks requiring less care.

However, the most important reason for respondeat superior is the fact mentioned that employees often cannot pay a tort judgment against them. Our point is not a deep-pocket point; it is that the employer can use the threat of termination as a substitute for employee tort liability in inducing employees to act with due care, and that he will do so only if the employee's carelessness is a cost to him. Making the employer liable for his employee's tort serves to enlist the employer as a substitute enforcer of tort law where the primary enforcement mechanism, a tort action against the immediate tortfeasor, is unworkable. They therefore are not very responsive to the threat of tort liability. The employer, however, can induce them to be careful, as by firing or otherwise penalizing them for their carelessness.... Making the employer liable for his employees' torts will give him an incentive to use such inducements.

The Prosser and Keeton treatise offers a similar explanation: What has emerged as the modern justification for vicarious liability is a rule of policy, a deliberate allocation of a risk. The losses caused by the torts of employees, which as a practical matter are sure to occur in the conduct of the employer's enterprise, are placed upon that enterprise itself, as a required cost of doing business. They are placed upon the employer because having engaged in an enterprise, which will on the basis of all past experience involve harm to others through the torts of employees, and sought to profit by it, it is just that he, rather than the innocent injured plaintiff, should bear them; and because he is better able to absorb them, and to distribute them, through prices, rates or liability insurance, to the public, and so to shift them to society, to the community at large. Added to this is the makeweight argument that an employer who is held strictly liable is under the greatest incentive to be careful in the selection, instruction, and supervision of his servants, and to take every precaution to see that the enterprise is conducted safely. Notwithstanding the occasional condemnation of the entire doctrine which used to appear in the past, the tendency is clearly to justify it on such grounds, and gradually to extend it.

In 1936, our own predecessor court explained the purpose of the doctrine as follows:

> The doctrine of respondeat superior is at best a harsh rule, dictated by considerations of public policy and the necessity for holding a responsible person liable for the acts done by others in the prosecution of his business, as well as for placing on employers an incentive to hire only careful employees.

In *Ira S. Bushey & Sons, Inc. v. United States*, one of the most cited respondeat superior cases involving an intentional tort, Judge Friendly rejected many of the traditional justifications for the doctrine, focusing instead on the activities of the business enterprise. In *Bushey*, a drunken sailor returned to his ship and opened valves that flooded a drydock, damaging both the ship and the drydock. Judge Friendly rejected many of the traditional policy arguments that have been offered in support of respondeat superior liability. He noted that even though the drunken sailor was not motivated by a purpose to serve his employer, respondeat superior liability was proper. This liability rested on the fact that the "business enterprise cannot justly disclaim responsibility for accidents which may be fairly said to be characteristic of its activities" and that the sailor's conduct "was not so unforeseeable as to make it unfair to charge the government with responsibility."

The Rule for Intentional Torts

Though the foregoing discussion is, no doubt, more academic than may seem necessary, an understanding of the competing rationales for the doctrine of respondeat superior is at least helpful, if not necessary, in determining the contours of the rule to be applied to the intentional torts of employees. As noted above, an employer's liability is limited only to those employee actions committed in the scope of employment. The central difficulty in applying the rule of respondeat superior focuses on this concept, especially when the tort in question was intentional (as opposed to merely the result of negligence). Thus, the question inevitably arises: What does "scope of employment" mean?

Judge Friendly applied the standard of foreseeability as the benchmark for scope of employment. He discussed foreseeability in the following manner: Here it was foreseeable that crewmembers crossing the drydock might do damage, negligently or even intentionally, such as pushing a Bushey employee or kicking property into the water. Moreover, the proclivity of seamen to find solace for solitude by copious resort to the bottle while ashore has been noted in opinions too numerous to warrant citation. Once all this is granted, it is immaterial that Lane's precise action was not to be foreseen.

The most prominent alternative to the foreseeability standard is the principle that an action is only within the scope of employment when the employee intends to further the employer's business or advance the employer's goal. Prosser and Keeton state that "in general, ... the master is held liable for any intentional tort committed by the servant where its purpose, however misguided, is wholly or in part to further the master's business." In explaining this principle, they offer the following example of the rule in action:

> Thus a railway ticket agent who assaults, arrests or slanders a passenger, in the belief that he has been given a counterfeit bill for a ticket, is within the scope of employment, although the employer has not authorized such conduct, or has even expressly prohibited it. But if he acts from purely personal motives, because of a quarrel over his wife which is in no way connected with the employer's interests, he is considered in the ordinary case to have departed from his employment, and the master is not liable.

Landes and Posner agree that this is the appropriate rule. They state that in the case of an intentional tort the court is likely to insist in addition that the employee in committing the tort have been trying, however misguidedly, to advance the employer's goals, as where the employee assaults a debtor of the employer in an effort to collect the debt. If the employee is actuated by purely personal motives, the employer's practical ability to prevent the tort will be slight. The employer should be able to ensure that the employee not only use due care but also avoid overzealous pursuit of the employer's goals, but it is much harder for the employer to screen and monitor employees for purely personal attitudes.

This rule differs significantly than the one proffered by Judge Friendly in that it depends on the employee's motivation in acting, not on whether his or her action is foreseeable. As the preceding discussion demonstrates, how one defines the scope of employment is the crucial inquiry. And while the opinions of the likes of Deans Prosser and Keeton and Judges Friendly and Posner on this issue are illuminating, we must ultimately turn to our precedent to define the standard to be applied in Kentucky.

In *Frederick v. Collins*, an employee of a neighborhood grocery shot and killed a frequent patron of the store who disguised his voice and said "Stick 'em up; this is a hold up." The employee turned around, hit the patron in the face with a gun, and shot him without realizing who it was. The employee was the store owner's son. The owner testified that he did not know his son had a gun and that he had frequently instructed all of his employees, including his son, never to resist a holdup. The question before the court was whether the owner could be held vicariously liable for the shooting, an intentional tort. The court noted that Prosser had recognized "that even intentional torts may be so reasonably connected with the employment as to fall within the scope of it. The present tendency is to extend the employer's responsibility for such conduct." The court then favorably cited Section 245 of the Second Restatement of Agency, which states that the master is liable "for the intended tortious harm by a servant to the person or things of another by an act done in connection with the servant's employment, although the act was unauthorized, if the act was not unexpectable in view of the duties of the servant."

In finding that the employee was acting within the scope of employment, the court placed great weight on his motive for the shooting. The court stated:

> In the case at bar Robert was admittedly the appellant's employee; moreover, he was in sole charge of the store at the time of the incident. Without doubt Robert Frederick was under obligation generally to manage and protect the appellant's store and its contents. There *is no evidence that Robert sought to serve any personal purpose in his activity* toward Collins. In fact, Robert asserted that he did not know whom he was shooting–that he acted in self-defense. He actually testified that he would have shot his father or brother under the same circumstances. So it is obvious that this case is not governed by any of the authorities which deny liability

> because the employee has acted in furtherance of a personal motive as distinguished from a motive connected with the employer's business.

Wood v. Southeastern Greyhound Lines, also contains a detailed discussion of respondeat superior. In *Wood*, after a car entered the highway, a bus driver for Southeastern Greyhound crowded the car and forced it off the road. After the car regained the highway, it continued traveling, eventually stopping in Williamstown. When the car stopped, the bus driver also stopped, leaving the bus in the middle of the road, and proceeded to assault the driver of the car. The court concluded that the bus driver was not acting within the scope of employment. The court explained:

> It is clear the rule of *respondeat superior cannot be invoked and the employer be held liable where the action of the employee was motivated by conceptions of personal wrong or the invasion of his private rights* [emphasis added]. And though there is some conflict of opinion, the trend of the decisions is to exonerate the principal where the act was not for the protection of his property or interests, but was to vindicate public justice or to redress an offense against society, or to punish an offender for something already done, although the wrongful act had its origin in some agency relation. (Citations omitted.)

The court then discussed other cases and authorities, synthesizing the rule in the following manner:

> And now, in collating these authorities and principles, it seems clear to us that in order to hold an employer responsible to a third person for the tortious act of an employee of the former, such act must have been committed while the employee was engaged in furthering his employer's business or interests, without any deviation by the employee to a pursuit of his own business or interest, and there must have been a general similarity between the tortious act committed and the usual, ordinary, everyday acts commonly pursued by the employee in prosecuting the regular routine of his employment.

The court further noted that we see no marked, or even faint, resemblance between the bus driver's fisticuffs, on the one hand, and the bus driver's customary duties of starting, guiding, stopping and safely operating appellee's busses, on the other hand, especially so in view of the fact that this assaulted appellant was not related to the bus driver's employer as a passenger, customer, employee or otherwise. This bus driver's attack and his usual bus driving employment bore no more similarity to each other than a plug horse bears to "Man O' War," according to our perspective of these two separate activities.

In *Osborne v. Payne*, a former husband sought to impose vicarious liability against a Roman Catholic Diocese for a priest's allegedly outrageous actions associated with an affair with his wife. This court held that the Diocese was not liable under respondeat superior and explained:

The critical analysis is whether the employee or agent was acting within the scope of his employment at the time of his tortious act. *Wood v. Southeastern Greyhound Lines*, provides that for it to be within the scope of its employment, the conduct must be of the same general nature as that authorized or incidental to the conduct authorized. A principal is not liable under the doctrine of respondeat superior unless the intentional wrongs of the agent were calculated to advance the cause of the principal or were appropriate to the normal scope of the operator's employment. In this situation, it is the abuse by the priest of his position that exceeds the scope of his employment. It is beyond question that Osborne was not advancing any cause of the diocese or engaging in behavior appropriate to the normal scope of his employment.

In discussing statutory civil rights actions relying on a theory of vicarious liability, this court recently noted:

> Vicarious liability, sometimes referred to as the doctrine of respondeat superior, is not predicated upon a tortious act of the employer but upon the imputation to the employer of a tortious act of the employee by considerations of public policy and the necessity for holding a responsible person liable for the acts done by others in the prosecution of his business, as well as for placing on employers an incentive to hire only careful employees. *Ordinarily, an employer is not vicariously liable for an intentional tort of an employee not actuated by a purpose to serve the employer* [emphasis added] but motivated, as here, solely by a desire to satisfy the employee's own sexual proclivities.

Despite the fact that this court has cited to varying authorities to explain its holdings in the area of intentional torts, we have, with few exceptions, focused on the motive of the employee in determining whether he or she was acting within the scope of employment. Although in certain cases we have paid lip service to the principle of the foreseeability of the misconduct that was advanced by Judge Friendly in *Bushey*, our substantive focus has remained on the servant's purpose or motive. It is quite possible that had *Bushey* been decided under Kentucky law, the employer would not have been held liable for the drunken sailor's conduct because the drunken sailor was "not actuated by a purpose to serve the employer." It is clear, however, that Kentucky law has rejected Judge Friendly's approach, which focuses exclusively on foreseeability and refuses to consider motive.

Instead, Kentucky's approach is precisely the standard advanced by Prosser and Keeton when they explained that "in general ... the master is held liable for any intentional tort committed by the servant where its purpose, however misguided, is wholly or in part to further the master's business." Thus, if the servant "acts from purely personal motives ... which [are] in no way connected with the employer's interests, he is considered in the ordinary case to have departed from his employment, and the master is not liable."

This sound approach also conforms to the economic theory of vicarious liability, discussed above, because when the employee acts for solely personal reasons, the employer's ability to prevent the tort is limited.

In fact, Kentucky's emphasis on employee motive has been embraced in the Tentative Draft of the Third Restatement of Agency. The Tentative Draft rejects formulations based on assessments of foreseeability and instead states that an "employee's act is not within the scope of employment when it occurs within an independent course of conduct not intended by the employee to serve any purpose of the employer."

In explaining this change from the Second Restatement of Agency, the commentators state that "although formulations that focus on an employee's intention may be difficult to apply in some cases, formulations based on assessments of foreseeability are potentially confusing and may generate outcomes that are less predictable than intent-based formulations."

A review of *Wood, Frederick* and *Osborne* makes clear that each of those cases focused on the servant's purpose for the intentional act that was perpetrated. Both the bus driver in *Wood* and the priest in *Osborne* committed acts based on purely personal motives, which were in no way connected with the employer's interests. On the other hand, in *Frederick*, the employee's misguided decision to shoot his supposed assailant was based solely on a business motive—to protect the store—and liability was proper even though the employer had forbidden such an action.

The court of appeals in this case relied on *Citizens Finance Co. v. Walton*, to support its holding that Blair, Jr., was not acting within the scope of employment when he confronted Patterson. In *Walton*, a finance company sent a debt collector to collect money from the plaintiff, and the employee struck and twisted the hand of the plaintiff. The court concluded that the employee was not acting within the scope of employment. The court ultimately rested its holding on foreseeability, explaining that "[t]he duty imposed upon Hensley to collect money did not carry with it as a reasonably contemplated act, the authority to assault Mrs. Walton." This holding *is* consistent with an example noted in the Second Restatement of Agency, which states:

> Thus, one who is sent to collect a bill does not normally make the employer responsible if he seizes money from the debtor, since this would be an unusual and unexpectable proceeding of a bill collector. On the other hand, one who is sent to recapture property is likely to come into contact with a possessor unwilling to surrender it, and persons sent to recapture goods are frequently the kind who would be not unlikely to attempt force.

Simply put, *Walton* is an aberration in our case law, and no Kentucky court has relied on it, at least any published decision, to find vicarious liability. In fact, in *Bingham v. Commercial Credit Corporation*, the court, when faced with an identical fact situation, declined to follow *Walton*. Instead, the court noted that there were divergent views on the issue among the states, and focused on another factor that survives today under all theories of determining respondeat superior liability, namely the effect of the criminal nature of the employee's activity. The *Bingham* court cited the Second Restatement of Agency for the proposition that whether the servant engaged in "a crime, especially if the crime is of some magnitude," should be considered in determining whether or not the act is within the scope of employment.

Prosser and Keeton also note that "where the conduct of the servant is unprovoked, highly unusual, and quite outrageous, there has been something of a tendency to find that this in itself is sufficient to indicate that the motive was a purely personal one, but it seems clear that this cannot hold true in all cases."

Application of the Rule

The following facts became apparent from an extensive review of the testimony offered at trial. Tommy Blair, Sr., was the sole owner and president of Courtesy. He had been in the automobile business for 35 years and had operated Courtesy for 22 years. His son, Blair, Jr., had worked for Courtesy for 22 years and was at the time of the incident the service manager for Courtesy. Blair, Jr., with his father's permission, represented himself as vice president of Courtesy. Blair, Jr., was a management employee and supervised employees within the service department.

On October 2, 1995, after attempting to work with Patterson to resolve the payment issue, Blair, Sr., became convinced that Patterson would not voluntarily give up the Jimmy. Shortly thereafter, two Courtesy employees, Michael Moore and Chris Wathen, tried to repossess the truck at Patterson's home, but they were unsuccessful because the key they had made did not work. Moore testified that Patterson confronted them during this attempted repossession and threatened to kill them. Moore informed Blair, Jr., that he thought Patterson was crazy and that he would not go back to attempt to retrieve the Jimmy. Blair, Sr., testified that Courtesy had several employees out trying to recover the truck from Patterson and that he knew his son was among those employees. In addition to the incident involving Moore, Wathen, and Patterson, there had been several other attempts to locate and retrieve the truck.

In explaining his decision to find Patterson on October 4, 1995, Blair, Jr., testified that the purpose of his confrontation with Patterson was to retrieve "our property" and repossess the vehicle for Courtesy. Chris Wathen accompanied Blair, Jr., to confront Patterson. Blair, Jr., also testified that he carried a gun with him anytime he was outside the office and that he made no attempt to hide the gun.

When Blair, Jr., went to repossess the truck, Blair, Sr. knew that: (i) his son was looking for the truck; (ii) Patterson would not voluntarily relinquish the truck; and (iii) Patterson had threatened other Courtesy employees during a failed attempt to repossess the truck. Blair, Sr., testified that Courtesy did not ordinarily finance vehicle loans, but he also testified that Courtesy sometimes had to repossess vehicles, noting only that it was a "rare occurrence." In fact, Blair, Jr., testified that another long-time employee, Mr. Dee, had handled repossessions for Courtesy up until the time of his death in June 1995, just a few months before the incident in this case. Thus, the record demonstrates that a reasonable juror could have concluded that Courtesy had previously repossessed cars. Furthermore, Blair, Sr.'s wealth of experience in the automobile business certainly made him aware of what can occur during automobile repossession.

Clearly, in confronting Patterson and shooting out the truck's tires, Blair, Jr., was acting to further the business interests of Courtesy. At the very least, his conduct was at least incidental to the conduct that was authorized by Courtesy. Here, just as in *Frederick*, Blair, Jr., was acting to protect his employer's property. In fact, Blair, Jr.'s testimony explicitly confirmed this motive. And perhaps most importantly, there is no evidence that he sought to serve any personal purpose by his actions. Quite simply, he engaged in the act to further his employer's business interests. This is clearly distinguishable from the acts of the employees in *Wood* and *Osborne*. And finally, although the act was criminal, it was not so outrageous to indicate that the motive was a personal one. Therefore, the jury's finding that Blair, Jr., acted within the scope of employment, thereby imposing vicarious liability on Courtesy, is supported by the evidence and the law of this Commonwealth.

Conclusion

The decision of the court of appeals on the issue of vicarious liability is reversed, and the case remanded for proceedings consistent with this opinion.

CASE COMMENT

This court decision provides an excellent historical and case precedent analysis of respondeat superior. In particular, the explanation used by the court should give the reader a good overview of the concept. This case, and its pointed analysis, serves as a useful introductory case to this subject matter.

As for the merits of the case, the court found that the international actions by the owner's son were done in the scope of his employment with the auto dealer. Even though shooting the tires was clearly wrong, and indeed resulted in the defendant's conviction in criminal court, the actions were not so personal as to take them outside of his scope of employment. In addition, there were adequate facts to illustrate that the attempted repossession may result in some violence. Because of such, the decision to carry the gun, and the attempt to disable the vehicle tires with it, was within the scope of employment.

167 S.W. 3d 580

Court of Appeals of Texas, Houston (14th Dist.)

ROBERT KNIGHT, APPELLANT v. CITY STREETS, LLC, APPELLEE.

June 28, 2005

Background

Nightclub patron brought action against nightclub for negligent supervision, hiring, and training, and for assault under theory of respondeat superior. The 55th District Court, Harris County, granted nightclub's Motion for Summary Judgment. Patron appealed.

Holdings

The court of appeals held that:

1. Nightclub employees were not acting within course and scope of their authority when they allegedly assaulted patron, and
2. Nightclub manager did not breach duty to supervise nightclub employees.

Affirmed

After a night out at City Streets, LLC, a Houston nightclub, appellant/plaintiff Robert Knight returned to his car in the parking lot of City Streets and found it had been burglarized. At around 3:30 a.m., Knight went back to the nightclub, which was then closed, to get help from Andrew Sanchez, an off-duty Houston police officer, Knight had seen working at the nightclub earlier in the evening. Knight banged on the door and yelled at Sanchez in an effort to get his attention. Sanchez and two other employees, Manuel Saenz and Chris Aquino, emerged from the nightclub. These three men allegedly assaulted Knight, and Sanchez arrested Knight for public intoxication and use of profane language. Knight allegedly sustained multiple injuries as a result of the incident.

Respondeat Superior

In its motion for summary judgment, City Streets asserted that it was not liable for the assault on Knight under the theory of respondeat superior because there was no evidence that Sanchez, Saenz, or Aquino were acting within the course and scope of their employment when they assaulted Knight. To hold an employer liable for the actions of its employee, a claimant must prove (1) an agency relationship existed between the employee (the tortfeasor) and the employer (the defendant); (2) the employee committed a tort; and (3) the tort was in the course and scope of the employee's authority.

A tort is within the course and scope of the employee's authority if his action (1) was within the employee's general authority; (2) was in furtherance of the employer's business; and (3) was for the accomplishment of the object for which the employee was hired.

Generally, committing an assault is not within the course and scope of an employee's authority. An assault by an employee will be found to be within the scope of his employment when the assault is of the same general nature as the conduct authorized by the employer or is incidental to the conduct authorized. Therefore, if the employer places his employee in a position that involves the use of force, so that the act of using force is in the furtherance of the employer's business, the employer can be found liable for its employee's actions even if the employee uses greater force than is necessary.

In response to City Streets' motion for summary judgment, Knight offered the following evidence: (1) a Houston Police Department offense report from the night of the alleged assault; (2) excerpts from Knight's deposition in which he described what happened that night; and (3) medical records related to the injuries Knight sustained as a result of the incident. The offense report describes Saenz as a City Streets employee and Sanchez as an off-duty police officer working a second job at City Streets. In his deposition, Knight stated that he was assaulted by three men he had seen on previous visits to City Streets. Knight also stated that he knew that the three men who assaulted him were City Streets employees because they were wearing black jeans and City Streets shirts. This evidence may raise a genuine issue of material fact as to whether Sanchez, Saenz, and Aquino were City Streets employees, but it does not create a fact issue as to whether the three men were acting within the scope of their employment when they allegedly assaulted Knight.

Knight presented no evidence that the use of force was within Sanchez, Saenz, and Aquino's scope of employment. In his deposition, Knight referred to each of the three men as a bouncer, a position that could involve the use of force. However, Knight did not provide any facts to support his belief that these men, in fact, were employed as bouncers. Conclusory statements, unsupported by facts that reasonably would support the inference, do not constitute probative summary-judgment evidence.

At one point in his deposition, Knight stated that he was not sure that all the men involved in the assault were bouncers. More importantly, however, Knight presented no evidence indicating the scope of the three men's authority or that the use of force was within their general authority as City Streets employees.

Knight failed to produce any summary-judgment evidence to raise a genuine issue of material fact as to whether Sanchez, Saenz, and Aquino were acting within the course and scope of their employment when they allegedly assaulted Knight. Therefore, we conclude the trial court did not err in granting summary judgment against Knight on his respondeat superior claim. Accordingly, we overrule Knight's first issue.

Negligent Supervision

In its motion for summary judgment, City Streets asserted that there was no evidence as to each of the essential elements of Knight's claims for negligent supervision, hiring, and training. On appeal, Knight concedes that there is no evidence proving that City Streets breached its legal duty to hire and train its employees. To prevail on his remaining claim of negligent supervision, Knight had to prove (1) City Streets owed him a legal duty to supervise its employees; (2) City Streets breached that duty; and (3) that breach proximately caused his injuries.

The components of proximate cause are cause-in-fact and foreseeability. To establish that City Streets' actions were the proximate cause of his injuries, Knight must show that City Streets' actions in supervising Sanchez, Saenz, and Aquino were the cause-in-fact of his injuries and that Knight's assault and resulting injuries were a foreseeable consequence of City Streets' supervision of these three individuals.

City Streets argues that a claim for negligent supervision cannot exist in the absence of a claim of negligent hiring. We need not address this issue because, even if a claim for negligent supervision could exist absent a claim for negligent hiring, Knight failed to produce any evidence that City Streets breached its legal duty to supervise its employees.

On appeal, Knight asserts there is a genuine issue of fact as to his negligent supervision claim because the summary judgment evidence allegedly shows that Chris Chelley, a City Streets manager, was present during the incident and failed to stop Sanchez, Saenz, and Aquino from assaulting Knight. Knight argues that Chelley, armed with managerial authority, had a duty to stop the assault. Knight also argues that Knight's injuries were foreseeable to Chelley because Chelley was allegedly present while Knight was being assaulted. Chelley's failure to intervene, Knight argues, was a substantial factor in bringing about Knight's injuries.

The summary judgment proof offered by Knight, however, fails to raise a genuine issue of material fact as to whether Chelley breached his alleged legal duty to supervise Sanchez, Saenz, and Aquino. There is no evidence that Chelley was actually present during the assault or that he had prior knowledge that these three men had a propensity for aggression. There is also no evidence that Chelley observed the assault or that he could have intervened to stop it. In the Houston Police Department offense report attached to Knight's summary judgment response, Chelley is described as a City Streets manager. The report also states that Chelley was offended by Knight's language, could identify Knight, and would testify in court, if needed. It does not, however, state that Chelley witnessed any alleged assault. In his deposition, Knight stated that there were four others present when the assault started and seven others present when the assault was over. He did not identify any of the individuals as Chelley and did not mention Chelley at any point in his deposition. In Knight's deposition, he asserted that Aquino stated that Saenz was an "aggressive bully." Even viewing this evidence in Knight's favor, we conclude it establishes nothing more than that Saenz may have been aggressive. It does not establish that Chelley or City Streets knew of Saenz's alleged propensity for aggression.

Because Knight did not produce any summary judgment evidence to raise a genuine issue of material fact that City Streets or Chelley breached a legal duty to Knight, the trial court properly granted summary judgment on Knight's negligent supervision claim. We overrule Knight's second issue.

Having overruled both of Knight's issues on appeal, we affirm the trial court's judgment.

CASE COMMENT

This case raises a number of relevant issues related to course and scope of employment. A key point, noted by the court, is that if the employer hires an individual for a job that entails the use of force, then the employer would be liable for the individual's use of excessive force. The logic behind this assertion is that because the employer knew that the job requires the use of force to perform the work, the employer cannot completely separate itself from situations whereby the individual performs the work in an excessive manner. Consequently, the use of excessive force, when force is part and parcel of the job, does not isolate the employer from liability. In this case, however, the plaintiff failed to show that the bouncers were actually employed by the bar. Further, the plaintiff failed to show that the bar supervisor was present at the time of the assault, thereby failing to demonstrate that the supervisor was negligent in his job.

312 F. Supp. 2d 505

United States District Court, S.D. New York

YVETTE ADORNO AND STEPHANIE WOMBLE, PLAINTIFFS v. CORRECTIONAL SERVICES CORPORATION, DEFENDANT.

March 30, 2004

Background

Female former inmates of a federal community confinement center operated by a private company under contract with the federal Bureau of Prisons (BOP), brought suit alleging that the company was negligent in hiring, retaining, training, and supervising an employee who allegedly sexually abused inmates.

Holdings

On a defense Motion for Summary Judgment, the district court held that:

1. Company could not be held liable under the doctrine of respondeat superior;
2. Inmates failed to show how any negligence of the company in failing to adhere to a one-year security experience requirement when transferring the employee to a resident advocate position proximately caused any of their harm; and
3. Genuine issues of material fact existed as to whether the company was on notice of the employee's sexually abusive behavior, and whether such behavior caused the harm alleged.

Motion granted in part and denied in part

Le Marquis Community Correctional Center was a "halfway house" for federal and state prisoners who had not yet completed their prison terms. It was operated by CSC, a private company, pursuant to a written contract with the BOP and in accordance with guidelines set forth by the BOP.

Plaintiffs Yvette Adorno and Stephanie Womble became residents at Le Marquis in August and September 1998, respectively. They claim that after arriving at Le Marquis, they were sexually assaulted by Miguel Correa, an employee of CSC who worked at Le Marquis as resident advocate.

On November 13, 1998, at approximately 7:00 or 8:00 p.m., Adorno reported to Correa's office to discuss an infraction she had allegedly incurred. As resident advocate, one of Correa's responsibilities was to investigate "incident reports" for each resident and to ensure that his or her rights were not being violated. Correa had a private office on the second floor of Le Marquis.

While in Correa's office, Adorno claims that Correa picked up her shirt, touched her breasts, made various inappropriate sexual comments, and initially refused to let her leave his office. Adorno states that she was permitted to leave Correa's office only because she had to be present in her room for roll call at 9:00 p.m. but that he instructed her to return to his office immediately thereafter. At approximately 10:00 p.m., following roll call, Adorno returned to Correa's office. When Adorno returned, Correa allegedly kissed her and pushed his body up against hers. Adorno claims that Correa let her leave only after she threatened to scream and promised not to report the incident.

Adorno did not report the incident to any CSC or BOP officials, including the facility administrator at Le Marquis, Josette Nelson-Dabo. The number to contact the BOP was posted throughout Le Marquis, including in the female recreation room and in the cafeteria. In addition, a representative from the BOP had explained to the residents at an orientation meeting that if they were having problems with a CSC employee they should call the BOP directly. Adorno testified that she did not report the incident because Nelson-Dabo had threatened to return any resident who complained about conditions at Le Marquis to federal prison. Adorno did tell another Le Marquis resident about the incident a day after it occurred. According to Adorno, this incident has caused her to experience anger, mood swings, feelings of distrustfulness toward men, and problems being intimate with men. Adorno has sought psychiatric counseling and therapy concerning these problems. According to one psychiatrist, Adorno suffers from post-traumatic stress disorder caused by Correa's actions.

Womble was a resident at Le Marquis from the end of September 1998 through December 1998. During her stay, she met with Correa in his office approximately 12 times to discuss various infractions. Womble alleges that over the course of these meetings, Correa made various sexually inappropriate remarks. On approximately three such occasions, Correa allegedly hugged Womble and placed his hands on her clothes over her breasts. In addition, Womble states that Correa touched her buttocks on one occasion.

After about the fifth such encounter, Womble told Ms. Arias, her Case Manager at Le Marquis and a CSC employee, that Correa had "been harassing me and putting his hands on me every time I go into his office." Pursuant to guidelines established by the BOP, CSC had instituted procedures by which case managers were required to report to their supervisors incidents of alleged sexual abuse, even if these allegations were unsubstantiated. At some point between her conversation with Womble and Thanksgiving Day 1998, Arias left her position at Le Marquis. There is no evidence that Arias ever reported Womble's complaint to her supervisors.

Womble alleges that, a day or two after Thanksgiving Day 1998, she was raped by Correa. According to Womble, Correa called her into his office at approximately 8:30 p.m. Correa rose from his chair, walked to Womble, and kissed her. Womble pushed him away, left his office, and went to a bathroom a few steps down the hall. Correa then entered the bathroom, grabbed Womble from behind, and raped her. When leaving the bathroom, Correa told Womble not to say anything to Nelson-Dabo about the encounter or else Womble would be sent back to federal prison.

Womble did not report the rape to Nelson-Dabo, to other Le Marquis officials, or to the police. She testified that she did not do so because Nelson-Dabo had threatened residents that if they engaged in any sexual activity or if they did not like the way Le Marquis was operated, they would be returned to federal prison. In addition, Womble testified that she believed these threats to be founded based on her recollection of an incident in which a resident voiced complaints and was subsequently docked various privileges.

Because of the rape and the others incidents with Correa, Womble states that she has suffered physical pain and emotional suffering. She has since been treated for chlamydia, a sexually transmitted disease that she states she did not have prior to the rape. She has sought psychiatric counseling and therapy. According to one psychiatrist, Womble suffers from post-traumatic stress disorder caused by Correa's sexual abuse and rape.

Hiring, Transfer, and Termination of Correa

CSC hired Correa for the position of resident supervisor at Le Marquis on November 20, 1997. CSC's requirements for the position of resident supervisor, whose responsibilities essentially were to monitor and supervise the activities of residents, were a high school diploma or GED and one year of "supervisory experience in a human service field."

By March 10, 1998, Correa had been transferred to the position of resident advocate. CSC's requirements for the position of resident advocate were a high school diploma or GED and one year of "experience in [the] area of security." In addition, applicants for the position had to successfully pass a security background investigation. The BOP, which approved these requirements, conducted a background investigation on Correa prior to his transfer. This check, which consisted of running Correa's social security number and fingerprints, revealed that Correa had attended college and had not been convicted of any crimes.

As resident advocate, Correa's responsibilities included meeting privately with residents in his office to discuss confidential matters. Correa was required to attend—and did attend—an ethics class provided by CSC. The class dealt with how a resident advocate should interact with residents to maintain a courteous relationship, how to avoid inappropriate behavior, and how to report any misconduct to management.

Correa's alleged sexual abuse of Adorno and Womble was reported to Mark W. Jensen, a BOP official, at the end of December 1998 by other Le Marquis residents who learned of the abuse from Adorno and Womble. Immediately upon learning of Correa's alleged misconduct from the BOP, CSC interviewed Correa and the plaintiffs. After conducting its investigation, CSC terminated Correa on January 4, 1999.

A. CSC's Vicarious Liability

CSC states that "Correa's alleged sexual misconduct was clearly outside the scope of his duties as [resident advocate] and the alleged conduct clearly did not serve any legitimate business purpose." Thus, CSC argues that it cannot be held vicariously liable for Correa's actions because they were taken outside the scope of his employment.

The doctrine of respondeat superior "renders a master vicariously liable for a tort committed by his servant while acting within the scope of his employment." However, "an employer will not be held liable under this doctrine for actions which were not taken in furtherance of the employer's interests and which were undertaken by the employee for wholly personal motives." Nevertheless, an employer is not excused from liability "merely because [its] employees, acting in furtherance of [its] interests, exhibit human failings and perform negligently or otherwise than in an authorized manner." Instead, the test is "whether the act was done while the servant was doing his master's work, no matter how irregularly, or with what disregard of instructions."

To be held vicariously liable, an "employer need not have foreseen the precise act or the exact manner of the injury as long as the general type of conduct may have been reasonably expected." Thus, "where the element of general foreseeability exists, even intentional tort situations have been found to fall within the scope of employment." This determination "is heavily dependent on factual considerations and is therefore ordinarily a question for the jury." However, where there is no conflicting evidence as to the material facts, a court may make this determination as a matter of law.

The Court of Appeals of New York has set forth the following guidelines for determining whether tortious acts have been committed within the scope of employment: (1) the connection between the time, place and occasion for the act, (2) the history of the relationship between employer and employee as spelled out in actual practice, (3) whether the act is one commonly done by such an employee, (4) the extent of departure from normal methods of performance, and (5) whether the specific act was one that the employer could reasonably have anticipated. "While all five factors are considered, New York courts generally place greater emphasis on the fifth factor, namely, whether the acts involved ... could reasonably have been anticipated by the employer."

After applying these factors and accepting as true all of plaintiffs' evidence, the court concludes that no reasonable jury could find that Correa's actions were within the scope of his employment. Of the above five factors, the only one that arguably favors the plaintiffs is the first—"the connection between the time, place and occasion for the act." This is because the "time, place and occasion for the act" show that Correa's status as a CSC employee in the position of resident advocate enabled him to commit the alleged sexual assault. Plaintiffs have testified that they were sexually assaulted after being required to report to Correa's private office as part of CSC's process for reviewing alleged infractions. Thus, there was a connection between the time, place, and occasion for the act and Correa's employment.

There is no evidence in the record concerning the second factor. The third and fourth factors, however, clearly favor CSC. Plaintiffs do not dispute that the act of sexual abuse and/or rape is not one that is commonly done by a resident advocate; nor do they dispute that Correa's actions substantially departed from normal methods of performance.

The court turns now to the fifth factor, which "New York courts generally place greater emphasis on ..., namely, whether the acts involved ... could reasonably have been anticipated by [the] employer." Employers have been found vicariously liable for an intentional assault where the nature of the employee's duties made it foreseeable that such an assault would take place. Here, however, the nature of Correa's duties as resident advocate in no way mandated any kind of physical contact, let alone sexually oriented physical contact.

Because tortious sexual activity generally is entirely divorced from the nature of an employment position, "New York courts consistently have held that sexual misconduct and related tortious behavior arise from personal motives and do not further an employer's business, even when committed within the employment context." Thus, New York courts have repeatedly found no vicarious liability for claims involving sexual misconduct, including sexual assault.

The applicability of these principles is not altered merely because CSC allegedly had notice of Correa's propensity to commit sexual acts through Womble's complaint to Arias. As the Second Circuit has explained:

What is reasonably foreseeable in the context of respondeat superior is quite a different thing from the foreseeably unreasonable risk of harm that spells negligence. When we talk of vicarious liability we are not looking for the employer's fault but rather for risks that may fairly be regarded as typical of or broadly incidental to the enterprise [the employer] has undertaken. In other words, while Womble's complaint to Arias is relevant to CSC's liability for negligence (as discussed below), it is not a consideration in determining whether CSC is vicariously liable for Correa's actions.

Because the factors applicable to the doctrine of vicarious liability favor CSC, the court grants it summary judgment with respect to this issue.

B. CSC's Direct Liability for Negligence

"Even where an employee does not act within the scope of his employment, an employer may be required to answer in damages for the tort of an employee against a third party when the employer has either hired or retained the employee with knowledge of the employee's propensity for the sort of behavior which caused the injured party's harm." "A cause of action for negligent hiring or retention requires allegations that the employer knew or should have known of the employee's propensity to commit injury, or the employer failed to investigate a prospective employee notwithstanding knowledge of facts that would lead a reasonably prudent person to investigate that prospective employee."

CSC argues that it is entitled to summary judgment on plaintiffs' claims of negligent hiring and negligent retention. We deal with each claim in turn.

1. Negligent Hiring

CSC argues that it could not have been negligent in hiring Correa because the BOP's background check and CSC's interview process "did not place CSC on notice of any potential propensity Correa might have had for violence or sexual abuse." Plaintiffs do not argue that the background check was somehow inadequate or that there is any evidence in the record that CSC should have been on notice of any propensity Correa might have had for violence or sexual abuse prior to his transfer to the position of resident advocate. Instead, plaintiffs' argument is that CSC was negligent in transferring Correa to the position of resident advocate without his having met CSC's own requirement for the position: possessing one year of "experience in [the] area of security."

The court will assume, *arguendo*, that Correa did not possess the necessary experience and that the failure by CSC to adhere to the one-year security experience requirement could constitute negligence on its part. The problem with plaintiffs' argument is that, even under these assumptions, CSC is still entitled to summary judgment because plaintiffs have not demonstrated how this negligence proximately caused any of their harm.

Plaintiffs argue that "security experience was obviously required because the resident advocate ... asserted extensive authority over residents, including of the opposite sex, in a confidential setting." No reasonable jury, however, could conclude that Correa's lack of having one-year security experience proximately caused the plaintiffs' harm. There is no reason to believe that "experience in [the] area of security" means anything other than its normal meaning: experience protecting persons or property from harm by others—not from harm caused by the very person performing the security function. As plaintiffs tacitly admit elsewhere in their argument, this is a case of an abuse of supervisory authority. There is no causal contention between Correa's alleged lack of security experience and the abuse of his supervisory authority over the residents. Accordingly, CSC is entitled to summary judgment on plaintiffs' negligent hiring claims.

2. Negligent Retention

CSC argues that it is entitled to summary judgment on plaintiffs' negligent retention claims because it had no notice of Correa's alleged actions or his propensity to commit such actions until the alleged rape of Womble was reported to CSC by the BOP, at which time CSC immediately conducted an investigation and terminated Correa.

As noted, an employer is "required to answer in damages for the tort of an employee against a third party when the employer has ... retained the employee with knowledge of the employee's propensity for the sort of behavior which caused the injured party's harm." Here, there is evidence that Womble told Arias that Correa had "been harassing me and putting his hands on me every time I go into his office." Womble's report came "a couple of weeks" after her arrival at Le Marquis in September 1998, and thus preceded the alleged rape by Correa near Thanksgiving Day 1998 and the alleged sexual abuse of Adorno on November 13, 1998. A jury would be entitled to conclude that the report to Arias put CSC on notice of "the sort of behavior which caused the injured party's harm." While CSC complains that the only evidence in the record of Womble's report to Arias is Womble's own testimony, this testimony is enough to create a genuine issue of fact as to whether that report occurred. Accordingly, CSC is not entitled to summary judgment on plaintiffs' negligent retention claims.

Conclusion

CSC's Motion for Summary Judgment is granted in part and denied in part. Plaintiffs may not assert at trial any theory of vicarious liability. Also, their negligent hiring claims are dismissed.

CASE COMMENT

This case also represents an excellent analysis of the relevant issues related to a respondeat superior claim. The court examined the factors relating to scope of employment. It found that the sexual assault was not within the scope of employment. While this conclusion may appear to be obvious, the analysis used by the court was necessary to properly respond to the plaintiff's assertions. In addition, the tort-based claims, which are often asserted in these fact patterns, were dealt with as follows. The negligent hiring claim was dismissed because the one year security experience required in the job description was not related to the sexual assaults. The negligent retention claim, however, may have merit because of the complaints made by the women prior to sexual the assaults.

615 S.E.2d 45

Court of Appeals of North Carolina

TERI HARVEY LITTLE AND FRANK DONALD LITTLE, JR., PLAINTIFFS v. OMEGA MEATS, INC., THOMAS A. CASSANO, AND RONALD LEE SMITH, DEFENDANTS.

July 19, 2005

Background

Victims of robbery and assault committed by independent contractor salesman for company that sold meat door-to-door sued company and its president for negligent hiring and retention. The Superior Court, Guilford County, granted directed verdict for company and president and certified the judgment for immediate appeal.

Holding

The court of appeals held that company that employed independent contractor did not have duty to plaintiffs.

Affirmed

Plaintiffs Frank and Teri Little resided in a single-family residence in the City of Greensboro. About midday on 23 March 2001, Frank was at work and Teri had left the residence to take a walk in a nearby neighborhood. While the Littles' were gone from their residence, defendant Smith drove into the neighborhood, operating a refrigerated Omega Meats truck. Smith parked the truck in the driveway of the Littles' next door neighbor, and proceeded to break into the side entrance of the Littles' residence. While Smith was still inside, Teri returned to the home and went inside. She was attacked by Smith, handcuffed, and robbed. Approximately twenty to thirty minutes later, Frank also returned home. Smith then further assaulted Teri, bound Frank, and attempted to asphyxiate him with a plastic bag. As Smith began to sexually assault Teri, Frank freed himself and grabbed a knife. A struggle ensued over the knife, during which Teri was able to flee from the home. Realizing that one of his victims had escaped, Smith fled from the Littles' residence and drove off in the Omega Meats truck. Smith was subsequently convicted of several counts of kidnapping, felony assault, robbery, and felonious breaking and entering.

Defendant Omega Meats, Inc., sells meat products using independent contractor salesmen. Defendant Thomas A. Cassano is the president of Omega. Salesmen rent refrigerated trucks from Omega on a daily basis, and attempt to sell consigned meats to customers, door to door. At the end of the day, the salesman pays Omega for the truck rental, and for any meat sold. Once a salesman leaves Omega's warehouse, he is not supervised or controlled by Omega. Each salesman develops his own customers and decides where to drive the truck to service his existing customers or attempt to acquire new customers.

Smith first worked for Omega in 1997. Prior to beginning work as an independent contractor salesman, Omega performed a driver's license check on Smith, but did not perform a criminal background check. Had a criminal background check been performed, it would have revealed that Smith had numerous convictions, including drug offenses and assault. During his first period as a salesman for Omega, Smith was convicted of common law robbery and kidnapping, and served an active prison sentence of 26 months. Following Smith's release from prison, he went back to work for Omega as an independent contractor salesman. It was during Smith's second term with Omega that the incident with the Littles' occurred.

We agree with plaintiffs that Smith's relationship with Omega was that of an independent contractor and not an employee. "Generally, one who employs an independent contractor is not liable for the independent contractor's [acts]." However, in certain limited situations an employer may be held liable for the negligence of its independent contractor. Such a claim is not based upon vicarious liability, but rather is a direct claim against the employer based upon the actionable negligence of the employer in negligently hiring a third party. "The party that employs an independent contractor has a continuing responsibility to ensure that adequate safety precautions are taken.... The employer's liability for breach of this duty 'is direct' and not derivative."

Because plaintiff's claim against Omega is a direct claim, there must be a legal duty owed by the employer to the injured party in order to establish the claim for negligent hiring. Once that duty is established, then the plaintiff must prove four additional elements to prevail in a negligent hiring and retention case: "(1) the independent contractor acted negligently; (2) he was incompetent at the time of the hiring, as manifested either by inherent unfitness or previous specific acts of negligence; (3) the employer had notice, either actual or constructive, of this incompetence; and (4) the plaintiff's injury was the proximate result of this incompetence." Most of our cases dealing with negligent hiring of an independent contractor have turned upon the third element, whether the employer had actual or constructive notice of the incompetence of the independent contractor. (Cases and citations omitted—holding defendant had no notice of her nephew's incompetence in tree removal; holding that a general contractor did not have notice of subcontractor's practices which led to a trench cave-in; holding that defendant school system did not have notice of a principal's pedophilic tendencies.) Since these cases turned on the notice question, they do not contain any significant discussion of the duty owed by the employer to the plaintiff.

However, other cases make it clear that there must be a duty owed by the employer to the plaintiff in order to support an action for negligent hiring. In the leading case of *Page v. Sloan*, our Supreme Court stated that the "duties thus imposed upon an innkeeper for the protection of his guests are non-delegable, and liability cannot be avoided on the ground that their performance was entrusted to an independent contractor." In *Kinsey*, this court stated that in cases where the independent contractor engages in ultra-hazardous or inherently dangerous work, that "the employer has a non-delegable duty for the safety of others."

The nature and extent of the duty owed by the employer to injured parties in negligent hiring cases has not been described with great precision in the case law of North Carolina to date. However, most jurisdictions accepting the theory of negligent hiring have stated that an employer's duty to select competent employees extends to any member of the general public who comes into contact with the employment situation. Thus, courts have found liability in cases where employers invite the general public onto the business premises, or require employees to visit residences or employment establishments. One commentator, in analyzing the requisite connection between plaintiffs and employment situations in negligent hiring cases, noted three common factors underlying most case law upholding a duty to third parties: (1) the employee and the plaintiff must have been in places where each had a right to be when the wrongful act occurred; (2) the plaintiff must have met the employee as a direct result of the employment; and (3) the employer must have received some benefit, even if only potential or indirect, from the meeting of the employee and the plaintiff.

Courts in other jurisdictions have generally, though not exclusively, declined to hold employers liable for the acts of their independent contractors or employees under the doctrine of negligent hiring or retention when *any one* of these three factors was not proven. It is only after a plaintiff has established that the defendant owed a duty of care that the trial court considers the other elements necessary to establish a claim for negligent hiring or retention of an independent contractor. "Thus, to be liable the employer must first owe the plaintiff a duty of care."

In the instant case Smith was not in a place where he had a legal right to be since he broke in to plaintiffs' home; Smith and plaintiffs did not meet as a direct result of Smiths' relationship with defendants, since he did not enter plaintiffs' home as a salesman; finally, defendants received no benefit, direct, indirect or potential, from the tragic "meeting" between Smith and plaintiffs. We have found no authority in North Carolina suggesting that defendants owed plaintiffs a duty of care on these facts, and we hold that in fact none existed.

We refuse to make employers insurers to the public at large by imposing a legal duty on employers for victims of their independent contractors' intentional torts that bear no relationship to the employment. We note that because this is a direct action against the employer, for the purposes of this appeal the result would be the same if Smith had been an employee of defendants instead of an independent contractor. Smith could have perpetrated the exact same crimes against these plaintiffs, in the exact same manner, and with identical chances of success, on a day that he was not selling Omega's meats and driving Omega's vehicle.

Because Omega did not owe plaintiffs a duty of care, plaintiffs had no legal cause of action against Omega grounded in negligent hiring or retention. Having so held, we must further hold that the same reasoning applies to defendant Cassano. Therefore, the trial court properly granted defendants' motion for directed verdict pursuant. Our holding should not be interpreted as limiting employers' duties to third parties in negligent hiring or retention claims to duties that are non-delegable. What is required, however, is a nexus between the employment relationship and the injury.

Assuming arguendo that defendants did owe plaintiffs a duty of care, we further hold there was insufficient evidence, taken in the light most favorable to plaintiffs, to prove that any negligence on the part of defendants was the proximate cause of plaintiffs' injuries.

> Proximate cause is a cause which in natural and continuous sequence, unbroken by any new or independent cause, produced the plaintiff's injuries, and without which the injuries would not have occurred, and one from which a person of ordinary prudence could have reasonably foreseen that such a result, or consequences of a generally injurious nature, was probable under all the facts as they existed. Thus, it is axiomatic that proximate cause requires foreseeability. Plaintiffs argue that it was foreseeable to defendants that sending a person such as Smith, with his recent, as well as long, record and propensity for violence, into residences could and likely would create an unreasonable risk of harm.

In support of this contention they cite the North Dakota Supreme Court case of *McLean v. Kirby Co.* While plaintiffs may be correct in their assertion that sending Smith into residences could foreseeably create an unreasonable risk of harm, the foreseeability of a risk of harm is insufficient unless defendants' negligent hiring or retention of Smith in some manner *actually caused* the injury in question.

In *McLean*, the victim "let Molachek into her apartment to demonstrate [defendant's] vacuum cleaner. Molachek also brought with him a set of knives, provided by the distributor, as a 'door opener' or 'gift offering' for allowing the in-home demonstration. After beginning the demonstration, Molachek used the knives in assaulting and raping [the victim]." In *McLean*, defendant's independent contractor was invited into the victim's home as a direct result of his position as a representative of defendant.

Further, he accomplished the assault and rape by utilizing knives provided to him by the defendant. The facts in *McLean* support a finding of proximate cause arising out of the employment or independent contractor relationship. This is not true in the instant case. As discussed above, though Smith was driving an Omega truck, his association with defendants did not advance his criminal endeavor in any manner. The same result would have occurred had he not been driving an Omega truck.

Therefore, even assuming arguendo that defendants were negligent in hiring Smith, this negligence was not the proximate cause of plaintiffs' injuries. The trial court correctly granted defendants' Motion for Directed Verdict.

Affirmed

CASE COMMENT

This case shows how courts view the actions of independent contractors in relation to the liability exposure of the employing company. In this case, the salesman was an independent contractor, who drove a truck owned by the company. During the course of his work, he sexually assaults a woman and assaults her husband. The court held that the assaults were not within the course and scope of the employment. The court further held that the tort claims of negligent hiring and retention failed due to the facts in the case. Significantly, the court held that "we refuse to make employers insurers to the public at large by imposing a legal duty on employers for victims of their independent contractors' intentional torts that bear no relationship to the employment."

131 Cal. App. 4th 464, 32 Cal. Rptr. 3d 151

Court of Appeal, Fourth District, Division 3, California

DONALD TILLEY, PLAINTIFF AND APPELLANT v. CZ MASTER ASSOCIATION, DEFENDANT AND RESPONDENT.

June 28, 2005

Background

Security guard employed by security firm sued homeowner's association which had contracted with the firm for security services, for injuries he suffered from an assault while responding to complaint about a youth party on association's premises. The Superior Court of Orange County entered summary judgment for association, and guard appealed.

Holdings

The court of appeal held that the property association was not liable on basis of retained control over premises, that it had no liability for the injuries suffered by the employee of an independent contractor, and it had no duty to restrict access or regulate parties.

Affirmed

Donald Tilley, a security guard employed by BonaFide Security Services, Inc., sued CZ Master Association, a homeowner's association which had contracted with BonaFide for security services, because of injuries he suffered from an assault while responding to a complaint about a youth party on CZ's premises. In essence, Tilley argued that CZ owed the security guards a duty to provide a safe premises for them to guard, including imposing restrictions to control youth parties, that it acted negligently by failing to do so, and that it increased the danger to the guards by requiring them to work unarmed and to respond personally to complaints about such parties.

The assault on Tilley, which is at the heart of this case, occurred in August 1998. At that time, Tilley was a 62-year-old former law enforcement officer, employed as a security guard by BonaFide. BonaFide had contracted with CZ to provide security for Coto de Caza, a private, gate-guarded community, and Tilley had been assigned to work there since at least 1996.

The circumstances surrounding Tilley's assault are undisputed. Ashley S., a 17-year-old resident of Coto, had a party. Substantially more guests attended her party than had been directly invited. The party got out of hand, and both Coto's security officers and the Orange County Sheriff's deputies were called. The party was broken up, and most of the guests dispersed. Unfortunately, they did not all stay dispersed.

One of the guests who returned was Robbie Carreno. He had earlier been assaulted by some other partygoers, and he returned to the S. residence with his brother, Nathan, intending to locate his assailants and perhaps retaliate. Robbie and Nathan located one of the perpetrators of Robbie's assault, and attacked him.

Meanwhile, Coto security personnel again received complaints about the goings on at the S. residence. When Tilley, along with another security officer, returned to the residence, 20 to 30 people remained in and around it. Nathan and Robbie Carreno, however, were already in Nathan's truck, preparing to leave. Tilley approached them, and informed Nathan he was "under arrest." Tilley then asked Nathan for his keys, and obtained them. As Tilley moved away from the truck, Nathan and Robbie came after him and assaulted him in an attempt to regain the keys. Tilley was severely injured in the assault, including a fractured skull. Deputies from the sheriff's department arrived after the assault.

Tilley obtained worker's compensation benefits from BonaFide on account of his injuries, and sued CZ, along with several other individuals and entities he alleged were responsible for the incident. He resolved his claims against all named defendants other than CZ.

According to Tilley's third amended complaint, "the primary function of BonaFide under its contract with CZ Master Association was to protect the privacy of the residents of Coto de Caza, by attempting to monitor and control traffic proceeding through the gates for Coto de Caza, [with] the goal of preventing entry by uninvited persons; CZ Master Association contracted with BonaFide to provide a roving patrol to monitor and report to CZ Master Association the violation of the rules and regulations issued by CZ Master Association relating to pets, parking, landscaping, signage, holiday decoration, and the like; Bona Fide personnel, to the extent they observed nuisances, disturbances, suspicious and/or criminal acts were to make a record and report such incidents and activities to CZ Master Association for further action, and call for local law enforcement; the contract between CZ Master Association and BonaFide expressly forbade BonaFide personnel from carrying firearms in the performance of their employment obligations; BonaFide personnel were not required nor expected to perform arrests or confront lawbreakers as part of their regular employment duties.... CZ Master Association made clear to BonaFide and its personnel that they did not have the authority, power or right to comport themselves or otherwise act as law enforcement officials in the performance of their employment duties and/or their interaction with the community. In a word, CZ Master Association originally retained BonaFide to man the gates and provide courtesy patrols, not perform law enforcement functions."

Tilley also alleges that by the time of his injury in August of 1998, Coto already had a long-standing problem with frequent and uncontrolled youth parties, many of which erupted into violence. He specifically alleges that the S. family, which hosted the party at which he was injured, had previously held summer parties in 1996 and 1997, both of which had spiraled out of control, including numerous uninvited guests, excessive drinking, and violence. There is evidence that Ashley's father, Richard S., was arrested at the 1996 party for allowing minors to consume alcohol at his residence. Tilley himself responded to complaints about the S.s' 1997 party, and found the S.s' other daughter, Torri, involved in a physical altercation with John Jesme, a young male resident of Coto. Tilley intervened on her behalf, and was struck by Jesme. That incident was the only one involving violence against any security guard in connection with a youth party prior to the incident at issue in this case.

Tilley alleged that CZ was aware of the many problems caused by out-of-control youth parties in Coto, and had authority to impose reasonable restrictions on the number of guests allowed, and to impose greater restrictions on access to the association's property. He also alleged CZ was aware of two non-party incidents in which young males had "savagely" attacked adult males who had attempted to curtail the youths' conduct within the association property, shortly prior to the S.s' 1998 party. He alleged that CZ "unreasonably increased the risk of harm to BonaFide personnel by instructing them to respond to reports of disturbances, instead of leaving such matters for law enforcement, and without instructing, training or equipping BonaFide personnel to handle such matters."

CZ moved for summary judgment, arguing that it owed Tilley no duty to provide a secure premises, that any duty it had was discharged by hiring BonaFide, that Tilley's injury was not foreseeable, that no causal connection existed between its alleged negligence and Tilley's injury, that the elements of premises liability could not be established, and that Tilley's claim was barred by the firefighter's rule, the primary assumption of risk doctrine, and the *Privette* doctrine.

Once the wheat of Tilley's response to the separate statement is separated from its considerable chaff, it turns out that the facts from CZ's motion are largely undisputed. With respect to fact No. 5 (i.e., "CZ relied on BonaFide and its officers to use their judgment and discretion in carrying out security related procedures [and on] BonaFide's policy for each officer to observe and report incidents and violations of law, rather than get in harm's way"), Tilley offers only evidence that CZ had complained to BonaFide on one occasion that its officers had ignored resident complaints about a "noise disturbance" at the "Jesme" residence (described as "several teenagers being loud and boisterous very late in the evening"), and that there appeared to be a recurring problem of BonaFide officers ignoring complaints about the Jesmes. According to the letter, BonaFide gate attendants had informed residents in the past *that they could not locate the Jesme residence to patrol it*. That letter does not signal any change in policy about juvenile parties in general. Instead, it appears to be focused on the Jesme residence in particular, and the concern that the guards are ignoring it. Tilley also relies upon evidence that one of BonaFide's "post orders" stated that "patrol of the property is to be aggressive, providing a feeling of omnipresence to the residents...." Again, however, that order in no way suggests the officers should put themselves in harm's way. It merely suggests the officers are expected to "see what is going on in the immediate patrol area and ... to be seen." It also makes clear that "[w]hen interaction is necessary with residents or guest, the greatest weapon an officer has is the quality of verbal delivery; *remain non-aggressive, professional and courteous.*

With respect to fact No. 7 (i.e., "Neither Merit no[r] CZ ever instructed plaintiff/BonaFide to carry out arrests or detentions"), Tilley merely responds that CZ knew or should have known that BonaFide officers sometimes did so, and thus must have impliedly encouraged it. However, the evidence he cites for the "knew or should have known" assertion establishes only that Tilley prepared a list of such incidents for Scott Myers, the BonaFide account representative, but not that the list was transmitted to CZ. In any event, the fact CZ may have known that BonaFide guards sometimes exercised their judgment to detain suspected wrongdoers, presumably when they felt it was safe to do so, does not equate to CZ itself imposing some change in policy.

The evidence cited includes Tilley's report of the assault perpetrated on Tilley by a young male resident of Coto at the S.s' 1997 party. In that report, Tilley described an

> extremely large youth party *with* more then [*sic*] enough parents/adults supervising. John Jesme attempted to enter the party area and was instructed to leave. He refused and grabbed the 16-year-old host by the neck throwing her to the ground. When I attempted to help he struck me in the face with a closed fist. I struck him back and pulled him off the girl and arrested him.

Tilley also testified that the incident with Jesme was the only time he could remember responding to a complaint about fighting in connection with a youth party. The primary problems for which the security guards were summoned to parties were excessive noise, overcrowding and parking violations. If the problem was overcrowding alone, he would do nothing other than file a report. If the problem was noise, Tilley would knock on the homeowner's door and ask that the noise be reduced or the party ended. If that was not successful, he had been instructed by BonaFide to "call the Orange County Sheriffs." Tilley testified that he understood his only responsibility in connection with youth parties was to "observe and report."

The court then turned to the merits: "the Court is persuaded that Plaintiff's claims fail under the doctrine explained in *Privette*. Those cases stand for the principle that, except in limited circumstances, an employee of a contractor may not sue the hirer of the contractor under tort theories.

The limited circumstances, recognized in *Hooker*, occur when the hirer retains control over the contractor's performance in such a manner as to 'affirmatively contribute' to the employee's injury. Thus, the issue here is whether or not there is a triable issue of fact as to whether CZ Master retained control of BFSS's work and, in so doing, affirmatively contributed to the injury suffered by Plaintiff.... Based upon the evidence presented in connection with this motion, the court finds that no reasonable trier of fact could [conclude] that CZ Master in any way affirmatively contributed to this incident. Plaintiff points only to Defendant's role in establishing policy for the admission of persons into the gated community. Any such role, would have been at most an oblique—as opposed to affirmative—contribution to the injury. Certainly, the residents of the community, acting through its homeowners' association (CZ Master), could determine gate-admission policy or even allow completely open access to the neighborhood. Such determinations, as a matter of law, do not affirmatively contribute to the injuries resulting from a criminal assault by a person entering through the gate.

In addition, the court finds that plaintiff's claims are barred by the doctrine of primary assumption of risk. Here, as in, "the particular risk of harm that caused the injury was the very risk plaintiff and [his] employer was hired to prevent."

Mr. Tilley's primary duties—as set by BonaFide—were to serve as post supervisor and to perform the roving patrol function demanded by CZ Master Association, in accordance with instructions and directions as issued by CZ Master Association and/or its sub-associations, and Merit Property Management, Inc.

In any event, Tilley failed to demonstrate any triable issue of fact with respect to the issue of a special employment relationship between himself and CZ. According to his own testimony, he took his directions strictly from BonaFide. The scope of his duties was set forth in "post orders" which he stated were provided by BonaFide. "There would be not [*sic*] post orders coming from CZ Masters [*sic*] or Merit. They would be just directives requesting this or requesting that. The post orders had to come from BonaFide." Tilley went on to explain that a post order had more authority than a directive from CZ, and that "a directive could override a post order only if it was approved by BonaFide." BonaFide provided the vehicles used by its officers to patrol Coto, and those vehicles were connected by radio to a dispatcher at BonaFide headquarters.

Tilley also testified about circumstances when he had implemented changes in the security procedures, explaining he discussed them with BonaFide personnel, but not with CZ. For example, Tilley stated he had implemented a policy that if a security guard came upon a situation involving a potentially violent person, the guard was to wait for backup before acting. He stated the policy was approved by BonaFide, but when asked if it had been approved by CZ, he responded "I didn't know if it was or not." He then explained "I didn't go to CZ Masters [*sic*] because that was my boss's responsibility." Tilley also testified that on approximately six occasions, members of the CZ board would request he alter some procedure, such as adding a special patrol in an area, and on those occasions he would inform them they would "have to go through BonaFide." He couldn't remember a single time when a CZ board member had asked him to do something and he had responded in any way other than simply referring them to BonaFide.

As Tilley's own testimony establishes, he had no substantial direct relationship with CZ. He took all his orders from BonaFide, and obtained BonaFide's approval for his actions. To the extent he became aware of directives from CZ, he understood they were subordinate to BonaFide's post orders. He relied upon BonaFide to resolve any concerns that CZ might have. Under those circumstances, there was no relationship of "special employment" between Tilley and CZ as a matter of law.

In this case, there was no evidence BonaFide relinquished any control over Tilley, or that CZ ever directly exercised such control. Instead, what this evidence demonstrates is a tripartite relationship, with BonaFide squarely in the middle. Tilley answered to his employer, BonaFide, and BonaFide endeavored to keep its client, CZ, satisfied with the services provided. The combined effect of those relationships was that CZ would have had some power to affect Tilley's work situation and activities, but only an indirect one, and its influence extended only so far as BonaFide chose to allow. Such a relationship cannot be characterized as creating an "employment" between CZ and Tilley directly.

> Under the peculiar risk doctrine, a person who hires an independent contractor to perform work that is inherently dangerous can be held liable for tort damages when the contractor's negligent performance of the work causes injuries to others. By imposing such liability without fault on the person who hires the independent contractor, the doctrine seeks to ensure that injuries caused by inherently dangerous work will be compensated, that the person for whose benefit the contracted work is done bears responsibility for any risks of injury to others, and that adequate safeguards are taken to prevent such injuries.

"A critical inquiry in determining the applicability of the doctrine of peculiar risk is whether the work for which the contractor was hired involves a risk that is 'peculiar to the work to be done,' arising either from the nature or the location of the work and 'against which a reasonable person would recognize the necessity of taking special precautions.'" The term *peculiar risk* means neither a risk that is abnormal to the type of work done, nor a risk that is abnormally great; it simply means "a special, recognizable danger arising out of the work itself."

In *Privette*, however, the supreme court went on to conclude that a landowner's liability under the peculiar risk doctrine did not extend to the employees of the independent contractor itself—in that case a roofing contractor—if the contractor had provided them with workers' compensation coverage. The court reasoned that in the absence of direct negligence by the landowner, causing the injury, then allowing the worker to recover tort damages against it, in addition to the workers' compensation remedy from the employer, would be a windfall.

In this case, the peculiar risk doctrine was generally applicable. BonaFide was an independent security company, and the services it performed for CZ, including controlling access to the premises, enforcing parking restrictions, responding to complaints and otherwise promoting and encouraging compliance with association rules, obviously presented peculiar risks.

The undisputed facts demonstrate that BonaFide was in control of how its work was performed, and that all decisions concerning the activities of its employees were ultimately its responsibility. As set forth in CZ's statement of undisputed facts, "BonaFide Security set the patrol routes and times, created security procedures, approved Security post orders and directives, trained and assigned officers, instructed its officers how to respond to parties and otherwise controlled the day-to-day operations of security for CZ within Coto. Individual officers used their discretion in determining whether to contact law enforcement or residents and visitors in responding to disturbances."

There is evidence that CZ and its property manager, Merit, may have had significant influence on how BonaFide made certain decisions concerning the work, but no more than would be expected in the case of a contractor seeking to keep its customer satisfied. There is no evidence that CZ had any power to *override* BonaFide's decisions concerning how its employees should conduct themselves. Tilley himself testified that he answered only to BonaFide, and that any changes CZ might wish to implement in the work he did had to be cleared through BonaFide.

There *was* evidence CZ retained control over certain aspects of the worksite—i.e., the association's property. BonaFide had no independent authority to change the scope of access to the property, or to impose restrictions on how the homeowners could use it. In this respect, the instant case presents an issue of retained control, as in *Hooker*.

The supreme court in *Hooker* concluded that such a claim would be sufficient to support liability, but only if the hirer "exercised the control that was retained in a manner that affirmatively contributed to the injury of the contractor's employee." It concluded that no such "affirmative" contribution could be shown in that case. Under the "active participation" standard, a principal employer is subject to liability for injuries arising out of its independent contractor's work if the employer is actively involved in, or asserts control over, the manner of performance of the contracted work. Such an assertion of control occurs, for example, when the principal employer *directs* that the contracted work be done by use of a certain mode or otherwise interferes with the means and methods by which the work is to be accomplished.

In this case, there is likewise no evidence that CZ's exercise of the authority it retained over the premises affirmatively contributed to Tilley's injuries. Like Caltrans in *Hooker*, CZ is accused of permitting others (in this case, residents and their guests) to have access to the premises for parties, thus increasing the danger to the contractor's employees. But that conduct is merely passive. CZ did not host the parties, did not direct anyone to have them, and according to the undisputed evidence, was not given advance notice of them. CZ's misconduct amounts to merely a failure to exercise its (presumed) power to restrict or impose controls over the parties. Such a failure cannot be the basis of liability.

Moreover, CZ did not direct Tilley to respond to the situation at the S.s' home by confronting and purporting to "arrest" a presumed wrongdoer. As Tilley himself alleged in his complaint, the basic premise of the agreement between BonaFide and CZ was that "BonaFide personnel were not required nor expected to perform arrests or confront lawbreakers as part of their regular employment duties.... CZ Master Association made clear to BonaFide and its personnel that they did not have the authority, power or right to comport themselves or otherwise act as law enforcement officials in the performance of their employment duties and/or their interaction with the community."

CZ asserted, as undisputed facts, that BonaFide guards were expected to use their judgment in responding to situations, CZ relied upon BonaFide's policy for each officer to observe and report incidents and violations of law, rather than get in harm's way, and it never instructed BonaFide guards to carry out arrests or detentions. Tilley's own testimony supported those alleged facts, and he failed to offer any evidence to dispute them. Under those circumstances, CZ cannot have any liability for Tilley's decision to step out of his "observe and report" function to confront the Carrenos. There is simply no evidence that CZ expected, let alone required, that he do so.

Finally, it is irrelevant that CZ knew or should have known that Tilley (or other guards) had confronted and detained or arrested wrongdoers in the past. The same type of argument was made in *Hooker*, and rejected by the supreme court: "there was no evidence Caltrans' exercise of retained control over safety conditions at the worksite affirmatively contributed to the injury of the crane operator. There was, at most, evidence that Caltrans' safety personnel were aware of an unsafe practice and failed to exercise the authority they retained to correct it."

Under the *Privette* doctrine, and its extension in *Hooker,* the undisputed facts of this case demonstrate CZ could not be held liable to Tilley based upon its alleged failure to exercise its retained control over the association property so as to restrict or control youth parties on the premises.

In addition to determining CZ had no liability to Tilley under the peculiar risk doctrine, we also conclude CZ owed Tilley no independent duty to restrict the parties thrown by its homeowners, or to control the number of non-residents allowed to attend those parties.

Duty, of course, is primarily a matter of law, not fact. In *Sakiyama* relied upon by CZ, the court concluded that defendant had no duty to refuse the use of its premises for an all-night rave party, even though drinking and drug use by partygoers was foreseeable. The court rejected the notion that such parties were "inherently dangerous" because no party-goers were required to engage in dangerous or illegal conduct, and explained that imposing "ordinary negligence liability on a business owner that has done nothing more than allow its facility to be used for an all-night party, even if we assume [it] knew that drugs would be used at the party, would expand the concept of duty beyond any current model."

In reaching its decision, the *Sakiyama* court considered the well-known factors set out in *Rowland* to determine whether a legal duty of care existed: "[1] the foreseeability of harm to the plaintiff, [2] the degree of certainty that the plaintiff suffered injury, [3] the closeness of the connection between the defendant's conduct and the injury suffered, [4] the moral blame attached to the defendant's conduct, [5] the policy of preventing future harm, [6] the extent of the burden to the defendant and consequences to the community of imposing a duty to exercise care with resulting liability for breach, and [7] the availability, cost, and prevalence of insurance for the risk involved."

While foreseeability is a primary issue in determining duty, "foreseeability alone is not sufficient to create an independent tort duty.... Because the consequences of a negligent act must be limited to avoid an intolerable burden on society the determination of duty recognizes that policy considerations may dictate a cause of action should not be sanctioned no matter how foreseeable the risk. There are clear judicial days on which a court can foresee forever and thus determine liability but none on which that foresight alone provides a socially and judicially acceptable limit on recovery of damages for [an] injury. In short, foreseeability is not synonymous with duty; nor is it a substitute."

In this case, the evidence supporting foreseeability was slight, at best. Despite Tilley's sweeping assertion concerning the numerous violent juvenile parties that took place regularly in Coto, the evidence established only one occasion in which a party had erupted into violence prior to the 1998 party at issue in this case. That incident was the S.s' 1997 party, when Tilley himself responded to a report involving an altercation between the S.s' daughter Torri, and John Jesme. According to Tilley's own report, the party, while large, was adequately supervised by adults. Moreover, the violence was not the product of homeowners allowing a party to grow too large, or of non-residents being allowed access to the premises. To the contrary, the problem was that Torri S. *was* attempting to restrict access to her party, and the person she was seeking to bar was a Coto resident.

There is evidence of two other incidents of youth violence against adults within Coto in the record, but they are not sufficiently similar to the incident at issue here to support foreseeability. Those incidents were not related to parties, and the perpetrators in both cases included Coto residents, accompanied by their friends. Nothing in any of these incidents suggested any problem which could be cured by limiting the size of residents' parties or imposing more stringent restrictions on access to such parties by non-residents of Coto.

Additionally, none of the other *Rowland* factors (other than perhaps the certainty of plaintiffs' injury) support imposing a duty in this case. The connection between the defendant's conduct—failing to impose restrictions on homeowner parties—and the injury suffered, is attenuated at best. Tilley was injured after the S.s' party was over, and the Carrenos were in their car attempting to leave. It was Tilley's attempt to detain them, not the fact that the party had taken place, which was the immediate cause of the assault. Of course, there is no moral blame attached to allowing a homeowner to host a party, and the policy of preventing future harm would be little served by restricting parties, as the typical problems associated with parties, according to Tilley's own testimony, were noise and parking violations—not violence.

Moreover, the burden to CZ and consequences to the community of imposing a duty to place restrictions on residents' parties, with resulting liability for breach, would appear to be enormous. Any mishap at a party within Coto would presumably give rise to at least a colorable claim against CZ. Additionally, the undisputed evidence is that the community's CC & R's gave CZ no specific power to regulate parties within the residents' own homes. While Tilley argues that CZ could have regulated parties through use of the CC & R provision prohibiting nuisances would not have been effective. The nuisance regulation did not declare that parties, or even large parties, constituted a nuisance. Instead, it merely stated that a "noise or other nuisance" which was "offensive or detrimental" to other residents, was prohibited. That would allow an overly loud or raucous party to be stopped (as BonaFide guards sometimes did), but included no authority to prevent it in the first place.

And finally, it is undisputed that BonaFide had already insured against the risks encountered by its employees during the course of their work, through the workers' compensation system.

Based upon all of those factors, we conclude CZ had no duty to restrict access to the community or to regulate the parties hosted by its residents. Like the *Sakiyama* court, we do not consider parties to be "inherently dangerous," even assuming that underage drinking would take place. They may be unwise, troublesome, nasty, brutish and long, but they are not "inherently dangerous." More specifically, there is no evidence these parties posed any significant danger to the BonaFide security guards who patrolled Coto, so long as those guards limited their involvement and avoided placing themselves in harm's way. The problem in this case was Tilley did not. He chose to confront and attempt to detain a partygoer who was leaving the scene. Such conduct was not a required or expected part of his job, and was not a circumstance CZ was obligated to protect against.

We have concluded Tilley offered no evidence to create a triable issue of fact on his claim CZ either expressly or impliedly required the security guards to act aggressively in confronting problems with youth parties, thus placing themselves at risk. However, even if he had, summary judgment would have been appropriate based upon the primary assumption of risk doctrine.

As explained by the supreme court in *Neighbarger* the primary assumption of risk doctrine, as applied in the employment context, provides that one who hires a person to confront a particular risk, owes no duty to protect the person against that risk. As explained in *Neighbarger* "it is unfair to charge the defendant with a duty of care to prevent injury to the plaintiff arising from the very condition or hazard the defendant has contracted with the plaintiff to remedy or confront."

Although Tilley argues the primary assumption of risk doctrine cannot be applied against a private (as opposed to public) safety officer, citing *Neighbarger*, that case establishes no such rule. Instead, as we have already explained in refusal to apply the doctrine (in that case specifically the "firefighter's rule") was based upon the fact that the plaintiffs' claims had been asserted against a third-party wrongdoer, and not the entity which had hired them to undertake the risk.

As *Neighbarger* explained, "if we focus on the defendant and the question of the defendant's duty toward plaintiff, we see that the third party defendant stands in a different relation to the private safety worker than members of the public stand to the public firefighter."

> When a safety employee is privately employed, a third party lacks the relationship that justifies exonerating him or her from the usual duty of care. The third party, unlike the public with its police and fire departments, has not provided the services of the private safety employee. Nor has the third party paid in any way to be relieved of the duty of care toward such a private employee. Having no relationship with the employee, and not having contracted for his or her services, it would not be unfair to charge the third party with the usual duty of care towards the private safety employee. (Citations omitted.)

In this case, however, CZ is itself the entity which is alleged to have engaged Tilley to confront potentially violent young partygoers in Coto—an extension of the more passive "observe and report" function normally required of BonaFide security guards. Assuming that allegation was proven, it would establish that CZ hired Tilley to confront the very hazard which resulted in his injury, and would thus exonerate CZ from any duty to protect him from that hazard. Under those circumstances as well, summary judgment would be appropriate.

The judgment is affirmed.

CASE COMMENT

This case demonstrates that the facts do not expose the property association to liability due to the acts of the security guard. The plaintiff sought to connect the actions of the security officer and his firm to the association. The association argued that the security firm was an independent contractor. The court examined the contract, the operational and administrative relationship, and the facts of the particular incident, and found that there was insufficient evidence of control to make the association liable for the acts of the security officer. In addition, the tort-based claims were also found lacking based the failure to show a duty by the association to the plaintiff or the security firm.

836 N.E.2d 893

Appellate Court of Illinois, First District, Third Division

TAMMY MACDONALD, AS PERSONAL REPRESENTATIVE OF THE ESTATE OF NICHOLAS MICHAEL JAMES, DECEASED, PLAINTIFF-APPELLANT v. WILLIAM HINTON, AKA BILL HINTON AND TAU, INC., D/B/A TROPHIES ARE US II, DEFENDANTS-APPELLEES.

Sept. 30, 2005

Background

Personal representative of estate of employee who was murdered by coworker brought action against employer for damages based on breach of duty to warn employee of danger posed by coworker. The Circuit Court, Cook County, granted employer's Motion to Dismiss for failure to state a claim. Plaintiff appealed.

Holdings

The appellate court held that:

1. Risk to employee did not arise from the particular nature of his employment, and thus employer did not have duty to warn employee;
2. Harm inflicted by coworker was not foreseeable; and
3. Personal representative failed to allege that coworker killed employee on employer's premises or with the instrumentalities of the employment.

Affirmed

Plaintiff alleged that in May 2003, defendant employed Maust and her 19-year-old son James at his trophy business, Trophies Are Us II, in Dolton, Illinois. Defendant also owned a residential apartment building in Hammond, Indiana, and leased an apartment to James and another to Maust. Occasionally, defendant also employed James and Maust to perform repair work at the apartment building. Maust befriended James at work and frequently provided James with transportation to and from their mutual places of residence and work.

Subsequently, Maust assaulted and killed James. Maust buried James's body in the basement of defendant's apartment building. The homicide did not occur while the men were engaged in the course of their employment at Trophies Are Us. Plaintiff alleged that defendant knew that Maust was "a convicted killer who constituted a mortal danger to young men such as [James] with whom he was able to make acquaintance through mutual employment or otherwise." Defendant also knew of the relationship that had developed between James and Maust, and that James was not likely to become aware of the "mortal danger" posed by Maust on his own. Therefore, plaintiff asserted, defendant was negligent insofar as he breached a duty to warn James that Maust was "a convicted killer," whose "previous victims were young males," and that "Maust had established an acquaintance or some other sort of personal relationship with his previous victims prior to killing them ... suddenly, brutally and without warning." Plaintiff concluded that James's death was proximately caused by defendant's breach of duty to warn James about Maust.

On appeal, plaintiff first contends that she stated a claim of negligence against defendant based on a breach of defendant's duty to warn James about Maust. Specifically, plaintiff relies on Section 471 of the Restatement (Second) of Agency to assert that defendant should have warned James that Maust was "a convicted murderer" with the "propensity to befriend boys and young men and then, having won their confidence, to kill them."

Ordinarily, a party owes no duty of care to protect another from the harmful or criminal acts of third persons. However, the law recognizes at least four exceptions to this rule: (1) when the parties are in a special relationship and the harm is foreseeable; (2) when an employee is in imminent danger and this is known to the employer; (3) when a principal fails to warn his agent of an unreasonable risk of harm involved in the agency; and (4) when any party voluntarily or contractually assumes a duty to protect another from the harmful acts of a third party.

The first exception to the rule is set forth in Section 314A of the Restatement (Second) of Torts (1965), which provides that when a special relationship exists between the plaintiff and the defendant, the defendant owes the plaintiff a duty to protect him from unreasonable risks of physical harm arising within the scope of the relationship. However, Illinois does not consider the employer-employee relationship to be one of the special relationships covered by the Section 314A exception.

The second exception to the rule against tort liability for the criminal activities of third persons comes from Section 521(1) of the Restatement (Second) of Agency. That exception imposes a duty on employers "to exercise reasonable care to protect an employee 'who comes into a position of imminent danger or serious harm and this is known' to the employer."

Another exception is based on an express assumption of duty. Here, plaintiff relies upon the third exception, which is based on Section 471 of the Restatement (Second) of Agency, to allege the existence of a duty. Section 471 of the Restatement (Second) of Agency discusses when a principal would be liable for a breach of his duty to warn his agent of a particular risk, resulting in injury to the agent.

Section 471 provides that: "A principal is subject to liability in an action of tort for failing to use care to warn an agent of an unreasonable risk *involved in the employment*, if the principal should realize that it exists and that the agent is likely not to become aware of it, thereby suffering harm (emphasis added by court)."

Accordingly, based on Section 471 of the Restatement (Second) of Agency, a duty for an employer to issue a warning to an employee would arise only where the risk is (1) unreasonable, (2) involved in the employment, (3) foreseeable, and (4) the employee is not likely to become aware of it on his own.

One issue presented by plaintiff's complaint is whether she pled that the risk posed by Maust was "involved in the employment" relationship between defendant and James. Our research has failed to yield any cases from any jurisdiction in the United States that have discussed whether a particular risk was "involved in the employment" as defined in Section 471 of the Restatement (Second) of Agency. However, we find instructive three cases from other jurisdictions which discuss similar issues.

The case that most closely resembles the factual scenario in the case at bar is the 80-year-old case of *Dell v. Lancaster*. In that case, the Court of Civil Appeals of Texas affirmed the dismissal of an employee's complaint because the employee failed to plead that injuries he sustained in an assault had any connection to his employment. The employee was hired by the defendant employer to paint railroad coaches during a strike; however, the employer did not inform the employee of the strike. Sometime after he began his employment, while walking in town with his wife, the employee "was, for some reason not disclosed, attacked while on the street by lawless characters for whose acts [the employer was] not responsible."

The employee claimed that his employer was liable for his injuries because the employer was "negligent in not informing [him] that a strike was on" before he began work. However, the court found that the employee should have known of the circumstances on his own and held that a strike-breaker assumed the risk of violence from strikers while off the premises of the employer and while the employee was off-duty. In so holding, the court observed that the complaint contained:

> no allegation that [the employee] was not protected from violence while work, ... [but] it is affirmatively stated that [the employee] and his wife were on the street and not on the premises of [the employer] when attacked. The cause of the attack is not given, and it is not alleged that [the employee] was a strike breaker, or what is known as a "scab," and that he was attacked on that ground. There is no allegation that in any manner connects the assault upon [the employee] with his service for [the employer]. The facts show a criminal assault upon [the employee] by lawbreakers on the streets of Marshall, but give no inkling of the cause of such attack.

Similarly, in *Slagle v. White Castle Systems, Inc.*, the Court of Appeals of Ohio declined to hold an employer liable for injuries sustained by an employee who was assaulted on his way home from work. The plaintiff-employee in that case sought to hold his employer liable under the Section 314A special relationship exception. The employee contended that his employer should have been held liable for the injuries he sustained in the assault because the employer assigned him to work the overnight shift, then allowed him to walk home by himself at 3:15 a.m. The court found the employer not liable because the assault occurred while the employee was traveling home from work, which was outside the course of the victim's employment. The court explained that an employer has no duty to protect an employee from harm arising outside the scope of the employment relationship under Section 314A.

In *Jackson v. Remington Park, Inc.*, the Court of Appeals of Oklahoma found an employer not liable when one of its employees assaulted the plaintiff after the plaintiff went to the defendant-employer's racetrack in order to repay a debt to the employee. Although the employee was at work at the time he committed the assault, the court found that the assault was not within the scope of his employment at the racetrack and absolved the defendant of liability. The court explained that even though the employer's business was a racetrack, the employee's efforts to collect an old personal debt could not have been said to further the business of the employer.

In each of the above cases, the assaults did not arise from the nature of the employment relationship. Although *Slagle* was a case about whether the plaintiff's injuries were sustained within the scope of his employment, and the phrase "involved in the employment" in Section 471 may have been meant to encompass a broader class of risks than those confined within the scope of the employment, *Slagle* emphasizes how there will be no employer liability for an employee's injuries where the injuries have no connection to the employment relationship. As demonstrated in *Jackson*, even where the employee is supposed to be working at the time he commits a criminal act, if the act is not related to the employer's business, it cannot serve as a basis for employer liability. As suggested in *Dell*, to state a claim for negligent failure to warn of a risk involved in the employment, the employee must allege some direct connection to the nature of the employment relationship. We therefore hold that in order for the risk to be "involved in the employment," it must arise from the particular nature of the employment.

Here, plaintiff's complaint fails to allege that James's injuries arose from the particular nature of his employment at Trophies Are Us. Plaintiff specifically alleged that the murder did not occur while the two men were engaged in the course of their employment at Trophies Are Us. The complaint also contains no allegations to suggest that the murder occurred on the premises of Trophies Are Us. Rather, plaintiff asserted that Maust buried James's body in the basement of their apartment building. The only connection to the employment plaintiff alleged in the complaint was that Maust and James became friends through work. However, friendship is not a risk peculiar to the employment at Trophies Are Us. Maust could have become acquainted with James under other circumstances. We therefore find that James's injuries were not involved in his employment relationship with defendant. Accordingly, defendant cannot be liable for James's injuries under Section 471.

Another issue posed by plaintiff's complaint is whether the harm inflicted by Maust was foreseeable. The risk of a criminal assault on an employee is foreseeable if the employer knew or should have known of facts evidencing a threat of harm particular to his employees, but not common to all persons in the area. For example, in *Blake v. Consolidated R. Corp.*, the Court of Appeals of Michigan found that an employer, a railroad, had a duty to protect its employees from assaults by one Rudy Bladel, who had murdered at least three other employees of the same branch of the railroad while they were working because of a "vendetta" he had against the railroad.

Where the harm is not confined to a particular group of employees, the harm is not foreseeable and the employer has no duty to warn of it. For instance, in *A.H.*, the Supreme Court of Virginia found that injuries sustained by the plaintiff, a paper carrier, when he was sexually assaulted by one of the patrons on his early morning route in Harrisonburg, Virginia, were not foreseeable. The court explained that even though the defendant publishing company knew of three prior sexual assaults on early morning paper carriers in the city in the five years prior to the plaintiff's assault, the defendant had no reason to believe that the plaintiff would be assaulted on his particular paper route.

Here, as in *A.H.*, although plaintiff alleged that defendant was aware that Maust was "a convicted killer who constituted a mortal danger to young men such as [James] with whom he was able to make acquaintance through mutual employment or otherwise," and that Maust's "previous victims were young males," with whom "Maust had established an acquaintance or some other sort of personal relationship with ... prior to killing them ... suddenly, brutally and without warning," plaintiff failed to allege that an employee such as James was particularly at risk. Plaintiff's allegation that Maust would kill individuals he befriended through "mutual employment *or otherwise*," leaves the threat of harm open to a very broad group of individuals who are not necessarily employees of Trophies Are Us, like James. Therefore, the harm inflicted by Maust was not foreseeable, and defendant is not liable for breach of a duty to warn James about Maust's background.

Plaintiff next contends that "defendants are directly liable for negligently hiring and retaining a violent person known to pose a risk to others, without issuing a simple warning to other employees." In support of that contention, plaintiff relies upon Section 213 of the Restatement (Second) of

Agency, which provides that a principal "is subject to liability for harm resulting from his conduct if he is negligent or reckless ... in the employment of improper persons or instrumentalities in work involving a risk of harm to others", and cases discussing employer liability for negligent hiring.

In order to state a claim for negligent hiring, a plaintiff must allege that the employer hired or retained an employee who he knew, or should have known, was unfit for the job in the sense that the employment would place the employee in a position where his unfitness would create a foreseeable danger to others. An action for negligent hiring can be maintained even where an employee commits a criminal or intentional act which is outside the scope of the employment if the employee is on the employer's premises or using the chattel of the employer, and the employer has reason to know of the need and opportunity for exercising control over the employee.

Here, plaintiff's complaint contains no facts that would support a negligent hiring claim. Plaintiff alleged that Maust killed James outside the scope of their employment at Trophies Are Us, but failed to allege that Maust killed James on defendant's premises or with the instrumentalities of the employment. Thus, plaintiff's complaint, even liberally construed, was insufficient to state a claim of negligent hiring. We therefore affirm the order of the Circuit Court of Cook County dismissing plaintiff's complaint.

Affirmed

CASE COMMENT

In an attempt to connect a terrible killing to the owner of a business where the victim and offender meet, the plaintiff's estate sought to hold the business liable for damages relating to the death. The plaintiff argued that the business owner had a duty to inform the victim (employee) of the fact that the offender was a convicted felon. Since the business owner failed to do so, the plaintiff contends he should be liable for the death.

The logic of this argument was grounded on an exception to the general rule that the principal had no duty of care against criminal acts of third parties. After a pointed review of the law and relevant facts, the court refused to acknowledge that this exception was applicable. The court gave great weight to the applicable duty of care. Duty must emanate from a risk that is particular to the nature of the employment. Since the business was a trophy store, there was no particular risk to the victim (plaintiff) that was tied to the employment. The mere fact that the victim and offender met and became friends as they worked together, was not itself, sufficient to impose a duty on the business owner. Finally, the court found the tort claims lacking due to the failure to show foreseeability, and that the killing did not involve any instrumentalities from the business.

As a postscript to this case, the offender, Maust, who was convicted of killing James and others and burying their bodies in his basement, committed suicide in the Lake County Indiana jail in January 2006. This is an ironic ending to a tragic case.

DISCUSSION QUESTIONS

Is it ethically proper to hold an employer liable for the actions of a contractor? State the public policy and legal reasons for and against this proposition. What factors constitute "course and scope of employment"? What single factor should carry the most weight? Explain why?

9

Contracts

A. INSURANCE

17 A.D.3d 1134, 796 N.Y.S.2d 204

Supreme Court, Appellate Division, Fourth Department, New York

ESSEX INSURANCE COMPANY, PLAINTIFF-APPELLANT v. LAWANDA YOUNG, DEFENDANT, DWIGHT HICKS, BRIAN J. NELSON AND 8-BALL LAUNDRY LOUNGE, INC., DOING BUSINESS AS GROOVE, DEFENDANTS-RESPONDENTS.

April 29, 2005

Background

Lounge owner's liability carrier commenced action seeking judgment declaring that it had no obligation to defend or indemnify bouncer or lounge owner in patron's underlying personal injury action. The Supreme Court, Erie County, declared that carrier had a duty to defend and indemnify, and carrier appealed.

Holding

The Supreme Court, Appellate Division, held that lounge patron's causes of action against lounge owner and bouncer arise out of the alleged assault and/or battery by bouncer, and thus fell within lounge's liability policy exclusions for claims arising out of assault and/or battery. Affirmed as modified.

Defendant Lawanda Young commenced an action to recover damages for injuries allegedly inflicted by defendant Dwight Hicks, a bouncer employed by defendant 8-Ball Laundry Lounge, Inc., doing business as Groove, in an incident at Groove. Hicks allegedly grabbed Young by the arm, put her in a chokehold, and threw her to the ground. Plaintiff, Groove's liability carrier, commenced the instant action seeking judgment declaring that it has no obligation to defend or indemnify Hicks, Groove or defendant Brian J. Nelson, the owner of Groove, in the underlying action, based upon exclusions in the policy for claims arising out of "Assault and/or Battery" and "any charges or allegations of negligent hiring, employment training, placement or supervision...." Hicks thereafter sought summary judgment declaring that plaintiff must defend and indemnify him in the underlying action on the ground that the negligence causes of action therein trigger the duty to defend and indemnify him with respect to all causes of action. In addition, Hicks contended that plaintiff failed to disclaim coverage in a timely manner and thus must both defend and indemnify Hicks on that ground as well.

Plaintiff cross-moved for summary judgment declaring that it has no duty to defend or indemnify Hicks, Nelson or Groove in the underlying action based on the policy exclusions. Nelson and Groove then cross-moved for summary judgment declaring that plaintiff must defend and indemnify them "with respect to the complaint allegations sounding in negligence, carelessness, and/or recklessness...." The supreme court erred in denying plaintiff's cross motion and granting the motion of Hicks and the cross motion of Nelson and Groove insofar as they sought summary judgment declaring that plaintiff must provide them with a defense and indemnify them if it is determined that they are entitled to coverage for their liability in the underlying action. We therefore modify the judgment accordingly. "If no cause of action would exist but for the assault, the claim is based on assault and the exclusion applies." Here, Young's causes of action for negligent and reckless conduct in the underlying action, including those alleging negligent training and supervision, arise out of the alleged assault and/or battery by Hicks, and thus fall within the policy exclusions. Because plaintiff owes no duty to defend Hicks, Nelson, or Groove in the underlying personal injury action, the court erred in awarding those defendants reasonable attorneys' fees and costs incurred in defending the underlying personal injury action and this declaratory judgment action. It is hereby ORDERED that the judgment granting the cross motion of plaintiff in its entirety and vacating the award of attorneys' fees and costs and as modified the judgment is affirmed without costs and judgment is granted in favor of plaintiff as follows:

It is ADJUDGED AND DECLARED that plaintiff has no duty to defend or indemnify those defendants in the underlying personal injury action.

CASE COMMENT

In this instance, the existence of the "assault and battery" exclusion was fatal to the case. Even though the complaint was framed alleging negligent training and supervision, since the cause of action arose from the assault and battery, the exclusion was applicable. Since the exclusion is applicable, the insurance company had no duty to defend the claim, and had no liability exposure stemming from the incident. Since the contract between the insurance company and the business contained this exclusion, there was no coverage tendered to the business.

393 F. Supp. 2d 860

UNITED STATES DISTRICT COURT, D. MINNESOTA, KIM GRUETZMACHER, PLAINTIFF v. ACUITY, A MUTUAL INSURANCE COMPANY, A WISCONSIN CORPORATION (F/K/A HERITAGE MUTUAL INSURANCE COMPANY), DEFENDANT.

March 23, 2005

Background

Insured brought breach of contract action against homeowner's insurer. Insurer moved for summary judgment.

Holdings

The district court held that:

1. Under Minnesota law, church employee's claim that insured intentionally interfered with employee's employment contract fell within scope of the personal liability coverage provision of homeowners' policy; and
2. Policy's intentional acts exclusionary provision did not relieve insurer of its duty to defend insured.

Motion denied

In June 2002, Gruetzmacher was insured under the terms of a homeowner's insurance policy issued by Acuity. Under the policy's Personal Liability coverage provision, where "a claim is made or a suit is brought against an insured for damages because of *bodily injury* ... caused by an *occurrence* to which this coverage applies," the policy will afford "a defense at [the insurer's] expense by counsel of [the insurer's] choice, even if the suit is groundless, false or fraudulent (emphasis added by court)." "Bodily injury" is defined as "bodily harm, sickness or disease, including required care, loss of services and death that results." "Occurrence" is defined as "an *accident*, including exposure to conditions, which results, during the policy period, in bodily injury (emphasis added by court)." The policy also includes an intentional act exclusion which provides that "Personal Liability [coverage does] not apply to bodily injury ... which is expected or intended by the insured." The policy also covers "personal injury," which is defined as "injury arising out of one or more of the following offenses:

a. False arrest, detention or imprisonment, or malicious prosecution;
b. *Libel, slander or defamation of character;* or
c. Invasion of privacy, wrongful eviction or wrongful entry."

On June 4, 2002, Randall Egan brought suit against Gruetzmacher and Hamline United Methodist Church in state court, alleging that he had been unlawfully fired from his job at Hamline because of his sexual orientation. Count III of the Egan Complaint stated a claim for "Tortious Interference with Employment" against Gruetzmacher. The complaint alleged that Gruetzmacher, a lay member of Hamline, had written a letter to Hamline's pastor expressing "his vehement, anti-homosexual views" and, in doing so, had "intentionally, willfully and without justification interfered with Egan's employment relationship with" Hamline.

The Complaint further alleged that: As a direct and proximate result of Gruetzmacher's tortuous [*sic*] interference with Egan's employment contract with [Hamline], Egan has suffered and will continue to suffer damages, including lost pay, lost earning capacity, *physical pain*, emotional suffering, as well as damage to his name and reputation.

Gruetzmacher tendered the defense of the Egan Complaint to Acuity in June 2002, which Acuity promptly rejected on the grounds that the policy did "not extend to bodily injury that is expected or intended by the insured." Acuity informed Gruetzmacher that the "only claim Mr. Egan asserts against you is that he alleges that you 'intentionally, willfully, and without justification' interfered with his employment relationship. Given that assertion, there is no coverage for damages from such a claim under the policy." Acuity cited the following "pertinent portions of the policy" in support of its rejection of Gruetzmacher's tender of defense: the definition of "bodily injury," the Personal Liability coverage provision, and the exclusion for injury "expected or intended by the insured." It also cited the policy definition of "personal injury," and concluded by pointing out that "the definition of personal injury ... does not include a claim for tortious interference with employment."

On July 10, 2002, Gruetzmacher responded, requesting that Acuity "please reconsider [its] position" and provide him a defense to the Egan Complaint. He wrote: I'm being sued for damages because I wrote a letter to Hamline United Methodist Church complaining about the way I was treated by Randy Egan. I never intended to harm him. All I wanted was an apology. I don't see how you can deny me a defense to this lawsuit when I never intended to injure anyone. Acuity replied that it had "reviewed [Gruetzmacher's] issues and concerns," and its "position concerning this matter remains the same." Gruetzmacher then retained his own counsel and, in January 2004, Egan's claim against Gruetzmacher was dismissed after a summary judgment ruling in Gruetzmacher's favor. This action followed.

Gruetzmacher alleges that Acuity breached the policy and its fiduciary duty to him by refusing to provide him with a defense to the Egan Complaint. He has now moved for summary judgment on his breach of contract claim. In response to Gruetzmacher's Motion for Summary Judgment, Acuity has requested that summary judgment be entered in its favor, contending that the policy did not cover the allegations in the Egan Complaint.

Analysis

Under Minnesota law, an insurer assumes two duties to its insured: the duty to defend and the duty to indemnify. The duty to defend under an insurance policy is broader than the duty to indemnify. Minnesota has established a difficult evidentiary burden which an insurance carrier must satisfy in order to avoid providing a defense to claims under its insurance policy; a duty to defend an insured on a claim arises when any part of a claim against the insured is arguably within the policy's scope. "If a complaint alleges several claims, and any one of them would require the insurer to indemnify, the insurer must provide a defense against all claims." Thus, "an insurer who wishes to escape that duty has the burden of showing that all parts of the cause of action fall clearly outside the scope of coverage." Further, "in determining whether there is a duty to defend, a court must give the benefit of the doubt to the insured" and, "[a]s a result, unless the pleadings and facts clearly establish that the claim falls outside the policy terms, the duty to defend arises."

In considering whether a duty to defend arises, a court considers the applicability of the duty as of the time the insured tendered the defense to the insurer. While the duty to defend is generally determined by comparing the allegations in the complaint with the language of the insurance policy, courts may look beyond the complaint to extrinsic facts to establish the existence or nonexistence of that duty. However, "where the insurer has no knowledge to the contrary, it may make an initial determination of whether or not it is obligated to defend from the facts alleged in the complaint against its insured."

Accordingly, Gruetzmacher is entitled to summary judgment on the issue of Acuity's duty to defend if any part of the claim alleged against him in the Egan Complaint "arguably" falls within the provisions of the policy. The Egan Complaint alleges: "As a direct and proximate result of Gruetzmacher's tortuous [*sic*] interference with Egan's employment contract with [Hamline], Egan has suffered and will continue to suffer damages, including lost pay, lost earning capacity, *physical pain*, emotional suffering, as well as damage to his name and reputation (emphasis added by court)."

Acuity makes three arguments in support of its decision not to assume the defense of the Egan Complaint: (1) Egan's alleged injury does not fall under the Personal Liability Coverage provision because the injury was not due to an "occurrence," (2) the policy's intentional acts exclusion applies, and (3) the personal injury coverage provision does not apply because the Egan Complaint did not state a claim against Gruetzmacher for defamation.

I. Occurrence

The Personal Liability Coverage provision of the policy provides that Acuity will provide a defense for Gruetzmacher if "a suit is brought against [him] for damages because of *bodily injury* ... caused by an *occurrence* to which this coverage applies." "Occurrence" is defined by the Policy as "an *accident*, including exposure to conditions, which results ... in bodily injury." Acuity argues that Egan's claim of tortious interference with his employment contract is not an "occurrence" because it alleges *intentional* (not accidental) conduct on the part of Gruetzmacher. Gruetzmacher responds by asserting that he did not intend to cause bodily injury to Egan. According to Gruetzmacher, his actions were covered by the policy because under Minnesota law the term "accident" or "occurrence" encompasses unintended consequences resulting from intentional acts.

"In interpreting the word accident, [the Minnesota courts] are guided by the maxim that in insurance contracts, coverage provisions are construed according to the expectations of the insured and exclusions are construed narrowly." "Accident" is generally interpreted to mean "an unexpected, unforeseen, or undesigned happening or consequence"; under Minnesota law, "where there is no intent to injure, the incident is an accident, even if the conduct itself was intentional." Accordingly, the question becomes whether Egan's alleged bodily injury was "caused by an incident in which the resulting harm was unintended or unexpected by [Gruetzmacher]."

The Egan Complaint did not allege that Gruetzmacher intended to cause bodily injury to Egan. Thus, Acuity rests its argument not on allegations that Gruetzmacher specifically intended to cause bodily injury to Egan, but on the fact that intentional conduct is a necessary element of a tortious interference claim. Acuity urges that because Egan alleged an "intentional act," any resulting injury did not stem from an accident or occurrence. This position, however, misses the point; the policy covers unexpected bodily injury even where there was an intent to act. Egan simply asserted that by writing a letter to Hamline, Gruetzmacher was intentionally interfering with his employment contract; he did *not* allege that Gruetzmacher specifically intended to cause him *bodily injury*. As the state court noted in its summary judgment order dismissing Egan's claims against him: Gruetzmacher "wrote a letter to his clergyman complaining about an employee. Nothing more. The letter can be characterized by some as distasteful, yet remains simply a letter from a parishioner." Acuity has failed to establish that these allegations fall clearly outside the scope of the policy. "The 'intent' required to exclude coverage is neither the 'intent to *act*' nor the 'intent to cause the *specific* injury complained of.' Rather it is the 'intent to *cause bodily injury*' even if the actual injury is more severe or of a different nature than the injury intended (emphasis in original)."

Finally, Acuity had information external to the Egan Complaint establishing that the claims against Gruetzmacher could arguably be covered under the policy. In his July 10, 2002 letter, Gruetzmacher clearly informed Acuity that he did not intend to injure Egan and stated that he "never intended to harm [Egan]" and that he did not "see how [Acuity could] deny him a defense to this lawsuit when he never intended to injure anyone." This letter clearly raised "a question as to whether he actually intended" to cause injury to Egan. Such "facts outside the complaint" are to be considered by the insurer in determining whether it has a duty to defend an insured, and "any ambiguity is resolved in favor of the insured." Accordingly, the court determines, under the facts of the present case, that the requirement that any bodily injury be caused by an "occurrence" for the Personal Liability coverage provision to apply does not negate Acuity's duty to defend the Egan Complaint.

II. Intentional Acts Exclusion

The court next considers whether the policy's intentional acts exclusionary provision relieves Acuity of its duty to defend. The exclusionary provision provides that "Personal liability [coverage does] not apply to bodily injury ... which is expected or intended by the insured." Acuity alleges that it has no duty to defend Gruetzmacher because the claim alleged against him is an intentional tort, and, accordingly, his intent must be inferred as a matter of law.

The Minnesota courts "have stated that the purpose of intentional act exclusions is to exclude insurance coverage for wanton and malicious acts by an insured, and therefore the court may, absent a finding of specific intent to injure, infer intent to injure as a matter of law." Cases where the courts have inferred intent to injure generally involve "insured who acted in a manner in which they knew or should have known that some harm was substantially certain to result; that is, they acted with deliberate and calculated indifference to the risk of injury." Statements outside the pleadings made by the insured may be considered in determining whether intent can be inferred as a matter of law. "If the insured tells the insurer of [facts indicating that there may be a claim], or if the insurer has some independent knowledge of such facts, then the insurer must either accept tender of the defense or further investigate the potential claim."

The acts charged in the Egan Complaint distinguish it from the cases relied upon by Acuity; the facts of those cases are more extreme than the facts presented here. In *Woida*, the court held that an intentional act exclusion applied where the insured shot a security guard. The court found that the insured "knew that the guards' truck was occupied at the time the shots were fired ... yet, they proceeded to fire through the windshield of the vehicle." In *Rulli*, the court held that an intentional act exclusion applied where the insured was charged with sexual assault and battery. The court stated that "it is the character of the nonconsensual sexual act that results in the mandatory inference [of intent]."

The facts presented here do not support the conclusion that Gruetzmacher acted with "deliberate and calculated indifference to the risk" of Egan's injury. In *Walser*, the Minnesota Supreme Court held that intent could not be inferred where the insured pulled on the ankles of a fellow student who was hanging onto the rim of a basketball-hoop causing that student to lose his grip and fall. The court specifically noted that *Woida* and cases involving "some type of sexual contact" were sufficiently extreme to justify inferring intent as a matter of law. In the instant case, however, while the underlying act (Gruetzmacher's writing of the letter to Hamline) was certainly intentional, it is clear that such an act was not done with deliberate and calculated indifference to any injury to Egan. There is no dispute that Gruetzmacher did not have the actual intent to cause bodily injury to Egan. Without the specific intent to cause injury, the writing of the letter to Hamline in and of itself is not so extreme as to warrant the inference of intent to injure as a matter of law. Because "it is the intent to injure rather than intent to act which triggers the [intentional acts] exclusion's applicability," the court determines that Acuity has not carried its burden and that the Egan Complaint alleged claims arguably within the Personal Liability coverage provision of the policy.

Based on the materials and record presented, the allegations in Count III of the Egan Complaint triggered Acuity's duty to defend Gruetzmacher under the policy. This ends the court's inquiry. (Case and citation omitted—stating that "if *any* part of a cause of action is arguably within the scope of coverage, the insurer must defend [emphasis added by court]);" (Case and citation omitted—"If *any* claim is arguably within the scope of coverage of the insurance policy, the insurer must defend [emphasis added by court].")

Conclusion

Based on the foregoing, and all the files, records and proceedings herein **IT IS ORDERED** that plaintiff Kim Gruetzmacher's Motion for Summary Judgment is **GRANTED** and Defendant Acuity's request for summary judgment is **DENIED.**

CASE COMMENT

In this case, the court held that the insurance company had a duty to defend the cause of action asserted against the insured. In reaching this decision, the court held that the occurrence and the intentional acts exclusions should not have prevented the insurance company from honoring its duty to defend the lawsuit. Stated another way, the contract exclusions were not applicable. Therefore, the insurance company had a duty to defend the insured in the lawsuit instituted against him. Indeed, the court found that the letter written by Gruetzmacher was pivotal. The letter clearly articulated that the plaintiff did not intend to harm anyone. The court held "without the specific intent to cause injury, the writing of the letter to Hamline in and of itself is not so extreme as to warrant the inference of intent to injure as a matter of law." Consequently, the insurance company was required to defend the plaintiff in the litigation instituted by Egan.

396 F. Supp. 2d 624

United States District Court, D. Maryland

KAMAKI SKIATHOS, INC., PANAGIOTIS AVRAMIS, AND CODY GABRIELE, PLAINTIFFS v. ESSEX INSURANCE COMPANY, DEFENDANT.

Oct. 27, 2005

Background

This declaratory judgment action presents the question of whether the defendant Essex Insurance Company ("Essex") is obligated to cover the plaintiffs' costs in defending against three lawsuits arising out of the actions of bouncers employed at Moby's Bar ("Moby's") in Baltimore. The parties have filed cross Motions for Summary Judgment.

Holding

For the reasons stated below, Essex's motion will be granted and plaintiffs' motion will be denied.

All three underlying complaints result from the actions of bouncers at Moby's in ejecting patrons from the premises. In all three cases, the ejected patrons filed suits for personal injury damages. In the King action, plaintiff Michael King alleged that the several agents, servants and/or employees of Moby's "suddenly and without warning … brutally attacked the plaintiff, kicking and beating him so severely, and without just cause," resulting in an "intentional and unpermitted application of trauma." King brought claim for vicarious liability to recover against Moby's principals for the alleged negligence of Moby's agents or servants in ejecting King.

In the Kraft action, Plaintiff Zachary Kraft alleged that Todd Schindeldecker, a bouncer at Moby's, forcibly threw Kraft from the bar and followed him down the street, then "came up from behind the plaintiff and punched him with tremendous force on the side of the head." Kraft brought claim alleging negligence against Schindeldecker.

In the Louard action, plaintiff Lamont Louard alleged that he was "forcefully detained," placed in a "full nelson," and carried out of Moby's by defendant Gabriele after having been found in the women's restroom. Louard alleged that Gabriele continued to "assail" him, and "held Louard's hands so tight that he could not protect himself and thrust him down onto the street." Louard brought claim alleging negligence against Gabriele.

The Essex Policies

The events giving rise to the underlying tort suits occurred while Moby's was insured under two different comprehensive liability policies issued by Essex, one covering the period from 12/01/01 through 12/01/02 (the "2001 Policy") and the other covering the period from 12/01/02 through 12/01/03 (the "2002 Policy"). Both policies were substantially the same.

Under both policies, the general grant of coverage was a blanket statement: We will pay those sums that the insured becomes legally obligated to pay as damages because of "bodily injury" or "property damage" to which this insurance applies.... However, we have no duty to defend the insured against any "suit" seeking damages for "bodily injury" or "property damage" to which this insurance does not apply.

For purposes of the parties' cross motion for summary judgment, however, the relevant aspects of the policies are found in their exclusions. Specifically, the policies exclude coverage of any intentional injuries or damage—the policies clearly state that "this insurance does not apply to: "Expected or Intended Injury, 'Bodily Injury' or 'property damage' expected or intended from the standpoint of the Insured." In addition, the policies exclude intentional torts such as assault and battery, although in slightly different ways.

The King Action occurred while Moby's was insured under the 2001 Policy. Under this policy, assault and battery were excluded from coverage by the following: This insurance does not apply to any claim, suit, cost or expense arising out of:

ASSAULT AND/OR BATTERY

Assault and/or battery or out of any act or omission in connection with the suppression of such acts, whether caused by or at the instigation or direction of any Insured, Insured's employees, patrons or any other person.

The Kraft and Louard Actions occurred while Moby's was insured under the 2002 Policy. This policy went into more detail in its provision excluding assault and/or battery, stating that:

The coverage under this policy does not apply to any claim, suit, cost or expense arising out of assault and/or battery, or out of any act or omission in connection with the prevention or suppression of such acts, whether caused by or at the instigation or direction of any Insured, Insured's employees, patrons or any other person.... Furthermore, assault and/or battery includes "bodily injury" resulting from the use of reasonable force to protect persons or property.

The 2002 Policy also contained an exclusion provision directed specifically at bars and restaurants, taverns, night clubs, and fraternal and social clubs, which again directly excluded assault and/or battery with almost identical language to that above.

Under Maryland law two inquiries are made to determine whether an insurer has a duty to defend its insured against tort suits. First, the court examines the coverage provided for in the policy and any defenses under its terms. Second, the court asks whether the allegations in the complaint potentially bring the claim within the coverage. Thus, the court inquires first as to the boundaries of coverage, and second as to the allegations made in the underlying suit.

In determining the boundaries of coverage, the court construes an insurance policy just as it does any other contract, by giving its terms their "customary, ordinary, and accepted meaning." If a term is ambiguous, extrinsic evidence may be admitted to show both intent of the parties and any possible special trade usage of terms. Here, however, it is not necessary to consider extrinsic evidence because the Essex policies use clear language and define any terms that might otherwise be found ambiguous. The resulting coverage excludes intentional injury and the torts of assault and battery. The 2002 Policy even explicitly confirms that this exclusion operates in the context of bars such as Moby's.

Once the court has determined the scope of coverage, the court considers the allegations in the tort suit to determine whether the claim is potentially covered by the policy. This test favors coverage, since, as the Maryland Supreme Court has noted, "representation from the insurer … is part of the bargained-for exchange in any insurance policy." Even where a tort plaintiff fails to allege facts that clearly bring the claim within coverage, the insurer must defend if the plaintiff shows a potentiality of coverage. If, based on the allegations in the underlying suit, the court is unsure about coverage, any doubts should be resolved in favor of the insured. In this case, however, the plaintiff has failed to show a potentiality for coverage. There is little room for doubt that the Essex policies do not cover the types of claims alleged in the King, Kraft, and Louard actions.

The King Action

Complaint alleges that "suddenly and without warning, several of defendant's agents, servants and/or employees, brutally attacked the Plaintiff ... without just cause…." Were it not for plaintiff King's caption "Negligence," and his allegation that the attack was caused "solely to [*sic*] and by reason of the negligence of the defendants' agents …," there would be no reason to expect that King was complaining of anything other than an assault and/or battery.

Plaintiffs seek to circumvent the intentional character of their allegation by characterizing it as a potential situation of defense of property or others. They contend that the bouncer Schindeldecker "reacted to King attempting to hit a female patron over the head with a beer bottle by striking him once and restraining him." This contention, if true, would effectively place the claim outside of the assault and/or battery exclusion under the 2001 Policy. However, this contention is clearly contradicted by the

King complaint itself. It affirmatively alleges that King did not contribute to the attack by any "negligence or provocation," and that the initial attack occurred "suddenly and without warning."

The Kraft Action

The Kraft complaint incorporates the "Facts Common to All Counts," and additionally asserts that the bouncer Schindeldecker owed a duty of care to Moby's patrons which he subsequently breached by "violently removing the plaintiff from the bar ... [and] negligently using additional force on the plaintiff...."

The "Facts Common to All Counts" described in the Kraft complaint include allegations that Schindeldecker "forcibly threw" Kraft from the bar, and "punched him with tremendous force on the side of the head," constituting an "unprovoked battery." As Essex argues, this incorporation of the common facts contributes to its appearance as an intentional tort. In addition, the allegations are inherently intentional acts. In fact, even plaintiffs portray Kraft's allegations as intentional, describing them as: "... Schindeldecker used physical force to remove Kraft from the tavern and that while outside, struck Kraft in the face causing him to hit his head on the sidewalk."

Plaintiffs acknowledge that the reference to the common facts incorporates allegations of intentional harm, but argue that there is still a potential for coverage. They do this by hypothesizing a scenario where the negligence occurred while Schindeldecker was inside the bar and acting as a bouncer ("on the premises and within the scope of employment"), and the intentional tort did not occur until Schindeldecker followed Kraft down the street ("outside the scope of employment"). Had this been stated, or even alluded to in Kraft's complaint, it would be a more arguable position. However, Kraft clearly alleges that Schindeldecker violently removed him from Moby's, and that such action, in addition to others, constituted a breach of the duty of care.

Thus, although titled "Negligence," in reality it alleges a battery. Battery, as an intentional tort, is explicitly excepted from coverage by the 2002 Essex Policy in question here. It clearly does not fall within the bounds of coverage, and the plaintiffs cannot demonstrate a potentiality of coverage.

The Louard Action

Louard's Count titled "Negligence," incorporates all the foregoing allegations, including "Facts Common to All Counts," and additionally alleges that: defendant Gabriele breached said duty of care by negligently (1) expelling plaintiff Louard from the establishment; (2) utilizing unreasonable force when expelling plaintiff Louard from defendant Moby's Bar; (3) detaining plaintiff Louard's arms in such a manner that he was incapable of defending himself; (4) placing plaintiff Louard in such a position that he was incapable of standing on his own; and (5) causing plaintiff Louard to fall to the roadway surface.

This count yields the most colorable claim for coverage, since it does appear on its face to allege some form of negligence. However, like Kraft's claim, although Louard used the right negligence "terminology," in reality his claim masks a simple battery claim. Like Kraft, Louard incorporates "Facts Common to All Counts," which make clear allegations of intentional harm. For example, the same events that are narrated above to appear as negligence are described in the common facts as: "Even after plaintiff Louard had been forced out of defendant Moby's Bar, defendant Gabriele continued to assail him. Defendant Gabriele held plaintiff Louard's hands so that he could not protect himself and thrust him down onto the street...." In fact, the very next paragraph begins, [w]hile plaintiff Louard was being assaulted.... Therefore, like Kraft's, Louard's misnamed negligence claim must be read as a battery claim and is excluded from the 2002 Policy.

ORDER

The claims for which all plaintiffs seek coverage fall outside the boundaries of the Essex policies, thereby grant Essex's Motion for Summary Judgment.

CASE COMMENT

The court articulated in a plain and pointed manner that each of the three lawsuits failed due to the "assault and battery" exclusion in the insurance contract. In its decision, the court first analyzed the language in the contract, finding the language to be unambiguous, with clearly defined terms within the document. Next, the court analyzed the allegations in the lawsuits. It found the lawsuit allegations clearly stemming from an underlying assault and battery. Even though the drafting within the lawsuit tried to make the language sound as it were based on a negligence claim, the court rejected their attempts to creatively craft the lawsuit. Indeed, the court asserted that "although Louard used the right negligence 'terminology,' in reality his claim masks a simple battery claim." Consequently, the court held that the insurance company had no duty to defend the lawsuits.

702 N.W.2d 492

Supreme Court of Iowa

IMT INSURANCE COMPANY, APPELLANT v. CRESTMOOR GOLF CLUB, D/B/A CRESTMOOR COUNTRY CLUB, GALEN KRIEGER AND TABITHA LYNNAE COTTRELL, APPELLEES.

Aug. 19, 2005

Background

Liability insurer brought declaratory-judgment action, asserting that it did not have duty to defend or indemnify insured or insured's employee concerning claims of former employee for negligent supervision and retention of supervisory employee, who allegedly sexually harassed and assaulted former employee. Following a bench trial on stipulated facts, the District Court, Union County, determined that coverage existed. Insurer appealed.

Holdings

The supreme court held that:

1. Clause of amendatory endorsement exclusion that stated that policy did not apply concerning damages arising out of misconduct by an insured did not apply; and
2. For purposes of amendatory endorsement exclusion, supervisory employee qualified as "any other person," and thus exclusion precluded coverage.

Reversed and remanded with instructions.

Tabitha Lynnae Cottrell, a former female employee of Crestmoor Golf Club d/b/a Crestmoor Country Club claims her supervisor, Galen Krieger, made inappropriate sexual comments to her, touched her inappropriately, and sexually assaulted her. She later complained to Crestmoor personnel. She alleges when she returned to work at Crestmoor, "other managers ridiculed her complaint and engaged in other improper conduct toward her." She further claims Crestmoor constructively discharged her. As a result of the actions of her supervisor and Crestmoor, she claims she suffered humiliation, alienation, severe emotional distress, and economic harm.

Relevant to this appeal, she alleged "Crestmoor knew, or should have known, that Krieger harassed and acted inappropriately toward other employees prior to Krieger's harassment and assault on [her]." Her allegation of negligent supervision claimed: "Crestmoor, its agents, board members, servants, and employees were negligent in failing to properly supervise and control the activities of Krieger." Her allegation of negligent retention claimed: "Crestmoor, its agents, board members, servants, and employees were negligent in retaining and failing to terminate Krieger." As a proximate cause of Crestmoor's negligent supervision and retention of Krieger, Cottrell asked for damages.

Crestmoor purchased a contract of insurance through IMT Insurance Company. This policy was in force at the time of the alleged incident. Although Crestmoor and Krieger timely requested IMT defend them from the claim, IMT denied the request asserting there was no coverage under the terms and provisions of the insurance contract existing between IMT and Crestmoor. IMT filed a petition for declaratory judgment requesting judgment that it did not have a duty to defend or indemnify Crestmoor or Krieger under its policy of insurance. IMT also named Cottrell as a defendant.

The parties submitted the coverage case to the court as a bench trial on stipulated facts. The parties stipulated the IMT insurance policy did not provide coverage for the claims against Krieger, individually, or for the claims against Crestmoor based on theories other than negligent supervision and retention. Therefore, the issue before the district court was whether the IMT policy provided coverage for the negligent supervision and retention claims brought against Crestmoor. The district court determined insurance coverage existed for the negligent supervision and retention claims requiring IMT to defend and indemnify Crestmoor on those claims. IMT appeals.

I. Analysis

We have long adhered to the following principles regarding interpretation and construction of insurance contracts:

> "The cardinal principle in the construction and interpretation of insurance policies is that the intent of the parties at the time the policy was sold must control. Except in cases of ambiguity, the intent of the parties is determined by the language of the policy. An ambiguity exists if, after the application of pertinent rules of interpretation to the policy, a genuine uncertainty results as to which one of two or more meanings is the proper one. Where neither party offers any extrinsic evidence concerning the meaning of the policy language, the process of construing or interpreting the meaning of the words used is a matter of law for the court to decide."

Because insurance policies are adhesion contracts, we construe ambiguous terms in the insured's favor. "It is therefore incumbent upon an insurer to define clearly and explicitly any limitations or exclusions to coverage expressed by broad promises." Even in cases of doubt as to whether a claim is covered by the policy, the doubt must be resolved in the insured's favor. The policy of insurance issued to Crestmoor contains an amendatory endorsement that states: this insurance does not apply under any of the coverages to damages arising out of: misconduct by an insured, or the liability of the insured for the misconduct of another insured or any other person.

The policy endorsement includes a definition of "misconduct": as used in this endorsement means sexual misconduct, sexual molestation, sexual abuse, non-consensual sexual activity, or the physical or mental abuse of any person. Cottrell claims she is entitled to damages because Krieger made inappropriate sexual comments to her, touched her inappropriately, and sexually assaulted her. These claims clearly constitute misconduct under the policy endorsement's definition. Paragraph (a) of the amendatory endorsement exclusion does not exclude coverage, however, because Cottrell is not alleging misconduct by Crestmoor. Her claims against Crestmoor are for negligent supervision and retention of Krieger, whose misconduct allegedly caused her damages. We hold under paragraph (b) of the amendatory endorsement exclusion, coverage for Crestmoor's negligent supervision and retention of Krieger is excluded. Crestmoor is liable for Cottrell's damages only if Krieger committed the underlying acts alleged by her. A necessary element of a claim for negligent supervision or retention is an underlying tort or wrongful act committed by the employee. In a claim of negligent retention and supervision, the cause of action arises from the employer's own tortious conduct. "The underlying tort or wrongful conduct is simply a link in the causal chain leading to compensable damages." Paragraph (b) of the amendatory endorsement exclusion applies "to damages arising out of ... the liability of the insured for the misconduct of ... any other person." We narrowly construe the phrase "damages arising out of" to mean only those injuries proximately caused by the liability of the insured. The phrase "the liability of the insured" refers to the theories of recovery alleged in the claim of the injured party. In the present case, the theories of recovery are negligent supervision and retention. The phrase "for the misconduct of ... any other person" means misconduct, as defined by the exclusion, caused by *any* person. In the present case, the misconduct is the inappropriate sexual comments, inappropriate touching, and sexual assault allegedly committed by Krieger, who qualifies as "any other person."

The claims of negligent supervision and retention, the basis of Crestmoor's liability, are dependent on the wrongful conduct of Krieger; consequently, the damages allegedly incurred by Cottrell arose out of the liability of Crestmoor and the wrongful conduct of Krieger. The alleged wrongful conduct of Krieger, the inappropriate sexual comments, inappropriate touching, and sexual assault, is misconduct under the amendatory exclusion. Therefore, the amendatory exclusion excludes coverage for Crestmoor, because Krieger qualifies as "any other person" under the exclusion.

The same result is required in the present case. Even though we are required to apply the amendatory endorsement exclusion solely from the viewpoint of Crestmoor, the plain language of the exclusion requires that we consider whether the claims made against Crestmoor include as an element misconduct, as defined by the exclusion, by *any* other person. Therefore, the damages that Cottrell seeks to recover from Crestmoor arise out of Krieger's misconduct, as defined by the amendatory endorsement exclusion; thus, the policy does not provide coverage. We reverse the decision of the district court requiring IMT to defend and indemnify Crestmoor because the amendatory endorsement exclusion precludes coverage for Cottrell's claims for negligent supervision and retention against Crestmoor based on the inappropriate sexual comments, inappropriate touching, and sexual assault committed by Krieger. Accordingly, we remand the case to the district court to enter judgment in favor of IMT.

CASE COMMENT

The court in this case used familiar logic to hold that the insurance company does not have the duty to defend or indemnify based on the relevant facts. In the lawsuit, the victim of the sexual assault asserted that the golf club negligently supervised and retained the employee who committed the assault. Since these are negligence-based claims, the question for the court was whether the "misconduct" exclusion negated insurance coverage. The court answered in the affirmative. In finding for the insurance company, the court asserted that the sexual assault was the misconduct underlying the negligent claims. Since the misconduct was directly connected to the alleged negligence claims, the misconduct exclusion precluded insurance coverage.

843 N.E.2d 427

Appellate Court of Illinois, Third District

L. A. CONNECTION, PLAINTIFF-APPELLANT v. PENN-AMERICA INSURANCE COMPANY, DEFENDANT-APPELLEE, AND MARVIN E. WHITE, ADMINISTRATOR OF THE ESTATE OF MARVIN E. WHITE, JR., DECEASED, DEFENDANT.

January 23, 2006

Background

Marvin E. White, Jr., was shot and killed on the dance floor of plaintiff L. A. Connection, a Peoria bar, on November 11, 2001. White's estate filed a wrongful death action against plaintiff, which tendered defense of the claim to defendant Penn-America Insurance Company. Penn declined to defend or indemnify plaintiff, primarily on the basis of an "assault and battery" exclusion contained in the commercial general liability policy issued to plaintiff. Plaintiff thereafter filed a declaratory judgment action to determine Penn's obligations under the policy. The trial court granted summary judgment to Penn and this appeal followed.

Holding

Appellate Court, Third District, finds no duty to defend claim as it stems from an assault and battery. The trial court's decision is AFFIRMED.

Plaintiff was served with a complaint by White's estate on May 28, 2002. The complaint alleged that Edward Jackson entered plaintiff's premises on November 11, 2001, armed with a handgun and thereafter shot and killed Marvin White. The complaint asserted that plaintiff was negligent in allowing Jackson to enter while armed, in failing to provide security, and in failing to search patrons for weapons.

Plaintiff tendered defense of the suit to Penn on or about June 5, 2002, and Penn denied coverage by letter on June 11. Plaintiff filed the instant declaratory judgment action on August 13, 2002. On August 24, 2004, plaintiff filed a motion for summary judgment, to which Penn responded by filing its own summary judgment motion on November 18, 2004. Under the uncontested facts presented, the court finds that the injuries were caused as a result of a "battery." The incident therefore was excluded by the insurance contract and was not covered by it.

Duty to Defend

The initial step in [our] analysis is determining whether a duty to defend exists. The duty to defend is determined solely from the language of the underlying complaint and the insurance policy. If the complaint alleges facts within or potentially within policy coverage, the insurer is obliged to defend its insured even if the allegations are groundless, false, or fraudulent, and even if the insurer knows that the allegations are untrue. The complaint and insurance policy must be liberally construed in favor of the insured, and an insurer may not justifiably refuse to defend unless it is clear from the face of the complaint that it fails to state facts which bring the case within, or potentially within, the policy's coverage.

In this case, the complaint alleged that plaintiff was negligent in allowing Edward Jackson to enter the bar while armed with a handgun and in failing to provide security. Thereafter, according to the complaint, Jackson "shot and killed" Marvin White. The general liability policy issued by Penn contained an exclusion for injury or damages "resulting from assault and battery or physical altercations that occur in, on, near, or away from" the insured premises, including damages arising out of the insured's failure to properly supervise or keep the premises in a safe condition. Plaintiff argues that the exclusion does not necessarily apply because the complaint does not allege an intentional shooting and could describe an accidental discharge of the firearm. We agree that, construed most liberally in favor of the plaintiff, the allegations of the complaint are not, on their face, clearly encompassed by the assault and battery exclusion and therefore are potentially within the policy's coverage. Accordingly, Penn had a duty to defend its insured which required it to either defend under a reservation of rights or seek a declaratory judgment of no coverage. The trial court ruled that this duty was discharged when Penn filed its answer and cross-claim in response to plaintiff's declaratory judgment action, and we agree.

Assault and Battery Exclusion

Finally, having determined that Penn is not estopped from raising policy defense, we consider the effect of the assault and battery exclusion contained in the insurance policy. In doing so, we are no longer limited to the allegations of the complaint, but may also consider extrinsic evidence gathered during the discovery process. Deposition testimony contained in the record establishes that Edward Jackson intentionally shot Marvin White while White was on the dance floor of L. A. Connection. After White fell to the floor, Jackson grabbed a bottle from a table and hit White on the head with it. Jackson was later arrested and he was subsequently convicted of first degree murder. Jackson's actions are clearly encompassed by the assault and battery exclusion, regardless of whether those terms are defined under the criminal code (720 ILCS 5/12-1), or by civil case law. Accordingly, the trial court properly granted summary judgment in favor of Penn.

Affirmed.

CASE COMMENT

Here again the lawsuit stems from an intentional act, a shooting at a nightclub. The insurance policy excluded coverage for "assault and battery." Because the shooting fits within this exclusion, the court held that the insurance policy precluded coverage. Of course, the shooting clearly stems from an assault and battery, which was specifically excluded in the insurance contract. The moral of these cases is that property and business owners must carefully review their insurance policies. Language designed to exclude coverage for intentional acts is common in the industry. For those property and business owners who seek coverage for intentional acts, it may be necessary to purchase a rider designed for this level of financial and liability protection.

B. SECURITY SERVICES CONTRACTS

---

255 F. Supp. 2d 497

United States District Court, E.D. Pennsylvania

ROYAL INDEMNITY COMPANY A/S/O DANA CORPORATION, PLAINTIFF v. SECURITY GUARDS, INC., DEFENDANT.

April 4, 2003

Background

Property insurer which paid insured for loss resulting from fire on insured's premises brought action against security guard service. This firm was contracted with insured to provide security services, seeks to recover portion of damages, based upon security service employee's alleged failure to respond to fire alarm on premises which led to spread of fire. Security service moved for summary judgment.

Holding

The district court held that the limitation of liability clause in contract between security service and insured did not apply to alleged losses caused by gross negligence or breach of contract, thereby precluding summary judgment.

Motion denied

This subrogation action arises out of a fire that occurred on August 11, 1999, at a truck frame manufacturing facility located in Reading, Pennsylvania. The facility was owned and operated by Dana Corporation, a Virginia corporation with its principal place of business in Toledo, Ohio. At all relevant times, Royal Indemnity Company, a Delaware corporation with its principal place of business in Charlotte, North Carolina, was Dana's property insurer.

At the time of the fire, defendant Security Guards, Inc., a Pennsylvania corporation with its principal place of business in Wyomissing, Pennsylvania, provided guard services to Dana at its Reading facility pursuant to a security services agreement between Dana and SGI executed on August 14, 1989, and renewed annually pursuant to its terms. At the time of the fire, the agreement was in full force and effect, subject only to the fact that the hourly rate for each guard had increased from $9 to $12.58.

SGI employee Hank Clarke was stationed at Dana's main security guard booth on August 11, 1999, from 2 p.m. to 10 p.m. Upon the sounding of a "critical alarm," or Point 51 alarm, SGI guards were required to immediately contact the maintenance supervisor located in the area where the alarm sounded and to contact ADT, the alarm company, which, in the case of a fire, would contact the Reading fire department. At 5:39 p.m., a critical alarm was activated by a fire in the paint shop in Section 104 of the Lewis building at the Dana plant. Royal alleges that Clarke failed to immediately contact the supervisor in the area of the alarm or upon the sounding of three subsequent critical alarms and attempted to instead reset the alarm. At 5:54 p.m., approximately fifteen minutes later, ADT automatically received a signal that Dana's fire alarm had been activated and notified the Reading fire department. Royal claims the fire department would have responded to the fire fifteen minutes earlier if Clarke had followed the appropriate security procedure and that the amount of damage to the plant would have been substantially less. As a result of the fire, Dana made a claim on Royal, and in accordance with its policy terms, Royal paid Dana $16,535,882.84.

Royal, as Dana's subrogee, initiated this action. The three-count Complaint alleges negligence, gross negligence, and breach of contract against SGI for its employees' failure to promptly respond to the critical alarm signal at the Dana plant by immediately contacting the maintenance supervisor and the alarm company, who would have alerted the Reading fire department. Royal alleges that as a result of SGI's alleged failure to respond to the critical alarm that the fire department could not respond to the fire at the Dana plant until approximately fifteen minutes after the first critical alarm sounded, resulting in greater damage to the plant. On each count, Royal claims damages of at least $7 million plus interest and costs of suit.

A. Limitation of Liability Clause

The limitation of liability clause in the contract between Dana and SGI states in relevant part: In the event of any bodily injury or property damage loss sustained by CLIENT [Dana] and caused solely by the negligence of CONTRACTOR [SGI] or its employees, CONTRACTOR [SGI] will indemnify and hold CLIENT [Dana] harmless for such loss to the extent of $50,000 per occurrence. By its terms, this clause is limited to claims based on negligence.

Under Pennsylvania law, "it is well established that the intent of the parties to a written contract is to be regarded as being embodied in the writing itself, and when the words are clear and unambiguous the intent is to be discovered only from the express language of the agreement." "In deciding whether contract language is unambiguous, a court not only asks whether the language is clear, but also hears the proffer of the parties and determines if there are objective indicia that, from the linguistic reference point of the parties, the terms of the contract are susceptible of different meanings." To be ambiguous, a contract provision must be capable of two reasonable, alternative meanings. To be unambiguous, a contract provision must be reasonably capable of only one construction. It is the court's function to determine if a provision is ambiguous. In doing so, the court must not "distort the meaning of the language or resort to a strained contrivance in order to find an ambiguity."

Defendant SGI moves for summary judgment and contends that pursuant to the terms of the agreement between Dana and SGI in effect at the time of the fire, that Royal's damages are limited to $50,000, which cannot satisfy the $75,000 amount in controversy requirement for diversity jurisdiction under 28 U.S.C. Section 1332(a), and therefore Royal's claim must be dismissed. SGI asserts that this provision was essential to the agreement. SGI maintains that this provision clearly and unambiguously limits its liability for any damages caused to Dana by SGI's negligence to $50,000. SGI notes that whereas exculpatory clauses are generally disfavored by courts and subject to strict construction standards, limitation of liability clauses are not disfavored and are construed under the general rules applying to contract interpretation. SGI seeks to enforce the $50,000 limitation of liability clause against Dana because it claims that the parties were aware of the potential multimillion-dollar exposure to SGI, and that the $50,000 amount is reasonable when considered against SGI's fees for providing security services, which amounted to $533,733.19 for 1999.

Plaintiff opposes summary judgment and contends that the limitation of liability clause is strictly limited to negligence, that the issues in this case raise the standard of gross negligence which is well founded under Pennsylvania law, and also the limitation of liability clause does not address the claims based on breach of contract.

This court previously has examined the scope of limitation of liability clauses in contracts in situations similar to the instant case. In (case and citation omitted), the plaintiff insurer brought a subrogation action against defendants ADT and others alleging that their negligence and gross negligence resulted in the burglary of a Rolex watch repair facility and the theft of $1.8 million in merchandise. After examining the plaintiff's evidence and limitation of liability clause in the contract between the plaintiff and defendants, the court concluded that the contract limited the defendants' liability for acts of negligence and gross negligence and granted summary judgment in favor of the defendants.

In *Neuchatel*, the limitation of liability provision in question was substantially broader than the provision in the instant case. The first provision provided:

> It is understood that ADT is not an insurer ... and that the amounts payable to ADT hereunder are based upon the value of the services and the scope of liability as herein set forth and are unrelated to the value of the customer's property or property of others located in customer's

> premises. ADT makes no guaranty or warranty, including any implied warranty of merchantability or fitness, that the system or services supplied, will avert or prevent occurrences or the consequences therefrom, which the system or service is designed to detect. It is impractical and extremely difficult to fix the actual damages, if any, which may proximately result from the failure on the part of ADT to perform any of its obligations hereunder. The customer does not desire this contract to provide for full liability of ADT and agrees that ADT shall be exempt from liability for loss, damage or injury due directly or indirectly to occurrences or consequences therefrom, which the service or system is designed to detect or avert; that if ADT should be found liable for loss, damage or injury due to a failure of service or equipment in any respect, its liability shall be limited to a sum equal to 100% of the annual service charge or $10,000, whichever is less, as the agreed upon damages and not as a penalty, as the exclusive remedy; *and that the provisions of this paragraph shall apply if loss, damage or injury irrespective of cause or origin results directly or indirectly to person or property from performance or nonperformance of obligations imposed by this contract* or from negligence, active or otherwise, of ADT, its agents or employees.

Similarly, the provision in the insured's contract with defendant Wells Fargo contained language limiting that defendant's liability:

> It is agreed that Wells Fargo is not an insurer and that the payments herein provided are based upon the cost to Wells Fargo of its services hereunder, and the extent of its liability as herein below limited; that in the event of a default on the part of Wells Fargo *in the performance of any of its obligations hereunder, either by way of non-performance or negligent performance or otherwise*, and as a resulting loss, or in any event resulting from the relationship hereby created, Wells Fargo's liability shall not exceed the sum of $50.00 and Subscriber's sole remedy at law or in equity shall be the right to recover a sum within such limit.

The court concluded that: The ADT and Wells Fargo contracts both contain clauses excluding, and/or placing a dollar ceiling on, liability; and in both instances those clauses are keyed to negligence and conduct that is "otherwise" wrongful. Accordingly, this court concludes that, notwithstanding plaintiffs' allegations of gross negligence, plaintiffs' potential recovery is limited by those clauses. In the instant case, the limitation of liability provision only limits liability for damages "caused solely by the negligence" of SGI or its employees. The court agrees with Judge Pollak's finding in *Neuchatel* "that if either an exculpatory clause or a limitation of liability clause excludes or limits only negligent conduct and is not broad enough to cover conduct that may be described as grossly negligent, willful or wanton, liability is neither excluded nor limited if the conduct alleged is found to be grossly negligent, willful, or wanton." Additionally, the limitation of liability provision makes no reference to liability for performance or non-performance under the contract, so liability is neither excluded nor limited for breach of contract.

B. Claims Based on Negligence

Royal claims that SGI's duty to Dana is undisputed. If a Point 51 critical alarm was triggered in the Dana paint shop, it was Dana's procedure for the SGI guard to immediately notify the Department 104 supervisor. A Point 51 critical alarm was triggered on August 11, 1999 at 5:39 p.m., approximately fifteen minutes before a fire alarm was triggered, and Clarke was monitoring the alarm panel for Dana in the control booth. Clarke knew that he was always required to call someone in response to a Point 51 critical alarm, and he was usually able to contact a Dana supervisor within a minute. Royal alleges that Clarke neglected his duty. Mr. Janisjewski, the Reading fire marshal, testified that the sooner a fire department responds to a fire, the less damage is done, and with regard to Dana's paint shop fire, he stated that there was an incipient stage to the fire, for approximately ten to fifteen minutes before it broke into full flame, but by the time the Reading fire department was alerted, the paint shop was engulfed in flames.

Royal's fire cause and origin expert, John F. Goetz, testified that it was likely that the fire started small before burning across the side and under the dip tank, and that it was likely that the fire burned for two to five minutes before triggering the Point 51 alarm. Mr. Goetz stated that the "delay in alerting the fire department resulted in significant additional fire damage to the Dana paint shop well in excess of one million dollars." Royal further supports its claim that the fifteen-minute delay resulted in the spread of the fire by pointing to the arrival of the deputy fire chief on the scene three minutes after the fire department was alerted. Royal also asserts that even if the alarm were placed in test mode, as SGI contends, SGI guards were not instructed to ignore all alarms, or specifically the Point 51 critical alarms, but would not respond if an alarm was in test mode only if specifically ordered not to do so. Mr. Clarke does not recall placing the alarm in test mode or being told by anyone to ignore the Point 51 critical alarm on the day of the fire. Although Clarke did not know what a "critical alarm" referred to, he knew that it could be "very, very serious" and that it was always his duty to call a supervisor when such an alarm sounded.

Royal, through affidavits and depositions, has pointed to genuine issues of material fact as to whether Clarke's failure to contact Dana personnel when the Point 51 critical alarm sounded constitutes negligence. SGI's Motion for Summary Judgment on this count will be denied. However, if a jury were to conclude that SGI was negligent, its liability would be limited to $50,000 as provided in the limitation of liability clause in the contract between Dana and SGI.

C. Claims Based on Gross Negligence

SGI contends that Count II of Royal's complaint, alleging gross negligence, must fail because the limitation of liability clause applies to negligence claims, and SGI cites numerous cases to support its argument that Pennsylvania does not recognize a cause of action for gross negligence. There are many decisions of the Pennsylvania and federal courts applying Pennsylvania law and which discuss the concept of gross negligence. Analyzing the holdings and the language of the numerous Pennsylvania cases on this issue is more similar to looking at multiple pellets from a shotgun as compared to a single bullet from a rifle. SGI points to (citation omitted), in which the Pennsylvania Supreme Court wrote that "there are no degrees of negligence in Pennsylvania." SGI also points to the Third Circuit's discussion of gross negligence in *Fialkowski*, in which the Court observed that "degrees of negligence are not generally recognized under Pennsylvania common law." Following *Fialkowski*, in *Jordan*, the District court dismissed a gross negligence count of a complaint in response to a Rule 12(b)(6) motion, finding that the plaintiffs could proceed with their claims under a general negligence theory with gross negligence as the alleged standard of care violated. However, it is not necessary to attempt to harmonize these many cases or to try to devise a uniform theory under Pennsylvania law in order to decide the summary judgment issue in this case.

In *Shouey*, the court addressed the concept of gross negligence having relevance under Pennsylvania law only as it pertains to different standards of care, which are not generally applicable in negligence cases. The court disregarded the claim of gross negligence and considered the complaint as simply having asserted a claim for negligence. SGI asserts that because the instant case does not involve any of the unique circumstances requiring a consideration of a different standard of care than that presented in an ordinary negligence case, that Royal's gross negligence claim is not cognizable under Pennsylvania law.

SGI also contends in the alternative that Royal's factual allegations do not meet Pennsylvania's standard for gross negligence. Pennsylvania courts generally view gross negligence as "a want of even scant care, but something less than intentional indifference to consequences of actions." Gross negligence also has been defined as a "failure to perform a duty in reckless disregard of the consequences or with such want of care and regard for the consequences as to justify a presumption of willfulness of wantonness." To find gross negligence, there must be "an extreme departure from ordinary care." SGI contends these cases demonstrate a focus on the defendant's conduct rather than on the results of the incident.

Royal contends that whether gross negligence is considered a standard of care violated under a negligence theory, or whether it is a separate cause of action, is a distinction with no practical relevance because Pennsylvania consistently has recognized that limitation of liability clauses which merely mention "negligence," such as the one in the instant case, do not limit damages arising out of gross negligence. This court concludes Royal's argument is supported by close analysis of case law.

The court agrees with Royal that the Third Circuit's discussion in *Fialkowski* that "degrees of negligence are not generally recognized under Pennsylvania common law" is dicta because other language in the case identifies Pennsylvania "cases holding that the allegations of the complaint were sufficient to state a claim for gross negligence." Royal deems inapposite the language in *Ferrick* that "there are no degrees of negligence in Pennsylvania" because that case concerned the standard of care applicable to bailment situations and did not specifically discuss gross negligence. As noted, though, in (citation omitted), there are numerous post-*Ferrick* opinions recognizing gross negligence as a theory or standard under Pennsylvania law. For example, in *Nicholson*, the court denied the defendant's motion for summary judgment on the plaintiff's claim of gross negligence and noted the following:

> Generally, "the issue of whether a given set of facts satisfies the definition of gross negligence is a question of fact to be determined by a jury." (Assessing "gross negligence" whether "defendant's actions demonstrate the lack of care required of gross negligence is a question of fact for the jury.) The court may decide the issue as a matter of law only when "the conduct in question falls short of gross negligence, the case is entirely free from doubt, and no reasonable jury could find gross negligence."

In *Douglas W. Randall*, a store security system triggered numerous false alarms, which the security company responded to by adjusting the system so that the alarms stopped. The court denied the defendant's motion for judgment notwithstanding the verdict, finding that if the defendant turned down the sensitivity level of the system to such a low level that it could not detect the entry of a person into the store, that the jury did not err in finding that the defendant's actions departed from the standard of ordinary care to the extent that they constituted gross negligence.

In *Newark*, the plaintiff insurance company, as subrogee of its insured, brought an action against the defendants ADT and Bell Atlantic alleging negligence, gross negligence, and breach of contract, among other claims, stemming from a burglary of videotapes from the insured's warehouse. Defendant ADT had installed and maintained the alarm at the warehouse, and the defendant Bell Atlantic had provided service on the telephone lines. The Court found that a genuine issue of material fact existed as to whether ADT was negligent or grossly negligent in allowing the warehouse alarm system to allegedly remain unmonitored for 56 days and in not performing certain tests required for particular alarm systems. The court denied ADT's motion for summary judgment, finding that if ADT were found negligent at trial, its liability would be limited to $1,000 as provided in the limitation of liability clause in its contract with the insured, but if it were found grossly negligent, its liability would not be contractually limited. On the breach of contract claim, the court found that a genuine issue of material fact existed as to whether ADT breached its contractual obligations to the insured but found that recovery was limited to $1,000 by the contract provision applying to injury resulting from performance or non-performance of contractual obligations.

Applying a gross negligence standard, SGI contends in the instant case that Royal has not produced any evidence suggesting that Clarke's failure to notify the maintenance supervisor in response to the Point 51 alarm constitutes gross negligence, but "was, at most, a failure to measure up to the conduct of a reasonable person and, therefore, perhaps negligence." SGI notes that there were no other critical alarms between 5:39 p.m. and 5:52 p.m. when the first alarm was received (citing Dana Alarm Records). One other critical alarm occurred after 5:54 p.m. after ADT responded to the fire alarm by calling the fire department. SGI emphasizes that the 5:39 p.m. critical alarm was not a fire alarm but was a supervisory alarm, which did not require contacting the fire department. It goes on to claim that Point 51 alarms were a common occurrence at Dana, and not once during the previous forty Point 51 alarms that had sounded in the weeks leading up to and including the day of the fire had there been a fire in the paint shop. SGI contends that even though Clarke did not remember putting the alarm into test mode that he must have done so, which would not require a response from Clarke or ADT.

Royal asserts that Clarke's ignoring of this alarm was reckless and that SGI's attempts to explain the Point 51 alarm as a common occurrence that allegedly sounded five times on the day of the fire are similar to the defense used in *Douglas W. Randall*, where the alarm company defendant, after numerous false alarms, turned down the system's sensitivity to the point that it could not detect the entry of a person into the store. Just as the jury found the defendant grossly negligent in that case, Royal argues that it would not be unreasonable for a jury to find that SGI was grossly negligent when its employee ignored an alarm that he understood could be "very, very serious."

In its reply brief, SGI submitted further evidence regarding the Point 51 alarms that had sounded in the days and hours leading up to the 5:39 p.m. alarm on August 11, 1999, in an attempt to show that such alarms were a common occurrence and that none of the prior alarms indicated a fire. SGI also points to records showing that Mr. Clarke ordered the alarm to be placed in test mode until 10 p.m. on August 11 even though he does not recall doing so. However, even if the alarm were placed in test mode, SGI guards were not instructed to ignore all alarms, or specifically the Point 51 critical alarms, but would not respond if an alarm was in test mode only if specifically ordered not to do so.

Royal, through affidavits and depositions, has pointed to genuine issues of material fact as to whether Clarke's failure to contact Dana personnel when the Point 51 critical alarm sounded constitutes gross negligence. SGI's Motion for Summary Judgment on this count will be denied. Construing the limitation of liability clause, the court concludes that if, under either a standard of care theory or a claim applying gross negligence, if SGI were to be found grossly negligent, its liability would not be limited to $50,000, and Royal has provided evidence upon which a jury could find that its damages far exceed the $75,000 jurisdictional amount in controversy.

D. Claims Based on Breach of Contract

Royal asserts that its claim for breach of contract is not subject to the limitation of liability provision in the contract between Dana and SGI because that provision relates to injury or damage caused solely by the negligence of SGI. Royal asserts that the provision is unambiguous and must be given its plain meaning, but that if the court finds the language ambiguous, that becomes a question of fact for the jury.

Under Pennsylvania law, courts "have routinely referred to the specific language of the contract in issue to determine the scope of an exculpatory/limitation of liability clause, and therefore, the type of conduct for which liability was excluded or limited." In *Neuchatel*, for example, the contracts at issue in that case clearly limited the defendants' liability for breach of contract by specifically referring to the defendant's duties according to their respective contracts. In the instant case, the limitation of liability provision makes no reference to liability for performance or non-performance under the contract, but only limits liability for damages "caused solely by the negligence" of SGI or its employees.

A cause of action for breach of contract is distinct from a cause of action for negligence. In Pennsylvania, "a contract action may not be converted into a tort simply by alleging that the conduct in question was done wantonly." Royal maintains that the breach of contract count of its complaint is based on SGI's failure to perform duties owed to Dana under the Agreement and is distinct from its negligence cause of action, which is based on duties SGI owes Dana "as a matter of social policy."

Plaintiff points to *Newark*, in which the court recognized a cause of action for both breach of contract and negligence and found that the plaintiff raised a genuine issue of material fact on both actions. Defendant relies on *Valhal*, in which the Third Circuit considered whether a cause of action, although arising out of a contractual relationship, should be brought in contract or tort. In *Valhal*, the court discussed two lines of reasoning: the "misfeasance/nonfeasance" approach and the "gist of the action" approach.

The first line comes from the Pennsylvania Superior Court's opinion in *Raab,* which involved a claim that the insurance company negligently failed to pay benefits under a no-fault automobile insurance policy and that an agent of the company maliciously interfered with the contractual relationship between the policyholder and the carrier. The court wrote:

> Generally when the breach of a contractual relationship is expressed in terms of tortious conduct, the cause of action is properly brought in assumpsit and not in trespass. However, there are circumstances out of which a breach of contract may give rise to an actionable tort. The test used to determine if there exists a cause of action in tort growing out of a breach of contract is whether there was an improper performance of a contractual obligation (misfeasance) rather than a mere failure to perform (nonfeasance).

Under the *Raab* line of reasoning, if there had been a complete failure to perform a contract, the action lies in assumpsit, while if there had been an improper performance, the action lies in tort. Under the second line, the misfeasance/nonfeasance distinction is not pursued. Rather, the nature of the wrong ascribed to the defendant "is the gist of the action, the contract being collateral." Thus, if the harm suffered by the plaintiff would traditionally be characterized as a tort, then the action sounds in tort and not in contract.

However, *Valhal* is unavailing to defendant. The Pennsylvania Superior Court has explained that "the important difference between contract and tort actions is the latter lie from the breach of duties imposed as a matter of social policy while the former lie for the breach of duties imposed by mutual consensus." In the instant case, a genuine issue of material fact exists on all three counts of plaintiff's complaint as to whether defendant's conduct constituted negligence, gross negligence, or breach of contract. The claim for breach of contract arises out of SGI's alleged failure to perform duties owed to Dana under the Agreement, and the negligence cause of action may be based on those duties as well as duties SGI may owe Dana as a matter of social policy. Here, the contract provision between Dana and SGI does not limit liability for breach of contract, and Royal has offered evidence that its damages exceed $75,000. Therefore, defendant's Motion for Summary Judgment on this count will be denied.

Conclusion

Royal has raised genuine issues of material fact for trial. Therefore, for the reasons discussed above, defendant's Motion for Summary Judgment will be denied.

CASE COMMENT

This case provides an excellent overview and analysis of security contracts. Notice the court compared limitation of liability clauses from other cases, with different language contained in each contract. This analysis distinguished the case at bar as compared to other cases. The key distinction involves the actual language in the contract. The court noted that the insurance company raised the question of whether gross negligence was included in the limitation of liability clause. The court stated if a jury found that the security provider was grossly negligent, then the limitation of liability clause would not be operative. In this way, the security firm may be liable far in excess of the contract clause. In addition, there was a legitimate question whether the security firm breached the contract by its failure to timely act following the fire alarm.

902 So.2d 46

Supreme Court of Alabama

SAIA FOOD DISTRIBUTORS AND CLUB, INC., D/B/A KLUB 280; AND NORMAN SAIA, JR. v. SECURITYLINK FROM AMERITECH, INC., AND ADT SECURITY SERVICES, INC.

Dec. 3, 2004

Background

Nightclub owners brought action against security alarm companies, after alarm system in the club failed to go off during a burglary and fire, which destroyed club. The Shelby Circuit Court entered summary judgment for security companies on claim that limitation-of-liability clause in contract capped liability at $5,800. Company and shareholder appealed.

Holdings

The supreme court held that:

1. Limitation-of-liability clause in security system contract was enforceable; and
2. Security companies' conduct did not amount to promissory fraud.

Affirmed in part, reversed in part, and remanded

In February 2000, Saia Food entered into a contract with SecurityLink pursuant to which SecurityLink was to provide alarm equipment and monitoring services to "Klub 280," a nightclub located in Shelby County and owned and operated by Saia Food. Saia Food agreed to purchase from SecurityLink the necessary monitoring equipment and to pay a monthly fee for the monitoring services. Saia Food purchased equipment totaling $5,800 from SecurityLink.

Although initially functional, shortly after it was installed the system began displaying a "zone-error" message. Saia allegedly reported the problem to SecurityLink. According to Saia, SecurityLink was unable to locate the problem and instructed Saia to hit the "bypass" button when arming the system in order to avoid the zone-error message. Saia Food and Saia alleged that Saia continued to operate the system using this "bypass" method.

On the night of October 31, 2000, Klub 280 was allegedly burglarized. After the alleged burglary, a fire was set inside the building. However, SecurityLink claimed that it never received a signal from the equipment at Klub 280 on that night indicating either a break-in or a fire. SecurityLink did not notify the proper authorities of the burglary and fire. The damage to the Klub 280 building was extensive. Saia alleges that SecurityLink was not monitoring Klub 280 on the night of the fire. Saia obtained records from SecurityLink; they interpreted those records to mean that SecurityLink had not been monitoring Klub 280 since October 21, 2000.

At the time of the fire, Klub 280 was insured with Seneca Insurance Company. Saia Food filed a claim under its insurance policy. When Seneca refused to pay the benefits under the policy, Saia Food sued Seneca. The lawsuit was settled for $920,000.

On January 11, 2002, Saia sued SecurityLink and ADT alleging breach of contract; negligent, wanton, and intentional failure to provide alarm and monitoring services; negligent or wanton failure to hire, train, and supervise their agents; and promissory fraud. ADT answered the complaint, denying that it had entered into a contract with Saia. ADT asserted that only SecurityLink had contracted with Saia Food and that, on or around July 2001, after the date of SecurityLink's contract with Saia Food, SecurityLink and ADT merged. ADT also asserted the affirmative defenses of contributory negligence, assumption of the risk, unclean hands, estoppel, and, as to the claims asserted by Norman Saia, individually, the failure to state a claim upon which relief could be granted. SecurityLink also denied the allegations, raising contract defenses, and asserting the same affirmative defenses raised by ADT.

In March 2003, ADT and SecurityLink filed a motion for a summary judgment. As a basis for their summary-judgment motion, ADT and SecurityLink relied on a paragraph of the SecurityLink contract, which contained a limitation-of-liability provision and an exculpatory clause. That provision provided:

> It is understood and agreed by and between the parties hereto that [SecurityLink] is not an Insurer, nor is this Agreement intended to be an insurance policy or a substitute for an insurance policy. Insurance, if any, will be obtained by [Saia Food]. Charges are based only on the value of the System and/or the services provided and are unrelated to the value of [Saia Food's] property or the property of others located in [Saia Food's] premises. The amounts payable by [Saia Food] are not sufficient to warrant [SecurityLink's] assuming any risk of consequential, collateral, incidental or other damages to [Saia Food] due to the System, its installation, or the use thereof, or any deficiency, defect or inadequacy of the System or services or due to [SecurityLink's] negligence or failure to perform, except as specifically provided for in this agreement. [Saia Food] does not desire this agreement to provide for the liability of

> [SecurityLink] and [Saia Food] agrees that [SecurityLink] shall not be liable for loss or damage due directly or indirectly to any occurrences or consequences therefrom which the System or service is designed to detect or avert. From the nature of the System provided hereunder, or the services to be performed, it is impractical and extremely difficult to fix the actual damages, if any, which may proximately result from the active or passive negligence of, or a failure on the part of, [SecurityLink] to perform any of its obligations hereunder, or the failure of the System to properly operate. If [SecurityLink] should be found liable for loss or damage due to a failure on the part of [SecurityLink] or the System or services, in any respect, such liability shall be limited solely with regard to any RECURRING SERVICE transaction, to an amount equal to 50 percent of one year's recurring service charge or the amount of $1000.00, whichever is less, or, solely with respect to a DIRECT SALE transaction, to an amount equal to the purchase price of the equipment with respect to which the claim is made, and regardless of the type of transaction, this liability shall be exclusive. The provisions of this paragraph shall apply in the event loss or damage, irrespective of cause or origin, results directly or indirectly to person or property from the performance or nonperformance of the obligations set forth by the terms of this Agreement or from the active or passive negligence of [SecurityLink], its agents or employees. In the event that [Saia Food] desires [SecurityLink] to assume greater liability under this Agreement, a choice is hereby given of obtaining full or limited liability by paying an additional amount in proportion to the amount of liability [SecurityLink] will assume. If this option is chosen, an additional rider shall be attached to this Agreement setting forth the additional liability of [SecurityLink] and the additional charge (capitalization in original).

On May 20, 2003, the trial court held that the limitation-of-liability clause was valid and enforceable and that it encompassed all of the claims asserted by Saia except for claims asserting intentional, willful, or wanton conduct. Therefore, the trial court held, to the extent ADT and SecurityLink's liability could be established for breach of contract and/or negligence, the maximum damages Saia could recover were capped by the limitation-of-liability clause at $5,800, which represented the purchase price of the equipment. The trial court also held that Saia had failed to establish by substantial evidence any of their claims alleging intentional, willful, and wanton conduct and granted SecurityLink and ADT's motion for a summary judgment as to those claims.

Enforceability of the Limitation-of-Liability Provision

This court has upheld a similar limitation-of-liability provision. In *American District Telegraph Co. of Alabama v. Roberts & Son, Inc.*, this court upheld a $50 limitation-of-liability clause found in a sprinkler-service contract. That clause provided:

"It is agreed by and between the parties hereto that the Contractor is not an insurer, and that the rates hereinbefore are based solely on the value of the service in the operation of the system described, and in case of failure to perform such service and a resulting loss its liability hereunder shall be limited to and fixed at the sum of $50.00 as liquidated damages, and not as a penalty, and this liability shall be exclusive." Without much explanation, the *American District Telegraph* court found the provision enforceable and modified the trial court's judgment in favor of the plaintiff to award $50, in conformity with the language of the limitation-of-liability provision.

The case of *Leon's Bakery, Inc. v. Grinnell Corp.*, provides additional explanation for upholding a limitation-of-liability provision. In *Leon's Bakery*, the United States Court of Appeals for the Second Circuit enforced a limitation-of-liability clause found in a contract between a fire-alarm-monitoring service and a bakery. The Second Circuit Court of Appeals stated:

> From all that the parties have cited to us and from all that our own research has unearthed, it appears that all of the courts that have considered the validity of limitation-of-liability clauses in contracts for the provisions of fire alarm systems have found those clauses to be permissible." Apparently, a greater number of courts have been concerned with the enforceability of such clauses in contracts for the installation and servicing of burglar alarm systems, and those courts have similarly upheld clauses limiting liability for the failure of such systems.

The rationale for upholding an agreement between the purchaser and the manufacturer of an alarm system to limit the liability of the manufacturer is that:

> Most persons, especially operators of business establishments, carry insurance for loss due to various types of crimes. Presumptively insurance companies who issue such policies base their premiums on their assessment of the value of the property and the vulnerability of the premises. No reasonable person could expect that the provider of an alarm service would, for a fee unrelated to the value of the property, undertake to provide an identical type coverage should the alarm fail to prevent the crime.

Even where the contract is not only for the sale and installation of a burglar alarm system but is also for its maintenance or monitoring, if the fee paid is not sufficiently high to include a premium for theft insurance, a clause limiting the alarm service company's liability in the event the alarm service does not function properly is not unconscionable.

> Though the events against which burglar alarms and fire alarms, respectively, are intended to provide protection differ somewhat, in that burglaries are always criminal interventions whereas fires may be either criminal or accidental, we think the rationale for permitting the

> provider of a burglar alarm system to limit its liability is equally applicable to the provider of a fire alarm system. The supplier of either type of system is paid for its equipment and services, and the price does not generally include a sum designed to anticipate the possible need to pay the purchaser the value of the property that the system is designed to protect. The owner or custodian of the property is in a far better position than the alarm system seller to know the property's value and to bargain with an insurance company for appropriate coverage and an appropriate premium, and, as the New York Court of Appeals noted, the alarm seller's limitations on liability help keep alarm services affordable....

We agree that an installer of security equipment or a supplier of fire- or security-monitoring services does not become an insurer of the property it is designed to help safeguard. Construing a security-equipment or security-monitoring contract as an insurance policy would render such a contract cost prohibitive. In fact, SecurityLink's contract, which Saia executed expressly recognized this: "The Company [SecurityLink] is not an insurer, nor is this Agreement intended to be an insurance policy or a substitute for an insurance policy." SecurityLink's contract limits its damages to, in this case, the costs of the equipment Saia Food purchased from SecurityLink. Finally, the contract specifically offered Saia Food the option of increasing SecurityLink's liability exposure by paying additional charges commensurate with the risk Saia Food wished SecurityLink to assume. Saia Food did not select this option.

Saia Food and Saia argue that this court should hold unenforceable the limitation-of-liability provision in Saia Food's contract with SecurityLink. They argue that the facts of *American District Telegraph,* are distinguishable from those presented in this case. However, we find nothing in this case that compels us to reach a result different from the result this court reached.

Saia also argues that, if we uphold the limitation-of-liability provision, we are allowing SecurityLink to limit its liability for negligence in the performance of the very duties it assumed under the contract. SecurityLink specifically agreed that it would provide monitoring services for Klub 280. However, Saia Food's contract with SecurityLink also specifically provided:

> If [SecurityLink] should be found liable for loss or damage due to a failure on the part of [SecurityLink] or the System or services, in any respect, such liability shall be limited ... solely with respect to a DIRECT SALE transaction, to an amount equal to the purchase price of the equipment with respect to which the claim is made, and regardless of the type of transaction, this liability shall be exclusive. The provisions of this paragraph shall apply in the event loss or damage, irrespective of cause or origin, results directly or indirectly to person or property from the performance or nonperformance of the obligations set forth by the terms of this Agreement or from the active or passive negligence of [SecurityLink], its agents or employees.

We do not interpret this language as allowing SecurityLink to escape all liability for any breach of its contract with Saia Food or for SecurityLink's negligence, if any. SecurityLink and Saia Food merely agreed to limit the amount of damages for which SecurityLink could be held responsible. The parties' agreement to limit SecurityLink's exposure is enforceable.

Intentional Tort Claims Asserted by Saia Food and Saia

Saia also appeals from the trial court's summary judgment in favor of ADT and SecurityLink on claims alleging willful, wanton, and intentional failure to monitor Klub 280; willful, wanton, and intentional failure to supervise and train their employees; and promissory fraud.

We address the claim of promissory fraud first.

> The elements of fraud are (1) a false representation (2) of a material existing fact (3) reasonably relied upon by the plaintiff (4) who suffered damage as a proximate consequence of the misrepresentation. To prevail on a promissory fraud claim such as that at issue here, that is, based upon a promise to act or not to act in the future, two additional elements must be satisfied: (5) proof that at the time of the misrepresentation, the defendant had the intention not to perform the act promised, and (6) proof that the defendant had an intent to deceive.

Saia claims that SecurityLink represented to them that it would monitor Klub 280 but that it failed to do so. However, we find nothing in the record to suggest that, at the time the contract was signed, SecurityLink intended not to perform the promised monitoring services. At most, the evidence suggests that SecurityLink negligently failed to monitor Klub 280. Negligently failing to perform services does not rise to the level of promissory fraud.

Saia also claims that SecurityLink represented that it would properly install the fire-alarm system at Klub 280 but that it failed to do so. However, Saia's own testimony established that the system operated properly, at least for a period. We find nothing in the record to suggest that, at the time it entered into the contract, SecurityLink intended not to install the system properly. The evidence in the record suggests at most that ADT and SecurityLink were negligent in repairing or locating the problem in the security system installed at Klub 280. Negligently repairing the system or failing to locate the problem in a system does not rise to the level of promissory fraud. The trial court properly entered a summary judgment for ADT and SecurityLink on the promissory-fraud claim.

We next address Saia's appeal from the summary judgment in favor of ADT and SecurityLink on claims of willful, wanton, and intentional failure to monitor Klub 280, and willful, wanton, and intentional failure to supervise and train their employees. However, after a review of the record, we find nothing to support the claims that ADT and

SecurityLink willfully, wantonly, and intentionally failed to monitor Klub 280, or that they willfully, wantonly, and intentionally failed to supervise and train their employees. The record contains evidence supporting, at most, claims of negligence and breach of contract. We affirm the summary judgment entered in favor of ADT and SecurityLink on the claims asserting a willful, wanton, and intentional failure to monitor, supervise, and train.

Conclusion

The limitation-of-liability provision contained in the SecurityLink contract is valid and enforceable as to the breach-of-contract and negligence claims. We affirm the trial court's ruling that the maximum amount of damages recoverable from ADT and SecurityLink for breach of contract and negligence is limited to $5,800. We affirm the summary judgment entered in favor of ADT and SecurityLink as to the intentional tort claims asserted by Saia.

AFFIRMED IN PART; REVERSED IN PART; AND REMANDED

CASE COMMENT

The court upheld the limitation of liability clause in this case. After analyzing the language in the contract coupled with the facts of the case, the court found that the security firms were not grossly negligent—which the court inferred would have pierced the limitation of liability clause. Finding that gross negligence was not shown, the court held that the language in the clause limited compensable damages to the cost of the equipment. Consequently, the negligence and breach of contract claims were limited to the amount stated in the limitation of liability clause.

On a personal note, I was previously employed by SecurityLink, as their legal counsel and operational auditor. I negotiated this limitation of liability clause on hundreds of occasions. I often echoed many of the same arguments made by the court. It seems ironic—and appropriate—that this language would appear in this book!

C. LANDLORD-TENANT

---

185 N.J. 100, 881 A.2d 719

Supreme Court of New Jersey

ANTONIO GONZALEZ, PLAINTIFF-RESPONDENT v. SAFE AND SOUND SECURITY CORP., DEFENDANT AND THIRD PARTY–PLAINTIFF, AND ATLANTIC CITY HOUSING & URBAN RENEWAL ASSOCIATES, LP D/B/A THE SCHOOLHOUSE APARTMENTS, DEFENDANT-APPELLANT, AND RAYMOND BUNN, SECURITY OFFICER, COMMUNITY REALTY MANAGEMENT CORPORATION AND INSIGNIA MANAGEMENT GROUP, DEFENDANTS, AND AHMID ABDULLAH, THIRD PARTY DEFENDANT.

Decided Sept. 19, 2005

Background

Gunshot victim brought action against apartment complex owner, managers, security guard, and company to recover for negligent failure to provide adequate security to common area where he was shot. The Superior Court, Law Division, Atlantic County, entered judgment in victim's favor, and owner appealed. The Superior Court, Appellate Division affirmed. Certification was granted.

Holdings

The supreme court held that the standard of care for the landlord was not adequately determined, thereby a new trial is required. Reversed and remanded.

On April 25, 1996, Ahmid Abdullah shot plaintiff Antonio Gonzalez in the common area of the Schoolhouse Apartments in Atlantic City. As a result of the shooting, plaintiff suffered a spinal cord injury that left him paralyzed from the mid-chest down. In 1997, plaintiff filed a lawsuit alleging that his injuries were caused by the negligence of various defendants who failed to provide adequate security to the apartment complex despite their knowledge that the complex was plagued by criminal activities. Plaintiff named as defendants (1) Atlantic City Housing & Urban Renewal Associates, LP (ACHURA), the owner of the Schoolhouse Apartments; (2) Safe and Sound Security Corporation (Safe and Sound), the company retained to provide security for the apartment complex; (3) Raymond Bunn, the Safe and Sound security guard on duty the night plaintiff was shot; (4) Community Realty Management Corporation (Community Realty), the company that provided management services to the apartment complex; and (5) Insignia Management Group (Insignia Management), a management company that succeeded Community Realty several weeks before the shooting. Safe and Sound filed a third-party complaint against Abdullah. Before trial, Community Realty and Insignia Management both settled with plaintiff for $100,000 each. Abdullah defaulted and judgment was entered against him.

At a jury trial in 2001, plaintiff and the remaining defendants presented evidence describing the shooting, its aftermath, and the security conditions at the apartment complex during the months leading up to and on the day of the shooting. On the evening of the shooting, plaintiff and his friend, Antoine Robinson, entered the Schoolhouse Apartments through an electronic gate after identifying themselves to a security guard in a booth. Once inside one of the buildings, Robinson became embroiled in a heated verbal exchange with Abdullah, who apparently had stepped on his sneaker. The war of words lasted three to five minutes and escalated into a fistfight. Plaintiff unsuccessfully attempted to restrain his friend from fighting. After several minutes of slugging each other, Robinson and Abdullah paused and agreed to take the fight outside. They resumed exchanging blows in a breezeway between two buildings, where twenty to twenty-five people gathered to watch. Before the increasingly noisy crowd, the fight continued for five to seven minutes until plaintiff and another man stepped in and separated the combatants.

Plaintiff grabbed Robinson and told him, "come on, let's leave," while the other man held on to Abdullah. As plaintiff pulled him away, Robinson threatened Abdullah, "I'll be back; I'm going to burn you." With Robinson out of earshot, Abdullah asked someone in the crowd for a gun, and within moments, Abdullah was armed with a .38 caliber revolver. He pursued Robinson who, along with plaintiff, had rounded the building's corner and was trying to get the guard to open the locked exit gate. Abdullah fired six rounds in Robinson's direction, striking plaintiff twice. At no time did the Schoolhouse Apartment security guard intervene to stop the fight or call the police for assistance.

Plaintiff and Robinson gave conflicting explanations for their presence at the Schoolhouse Apartments that night. After identifying himself as Antonio Gomez, plaintiff told a police officer that he and Robinson were "looking for a female by the name of Shakima in room 207." In contrast, Robinson told the officer that they were there to visit a woman named "Kimmy" in "apartment 322." In yet another version, plaintiff stated at his deposition that he and Robinson "were about to go to [Robinson's] house." In his deposition testimony, plaintiff estimated that the entire incident lasted twenty minutes and that he and Robinson were at the gate trying to get out "for about five minutes."

Plaintiff presented evidence that, in the years before the shooting, ACHURA did not commit sufficient resources to combat the crime that had become commonplace on its premises. Detective Sergeant Charles Love, an Atlantic City police officer, testified that from 1994 to 1996, police officers responded to "numerous calls" concerning fights at the Schoolhouse Apartments. He described a "consistent level of problems" at the apartments that included drugs, violence, and guns. In his opinion, the in-house security was not staffed properly to cope with the criminal activities at the apartment complex.

Christopher Harty testified as an expert regarding the way the security guard should have conducted himself that day. Harty concluded that the fight could have been prevented had the security guard followed "established" protocol, used "common sense," and called the police immediately. Instead, according to Harty, the guard became just another spectator in the crowd, exhibiting no "command presence."

Leslie Cole, another security expert, testified that Safe and Sound deployed the guard on duty at the Schoolhouse Apartments without providing him with even "minimal training" or supervision. In Cole's opinion, had the guard "made his presence known" to the crowd and announced "that he was calling the police," the shooting could have been averted. Moreover, he found that a single guard on duty without "proper equipment" was insufficient to deal with the security needs of the apartment complex.

Representatives of ACHURA, Community Realty, Insignia Management, and Safe and Sound all acknowledged that security was inadequate to deal with the criminal activity at the beleaguered Schoolhouse Apartments. The apartment complex was the scene of drug offenses, assaults, burglaries, and shootings. ACHURA, the property managers, and the security agency agreed that there was a clear need for increased security, but differed on who was responsible for providing it, pointing fingers at one another and directing blame away from themselves.

Lawrence Sherman, Safe and Sound's expert in "the scientific study of the causes, prediction and prevention of crime," testified that nothing in the evidence suggested that additional security measures, such as a risk analysis study, additional guards, or even calling the police, would have prevented the shooting. Based on his review of empirical data, he asserted that such measures have not been shown to "reduce gun violence among angry young men." ACHURA's security expert, Ira Somerson, conceded that the "overall security program" at the Schoolhouse Apartments was a "nightmare" and that there should have been two armed security officers on duty "around the clock." He concluded, however, that the events that led to the shooting happened in a span of no more than five minutes and, consequently, there was little that any security guard could have done to prevent the tragedy. Although he found the shooting to be "foreseeable," he emphasized that security cannot guarantee protection from random violence.

The jury rendered a verdict finding that the negligence of ACHURA and Community Realty was the proximate cause of plaintiff's injuries and that Community Realty was acting as ACHURA's agent. The jury also found that Safe and Sound and Insignia Management was not liable and that plaintiff was not comparatively negligent. The jury assigned the following percentages of liability to those responsible for plaintiff's injuries: 40 percent to ACHURA; 30 percent to Community Realty; and 30 percent to Abdullah, against whom the court had entered judgment due to his default. The court granted plaintiff's motion to allocate Community Realty's percentage liability to ACHURA.

The jury awarded plaintiff $2,364,331.45 in total damages: $1,140,000 for future care expenses; $1,000,000 for pain, suffering, and loss of enjoyment of life; $142,272 for loss of past and future earnings; and $82,059.45 for past medical expenses. In addition, the court awarded plaintiff $782,496.55 in prejudgment interest. ACHURA appealed.

The appellate division affirmed. The panel disagreed with ACHURA's contention that the trial court should have charged the jury not only on a property owner's duty to a business invitee, but also on the lesser duties of care applying to a social guest or trespasser. The panel observed that plaintiff was injured in a "public area of a commercial apartment complex" and that there was no evidence that plaintiff was trespassing. Because owners of multi-unit dwellings, like ACHURA, owe the same duty of care to anyone legally in the common areas, the panel concluded that plaintiff's status on the property was irrelevant.

We agree with both the trial court and the appellate division that there was no evidence in the record that plaintiff was a trespasser. That plaintiff and his friend were "buzzed" in to the apartment complex by the security guard makes it difficult for ACHURA to argue that plaintiff did not have a right or privilege to be there. Admittedly, there were discrepancies in plaintiff's and Robinson's accounts of who they were there to visit. That, however, does not detract from the fact that ACHURA's security guard opened the gate and permitted plaintiff to enter.

Moreover, it is undisputed that the fight between Abdullah and Robinson and the shooting of plaintiff occurred in common areas of the Schoolhouse Apartments. As the landlord, ACHURA had the responsibility to render those areas reasonably safe for the use of both tenants and their guests. In the common areas of an apartment complex, tenants and their social guests are deemed to be business visitors of the landlord. For business visitors, the landowner owes a duty "to conduct a reasonable inspection to discover latent dangerous conditions as well as to guard against any dangerous conditions ... that the owner either knows about or should have discovered."

A landlord also has a duty to take reasonable security precautions to protect tenants and their guests from foreseeable criminal acts. Liability imposed on landlord for failure to "take reasonable security measures for tenant protection on the premises."

Supermarket could be liable to customer who was mugged in supermarket's parking lot because of its knowledge of other muggings on premises during preceding year. Landlord could be liable for burglary of tenant's apartment because landlord had breached duty of care by failing to provide functioning deadbolt lock.

When a landlord knows or should know of a pattern of criminal activity on his premises that poses a foreseeable risk of harm to his tenants and their guests and does not take reasonable steps to meet the danger, he cannot escape liability merely because the criminal act was committed by a third party who was not within his control. For example, *Scully v. Fitzgerald*, holds that landlord owes a duty "to take reasonable steps to curtail the dangerous activities" on premises "of which he should be aware and that pose a hazard to the life and property of other tenants." Landlord has duty to protect tenant from other tenant's foreseeable criminal acts.

We realize that based on new evidence at the retrial, ACHURA may attempt to make out a case that plaintiff was a trespasser and request a different jury charge. We do not suggest that, given the conditions at the Schoolhouse Apartments and the peculiar circumstances of this case, the duty of ACHURA would be different even if plaintiff were a trespasser. It is true that a landowner owes a lesser duty of care to a trespasser "under most circumstances" and is required "to warn 'only of artificial conditions on the property that pose a risk of death or serious bodily harm.'" However, "landowners owe a higher duty even to trespassers when their presence is foreseeable." The Restatement (Second) of Torts Section 336 explains that "a possessor of land who knows or has reason to know of the presence of [a trespasser] is subject to liability for physical harm thereafter caused to the trespasser by the possessor's failure to carry on his activities upon the land with reasonable care for the trespasser's safety.

We recognize that "in many instances, a landowner's liability for injuries is no longer based exclusively on the status of the injured party." "The question of whether a duty to exercise reasonable care to avoid the risk of harm to another exists is one of fairness and policy that implicates many factors." In light of those considerations, the trial court should exercise its sound judgment on a fully developed record and determine the applicable standard of care and the appropriate charge to be given to the jury.

We reverse and remand to the trial court for proceedings in accordance with this opinion.

CASE COMMENT

Here the court struggled with the question of the security responsibility and standard for liability landlord liability. In this tragic case, the court noted there was insufficient evidence to answer this question. The analysis offered by the court was illustrative of the law and fact questions which are underlying these cases. In this analysis, the court asserted the standard as "when a landlord knows or should know of a pattern of criminal activity on his premises that poses a foreseeable risk of harm to his tenants and their guests and does not take reasonable steps to meet the danger, he cannot escape liability merely because the criminal act was committed by a third party who was not within his control." The case was remanded back to the trial court to determine the applicable standard of care in light of the relevant facts.

802 N.Y.S.2d 306

Supreme Court, Kings County, New York

PO W. YUEN, GUARDIAN OF PLAINTIFF WING CHEONG WOO, AN INCAPACITATED PERSON, ET AL., PLAINTIFFS v. 267 CANAL STREET CORP., DEFENDANT.

July 13, 2005

Background

Commercial tenant's employee brought action against landlord to recover for personal injuries sustained when he was assaulted in building. Landlord filed third-party complaint against tenant seeking common law contribution/indemnification. Parties filed cross motions for summary judgment.

Holdings

The Supreme Court, Kings County, held that the landlord was not liable for injuries inflicted upon employee during assault.

Motions granted in part, and denied in part

On December 1, 2000, shortly after noon, Mr. Woo was assaulted by Eric McClendon on the sixth floor of the building located at 265–267 Canal Street in Manhattan. At the time of the assault, Mr. Woo was the president and sole shareholder of GBT and J & J, which were clothing manufacturing businesses that operated in the same space on the sixth floor of the building. GBT, rented this space from the owner of the building, 267, pursuant to a written lease agreement that became effective on January 1, 2000.

The building was a six-story commercial "garment factory" located in the Chinatown section of Manhattan. In fact, several different clothing manufacturing businesses, including GBT, leased space and manufactured apparel in the building. During business hours (i.e., when the assault took place), the front door of the building, which led to the lobby, remained open. Inside the lobby, there were two elevators, both of which accessed all six floors of the building. One of these elevators was used for freight and was operated by two elevator operators. If the elevator operators did not recognize a person seeking to use the freight elevator, they would ask to see a receipt or bill before taking the person to the desired floor. The other elevator in the lobby, which was for passenger use, was not assigned an elevator operator. Instead, passengers merely pressed the button for the floor they wished to reach. However, each tenant in the building was given a key which they could use to prevent the passenger elevator from opening in their leased area.

In addition to the two elevators, the building also had two stairways, one of which led to the area leased by GBT on the sixth floor of the building. The street-level doors of these stairways were kept locked and tenants and their employees were provided with keys to open these doors.

The area of the sixth floor leased by GMT consisted of an open area, where approximately 20 employees worked at sewing machines, and an enclosed office area where Mr. Woo worked. The freight elevator opened directly inside the leased area. However, in order to gain access to the leased area from the passenger elevator, one had to pass through a cage-like metal door that was supposed to be kept closed and locked at all times. This door could be opened with a key that was given to GMT's employees, or it could be opened by pushing a "buzzer" button inside the leased area which released the lock on the doors. There was also a separate steel cage door which prevented persons in the stairwell from gaining access to the leased area unless they had a key or were "buzzed in" by a person inside the leased area.

According to McClendon's affidavit and deposition testimony, on December 1, 2000, he entered the building through the open front door and proceeded to passenger elevator in the lobby. McClendon testified that he intended to go through the building starting at the top floor and buy merchandise, which he would resell for a profit. Accordingly, McClendon entered the passenger elevator and pushed the button for the sixth floor.

Although an operator for the freight elevator was in the lobby at the time, McClendon stated that he was too busy to notice McClendon. At the sixth floor, McClendon exited the elevator and proceeded to the steel cage door, which, according to McClendon's testimony, was ajar. McClendon then walked into the leased area and entered the office, where he noticed a boy sitting on a couch with a cashbox in his lap. According to McClendon, although he was tempted to steal the cashbox, he exited the office without taking anything. Upon leaving the office, Ms. Woo saw McClendon, screamed, and ran into the office. McClendon testified that he attempted to leave the leased area but Mr. Woo grabbed him. McClendon then struck Mr. Woo in the face with his fist. As a result, Mr. Woo fell, struck his head on the ground, and sustained a catastrophic brain injury.

Thereafter, McClendon returned to the lobby using the passenger elevator and exited the building. Shortly after the attack, Eric Chong, the managing agent for the building at the time of the accident, inspected the steel cage door and discovered that if the door was opened a full 180 degrees, it would not fully close and lock as it was designed to do. According to Mr. Chong, GBT employees were aware of this problem and it is undisputed that a sign was placed inside the leased premises which told employees (both in English and Chinese) to make sure that they fully closed the door when entering and leaving the leased premises.

Some three months later, McClendon was arrested while attempting to burglarize another garment factory building. McClendon eventually pled guilty to attempted assault in the first degree for his actions on December 1, 2000, and was sentenced as a persistent violent felony offender to 16 years–to life in prison.

Plaintiffs' Claims Against 267

[Defendant] 267 now moves for summary judgment dismissing plaintiffs' claims against it. In so moving, 267 argues that the criminal assault upon Mr. Woo was an unforeseeable act given the lack of any similar incidents preceding the attack. Under the circumstances, 267 maintains that the security measures in the building—including the steel cage doors protecting the area leased by GBT, the screening of delivery personnel by the freight elevator operators, the locked doors to the stairwells, and the ability to lock-out the passenger elevator from specific floors—were adequate as a matter of law, thereby precluding any finding of liability against 267.

In support of this argument, 267 points to the deposition testimony the building's current and former managing agents. In particular, Shun K. Fung, the managing agent for the building between 1985 and August 2000, testified that he was unaware of any mugging incidents or assaults occurring in the building during his tenure and he never received any complaints from tenants about inadequate security in the building. Similarly, Mr. Chong, the managing agent for the building from August 2000 to the present, testified that before the attack on Mr. Woo, he was unaware of any robberies or assaults taking place in the building prior and he never received any complaints from GBT regarding unauthorized persons gaining access to the leased area.

In addition to the building's managing agents, 267 points to the testimony of Peter Wong, the president of another garment manufacturing company which also leased space on the sixth floor of the building. According to Mr. Wong, the steel cage doors such as those present in the building were customary in the garment industry in Chinatown. Mr. Wong also testified that he was unaware of any violent crimes taking place in the building prior to the assault upon Mr. Woo and he characterized security in the building as "fairly safe."

[Defendant] 267 also points to the affidavit and deposition of McClendon. In particular, 267 notes the fact that McClendon testified that the steel cage door leading to the leased area was ajar when he exited the passenger elevator. Thus, 267 reasons that assault upon Mr. Woo was not caused by a lack of adequate security features in the building, but rather, was caused by the failure of one of GBT's employees to close this door behind them when they entered or exited the leased premises. Finally, to the extent that the door was not functioning properly, 267 argues that it did not have notice of any problems with the door and that under the terms of the lease agreement, GBT was responsible for maintaining the door.

In opposition to 267's motion, plaintiffs argue that 267 has failed to establish that it met its duty of providing adequate security at the building. In support of this argument, plaintiffs point out that prior to the assault the building had a serious problem whereby vagrants and homeless people gained access to the building's stairwells where they slept during the winter months. Plaintiffs also point out that Ms. Woo testified that two or three months prior to the underlying assault, she discovered an intruder in the office who fled when she saw him. In addition, plaintiffs have submitted a New York City Police Department "complaint address tracking system" sheet for the building's address which indicates that robberies took place there in March and May 2000, and a burglary occurred there in February 2000. Plaintiffs have also submitted a 1997 NYPD "compstat" sheet for the precinct in which the building is located which indicates that there were 352 robberies, 227 felony assaults, 394 burglaries, 965 grand larcenies, 159 aggravated grand larcenies, 6 rapes, and 4 murders in the precinct during the subject year. According to plaintiffs, this indicates that the building was located in a high crime area.

Given this evidence of crime in and around the building, as well as the history of intruders gaining access to the building, plaintiffs maintain that the security measures in the building were clearly inadequate. In support of this claim, plaintiffs have submitted an expert affidavit by Leslie N. A. Cole, a professional security consultant. According to Mr. Cole, adequate security at the building would have consisted of a closed-circuit television system in the building to monitor activity, as well as appropriate signs notifying persons in the building that the premise that they were being monitored on closed-circuit television. Mr. Cole further maintains that an elevator operator and/or security guard should have been placed in the lobby of the building to control access to the passenger elevator. In addition, Mr. Cole argues that the front door of the building should have been kept locked. Finally, Mr. Cole claims that, as the owner of the building, 267 had a responsibility to ensure that the steel cage door leading to the leased premises on the sixth floor of the building functioned properly by automatically closing and locking after a person passed through the door.

"Landlords have a 'common-law duty to take minimal precautions to protect tenants from foreseeable harm' ... including a third party's foreseeable ... conduct." "Foreseeability and duty are not identical concepts. Foreseeability merely determines the scope of the duty once the duty is determined to exist." "In order to establish the element of foreseeability, [a plaintiff is] required to present proof that the criminal conduct at issue was 'reasonably predictable based on the prior occurrence of the same or similar criminal activity at a location sufficiently proximate to the subject location.'" Thus, evidence of dissimilar criminal activity is insufficient to establish foreseeability. For example, evidence of prior shoplifting incidents at a shopping mall does not render a subsequent assault at the premises foreseeable. Similarly, evidence of vagrants being removed from a hotel lobby and of automobile break-ins occurring in a hotel parking lot do not establish that an assault that took place on the sixth floor of the hotel was foreseeable. Moreover, "ambient neighborhood crime alone is insufficient to establish foreseeability."

Here, 267 has presented sufficient evidence in the form of Mr. Fung, Mr. Chong, and Mr. Wong's deposition testimony to establish that, prior to the assault on Mr. Woo, there was no similar criminal activity on the sixth floor of the building, or in any of the other garment manufacturing businesses on the upper floors of the building. Accordingly, 267 has met its initial burden of demonstrating that it provided adequate security in the building given the unforeseeable nature of the assault. Under the circumstances, the burden shifts to plaintiffs to submit sufficient evidence to raise a triable issue of fact in this regard.

Plaintiffs have not met this burden. With regard to the issue of foreseeability, the overall crime statistics for the precinct in which the building is located is insufficient to demonstrate that an assault on the sixth floor of the building was foreseeable. Furthermore, the fact that vagrants managed to gain entry to the stairwells in the building prior to the incident does not support plaintiffs' claim that the assault on Mr. Woo was foreseeable. There is no evidence that these vagrants ever threatened tenants or their employees, and, in any event, McClendon did not use the stairs to gain access to the area leased by GBT. The NYPD complaint address tracking sheet submitted by plaintiffs is also insufficient to establish that the underlying assault was foreseeable since this report does not indicate whether the listed crimes took place inside or outside the building. At the same time, Ms. Woo's testimony that she discovered an intruder in the office several months before the assault is insufficient to establish foreseeability since there is no admissible evidence that 267 was notified of this incident. Ms. Woo admitted that she did not report this event to the police and her testimony that she told her husband what happened, and he in turn informed 267 of the event, is inadmissible hearsay.

Given the lack of prior similar criminal acts in the building, plaintiffs' expert's claim that 267 had a duty to provide enhanced security in the form of a closed-circuit television system, the posting of a security guard and/or additional elevator operator to screen persons entering the passenger elevator, and to lock the front door of the building during business hours is without merit. An after-the-fact realization that one or more of these measures might have prevented the tragedy that ultimately occurred does not establish that 267 breached its duty to provide minimal security precautions. 267 merely owed Mr. Woo a duty to adopt adequate security measures given the foreseeable risks, it was not an insurer of his safety. Finally, the fact that the steel cage door separating the leased premises from the passenger elevator did not always close automatically is insufficient to raise an issue of fact regarding 267's negligence. It is undisputed that GBT was responsible for maintaining this door under the terms of the lease agreement. Moreover, 267 did not have notice of this problem prior to the assault.

Accordingly, 267's motion for summary judgment dismissing plaintiffs' complaint is granted.

Summary

In summary, 267's Motion for Summary Judgment dismissing plaintiffs' complaint is granted. This constitutes the decision and order of the court.

CASE COMMENT

In another excellent example of security law, the court analyzed the facts and applicable law in finding that the landlord was not liable for the damages stemming from the crime. Notice the emphasis placed by the court on foreseeability. In the end, the court found insufficient foreseeability to hold the landlord liable. Indeed, the court noted that the landlord was not acting as an insurer simply by entering into the lease with the tenant. This same logic applies to the operative balance between security and contract provisions.

Notice, the variation of the "prior similar incidents" standard, adhered to in New York, was not met by the plaintiffs. In this analysis, the court assessed the amount and types of crime committed prior to this incident. While there were some criminal acts prior to this incident, the court held that the plaintiff failed to establish that the security methods employed by the building were inadequate to prevent the crime. Stated another way, while there was some evidence of prior crimes, the security methods used were adequate in light of these prior crimes. Consequently, the plaintiff's cause of action failed.

162 S.W.3d 547, 48 Tex. Sup. Ct. J. 556

Supreme Court of Texas

WESTERN INVESTMENTS, INC., FRONT ROYALE APARTMENTS, WESTERN INVESTMENTS D/B/A FRONT ROYALE APARTMENTS, RON DEUTSCH, WARREN DEUTSCH, AND KATE MICHON, PETITIONERS v. MARIA URENA, INDIVIDUALLY AND AS NEXT FRIEND OF L. U., A MINOR, RESPONDENT.

April 8, 2005

Background

Tenant at apartment complex brought claims against landlord in connection with sexual assault on tenant's minor son by another tenant. The 269th District Court, Harris County, granted summary judgment to landlord. Tenant appealed. The Houston Court of Appeals, First District, reversed and remanded. Review was granted.

Holdings

The supreme court held that:

1. Landlord's alleged breach of duty, in failing to provide security guards to patrol apartment complex, was not proximate cause of tenant-on-tenant sexual assault;
2. Landlord's alleged breach of duty, in failing to obtain police reports of calls related to criminal activity in the area, was not proximate cause of sexual assault; and
3. Landlord's alleged breach of duty, in failing to require certain documents from prospective tenants, was not proximate cause of sexual assault.

Court of appeals reversed; judgment rendered

Maria Urena and her 10-year-old son, L. U., lived in the Front Royale Apartments in Houston. L. U. has the mental capacity of a 4-year-old. One day in November 1999, Urena left L. U. under the care of his aunt, who also lived in the complex. At around 10:00 in the morning, L. U. left his aunt's apartment, unsupervised, to retrieve some toys from his home. On the way back, another Front Royale resident, Michael Zuniga, lured L. U. into his apartment with the promise of a $1 bill and sexually assaulted him. L. U.'s aunt discovered the assault immediately, confronted Zuniga, and called the police. Zuniga fled and has never been apprehended.

Citing a series of violent crimes such as attempted sexual assault, robbery, and murder occurring in and around the Front Royale complex over a two-year period preceding L. U.'s assault, the court of appeals held that these crimes, which were violent and personal in nature, created a fact question as to whether the risk of other violent crimes in the apartment complex was foreseeable. Applying this court's decision in *Timberwalk Apartments, Partners, Inc. v. Cain*, the court of appeals held that summary judgment was improper and a fact issue remained with regard to whether Front Royale owed Urena and her family a legal duty to provide protection from the criminal acts of third parties.

The court of appeals also held that the plaintiff presented evidence sufficient to raise a fact issue as to whether Front Royale breached that duty. The court relied on the following evidence to support its conclusion: (1) Front Royale had not replaced its previously terminated security company at the time of the attack; (2) the apartment manager's testimony that she did not request or obtain police reports of calls related to criminal activity in the area as the Texas Apartment Association's "Red Book" recommended; and (3) although various witnesses testified that Front Royale required prospective tenants to provide certain documents such as Social Security cards and drivers licenses, and performed criminal background checks on at least some tenants, these documents were missing from a number of the tenants' files. The defendants argue that Urena failed to present any evidence that Front Royale's acts or omissions proximately caused L. U.'s injuries and therefore the trial court properly granted summary judgment in its favor.

Urena contends she presented evidence that Front Royale proximately caused L. U.'s injuries by failing to provide appropriate security personnel and security measures, failing to implement sufficient security policies and procedures, and failing to warn the other tenants of Zuniga's dangerous tendencies. These failures, Urena claims, constitute negligence in managing the complex as well as a breach of a duty to remedy a premises defect about which Front Royale knew or should have known.

We analyze Urena's negligence and premises-liability claims together. To prevail on her negligence cause of action, Urena must establish the existence of a duty, a breach of that duty, and damages proximately caused by the breach. Premises liability is a special form of negligence where the duty owed to the plaintiff depends upon the status of the plaintiff at the time the incident occurred. Here, because the Urenas were invitees, the premises liability inquiry focuses on whether Front Royale proximately caused L. U.'s injuries by failing to use ordinary care to reduce or to eliminate an unreasonable risk of harm created by a premises condition that it knew about or should have known about.

Negligence and premises liability, therefore, involve closely related but distinct duty analyses. But we need not delve into this distinction to resolve this case because recovery under either cause of action is foreclosed in the absence of evidence that Front Royale's acts or omissions proximately caused L. U.'s injuries. Even if we were to assume that Front Royale owed the Urenas a duty to provide security guards, obtain police reports of calls related to criminal activity in the area, and investigate its tenants, as Urena contends, and further assumed that Front Royale breached these duties, there is no evidence that such a breach proximately caused the tragic occurrence here. Proximate cause has two elements: cause in fact and foreseeability. "These elements cannot be established by mere conjecture, guess, or speculation." The test for cause in fact is whether the act or omission was a substantial factor in causing the injury without which the harm would not have occurred. If the defendant's negligence merely furnished a condition that made the injuries possible, there can be no cause in fact.

Urena points to three areas in which Front Royale allegedly breached its duty and argues that these breaches caused L. U.'s assault. First, Urena relies on deposition testimony showing that at the time of the assault, Front Royale did not employ a security company to patrol the complex. Urena alleges that had Front Royale provided adequate security, the assault would not have occurred. She presented no evidence, however, that increased security would have prevented this crime. Zuniga was a tenant authorized to be on the property. As such, security guards could not have prevented him from moving freely about the complex and interacting with other residents, nor would security guards have had the ability to monitor the goings-on inside Zuniga's own apartment. Zuniga approached L. U. at 10:00 in the morning, calling L. U. by his name. When Zuniga asked him to come into the apartment he did so, apparently willingly. There was no evidence of a struggle or physical confrontation in the common areas of the complex, nor was there evidence that L. U. raised an outcry that would have been heard outside of Zuniga's apartment once the assault was underway. In sum, nothing transpired that reasonably would have alerted security guards had they been present.

Second, Urena relies on the apartment manager's testimony that she did not obtain police reports of calls related to criminal activity in the area, even though the guide she used in operating the apartments recommended it. But there is no evidence that the police reports would have alerted management that its tenant was likely to sexually assault a young child. Police reports about criminal activity in the area would have done nothing to alert management that Zuniga was a pedophile, or to suggest that an attack by a pedophile tenant was likely to occur.

Third, Urena claims that although Front Royale required certain documents from prospective tenants like social security cards, driver licenses, and criminal-background checks, these documents were missing from a number of tenants' files. But there is no causal connection between this alleged breach of duty and L. U.'s injury. None of the tenants whose files were allegedly incomplete committed the crime here. Furthermore, a background check performed on Zuniga revealed only driving infractions, nothing that would have alerted a reasonable landlord to the possibility that he posed a danger to others.

Simply stated, Urena presented no evidence that L. U.'s sexual assault could have been prevented if Front Royale had done the three things the plaintiff claims it should have done. Even assuming Front Royale's acts or omissions constituted breach of a duty owed to the Urenas, as they allege, the Urenas presented no evidence that such acts or omissions were a substantial factor in causing L. U.'s injury.

We reverse the judgment of the court of appeals and render judgment in favor of Front Royale.

CASE COMMENT

This case is a classic factual situation where the crime victim seeks recovery for the actions of a criminal, asking the landlord to pay for the crime. The court held against the plaintiff and in favor of the landlord, as the proximate cause element was not sufficiently demonstrated. In addition, the court held that leasing issues and provisions, such as providing security patrols and conducting background checks of tenants, had not been shown to have prevented the crime. Plaintiff simply asserted these measures should have been taken, but failed to show they would have prevented the crime. Consequently, the landlord could not have held liable for failing to implement security measures that were unrelated to the incident.

Part Four

Legal Authority and Liability

The question of legal authority is raised by a number of issues relating to crime and misconduct. Most of the jurisprudence in this area has focused on the police. There have been thousands of court cases relating to police legal authority. These cases have been presented and analyzed in numerous casebooks and treatises. Most of the legal issues related to what one typically thinks of as police matters go beyond the scope of this book. Instead, this book relates to the legal authority of security personnel, or of police officers serving in a security capacity. Thus, Part IV will examine the relevant issues faced by these security service providers.

It may be helpful to begin this section by defining the scope of this examination of legal authority. There are two basic issues that relate to legal authority: arrest powers and the application of constitutional rights (e.g., the Bill of Rights). When acting as a security officer, the typical legal authority afforded is of a private citizen. Similarly, as a private citizen, constitutional prohibitions are generally not applicable. This is because the Constitution was designed as a check of government power, not private parties. While these are general principles, the distinctions between private security officers and public police are closer than one may realize. Indeed, trends both in the legal environment and in contemporary American society are creating conditions that will bring security personnel and the police closer together.[1] While much of these trends are beyond the scope of this book, there are important and relevant factors that illustrate this assertion. Consider this quote from Center for Disease Control relating to public police and private security:[2]

> The shift in risk for public police and private security guards is particularly noteworthy, as the data reveals a decline in rates among public police officers and a dramatic increase among private security guards. We do not know the extent to which these findings are attributable to efforts among public police forces to reduce risks through training and use of protective equipment, the employment of private security guards

> by businesses and communities that had previously relied solely on public safety personnel, and the level of training and background of private security officers. However, further research is warranted.

When one considers the questions posed in this quote, there are a number of factors that could be emphasized. In my mind, the key assertion is the notion of *public safety personnel.* Without saying so, the term *public safety personnel* seems to separate public safety (police) from private security. Notwithstanding this apparent distinction, the facts and trends noted within the quote belie the existence of this distinction. While the need for further research is correctly noted, I contend that police and security are increasingly considered public safety providers. The significance of this assertion relates directly to the legal issues addressed in this book.

There are two basic issues relating to legal authority. While we will deal with each separately, it is important to note that legal authority and constitutional protections are often interrelated. For example, if a private security officer makes an arrest, his or her authority to make the arrest may be questioned. Typically, this inquiry goes to the *legal power* to affect the arrest. Conversely, in the prosecution of the arrestee, there will often be an inquiry as to whether any search or seizure of the arrestee is constitutionally proper.[3] In this inquiry, the question is not about the power to affect the arrest, but whether the search and seizure conforms to the confines of the Fourth Amendment.[4] While this may seem like splitting hairs, it is a rather distinct legal inquiry. In the former example relating to the power of arrest, the legal inquiry typically goes to whether private security officer had the power to arrest the individual.[5] In the latter example relating to the search and seizure, the legal inquiry goes to whether the search and seizure of the arrestee was constitutionally proper.[6] With this caveat established, these issues will be examined separately.

ARREST POWERS

The ability to make an arrest is inevitably tied to the authority of the state. Throughout much of recorded history, the act of affecting an arrest, even if performed by private citizens, was done on behalf of the state.[7] The notion of making a "citizen's arrest" is illustrative. Government has long allowed, and often encouraged, citizens to act to affect an arrest when warranted. Upon the advent of public police, this practice was slowing and inevitably discouraged. After many generations, the incident of citizen arrests is now quite rare. However, with the rise of private security personnel, the frequency of arrests by security personnel is much more frequent. Consequently, there appears to be two trends going in opposite directions.

As the average citizen is less inclined to make an arrest, the inclination of security personnel to make arrests becomes more common. While I make this assertion, I do not necessarily see a correlation in them. Instead, the increase in the number and scope of private security personnel may be the key factor in any increase in the number of arrests. Indeed, the more security personnel employed, the more likely arrests will be made. It becomes a function of probability based on the sheer size and scope of the security industry. Further, consider the number of shoplifting arrests that occur on an annual basis. It is safe to assume that many, if not most, of these arrests are made by security personnel. In any case, whenever an arrest is made, it inevitably involves the power of the state. The arrestee is typically processed by the police, charged by prosecutors, and tried in a state or federal court.

Even when one understands that the power of arrest is available to all citizens, it is commonly believed that the police have broad arrest powers, while private citizens have much more limited powers. This is generally false. While each state has differing laws relating to the power to affect arrest, there is some commonality throughout the country. Almost all states give citizens power to affect arrests for felonies, and for misdemeanors committed in their presence.[8] Indeed, the slight distinction relating to arrest powers between police and private citizens can be illustrated by the language of arrest powers for all citizens:[9]

"Any person may arrest another when he has reasonable grounds to believe that an offense other than an ordinance violation is being committed."

The legal powers derived from this statute reveal the following elements. First, the timing of the arrest—*is being committed*—entails while the criminal act is in progress, or *immediately after* the criminal act has been completed.[10] Second, private citizens can arrest for a felony and a misdemeanor, but not an ordinance violation. Obviously, this gives private citizens wide authority to make an arrest. This is particularly true when one considers most ordinance violations relating to criminal acts also have a corresponding misdemeanor charge. In this sense, there is little distinction between arrest powers of ordinances and misdemeanors. A classic example of this empty distinction is disorderly conduct, which is often sanctioned in both municipal ordinances and in state misdemeanor statutes.

Thus, the most common distinction between the arrest powers of police and security is that police can arrest on the authority of court issued warrants and after the crime has been committed. In addition, there are some distinctions related to being in the presence of the crime and other technical matters.[11] That being said, the power of arrest is often a legal question for the court. This inquiry typically goes to the power, not the conduct, of the person making the arrest. Conversely, the conduct related to search and seizure is typically a fact question based on legal standards.[12]

CONSTITUTIONAL PROTECTIONS

It is generally understood that the constitutional prohibitions contained in the Bill of Rights were designed to limit the power of the government.[13] These rights, such as the Fourth Amendment prohibition against unreasonable searches and seizures, are applicable only when government is involved.

In legal parlance, the applicability of these protections is triggered when a "state actor" was involved in the arrest. *State actor* is a legal term to describe government employees, agents, or officials, such as a police officer or some other law enforcement official.

The question of whether an individual acts as a state actor is not as clear-cut as it may appear. When this involves police and law enforcement officials performing a public function, the answer is usually straightforward: constitution protections are applicable. When private security personnel are involved, the answer is more complicated. There are a number of criteria that courts use to assess if security personnel acted as a "state actor," including the following:[14]

1. Whether the security personnel are licensed by the state (or other governmental entity)
2. Whether the security personnel acted in cooperation with or by the supervision of public police
3. Whether the security personnel were the police working secondary employment (moonlighting)
4. Whether the security personnel were designated with "special police" powers
5. Whether a "nexus" exists, meaning a significant connection or contact with government
6. Whether security personnel were performing a public function, a question that typically hinges on whether the individual was
   (a) Acting to enforce the law versus merely serving a private interest,
   (b) Wearing a "police-like" uniform, firearm, and other police equipment,
   (c) Identified as the "police,"
   (d) Arrested on private or public property.

Once this assessment is made, the applicability of constitutional prohibitions is determined. If the individual in question acted as "state actae" under the color of law, then Constitutional protections apply. The next inquiry is to assess if governmental immunity applies. Generally, government officials performing discretionary functions typically are granted qualified immunity. Qualified immunity is available to police supervisors, if involved in discretionary activity tasks that require deliberation or judgment, such as policy making. It is also available to police officers, generally, if[15]

1. The action was not a breach of clearly established right at that time, and
2. The officer's conduct was objectively reasonable.

Whether qualified immunity applies is a question of law for the court to consider.[16] If qualified immunity attaches, then no liability exists. Assuming qualified immunity does not attach, there are various statutory remedies available to the plaintiff in civil cases. In criminal cases, immunity typically is not at issue. Hence, there are two aspects of this determination that have application in both criminal and civil courts.

In a criminal context, the remedy is to prevent evidence obtained in violation of the constitution from being used at trial. This is known as the exclusionary rule, which is designed to *exclude* evidence that was improperly—or illegally—obtained.[17] This rule seeks to prevent, or at least diminish, the incidence of constitutionally violative actions by not rewarding bad police conduct. The aim is to dissuade police from such conduct by excluding the evidence at trial. The logic is that police will be less likely to commit bad acts if they are prevented from using the fruits of the constitutional violation, such as a coerced confession or illegally recovered contraband, from being used at the trial. In this sense, the remedy is defensive in that it protects the integrity of the trial (and constitutional rights of the individual) by refusing to allow tainted evidence in a criminal proceeding.[18]

In a civil context, the remedy is to assert causes of actions against the offending officer(s) and the employing entity. These causes of action seek compensatory and punitive damages, injunctions, changes in policy and practice, and other relevant remedies. Here the aim is to "make the plaintiff whole" by awarding compensatory damages, or to punish and deter bad actions through the assertion of punitive damages. Typically, the lawsuit asserts some deprivation of rights, either statutory or constitutional.

To defend against a claim based on the Fourth Amendment protection against unreasonable searches and seizures in either a criminal or civil case typically requires establishing probable cause for the arrest. Probable cause means that the facts and circumstances within the officer's knowledge are sufficient to warrant a prudent person, or one of reasonable caution, to believe, in the circumstances shown, that the suspect has committed, is committing, or is about to commit an offense.[19] Establishing probable cause also requires that the arresting officer articulate concrete and objective facts from which they inferred criminal conduct.

The most common statutory claim is Section 1983. This statute was patterned after the Civil Rights Act of 1871. This act was seldom used. It was used only about 36 times in the 90 years prior to 1960. Later this act was codified as Title 42 Section 1983, which states:[20]

> Every person, who under color of any statute, ordinance, regulation, custom, or usage, of any State or territory, subjects, or causes to be subjected, any citizen of the United States or other persons within the jurisdiction thereof to the deprivation of any right, privilege, or immunity secured by the Constitution and laws, shall be liable to the party injured in the action at law, suit in equity, or other proper proceeding for redress.

To state a Section 1983 claim, the plaintiff must allege the violation of a constitutional right, and show that the alleged violation was committed by a person acting under color of state law. Acting under color of state law requires that the defendant exercise power possessed by virtue of state law, and made possible only because he or she is clothed with the authority of state law.

In the context of private security, common allegations relate to searches and seizures, improperly obtained confessions, and improper use of force. Early cases involving security personnel held that these constitutional prohibitions did not apply. However, over time many courts have tended to make these prohibitions applicable. A brief history of some relevant cases may help to illustrate this point.

The classic case dealing with the application of constitutional prohibitions for private security is *Burdeau v. McDowell.*[21] In *Burdeau*, the case involved an investigation into fraudulent activities of a company executive. The executive, McDowell, occupied an office where he kept personal and company documents. The office was searched by company personnel, while police detectives secured the area. The improperly recovered documents were later turned over to Burdeau, who was a Special Assistant to the U.S. Attorney General. McDowell was then indicted based on information derived from the documents. Significantly, the court determined that if this search was conducted by police officials, it would have been violative of the Fourth Amendment.

The *Burdeau* court emphasized that the origin and the history of the Fourth Amendment manifested an intention to act as a restraint upon the activities of the government. Since the documents used to prosecute McDowell came into possession of the government without any direct violation by any governmental official, the court reasoned that the constitutional protections against unreasonable searches and seizures were not applicable. This decision, therefore, had the affect of excluding constitutional protections, when the purported violation was done by private security personnel. The *Burdeau* court stated in pertinent part:[22]

> "We see no reason why the fact that individuals, unconnected with the government, may have wrongfully taken [documents] should prevent them from being held for use in prosecuting an offense where the documents are of an incriminating character."

Over time, courts began to move away from the proposition established in *Burdeau*. One such case, *Commonwealth v. Leone*, stands for the proposition that private security personnel who are recognized as "special police" by a governmental entity are more likely to be deemed as state actors, thereby making constitutional prohibitions applicable.[23] The term special police relates to a special license provided by a governmental entity, which confers arrest or police powers similar to those conferred on sworn police officers.[24]

This case deals with a search by the security guard of the sleeping compartment of a commercial truck as it entered a facility owned by General Electric. The search revealed the truck driver to be in possession of a stolen firearm. The security guard then turned over the arrestee and the weapon to the police, who formally charged the defendant.

The *Leone* court observed, as did the court in *Burdeau*, that the Fourth Amendment and the exclusionary rule apply only to governmental action. In this way, the court deemed evidence discovered and seized by private parties admissible without regard to the methods used. However, this court provided an exception to this general principle. The exception includes situations where state officials have instigated or participated in the search. If this exception can be shown, then constitutional protections would apply.

In developing this exception, the court struggled with the fact that privately employed security forces pose a difficult problem in distinguishing between state and private action. It articulated a distinction based on the protection of their employer's or client's property. This primary function of private security was contrasted with public police, who are generally more concerned with the arrest and conviction of wrongdoers. Significantly, the *Leone* court noted that "private security forces have come into increasing use as supplements to police protection, and perform functions much like those of ordinary police."[25]

The *Leone* court then articulated the appropriate legal standard involving searches and seizures by special police. Since special police are commissioned officers by the government, and generally possess authority beyond that of an ordinary citizen, they may be treated as agents of the state, thereby subject to the constraints of the Fourth Amendment. The court, however, further distinguished special police from sworn public police personnel. This regards the motivations for the respective officer. The key question for the court was whether the officer acted in accord with the interests of the public or for his/her employer. The *Leone* court articulated this distinction by asserting:[26]

> [T]he guard's private function adds a new aspect to his activities, which we believe is relevant to the proper application of the Fourth Amendment. The action he [guard] takes on behalf of his employer may be a lawful and necessary means of protecting the employer's property, although it would be impermissible if taken on behalf of the state in pursuit of evidence. When the guard's conduct is justified by his legitimate private duties, it should not be treated as lawless, or "unreasonable" search and seizure.

The court also reasoned that security officers may intrude upon an individual's privacy and discover some contraband. When a subject is on private property, he or she has reason to expect some scrutiny or interference by the agents of the private party. When the guard takes legitimate steps for the protection of the employer's property, there is no cause for the deterrent sanction of the exclusionary rule. Exclusion of the evidence, the court reasoned, would serve only to frustrate prosecution of crimes which happen to come to light in the course of a routine inspection by a security guard. For these reasons, the *Leone* court concluded:[27]

> that an investigation by a special police officer privately employed as a security guard does not violate the Fourth Amendment when it is conducted on behalf of the private employer, in a manner that is reasonable and necessary for protection of the employer's property. If, on the other hand, the officer [guard] steps outside this sphere of legitimate private action, the exclusionary rule applies as it would to any state officer.

In *United States v. Francoeur*, the case dealt with the indictment of three individuals for counterfeiting charges stemming from the use of bogus currency at Walt Disney World.[28] The defendants were observed passing counterfeit bills by security personnel while shopping at stores within the park property. The defendants were confronted by the security personnel and were taken to the security office. Once in the office, nine counterfeit bills were recovered. While still being held by security personnel, the defendants were identified by store cashiers. Following these positive identifications, the U.S. Secret Service was called. A search warrant was obtained which resulted in the recovery of additional counterfeit bills. During the criminal trial, the defendants sought to preclude the admission of the evidence based on the initial detention and recovery by the security personnel as being violative of their constitutional rights.[29]

The court in *Francoeur* asserted that the Fourth Amendment gives protection only against "unlawful governmental action." Recognizing this principle, the defendants argued that the security personnel of Disney World are "in truth and in fact" government officials. The court disagreed. It noted that the amusement park was on "private property" where admission is charged. In this way, no one is permitted to enter the outer gates except by implied or actual consent of the owners. If agents of the property committed an illegal act against park guests, civil remedies could be asserted against the owners. The court construed, however, that an illegal search or other improper conduct would not give the guests protection of the Fourth Amendment or the exclusionary rule that has developed from it. In ruling against the defendants, the court stated:[30] "[T]he Supreme Court has in no instance indicated that it would apply the exclusionary rule to cases in which evidence has been obtained by private individuals in a manner not countenanced if they were acting for state or federal government."

In *People v. Stormer*, the case dealt with another arrest by private security personnel in a confined semi-public area.[31] The defendant was a Sagamore Hotel maid, who was employed by the hotel. The hotel was located on Green Island, which is comprised within the corporate limits of the Town of Bolton in Warren County, New York. The only connection to the main land is a causeway between the town landing and Green Island.

Based partly on the remote nature of the island, the Sagamore Hotel security force previously advised the Warren County Sheriff's Department that routine patrols to the island were unnecessary. This request noted that in the future their presence on the island would be required only upon special request. Subsequently, Sagamore Hotel security personnel investigated a theft at the hotel. As a result of the investigation, security personnel searched the vehicle of the defendant, without her knowledge or consent. This search recovered money missing from a hotel room. The defendant was then held by security personnel until she was placed in custody with the Warren County Sheriff's Department.[32]

The defendant sought to suppress the money from being admitted into evidence. She asserted that it was obtained from an unreasonable search and seizure by security personnel. The prosecution, on the other hand, asserted that the prohibitions regarding unlawful search and seizure "do not require exclusion of evidence because a private individual has gathered it by unlawful means." The court considered these conflicting assertions, and related the following in pertinent part:[33] "Given the proliferation in this country of privately-employed security personnel as a supplement to or, as in this case, a replacement for local law enforcement authorities, the privacy rights of a citizen of this State may be increasingly jeopardized."

The court determined that the security personnel were performing a public function. This determination was largely due to the self-contained nature of the property, and that the security force essentially functioned as an autonomous entity. Both of these factors illustrated that the security force performed a "public function." After making this finding, the court must then determine if two other conditions were met:

- The security officer must have a strong interest in obtaining convictions; and
- The security officer must commit searches and seizures regularly in order to be familiar enough with the rules to adopt his methods to conform to them [rules].

The *Stormer* court assessed the aforementioned criteria in light of the facts in the case. The court held that the hotels' interests could have been vindicated by the confiscation of the money and the termination of her job. By going further and detaining her for criminal charges, hotel security personnel went beyond simply asserting the interests of the hotel. Instead, by prosecuting the defendant, they asserted a larger public interest. With the arrest and prosecution, the safeguards provided by the Fourth Amendment were activated. As such, the court held the seizure of the money was unlawful, and was suppressed as unconstitutionally seized.[34]

In yet another private search case, *Mancusi v. DeForte*, a district attorney issued a subpoena to a union for production of certain books and documents. The union refused to comply with the subpoena. Instead of pursuing other legal procedures, union officials seized the books and documents, giving them to the district attorney. The evidence was then used against the defendants at trial.[35]

The court held that the seized materials were not admissible, as their seizure was violative of the Fourth and Fourteenth Amendments. Thus, this court deemed the constitution applicable to security personnel. This was so even though the facts were strikingly similar to those in *Burdeau v. McDowell.* In both cases, the evidence was initially seized by private non-governmental personnel, and then turned over to prosecutors. Each court took a different approach. The *Mancusi* court did not anguish over the actions of private security personnel in relation to the constitution. Indeed, *Burdeau* established that the Constitution does not apply to non-governmental actors. In contrast, the *Mancusi* court was more focused on the protections provided by the Constitution. As an illustration of this emphasis, the *Mancusi* court declared that[36]

> it is, of course, immaterial that the state might have been able to obtain the same papers by means which did not violate the Fourth Amendment. As Justice Holmes stated in *Silverthorne Lumber v. U.S.,* the rights ... against unlawful search and seizure are to be protected even if the same result might have been achieved in a lawful way.

These cases illustrate the growing tendency of the courts to apply constitutional protections to private security personnel. This is due to a number of factors, including the increasing scope of the private security industry, the changing functions of private security personnel, and the nature and location of the service provision. In making this decision, the following tests are assessed for determining the existence of state action:[37]

1. Public function test: the private parties performed a public function that was traditionally the exclusive prerogative of the State.
2. State compulsion test: the State has coerced or at least significantly encouraged the action alleged to violate the Constitution.
3. Nexus test: the State had so far insinuated itself into a position of interdependence with the private party or entity that it was a joint participant in the enterprise (viewed as symbiotic relationship/connection between public and private actors).

The presented cases provide a more contemporary view of these tests. It is my belief that in light of the current terrorist threat, these legal authority and liability questions will prove to be significant concerns as we go forward.

PUBLIC AND PRIVATE POLICING PRINCIPLES

This analysis goes to what would traditionally be deemed "police methods," as this discussion in many ways speaks to the distinction between a security officer, a special police officer, and a peace officer. In this sense, a more vigorous application of the law is typical, as compared to the job of most security officers. This is not to imply that security officers do not regularly invoke the law. Clearly they do. This is particularly true when you consider retail security personnel, and to a lesser extent, hospital security personnel.

Security personnel often take an active enforcement role. This statement does not advocate turning security personnel into law enforcement officers. Instead, this argues, or at least acknowledges, that in some instances, security personnel have taken on more aggressive law invoking functions.[38] Indeed, many cases in this section validate this assertion.

With this in mind, the initial question is whether security officers are "state actors" operating under color of law? As the cases will illustrate, this is a legal conclusion based on a factual assessment. The better question in this context is: should security officers function as if they are "state actors," thereby making constitutional prohibitions applicable to their actions. As asserted in other chapters of this book, it is my opinion that they should. The reasons for this assertion will become clear.

Even if one disagrees with this assertion, some legal principles relative to private policing should be illustrative. While the authority to affect an arrest is largely a legal question, the application of constitutional prohibitions is very fact specific. In this light, a security officer who engages the public in any meaningful manner, may have to address the legal perimeters of his or her authority.

Based on the issues and cases developed in this section, it is my assertion a new model of policing is emerging. While this model is in its infancy, the appropriate use of force and other legal standards, such as exceptions to warrant requirements, are likely to play an increasingly larger role in the private security industry. While the model is developing, certain assumptions can be made on what a future model of policing will look like. An illustrative description of this "public safety" policing model is shown in Figure IV-1.

While this figure excludes certain police functions (such as investigative and administrative units), it captures the essence of the three key aspects of policing. Tactical operations would include heavy weapons/ SWAT teams, gang and drug tactical teams, and saturation units. The use of these units would likely be much more militarized than the current operations of most municipal police agencies. This function will focus on tactical techniques, accomplished by highly trained public police officers.

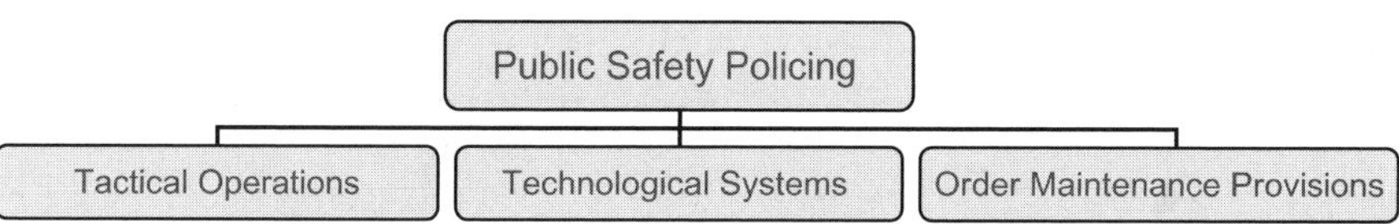

Figure IV-1 Policing model components.

The technological functions will also be greatly expanded as from current policing practices. As many readers are quite familiar, the security industry has extensively used technologies for access controls, surveillance, identification measures, and the like for many decades. The distinction as we go forward is that many commonly used security technologies will be emphasized within police agencies—and on the public way. This includes: the extensive use of networked cameras and access control systems, highly predictive crime-mapping software, and integrated identification systems. These technologies will improve the "eyes and the ears" as well as the "feel" of policing agencies, enabling them to better respond to and even predict criminal or terrorist behavior. The key to this approach is one of surveillance for both crime prevention and apprehension.

Finally, as asserted in Chapter 1, order maintenance operations have played a key role in crime prevention strategies. The extensive use of order maintenance is costly both in personnel and time expenditures. Simply stated, order maintenance, while critical to crime prevention, is difficult to operationalize—due to budgetary and resource constraints. Because of such, I contend that public police will gradually shift this key component to private policing as alternative service providers. In this function, the focus will be to control the environment. This entails emphasis on both physical and social incivilities. The primary tasks of these service providers are to provide certain routine service functions, such as reports, alarm response, traffic control, and "street corner security." Each of these tasks relates to either order maintenance or "observe and report" functions. In these ways, these alternative service providers will also enhance the "eyes and ears" of policing agencies. It is my belief that the majority, if not the vast majority, of alternative service providers will be private police employed by security firms.

EXCEPTIONS TO THE FOURTH AMENDMENT

As with public police, critical questions relating to authority are derived from exceptions to the warrant requirement of the Fourth Amendment. While not usually thought of as an "exception," the notion of a "stop and frisk" (or a Terry stop) has been widely used by street police officers. This allows the officer to stop an individual and conduct a protective pat down—or frisk, to determine if the individual has a weapon that could harm the officer or others. This is lawful when the officer has reasonable suspicion that "criminal activity is afoot," and that safety concerns exist.[39] As security personnel expand into more and more public environments, these "Terry stops" will be addressed by the courts.[40] Suffice to state at this point, the standard for stop and frisk should be articulated to and by security officers.

The other more commonly accepted exceptions to the Fourth Amendment requirements are as follows:[41]

1. Search incident to arrest: this allows the officer to search the arrestee and the area immediately around him/her after affecting a lawful arrest.
2. Emergency: this allows the officer to undertake a prompt inspection (or search) based on a compelling urgency, such as a bomb threat.
3. Plain view: allows the officer to seize contraband when he or she was lawfully in the place to observe the contraband.
4. Found property: allows the officer to take the property in possession consistent with the business practice of the entity for the purpose of minimizing liability, returning the property to its proper owner, and for clearing the environment of discarded items.
5. Inventory: allows the officer to take evidence into custody as part of a proper investigation.
6. Consent: allows the officer to search the property of another based on either actual or implied consent. The consent is typically found in a company policy, in an instrument or consent form, or by verbal acknowledgement.
7. Special needs or safety sensitive: usually involves drug testing, typically based on employment position that affects public safety.

USE OF FORCE PRINCIPLES

The legal standard to assess whether the use of force used was "reasonable" under the Fourth Amendment requires a careful assessment of objective facts as perceived by the officer at the time of the incident.[42] This also is a factual driven assessment. Regardless of the result of this assessment, "the right to make an arrest ... necessarily carries with it the right to use some degree of physical coercion."[43] The assessment of what is reasonable depends upon many particular facts and circumstances, including "the severity of the crime, whether the suspect poses an immediate threat to the safety of the officers or others, and whether the suspect is actively resisting arrest or attempting to evade arrest by flight."[44] In addition, what is reasonable "must be judged from the perspective of a reasonable officer on the scene, rather than with the 20/20 vision of hindsight."[45]

With this legal standard in mind, the application of use of force principles is critical to both prudent policing and to legal exposure. In this sense, the key determination is what level of force (if any) is reasonable under the circumstances. Force may only be used to control the situation, and must cease immediately once the threat is ceased.[46]

It is important to note that force is not just physical. It can include intimidating words and acts which place a person in fear of receiving a battery. Force can also be implied to restrict an individual's freedom of movement. This can be accomplished by the physical presence of authority figures, the use of verbal commands, the tone of the verbal commands, the body gestures used in an encounter, the positioning of those involved, and in various other mannerisms.

When assessing the proper level of force, the objective standard looks at what is "reasonable under the circumstances" as perceived by the officer at the time of the incident. In this way, the "Monday-morning quarterbacking" or the 20/20 hindsight arguments must be tempered by the facts and perceptions as they were at the time of the incident. Sometimes this assessment can literally require a reaction based on a second, or even in factions of a second. This is particularly true in shooting incidents. As one can image, this is a difficult assessment to make. Numerous stimuli and perceptions must be processed quickly and accurately. Sometimes this must be accomplished under tense and dangerous situations. Fortunately, courts have articulated some factors to help determine the appropriateness of the extent and level of force. These factors include the following:[47]

- Seriousness of the threat
- Immediacy of the threat (in terms of time and distance)
- Weapons or methods used (or threatened to be used) by the suspect or offender
- Whether escape or retreat was possible
- Safety of innocent third parties (the public at large)

In making this assessment, the use of force sometimes is triggered by an act of self-defense. For example, if an officer seeks to affect an arrest, but the individual resists the arrest, often the officer will be required to protect his or her personal safety—in conjunction with the application of an arrest. In this way, the level of cooperation of the "arrestee" is an important factor in the application of force. The arrestee classifications stem from compliant to passive resistant to active resistant to assaultive.

When attempting an unlawful attack, the person being attacked may repel the force with responsive force to the extent that it seems reasonable under the circumstances. As stated above, however, all force must cease when the offender is under control. It is important to note that in defense of property, it is only appropriate to use reasonable force to affect arrest. It is never justified to use deadly force when protecting only property.

ARREST POWER STANDARDS

The legal issues and limitations of private police related to arrest powers and the use of force have been demonstrated. Given this analysis, it is recommended that private police officers be vested with some governmental authority. There are three basic alternatives.

Consider Figure IV-2 as a continuum. On one side, are the arrest powers of private citizens. On the other are peace officer arrest powers. In the

Figure IV-2 Arrest power continuum.

middle, are the arrest powers of special police. Special police combines the private citizen role (i.e., not an employee of government) with the arrest powers of a peace officer (public police officer). Typically, peace officer arrest powers are only available to the special police officer during the tour of duty. This "on-duty" limitation, logically, will not affect the work they are paid to perform.

Without instituting this "special police" designation, private police officers will have the same arrest powers as a private citizen. While there is not a great distinction between the arrest powers of a private citizen and of a peace officer, there are certain benefits of being "blessed" by government. This includes a sense of moral and legal authority that most citizens tend to respect. In this way, the pronouncements and actions of an officer with some governmental authority is much more likely to be complied with. For example, the common response "I don't have to listen to you, you are not the police" would largely be negated with an official connection to governmental authority. With this legal authority derived from government, it would not be one private citizen (e.g., private police officer) telling another private citizen what to do. Consequently, a special police designation would give private police officers a much greater level of moral and legal authority, which is often an important element of an effective police officer.

The benefits of this designation, however, are larger than just authority. Since special police officers have the same police powers as peace officers *while performing their job,* this "on-duty" authority would give municipal police departments a larger "police force" without the economic and operational constraints caused by employing more police officers. Since wages of private police are much less than public police, there would be a direct economic benefit to those policing agencies or communities that employ them.[48]

In addition, the designation of special police would carry with it the protection of "qualified immunity" which is afforded public police officers. As discussed above, qualified immunity essentially acts as a liability shield to protect the officer (and his/her employer) from civil lawsuits. While this shield is not available for reckless or malicious conduct, it does serve to protect the reasonable and prudent officer who makes a mistake in judgment or behavior. Further, having qualified immunity attach to private police officers serves to reduce the legal exposure of the security firm, and accordingly, the insurance costs associated with the service provision. For all these reasons, the use of the special police designation is strongly recommended.

LICENSING STANDARDS

Licensing standards directly relate to the issue of legal authority. In order to perform the work of the "police," private officers (also called "para-police") should be trained and selected in a manner commensurate with their functional work product. Stated another way, training and selection standards must prepare these officers for the complexities of policing. In response to this need for training and selection standards, ASIS International has developed *The Private Security Officer Selection and Training* guideline. According to the authors of this guideline, "security officers ... must also be able to work closely and effectively with public safety personnel." This is directly in line with the thesis of this section.[49]

These guidelines are, by far, the most comprehensive approach to addressing the training and selection needs of security officers to date. While these guidelines are designed for private security officers generally, their application to private police officers is both relevant and pointed. They provide recommended guidelines for state regulation in such areas as background investigations, training, continuing education, insurance, licensing, and oversight bodies. In addition, the guidelines suggest certain selection criteria, including: criminal history, education, citizenship, finger-printing, photographs, drug screening, and other personal information related to the applicant.[50] Without getting into the details of these criteria, it suffices to say that each of these factors will go a long way in establishing more professionalism in the security industry generally. This may be of particular importance to those private police officers who operate within the public realm. Indeed, since the actions of private police officers are likely to be much more visible in the public realm, the need to meet or exceed these criteria is critical—for both operational and liability reasons.

This being said, it is not necessary that the training and selection standards of private police equal those of a public police officer—who typically receive 600 to 800 hours of training. Instead, the best practice would be to develop a training curriculum which focuses on the particular role or function to be performed.[51] The different levels and types of training should be regulated by a particular type of license issued by the state (or other government entity). The proposed training and licensing continuum is illustrated in Figure IV-3.

In this figure, as the functional complexity of the work increases, or as the critical nature of the task increases, the level of training and licensing should commeasurably increase. An excellent example of this continuum can be found in vehicle licensing standards. For passenger vehicles, the typical training and licensing requirements are rather basic. As the nature of the vehicle increases (e.g., larger tracker trailers), or as the nature of the cargo changes (e.g. passengers in a bus or dangerous chemicals in a tank car), the need for better trained and higher skilled drivers also increases. In this sense, the key is to train and license the private officer in a manner that adequately prepares them for the expected work product.

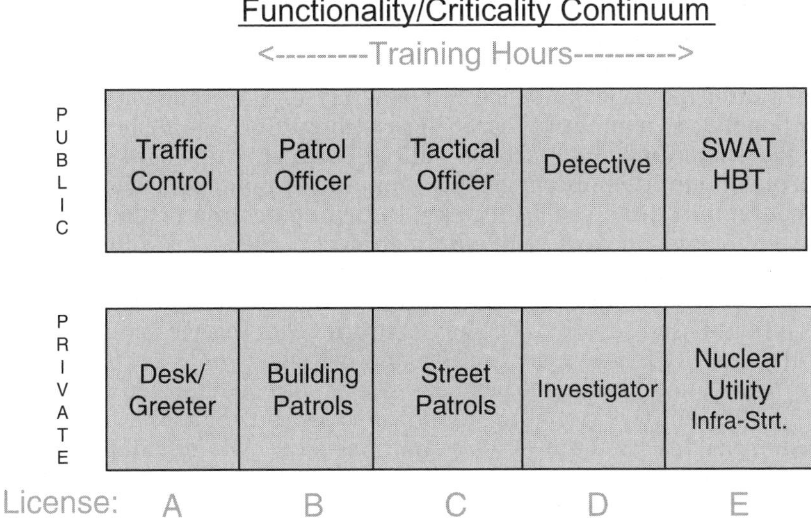

Figure IV-3 Skills and training gradations (HBT—hostage, barricade, and terrorist unit).

Few would argue that the tasks of a desk greeter vary substantially from the tasks of a security officer at a nuclear power plant. It stands to reason that each position should be trained and licensed at a different level. The licensing should range from class "A" to "D" or "E," depending upon the legislative analysis. Similarly, training hours should range from 20 or 40 minimum, and rise to 200 to 600 hours for street patrols and critical infrastructure security. Accordingly, this licensing and training standard is both logical and consistent with the legal standards for text claims, where the level of care is consummate with the risk of harm.

ACCOUNTABILITY STANDARDS

The issue of accountability of private police is often overlooked outside of civil courts. As evidenced by the cases in this chapter, this is a critical, yet difficult undertaking. Simply stated, it is critical that private security personnel be perceived as accountable to the community, the law, and the larger society. This must be more than a perception. Real and specific mechanisms must be in place.[52]

There are several ways to enhance accountability. First and foremost, specific operating procedures must be developed which address the realities of the job. Just as post orders are critical to a protected facility, so is the need for policies and procedures which will guide the officer through the expectations of the work. This also includes specific job descriptions on top of those described in post orders. Particularly in the public domain, without specific guidance, there is simply too much discretionary decision making in the fluid environment of the "street." Indeed, discretion without judgment, which was formed through proper guidance and experience, is a recipe for disaster.

Second, a community based board should be established that oversees the operations of the private policing firm(s). This board parallels the logic of community policing. Just as community policing is designed to get the community involved in the day to day operations of the police, this oversight board can work with administrators of the security firm for direction and guidance in addressing the problems within the community. In this sense, because of the nature of the contractual relationship, this is a true "client-based service." The key to this level of service is due to the fact that the security firm can be fired. The police agency does not face this ultimate "sanction." Frankly, it has been my experience that too much of the current "community policing" model is based on rhetoric of community decision making, without much actual decision making authority. It may be more realistic to have local police administrators work with this oversight board, thereby helping to coordinate the activities of both the public and private police officers. Consequently, this model would actually increase the community decision making powers relative to the work product of the private policing services.

Another critical element of accountability is to have some well-defined process to address citizen complaints. This should be done by a separate board, specifically mandated with investigatory and quasi-judicial powers to impose discipline and other sanctions. This body should be vested with subpoena powers, and the ability to conduct hearings. These hearings should be designed to assess the substance of any allegation or complaint, and if deemed warranted, have the legal authority to levy warnings, fines, and other employment and contractual remedies. These hearings could be conducted by a number of existing governmental agencies, including the Department of Professional Regulation, or a civilian oversight board that monitors police misconduct. However this board is constituted, it must be able to deal with the type of complaints common to police departments.

In summary, there is a growing trend toward public-private policing. In the coming years, many challenges lie ahead. Varying levels of operational and financial constraints, coupled with the threat of violence and terrorism will foster increased viability of this trend. As with any problem, opportunities for new ways of thinking, innovative techniques, and thoughtful solutions are manifest. Hopefully, this discussion and the following cases will serve to guide this development.

NOTES

1. See Pastor, James F. (2003). *The Privatization of Police in America: An Analysis and Case Study.* Jefferson, NC: McFarland and Company; Clifford,

Mary (2004). *Identifying and Exploring Security Essentials.* Upper Saddle River, NJ: Prentice Hall; Inbau, Fred E., Bernard J. Farber, and David W. Arnold (1996). *Protective Security Law,* 2nd ed.. Burlington, MA: Butterworth-Heinemann; and Nemeth, Charles (2005). *Private Security and the Law,* 3rd ed. Burlington, MA: Butterworth-Heinemann.

2. Taken from www.cdc.gov/niosh/violhomi.html on 9-16-2002.
3. See, for example, Inbau et al. op cit. at 31–44; and Nemeth op cit. at 67–69. See also Holtz, Larry E. (2001). *Contemporary Criminal Procedure,* 7th ed. Longwood, FL: Gould Publications.
4. Inbau et al. op cit. at 31–44; Nemeth op cit. at 68–72; and Holtz op cit. at 199–200.
5. Pastor op cit. at 77–83; Nemeth op cit. at 69–85; and Inbau et al. op cit. at 18–29.
6. Pastor op cit. at 67–77; and Holtz op cit. at 199–200.
7. Inbau et al. op cit. at 21–22; and Pastor op cit. at 33–41.
8. Nemeth op cit. at 78.
9. See Chapter 39/107-3 of Illinois Compiled Statutes.
10. Nemeth op cit. at 72–79; and Pastor op cit. at 77–83.
11. See, for example, Nemeth op cit. at 78.
12. Holtz op cit. at 199–200.
13. Nemeth op cit. at 83–85; and Pastor op cit. at 67–72.
14. Nemeth op cit. at 89–94; and Pastor op cit. at 81–83.
15. Holtz op cit. at 831–832.
16. Ibid at 831–832.
17. Inbau et al. op cit. at 31.
18. In regard to the application of the exclusionary rule to private policing, see for example, Joh, Elizabeth E. (2004). The Paradox of Private Policing. *The Journal of Criminal Law and Criminology,* Vol. 95 (1), Northwestern University School of Law, Evanston, IL: pp. 49–132, who stated, "with regard to searches, lower courts have generally found that the Fourth Amendment and its accompanying exclusionary rule do not apply to private police, unless they have been accorded specialized deputized powers."
19. Holtz op cit. at 1–7.
20. Ibid at 831.
21. *Burdeau v. McDowell,* 256 U.S. 465 (Supreme Court, 1921).
22. Pastor op cit. at 71–72.
23. *Commonwealth v. Leone,* 435 N.E. 2d 1036 (1982).
24. Pastor op cit. at 74; and Inbau op cit. at 18–19.
25. Pastor op cit. at 74.
26. Pastor op cit. at 73.
27. Pastor op cit. at 74.
28. *United States v. Francoeur,* 547 F. 2d 891 (1977).
29. Pastor op cit. at 75.
30. Ibid.
31. *People v. Stormer,* 518 N.Y.S. 2d 351 (1987).
32. Pastor op cit. at 75–76.
33. Ibid.
34. Ibid.
35. *Mancusi v. DeForte,* 392 U.S. 364 (U.S. Supreme Court, 1968).
36. Pastor op cit. at 77.

37. Nemeth op cit. at 68.
38. Joh op cit. at 112, stated: "private police are more like public police and less like private citizens."
39. Nemeth op cit. at 71; Holtz op cit. at 497–500; and Inbau op cit. at 36–37.
40. For examples of Terry stop litigation in the private sector, see *DeBroux v. Commonwealth of Virginia,* 528 S.E. 2d 151 (2000); *Payton v. Rush-Presbyterian St. Luke's Medical Center,* 82 F. Supp. 2d 901 (2000); and *Woods v. State,* 970 S.W. 2d 770 (1998).
41. See, for example, Holtz op cit. at 199–359.
42. See *Graham v. Connor,* 490 U.S. 386 (1989), holding that "reasonableness of particular use of force must be judged from perspective of reasonable officer on the scene, and the calculus of reasonableness must allow for fact that police officers are often forced to make split-second judgments, in circumstances that are tense, uncertain and rapidly evolving, about amount of force that is necessary in a particular situation."
43. See *Tennessee v. Gardner,* 471 U.S. 1 (1985), holding that use of force, including deadly force, is a "seizure" pursuant to the Fourth Amendment.
44. See *Graham* supra.
45. See *Johnson v. LaRabida,* 372 F. 3d 894 (2004).
46. Connor, G. (1995). *Law Enforcement Officer Use of Force Model,* Integrated Force Management.
47. Ibid.
48. Pastor op cit. at 47–51.
49. See The Private Security Officer Selection and Training Guidelines (2004), drafted and adopted by ASIS International.
50. Ibid.
51. See *Security Director's Report* (2006), IOMA, www.ioma.com/secure, 06-03, March, citing "A Taxonomy for Security Assignments" by Edward G. Blitzer and Roger G. Johnston.
52. See Pastor op cit. at 166–173, where one conclusion from my research is that privatized policing arrangements must develop formal accountability standards and methods.

10

Off-Duty Police

03 CV 2571 (N.D. Ohio)

United States District Court, N.D. Ohio, Eastern Division

JEFFREY SWIECICKI, ET AL., PLAINTIFFS v. JOSE DELGADO, DEFENDANT.

July 13, 2005

Background

Plaintiffs Jeffrey Swiecicki and Scott Swiecicki filed suit in this court against Jose Delgado, alleging various constitutional violations under 42 U.S.C. Section 1983. Jeffrey Swiecicki and Scott Swiecicki both allege four identical Section 1983 claims: freedom of speech, freedom from seizure of person, arrest, or imprisonment without probable case, freedom from excessive force, and freedom from malicious prosecution.

Holding

Officer Delgado's Motion for Summary Judgment will be granted as to all of the plaintiffs' Section 1983 claims.

On 25 September 2001, plaintiffs Jeffrey Swiecicki and Scott Swiecicki were seated in the outfield bleachers of Jacobs Field, a baseball stadium in Cleveland, Ohio, attending a baseball game between the Cleveland Indians and the Toronto Blue Jays. They were seated in a group of between fifteen and twenty people. During the game, Jeffrey Swiecicki heckled the left fielders, both from the Indians and the Blue Jays. While approximately half of his group was heckling the players throughout the game, Jeffrey Swiecicki admits to leading the heckling. Jeffrey Swiecicki also admits to drinking two full beers with a group of his friends, but Scott Swiecicki denies drinking any beer at the game. During the criminal proceedings, Officer Delgado testified that he observed Jeffrey Swiecicki carrying beers back to his seat several times during the game; specifically, he saw Jeffrey Swiecicki holding a beer when he yelled at Russell Branyan, the Cleveland Indian's outfielder and third baseman.

At the time, defendant Jose Delgado, a City of Cleveland police officer, was working his authorized secondary employment as a security guard at Jacobs Field, and he was stationed at a tunnel near the bleachers along with Wilfred Labrie, a host greeter. While technically off-duty as a police officer, Officer Delgado was wearing his official City of Cleveland police officer uniform and was armed with his official City of Cleveland police weapons.

Sometime around the seventh inning, both Mr. Labrie and Officer Delgado heard foul and abusive language coming from the bleachers. While Jeffrey Swiecicki admits to heckling the players, he denies using profanity at any point during the game. In contrast, Officer Delgado claims that he heard someone call out, "Branyan, you suck. Branyan, you have a fat ass," and he identified Jeffrey Swiecicki as the speaker. Officer Delgado also claims that there were younger children in the bleachers; specifically, a ten-year-old girl was sitting behind Jeffrey Swiecicki along with an older gentleman. Jeffrey Swiecicki does not recall seeing any children sitting close by.

The owners of Jacobs Field prohibit fans from using abusive or foul language during games, so Officer Delgado stood in front of the bleachers and motioned for Jeffrey Swiecicki to "cut it out." When Officer Delgado told Jeffrey Swiecicki to cut it out, he claims that the older gentleman thanked him. Apparently, Jeffrey Swiecicki did not see Officer Delgado's signal. When Jeffrey Swiecicki seemed to be ignoring his command, Officer Delgado went up to his row and asked Jeffrey Swiecicki to come with him. At first, Jeffrey Swiecicki did not comply; instead, he repeatedly asked Officer Delgado what he had done wrong. Officer Delgado said, "We can do this the easy way or we can do this the hard way." Jeffrey Swiecicki ultimately complied with the orders and exited the row. Once he did, Officer Delgado grabbed him in the "escort position," holding him by one arm with both hands, and escorted him down into the tunnel with the intent of ejecting him from the stadium. As they were traveling through the tunnel, Jeffrey Swiecicki continued to ask, "What have I done?"

While Officer Delgado was escorting Jeffrey Swiecicki into the tunnel, Jeffrey's brother Scott Swiecicki along with companions Matthew Hlabac, Jason Kulwicki, and Ralph Sapolla, followed them on foot. Scott Swiecicki also asked, "Officer, what has my brother done?" At this time, Officer Delgado claims that Jeffrey Swiecicki jerked, pushed his arm away, and turned around to face him. Then, Officer Delgado told Jeffrey Swiecicki that he was under arrest, turned him around, pushed him against a concession stand door, and put his arms behind his back. At the criminal trial,

Delgado admitted that he "was just going to escort him [Jeffrey Swiecicki] out until he jerked away from my hold and pushed my arm away. That's when I said he was under arrest." As he was about to put handcuffs on Jeffrey Swiecicki, Officer Delgado claims that Scott Swiecicki approached him too closely, yelling, and interfering with his safety. When Officer Delgado let go of one of Jeffrey Swiecicki's hands in order to stop Scott Swiecicki, Jeffrey Swiecicki again pushed his arm away and turned around to face him.

Officer Delgado claims that he felt unsafe given the situation and the small area, so he grabbed Jeffrey Swiecicki's shoulders and ordered him to the ground. Officer Delgado told him to get down and stop resisting, but he claims that Jeffrey Swiecicki continued to resist, so Officer Delgado put him in an "arm bar," grabbing Jeffrey Swiecicki's left arm and twisting it to lock it into a bond. Officer Delgado was then able to bring him down to the ground without resistance.

Jeffrey Swiecicki does not himself remember what happened, but he believes that Officer Delgado slammed him into the door because the officer was tired of him asking what he had done wrong. Jeffrey Swiecicki claims he never pulled his arm away from Officer Delgado's grasp. In fact, he alleges that he fell to his knees because Officer Delgado had pushed him so hard against the door that he suffered an injury on the right side of his head.

As soon as Officer Delgado was able to handcuff Jeffrey Swiecicki, he radioed for backup. Once backup arrived, he had the other officers arrest Scott Swiecicki. Next, the officers moved the plaintiffs to a holding area in the basement of Jacobs Field and eventually escorted them to the Justice Center where they were both charged with aggravated disorderly conduct pursuant to Cleveland Code Section 605.03, and resisting arrest pursuant to Cleveland Code Section 615.08. The Cleveland Municipal Court found Jeffrey Swiecicki guilty of the lesser included offense of disorderly conduct and resisting arrest; however, the judge acquitted Scott Swiecicki of all charges. Later, the Ohio Court of Appeals granted Jeffrey Swiecicki's motion for direct acquittal and dismissed all criminal charges against him.

A. Acting Under Color of Law

In his Motion for Summary Judgment, Officer Delgado alleges that he was acting in a private capacity when he attempted to eject Jeffrey Swiecicki from Jacobs Field, insinuating that he was not acting under color of state law. Plaintiffs point out the inconsistency of Officer Delgado arguing that he was acting as a private security guard at one moment and a police officer the next.

To state a Section 1983 claim, a plaintiff must allege the violation of a Constitutional right and show that the alleged violation was committed by a person acting under color of state law. Acting under color of state law requires that the defendant exercise power possessed by virtue of state law and made possible only because he or she is clothed with the authority of state law. The nature of the act performed, not the clothing of the actor or even the status of being on duty or off duty determines whether the officer has acted under color of law.

In this case, Officer Delgado stipulated that on 25 September 2001 he was wearing his official City of Cleveland police uniform and carrying his official City of Cleveland police weapons. Although Officer Delgado may have been acting as a private actor when he began escorting Jeffrey Swiecicki out of the stadium pursuant to the rules and regulations of Jacobs Field, he asserted his official state power when he placed Jeffrey Swiecicki under arrest. Therefore, this court will only consider Jeffrey Swiecicki's Section 1983 claims that turn not on the wrongfulness of being escorted out of the stadium but the unlawfulness of his arrest and subsequent prosecution.

Officer Delgado is potentially liable as a state actor under Section 1983 for any constitutional violations that arose from his exercise of his state power in arresting, detaining, and aiding in the prosecution of Jeffrey Swiecicki. However, because Officer Delgado was acting in his private capacity when he began escorting Jeffrey Swiecicki out of the stadium, the Officer will not be liable for any potential constitutional violations that may have occurred before he asserted his official state power by beginning to place Jeffrey Swiecicki under arrest.

B. Qualified Immunity

Officer Delgado claims he is entitled to qualified immunity for all of Jeffrey Swiecicki's Section 1983 claims because he reasonably believed there was probable cause to arrest Jeffrey Swiecicki for aggravated disorderly and resisting arrest. On the other hand, Jeffrey Swiecicki claims that Officer Delgado was unreasonable in determining that there was probable cause for his arrest.

Government officials performing discretionary functions generally are granted qualified immunity, which shields them from liability for civil damages as long as their conduct does not violate clearly established statutory and constitutional rights of which a reasonable person would have known. Qualified immunity is an entitlement not to stand trial, not a defense from liability. Whether qualified immunity applies is a question of law for the court to consider.

1. Freedom of Speech

Jeffrey Swiecicki argues that Officer Delgado impermissibly arrested him for the content of his speech in violation of his First Amendment rights.

Specifically, he alleges that Officer Delgado arrested him for saying, "you suck, and you have a fat ass," and for continually asking what he had done wrong when the Officer began escorting him out of the stadium.

First, this court must determine whether Jeffrey Swiecicki has alleged facts sufficient to establish the violation of a constitutional right. The Sixth Circuit Court of Appeals has held that protected speech cannot serve as the basis for a violation of municipal ordinances. The First Amendment protects a significant amount of verbal criticism and challenges directed at police officers. The only type of language that is denied First Amendment protection is "fighting words" which "by their very utterance inflict injury or tend to incite an immediate breach of the peace."

If Officer Delgado arrested Jeffrey Swiecicki even partially because of the content of his speech, then Officer Delgado would have violated Jeffrey Swiecicki's constitutional right to freedom of speech. Since Jeffrey Swiecicki has alleged that Officer Delgado arrested him at least in part because of the content of his heckling and his repeated questions about why he was being asked to leave the stadium, he has alleged sufficient facts to implicate the violation of his constitutional right to freedom of speech.

Next, this court must determine whether Jeffrey Swiecicki's right to freedom of speech was clearly established such that a reasonable officer would have known that his conduct was unlawful in this particular situation. Ohio courts have recognized that a violation of the statute does not necessarily depend upon the particular context of the speech involved. Rather, a violation can be based upon the defendant's actions if he is creating enough noise and commotion to cause annoyance and alarm regardless of the content of his speech.

At the criminal trial, Officer Delgado testified that he saw a ten-year-old girl with an older man who appeared to be disturbed by Jeffrey Swiecicki's behavior and who subsequently thanked the Officer when he motioned to Jeffrey Swiecicki to cut it out. Under these circumstances, a reasonable officer could have believed that Jeffrey Swiecicki was, in public, engaged in conduct—not simply speech—likely to be offensive or to cause inconvenience to others. In other words, a reasonable officer could have believed that he or she had probable cause to arrest Jeffrey Swiecicki for aggravated disorderly conduct based upon the loudness and disruptiveness of his heckling and the apparent discomfort of fellow patrons. Under these circumstances, it would not have been clear to a reasonable officer that he or she was violating Jeffrey Swiecicki's First Amendment rights because there was evidence that the manner, not the content, of his speech violated the statute. Ultimately, Officer Delgado's arrest of Jeffrey Swiecicki for disorderly conduct was not plainly incompetent, nor is it shown he knowingly violated the law.

Moreover, Officer Delgado testified that he did not charge Jeffrey Swiecicki with resisting arrest for the reason that Jeffrey Swiecicki constantly questioned being arrested. Rather, Officer Delgado claimed that he charged

Jeffrey Swiecicki with resisting arrest because Jeffrey Swiecicki physically jerked his arm away out of the officer's hold. According to (citation omitted), which defines the crime of resisting arrest, "No person, recklessly or by force, shall resist or interfere with a lawful arrest of himself or another." A reasonable officer could have believed that Jeffrey Swiecicki's action of jerking his arm out of Officer Delgado's hold constituted a resistance or interference requisite for a charge of resisting arrest. Therefore, a reasonable officer would not have thought that he or she was violating Jeffrey Swiecicki's constitutional right to free speech because there were grounds for the resisting arrest charge that involved physical action and had nothing to do with the content of Jeffrey's Swiecicki's speech. As a result, Officer Delgado will be granted qualified immunity on Jeffrey Swiecicki's First Amendment claim.

2. Freedom from Seizure, Arrest, and Imprisonment Without Probable Cause

Jeffrey Swiecicki also argues that Officer Delgado violated his right to be free from seizure, arrest, and imprisonment without probable cause. First, he alleges that Officer Delgado did not have probable cause to arrest him for disorderly conduct because there was no evidence to believe that he was intoxicated and the only evidence of him offending others relates to the content of his speech, which is protected by the First Amendment. Second, he alleges that Officer Delgado did not have probable cause to arrest him for resisting arrest because the prerequisite for such a charge is a lawful arrest.

Again, this court must first determine whether Jeffrey Swiecicki has adequately alleged a constitutional violation. To satisfy a citizen's Fourth Amendment right against unreasonable searches and seizures, police officers must have probable cause to support a full-fledged arrest. "Probable cause justifying an arrest means facts and circumstances within the officer's knowledge that are sufficient to warrant a prudent person, or one of reasonable caution, in believing, in the circumstances shown, that the suspect has committed, is committing, or is about to commit an offense." Probable cause also requires that officers articulate concrete and objective facts from which they infer criminal conduct. Protected speech, however, cannot serve as the basis for a violation of any municipal ordinance and cannot be relied on for probable cause.

If Officer Delgado did not have probable cause to arrest Jeffrey Swiecicki for aggravated disorderly conduct or resisting arrest, then he would clearly be violating Jeffrey Swiecicki's Fourth Amendment right against illegal searches and seizures. Ultimately, Jeffrey Swiecicki has sufficiently alleged a constitutional violation to get past the first element of the qualified immunity test.

Next, this court must consider whether a reasonable officer in the same situation would have known that there was no probable cause for

Jeffrey Swiecicki's arrest, and that it was, therefore, unconstitutional. "Officers can have reasonable, but mistaken, beliefs as to the facts establishing the existence of probable cause or exigent circumstances, for example, and in those situations courts will not hold that they have violated the Constitution."

First, Jeffrey Swiecicki argues that Officer Delgado did not have sufficient evidence that he was intoxicated in order to arrest him lawfully for aggravated disorderly conduct. In contrast, Officer Delgado was presented with evidence that Jeffrey Swiecicki was intoxicated. He had seen Jeffrey Swiecicki and others in his group bringing beers back to their seats, and Jeffrey Swiecicki himself admitted that he drank two full beers during the game. While the Ohio Court of Appeals may have found that the prosecution had presented insufficient proof of intoxication to support a conviction, a reasonable police officer could have believed that there was enough probable cause of intoxication to arrest Jeffrey Swiecicki for aggravated disorderly conduct. In addition, for the reasons stated in the previous section, a reasonable police officer could also have believed that there was probable cause based on Jeffrey Swiecicki's loud and rowdy manner to support an arrest for aggravated disorderly conduct. Finally, a reasonable officer could have found that Jeffrey Swiecicki's failure to stop heckling after Officer Delgado signaled to him to "cut it out" constituted probable cause for the aggravation of the charge.

Jeffrey Swiecicki further argues that Officer Delgado had no probable cause to arrest him for resisting arrest since his first arrest was unlawful. However, since a reasonable officer could have believed that Jeffrey Swiecicki's arrest for aggravated disorderly conduct was constitutional, a reasonable officer could also believe that his arrest for resisting arrest was lawful. Whether or not Jeffrey Swiecicki intended to jerk his arm away from Officer Delgado's grasp, a reasonable officer could interpret that movement as an attempt to resist arrest. Accordingly, Officer Delgado will be granted qualified immunity on Jeffrey Swiecicki's false arrest and imprisonment claim.

3. Freedom from Malicious Prosecution Without Probable Cause

Plaintiffs also urge this Court to find that Officer Delgado violated their right to be free from malicious prosecution. Following the elements necessary to establish a malicious prosecution claim, as laid out in (citation omitted), the Swiecicki's insist that Officer Delgado lacked probable cause for instituting the lawsuit and harbored malice in initiating the proceedings.

Neither allegation bears the weight of scrutiny. First, as this court has indicated in its analysis of the plaintiffs' false arrest and imprisonment claim, a reasonable officer in defendant Delgado's position could have believed there existed enough probable cause of intoxication to detain Jeffrey Swiecicki for aggravated disorderly conduct.

Second, whether Officer Delgado possessed the malice necessary for the plaintiffs' malicious prosecution claim is a question of state law which, pursuant to long-standing precedent, will not support a finding of malice where the court has determined that an officer acted upon a reasonable belief that probable cause existed for the prosecution (noting "if the defendant entertained an honest belief that plaintiff had committed a violation of the law in acting on that belief, caused the prosecution to be instituted from a desire to bring a supposed public offender to justice, then he is not liable in action for malicious prosecution"). Accordingly, this court will grant Officer Delgado's Motion for Summary Judgment with regard to plaintiff's malicious prosecution claim.

Conclusion

For the reasons set forth above, defendant Officer Delgado's Motion for Summary Judgment is granted against both plaintiffs Jeffrey Swiecicki and Scott Swiecicki, and those counts are dismissed with prejudice.

IT IS SO ORDERED.

CASE COMMENT

In this case, the court analyzed the facts to the law in a very appropriate step-by-step fashion. Significantly, the court found that the police officer was initially acting as a private person when he began escorting the plaintiff from the stadium. However, when the plaintiff attempted to jerk away from the officer, the officer stepped away from his role as a private security officer and into the role of a police officer. Based on this finding, the court reasoned that Delgado performed all subsequent actions under color of law in his role as a Cleveland police officer. In making this determination, the court found that qualified immunity attached to the actions he took as a police officer, thereby requiring summary judgment of each constitutional claim asserted by the plaintiff.

830 N.E.2d 1266

Hamilton County Municipal Court, Ohio

THE STATE OF OHIO, PLAINTIFF v. UNDERWOOD, DEFENDANT.

Decided March 22, 2005

Background

Defendant was charged with obstructing official business.

Holding

The Municipal Court, Hamilton County, held that as an issue of first impression, police officer was a public official when he was working private-duty security detail at store, and thus defendant was guilty of obstructing official business when he defied officer's orders to stop after having left store without paying for merchandise.

Judgment of conviction entered.

Defendant Joseph Underwood is charged with obstructing official business in violation of (citation omitted), which states as follows:

No person, without privilege to do so and with purpose to prevent, obstruct, or delay the performance by a public official of any authorized act within the public official's official capacity, shall do any act that hampers or impedes a public official in the performance of the public official's lawful duties.

Defendant's encounter with police on February 2, 2005, began when Joshua Younger, a cashier at a Kroger store, alerted a police officer working a security detail that defendant had left the store without paying for store merchandise. When Officer Eric Carpenter heard the cashier shout "shoplifter," he ran after defendant. There is no doubt that defendant knew he was being pursued by a police officer. Defendant ran across the Kroger parking lot and Warsaw Avenue and kept running after the officer had ordered him to stop five times. The officer also shouted that he would use his taser on defendant if he did not stop.

Officer Carpenter strained a muscle in his calf while chasing defendant, so he called for other officers to assist him. After a pursuit of two to three minutes and then a brief struggle, Officer Carpenter arrested defendant and charged him with theft and obstructing official business.

Officer Carpenter, a veteran Cincinnati police officer, was in full uniform and equipped with a firearm when these events occurred.

He was working a private-duty security assignment in a Kroger store in Cincinnati.

Defendant does not dispute that he ran when the officer ordered him to stop and that as a result, he obstructed the officer's efforts to subdue him. Rather, his defense to this charge is that since the officer was on the payroll of a private entity, namely, the Kroger Company, he was not a "public official" performing "any authorized act," as must be shown to sustain a conviction for obstructing official business. Thus, the defense urges, if an alleged thief runs from a uniformed officer who is working a private detail, he cannot be found guilty of obstructing official business in violation of the statute.

The question of whether an officer in full uniform, working a private security detail is a "public official" has not been determined in Ohio with regard to a charge of obstructing official business. Nevertheless, Ohio has statutes and case law that shed light on this issue.

"Public officials" include law-enforcement officers. In addition, a number of Ohio appellate courts have determined in other contexts, most notably in relation to charges of resisting arrest, that a sworn officer, performing valid police duties is a "public official," even if he is being paid by a private business.

The leading case in this area is *State v. Glover*. In *Glover,* the defendant was arrested at a supermarket by an officer of the Columbus Police Department who was off duty, out of uniform, and working as a Kroger employee. When the officer saw Glover exit the store with merchandise he had not paid for, the officer stopped him, showed him his Columbus-police-officer badge, and informed him that he was under arrest. A scuffle ensued, which gave rise to a charge of resisting arrest.

Assessing the status of the officer to determine whether the charge could stand, the Tenth District Court of Appeals reasoned:

> A duly commissioned police officer holds a public office upon a continuing basis. The officer here remained an officer of the law, and his obligation to preserve the peace was not nullified by the fact he was working for Kroger in this case. Notwithstanding, the officer, even though acting as a private security policeman, had the right and duty to arrest and detain a person who was violating a law of this state or an ordinance of the city of Columbus until a warrant could be obtained.

In *Duvall,* off-duty, uniformed officers who were paid by a school system to provide security at a football game were assaulted by defendants, Fred and Jason Duvall. Charges of assault on a peace officer were filed. To sustain this charge, the state needed to show that the peace officer in question was performing his official duties when assaulted. Specifically, the court had to determine whether a uniformed, off-duty peace officer is performing "official duties" when he serves as a private security guard paid by a local school system. As in this case, the defense argued that "official duties" should be interpreted only to include those times when a peace officer is officially "on duty" or "on the clock."

Discussing this issue in detail, the Eleventh District Court of Appeals referred to a police officer's duties as defined by state statute, rule, regulation, and usage, noting that creates many duties for peace officers to perform without regard to their duty status.

Noting that several Ohio courts, including the court in *Glover*, have held that an officer has an obligation to observe and enforce the laws of this state when off duty, the court concluded:

> To determine what comprises a peace officer's "official duties," the court must look at the activities in which the peace officer was engaged when he was assaulted. If the peace officer was engaging in a duty imposed upon him by statute, rule, regulation, ordinance or usage, regardless of his duty status, that officer is "in the performance of [his] official duties" for purposes of [the assault-on-a-police-officer] section. This general precept is limited to activities occurring within the peace officer's territorial jurisdiction, while the peace officer is in uniform.

The court thus decided that under the facts in *Duvall*, the officers were pursuing their official business when they patrolled or monitored the crowd and were working to "preserve the peace." Accordingly, the defendants were properly charged with and convicted of assaulting a peace officer in the performance of his official duties.

The statute cited states: "The police force of a municipal corporation shall preserve the peace, protect person and property, and obey and enforce all ordinances of the legislative authority of the municipal corporation, all criminal laws of the state and the United States ..." Other Ohio courts have determined that a police officer is always on duty for other purposes as well (off-duty police officer who was injured when out of uniform and working a private detail and while attempting to arrest a shoplifting suspect is entitled to workers' compensation benefits; off-duty drug involvement is valid reason for dismissal of police officer, since officer has continuing duty to obey and enforce the criminal law, even when off duty; off-duty officer has a continuing right and obligation to enforce the law; a police officer, not in uniform, can testify in court about a traffic violation observed while not officially on traffic duty.)

Turning to the facts of this case and applying the criteria cited in *Duvall* and *Glover*, the court finds that on the date in question, Officer Carpenter, a Cincinnati police officer working a security detail in Cincinnati, was a public official performing an authorized action within his official capacity as must be shown to secure a conviction. Defendant, by his own testimony, was aware that a police officer in full uniform had ordered him to stop. When defendant ran, he was obstructing and delaying the officer in his attempt to legitimately arrest him for shoplifting. Officer Carpenter was injured while chasing defendant, and he was also required to call for additional police assistance to carry out the stop. Based on these facts, the court finds defendant guilty of obstructing official business.

CASE COMMENT

This court provided an excellent overview of precedent in assessing the question of whether Officer Carpenter was acting as a police officer or a security officer at the time of the shoplifting and obstructing justice arrest. In its analysis, the court correctly determined that Officer Carpenter was acting as a police officer based on a number of factors. These include being in full uniform with his firearm, ordering the shoplifter to stop, and his having to call for additional police assistance. These facts coupled with the prior court decisions left no doubt that the officer was performing a public function as a police officer.

361 F. Supp. 2d 740

United States District Court, Northern District Illinois, Eastern Division

REGGIE COLES, PLAINTIFF v. THE CITY OF CHICAGO, A MUNICIPAL CORPORATION, TIMOTHY THOMAS, MAXINE THOMAS JACKSON, D/B/A ROSE COCKTAIL LOUNGE, DEFENDANTS.

March 11, 2005

Background

Bar patron filed Section 1983 action to recover for injuries sustained when he was allegedly shot by off-duty city police officer during altercation. City moved for summary judgment.

Holding

The district court held that fact issues remained as to whether city was liable for shooting.

Motion denied

On the night of December 31, 2001, and the early morning of January 1, 2002, Mr. Coles and Mr. Thomas were both at the Rose Cocktail Lounge. Mr. Thomas was employed as a police officer of the City of Chicago, and was off duty.

Shortly after midnight, a fight broke out among some of the patrons—first at the back of the nightclub (the "initial disturbance"), and then at the front entrance to the nightclub. Both Mr. Coles and Mr. Thomas, for different reasons and from different places in the nightclub, walked to the front entrance, toward the fight. Mr. Thomas was not wearing a police uniform or a police badge of any kind, but rather was dressed in plain clothes. Mr. Coles has testified that he heard the person who injured him at the front entrance shout, "police, police, police!" For his part, Mr. Thomas has testified that he shouted to the crowd at the front door that he was the police "at least once," for the purpose of establishing his authority to tell the patrons to "get out of" and/or to "get [the fight] out of" the club. The General Orders of the Chicago Police Department require an off-duty officer to take some action when he observes a crime being committed.

The parties agree that an altercation took place. And, although they disagree about precisely what happened during that altercation, they agree that a 911 call was made from the nightclub. The individual making that call, Sonya Remus, told the telephone dispatcher that shots had been fired inside the lounge, that three women were stabbed and one man was shot, and that everyone was running for cover.

Thereafter, Mr. Coles was taken to the Loretto Hospital emergency room, where it was documented that he had active bleeding from the mouth. A man named "Dorsey" made a 911 call from Loretto Hospital to report a possible gun shot victim who was unable to give any information. Mr. Dorsey further reported that "someone ... came in with him but ran out of the building before [they] could get any information from him." A female named "Carey" made a 911 call from Mount Sinai Hospital. Ms. Carey reported that Mr. Coles had been shot at the Rose Cocktail Lounge by a bouncer. Ms. Carey further reported that the bouncer fired shots in the nightclub.

Mr. Coles claims that during the altercation at the nightclub in the early morning hours of January 1, 2002, Mr. Thomas shot him at point-blank range after first shouting "police, police, police!" Mr. Coles claims that Mr. Thomas did this within the scope of his employment as a police officer. Conversely, the City claims that Mr. Thomas did not shoot Mr. Coles; and that while Mr. Thomas "perhaps" announced his office "once," he was not acting as a police officer or within the scope of his employment at any time during the incidents in question. We find a number of genuine, material fact disputes on these points, which we summarize below.

First, the parties do not dispute that Mr. Thomas announced himself as a police officer to the fighting crowd. The dispute appears to center on the manner, frequency, and purpose of the announcement. That dispute is relevant to the questions of color of state law, and scope of employment.

Second, Mr. Coles points out that Mr. Thomas has admitted that he assisted another security guard to restore peace inside the nightclub when the fight at the front door of the club broke out. The City's principal response is to emphasize all the things that Mr. Thomas allegedly did not do: he did not aid the security guards in removing any of the patrons from the nightclub; he "did not attempt to break up the fight at the front of the nightclub"; he did not call 911 from his cell phone; he did not restrain the person who allegedly hit him; he did not arrest anyone or attempt to arrest anyone that evening; he never showed his badge to anyone other than to the responding officers who arrived at the nightclub after the fight had occurred; and, he did not investigate the crime that occurred in the night-club that evening. The City also denies that Mr. Thomas was working as a security guard at the time of the fight. However, none of that evidence directly refutes Mr. Thomas's deposition testimony that he assisted security in restoring peace. These factual issues bear on the purpose for Mr. Thomas's actions, which is relevant to both color of the state law and scope of employment.

Having identified the genuinely disputed issues of material fact, the court turns to the substantive legal standards that make these disputed facts material, and that govern resolution of the City's motion.

Mr. Coles alleges that Mr. Thomas deprived him of his Fourth and Fourteenth Amendment rights to be secure in his person against unreasonable seizure; not to be deprived of life, liberty or property without due process of law; and to be accorded equal protection of the laws. Mr. Coles alleges that the deprivation of these rights violated Section 1983, causing him damage.

To establish Mr. Thomas's liability under Section 1983, Mr. Coles must show: (1) that Mr. Thomas deprived Mr. Coles of a right secured by the Constitution and laws of the United States, and (2) that Mr. Thomas acted under color of state law when he did so.

There is no doubt that a judgment under Section 1983 constitutes a "tort" judgment. Moreover, we note that it is common, and indeed advisable, for a plaintiff who expects a public entity to indemnify a Section 1983 judgment to add that entity as a defendant on the indemnity claim during the pendency of the Section 1983 case.

Thus, in order for Mr. Coles to establish the City's responsibility for indemnity on Count II, he must establish: (1) his Section 1983 claim against Mr. Thomas, by showing that Mr. Thomas wrongfully deprived him of a protected right, while acting under color of state law, and (2) that Mr. Thomas was acting within the scope of his employment at the time of the wrongful conduct.

The two elements of "under color" and "scope of employment" should not be confused. The under color requirement is necessary for liability against the individual officer; the scope of employment requirement is necessary to hold the City that employs this officer responsible.

We turn to the question of whether the undisputed material facts show that Mr. Thomas was not acting under color of law during any encounter he had with Mr. Coles at the nightclub. Throughout this opinion, we have referred to Mr. Thomas without using his official title for a reason: we do not wish to have been thought to prejudge the question of whether Mr. Thomas, who was indisputably "off-duty" at the time of Mr. Coles's alleged injury, acted "under color of law."

The question of whether Mr. Thomas acted under color of law is a highly fact-specific inquiry that is not susceptible to an easy, formulaic analysis. In considering the factors relevant to that inquiry, we find helpful the treatment of this question in which we quote at length:

Traditionally, the courts have held that a defendant acts under the color of state law when he exercises power "possessed by virtue of state law and made possible only because the wrongdoer is clothed with the authority of state law." Thus, government employees who act in their official capacity or exercise their responsibilities pursuant to state law act under color of state law. Conversely, government employees who act without the cloth of state authority do not subject themselves to liability under Section 1983.

Although most police officers are state officials for purposes of Section 1983, the mere fact that the defendant is a police officer does not mean that the defendant acted under color of state law. Indeed, the Supreme Court has observed that "acts of officers in the ambit of their personal pursuits are plainly excluded." On the other hand, "acts of officers who undertake to perform their official duties are included whether they hew to the line of their authority or overstep it."

Notably, the Supreme Court has stated that "under color of state law" also means under "pretense" of state law. Thus, a police officer who purports to exercise official authority to further private interests is generally considered to be acting under color of state law. As Judge Conlon has noted, no bright line distinguishes a police officer's personal pursuits from actions taken under color of state law. Thus, the question of whether a police officer acted under color of state law is not answered by whether the officer was on or off duty at the time. Further, the accouterments of state authority, such as the police uniform, patrol car, badge, or gun, are not dispositive.

Instead, the essential inquiry is whether the police officer's actions related in some way to the performance of a police duty ("the specific nature of the acts performed must be considered and their relationship to the officer's performance of his or her official duties"; and "even acts committed while a police officer is on duty are not committed under color of state law unless they are in some way related to the performance of police duties").

In *Zienciuk*, summary judgment was granted in favor of two off-duty Chicago police officers, holding that they did not act under color of state law when they engaged in a bar fight prompted by an alleged derogatory racial remark. The decision noted that "not only were [the defendants] off-duty, but they were not wearing police uniforms and they did not identify themselves to [the plaintiff] as police officers when they initially approached him." Further, neither officer "asserted their police authority over [the plaintiff] by arresting him, and they behaved the same way non-police officers would behave after they got into a brawl." Because the case involved "a bar fight, plain and simple," the court concluded that the two officers did not act under color of state law.

Unlike the case in *Zienciuk*, we do not think that the undisputed facts here show that the actions allegedly taken by Mr. Thomas amounted to "a bar fight, plain and simple." Mr. Thomas announced his presence as a police officer—"at least once" according to his own testimony, and three times according the Mr. Coles's testimony. The record here indicates that, unlike the case in *Zienciuk*, Mr. Thomas did so *before* he began to take the actions Mr. Coles alleges as the deprivation of his constitutional rights (i.e., *before* he allegedly raised his gun and shot him at close range in the face). And, there is evidence that the alleged shooting occurred immediately after Mr. Thomas shouted "police, police, police!"

Moreover, Mr. Thomas has testified that while he was at the front door, and after he notified the crowd that he was a police officer, he assisted the security guards who were present in trying to restore the peace among the fighting patrons. Mr. Thomas's testimony indicates that as he entered the fighting crowd he announced his presence as a police officer and told the crowd to "get out of" the nightclub. Mr. Thomas also says that he directed his mother to call the police before he entered the crowd. To be sure, the undisputed facts show Mr. Thomas was off-duty and he did not wear a uniform that night; nor did he carry or show the crowd a badge. Although such "accouterments of state authority... are not dispositive," they are factors a jury may consider in determining whether Mr. Thomas was acting under color of law. At the same time, according to Mr. Thomas, his actions satisfied the General Orders of the Chicago Police Department to take "some action when he observes a crime being committed." And, Mr. Thomas has testified that when he is fulfilling this duty to take "some action" in response to a crime, then he is taking "police action" which means he is "doing police work."

This disputed factual record is significantly different from the record presented in *Zienciuk*. There, the off-duty police officers began to strike the plaintiff well before they told the plaintiff they were police officers. In addition, the way in which the officers in *Zienciuk* revealed their police officer status might suggest an intent different than Mr. Thomas's intent here. In *Zienciuk*, the off-duty officers revealed their status to the plaintiff, not for the purpose of motivating or ordering him to act or refrain from acting in a way that potentially violated a criminal law, but rather as a jeer in response to the plaintiff's assertion that someone should call the police. By contrast, the record here could support the inference that Mr. Thomas made an announcement of his office that was not directed to plaintiff alone, and that was motivated (at least in part) by a desire to perform the police duties of breaking up the fighting crowd, and restoring peace.

This record does not allow the court to make that determination on summary judgment. Accordingly, the court concludes that there is a triable issue on whether Mr. Thomas acted under color of law.

Because this motion is brought by the City, there is one more issue to discuss. As stated, the City can be held liable for indemnity under Section 10/9-102 only if Mr. Thomas's alleged actions fell within the scope of his employment as a City of Chicago police officer. In *Pyne*, the Illinois Supreme Court noted that while "[n]o precise definition has been accorded the term 'scope of employment,'" broad criteria have been enunciated:

(1) Conduct of a servant is within the scope of employment if, but only if:
   (a) it is of the kind he is employed to perform;
   (b) it occurs substantially within the authorized time and space limits;
   (c) it is actuated, at least in part, by a purpose to serve the master, ...

(2) Conduct of a servant is not within the scope of employment if it is different in kind from that authorized, far beyond the authorized time or space limits, or too little actuated by a purpose to serve the master.

Facts related to the subjective intent of the employee are highly relevant to the scope of employment issue. For purposes of this motion, the City concedes that Mr. Thomas's conduct was of the kind he is employed to perform, and occurred within authorized space and time limits. The City argues that the undisputed material facts show that an indemnity claim nonetheless must fail, because Mr. Thomas's actions were not "actuated, at least in part, by a purpose to serve the master." To support this assertion, the City recites the testimony of Mr. Thomas indicating that he moved toward the front door of the nightclub to determine whether his brother was involved in the disturbance, and that "at no time did [Mr. Thomas] assist the security guards in removing the participants in the fight from the club" and "he did not even attempt to break up the fight."

In making this argument, the City ignores Mr. Thomas's testimony that he went to the front door to help security restore the peace and to tell the fighting patrons to leave the nightclub. He also testified that he perceived himself as taking police action to stop the commission of a crime and that is why he shouted "police!"—"at least once"—into the general crowd as he approached. And, although he did not personally summon the police by calling 911 from his cell phone, as the City asserts, he testified that he directed his mother to do so. This evidence is consistent with Mr. Thomas having an intent to advance the City's interest in seeing an altercation ended quickly. And, if that was his intent (at least in part), then that could be read as consistent with the admonition that even if off duty, an officer is expected to take "some action when he observes a crime being committed." The City is correct that there are no facts indicating that Mr. Thomas was in uniform, arrested anyone, or investigated the fight beyond those facts which we have summarized above. It is also undisputed that Mr. Thomas was off-duty at the time he and Mr. Coles interacted. However, these facts tell us nothing about Mr. Thomas's purpose when he moved toward the front door of the nightclub during the fight. Even if Mr. Thomas did not do all he might have done, the disputed facts could lead a jury to conclude that his actions were calculated—at least in part—to serve the City's interests. Finally, we are aware that Mr. Thomas may have an interest in recalling his conduct in a way that brings him within the scope of his employment during the fight at the nightclub, so as to ensure that if Mr. Coles were to obtain a compensatory damages judgment on the Section 1983 claim, that judgment would be paid out of the City's pocket and not Mr. Thomas's pocket. However, that potential interest goes to the credibility of Mr. Thomas's rendition of events, a matter that is for a jury to resolve at trial and not the court to resolve on summary judgment.

Conclusion

IT IS THEREFORE ORDERED that the defendant City of Chicago's Motion for Summary Judgment be DENIED.

CASE COMMENT

This case illustrates the factual difficulties in extrapolating whether an off-duty police officer acted in a public capacity or as a private citizen for purposes of a 1983 claim. This is a particularly difficult assessment when the off-duty police officer is not working in a security capacity. Indeed, the fact that the officer identified himself as the "police" and tried to assist the bouncers (as security personnel) served as the basis for the court's assertion that summary judgment was improper. In this decision, the court presented the factors related to scope of employment to assess whether the city would be liable for the actions of the police officer. In this assessment, the court noted that even if the police officer "did not do all he might have done, the disputed facts could lead a jury to conclude that his actions were calculated—at least in part—to serve the City's interests." Consequently, the court held that the police officer may have acted under color of law, and may have acted within the scope of his employment, thereby making summary judgment inappropriate.

386 F. Supp. 2d 277

United States District Court, Southern District New York

ELIEZER WAHHAB, AND AMEHRA BROWN, PLAINTIFFS v. THE CITY OF NEW YORK, CERTAIN NEW YORK CITY POLICE OFFICERS, THE GALLERY AT FULTON ST., LLC, TOP POTATO PLUS CORP., THEODORE PRIFTAKIS, INDIVIDUALLY AND AS OWNER/MANAGER OF TOP POTATO PLUS CORP., CANNADY SECURITY CO., HENRY CANNADY, INDIVIDUALLY AND AS OWNER OF CANNADY SECURITY CO., SECURITY GUARD JOVAN ROUSE, AND SECURITY GUARDS DOE ONE THROUGH FIVE, NOT YET IDENTIFIED, DEFENDANTS.

Feb. 10, 2005

Background

Shopper, who was assaulted by security guards while at a restaurant in shopping mall food court, filed a lawsuit raising claims under Section 1983 against the restaurant, its manager, various security guards, the guards' security company, the security company's owner, the mall, and city. Defendants filed Motions for Summary Judgment.

Holdings

The district court held that:

1. City was not entitled to summary judgment on shopper's Section 1983 claim based on the custom and practice of the city and on its failure to train its employees;
2. Uniformed police officers had probable cause to arrest shopper;
3. Off-duty police officers moonlighting as mall security guards had probable cause to arrest;
4. City was not entitled to summary judgment on shopper's Section 1983 claims that officers were not acting under color of law; and
5. City was not entitled to summary judgment on shopper's respondeat superior claims.

Motions granted in part and denied in part

Plaintiffs Eliezer Wahhab and Amehra Brown claim that Wahhab was assaulted by security guards while they and their family were at a restaurant in the food court of a shopping mall. After an altercation arose between Wahhab and the restaurant manager over food quality, security guards, some of whom were off-duty police officers and some of whom were civilian guards responded. Wahhab alleges that he was forced to accompany the guards to a security room toward the rear of the mall, where he was severely beaten and suffered injuries including a shattered jaw.

The incident leading to the present action occurred in the afternoon of October 8, 2001, at The Gallery at Fulton Street, a shopping mall in Brooklyn. Plaintiffs Eliezer Wahhab and Amehra Brown, along with one or two of their children, were at the Top Potato concession stand in the food court of The Gallery at Fulton Street. Wahhab and Top Potato Manager Theodore Priftakis became involved in a quarrel concerning unsatisfactory food and soft drinks. Wahhab requested but was denied a refund, and, upset with the service, knocked a container of straws off a counter and onto the floor.

Virtually all of the facts that follow are in dispute. Plaintiffs claim that as Wahhab was preparing to leave, defendants Rushing and Martin, who were off-duty police officers moonlighting as security guards at the Gallery, appeared. "One of them showed a badge of some sort" and bumped chests with Wahhab, blocking his path. They were in plainclothes on the date of this incident. Plaintiffs allege that when Wahhab requested them to identify themselves and leave him alone, the response was less than conciliatory: "We have a smart ass here.... You're not going anywhere." Defendant Rushing, though, testified in his deposition that he identified himself to Wahhab by stating "I'm from security" and that Wahhab did not ask Rushing or Martin to identify themselves. Jovan Rouse ("Rouse"), lead security guard present at the time, gave corroborating testimony averring that Rushing and Martin identified themselves as mall security.

Defendants' version of the initial encounter between plaintiff Wahhab and defendants Rushing, Martin, and other security personnel begins with a call from Top Potato management to security, to which Rouse responded. Rouse was apparently the first to address Wahhab, although from what can be gleaned from the record Rouse, Rushing, and Martin arrived on the scene nearly simultaneously. Defendants allege that Rouse approached Wahhab and asked him to step aside to speak with him. Wahhab allegedly answered: "[F]uck you and fuck security." Rouse maintains that he clarified to Wahhab that he was not intending to be disrespectful and assured Wahhab that he was in no "trouble" but that he must "sign a paper not to come back to the mall," which stated that if were to return, he would be treated as a trespasser. Defendants maintain that Wahhab responded once again with obscenities. Rouse then decided to call and wait for the undercover security and stepped back from Wahhab to allow them to handle the situation.

According to the depositions of Rushing and Martin, they each received a transmission over mall-issued radios requesting assistance in the food court from "red coats," or off-duty police officers. As Martin reached the food court, he observed that all the people in the food court were standing still, indicating to him that a serious incident had occurred. Rushing heard "yelling and screaming" coming from Wahhab and Top Potato manager Priftakis, who said, "Get that guy, get that guy, he just threw a bottle at me," pointing at Wahhab.

Defendants allege that directly thereafter, Martin noticed other individuals, whether patrons or employees, gesturing towards Wahhab. Martin, who was the first undercover security guard to address Wahhab, approached Wahhab and inquired as to what the problem was. Wahhab allegedly replied "I have to go, I have to go." Rushing avers that he then arrived, walked up to Wahhab and said, "Calm down, calm down, we don't know what happened. You're yelling, screaming, and swearing. I need to know what's going on, calm down." Wahhab answered "Get the fuck out of my face. I don't want to talk to you. Fuck you, fuck everybody. Get out of here."

Rushing alleges that he told Wahhab he needed to "go in the back with [them]," referring to a security office separated from the public area. According to defendants, three or four more security guards then joined Rushing and Martin, including Rouse (who was in the immediate vicinity), at which time Wahhab voluntarily accompanied the group to the security office in the back of the mall.

Plaintiffs, in contrast, allege that Wahhab was repeatedly pushed "hard" in the direction of the security office. Just inside the security office door, Wahhab heard plaintiff Amehra Brown's voice and noticed that she was being blocked from entering the security office by one of the security guards. Wahhab allegedly turned around and asked that she be allowed to enter, at which point Rushing allegedly punched Wahhab in the face and put him in a headlock. As Wahhab was attempting to pry Rushing's arms from around his neck, Rushing allegedly stated, "Now you're under arrest, asshole, you just assaulted a police officer." Rushing and several officers then allegedly forced Wahhab to the ground, punching and kicking him in the process, immobilizing his arms behind him, and repeatedly stating, "You're going to jail."

Defendants also claim that Wahhab was punched, but only once, and relate a different set of circumstances giving rise to the blow. Rouse alleges that he was struck by Wahhab "in the back of the neck, shoulder area" as the group was entering the security office. It was then that Rushing and Martin allegedly grabbed Wahhab and, with Rouse's assistance, brought Wahhab to the ground. Rouse alleges that at that time Wahhab was again instructed that he was in no trouble, would not go to jail, and that all that was required of him was to sign a paper stating he would not come back to the mall. Wahhab was allegedly then seated on a two-seated couch in the security office, while Martin went to an adjacent room to find handcuffs. According to Rushing, Rushing turned his back to Wahhab, and despite the earlier assurances that Wahhab was "in no trouble," began to call 911 to request Wahhab's arrest. Rouse, the only other person then in the room with Rushing and Wahhab, was facing Rushing. Rushing alleges that while Wahhab was seated on the couch, Wahhab became more and more irate, stating, "I don't care if you guys got guns. I have guns. I'll come back here. I will do this." As Rushing was attempting to dial 911 and simultaneously turning back around to face Wahhab, Wahhab jumped from his seat and struck Rushing in the shoulder and neck, breaking the chain that held Rushing's badge. Rushing instantly returned the blow, connecting with Wahhab's jaw. Rushing alleges that he then left the room. Soon thereafter, uniformed police officers arrived and Rushing gave an account of the crime he witnessed. Wahhab was arrested and taken to Kings County Hospital.

Plaintiffs' account of this episode differs dramatically from defendants' version. Plaintiffs allege that while seated on the couch in the security office, and after being told to "shut up" and that he was "going to jail," Wahhab stated, "But you think that I should be intimidated by you because you have a badge and a gun? Just because you have a badge and a gun doesn't mean that people should live in fear. You're not the only person I know that has a gun." Enraged at this, Rushing retaliated, "Are you threatening me? Are you threatening me?" and proceeded to grab Wahhab, push his head into the couch so the left side of his face was exposed, and sit on top of him to prevent his moving. Wahhab alleges that he was then struck in the face and body repeatedly, and then bodily thrown, several times, into another room. Just after the beating, Wahhab, wavering in and out of consciousness, maintains he heard someone say, "Let's say he's not a cop. Let's say he's a security officer."

Wahhab alleges that he spent five days in the hospital, where surgery was performed to re-attach his left jaw back to the side of his face and to pin his jaw together in the middle where it had been broken in two. He alleges that he has had three surgical procedures since then, one to remove the wiring and pins from his jaw, another to re-open the wound because of an infection, and another to have a root canal because of damage to his teeth. Other conditions Wahhab attributes to the incident in question are sharp pains in his left shoulder, numbness in his chin and lip, biting his lip when he speaks, loss of sensation in the left side of his neck, loose teeth, two broken teeth, and diminished eyesight.

1. Policy or Custom Under the Monell Doctrine

Defendant City of New York moves this court to grant summary judgment in its favor, arguing that plaintiffs have not proffered evidence showing that a custom or policy of the City caused the alleged deprivation of plaintiffs' civil rights. It is well settled that in a 42 U.S.C. Section 1983 suit a municipality may not be held liable on a theory of respondeat superior. However, a municipality may be liable for damages under section 1983 "when execution of [its] policy or custom, whether made by its lawmakers or by those whose edicts or acts may fairly be said to represent official policy, inflicts the injury...." The plaintiff alleging constitutional harm attributable to a municipality under Section 1983 "must also demonstrate that, through its *deliberate* conduct, the municipality was the 'moving force' behind the injury alleged."

There are four situations in which a municipality can be held liable under 42 U.S.C. Section 1983:

1. an officially promulgated policy endorsed or ordered by the municipality,
2. a custom or practice that is so pervasive and widespread that the municipality had either actual or constructive knowledge of it,
3. actions taken or decisions made by the municipal employee who, as a matter of state law, is responsible for establishing municipal policies with respect to the area in which the action is taken, or
4. where the failure of the municipality to train its employees rises to the level of deliberate indifference to the constitutional rights of others.

Plaintiffs' allegations of the liability on the part of the City fall under the second and fourth bases. The court addresses each of these in turn.

Under the second basis, causation may be found where a municipal policymaker's "acquiescence in a longstanding practice or custom..." constitutes the "standard operating procedure" of the local governmental entity." Here, an act performed pursuant to custom, although not formally approved, "is so widespread as to have the force of law." In *Sorlucco*, the court found that the municipality was liable because the injurious conduct of the lower echelon employees was so manifest as to have been "constructively acquiesced" in by higher-ranking policymakers.

To bolster plaintiffs' claim, plaintiffs reference reports and statistical information that suggests a widespread pattern of police misconduct. Specifically, plaintiffs cite the *Commission to Investigate Allegations of Police Corruption and the Anti-corruption Procedures of the Police Department*, known commonly as the "Mollen Commission Report," which describes a New York City Police Department ("NYPD") policy of reacting to officer misconduct with "tolerance or willful blindness." Plaintiffs also refer to statistical information obtained from the Civil Complaint Review Board's 2002 Annual Report, which reveals that in 2000, one year before the incident in question—4,113 complaints alleging misconduct were filed against New York City police officers, of which 233 were recommended for discipline. In 2001, 203 disciplinary penalties were imposed by the New York City Police Department, only one of which received termination, and only one of which received a suspension of 31 days or more or loss of vacation plus a one-year probation. Between 1999 and 2001, a total of 13,171 complaints were filed, resulting in the termination of five officers and two others receiving penalties greater than suspension for 30 days with probation for one year. Lastly, plaintiffs state that defendant Rushing has been accused of misconduct in various forms four times during the years 1998 to 2000, including use of an ethnic slur, stealing money during a stop and frisk, unjustifiable use of force, and improper threats of force and arrest.

Plaintiffs' claim that the lack of discipline with regard to complaints issued against Rushing as well as the rest of the department, together with the conclusions of the Mollen Commission Report regarding lack of discipline, could have permitted defendant Rushing to believe that his actions denying plaintiff Wahhab his civil rights would go unpunished.

In accordance with the liberal pleading requirements of the Federal Rules of Civil Procedure, a "plaintiff is not required to 'state or establish' exactly the policy by which he alleges the defendants violated his rights, nor is he required to plead more than a single instance of misconduct." Although a complaint may assert "conclusorily the existence of a policy without allegations of fact beyond the single incident alleged in the complaint," plaintiffs here have alleged statistical evidence that along with the incident alleged and prior complaints against a particular defendant, raises a material question of fact regarding an NYPD policy or custom of acquiescence in unconstitutional conduct. Therefore, defendant City of New York's Motion for Summary Judgment on the claim that a custom or policy of the City caused the alleged deprivation of plaintiffs' civil rights is denied.

2. Negligent Hiring, Screening, Retention, Supervision, and Training

Defendant City of New York argues that plaintiffs cannot establish a prima facie case of negligent hiring, screening, retention, supervision and training against the City, because Rushing and Martin were not working as NYPD officers at the time of the events at issue here. City of New York submits in support of this contention that Rushing and Martin were off duty working as mall security guards, they were in plain clothes, they were using mall-issued radios, and they acted in response to a call from a fellow member of mall security.

The City of New York's argument here is precluded by the conclusions reached in other sections of this opinion which do not relieve the City from liability for the actions of defendants Rushing and Martin. It has yet to be established whether defendants Rushing and Martin acted under color of law. Therefore, the question of whether defendant City may be liable for their negligent hiring, screening, retention, supervision and training is unresolved, and the City therefore is not entitled to summary judgment on this issue.

3. False Arrest

Defendant City of New York asserts that plaintiff Wahhab's false arrest claim should be dismissed because the uniformed NYPD officers who responded to the 911 call had probable cause to arrest him. Plaintiffs' false arrest claim is alleged against the City of New York as well as individual defendants, including Rushing and Martin. Consequently, the City of New York is potentially subject to liability in both possible arrest scenarios, either by means of actions of the uniformed officers in effecting an arrest on Mr. Wahhab, or via Rushing and Martin's actions in initially detaining and allegedly arresting Wahhab.

A Section 1983 claim for false arrest derives from the right to be free from unreasonable search and seizure, including the right to be free from arrest absent probable cause. The law of the forum state controls the elements of a Section 1983 false arrest claim. Under New York law, a plaintiff must show that (1) the defendant intentionally confined the plaintiff, (2) the plaintiff was aware of the confinement, (3) the plaintiff did not consent to the confinement, and (4) the confinement was not justified or privileged.

"There can be no federal civil rights claiming false arrest where the arresting officer had probable cause." Accordingly, probable cause is a complete defense to an action for false arrest. Probable cause is established "when the arresting officer has 'knowledge or reasonably trustworthy information', sufficient to warrant a person of reasonable caution in the belief that an offense has been committed by the person to be arrested." The focus with regard to probable cause is not on certitude, but the likelihood of criminal activity. The establishment of probable cause requires a fact-based determination that considers the "totality of the circumstances."

Probable cause will generally be found to exist when an officer is advised of a crime by a victim or an eyewitness. Where there is no dispute as to the knowledge of the officers, whether probable cause existed may be determined as a matter of law. Here, with regard to the uniformed NYPD officers' arrest of Wahhab, the facts are not in dispute as to the information upon which the uniformed officers acted. Plaintiffs' complaint alleges that Wahhab was "[a]rrested by other police officers who were called in." The uniformed officers came on the scene in response to a 911 call placed by defendant Security Guard Jovan Rouse who reported an "emergency going at [*sic*] ... the Galleria...." Upon the officers' arrival, Rushing reported to them that a crime had been committed and gave a brief description of the altercation that had occurred. The court finds this information, which was before the uniformed officers, sufficient to warrant a person of reasonable caution in the belief that a crime had been committed. Therefore, the court concludes that the uniformed NYPD officers had probable cause to arrest Wahhab, and plaintiffs' false arrest claim arising out of the uniformed officers' arrest of Wahhab is dismissed.

As to the alleged arrest by Rushing and Marin, plaintiffs state a claim as to the first three elements. According to Wahhab, he was intentionally confined upon first contact with defendants Rushing and Martin. Wahhab alleges that he was aware of this confinement and did not consent because he requested to be left alone. The last element, however, is determinative. Reading the facts in the light most favorable to the plaintiff, the information upon which Rushing and Martin acted was a call to the food court area of the Gallery requesting assistance; there was an altercation between Priftakis and Wahhab, who became agitated and knocked straws off a Top Potato counter. The court finds that a person of reasonable caution would be warranted in the belief that an offense had been committed based on these facts. Therefore, defendant City of New York's Motion for Summary Judgment as to the alleged false arrest of plaintiff Wahhab by defendants Rushing and Martin is granted.

4. Under Color of Law

For liability to attach to defendant City of New York on plaintiffs' Section 1983 claims, Rushing and Martin must have acted under color of law. It is axiomatic that "color" of law means "pretense" of law, and additionally that "acts of officers in the ambit of their personal pursuits are plainly excluded." The court of appeals in *Pitchell*, explained that although there is no bright line test for distinguishing personal pursuits from actions under color of law, more is required than the simple determination of whether the officer was on or off duty at the time of the contested actions. Liability may exist where an off-duty officer invokes the real or apparent power of the police department, or performs duties prescribed generally for police officers.

For guidance in its analysis, *Pitchell* cited *Stengel*, in which an off-duty police officer shot three men, killing two and paralyzing a third in a barfight. A jury found Belcher guilty, implicitly finding that Belcher acted under color of state law at the time of the incident. There were several facts supportive of this finding. "The chemical mace which Belcher sprayed was issued to him by the Columbus police department. Belcher carried his pistol pursuant to a regulation of the police department which required off-duty officers to carry pistols as well as mace at all times." There was also evidence that permitted the inference that Belcher intervened in the dispute pursuant to a duty imposed by police department regulations, such as the former police chief's testimony that Belcher acted under the authority of regulations requiring an officer to take action "in any type of police or criminal activity 24 hours a day," and a letter from the Director of the Department of Public Safety which closed the inquiry of the Police Firearms Board of Inquiry by exonerating Belcher because his actions were "in the line of duty."

In *Pitchell*, defendant police officers Callan and Sargis went to a bar after their shifts ended at midnight on June 18, 1987 and began drinking with Pitchell and another individual. When the bar closed, they went to Callan's apartment to continue drinking. At approximately 3:00 a.m., after discussion on a variety of topics, Callan went into another room and emerged with a gun, which he then used to shoot and seriously injure Pitchell because of something Pitchell said about former President Kennedy.

The court concluded that the defendants were not acting under color of law. Callan was not "acting in accordance with police regulation, as was the off-duty officer in *Stengel* ... nor was he invoking the authority of the police department...." He was an off-duty cop, "who while drunk in his own home, used his own personal weapon to shoot a guest."

In *Manning*, also cited by *Pitchell*, the court outlined facts to be weighed when determining whether a party acted under color of law. They included: whether defendants identified themselves as police officers at any time during the incident; if plaintiff was aware that the defendants were police officers; whether defendants detained or questioned the plaintiff in the line of duty or scope of employment as police officers; if defendants drew a firearm or arrested the plaintiff; whether defendants were engaged in any investigation or any aspect of the traditional public safety functions of police work. There, the court found that the fact that the altercation arose out of a personal matter in which the defendants were not acting in the performance of their duties militated against a finding that the defendants were acting under color of law.

The facts upon which a resolution of this issue in the instant case must rely are in conflict. For example, it is disputed whether Rushing or Martin identified themselves as police officers, whether by stating so, by showing identification, or otherwise indicating. Plaintiffs claim that Rushing or Martin "flashed his badge" upon approaching Wahhab at Top Potato. Contrarily, defendants maintain that neither Rushing nor Martin identified themselves as police officers, and Rushing introduced himself as being from security. Defendants state that a "badge of some sort" was shown to Wahhab, while Wahhab could not recall any details regarding the badge, but had seen security guards wearing shields. Further, it is not evident at this point whether there was a NYPD regulation in place requiring twenty-four–hour duty.

The use of handcuffs is also disputed. Plaintiff Wahhab contends his arms were "mechanically immobilized behind him," while Rushing alleges that he had no handcuffs on him, but normally did, and had handcuffed persons at the Gallery mall in the past. It is also disputed whether Wahhab was physically seized and transported from the food court to the security room, from the floor outside the security room to the couch in the security room, or to an adjacent room by being thrown, or whether he went voluntarily during the incident. The parties likewise disagree over whether Rushing and Martin engaged in any investigation. Plaintiffs claim two men in plain clothes "bumped chests" with Wahhab, asking "What's the problem?" In response to Wahhab's attempt to ascertain their identities, Wahhab alleges that the men "grasp[ed] him about the body and ... propel[led] him toward the food court exit." Rushing alleges in his deposition, however, that he merely attempted to calm Wahhab down, and indicated his desire to "find out what happened."

The case *Lizardo* is instructive. There, an off-duty officer working for a Denny's restaurant was found to have acted under color of law when he threatened to arrest the plaintiff for disorderly conduct. The relevant factors analyzed by the court in *Lizardo* were similar to those in each of the above cases. The court stated that "an officer can purport to exercise official authority by flashing a badge, identifying [himself] as an officer, placing an individual under arrest, or intervening in a dispute involving others pursuant to a duty imposed by ... department regulations."

In *Lizardo*, similar to Wahhab's claim that Rushing told Wahhab he was under arrest for assaulting a police officer, "in the course of escorting [the plaintiff] from the Restaurant, [the off-duty officer] threatened to arrest him for disorderly conduct. [The officer] possessed that power under state law." The court concluded that "because the officer threatened to invoke his official authority to arrest [the plaintiff], a reasonable jury could find that [the officers] purported to act pursuant to their official duties at the time of the incident."

Considering the foregoing in the light most favorable to the non-movant, because Rushing threatened to invoke his official authority, and the additional relevant factors dispute, such as whether the off-duty officers identified themselves in any manner, whether they carried or used handcuffs, whether plaintiff was aware that the defendants were police officers, and whether defendants engaged in any investigation, the court finds that defendants have not met their burden of establishing that there is no genuine issue of material fact such that they are entitled to judgment as a matter of law. Accordingly, the City of New York's Motion for Summary Judgment on this issue is denied.

5. Respondeat Superior

New York law holds employers liable where the employee acts in furtherance of the employer's business and the employer was or could have been exercising some control, either directly or indirectly, over the employee's activities.

The City of New York argues that because Rushing and Martin were not acting under color of law, liability under respondeat superior is precluded. This statement is inaccurate because although similar factual questions are involved, the inquiries are distinct, and a plaintiff may proceed on state law claims even though Section 1983 claims under *Monell* may be barred. As the court in *Mahmood* held, "The fact that a police officer uses, or abuses, his authority may be relevant in deciding whether he was acting under color of state law. It is not relevant, however, in determining whether the actions taken were within the scope of his employment."

The rules concerning scope of employment dictate that "where an employee's conduct is brought on by a matter wholly personal in nature, the source of which is not job-related, his actions cannot be said to fall within the scope of his employment." In *Mahmood*, plaintiff Mahmood, while stopped behind off-duty officer Thomas Fitzgibbon at a red light, honked his horn to alert Fitzgibbon when the light turned green. Fitzgibbon then exited his vehicle, approached Mahmood's vehicle, and attempted to punch Mahmood through the open driver's side window. After ordering Mahmood to pull over, which he did, Fitzgibbon proceeded to pull Mahmood from his vehicle and assault, yell at, and beat him. Mahmood argued that Fitzgibbon was acting in the scope of his employment as an officer when he verbally identified himself as a police officer, showed plaintiff his badge, and ordered him to pull over to the side of the road. The court stated, however, that the officer's identification "does not, by itself, establish that he was furthering the City's interest in maintaining law and order." The *Mahmood* court concluded that Fitzgibbon acted out of personal rage and that the city could therefore not be vicariously liable.

This court finds that material factual issues involved in this inquiry are in dispute. Accordingly, defendant City of New York's Motion for summary judgment as to plaintiffs' respondeat superior claim is denied.

Conclusion

In sum, defendants Cannady Security, Cannady, and Rouse's Motion for Summary Judgment is granted with respect to plaintiffs' false arrest claim. Defendants Cannady Security, Cannady, and Rouse's Motion for Summary Judgment is denied as to defendant Rouse's liability and whether Rushing and Martin (and thereby Rouse) acted under color of law.

CASE COMMENT

This case again provides an excellent illustration of the difficult factual and legal analysis required of the court. As with many cases, there were significant differences between the respective parties' version of the events that led to the arrest. Notice that the court noted and contrasted these versions in its decision. Ultimately, the court held that for purposes of summary judgment, certain key questions must be addressed. These include the existence of custom and practice, whether the arresting officers acted under color of law, and whether the city should be liable under respondeat superior. In regard to the actual arrest, the court held that the arresting officers had probable cause to make the arrest. As a practical matter, this decision on probable cause is significant because it gives the city a basis for arguing at the trial that the underlying arrest, which resulted in this lawsuit, was proper. However, if the court finds that the officer's actions subsequent to the arrest—which led to the plaintiff's injuries—could be attributable to the city, then the bad acts of the police officers would accrue to the city. In any event, these cases illustrate that the municipal government, as well as a private employer, can be liable for the actions of off-duty police officers who are either employed by or acting for a private entity.

DISCUSSION QUESTIONS

What factors do courts use to assess whether an off-duty police officer acted as a private or public actor? What factor or factors are dispositive? When a police officer is employed by a private entity, is it helpful to the business for the officer to be deemed a public actor? Why or why not? If you were a city administrator, what would you do to reduce your liability exposure from off-duty police officers working secondary employment? If you were a business owner, what would you do to reduce your liability exposure in hiring off-duty police officers?

11

Special Police/Private Security

341 U.S. 97, 71 S. Ct. 576

Supreme Court of the United States

WILLIAMS v. UNITED STATES.

Decided April 23, 1951

Background

Jay G. Williams was convicted in the District Court of the United States for the Southern District of Florida for a violation of the statute providing that whoever under color of any law willfully subjects inhabitants of a state to deprivation of rights, privileges, or immunities secured by the Constitution and laws of the United States shall be guilty of an offense, and he appealed. The United States Court of Appeals for the Fifth Circuit, affirmed the judgment, and the defendant brought certiorari.

Holding

The United States Supreme Court held that a jury could properly find that a private detective who held a special city police officer's card and obtained confessions from suspects through the use of force and violence was acting under color of law within the meaning of the civil rights statute. Judgment affirmed.

The question in this case is whether a special police officer who in his official capacity subjects a person suspected of crime to force and violence in order to obtain a confession may be prosecuted.

The statute provides in pertinent part: "Whoever, under color of any law, statute, ordinance, regulation, or custom, willfully subjects, or causes to be subjected, any inhabitant of any State, Territory, or District to the deprivation of any rights, privileges, or immunities secured or protected by the Constitution and laws of the United States ... shall be fined not more than $1,000, or imprisoned not more than one year, or both."

The facts are these: The Lindsley Lumber Co. suffered numerous thefts and hired petitioner, who operated a detective agency, to ascertain the identity of the thieves. Petitioner held a special police officer's card issued by the City of Miami, Florida, and had taken an oath and qualified as a special police officer. Petitioner and others over a period of three days took four men to a paint shack on the company's premises and used brutal methods to obtain a confession from each of them. A rubber hose, a pistol, a blunt instrument, a sash cord, and other implements were used in the project. One man was forced to look at a bright light for fifteen minutes; when he was blinded, he was repeatedly hit with a rubber hose and a sash cord and finally knocked to the floor. Another was knocked from a chair and hit in the stomach again and again. He was put back in the chair and the procedure was repeated. One was backed against the wall and jammed in the chest with a club. Each was beaten, threatened, and unmercifully punished for several hours until he confessed. One Ford, a policeman, was sent by his superior to lend authority to the proceedings. And petitioner, who committed the assaults, went about flashing his badge.

The indictment charged among other things that petitioner acting under color of law used force to make each victim confess to his guilt and implicate others, and that the victims were denied the right to be tried by due process of law and if found guilty to be sentenced and punished in accordance with the laws of the state. Petitioner was found guilty by a jury. The court of appeals affirmed.

We think it clear that petitioner was acting under color of law, or at least that the jury could properly so find. We interpreted the phrase "misuse of power, possessed by virtue of state law and made possible only because the wrongdoer is clothed with the authority of state law, is action taken under color of state law." It is common practice for private guards or detectives to be vested with policemen's powers. We know from the record that that is the policy of Miami, Florida. Moreover, this was an investigation conducted under the aegis of the State, as evidenced by the fact that a regular police officer was detailed to attend it. We need go no further to conclude that the lower court, to whom we give deference on local law matters, was correct in holding that petitioner was no mere interloper but had a semblance of policeman's power from Florida. There was, therefore, evidence that he acted under authority of Florida law; and the manner of his conduct of the interrogations makes clear that he was asserting the authority granted him and not acting in the role of a private person.

The main contention is that the application of [the statute] so as to sustain a conviction for obtaining a confession by use of force and violence is unconstitutional. The argument is the one that a clear majority of the Court rejected in *Screws v. United States*, and runs as follows:

Criminal statutes must have an ascertainable standard of guilt or they fall for vagueness. The statute, it is argued, lacks the necessary specificity when rights under the Due Process Clause of the Fourteenth Amendment are involved. We are pointed to the course of decisions by this Court under the Due Process Clause as proof of the vague and fluid standard for "rights, privileges, or immunities secured or protected by the Constitution" as used in [the statute]. We are referred to decisions where we have been closely divided on whether state action violated due process. More specifically we are cited many instances where the Court has been conspicuously in disagreement on the illegal character of confessions under the Due Process Clause. If the Court cannot agree as to what confessions violate the Fourteenth Amendment, how can one who risks criminal prosecutions for his acts be sure of the standard? Thus it is sought to show that police officers such as petitioner walk on ground far too treacherous for criminal responsibility.

Many criminal statutes might be extended to circumstances so extreme as to make their application unconstitutional. Conversely, as we held in *Screws v. United States*, a close construction will often save an act from vagueness that is fatal. The present case is as good an illustration as any. It is as plain as a pikestaff that the present confessions would not be allowed in evidence whatever the school of thought concerning the scope and meaning of the Due Process Clause. This is the classic use of force to make a man testify against himself. The result is as plain as if the rack, the wheel, and the thumbscrew—the ancient methods of securing evidence by torture, were used to compel the confession. Some day the application of [the statute] to less obvious methods of coercion may be presented and doubts as to the adequacy of the standard of guilt may be presented. There may be a similar doubt when an officer is tried under [the statute] for beating a man to death. That was a doubt stirred in the *Screws* case; and it was the reason we held that the purpose must be plain, the deprivation of the constitutional right willful. But where police take matters in their own hands, seize victims, beat and pound them until they confess, there cannot be the slightest doubt that the police have deprived the victim of a right under the Constitution. It is the right of the accused to be tried by a legally constituted court, not by a kangaroo court. Hence when officers wring confessions from the accused by force and violence, they violate some of the most fundamental, basic, and well-established constitutional rights which every citizen enjoys. Petitioner and his associates acted willfully and purposely; their aim was precisely to deny the protection that the Constitution affords. It was an arrogant and brutal deprivation of rights which the Constitution specifically guarantees. The statute would be denied the high service for which it was designed if rights so palpably plain were denied its protection. Only casuistry could make vague and nebulous what our constitutional scheme makes so clear and specific.

The indictment charged that petitioners deprived designated persons of rights and privileges secured to them by the Fourteenth Amendment. These deprivations were defined in the indictment to include "illegal" assault and battery. But the meaning of these rights in the context of the indictment was plain: immunity from the use of force and violence to obtain a confession. Thus Count 2 of the indictment charges that the Fourteenth Amendment rights of one Purnell were violated in the following respects:

> [T]he right and privilege not to be deprived of liberty without due process of law, the right and privilege to be secure in his person while in the custody of the State of Florida, the right and privilege not to be subjected to punishment without due process of law, the right and privilege to be immune, while in the custody of persons acting under color of the laws of the State of Florida, from illegal assault and battery by any person exercising the authority of said State, and the right and privilege to be tried by due process of law and if found guilty to be sentenced and punished in accordance with the laws of the State of Florida; that is to say, on or about the 28th day of March, 1947, the defendants arrested and detained and caused to be arrested and detained the said Frank J. Purnell, Jr., and brought and caused him to be brought to and into a certain building sometimes called a shack on the premises of the Lindsley Lumber Co., at or near 3810 N.W. 17th Avenue, in said City of Miami, Florida, and did there detain the said Frank J. Purnell, Jr., and while he was so detained the defendants did then and there illegally strike, bruise, batter, beat, assault and torture the said Frank J. Purnell, Jr., in order illegally to coerce and force the said Frank J. Purnell, Jr., to make an admission and confession of his guilt in connection with the alleged theft of personal property, alleged to be the property of said Lindsley Lumber Co., and in order illegally to coerce and force the said Frank J. Purnell, Jr., to name and accuse other persons as participants in alleged thefts of personal property, alleged to be the property of the said Lindsley Lumber Co., and for the purpose of imposing illegal summary punishment upon the said Frank J. Purnell, Jr.

The trial judge in his charge to the jury summarized Count 2 as meaning that the defendants beat Purnell for the purpose of forcing him to make a confession and for the purpose of imposing illegal summary punishment upon him. He further made clear that the defendants were not here on trial for a violation of any law of the State of Florida for assault or for assault under any laws of the United States. There cannot be the slightest doubt from the reading of the indictment and charge as a whole that the defendants were charged with and tried for one of the most brutal deprivations of constitutional rights that can be imagined. It therefore strains at technicalities to say that any issue of vagueness of [the statute] as construed and applied is present in the case. Our concern is to see that substantial justice is done, not to search the record for possible errors which will defeat the great purpose of Congress in enacting [the statute].

Affirmed

CASE COMMENT

In this case, the private security officer vested with "special police" powers used his powers to coerce confessions from a prisoners. The U.S. Supreme Court held that the special police officer was a state actor who exercised the coercive punishment under color of law. Since the actions were done under color of law, the Fifth Amendment prohibition against coercive punishment applies. Notice that the Fifth Amendment would therefore have precluded the punishment from being used against the prisoner (Purnell) at his criminal trial. In this case, however, the security officer, Williams, was being tried in criminal court for the constitutional deprivations. The court upheld Williams's criminal conviction for the Fifth Amendment deprivation.

378 U.S. 130, 84 S. Ct. 1770

Supreme Court of the United States

WILLIAM L. GRIFFIN ET AL., PETITIONERS v. STATE OF MARYLAND.

Decided June 22, 1964

Background

Defendants were convicted of criminal trespass upon premises of private amusement park. The Circuit Court for Montgomery County, Maryland, rendered judgment, and defendants appealed. The Maryland Court of Appeals affirmed the convictions. Certiorari was granted.

Holding

The Supreme Court held that person deputized as sheriff and was employee of park, under contract to protect and enforce racial segregation policy, in ordering Negroes to leave park and arresting them for trespassing denied them equal protection of the laws secured by the Fourteenth Amendment. Their convictions were required to be set aside.

Reversed

Petitioners were convicted of criminal trespass for refusing to leave a privately owned and operated amusement park in the State of Maryland at the command of an employee of the amusement park acting under color of his authority as a deputy sheriff.

The Glen Echo Amusement Park is located in Montgomery County, Maryland, near Washington, D.C. Though the park through its advertisements sought the patronage of the general public, it was (until recently) the park's policy to exclude Negroes who wished to patronize its facilities. No signs at the park apprised persons of this policy or otherwise indicated that all comers were not welcome. No tickets of admission were required. In protest against the park's policy of segregation a number of whites and Negroes picketed the park on June 30, 1960. The petitioners, five young Negroes, were participating in the protest. Hopeful that the management might change its policy, they entered the park, and encountered no resistance from the park employees, boarded the carousel. They possessed transferable tickets, previously purchased by others, entitling the holder to ride on the carousel.

The park employed one Collins as a special policeman by arrangement with the National Detective Agency. Although Collins was formally retained and paid by the agency and wore its uniform, he was subject to the control and direction of the park management. Apparently at the request of the park, Collins had been deputized as a sheriff of Montgomery County, wearing this badge on the outside of his uniform.

When Collins saw the petitioners sitting on the carousel waiting for the ride to begin, he reported their presence to the park manager. The manager told Collins that petitioners were to be arrested for trespassing if they would not leave the park. Collins then went up to the petitioners and told them that it was the park's policy "not to have colored people on the rides, or in the park." He ordered petitioners to leave within five minutes. They declined to do so, pointing out that they had tickets for the carousel. There was no evidence that any of the petitioners were disorderly. At the end of the five-minute period Collins, as he testified, went to each defendant and told them that the time was up and that they were under arrest for trespassing. Collins transported the petitioners to the Montgomery County police station. There he filled out a form titled "Application for Warrant by Police Officer." The application stated:

> Francis J. Collins, being first duly sworn, on oath doth depose and say: That he is a member of the Montgomery deputy sheriff Department and as such, on the 30th day of June, 1960, at about the hour of 8:45 p.m. he did observe the defendant William L. Griffin in Glen Echo Park which is private property. On order of Kebar Inc. owners of Glen Echo Park the defendant was asked to leave the park and after giving him reasonable time to comply the defendant refused to leave (and) he was placed under arrest for trespassing.... Whereas, Francis J. Collins doth further depose and say that he, as a member of the Montgomery County Police Department believes that [arrestee] is violating Sec. 577 Article 27 of the Annotated Code of Maryland.

Art. 27, Sec. 577, is a criminal trespass statute. On the same day a Maryland Justice of the Peace issued a warrant which charged that petitioner Griffin "did enter upon and pass over the land and premises of Glen Echo Park ... after having been told by the Deputy Sheriff for Glen Echo Park, to leave the Property, and after giving him a reasonable time to comply, he did not leave ... contrary to the ... [Maryland criminal trespass statute] and against the peace, government and dignity of the State." The warrant recited that the complaint had been made by "Collins Deputy Sheriff." An amended warrant was later filed. It stated that the complaint had been made by "Collins, Deputy Sheriff" but charged Griffin with unlawfully entering the park after having been told not to do so by "an Agent" of the corporation which operated the park. Presumably identical documents were filed with respect to the other petitioners.

Petitioners were tried and convicted of criminal trespass in the Circuit Court of Montgomery County. Each was sentenced to pay a fine of $100. The Maryland Court of Appeals affirmed the convictions. That court, rejecting the petitioners' constitutional claims, reasoned as follows:

> The appellants in this case ... were arrested for criminal trespass committed in the presence of a special deputy sheriff of Montgomery County (who was also the agent of the park operator) after they had been duly notified to leave but refused to do so. It follows—since the offense for which these appellants were arrested was a misdemeanor committed in the presence of the park officer who had a right to arrest them, either in his private capacity as an agent or employee of the operator of the park or in his limited capacity as a special deputy sheriff in the amusement park ... the arrest of these appellants for a criminal trespass in this manner was no more than if a regular police officer had been called upon to make the arrest for a crime committed in his presence.... The arrest and conviction of these appellants for a criminal trespass as a result of the enforcement by the operator of the park of its lawful policy of segregation, did not constitute such action.

Collins—in ordering the petitioners to leave the park and in arresting and instituting prosecutions against them—purported to exercise the authority of a deputy sheriff. He wore a sheriff's badge and consistently identified himself as a deputy sheriff rather than as an employee of the park. Though an amended warrant was filed stating that petitioners had committed an offense because they entered the park after an "agent" of the park told them not to do so, this change has little, if any, bearing on the character of the authority which Collins initially purported to exercise. If an individual is possessed of state authority and purports to act under that authority, his action is state action. It is irrelevant that he might have taken the same action had he acted in a purely private capacity or that the particular action which he took was not authorized by state law. Thus, it is clear that Collins's action was state action. The only question remaining in this case is whether Collins's action denied petitioners the equal protection of the laws secured to them by the Fourteenth Amendment. If it did, these convictions are invalid.

It cannot be disputed that if the State of Maryland had operated the amusement park on behalf of the owner thereof, and had enforced the owner's policy of racial segregation against petitioners, petitioners would have been deprived of the equal protection of the laws.

In the *Board of Trusts* case we were confronted with the following situation. Stephen Girard by will had left a fund in trust to establish a college. He had provided in his will, in effect, that only "poor white male orphans" were to be admitted. The fund was administered by the Board of Directors of City Trusts of the City of Philadelphia as trustee. In accord with the provisions of the will it denied admission to two Negro applicants who were otherwise qualified. We held:

"The Board which operates Girard College is an agency of the State of Pennsylvania. Therefore, even though the Board was acting as a trustee, its refusal to admit Foust and Felder to the college because they were Negroes was discrimination by the State. Such discrimination is forbidden by the Fourteenth Amendment." The Board of Trusts case must be taken to establish that to the extent that the State undertakes an obligation to enforce a private policy of racial segregation, the State is charged with racial discrimination and violates the Fourteenth Amendment.

It is argued that the State may nevertheless constitutionally enforce an owner's desire to exclude particular persons from his premises even if the owner's desire is in turn motivated by a discriminatory purpose. The State, it is said, is not really enforcing a policy of segregation since the owner's ultimate purpose is immaterial to the State. In this case it cannot be said that Collins was simply enforcing the park management's desire to exclude designated individuals from the premises. The president of the corporation which owned and managed the park testified that he had instructed Collins to enforce the park's policy of racial segregation. Collins was told to exclude Negroes from the park and escort them from the park if they entered. He was instructed to arrest Negroes for trespassing if they did not leave the park when he ordered them to do so. In short, Collins, as stated by the Maryland Court of Appeals, was "then under contract to protect and enforce ... [the] racial segregation policy of the operator of the amusement park...." Pursuant to this obligation Collins ordered petitioners to leave and arrested them, as he testified, because they were Negroes. This was state action forbidden by the Fourteenth Amendment. Reversed.

CASE COMMENT

The racial segregation policy of the park, which was enforced by a special police officer, violated the Fourteenth Amendment. The court noted that the special police officer acted under color of law, even though he could be construed as acting as an agent for the business owner. By contemporary standards, this is an "easy" decision. Such racially discriminatory policies are reprehensible. The use of a special police officer to enforce these policies placed the state in the position of aiding and abetting the constitutional deprivation.

834 N.E.2d 760

Appeals Court of Massachusetts, Suffolk

CHRISTOPHER YOUNG v. BOSTON UNIVERSITY.

Decided Sept. 22, 2005

Background

Arrestee, who was arrested by university police officer for alleged violation of abuse prevention order requiring him to stay at least 30 yards away from a certain university student, brought action against the university, alleging assault and battery, false imprisonment, civil rights violations, and other claims based on allegation that university police lacked authority or probable cause to arrest him. The Superior Court Department, Suffolk County, granted summary judgment in favor of university. Arrestee appealed.

Holdings

The appeals court held that:

1. University police officer had authority to arrest arrestee on public street near campus; and
2. Officer had probable cause to make the arrest.

Affirmed

We summarize the undisputed facts, drawing inferences in favor of Young where they may reasonably be drawn from the facts. On February 27, 1996, Courtney Cronin, a BU student, obtained a G.L. c. 209A abuse prevention order against Young, a BU alumnus, requiring Young to stay at least 30 yards away from Cronin. On October 9, 1996, as Cronin left a BU building located at 1 University Road, she saw Young parked in his vehicle across the street. She immediately went back inside and called the BU police department to report an apparent violation of the c. 209A order, providing a description of Young's vehicle. During this time, Young drove away from the area. Officers

Daniel DiGiovine and Richard Camillo responded to Cronin's call. Officer DiGiovine confirmed that there was a c. 209A order in place; he also observed that the area where Cronin stated Young was parked was within thirty yards of where Cronin left the building. Two hours later, the dispatcher informed a patrolling BU officer, Robert Casey, that Young was wanted for violating a c. 209A order and gave Officer Casey a description of Young's car. When Officer Casey thereafter observed the vehicle on Commonwealth Avenue, he stopped and arrested Young, who was driving, near the intersection of Commonwealth Avenue and Babcock Street. Soon after the arrest, BU indefinitely barred Young from its property.

Arrest-Related Claims

Young argues that it was not established as a matter of undisputed fact that Officer Casey held an appointment as a special State police officer or a deputy sheriff in Suffolk County at the time of the arrest. Officer Casey's affidavit, stating that on the day of the arrest he held an appointment as a special State police officer under G.L. c. 22C, Section 63, and a commission as a Suffolk County deputy sheriff, is unrebutted by sufficient evidence. In order to defeat a motion for summary judgment, a plaintiff cannot rely merely on allegations set forth in his pleadings or on bald assertions that facts are disputed.

Young next argues that, as matter of law, the officer lacked authority or jurisdiction to arrest Young on a public street near BU for an alleged violation of a c. 209A order occurring on BU property. General Laws provides that employees of a university who are appointed as special State police officers "have the same power to make arrests as regular police officers for any criminal offense committed in or upon lands or structures owned, used or occupied by such ... university." We conclude that, as a special State police officer, a BU police officer's authority extends to the environs surrounding the campus when the "special vigilance of an officer might be required to keep the peace and preserve order amongst those frequenting the [university and] those carrying persons to and from it." This case is similar to *Commonwealth v. Mottola*, where we held that police officers of the Massachusetts Bay Transportation Authority (MBTA) had the "authority to question and arrest the defendant at the East Boston High School, at least where ... the offense originated on MBTA property and related to the protection of an MBTA passenger."

We similarly reject Young's argument that the officers did not have probable cause to arrest him. On the undisputed facts, the BU police had a reasonable belief that Young had violated the c. 209A order based on Cronin's statements to the officers, the officers' observations that the area where Cronin said Young was parked was within 30 yards of Cronin, and Officer DiGiovine's confirmation of the existence of the restraining order.

The arresting officer was justified in his reliance on the information gathered by other officers, as the knowledge of one officer is the knowledge of all.

We affirm the summary judgment.

CASE COMMENT

In this case, the fact that the university police officer has "special police" power gave him the legal authority to stop the driver and arrest him for the order of protection. The probable cause to affect the arrest was based on information obtained from other university police officers. As such, the stop and the subsequent arrest were valid, as they were within the authority vested in special police officers. In addition, the arresting officer reasonably relied on information from objective facts verified by other officers to substantiate the arrest.

428 F.3d 629

United States Court of Appeals, Sixth Circuit

STELLA ROMANSKI, PLAINTIFF-APPELLEE v. DETROIT ENTERTAINMENT, LLC, D/B/A/ MOTORCITY CASINO, A MICHIGAN LIMITED LIABILITY COMPANY; MARLENE BROWN, DEFENDANTS-APPELLANTS, GLORIA BROWN; ROBERT EDWARDS; AND JOETTA STEVENSON, DEFENDANTS.

Oct. 28, 2005

Background

Casino patron sued casino and casino security officer in state court under Section 1983 and state law for unlawful and false arrest, which occurred when she took a 5-cent token from the tray of one slot machine and played it in another. Following a jury trial, the United States District Court for the Eastern District of Michigan entered judgment for patron, which included an $875,000 punitive damages award.

Holdings

The court of appeals held that security officer was a state actor as a matter of law.

Affirmed in part, vacated in part, and remanded

On August 7, 2001, Romanski, then 72 years old, and her friends Dorothy Dombrowski and Linda Holman, went to Defendant Detroit Entertainment's Motor City Casino in Detroit, Michigan, to gamble and enjoy lunch at the buffet. After a spate of unsuccessful tries at the slot machines, Romanski took a walk around the gaming floor. During her walk, Romanski noticed a 5-cent token lying in a slot machine's tray. Seeing no chair at the machine, she picked up the token and returned to the machine at which she had earlier played, intending to use the token there. Soon a uniformed male casino employee approached and asked that she accompany him to the office. She asked why but he did not answer. Romanski then noticed there were also three female casino employees, not in uniform, surrounding her; she felt she could not move.

One of these plain-clothed security officers was Defendant Marlene Brown, who had been assigned to patrol the casino floor at that time. Brown testified that she approached Romanski, displayed her casino security badge, and began to explain it was the casino's policy not to permit patrons to pick up tokens, which appeared to be abandoned, found at other slot machines, a practice known as "slot-walking." Romanski could not have known this at the time because the casino does not post the so-called policy anywhere. It is undisputed, therefore, that Romanski did not have—and could not have had—notice of the casino's purported policy on slot-walking.

According to Brown, Romanski became loud and belligerent, so, at the advice of Brown's supervisor, JoEtta Stevenson, Brown escorted Romanski to an off-the-floor room where Brown intended to explain the policy in detail. For her part, Romanski testified that Brown did not detain her because of her attitude but rather because Brown suspected her of theft.

It is undisputed that Brown and her colleagues escorted Romanski to what defendants alternately call the "security office" and the "interview room." Whatever its name, the room is small and windowless, located off the casino's floor. According to Romanski, once they had taken their seats, Brown accused Romanski of stealing the token, whereupon Brown counted Romanski's money and removed one nickel from Romanski's winnings. Stevenson asked Romanski to turn over her social security card and driver's license. Romanski complied and these items were photocopied. Romanski was then photographed. Romanski testified that she acquiesced to these requests because Brown said she was a police officer, had a badge, and appeared to have handcuffs. Brown admitted having presented her badge and possessing handcuffs but testified that she identified herself only as a "security police officer," not as a bona fide police officer. There is no dispute that a uniformed casino security officer stood just outside the room for the duration of the questioning.

Romanski was ejected from the casino for a period of 6 months. Stevenson made the final decision to eject, or "86," Romanski. The precise ground for ejecting Romanski is unclear from the record. Although unknown to Romanski at the time, it is now undisputed that Brown and some of her colleagues on the casino's security staff were licensed under state law as "private security police officer[s]." By virtue of being so licensed, a private security police officer has "the authority to arrest a person without a warrant as set forth for public peace officers ... when that private security police officer is on the employer's premises." The statute additionally requires that private security police officers make arrests only when they are on duty and in "the full uniform of their employer." It is undisputed that Brown was on duty during the events of this case. It is also undisputed that Brown was not wearing the uniform worn by some of the other security guards, but defendants have never contended that this rendered Brown out of uniform for purposes of the statute. Indeed, defendants have conceded from the beginning that the statute applies in this case. Their argument is simply that the power admittedly conferred on Brown by the statute did not make her actions under color of state law.

Brown was in charge of escorting Romanski to the valet parking area of the casino, where Romanski was to wait for her 3 p.m. bus home. Brown and her colleagues denied Romanski's request to meet her friends for lunch at the buffet—indeed, they did not permit Romanski to eat lunch at all. In addition, they did not permit Romanski to enter the restroom by herself. Brown accompanied Romanski into the restroom and waited outside the stall. At 3 p.m., Romanski exited the valet area to board what she thought was her bus; it turned out not to be but instead of returning to the valet area she ran into her friends and stayed outside. It was extremely hot and humid and Dombrowski and Holman persuaded Romanski to return to the casino. Upon entering, the three were confronted by casino employees, who directed them to return to the valet area, which is air-conditioned; they waited there until the bus arrived.

It is undisputed that Brown prepared an incident report following Romanski's ejection in which Brown referred to Romanski as a "suspect." Romanski introduced the casino's security manual into evidence; it instructs security employees to refer to patrons as "suspects" only if the employee arrested the patron and otherwise to refer to the patron as a "subject." Stevenson confirmed that this policy was in effect when Romanski was ejected. Finally, it is undisputed that as a matter of course, the casino notifies the Michigan State Police when it ejects someone. The casino notified the Michigan State Police of Romanski's ejection.

As these facts reflect, defendants' treatment of Romanski was inexplicable and egregious. The district court aptly expressed the egregiousness of defendants' conduct in its opinion denying defendants' motion for summary judgment:

> There is sufficient evidence to allow a jury to find that after [Romanski] picked up an abandoned token that defendants—by using the authority vested in them by the State of Michigan—surrounded her, arrested her, led her to the security office, prevented her from leaving the security office, and stole the 5 cents that she found from her. Afterwards, they surrounded her as they threw her out of the casino, and refused to let her use the restroom by herself. Defendants also prevented her from having lunch with her friends [and] falsely told her friends that she had stolen from them.... [A] jury could certainly exclaim "Outrageous."

Indeed, a jury *did* make such an exclamation: it found in Romanski's favor and made a substantial punitive damages award.

The plaintiff's complaint asserts a claim under 42 U.S.C. Section 1983 that defendants had violated Romanski's Fourth Amendment rights. Specifically, Romanski alleged that defendants, acting under color of state law, had arrested her without probable cause because the token she picked up was abandoned, i.e., not the casino's property. The district court issued an order to show cause "as to whether defendants' conduct was 'under color of law' for purposes of 42 U.S.C. Section 1983." The court concluded that Brown was acting under color of state law because she possessed the same authority to make arrests that the police enjoy. Having determined that there was a proper basis for federal jurisdiction, the district court exercised its supplemental jurisdiction over Romanski's state law claims.

The court held as a matter of law that defendants had acted under color of state law during the events of this case because Brown, the defendant who initiated Romanski's detention, did so while on duty in her capacity as a licensed private security police officer empowered with the same arrest authority as a public police officer. The court further held that genuine factual disputes precluded summary judgment on the Fourth Amendment claim and Romanski's state law claims.

State Action

Section 1983 makes liable only those who, while acting under color of state law, deprive another of a right secured by the Constitution or federal law. A private actor acts under color of state law when its conduct is "fairly attributable to the state." "The Supreme Court has developed three tests for determining the existence of state action in a particular case: (1) the public function test, (2) the state compulsion test, and (3) the symbiotic relationship or nexus test."

The district court concluded that Brown and any of her colleagues similarly licensed as private security police officers were state actors under the public function test. Consistent with this holding, the district court took the state action issue out of the case, granting in effect judgment as a matter of law to Romanski on that issue.

Under the public function test, a private entity is said to be performing a public function if it is exercising powers traditionally reserved to the state, such as holding elections, taking private property under the eminent domain power, or operating a company-owned town. The Supreme Court has expressly left open the question whether and under what circumstances private police officers may be said to perform a public function for purposes of Section 1983. Nevertheless, as the district court observed, there is a growing body of case law to consult for guidance on this question.

For example, in a decision deemed by both parties and the district court to bear directly on the issue presented in this case, the Seventh Circuit held that private police officers licensed to make arrests could be state actors under the public function test. To be sure, *Payton* held that by virtue of their status as on-duty special police officers, licensed by the city of Chicago, the defendants enjoyed "virtually the same power as public police officers." Indeed, the defendants in *Payton* operated under an ordinance which provided that special police officers "shall possess the powers of the regular police patrol at the places for which they are respectively appointed or in the line of duty for which they are engaged."

This broad delegation of power, the Seventh Circuit reasoned, distinguished *Payton* from an earlier case in which the court had held that a private security guard endowed with more limited police-type powers was not a state actor. See *Wade v. Byles*. The defendant in *Wade* was permitted to carry a handgun and to use deadly force in self-defense but could arrest someone only for "trespass pending the arrival of the police" and could exercise these powers only in the lobbies of properties owned by the public housing authority for which he worked. The defendant was not a state actor because, as the court put it in *Payton*, "none of these powers had been exclusively reserved to the police—citizen's arrests and the rights to carry handguns and use them in self-defense are available to individuals outside of the law enforcement community."

Payton illustrates a line that has been drawn in the case law. The line divides cases in which a private actor exercises a power traditionally reserved to the state, but not exclusively reserved to it, e.g., the common law shopkeeper's privilege, from cases in which a private actor exercises a power exclusively reserved to the state, e.g., the police power. Where private security guards are endowed by law with plenary police powers such that they are de facto police officers, they may qualify as state actors under the public function test. (Cases and citations omitted.) The rationale of these cases is that when the state delegates a power traditionally reserved to it alone—the police power—to private actors in order that they may provide police services to institutions that need it, a "plaintiff's ability to claim relief under Section 1983 [for abuses of that power] should be unaffected."

On the other side of the line illustrated by *Payton* are cases in which the private defendants have some police-like powers but not plenary police authority. These are cases in which a private institution's security employees have been dispatched to protect the institution's interests or enforce its policies. The canonical example here is when a store avails itself of the common law shopkeeper's privilege, the privilege at issue in this Court's decision in *Chapman v. Higbee Co.*, and the Fifth Circuit case upon which *Chapman* relied.

Like the district court, we think this case falls on the *Payton* side of the line. It is undisputed that Brown (and some of her colleagues) were private security police officers licensed under the state statute. This means that Brown's qualifications for being so licensed were vetted by Michigan's department of state police, and that Brown was subject to certain statutes administered by that department. More critical for present purposes are the undisputed facts that Brown was on duty and on the casino's premises at all times relevant to this case. These undisputed facts lead to an inescapable conclusion of law—namely, that at all times relevant to this case, Brown "had the authority to arrest a person without a warrant as set forth for public peace officers...." One consequence of Brown's possession of this authority, the authority to make arrests at one's discretion and for any offenses, is clear: at all times relevant to this case, Brown was a state actor as a matter of law.

Unlike the common law privileges at issue in *Wade* (the use of deadly force in self-defense, the right to detain for trespass, and the right to carry a weapon) and *Chapman* (the shopkeeper's privilege), which may be invoked by any citizen under appropriate circumstances, the plenary arrest power enjoyed by private security police officers licensed pursuant to the statute is a power traditionally reserved to the state alone.

Instead, a licensed private security officer's arrest power is plenary in the sense that while on her employer's property during her working hours, a private security officer can make warrantless arrests to the same extent as a public police officer. The instant case closely resembles *Henderson*, a case where the court found state action when the state delegated to university police officers a full power of arrest limited to campus property.

In contrast, the private security officers in *Wade* only had the power to "arrest people for criminal trespass...." As the Seventh Circuit later pointed out, the private security officers in *Wade* would have to "dial 911" if they witnessed a crime other than criminal trespass. Under Michigan law, a private security officer has no such limitation.

Defendants contend that *Wade* ought to control here because, as in that case, private security police officers' power to make arrests is subject to spatial or geographic limits. But the spatial or geographic limitation in *Wade* was profound—it prohibited housing authority security guards from exercising their (already minimal) powers anywhere except in the lobbies of buildings operated by the housing authority. By contrast, [Michigan statute citation] invests private security police officers with full arrest authority on the entirety of their employer's premises, which makes this case distinguishable from *Wade* and similar to *Payton* and *Henderson*, each of which involved a statute or ordinance that imposed or contemplated some spatial or geographic limits on the private defendants' police powers. Furthermore, as we have discussed, private security police officers in Michigan are endowed with plenary arrest authority, while the defendant in *Wade* was permitted to exercise only what were in effect citizens' arrests.

Finally, we address defendants' repeated representation that although empowered to make arrests under [Michigan statute citation], Brown and the other casino employees licensed under the statute are, as a matter of casino policy, not permitted to exercise this statutory authority to effectuate arrests. For this argument defendants again rely on *Wade*, in which the very document that was the source of the defendant's police-type powers, his contract with the public housing authority, at the same time imposed profound limits on those powers. Here the source of Brown's power to make arrests is a statute that includes no qualitative limits on that power, so *Wade* is inapplicable. Defendants do not cite a case in which a private security officer licensed to make arrests as under [Michigan statute citation] was held not to be a state actor on the ground that the officer's employer substantially circumscribed the arrest power conferred on the officer by having been licensed. The only arguable support we have found for defendants' argument is the concurring opinion in *Payton*, in which Judge Ripple opined that while for pleading purposes the plaintiff's claim of state action was viable, it might ultimately fail because "further development of the record might well establish ... that the guards' responsibilities were significantly circumscribed by their employer and that they performed well-defined functions quite narrow in scope...."

In this case, whatever development of the record occurred did not reveal circumscriptions of Brown's authority, let alone circumscriptions of the sort contemplated by Judge Ripple in *Payton*. Indeed, it is noteworthy that defendants did not even make this argument at the summary judgment stage of the proceedings, arguing instead that while Brown and some of her colleagues *do* have the power to make arrests, Brown did not use it in this case. It is not surprising then, that in their brief to this court, defendants do not offer a single citation to the record in support of the contention that Brown's arrest authority was substantially circumscribed. Furthermore, the jury found that defendants had in fact arrested Romanski and this aspect of the judgment is not on appeal (defendants' jury instruction claim goes to whether probable cause existed, not whether an arrest occurred). Under these circumstances, we decline defendants' invitation to look past [Michigan statute citation] express grant of plenary arrest authority to private security police officers. We similarly find unpersuasive the representation made on appeal that Brown was not acting pursuant to her [Michigan statute citation] authority when she initiated the unlawful arrest of Romanski, but rather was merely protecting the casino's self-interest—conduct, defendants maintain, that was more in the nature exercising the shopkeeper's privilege. Quite apart from the question whether Michigan's version of the shopkeeper's privilege even applies to casinos, there is no evidence in the record that could support the self-protection narrative defendants urge us to adopt. Indeed, all of the evidence was to the contrary: Brown was employed by the casino as a private security police officer and was on duty in that capacity when she initiated the detention of Romanski.

Consistent with the Seventh Circuit's approach in *Wade* and *Payton*, we have focused on the specific powers that Brown, in her capacity as an on-duty and duly licensed private security police officer, had at her disposal. Because at least one of these powers, the plenary arrest power, is "traditionally the exclusive prerogative of the state," and because it is undisputed that Brown was in fact duly licensed under [Michigan statute citation] and was in fact on duty at all times relevant to this case, the district court correctly held that Brown was a state actor as a matter of law.

Conclusion

We **VACATE** the punitive damages portion of the district court' s judgment, **AFFIRM** the judgment in all other respects, and **REMAND** for proceedings consistent with this opinion.

CASE COMMENT

In this case, the Michigan statute providing arrest powers as a "private security police officer" is analogous to a "special police" officer noted in other cases. In its decision, the court provides an excellent overview of the distinction between a private security officer and a police officer. A key distinction relates to the question of whether the officer acted as a state actor under color of law. In this case, the Michigan statute provided plenary power to "private security police officers," giving them broad arrest powers on the par with police (peace) officers. Given this broad legal authority afforded by the legislature, the court had no trouble finding that the officer was a state actor. Because the court reached this conclusion, the 1983 claim asserted by the plaintiff was actionable.

The jury award of $870,000 in punitive damages (reduced by the court to $600,000) to the plaintiff in a case that arose from a dispute over a nickel token from a slot machine serves as an ironic and instructive footnote to this case. Obviously when considered in light of the potentially enormous ramifications of a misstep by a security guard, the importance of clearly defined security policies and procedures cannot be overstated.

340 F. Supp. 2d 308

United States District Court, E.D. New York

CLAUDIE PIERRE, ON BEHALF OF HERSELF AND AS A REPRESENTATIVE OF SIMILARLY SITUATED INDIVIDUALS, PLAINTIFF v. J. C. PENNEY COMPANY, INC., ET AL., DEFENDANTS.

Nov. 3, 2004

Background

Black customer brought action against store, alleging store security guards denied her equal benefit of the law under Section 1981 and violated Fourth Amendment when they detained her on suspicions of shoplifting. Store moved to dismiss.

Holdings

The district court held that:

1. Customer sufficiently alleged nexus between store and a state law for the protection of persons and property to support equal benefit claim under Section 1981, but
2. Fourth Amendment constrains state action, not purely private action.

Motion granted in part and denied in part

Plaintiff's allegations arise out of an incident that occurred on September 20, 2002, at a J. C. Penney store in Queens, New York. After leaving the store without making a purchase, plaintiff was approached by J. C. Penney security guards on the street. She claims that they accused her of shoplifting and forced her to return to the store. She alleges that she was verbally and physically abused. It is undisputed that a search revealed no stolen merchandise. Plaintiff became increasingly upset, but was not allowed to leave the detention area for nearly three hours. She claims that the security guards attempted to force her to sign a false confession, which she refused to do. Plaintiff requested a copy of the incident report but never received one. Security personnel did not call the police or file a complaint against her. Plaintiff, however, filed a police complaint against the store on September 23, 2002.

Plaintiff alleges that she was singled out because she is black. She also claims that she saw only nonwhite shoppers in detention, although she had seen many white customers shopping in the store.

J. C. Penney moves to dismiss claiming that (1) plaintiff has not stated a Section 1981 equal benefit claim because there is no nexus between defendant's actions and the state, and (2) that plaintiff cannot raise a Fourth Amendment claim against a nongovernmental actor.

A. Section 1981 Equal Benefit Claim

Section 1981(a) provides in relevant part that "all persons ... shall have the same right ... to the full and equal benefit of all laws and proceedings for the security of persons and property as is enjoyed by white citizens...." To state a claim under Section 1981, a plaintiff must allege "(1) [membership in] a racial minority; (2) defendants' intent to discriminate on the basis of race; and (3) discrimination concerning one of the statute's enumerated activities."

1. Nexus to the State

Few cases in this circuit or elsewhere arise under the "equal benefit" clause of Section 1981. Although a number of circuits require allegations of state action for purposes of the equal benefit clause, the Second Circuit recently rejected this interpretation. The Second Circuit concluded that "although the phrasing of the equal benefit clause does suggest that there must be some nexus between a claim and the state or its activities, the state is not the only actor that can deprive an individual of the benefit of laws or proceedings for the security of persons or property."

Other circuits have expressed concern that an attenuated connection between a private defendant and the state risks federalizing large areas of state tort law. The Third Circuit warned that not requiring state action would create a federal cause of action "whenever a white man strikes a black in a barroom brawl."

The *Phillip* court was not persuaded by these concerns. The court emphasized that the equal benefit clause requires that a plaintiff demonstrate that the defendant's actions were motivated by race. Furthermore, the court highlighted that nothing in the legislative history suggested Congress intended to limit the reach of the statute. As the court noted, the contract clause of Section 1981 prohibits racially motivated private conduct that interferes with rights under state contract law. There was no principled reason to suggest that Congress favored federalizing state *contract* law but not state *tort* law.

That said, *Phillip* provides little guidance on what type of link between a private actor and a state law or proceeding will satisfy the nexus requirement. In *Phillip*, the nexus was rather explicit. Private university security officers had summoned the police to help disperse a group of black students gathered on university property. Although the police arrested and held four black students overnight, all charges were subsequently dismissed. The university admitted that its security officers had treated the students in a racist manner. The court held that "assuming that Section 1981 requires a nexus to state proceedings or laws but not state action, plaintiffs' allegations are sufficient because plaintiff's claim that defendants attempted to trigger a legal proceeding against plaintiffs but would not have taken the same action had white students engaged in the same conduct" (private security guard "acted in concert *with the authorities* to cause plaintiff to be falsely arrested and maliciously prosecuted because of his race").

J. C. Penney argues that under *Phillip*, this case should be dismissed because the store did not call the police, file a criminal complaint, or trigger a legal proceeding against plaintiff. The court agrees that plaintiff has not alleged a nexus to a state legal *proceeding* for the purposes of Section 1981 liability. However, the more difficult question is whether plaintiff's claims are sufficient to allege a nexus between defendants and a state *law* for the protection of persons and property.

2. Nexus Established by Allegations of State Law Violations

Plaintiff points to a number of state laws, the violation of which might satisfy the nexus requirement. For instance, plaintiff argues that the store violated (citation omitted) when it detained her. That section creates an affirmative defense for shopkeepers in civil actions who detain customers for a "reasonable time" if the store has "reasonable grounds" to believe the customer shoplifted. Defendant argues that Section 218 cannot supply the nexus, citing a handful of cases holding that a store's actions pursuant to this type of statute are not "state action" for purposes of Section 1983 liability. However, as defendant itself acknowledges, Section 1981 does not require traditional state action. Thus, these cases are inapposite.

Plaintiff also alleges that defendants violated state laws against assault, battery, and false imprisonment. J. C. Penney does not address whether these state laws could provide the necessary nexus.

Thus, the question is whether allegations of standard-fare tort law, with no involvement by state actors, will suffice for purposes of the nexus element. The legislative history of Section 1981, reviewed by the *Phillip* court, offers some insight as to the types of state torts actionable under the equal benefit clause. The legislative history reflects particular "concern over *private* acts motivated by racial discrimination" (emphasis added). For instance, Congress considered reports that the "hatred toward the Negro as a freeman is intense among the low and brutal, who are the vast majority. Murders, shooting, whippings, robbing, and brutal treatment of every kind are daily inflicted upon them." Senator Trumbull, who sponsored the legislation, identified "fundamental rights" to be protected by the statute, including "the enjoyment of life and liberty" and the freedom to "pursue and obtain happiness and safety." Similarly, "during the Congressional debates, assaults on blacks by private citizens were referred to on several occasions. These private attacks were clearly viewed as the type of evil the [section] was designed to prevent."

The two primary private-defendant Section 1981 cases involve this type of violent, racially motivated attack. Hawk and his cousin were attacked by a group of white men shouting racial epithets. Among other claims, the *Hawk* plaintiffs alleged violation of their equal benefit rights under Section 1981. Defendant Timothy moved to dismiss the equal benefit claim on the grounds that the plaintiffs failed to allege state action. The court denied the motion, concluding that "nothing in the wording of the statute compels the conclusion that state action is a prerequisite to Section 1981 liability." The court emphasized that Congress's intent was to reach "not only official acts of racial discrimination, but purely private injustices as well." Similarly, *Carey v. Rudeseal* involved a violent attack on plaintiff by a defendant attending a nearby Ku Klux Klan gathering. Carey brought suit in federal court under 42 U.S.C. Section 1981 and Georgia tort law. The court concluded that "Section 1981 provides a cause of action against private individuals for racially motivated, intentionally-inflected injury and does not require state action in the deprivation of rights."

Based on these cases, the court concludes that defendant's motion to dismiss must be denied. Plaintiff alleges that defendants violated various state laws against assault, battery, and false imprisonment—laws clearly intended for the "security of persons." To be sure, plaintiff does not allege the type of violent attack that originally concerned Congress. However, the severity of the harm does not offer a principled way to distinguish the cases. Furthermore, the racially motivated acts alleged here are examples of the more subtle, but no less invidious, type of private discrimination that seeks to deprive African Americans, and other people of color, of their civil rights. There is nothing in the text of the clause, or in the legislative history, to suggest that Congress did not intend to reach this form of invidious discrimination.

B. The Fourth Amendment Claim

Plaintiff contends that defendants violated her Fourth Amendment rights against search and seizure. Plaintiff appears to raise this claim both in the context of her Section 1981 claim and as an independent cause of action. J. C. Penney argues that these claims must be dismissed because the Fourth Amendment constrains state action, not purely private action. The court agrees.

Conclusion

For the foregoing reasons, J. C. Penney' s Motion to Dismiss the Section 1981 Equal Benefit claim is denied. The motion is granted with respect to plaintiff's Fourth Amendment claim.

SO ORDERED.

CASE COMMENT

In this case, the plaintiff asserted a Section 1981 claim, instead of using the more common Section 1983 claim. Using Section 1981 to address allegations of racial discrimination proved to be a wise pleading decision. Notice that the court acknowledged that Section 1983 claims require state action. However, Section 1981 claims, which are designed to remedy racially motivated private action, logically does not require state action. While the court noted that traditionally Section 1981 claims were instituted in cases with extreme violence directed blacks motivated by racial discrimination, the court observed that the facts of this case do not preclude a Section 1981 action. Further, the court quickly dismissed the Fourth Amendment claim, as no state action was associated with this case. This was at least partly based on the fact that the security officer was not granted with any "special police" designation—as illustrated in previous cases.

372 F.3d 894

United States Court of Appeals, Seventh Circuit

PAMELA JOHNSON, PLAINTIFF-APPELLANT v. LARABIDA CHILDREN'S HOSPITAL, DEFENDANT-APPELLEE.

June 22, 2004

Background

Former employee brought civil rights action against hospital under Fourth Amendment alleging use of excessive force. The United States District Court for the Northern District of Illinois dismissed action. Employee appealed.

Holdings

The court of appeals held that:

1. Hospital security guard was not "state actor," and
2. Single blow from walkie-talkie of hospital security guard to head of former employee was reasonable use of force to detain employee.

Affirmed

On March 23, 1999, plaintiff-appellant Pamela Johnson entered the lobby of her former employer, the LaRabida Children' s Hospital to discuss a negative recommendation a potential employer allegedly received from LaRabida while she was applying for a new job. The stated purpose of her visit to the hospital that day was to review her personnel file with the director of the human resource department, Bill Koulias. Upon arrival, Johnson requested access to the human resources department and Koulias, but her request was denied by the hospital's receptionist, Willie Williams. At this point, Johnson began to threaten Williams, allegedly screaming "Call the police [explicative] because I am going to kill you!" This prompted Williams to again deny Johnson's requested audience with Koulias and place a call to hospital security. Prior to security arriving Johnson continued her tirade, allegedly threatening to beat and kill Williams and Koulias.

When security guard Tommy Stephens arrived on the scene, in the midst of Johnson's ranting, he directed Williams to call 911. Stephens also told Johnson that she would not be allowed to go up to the human resource department to see Koulias. Johnson responded by asking whether Stephens had a gun. When Stephens told her that he did not, Johnson warned Stephens that he would need to find some people with guns to stop her. According to Stephens and Williams, Johnson claimed to have a gun.

As Johnson became more enraged, she attempted to walk around Stephens and proceed to the human resource department. Stephens grabbed Johnson to impede her advance and was subsequently kicked in the leg. Stephens responded by screaming out "that bitch kicked me." Then, in an attempt to prevent Johnson from possibly doing harm to herself or others, Stephens, using a downward motion, struck Johnson in the head with the walkie-talkie he was holding in his left hand. It was only after Stephens struck Johnson that her verbal and physical barrage ceased and she left the hospital's lobby, where she was met at the door by Chicago police called to the scene by Williams. Police took Johnson to a local hospital where she received thirteen stitches for her wound. While neither Johnson nor Stephens were arrested the day of the incident, Johnson was issued a citation for assault, battery, and disorderly conduct.

Although Johnson filed criminal battery charges against Stephens, the State's Attorney's Office elected not to pursue charges. Subsequently, Stephens, Koulias, and two other hospital employees prepared and signed misdemeanor criminal complaints against Johnson alleging disorderly conduct, telephone harassment, assault, and battery. The assault and battery charges were dismissed on April 4, 2000, and never reinstated. In return for the dismissal of those charges, Johnson pled guilty to the misdemeanor disorderly conduct and telephone harassment charges. She was sentenced to, and completed, one year of conditional supervision. In her plea agreement, Johnson admitted that she (1) acted in "an unreasonable manner"; (2) "threatened bodily harm" to persons at the hospital; (3) "provoked a breach of the peace"; (4) "battered Stephens"; and (5) "created dismay."

Title 42 U.S.C. Section 1983 provides in pertinent part that "[e]very person who, under color of any statute, ordinance, regulation, custom, or usage, of any State ... subjects, or causes to be subjected, any citizen of the United States ... to the deprivation of any rights, privileges, or immunities secured by the Constitution and laws, shall be liable to the party injured in an action at law." While generally employed against government officers, the language of Section 1983 authorizes its use against private individuals who exercise government power; that is, those individuals who act "under color of state law." This court held in *Payton v. Rush-Presbyterian-St. Luke's Medical Center* that a private party will be deemed to have acted under "color of state law" when the state either (1) "effectively directs or controls the actions of the private party such that the state can be held responsible for the private party's decision"; or (2) "delegates a public function to a private entity." Johnson argues, in accord with the latter theory, that Stephens should be considered a state actor due to his status as a special policeman, duly appointed under Chicago Municipal Code Section 4-340-100.

Chicago Municipal Code Section 4-340-100 declares that "[s]pecial policemen shall possess the powers of the regular police patrol at the places for which they are respectively appointed." Furthermore, "for purposes of determining whether an individual is a state actor ..., no legal difference exists between a privately employed special officer *with full police powers* and a regular Chicago police officer (emphasis added)." If, however, the privately employed special officers are "no substitute for the police" in that they are not "entrusted with all powers possessed by the police," then the special officer is not considered a state actor. When, for example, a special officer's only recourse in a given situation is to call the police for help, it is "a far cry from delegating all of the powers of the regular police patrol to the special officer."

In *United States v. Hoffman*, for example, we held that privately employed railroad policemen, who were also Chicago special police officers, were state actors when they brutally beat vagrant trespassers. Of particular importance was the fact that the policemen were "authorized on a continuing and full-time basis to search actively for criminals and ... to use the powers of the state when their search was successful."

In *Wade v. Byles*, on the other hand, we held that a security guard working under contract with the Chicago Housing Authority ("CHA") was not a state actor when, while on duty, the security guard got into an altercation with an individual at a CHA security checkpoint, and shot the man in the groin. Like the railroad policemen in *Hoffman*, the CHA had been officially delegated police authority. Unlike the situation in *Hoffman*, however, we held that *Wade* was not a case "where the state had delegated its entire police power to a private police force." For that reason, the guard in *Wade* was not a state actor.

Under this standard, the district court did not err in finding that Stephens was not a state actor. Initially, it should be noted that Stephens did not, and was not authorized to, carry a firearm. Also, at the time of the incident, Stephens was not expected or authorized to carry out the functions of a police officer. Stephens was merely responsible for routine security duties only such as patrolling the interior and exterior of the hospital, observing potential safety hazards, manning an information desk, monitoring the alarm system, and providing escorts for patients and staff. In the event that a visitor to the hospital was to become unruly or disruptive, as Johnson clearly did, it was within Stephen's discretion to ask that person to leave the premises. However, per hospital policy, when Johnson began acting belligerent and hostile and refused to leave, the only recourse Stephens had was "to call 911 for assistance in having the individual removed." This is "a far cry from delegating all of the powers of the regular police patrol to ... special officer [Stephens]."

Indeed, Stephens precisely followed this procedure on March 23, 1999. For when Stephens arrived on the scene (after responding to an assistance call from Williams) and perceived the threat that Johnson posed, he immediately directed Williams to dial 911. It was only after Stephens had been physically assaulted by Johnson, and legitimately feared for his safety and the safety of others present, that he used force to subdue Johnson, striking her once in the head with the only "weapon" he had, his walkie-talkie. Much like *Wade*, therefore, this is not a case "where the state had delegated its entire police power to a private police force." Stephens was no substitute for the police and, therefore, not a state actor.

Nonetheless, assuming arguendo, that Stephens was a state actor, Johnson would still need to establish that Stephens deprived her of a constitutional right. She cannot do so. In her complaint, Johnson claims that Stephens used excessive force in seeking to detain her in violation of the Fourth Amendment. We disagree. Stephens' use of force was reasonable as a matter of necessity and law.

"Determining whether the force used to affect a particular seizure is 'reasonable' under the Fourth Amendment requires a careful balancing of the nature and intrusion on the individual's Fourth Amendment interests against the countervailing governmental interests at stake." Furthermore, it is clear that, under the Fourth Amendment, "the right to make an arrest ... necessarily carries with it the right to use some degree of physical coercion." What is reasonable depends upon the particulars of a given case, including "the severity of the crime at issue, whether the suspect poses an immediate threat to the safety of the officers or others, and whether [s]he is actively resisting arrest or attempting to evade arrest by flight." In addition, what is reasonable "must be judged from the perspective of a reasonable officer on the scene, rather than with the 20/20 vision of hindsight."

Under this standard, it is clear that Stephens exercised reasonable force in attempting to detain Johnson. By her own admission, Johnson (1) acted in "an unreasonable manner"; (2) "threatened bodily harm" to persons at the hospital; (3) "provoked a breach of the peace"; (4) "battered Stephens"; and (5) "created dismay." These admissions alone demonstrate that Stephens had reason to exercise physical coercion and that the single blow from his walkie-talkie was reasonable force given the situation. As such, even if we were to hold that Stephens was a state actor, he did not deprive Johnson of her Fourth Amendment right to be free from excessive force.

The judgment of the district court is AFFIRMED.

CASE COMMENT

This case again distinguishes the factual circumstances to determine when a special police officer is a state actor. In assessing this question, the court noted several cases which provide guidance. The key determination is whether the special police officer is "entrusted with all powers possessed by the police." If so, the special police officer will then be construed as a state actor. In this case, the special police officer was not deemed a state actor. In reaching this conclusion, the court noted that the policy of the hospital was for the special police officer to call Chicago police when an individual refused to leave the hospital. In addition, the hospital security personnel did not possess firearms. Based on this conclusion, the Section 1983 claim was dismissed, as the plaintiff could not show her constitutionally protected rights were violated by a state actor. Finally, the Fourth Amendment claim based on allegations of excessive use of force was also dismissed, as the court found the force used by the hospital security officer as reasonable under the circumstances. This is particularly relevant given the outrageous conduct exhibited by the plaintiff.

144 S.W.3d 574

Court of Appeals of Texas, Austin

LAURA RAMIREZ AND ADOLFO RAMIREZ/FIFTH CLUB, INC. AND DAVID A. WEST, APPELLANTS v. FIFTH CLUB, INC.; DAVID A. WEST; AND LUIS A/K/A LOUIS MEDRANO/ROBERTO RAMIREZ, APPELLEES.

April 29, 2004

Background

Three nightclub patrons brought action against nightclub and nightclub security personnel following altercation, alleging assault, false imprisonment, malicious prosecution, intentional infliction of emotional distress, and malice. The 353rd Judicial District Court, Travis County, entered judgment on jury verdict in favor of one patron, and against other two patrons. Parties appealed.

Holdings

The court of appeals held that:

1. Nightclub security personnel who were also employed as campus police officers at private college were entitled to official immunity for warrantless arrests at off-campus nightclub;
2. Evidence supported finding that security guard was not acting as peace officer when he slammed patron's head into a wall while making arrest; and
3. Nightclub was liable for acts committed by security personnel.

Affirmed

The facts of this case were hotly contested at trial. What is undisputed is that on September 16, 2000, Roberto Ramirez and his brother, Adolfo Ramirez, attended a party to celebrate the baptism of their cousin. After the party, around 12:30 or 1:00 a.m. on September 17, Roberto and Adolfo arrived at Club Rodeo with some friends. Roberto and Adolfo were, at some point, denied admission into Club Rodeo. West and Medrano, both of whom were working security in the Club Rodeo parking lot, were signaled by the Club

Rodeo doorman and proceeded to the doorway of the club. An altercation between Roberto and West ensued, during which Roberto's head struck a wall, fracturing a bone in his skull. Apparently, Adolfo intervened in the altercation between Roberto and West, causing Medrano to restrain Adolfo.

It should be noted, West and Medrano were employed as full-time campus police officers at Huston-Tillotson College. The night of the incident pertinent to this case, both were working as security for Fifth Club at Club Rodeo. They were wearing their duty belts and black shirts that stated "POLICE."

Eventually, West and Medrano took Roberto, who was unconscious, and Adolfo into the parking lot and handcuffed them. Laura Ramirez, who was dropping off another brother at Club Rodeo, soon arrived to find her brothers Roberto, who had regained consciousness, and Adolfo lying handcuffed on the parking-lot pavement. She and West became embroiled in a verbal altercation, and West eventually handcuffed Laura and placed her under arrest as well. Both Medrano and an eyewitness called 911. Austin Police Department (APD) officers soon arrived and transported Roberto, Adolfo, and Laura Ramirez to the city jail.

West and Medrano asserted the affirmative defense of official immunity. At the time of this incident, peace officers outside of their jurisdiction could make a warrantless arrest of a person who commits a felony, a breach of the peace, or public intoxication within the officer's presence or view. West and Medrano argued that they observed Roberto, Adolfo, and Laura commit felonies, breaches of the peace, public intoxication, or some combination thereof. Because West and Medrano were commissioned by Huston-Tillotson College to function as peace officers, they assert they were entitled to function as peace officers and were therefore entitled to official immunity (permitting private institutions of higher education to commission campus security personnel).

Based on its official-immunity findings, the jury did not reach any liability questions stemming from Laura's and Adolfo's complaints. The jury did, however, find both West and Fifth Club liable to Roberto and awarded him $80,000 for physical pain and mental anguish sustained in the past, $20,000 for mental anguish that he will reasonably sustain in the future, $2,100 for loss of earning capacity in the past, $7,000 for physical impairment sustained in the past, $1,198 for medical care in the past, and $35,000 as exemplary damages against Fifth Club.

Authority to Act as "Peace Officers"

Laura and Adolfo argue in one issue that they are entitled to a remand because the district court improperly submitted to the jury a question regarding official immunity for West and Medrano. West and Medrano were both employed by Huston-Tillotson College, a private institution of higher education, as campus security personnel. In empowering private institutions to hire security personnel, the legislature provided:

The governing boards of private institutions of higher education, including private junior colleges, are authorized to employ and commission campus security personnel for the purpose of enforcing the law of this state on the campuses of private institutions of higher education. Any officer commissioned under the provisions of this section is vested with all the powers, privileges, and immunities of peace officers *while on the property* under the control and jurisdiction of the respective private institution of higher education *or otherwise in the performance of his assigned duties* (emphasis added). Because this section states that a campus officer has the powers, privileges, and immunities of peace officers "while on the property ... or otherwise in the performance of his assigned duties," Laura and Adolfo argue that West and Medrano could not function as peace officers while working at Club Rodeo.

However, the statute unambiguously defines "officers commissioned under ... Subchapter E, Chapter 51, Education Code" as "peace officers."

A peace officer *who is outside his jurisdiction* may arrest, without warrant, a person who commits an offense within the officer's presence or view, if the offense is a felony, a [disorderly conduct and related offenses], a breach of the peace, or public intoxication. A peace officer making an arrest under this subsection shall, as soon as practicable after making the arrest, notify a law enforcement agency having jurisdiction where the arrest was made. The law enforcement agency shall then take custody of the person committing the offense and take the person before a magistrate.

We believe the interaction between these statutes is clear, establishing the jurisdiction for campus security personnel. Within this jurisdiction, campus security personnel are "vested with *all* the powers, privileges, and immunities of peace officers" (emphasis added). But the former statute acts as an exception to the general rule that a peace officer's authority to act is limited to his own geographic jurisdiction. Outside of their primary jurisdiction, officers are vested with the *limited* authority to arrest for certain enumerated offenses committed within the officer's presence or view.

After thoroughly analyzing the education code, the code of criminal procedure, and Texas case law, Laura and Adolfo argue that interpreting former to include campus security personnel commissioned under would lead to absurd results. First, they argue that expressly addresses the limited circumstances under which officers commissioned by private institutions may act as peace officers outside their ordinary jurisdiction. This section provides in part:

> (a) Within counties under 200,000 population, the chief of police of a municipality or the sheriff of the county, if the institution is outside the corporate limits of a municipality, that has jurisdiction over the geographical area of a private institution of higher education, provided the governing board of such institution consents, may appoint up to 50 peace officers who are commissioned under, and who are employed by a private institution of

higher education located in the municipality or county, to serve as adjunct police officers of the municipality or county. Officers appointed under this article shall aid law enforcement agencies in the protection of the municipality or county in a geographical area that is designated by agreement on an annual basis between the appointing chief of police or sheriff and the private institution.

(b) The geographical area that is subject to designation under Subsection

  (a) of this article may include only the private institution's campus area and an area that:

    (1) is adjacent to the campus of the private institution;

    (2) does not extend further than a distance of one mile from the perimeter of the campus;

    (3) is inhabited primarily by students or employees of the private institution.

(c) A peace officer serving as an adjunct police officer may make arrests and exercise all authority given peace officers under this code only within the geographical area designated by agreement between the appointing chief of police or sheriff and the private institution.

(d) A peace officer serving as an adjunct police officer has all the rights, privileges, and immunities of a peace officer but is not entitled to state compensation and retirement benefits normally provided by the state to a peace officer.

Laura and Adolfo argue that this specific section, which explains the circumstances under which a campus security officer at a private educational institution may function outside of his jurisdiction, should control over the more general former former ("more specific statute controls over the more general"). However, this rule of statutory construction only applies when different code provisions are "irreconcilable."

Here, we do not find that [the two statutes] conflict. The fundamental difference between these two articles is that [the current statute] provides the specific circumstances, including geographic restrictions, for when a campus security officer may exercise *all* the rights, privileges, and immunities of a peace officer, while former statute provides an additional situation where a peace officer, including a campus security officer, can exercise the *limited* function of arresting an individual for specific offenses committed within the officer's presence or view.

The current statute allows a campus security officer functioning as an adjunct officer to make *all* arrests, but only within a specified geographic area. The former statute, on the other hand, allows a campus security officer to make a warrantless arrest without regard to geographic boundaries within the state *only if* the offense is committed "within the officer's presence or view" and *only if* the offense observed is specifically listed. We conclude that the plain language of these two articles does not conflict, and we overrule Laura's and Adolfo's issue insofar as it is based on this reasoning.

Next, Laura and Adolfo point to [education statute] to support their argument that West and Medrano were not entitled to official immunity. This statute provides in part:

> (a) The governing boards of each state institution of higher education and public technical institute may employ and commission peace officers for the purpose of carrying out the provisions of this subchapter. The primary jurisdiction of a peace officer commissioned under this section includes all counties in which property is owned, leased, rented, or otherwise under the control of the institution of higher education or public technical institute that employs the peace officer.
>
> (b) Within a peace officer's primary jurisdiction, a peace officer commissioned under this section:
>
> (1) is vested with all the powers, privileges, and immunities of peace officers;
>
> (2) may, in accordance with Chapter 14, Code of Criminal Procedure, arrest without a warrant any person who violates a law of the state; and
>
> (3) may enforce all traffic laws on streets and highways.
>
> (c) Outside a peace officer's primary jurisdiction a peace officer commissioned under this section is vested with all the powers, privileges, and immunities of peace officers and may arrest any person who violates any law of the state if the peace officer:
>
> (1) is summoned by another law enforcement agency to provide assistance;
>
> (2) is assisting another law enforcement agency; or
>
> (3) is otherwise performing his duties as a peace officer for the institution of higher education or public technical institute that employs the peace officer.

Laura and Adolfo argue that construing former statute to include campus security personnel commissioned by *private* institutions under (citation omitted) would empower such officers with *more* power than similar officers commissioned by *public* institutions of higher education. This argument stems from the fact that limits the instances when an officer commissioned by a *public* institution may act outside of his primary jurisdiction, yet [the statute] contains no such restrictions. Therefore, according to Laura and Adolfo, construing former [statute] to include campus security personnel at private institutions would grant them *more* power than similar officers at public institutions, who can only act outside of their jurisdiction when the limited circumstances described in apply.

We disagree with Laura's and Adolfo's reading of the statutes in question. Indeed, in at least three instances courts have held when a campus officer at a public institution who is outside of his primary jurisdiction is "vested with *all* the powers, privileges, and immunities of peace officers and may arrest any person who violates *any* law of the state (emphasis added)." Section 51.203(c) is narrowly tailored to describe the circumstances under which a campus police officer maintains *full* peace-officer status, even if outside the officer's jurisdiction. This does not conflict with former article 14.03(d), which empowers campus police officers—those employed by public and private institutions alike—to make warrant-less arrests for a small number of offenses committed within the officer's presence or view. Because Section 14.03(d) applies equally to campus officers employed by public institutions and campus officers employed by private institutions and is not in conflict with Section 51.203, we overrule Laura's and Adolfo's issue insofar as it is based on this statute.

Finally, Laura and Adolfo cite numerous cases in support of their argument that former article 14.03(d) cannot apply to West and Medrano, but these cases are easily distinguishable from the situation now before us. In citing these cases, Laura and Adolfo focus on where West and Medrano were empowered to function with *full* peace-officer authority, yet they fail to address that the legislature specifically provided for *limited* situations in which peace officers, *outside of their jurisdiction*, may make warrantless arrests for a limited number of offenses committed within their presence or view.

We conclude that article 2.12(8) and former article 14.03(d) of the code of criminal procedure are clear and unambiguous and do not conflict with Section 51.203 or 51.212 of the education code, or with article 2.123 of the code of criminal procedure. We therefore hold that the district court properly submitted the question of official immunity to the jury. We overrule Laura's and Adolfo's sole issue.

Because all seven issues turn on an examination of the evidence presented at trial, a recounting of the evidence before the jury is necessary. The parties hotly contested what actually happened at Club Rodeo, and we will address their different accounts of the incident in turn.

Roberto and Adolfo both testified that when they were waiting in line in a front hallway to enter Club Rodeo, the club doorman allowed two men to cut in front of Roberto and Adolfo. Adolfo complained to the doorman, who then said Adolfo was not getting in. Adolfo apologized and showed his identification to the doorman, who said, "Get the [expletive] out of here." Roberto told the doorman not to speak to Adolfo that way, and the doorman then said Roberto was not getting into Club Rodeo either.

At this point, Roberto was under the impression that his friends, who were at the cash register, had already paid for his and Adolfo's admission. He told the doorman that if their money was returned, he and Adolfo would leave. Upon learning that their friends had not, in fact, already paid for their admission, Roberto and Adolfo turned around to leave. As Roberto was walking toward the exit, West approached from behind and grabbed his hands. When Roberto resisted West's effort to restrain Roberto's hands,

West allegedly "got very mad" and pushed Roberto's face against a limestone or concrete wall, fracturing a bone in Roberto's skull and rendering him unconscious. When Roberto regained consciousness, he was lying handcuffed in the parking lot.

Adolfo testified that after West pushed Roberto into the wall, West "was beating [Roberto] several times," prompting Medrano to tell West "that was enough." When Adolfo tried to push West away from Roberto, Medrano grabbed Adolfo by the neck and threw him to the floor. Medrano dragged Adolfo outside, where Medrano and West allegedly kicked both Adolfo and Roberto after they had been handcuffed.

Laura Ramirez, who was dropping off another brother at Club Rodeo, soon arrived to find her brothers Roberto and Adolfo lying handcuffed on the parking-lot pavement. She exited her vehicle and attempted to ascertain what had happened from West, who was initially non-responsive. West told Laura to move her car, but Laura attempted to move closer to Roberto, whose face was swollen and bleeding. West again told Laura to move her car, allegedly telling her "it wasn't [her] [expletive] business what was happening there."

Laura inquired about Roberto's injuries, which West admitted to causing. Laura stated she was going to call an attorney and returned to her truck to get her cellular phone. When Laura obtained her phone, West grabbed her from behind, threw her against a car, handcuffed her, told her she was under arrest, and pushed her to the ground. While Laura was handcuffed on the ground, Thomas Romero, Club Rodeo's manager at that time, purportedly laughed at and mocked Laura's predicament. Laura testified that at no point did West ever identify himself as a police officer, and at no point did she touch West or Medrano.

APD officers arrived after being called by both a witness to the incident and Medrano. APD officers transported Adolfo, Roberto, and Laura to jail. Roberto and Adolfo spent two days in jail, and were subsequently no-billed by the grand jury for assault on a police officer, the only crime with which they were charged. Laura spent three days in jail, purportedly for assault on a police officer, but was never charged with any crime.

Fifth Club, West, and Medrano present a much different account of the events of September 17. Fifth Club's doorman testified that when he asked for Roberto's identification to get into the club, Roberto seemed intoxicated and shoved his ID against the doorman's chest. The doorman asked Roberto to leave, and Roberto refused. The doorman threatened to call the police if Roberto did not leave, and Roberto again refused. The doorman then signaled with a flashlight to West and Medrano that they were needed inside the club.

West was sitting in his car in the parking lot when the doorman signaled that he and Medrano, who was near the entrance, were needed inside the club. West and Medrano proceeded inside the club, where the doorman informed them that Roberto was intoxicated and should not enter the club. Roberto and Adolfo refused to leave, at which point Medrano grabbed Roberto by the wrist or hand to escort him out. Roberto pulled away and was then grabbed by West. As West was escorting Roberto to the door, Roberto kneed West in the groin, and West lost his grip on Roberto. West then pushed Roberto against a wall. Roberto attempted to strike West, at which point West began to throw a forearm at Roberto. Adolfo then punched West in the head, causing West and Roberto to fall either against the wall or onto the floor. Roberto was not moving, and West surmised he may have passed out. West handcuffed Roberto and moved him outside.

After Adolfo punched West, Medrano pushed Adolfo out the door of the club, and Adolfo tried to kick and punch Medrano. Both Medrano and Adolfo fell to the ground outside the door to the club. Adolfo repeatedly kicked Medrano while Adolfo was on the ground, causing Medrano to strike Adolfo with a flashlight several times while saying, "Police, stop kicking me." Medrano eventually subdued and handcuffed Adolfo.

Laura soon arrived, parking her car where it would block APD efforts to arrest and transport Roberto and Adolfo. She immediately threatened to sue West, who repeatedly asked her to move her car. West escorted Laura by the elbow to her car, and Laura snatched her elbow away from West and elbowed him. West then informed Laura she was under arrest and handcuffed her. Romero, Club Rodeo's manager, testified via deposition that he simply told Laura, "If you calm down, they'll probably let you go." APD officers then transported Roberto, Adolfo, and Laura to jail.

Whether West Was Entitled to Official Immunity

Fifth Club and West argue that West was entitled to official immunity as a matter of law because he was functioning as a peace officer during the early morning hours of September 17. This argument, however, presupposes that Roberto committed one of the enumerated offenses in former article 14.03(d) within West's presence or view, thereby entitling West to function as a peace officer. To be entitled to immunity, West was required to show that he was acting at all relevant times pursuant to his authority as a peace officer and that his actions were discretionary and in good faith.

The jury was essentially asked to determine two questions. First, whether West was entitled to "switch hats" and transform from his role as private security for the club into a separate role as a peace officer. Next, if West was acting within his authority as a peace officer, the jury was asked to determine whether his actions were in good faith. Fifth Club and West argue that the evidence conclusively shows that West acted as a "reasonably prudent officer" and was entitled to immunity, but they ignore that the jury, from the evidence presented, could have concluded that Roberto never committed a crime within West's presence or view that entitled him to function as a peace officer under former article 14.03(d) and arrest Roberto. There is, at best, conflicting evidence of whether Roberto committed any crimes at all, and the jury is the sole judge of the credibility of witnesses and the weight to be given to their testimony.

Additionally, Fifth Club and West assert that because West and another one of their witnesses testified that West's actions were reasonable, the jury's refusal to grant official immunity to West was based on factually insufficient evidence. We disagree. Even Officer Payne, an expert witness for Fifth Club and West, testified that he had never seen an officer slam someone's head into a wall, and had never seen an officer hit a suspect who was already handcuffed, as West was alleged to have done. Officer Tidwell, an expert witness for Roberto, testified that the crimes allegedly committed by Roberto would not justify an officer slamming a suspect's head against a wall. Officer Tidwell also testified it would not have been reasonable for West to grab Roberto's arms from behind without announcing his presence as a police officer. We hold the evidence was both legally and factually sufficient to support the jury's finding that West was not entitled to official immunity for his actions toward Roberto, and we overrule Fifth Club's and West's seventh issue.

Whether Fifth Club Is Responsible for West's Actions

The district court submitted to the jury the following question: "On the occasion in question was David West acting in the furtherance of a mission for the benefit of Fifth Club, and subject to control by Fifth Club, as to the details of the mission?" The jury answered, "Yes." Fifth Club now asserts that it is not responsible for West's actions because he was acting as a peace officer.

This court has previously explained the process for determining when a security guard ceases functioning as an employee and functions instead as a peace officer:

In determining the status of a police officer, we ask,"[I]n what capacity was the officer acting at the time he committed the acts for which the complaint is made?" If the officer is performing a public duty, such as the enforcement of general laws, the officer's private employer incurs no vicarious responsibility for that officer's acts, even though the employer may have directed the activities. If the officer was engaged in *protecting the employer's property, ejecting trespassers, or enforcing rules and regulations promulgated by the employer*, however, the trier of fact decides whether the officer was acting as a public officer or as a servant of the employer (emphasis added). As explained above, there is both legally and factually sufficient evidence to support a conclusion that West was not acting as a peace officer under former article 14.03(d) when Roberto's injuries were inflicted. We therefore reject Fifth Club's contention that it is not responsible for West's actions because he was functioning as a peace officer.

Fifth Club also asserts it is not responsible for West's actions because he was an independent contractor. In the employment context, it is the right of control that commonly justifies imposing liability on the employer for the actions of the employee, and an employer may be vicariously liable for his independent contractor's acts if he retains the "right to control the means, methods, or details of the independent contractor's work."

An employer can also be liable for the acts of an independent contractor if the "personal character exception" applies. If the duties being carried out by an independent contractor are of a personal character owed to the public by one adopting measures to protect his property, owners and operators of enterprises cannot, by securing independent contractors for the purpose of protecting property, obtain immunity from liability for at least the intentional torts of those hired.

Here, the uncontroverted evidence established that the doorman signaled West and Medrano to enter the club and remove Roberto and Adolfo. The doorman then directed West and Medrano to eject Adolfo and Roberto, which they did. Salim Salem, one of Fifth Club's owners, testified that it was the club's responsibility to ensure the safety of patrons and that one of the reasons for hiring outside security like West was to deter crime, both inside and outside the club. This is evidence that West was carrying out the exact functions he was hired to perform, and was performing those functions at the direction of Club Rodeo employees. We hold that the record contains both legally and factually sufficient evidence that West was acting in the furtherance of a mission for the benefit of Fifth Club and subject to control by Fifth Club as to the details of the mission. We overrule Fifth Club's and West's first issue.

Malice Finding and Exemplary Damages

Fifth Club challenges the jury's award of exemplary damages against Fifth Club and the jury's finding that both Fifth Club and West acted with malice. Here, Roberto's expert testified that Fifth Club acted with gross negligence in hiring and retaining West. An employer can also be liable for exemplary damages due to the malicious acts of an employee if the employee was unfit and the corporation was grossly negligent in employing him. We conclude the evidence was legally and factually sufficient to support an award of exemplary damages.

Fifth Club also argues that the amount of $35,000 in exemplary damages is excessive. Exemplary damages must be reasonably proportioned to actual damages. There is no set rule of ratio between the amount of actual and exemplary damages that will be considered reasonable. An award of exemplary damages rests largely in the discretion of the fact finder and will not be set aside as excessive unless the amount is so large as to indicate that it is the result of passion, prejudice, or corruption, or that the evidence has been disregarded. Factors to consider when determining whether an exemplary-damages award is reasonable include: (1) the nature of the wrong, (2) the character of the conduct involved, (3) the degree of culpability of the wrongdoer, (4) the situation and sensibilities of the parties concerned, and (5) the extent to which such conduct offends a public sense of justice and propriety.

Here, the jury awarded over $110,000 in actual damages and $35,000 in exemplary damages. Examining the above factors to determine whether this proportion is reasonable, we note first that the nature of the wrong consists of serious bodily injury inflicted by Fifth Club personnel to Roberto, who subsequently spent two days in jail for crimes for which he was later no-billed. We concluded above that the evidence is legally and factually sufficient to support the jury's findings that Fifth Club is responsible for West's actions and that Fifth Club was itself grossly negligent.

Second, Fifth Club delegated the hiring of security officers to a third party, failed to perform background checks, did not require applications to be completed, did not provide policy manuals or instructions to outside security personnel, and was not even aware of the identities of the security personnel it was employing. Moreover, there is evidence in the record that Club Rodeo's manager laughed at and mocked Laura while she was handcuffed. It is undisputed that West and Medrano were paid in full at the end of their shift and that Fifth Club took no action as a result of this incident.

Third, regarding Fifth Club's culpability, the jury heard expert testimony that Fifth Club's conduct constituted gross negligence and proximately caused Roberto's injuries.

Fourth, considering the situation and sensibilities of the parties concerned, we concluded that the evidence is legally and factually sufficient to support the conclusion that Roberto suffered, and continues to suffer from, injuries proximately caused by Fifth Club's gross negligence.

Finally, Fifth Club's conduct offends a public sense of justice and propriety. Fifth Club representatives testified that personnel such as West were hired, in part, to protect its patrons. However, Fifth Club did nothing to ensure that the security personnel hired were qualified for employment. Furthermore, Fifth Club failed to inform its outside security personnel of club policies, as it did with other club employees. This is the type of conduct exemplary damages are meant to punish and deter. In light of these factors, the jury's award of exemplary damages equal to approximately one third the amount of actual damages is not clearly wrong and unjust. We therefore overrule Fifth Club's exemplary-damages issue.

Conclusion

The final judgment of the district court is therefore affirmed.

CASE COMMENT

This case provides another pointed analysis between the issue of legal authority, but with an additional element relating to this application of qualified immunity. The initial question regarding legal authority was largely a technical analysis of the statutes that imbue peace powers to officers similarly situated as West and Medrano. Next, the court held that even assuming that peace powers were conferred on these individuals, their physical maltreatment of the plaintiff does not make qualified immunity applicable. In essence, the court held that such bad conduct is not subject to the spirit and purpose of qualified immunity. Finally, while the punitive damage claim is beyond the scope of this chapter, I left the discussion largely intact due to the excellent analysis provided by the court. This discussion, again, serves to remind security professionals of the costly nature of bad actions and excessive force.

697 So. 2d 880

District Court of Appeal of Florida, Fifth District.

ROBERT W. SIPKEMA, II AND KATHLYN K. SIPKEMA, ETC., APPELLANTS v. REEDY CREEK IMPROVEMENT DISTRICT, ETC., ET AL., APPELLEE.

June 20, 1997

Background

Plaintiffs file action complaining about the "law enforcement" services provided by its property association. The trial court held that Disney's creation of Reedy Creek was not designed to provide "law enforcement" services.

Holding

The appellate court held there is no support for the proposition that Disney was providing law enforcement on behalf of Reedy Creek. Reedy Creek did not create or participate in the creation of Disney. To the contrary, Disney prevailed upon the legislature to create Reedy Creek for the benefit of its property and for the benefit of neighboring property.

In the present case, however, not only was the Reedy Creek Development District not created for the purpose of providing law enforcement services for the inhabitants of the district, but its enabling act does not authorize it to perform that function. Reedy Creek is neither a county nor a city nor a substitute thereof. Reedy Creek does have the authority under its charter to "enter into agreements with any ... firm ... for the furnishing by such ... firm ... any facilities and services of the type provided for in this Act to the District and *for or on behalf of the District to persons, firms, corporations and other public or private bodies and agencies to whom the District is empowered under this Act to furnish facilities and services....*" It seems to follow that if the District is not empowered to provide police protection to the inhabitants of the district, it cannot contract for others to provide it in its stead. One can only imagine the outcry of the owners of the 3 percent of the property within the boundaries of Reedy Creek not owned by Disney if they were suddenly assessed their proportionate share of the costs of the 800 security personnel now serving Disney at its complex located within the Reedy Creek Development District.

Appellants point to the contract between Reedy Creek and Disney which provides that Disney will perform "such other services as the District may, from time to time, deem necessary to meet its needs for security...." It is urged that by this agreement, Disney has agreed to perform law enforcement on behalf of Reedy Creek throughout the district. The stretch is simply too great. First, the trial court found that security services referred to by the agreement meant "routine premises security in the nature of what is generally termed 'night watchman' services." The record supports this finding. Appellants have not sought the records relating to this night watchman service. If they had, a different analysis might be required. Second, while the District inherently has the same right as any property owner to protect its own property, it has, as indicated above, no authority to provide law enforcement for anyone. This is consistent with the court's interpretation of the word "security" in the agreement. Third, Disney simply does not provide "law enforcement" services. As the trial judge found, Disney issues only Mickey Mouse traffic citations.

Such citations are issued only to Disney employees, in order to encourage them to obey the speed limits and to otherwise drive safely on Disney property. The citations have no force of law—no fines are authorized and no points are assessed. The citations are placed in the employee's personnel file for appropriate action based on the number and severity of the violations. Non-employees may be stopped by Disney security employees in order for the employees to caution such persons to slow down or otherwise drive more safely, but citations are not issued to non-employees. The actions of repeat or continuing non-employee offenders are reported to deputies of the Orange County Sheriff's Department. This is no more law enforcement than the action of one asking his teenage neighbor to slow down while driving in the neighborhood because there are small children playing.

Indeed, the law imposes on Disney the obligation to take such action as it appropriately can in order to reduce the hazards within its complex. For example, the Howard Johnson Motor Lodge was held civilly liable in *Orlando Executive Park, Inc. v. Robbins*, because it failed to have sufficient security personnel on its own property under the circumstances of that case. Municipalities across the state have enacted ordinances requiring 24-hour convenience stores to provide security, usually in the form of additional personnel. It cannot be said that private employers who provide additional security on their own property, whether gratuitously, pursuant to a labor agreement, or in compliance with governmental action, are somehow providing "law enforcement" on behalf of the local police department or the county sheriff's office and thereby subject their records to public scrutiny.

There is no evidence of public funding of the Disney security force. Although a relatively small amount is paid by Reedy Creek for the "night watchman" services performed by Disney, there is no evidence of a contribution toward the greater "law enforcement" services relied on by appellants herein.

Although a portion of Disney's security activities is conducted on roads belonging to Reedy Creek, such activity is not law enforcement.

But it is more in the nature of the duty imposed by the court in *Gunlock v. Gill Hotels Co. Inc.*: the "duty to provide its guests with reasonably safe passage across the highway."

The greater security role assumed by Disney and provided on its complex is not a part of Reedy Creek's decision-making process. Indeed, Reedy Creek has no authority to make a decision about providing security or law enforcement for others.

The greater security activities performed by Disney would not be provided by Reedy Creek if Disney failed or ceased to provide it. Reedy Creek simply has no authority to provide such services for the inhabitants of its district.

Reedy Creek does not control Disney. In fact the contrary is true. Because Reedy Creek is governed by a one acre, one vote rule and because Disney owns 97 percent of the acres in Reedy Creek, Disney has substantial control over the operation of Reedy Creek. But this, standing alone, is not a *Schwab* factor. Certainly *if* Disney exerted its control to obtain a contract that met the *Schwab* test, then its records as they relate to that activity would be subject to the public records disclosure requirements. For example, if Disney, under an agreement with the Reedy Creek Development District Board of Supervisors, undertook to do the reclamation, drainage and erosion control activities throughout the district which the Reedy Creek charter provided that Reedy Creek would do, and certainly if Disney received public funds for this activity and used publicly owned facilities and equipment to do it, the Disney records relating to this activity would be open for inspection. Such is not the case here.

The trial judge was right in his analysis and ruling, and I concur in the affirmance of his judgment.

CASE COMMENT

In this case, the question is whether Disney performed a public function sufficient to require it to respond to a freedom of information request by a Reedy Creek property owner. In addressing this issue, the court provided a good overview of the issues involved when a private entity takes upon itself to perform a public function. In this case, the public function was law enforcement. Because Disney employed about 800 security officers, and provided certain security services to the Reedy Creek development, the plaintiffs assert that Disney was providing law enforcement services, thereby serving a public function. After analyzing the facts and the law, the court held to the contrary. Disney did not perform a law enforcement function, thereby implying that its security officers were not police officers.

316 F. Supp. 2d 1254

United States District Court, M.D. Florida, Orlando Division

DAVID GREEN AND JENNIFER GREEN, PLAINTIFFS v. ABONY BAIL BOND, AMERICAN SURETY COMPANY D/B/A AMERICAN UNDERWRITERS SURETY COMPANY, RONALD R. JOHNSON, EDWARD WILLIAMS, JAMES V. BROWN, AND JOHN L. SPEAKE, DEFENDANTS.

March 30, 2004

Background

Principal arrested by bail bondsmen, and principal' s wife, brought Section 1983 action against bail bond agency, agency's underwriter, and individual bondsmen, alleging that couple had been assaulted by bondsmen in their attempt to arrest principal. Defendants moved to dismiss.

Holdings

The district court held that:

1. State right or privilege prong of state action requirement was satisfied, but
2. Bondsmen were not state actors under "nexus/joint action" test.

Motion granted

After being arrested on misdemeanor charges, Mr. Green procured a $500.00 bond from Abony. He was then released from custody on the condition that he appear before a court. On the scheduled date and time, however, Mr. Green inadvertently failed to appear. Accordingly, the defendants set out to arrest their principal.

On the night of November 11, 2003, Mr. and Mrs. Green heard a knock at their door. Shortly thereafter, the defendants busted through the front entranceway of their home with guns drawn. Although the Greens were unarmed, the defendants aimed their weapons directly at the plaintiffs' heads. At no time, did the defendants announce their presence or properly identify themselves.

Startled by the turbulence, the Green's dog began barking. In response, one of the defendants threatened to shoot the animal. When Mrs. Green attempted to contain her pet, a defendant forcibly grabbed her. That prompted Mr. Green to warn the defendants not to touch his wife or treat her in that manner.

At that time, the defendants converged on Mr. Green, striking him repeatedly with fists, batons, and flashlights. When Mr. Green went to his knees, the defendants continued their onslaught. In fact, they intensified their attack by incorporating stun guns.

Horrified by the events taking place in his residence, Mr. Green pleaded to the defendants for his life. In addition, he begged for his wife's assistance. The defendants staved off Mrs. Green by threatening to kill her if she moved any closer toward her husband.

Eventually, the defendants handcuffed Mr. Green, yet, they continued to administer punishing blows and tasers. As a consequence, Mr. Green stood up. When he got to his feet, however, he was thrown into a wall and strangled. This continued until he again fell to the floor.

At the conclusion of the second struggle, Mr. Green found himself on the ground severely hemorrhaging from wounds to his head, back, and face. The violence left blood spattered all over the walls and floors of the house. Seeing her husband in agony, Mrs. Green again attempted to render assistance. When she moved towards her companion, however, a defendant struck her on the right thigh.

Once the turmoil subsided, Mr. Green informed the defendants that he was having difficulty breathing, and that he desperately needed an ambulance. A defendant responded by cavalierly stating "good, die!" Mrs. Green then attempted to call for medical assistance, but the defendants issued her another stern warning: "step back bitch." On the threat of legal action, the defendants finally relented, permitting Mrs. Green to call 911.

As a result of his injuries, Mr. Green was rushed to a hospital. There, he was treated for trauma to his head, neck, arms, shoulders, and legs. In addition, a CAT scan was administered to determine if Mr. Green sustained brain damage. Ultimately, Mr. Green required hospitalization for twenty-three days. The severity of his injuries spawned a criminal investigation by an Assistant State's Attorney.

Title 42 U.S.C. Section 1983 affords a remedy to plaintiffs deprived of rights, privileges, or immunities secured by the United States Constitution by one acting under color of state law. Accordingly, for a plaintiff to recover under Section 1983 there must be a showing of state action. Merely private conduct, nor matter how wrongful, is not actionable under Section 1983.

To satisfy the state action requirement, a plaintiff must demonstrate that the conduct at issue is "fairly attributable to the State." Conduct is fairly attributable to a state where: (1) it is "caused by the exercise of some right or privilege created by the State or by a rule of conduct imposed by the State or by a person for whom the State is responsible"; and (2) where the party charged with the deprivation is a person who may "fairly be said to be a state actor."

A. The State Right or Privilege Prong

In accordance with the "fairly attributable" test, this court will first consider whether the conduct alleged in the amended complaint was caused by the exercise of some right or privilege created by Florida law.

According to the complaint, the individual defendants here are bail bondsmen, employed by defendant, Abony, a bail bond agency. Bail bondsmen and bail bond agencies are heavily regulated in the State of Florida. In fact, "[a] person may not act in the capacity of a bail bond agent ... or perform any of the functions, duties, or powers prescribed for bail bond agents ... unless that person is qualified, licensed, and appointed as provided [by Florida law]."

Indeed applicable Florida statutes provide:

> It is the public policy of this state ... that a bond for which fees or premiums are charged must be executed by a bail bond agent licensed pursuant to this chapter in connection with the pretrial or appellate release of a criminal defendant and shall be construed as a commitment by and obligation upon the bail bond agent to ensure that the defendant appears at all subsequent criminal proceedings.... A person, other than a certified law enforcement officer, may not apprehend, detain, or arrest a principal on a bond, wherever issued, unless that person is qualified, licensed, and appointed as provided [by Florida law].

Since the defendants' authority here—to affect the arrest of Mr. Green—was derived from Florida law, this court finds that the plaintiffs have satisfied the first prong of the "fairly attributable" test. They have alleged a constitutional deprivation (violations of the Fourth, Fifth, Sixth, Eighth, and Fourteenth Amendments) caused by the exercise of a right (a bail bondsman license) created by Florida law.

B. The State Actor Prong

Since the plaintiffs have satisfied the first prong of the "fairly attributable" test, this court will next consider whether the defendants were State actors for purposes of Section 1983.

A private party may be considered a State actor only when one of the following three conditions is met:

> (1) [T]he State has coerced or at least significantly encouraged the action alleged to violate the Constitution ("State compulsion test"); (2) the private parties performed a public function that was traditionally the exclusive prerogative of the State ("public function test"); or (3) the State had so far insinuated itself into a position of interdependence with the [private parties] that it was a joint participant in the enterprise ("nexus/joint action test").

In this instance, the plaintiffs have not alleged sufficient facts indicating that the State of Florida coerced or significantly encouraged the action alleged in the complaint. Florida law enforcement officers were not present when the defendants engaged in the knock-down-drag-out struggle at the plaintiffs' residence. Nor have the plaintiffs established that the defendants were performing a public function that was traditionally within the exclusive prerogative of this State. Instead, it is apparent that bail bonding is a private function. The right of bail bondsmen to apprehend their principals, after all, "arises out of a contract between the parties and does not have its genesis in statute or legislative fiat." In any event, history indicates that bail bonding has never been an exclusive privilege of the sovereign. Rather, since the inception of the American legal system, bail was administered by private citizens and businessmen. As such, this Order will concentrate on whether the State of Florida has so far insinuated itself into a position of interdependence with the defendants that it could be considered a joint participant in the alleged deprivation of plaintiffs' constitutional rights.

The American system of bail, and the right of bounty hunters to search for and arrest criminal defendants, descends directly from the English common law. The origins of the practice of release on bail pending trial, antedating pre-Norman England, are unknown. Initially, sureties were literally bond body for body. If the defendant failed to appear for trial, the surety was liable to suffer the punishment that was hanging over the head of the released prisoner. Alternatively, sometimes an entire township served as surety for one of its citizens, and thus its populace was collectively responsible for the appearance of the accused.

By the thirteenth century, however, the system of bail had evolved to resemble its present state. Magistrates traveled between counties and were present in any particular locality for only a few months each year. To prevent prolonged detention of untried suspects, the sheriff often released the prisoner into the custody of a surety. Generally, a surety was a responsible individual from the community and an acquaintance of the accused who promised to pay the sheriff a certain sum, sometimes by the forfeiture of real property, in the event of the prisoner's nonappearance at trial.

In spite of increased state regulation over bail bondsmen, the majority of courts continue to hold that they are not state actors for purposes of Section 1983. In *Landry*, for example, the Fifth Circuit Court of Appeals concluded that a bail bondsman was not a state actor under Section 1983 because "he neither purported to act pursuant to a warrant, nor enlisted the assistance of law enforcement officials in executing a warrant." Likewise, the Ninth Circuit Court of Appeals concluded that a bail bondsman was not a state actor because bail bondsmen are "in the business in order to make money and are not acting out of a high-minded sense of devotion to the administration of justice."

While the Eleventh Circuit Court of Appeals has yet to address the issue of whether bail bondsmen are state actors for purposes of Section

1983, the appellate court's decision in *Jaffe* is instructive on this point. In *Jaffe*, Florida bounty hunters operating in Canada abducted the defendant and returned him to the State of Florida. There, he was tried and convicted on twenty-eight counts of unlawful land sale practices. The defendant then filed a writ of habeas corpus petition arguing that Florida authorities had no jurisdiction to try, convict, or incarcerate him because his abduction from Canada violated the 1971 Treaty on Extradition between the United States and Canada. That treaty affords Canada the right to either surrender fugitives or grant them asylum. "Absent governmental action," however, "either through a direct violation of a treaty or through circumvention of the treaty, a fugitive has no basis upon which to challenge his/her return to the prosecuting jurisdiction."

Characterizing bounty hunters as "individual citizens acting outside the parameters of the treaty," the Eleventh Circuit affirmed the district court's denial of the defendant's habeas corpus petition. In doing so, the appellate court accepted the factual findings of a lower state court which concluded that the bail bondsmen were not state actors because they received no "instructions, directions, aid, comfort, succor or anything else from any authorized agency of the ... State of Florida."

Following *Jaffe*, this court finds that the defendants were not state actors for purposes of Section 1983 when they attempted to affect the arrest of Mr. Green. Although their authority to arrest the plaintiff derived from the State of Florida, the complaint is bereft of allegations indicating that they received instructions, directions, aid, comfort, succor, or anything else from the State in pursuing their principal. Instead, the complaint indicates that they were acting unilaterally for their private financial interest. "When bondsmen unilaterally apprehend their principals without any assistance from law enforcement officials, courts have consistently found them not to be state actors." This is especially the case where bail bondsmen do not identify themselves as agents of the state.

The fact that the State of Florida qualifies, licenses, and appoints its bail bondsmen is unavailing. If that were the litmus test, then doctors, engineers, lawyers, private investigators, and even concealed weapons holders would be considered state actors violating the proscription that "only in rare circumstances can a private party be viewed as a 'State actor' for Section 1983 purposes."

Conclusion

Based on the foregoing, it is **ORDERED** that the defendants' Motion to Dismiss Complaint is **GRANTED.** Since bail bondsmen are not state actors, the plaintiffs have no cause of action against the defendants pursuant to 42 U.S.C. Section 1983.

CASE COMMENT

This case takes a different twist, analyzing bail bondsmen as state actors. Of course, since the plaintiffs allege a Section 1983 cause of action, they must show the bail bondsmen were state actors. They failed to do so. The court initially examined the level of state involvement in the bail bondsmen business. Finding rather substantial government regulation, the court held it satisfied the State Right or Privilege Prong. However, the State actor requirements were not met in light of the three tests previously set out by the Supreme Court. Consequently, the case was dismissed.

DISCUSSION QUESTIONS

What factors distinguish special police from peace officers? Is one factor more important than any other? What test used to assess whether an individual is a "state actor" has the most application in contemporary America? In light of terrorism, does the need for government to provide for public safety impact the usage of special police officers? Explain your answer, regardless of your conclusion. Finally, consider a hypothetical case in which a terrorist may have information regarding a "dirty bomb" that is set to explode in a downtown business district. Please discuss the prohibition of the Fifth Amendment coerced confession and the Eighth Amendment prohibition against cruel and unusual punishment in light of the potential for massive death, financial dislocation, and property destruction that such a case would pose. Specifically, when is coerced confession or even certain torture appropriate, if at all?

Part Five

Terrorism and Future Issues

Terrorism is a very complicated concept. There are many elements and levels associated with the concept. This book cannot delve deeply into these matters. Instead, the key elements of terrorism will be highlighted and discussed.

As compared to terrorism, the impact of crime is well known. Those in the security industry make their living from the impact of crime, and from the fear generated from it. It is not necessary to "sell" the readers on the relationship between crime and security. The relationship, indeed, is compelling. The same logic holds true for terrorism. In fact, the connection between fear and terrorism is more pronounced than with crime.

TERRORISM ISSUES AND IMPLICATIONS

An underlying purpose of terrorism, unlike that of "normal" crime, is to instill fear.[1] The impact of terrorism in creating fear, with the resulting desire for security, cannot be ignored. The relationship between terrorism and fear has been widely studied and developed.[2] Without getting into the complexities of this relationship, it is clear that one of the principles of terrorism is to foster fear in the targeted society.[3] Indeed, one of the basic principles of terrorism is that the "audience" (society) is the true target. Unlike crime, where the victim is the target of the attack, terrorism is designed to attack the larger society, not just actual victims of the attack(s). In this sense, terrorism has been described as being primarily theater.[4]

The relationship of terrorism to the amount of fear in society is difficult to predict. Studies of crime and fear discussed in Chapter 1 have largely focused on "ordinary crime." Of course, even ordinary crime creates fear. However, while fear is the inevitable result of crime, terrorism is *designed* to create fear—and at a much deeper level. The intent is to break the "inertial relationship" which binds the citizen to the government.[5] This disorientation is often coupled with the disruption of the stableness of daily life.[6]

At this level, terrorism upsets the framework of trust and security, on which people depend. This creates more anxiety and uncertainty, due in part to the unpredictability of violence. People may become so paranoid and isolated that they are unable to draw strength and security from their usual social supports, causing them to rely entirely upon their own resources. Ultimately, Greisman contends, the watchword for the stricken masses becomes: "Don't wait to be hunted to hide."[7] This impact of terrorism is summed up in a pointed assertion by Graham, who states that "terrorism destroys the solidarity, cooperation, and interdependence on which social functioning is based, and substitutes insecurity and distrust."[8] This is echoed by Ganor, who stated "the aim is to isolate the individual from the group, to break up a society into many frightened individuals hiding in their homes and unable to go about their daily lives."[9] Clutterbuck uses the descriptive term "climate of collapse" to refer to the cycle of violence and fear in which the political balance begins to favor the terrorists, instead of the government or the police.[10]

As this illustrates, the impact of terrorism upon society is substantial. Accordingly crime (and terrorism) may be increasingly based on "environmental scarcity, cultural and racial clashes, and geographic destiny."[11] Kaplan maintains that "as crime continues to grow in our cities, and the ability of government and criminal justice systems to protect their citizens diminishes, urban crime may develop into low-intensity conflict by coalescing along racial, religious, social, and political lines, resulting in a 'booming private security business.'"[12]

This description, while admittedly disconcerting, is quite probable in the next few years (see Chapter 14 for additional explanation).

TERRORISM DEFINITIONS

One of the problems in countering terrorism is that there is no single definitive definition of "terrorism." The statement, "One man's terrorist is another man's freedom fighter," has become a frequency cited cliché. It also is one of the most difficult obstacles in coping with terrorism. This is so because it makes understanding terrorism a very subjective consideration. Furthermore, some may feel that the definition and conceptualization of terrorism is only a purely theoretical issue—a mechanism for scholars to work out the appropriate set of parameters for the intended research. However, when dealing with terrorism, the implications of defined terms tend to transcend the boundaries of theoretical discussions. In the struggle against terrorism, Ganor contends "the problem of definition is a crucial element in the attempt to coordinate international collaboration, based on the currently accepted rules of traditional warfare."[13]

For these reasons, it is valuable to define terrorism. In its most basic form, terrorism is the "systematic use of violence, terror, and intimidation to achieve an end."[14] The U.S. Department of Defense uses a more pointed definition with a number of critical elements. It states terrorism is "the calculated use of violence or the threat of violence to inculcate fear; intended to coerce or to intimidate governments or societies in the pursuit of goals that are generally political, religious, or ideological."[15] Similarly, the Federal Bureau of Investigation defines terrorism as "the unlawful use of force or violence against persons or property to intimidate or coerce a government, the civilian population, or any segment thereof, in furtherance of political or social objectives."[16]

The FBI further breaks down terrorism as either domestic or international, depending on the origin, base, and objectives of the terrorist organization. Based on these distinctions, the FBI uses the following definitions of terrorism.

Domestic terrorism refers to "activities that involve acts dangerous to human life that are a violation of the criminal laws of the United States or of any state; appear to be intended to intimidate or coerce a civilian population; to influence the policy of a government by mass destruction, assassination, or kidnapping; and occur primarily within the territorial jurisdiction of the United States."[17]

International terrorism "involves violent acts or acts dangerous to human life that are a violation of the criminal laws of the United States or any state, or that would be a criminal violation if committed within the jurisdiction of the United States or any state. These acts appear to be intended to intimidate or coerce a civilian population; influence the policy of a government by intimidation or coercion; or affect the conduct of a government by mass destruction, assassination, or kidnapping and occur primarily outside the territorial jurisdiction of the United States or transcend national boundaries in terms of the means by which they are accomplished, the persons they appear intended to intimidate or coerce, or the locale in which their perpetrators operate or seek asylum."[18]

While these definitions are necessary to understand the concept, they are not widely accepted beyond the United States. Even if the definitions were widely accepted, they do not solve the problems posed by terrorism. The problems and implications are substantial. With such definitions and implications presented, we will now shift the focus to cases and statutes related to terrorism.

NOTES

1. See for example, Poland, James M. (2005). *Understanding Terrorism: Groups, Strategies and Responses.* Upper Saddle River, NJ: Prentice Hall; Ganor, Boaz (2005). Violence and Terrorism. *Terror as a Strategy of Psychological Warfare,* Thomas J. Badey (ed.), 05/06, McGraw-Hill/Dushkin; and Wardlaw, Grant (1982). *Political Terrorism: Theory, Tactics, and Counter-Measures.* Cambridge: Cambridge University Press.

2. Wardlaw op cit. at 36; Poland op cit. at 17; Ganor op cit. at 16. In addition, see Ezeldin, Ahmed Galal (1987). *Terrorism and Political Violence.* Chicago: University of Illinois at Chicago Press; Clutterbuck, Richard (1975). The Police and Urban Terrorism. *The Police Journal*; Wolf, John B. (1981). *Fear of Fear: Survey of Terrorist Operations and Controls in Open Societies.* New York: Plenum Publishing; and Davis, James R. (1982). *Street Gangs: Youth, Biker & Prison Groups.* Dubuque: Kendall-Hunt Publishing.
3. Wolf op cit. at 107; Clutterbuck op cit. at 206; Ganor op cit. at 6; and Poland op cit. at 16–17. For similar assertion see also Greisman, H. C. (1979). Terrorism and the Closure of Society: A Social Impact Projection. *Technological Forecasting and Social Change.* Vol. 14; and Tucker, Jonathan B. (2003). Strategies for Countering Terrorism: Lessons from the Israeli Experience. *Journal of Homeland Security*, March 26.
4. Wardlaw op cit. at 38; Poland op cit. at 10; and Ganor op cit. at 5–6.
5. Ganor op cit. at 6; Tucker op cit. at 18; Poland op cit. at 209; Ganor op cit. at 5–6; Wardlaw op cit. at 10; and Clutterbuck op cit. at 286. For similar assertion see also Waugh, William L. (1982). *International Terrorism.* Salisbury. NC: Documentary Publications; and Crenshaw, Martha ed. (1983). *Terrorism, Legitimacy and Power: The Consequences of Political Violence.* Middleton, CN: Wesleyan University Press.
6. Ganor op cit. at 6; Tucker op cit. at 18; Wolf op cit. at 282; and Greisman op cit. at 138. For similar assertion see also Young, R. (1977). Revolutionary Terrorism, Crime and Morality. *Social Theory & Practice,* Vol. 4.
7. Greisman op cit. at 41.
8. Graham, Thomas, and Tedd Gurr, eds. (1971). *A History of Violence in America*, Princeton, NJ: Princeton University Press.
9. Ganor op cit. at 6.
10. Clutterbuck op cit. at 206.
11. Kaplan, Robert (1994). The Coming Anarchy. *The Atlantic Monthly,* February.
12. Ibid at 74.
13. Ganor, Boaz (2005). *Is One Man's Terrorist Another Man's Freedom Fighter?* Taken from http://www.ict.org.il/articles/define.htm on December 16, 2005.
14. Payne, Carroll (2005). *World Conflict Quarterly.* Taken from http://www.globalterrorism101.com/UTDefinition.html on December 16, 2005.
15. See *Terrorism 2000/2001* taken from http://www.fbi.gov/publications/terror/terror2000_2001.htm on December 16, 2005.
16. Ibid. See also 28 C.F.R. Section 0.85 in the *Code of Federal Regulations.*
17. See 18 U.S.C. Section 2331(5).
18. See 18 U.S.C. Section 2331(1).

12

Terrorism Cases

776 N.Y.S. 2d 713

Supreme Court, New York County, New York

IN THE MATTER OF WORLD TRADE CENTER BOMBING LITIGATION.

Jan. 20, 2004

Background

In consolidated actions against Port Authority of New York and New Jersey, in its capacity as owner of World Trade Center (WTC), alleging that negligent security resulted in injuries due to 1993 terrorist bombing in parking garage of WTC, Port Authority moved for summary judgment.

Holdings

The Supreme Court, New York County, held that

1. Port Authority was not entitled to sovereign immunity, and
2. Triable issues of fact existed as to whether bombing was foreseeable.

Motion denied in part and granted in part.

The World Trade Center was a commercial office complex, covering 16 acres, in downtown Manhattan. As many will recall, on February 26, 1993, a bomb exploded in the public parking garage located beneath the concourse of the buildings, killing six people, injuring many others, and disrupting businesses. The explosives were placed in a van which was driven in and parked in the public parking area of the garage, the perpetrators left the garage, and then detonated the bomb. In March 1994, four individuals were convicted of placing and detonating the explosive device. Plaintiffs basically contend that the Port Authority failed to implement security measures by keeping the parking garage open to public transient parking, which would have kept the bomb out of the garage, and failed to mitigate the resulting injuries and destruction.

The Port Authority was created in 1921 when Congress consented to a compact between New York and New Jersey to develop and coordinate the terminal, transportation, and other facilities of commerce in, about, and through the port of New York. The Port Authority owns and/or operates many such facilities, including three major airports, interstate bridges and tunnels, an inter-city rail system known as the Port Authority Trans-Hudson rail (PATH), bus stations, and, before its destruction on September 11, 2001, the World Trade Center (WTC), one of the city's largest commercial office complexes.

The WTC, constructed by the Port Authority, was a multi-building commercial and office complex. It was built to bring together facilities such as customs houses, commodity and security exchanges, exporters and importers, freighters, other offices, and exhibition facilities, with portions of the buildings which "may not be devoted to purposes of the port development project other than the production of incidental revenue" to support the port development project. In carrying out the provisions of the law, the Port Authority "shall be regarded as performing an essential government function."

The WTC consisted of two 110-story office towers (One and Two WTC), a 47-story office building (Seven WTC), two nine-story office buildings (Four and Five WTC), an eight-story U.S. Customs House (Six WTC), and a 22-story hotel (Three WTC). The Concourse, with many shops, restaurants, and services, sat directly below the plaza that connected many of the buildings, and provided direct access to the Twin Towers. The WTC was served by the PATH system and the New York City subway system.

Beneath the Concourse, below grade level, there were six sub-levels, identified as B-1 to B-6. These sub-grade areas included: parking facilities for the public and tenants; tenant storage areas; a truck dock; mechanical equipment rooms; utility mains and connections; operations and maintenance support facilities; the WTC terminal of the PATH, with tracks and equipment; emergency generators; communication systems; fire standpipes; main feeder lines for electrical power; and the chiller plant for the air conditioning system. The Operations Control Center, which served as the center for fire alarm communications, the public address system and other systems alarms, as well as a communications center and a routing center for critical maintenance facilities and functions, was located off the truck loading dock, on the B-1 level.

1. Parking at WTC

The parking areas in the B-2 level were accessible to the public from two vehicle entry ramps on West Street, ramps A and B, which had no barriers, and two exit ramps, ramps C and D, which permitted exit back onto West Street. There were 400 public parking spaces, and approximately 1,600 tenant spaces. The sub-grade areas were also accessible through the truck dock entrance, located on Barclay Street, and this entrance was manned.

The passenger car entrances on West Street were not manned, but there was a ticket office, off the main ramp or road, run by the parking manager. The truck entrance had a gate and a guard post at which the truck, and its destination and contents, would be logged. Tenant parking was also accessible through the truck dock entrance, but if they used that entrance they had to present identification. Transient public parkers who attempted to use the truck dock entrance were directed to the West Street entrances. It was possible for a car to come in an entrance to the garage on West Street and then to leave the garage, essentially driving in a "U" or a circle, without encountering a security checkpoint, either barriers or security personnel.

2. Security at the WTC

The WTC was run by the World Trade Department of the Port Authority, which determined whether to open parts of the WTC to the public, whether public parking should be offered, and what security should be provided for the buildings and the garage. Civilian management personnel had responsibility for the day-to-day administration of security guards assigned to the WTC. The Port Authority Police had a command post on the B-1 level, and was responsible for public safety. The civilian security guards were not police officers, did not carry weapons or handcuffs, and reported to the World Trade Department, not to the Port Authority police. They provided security, were information agents (providing information and directions to the public), monitored access to the complex, reported accidents to the police, and detected intruders. The police were responsible for criminal investigations and accidents.

The Port Authority Establishes a Terrorism Planning Office

In the early 1980s the Port Authority was aware of terrorist activities occurring in other areas of the world, and that the WTC, as a highly symbolic target, was vulnerable to terrorist attack. Terrorist bombings, including car bombs, were becoming more prevalent, not only in the world but in the United States as well. In fact, the Port Authority recognized that, in 1983–84, two thirds of domestic terrorist incidents occurred in the New York–New Jersey metropolitan region.

In response, the Port Authority created a Terrorist Planning and Intelligence Section, and assigned Detective Sergeant Peter Caram the tasks of identifying terrorist groups and Port Authority targets, and to assess the vulnerability of Port Authority facilities to terrorist attack. The Terrorist Planning Section submitted its report in 1984, in which it warned that the threat of domestic terrorism was rising, that the WTC was vulnerable to terrorist attack, and that the underground public parking garage was highly vulnerable, easily accessible, and, if attacked, could critically affect the WTC's infrastructure.

In another report, entitled "Terrorist Assessment World Trade Center 1984," prepared at the request of the Port Authority Superintendent of Police, the Port Authority was warned that, more than at any time in its history, the WTC should be considered a prime target for domestic and international terrorists. The report also specifically warned that the parking lots "are accessible to the public and are highly susceptible to car bombings."

Later that year, again in 1984, the Port Authority created the Office of Special Planing (OSP) to address and evaluate the vulnerabilities of Port Authority facilities to terrorist acts, and to formulate recommendations to prevent and minimize the risks of such acts. Port Authority Executive Director Peter Goldmark, in a memorandum to Vic Strom, Director of the Port Authority's Public Safety Department, Edward O'Sullivan, Director of OSP, and Hank DeGeneste, the Assistant Superintendent of Port Authority Police, noted the particular concern the authorities at Scotland Yard, expressed to Port Authority officials in August 1984, about the vulnerability of the WTC parking garage to terrorist attack. He stated that those at Scotland Yard "are appalled to hear we had transient parking directly underneath the towers."

The OSP staff included Port Authority civilian or police personnel with experience in terrorism, operational security, tactical technology, bomb investigation, operations, and military operations. OSP's Director, Mr. O'Sullivan, was experienced in terrorism and counter-terrorism from his ten-year career in the Navy and Marine Corps. OSP's mission was "to study and prepare measures which would make Port Authority facilities less vulnerable to terrorist attack, to improve the organization's prevention and defensive capabilities, to establish liaison with foreign and domestic units engaged in counter-terrorism activities and to develop an awareness among staff of the potential terrorist threat and the need for vigilance and preparedness." OSP consulted with the FBI, the CIA, the National Security Agency, U.S. Secret Service, U.S. Department of Transportation, Department of State, Department of Defense, and security officials from the governments of France, England,

Italy, Switzerland, and Israel, as well as private consultants. The scope of OSP's activities included reviewing and addressing vulnerabilities, identifying alternatives and solutions, presenting recommendations to the facility's management, and obtaining responses from each facility that would be coordinated with the Director of Public Safety.

OSP's Study of the WTC

The OSP spent four to six months studying the WTC, including its building design through examination of photographs, blueprints, diagrams, and plans. OSP brought in experts, such as those who built the WTC, and those who operated it, as well as experts familiar with sabotage and explosives, and had them walk through to assess what was vulnerable, and identify critical areas of the WTC that, if damaged, could impair the building's ability to function or require it to shut down. The OSP visited other large commercial buildings in the City, reviewing their security and the way they handled and responded to bomb threats.

To formulate its recommendations, OSP conducted a "target analysis" in which it analyzed Port Authority targets in terms of "criticality, accessibility, vulnerability, recuperability and extended effect that destruction of the specific target" would have. Criticality is the measure of the impact on the normal flow of events by the target's destruction. Accessibility refers to the terrorist's ability to reach and attack a vincible point. Vulnerability is the extent to which the target would be damaged. Recuperability is the speed at which normal operation would resume after an attack. Finally, OSP evaluated the extended effect of destruction of the target.

In a preliminary report entitled "WTC Study Brief," OSP staff considered several attack scenarios, including, most significantly, a "bomb-laden truck attack." In the report, it was stated that, given the recent truck bombings in Lebanon, it was important to consider this possibility, and that a "strategically positioned truck or van could cause extensive structural damage to the Trade Center as well as a large number of casualties." OSP raised questions about this scenario, including which areas, i.e., across the street or in the parking lot below, provide the greatest "bang for the buck," what security exists for a truck bombing at WTC, and what other security measures against this scenario are viable.

In 1985, before the OSP issued its report, the Port Authority hired an outside security consultant, Charles Schnabolk, to review the WTC's security systems. Schnabolk's report focused on the threat of terrorism to the WTC. Schnabolk, in a letter to O'Sullivan, urged that action be taken as soon as possible to implement his recommendations. In the report, the terrorist threat of "bombing attempts" was placed in the "probable" category, and the report warned that the WTC "is highly vulnerable through the parking lot.... With little effort terrorists could create havoc without being seriously deterred by the current security measures." The report also made specific recommendations regarding security in the sub-grade levels:

1. The parking area needs better surveillance. This can be accomplished through the control systems which are proposed to operate at a sub-grade level. The parking lots also require CCTV and mirrors for security and safety purposes.
2. Vehicles coming to Port Authority parking areas may be screened for the presence of explosives. This can be done by inspecting trunks of cars and examining the undersides of vehicles.

The procedures would not substantially slow down the parking of vehicles in these areas. While it may be considered security overkill to establish such a security check, the measure can be instituted easily with the use of CCTV and mirrors placed in a trough over which the vehicles drive.

The OSP Report

In November 1985, OSP issued its report entitled *Counter-terrorism Perspectives: The World Trade Center* (the OSP Report). The OSP Report recognized that the WTC was a "most attractive terrorist target" based on its symbolic value, its visibility, and the fact that it is immediately recognizable to people from around the world. The report listed 25 bombing incidents that took place in and around New York City from 1980 to1984, including several car-bombing incidents. It also listed a bombing at the beginning of 1985 in an office building just a few blocks from the WTC, and the Port Authority was aware of three bombs that had been placed in downtown buildings in August of 1985. The OSP Report specifically warned that "[t]he car bomb is fast becoming the weapon of choice for European terrorists and the fact that parking an explosives-laden vehicle provides substantial escape time for the driver is ample justification to take decisive target hardening measures in this area."

The underground public parking garage was particularly singled out as a "definite security risk." The OSP report specifically found that "parking for 2,000 vehicles in the underground areas presents an enormous opportunity, at present, for terrorists to park an explosive-filled vehicle that could affect vulnerable areas." It warned that the garage was so vulnerable because it afforded "unimpeded access for someone bent on putting a car bomb into the World Trade Center parking lot," which would affect "virtually all of the important building systems, such as power, water, heating, [and] cooling," because those systems all were located in and around the parking areas.

In proposing potential terrorist scenarios at the WTC, the OSP Report predicted nearly precisely how the February 26, 1993 bombing would occur:

A time bomb-laden vehicle could be driven into the WTC and parked in the public parking area. The driver could then exit via an elevator into the WTC and proceed with his business unnoticed. At a predetermined time, the bomb could be exploded in the basement. The amount of explosives used will determine the severity of damage to the area.

With respect to the public parking, the OSP Report recommended taking "decisive target hardening measures in this area" by eliminating all public parking, because "explosives may be readily concealed within a vehicle parked within the core of the complex." OSP's Director, O'Sullivan, testified at his deposition, that because terrorists conduct surveillance of potential targets to determine the one with the greatest impact with the least risk to themselves, they can be deterred if they get a sense that the facility is protected, guarded, and presents some risk to them. OSP also recommended: providing manned entrances to the public parking area; restricting pedestrian entry into the parking areas via the ramps; subjecting vehicles to random inspections; and providing a police patrol with an explosives-detection dog. The OSP Report was submitted to the Executive Director of the Port Authority, the Director of Public Safety of the Port Authority, the Superintendent of the Port Authority Police, and the Director of the World Trade Department.

Port Authority's Actions with Respect to OSP'S Recommendations

Guy Tozzoli, the Director of the World Trade Department, in February 1986, in a letter to Stephen Berger, the Port Authority's Executive Director, addressed the OSP's recommendations. With respect to the subgrade levels and OSP's recommendation to ensure proper venting of smoke evacuation devices, Tozzoli responded that adequate ventilation was being provided by the sub-grade exhaust fans. As to the public parking recommendations, Tozzoli responded that: (1) the elimination of transient parking would not be implemented, because of the inconvenience to tenants and the loss of revenues; (2) manning the public parking would be too expensive and would not deter a terrorist; (3) restricting pedestrians is impractical because there are many other ways to gain access to the areas; and (4) random inspections of vehicles could not be done without probable cause.

The SAIC Report

The Port Authority sought a second opinion about the OSP's recommendations, and hired an outside consultant, Science Applications International Corporation (SAIC), to conduct a general security review of the WTC. SAIC was given a copy of the OSP Report as well as Tozzoli's letter to Berger rejecting OSP's recommendations about the subgrade level. SAIC's Report rated the attractiveness of the WTC's public areas to terrorist attack as "very high." It identified the vehicle ramps as vulnerable areas. It specifically noted that vehicle access for security purposes is uncontrolled. The report found that a "well-placed vehicle bomb in each of these locations [the vehicle ramps] would likely damage at least half of the support services (fresh water, steam, cooling water, electrical and telephone) to the WTC users." The SAIC Report found that an adversary would have "little difficulty" in procuring explosives which are "readily available" in the quantities envisioned in the report. Like the OSP Report, the SAIC Report described an attack scenario, remarkably like the one which occurred, in which a small delivery truck with explosives could be positioned on a ramp to the complex, and detonated following a short time delay for the driver's escape. It recommended certain possible upgrades, including installing blast deflectors around critical support service components (water, electrical, phone), eliminating parking in subgrades, conducting vehicle searches at truck entrances, conducting random searches of all vehicles, and developing redundant support service capabilities. These upgrades, however, had been deemed "very costly either in terms of operational impact, public acceptance, or monetary cost," though SAIC admitted that it had not provided any cost analysis to the Port Authority, and that the costs were not further analyzed. In SAIC's presentation to the Port Authority's Executive Director in October 1986, SAIC featured "barriers to deter car bomb attempts" at a cost of $83,000, as an upgrade "for immediate implementation" to counter a terrorist attack, with a risk reduction figure of 40 percent. The presentation also included a comparison of OSP's recommendations about eliminating parking, or instituting more stringent controls and monitoring, and SAIC's recommendation that these actions were "considered but not recommended" based on discussions with the Port Authority.

The Burns and Roe Securacom Report

In 1991, because of the Gulf War and the increased risk of terrorism to United States targets, the Port Authority commissioned another security consulting firm, Burns and Roe Securacom to prepare reports. Securacom was told by the Port Authority that the WTC was a terrorist target, and the report would help it plan its capital expenditures to maintain its competitive status with nearby buildings that offered more advanced security features. Securacom's draft report recognized that in the "aftermath of Mideast events," there would be a significant increase in "international activities." It included the subgrade utilities and the parking garage as areas of vulnerability. Its final report recommended that the WTC adopt a master plan approach to the development of security systems.

On January 23, 1993, one month before the bombing, the Port Authority received an intelligence report from the FBI that there was a threat from the Mideast to blow up a major office building in New York. Some heightened security measures were implemented over that weekend (January 23 was a Friday) as a result, including some increased patrols around the perimeter, which patrols also drove through the underground areas, but these were scaled back after the weekend was over.

The Bombing

On February 26, 1993, at 12:18 p.m., a bomb exploded beneath the WTC, on the B-2 level of the underground parking garage, on a ramp that leads toward an exit from the garage. The explosion had the force of 1,500 pounds of dynamite. The investigation revealed that the bomb had been detonated in a yellow van parked on the ramp of the public parking garage. Six people were killed, and many, many more were injured, mostly from smoke inhalation. There was evidence that the perpetrators had made several surveillance visits to the garage, and drew maps of the garage. The explosion made a crater six stories deep, compressed several levels of concrete slab, blew down a wall onto the PATH concourse, and destroyed the walls of a number of elevator shafts. The explosion destroyed the communications system, the police area and operations control center, and vital utility systems, including water and electrical, and fire standpipes. Because of the loss of the operations control center, the Port Authority lost the ability to communicate with tenants and their employees in the complex, and to institute its emergency evacuation procedures.

Plaintiffs' Claims

Plaintiffs' claims are based on their allegations that the Port Authority was negligent with respect to security: in failing to adopt, implement, and follow the recommendations in the security reports; in failing to restrict public access to the parking levels; in failing to have an adequate security plan; in failing to provide an electronic security system; in failing to institute a manned checkpoint at the garage; in failing to subject vehicles to inspection and to have security signs; in failing to have adequate security personnel; in failing to employ recording devices concerning vehicles, operators, occupants, and pedestrians; and in failing to conduct studies of the possible results of a bombing of the complex. The claims also are based on alleged failures with respect to the ventilation system, that is, in failing to have a proper and adequate regular and emergency ventilation system in case of fire and explosion. Plaintiffs also claim that the Port Authority failed to provide adequate lighting, to use air-cooled emergency generators, and to have adequate communications and backup communications systems. They further claim that the Port Authority failed to properly train and communicate with the fire wardens, and train employees on proper evacuation procedures.

Motion for Summary Judgment

The Port Authority is moving for summary judgment dismissing plaintiffs' negligence claims. First, it argues that it cannot be held liable in negligence as a matter of law for failing to protect plaintiffs from the criminal acts of third parties, because providing such protection is a governmental function. The Port Authority contends that plaintiffs' claims are based on the failure to provide security, which it urges is a governmental function. It points to the legislation establishing the Port Authority, as proof that it was performing an essential governmental function in undertaking to provide safety and security to the patrons at the WTC. It asserts that the activities for which plaintiffs want to hold the Port Authority liable essentially involve, or grow directly out of, the failure to allocate police resources. The Port Authority also urges that the principle that a government agency owes no duty to a victim of crime on government premises extends beyond the deployment of police officers to other security contexts, including those set forth in plaintiffs' claims here. It contends that plaintiffs are challenging the Port Authority's decisions regarding the allocation of resources to address potential vulnerabilities identified in the OSP and follow-up reports, which decisions, it contends, are legislative-executive ones, and are not for the courts. The Port Authority further contends that plaintiffs cannot establish a special relationship which might give rise to liability, because there was no direct communication between plaintiffs and the Port Authority in which plaintiffs sought and obtained promises from the Port Authority to provide protection from the events that happened on February 26, 1993.

Second, the Port Authority contends that even if it is determined that it was not performing a governmental function, it still would not be liable, because the bombing was not foreseeable as a matter of law. It points to the lack of evidence of similar criminal acts at the WTC. The Port Authority claims that the prerequisite for liability is the likelihood of crime, not the mere possibility. It urges that the courts have repeatedly held that the existence of ambient crime in the neighborhood is not a sufficient basis for holding a building owner liable for the criminal acts of third parties on the premises. It contends that the alleged basis for the predictability of the bombing, a security report, is not the equivalent of crime on the premises or actual crime in the neighborhood. The Port Authority maintains that plaintiffs have failed to present any evidence that an explosive-laden vehicle had been placed in the WTC prior to February 26, 1993, and that, therefore, plaintiffs have failed to establish a predicate for holding the Port Authority liable. It asserts that the OSP report raised the possibility of a bombing, not the likelihood of its occurrence.

In opposition, plaintiffs make several arguments. They counter the Port Authority's governmental immunity argument by citing (citation omitted) in which the Port Authority waives such immunity, and consents to liability in suits for tortuous acts committed by it "to the same extent as though it were a private corporation." Plaintiffs assert that this statute waives the Port Authority's potential immunity more broadly than other waiver statutes applicable to other governmental entities. They contend that they are seeking damages for the Port Authority's negligent failure to implement appropriate safety precautions in the parking facilities at the WTC, and that, the plaintiffs are entitled to bring their actions against the Port Authority.

Plaintiffs further argue that, even assuming that the Port Authority could still assert some kind of governmental immunity defense, the Port Authority's liability here arises from its negligent failures in operating a commercial office building, leased to commercial tenants, and to retail stores, which they claim were clearly proprietary, not governmental, functions. Plaintiffs assert that the facts show that the WTC complex, and in particular, its parking facilities, were commercial facilities, and that the Port Authority's operation of those facilities was not fundamental to its nature as a governmental entity. Further, they contend that security at the WTC was principally provided by civilian managers, and private security guards, not police officers. Thus, plaintiffs assert that the Port Authority's negligence falls along the continuum of responsibility to individuals and society deriving from its proprietary functions, in the sense that the negligence derives from its ownership, maintenance, and care of the WTC complex, including the garage and parking facilities. They claim they are seeking to hold the Port Authority liable, as a private commercial landlord, for its failure to either close the WTC parking garage to transient parking, or to implement any reasonable security measures in the face of a known threat. Plaintiffs distinguish these actions from those involving the failure to allocate police resources, such as the absence of police surveillance and the failure to warn of criminal activity. They assert that the fact of the size and complexity of the WTC, and that it serves a great number of people, does not require the conclusion that precautions taken for the security of the facility are transformed into governmental functions. They urge that the omissions complained of involve the provision of basic security measures, and that the Port Authority made such omissions in its capacity as a private landlord.

Alternatively, if the Port Authority's negligence arises from its exercise of a governmental function, plaintiffs maintain that the Port Authority had special relationships with them, and that it therefore may be held liable for its negligence in the performance of that function. They claim that whether there was a special relationship is a question of fact not resolvable on a motion for summary judgment.

Finally, plaintiffs argue that the Port Authority could not possibly argue that the bombing was unforeseeable as a matter of law, because, in fact, not only was it foreseeable, but it was actually foreseen. They urge that the undisputed facts show that domestic terrorism was on the rise, car bombs were the preferred method, the WTC was a prime target for a terrorist attack, and the parking garage was highly vulnerable. They contend that the record establishes that the Port Authority knew, or at the least, should have known, that there was a likelihood that third parties would engage in conduct that would endanger the safety of those using the premises, and that it was obligated to take measures to safeguard against that risk. Plaintiffs contend that, contrary to what the Port Authority is arguing, a landlord does not have to have past experience with the precise sort of criminal activity in the same place before a landlord could be found negligent in failing to take precautions that would have prevented the crime. Plaintiffs point to the evidence in the record that prior to the WTC bombing there had been successful terrorist bombings of buildings in the immediate neighborhood ... and that the FBI had warned, just a month before, that Middle Eastern terrorists had threatened to blow up a major office building in New York, to show that the bombing was foreseeable. They aptly assert that the law does not permit, as the Port Authority appears to claim, a landlord one free catastrophic event, particularly where, as in this case, the Port Authority was aware of the threat of terrorism, was aware that the WTC was a potential target, and was specifically warned by its own experts, as well as by other terrorist experts, of exactly the type of attack that occurred in 1993. Plaintiffs further contend that, at the least, the issue of foreseeability is a question for the jury. Plaintiffs urge that the Port Authority failed to implement reasonable safety precautions in the underground parking garage, leaving it completely open and accessible, and that the issue of the reasonableness of safety precautions is almost always a factual issue for the jury.

In reply, the Port Authority concedes that the reasonableness of safety precautions cannot be decided on a motion for summary judgment, but maintains that the bombing was not foreseeable as a matter of law. It asserts that courts have held that a landlord may not be held liable unless it had notice of the likelihood of such crime on the premises, based on a history of actual crimes on those premises sufficient to alert the landlord that the crime injuring the plaintiff was likely to occur on the property. It contends that plaintiffs cannot point to any previous cases in which the courts have relied on proof such as plaintiffs', e.g., the reports, which it claims are general statements, as opposed to actual crime on or near the premises, at times, and of such number, as to put a landlord on notice of the likelihood of similar crime being perpetrated on the plaintiffs. On the issue of governmental immunity, the Port Authority argues that the Port Authority waives sovereign immunity to suit in tort, it has not given up its substantive defense of governmental immunity. On the substantive defense, it urges that plaintiffs cannot show a duty owed by the Port Authority to them for the alleged negligence in providing security against crime in government facilities, such as the WTC. It contends that government immunity is not limited to the deployment of police resources, as plaintiffs argue. Finally, it contends that no special relationship was created by virtue of plaintiffs' entry into the WTC.

For the reasons delineated below, the court concludes that, based on statutes and case law, the Port Authority was not immune from liability for at least some of plaintiffs' negligence allegations, and that, based on the deposition testimony, the documentary evidence and affidavits, plaintiffs have provided sufficient evidence to demonstrate that there are triable issues of fact with respect to the foreseeability of plaintiffs' damages and injuries.

Governmental Immunity

To analyze the Port Authority's assertion that it is immune from plaintiffs' negligence claims because it was performing a governmental function, the applicable statutes must be examined. The Port Authority is a joint and common governmental agency of the States of New York and New Jersey. Although the Port Authority serves a governmental function in many of its undertakings, it is not immune from suit. In 1950 and 1951, the legislatures of New York and New Jersey enacted statutes with identical provisions pursuant to which the Port Authority waived its sovereign immunity to tort claims. Before these statutes, the Port Authority, as a direct agency of the State of New York, absent any consent by the State, was completely immune from suits of any kind. In the statutes, the states of New York and New Jersey consented to suits against the Port Authority, and provided, with exceptions not relevant here, that "although the port authority is engaged in the performance of governmental functions," it shall be liable "in such suits, actions or proceedings for tortuous acts committed by it and its agents to the same extent as though it were a private corporation." This consent to suit, and waiver of sovereign immunity, was expressed in expansive terms.

Applied to the instant case, the unambiguous language controls and confirms that the Port Authority has consented to this suit and may not assert the defense of sovereign immunity. These claims fall within the broad coverage of the statute, are not specifically excluded, and therefore are authorized under the terms of those sections.

The next step in the analysis is to determine if the Port Authority owed a duty to plaintiffs. As in the case of an action against a private corporation, it is necessary to decide whether the Port Authority is under a duty to these plaintiffs, irrespective of sovereign immunity. "Absent the existence and breach of such a duty, the abrogation of governmental immunity, in itself, affords little aid to a plaintiff seeking to cast a municipality in damages." Moreover, to establish liability against a municipality or government agency, the duty breached must be more than a duty owed to the general public, such as the failure to provide police or fire protection.

The Port Authority urges that plaintiffs' negligence claims of failing to close or provide adequate security in the WTC parking garage, are simply claims for the failure to provide police protection, a governmental function for which it cannot be held liable absent a special relationship with the plaintiffs. This argument is rejected. The court holds that the plaintiffs' allegations of the Port Authority's negligent acts essentially involve proprietary functions for which the Port Authority owes a duty to them.

Contrary to the Port Authority's contentions, the WTC and its public parking garage were primarily commercial facilities, the security was determined and provided by the civilian management and private security guards, and the actions and failures to act involved predominantly the Port Authority's maintenance and security of the property as a commercial landlord of an office and retail complex, rather than its governmental-executive decision making regarding the provision of resources for police protection.

It is well settled that when a public entity acts in a proprietary capacity as a landlord, it is subject to ordinary tort liability. The entity, however, remains immune from negligence claims arising out of governmental functions, such as police protection, unless a special relationship creates a duty to protect, and the plaintiff relies on the performance of that duty.

This dichotomy between proprietary and governmental functions was discussed and analyzed by the court of appeals in *Miller v. State of New York*.

A governmental entity's conduct may fall along a continuum of responsibility to individuals and society deriving from its governmental and proprietary functions. This begins with the simplest matters directly concerning a piece of property for which the entity acting as landlord has a certain duty of care, for example, the repair of steps or the maintenance of doors in an apartment building. The spectrum extends gradually out to more complex measures of safety and security for a greater area and populace, whereupon the actions increasingly, and at a certain point only, involve governmental functions, for example, the maintenance of general police and fire protection.

In determining whether the alleged negligent acts qualify as a governmental activity deserving of immunity, or a proprietary act subjecting the public entity to tort liability, "it is the specific act or omission out of which the injury is claimed to have arisen and the capacity in which that act or failure to act occurred which governs liability."

Miller involved negligence claims by a student at the State University of New York at Stony Brook, who was criminally assaulted in the laundry room of her dormitory. Plaintiff presented proof of reports to campus security of strangers in the hallways of the dorms, and of men present in the women's bathrooms; news reports of crime in the dorms; and proof that, notwithstanding these reports, the doors at all ten entrances to the dorm were concededly kept unlocked at all hours, though they contained locking mechanisms. In analyzing the claim, the court of appeals stated that "when the State operates housing, it is held to the same duty as private landlords in the maintenance of physical security devices in the building itself." It found that the student may recover damages against the State in its capacity as a landlord, upon a showing that "there was a reasonably foreseeable likelihood of criminal intrusion into the building, that the State negligently failed to keep the outer doors locked, and that the failure was a proximate cause of the injury." The court noted that the student was not proceeding on a theory of the failure to provide police protection. Instead, she was proceeding on her theory that the State failed as a landlord to properly maintain the dorm, by failing to maintain reasonable security, specifically, by failing to lock the entrances. The court, while recognizing the defendant's dual role, held that the "ownership and care relating to buildings with tenants has traditionally been carried on through private enterprise, specifically by landlords and thus constitutes a proprietary function when performed by the State."

The *Miller* court described the State's duty to act as a reasonable person by maintaining the premises in a reasonably safe condition, under all the circumstances, such as the likelihood of injury to others, the seriousness of the injury, and the burden of avoiding the risk. Thus, a landlord "has a duty to maintain minimal security measures, related to a specific building itself, in the face of foreseeable criminal intrusion upon tenants."

The *Miller* court was following the framework set out in *Weiner v Metropolitan Transp. Auth.* In *Weiner*, decided several years before *Miller*, the plaintiff was assaulted while attempting to enter an unmanned entrance to a subway station. The activities for which plaintiff sought to hold the Transit Authority liable included the absence of police surveillance at the entrance, and the failure to warn of criminal activity in the area, or to close the entrance when police protection was not available. The court held that the Transit Authority owed no duty because the plaintiff sought to hold it liable on the limited theory that it failed to allocate police resources.

In *Crosland v. New York City Transit Auth.*, the court of appeals looked again at *Weiner* and clarified that "*Weiner* did not ... absolve publicly owned common carriers ... from liability for assaults on their passengers by third parties in all cases." In *Crosland* a student was beaten to death by a group of teens at a train station. The court found that the Transit Authority could be held liable, because the complaint alleged that the Authority's employees had watched the beating from a position of safety, but failed to summon aid. This, the court found actionable, and outside the boundaries of the policy-based immunity established in *Weiner.*

The New Jersey Supreme Court's decision in *Lieberman v. Port Auth. of New York and New Jersey*, is particularly instructive with respect to the Port Authority's immunity for governmental functions. In *Lieberman*, the court concluded, relying on both New York and New Jersey law, that the plaintiff, a commuter, stated a claim against the Port Authority for injuries she sustained when a homeless man robbed her in the Port Authority bus terminal. The *Lieberman* court, while considering *Weiner* and *Crosland*, noted important differences between these cases and the case at bar. "First, although both serve to assist commuters in getting to their destinations, the Port Authority does much more. Not only does it operate a bus depot at the Terminal, but it also rents space to shops, businesses, and restaurants." This distinction is also appropriate here, since the Port Authority was operating a commercial office complex, with many diverse tenants, shops, and restaurants, as well as a parking garage open to the tenants and the public.

Second, the *Lieberman* court recognized that the New York City Transit Authority's waiver statute is not as broad as the Port Authority's, and concluded that the burdens and duties of the two Authorities are not completely analogous. The *Lieberman* court found the *Miller* case to be the more applicable precedent. It found that the duty to provide reasonably safe premises does not automatically translate into the duty to provide greater police protection. "Rather, the inquiry is directed to whether the Port Authority as the landlord of the Terminal had the duty to provide better lighting, signs, security cameras, and other measures to increase commuter safety." To the extent that the plaintiff's claims were questioning the Port Authority's management of the homeless, the *Lieberman* court held that those claims failed if they involved legislative or governmental decisions.

In this case the difficulty, as in *Miller*, arises from the Port Authority's dual role. While the Port Authority had governmental functions in connection with its operation and control of the WTC, such as the provision of police protection provided by the Port Authority police, it also had proprietary functions as a commercial landlord, maintaining an office building which included numerous retail stores in an enclosed shopping mall. As instructed by *Miller*, the focus is on the specific act or omission out of which the plaintiffs' injuries are claimed to have arisen, and the capacity in which that act, or failure to act, occurred. Contrary to the Port Authority's contention, the duty to provide security in the WTC, and to provide reasonably safe premises for its invitees, does not automatically constitute the duty to provide greater police protection.

Plaintiffs are seeking to hold the Port Authority liable for its failure to either close or restrict public access to the parking garage. They also seek recovery for the Port Authority's failure to implement other security measures recommended to it by its own security department, as well as outside consultants, including installing barriers to the entrance in the garage, having an electronic security system, having a manned checkpoint at the public garage entrance, inspecting vehicles, posting security signs, and employing recording devices, such as CCTV. These alleged negligent acts fall along the proprietary side of the continuum of responsibility. They stem from the Port Authority's failure as the commercial landlord of this building to physically maintain the building, more particularly the garage, by failing to install security features, and barriers. The ownership and care of a publicly accessible paid parking facility under an office tower and shopping mall, and the provision of these basic security measures, for the commercial tenants, business invitees, and the public, are activities which have traditionally been carried on through private enterprise, specifically by commercial landlords, and thus constitute proprietary functions when performed by the Port Authority. The activities are more analogous to a failure by the State in its proprietary capacity to maintain minimum security measures, such as exterior locks on a building (see *Miller v. State of New York,* supra), than to the failure to have police patrolling a subway station (see *Weiner v. Metropolitan Transp. Auth.*, supra). This duty does not necessarily implicate the Port Authority police, and, therefore, does not invoke the Port Authority's governmental functions. The alleged negligent actions do not implicate legislative-executive decision making regarding the allocation of police resources.

The Port Authority's reliance on cases finding that the acts alleged involved a public entity engaged in governmental functions, are misplaced. Those cases did not involve the entity's operation of a commercial office building, parking garage, and shopping mall. Rather, they involved, for example, the operation of a bus terminal which was a governmental function. The Port Authority's other cases involved safety in public schools in terms of the allocation of police resources, a function which has traditionally been governmental.

To the extent that any of plaintiffs' allegations, not being pursued by them on this motion, could be construed as the failure to have more Port Authority police patrolling the WTC and the garage, for example, the allegation that the Port Authority failed to have bomb-sniffing dogs patrolling with police officers, those allegations must be and are dismissed as falling within the Port Authority's governmental function, and plaintiffs fail to show a special relationship. To demonstrate a special relationship sufficient to cast a governmental entity in liability for failure to prevent harm from a third party's criminal acts, a plaintiff must show (1) that the agency assumed an affirmative duty to protect him or her through promises or actions; (2) knowledge by the agency that inaction could lead to harm to plaintiff; (3) direct contact between the agency's representative and the plaintiff; and (4) reliance by plaintiff on the agency's affirmative undertaking to provide protection to him or her. Plaintiffs fail to demonstrate any evidence of promises, direct contact, or any reliance. Accordingly, there is no basis for liability by the Port Authority under the special relationship exception.

Because this court holds that the negligent acts that plaintiffs are pursuing involve the Port Authority's proprietary functions, there is no basis as to those acts to grant the Port Authority summary judgment on its governmental immunity defense.

Foreseeability

The next ground for the Port Authority's motion is its contention that the WTC bombing was unforeseeable as a matter of law, and that therefore, the Port Authority cannot be held liable. To obtain summary judgment, the Port Authority must meet a high threshold: only one conclusion can be drawn from the undisputed facts, and that, as a matter of law, the injuries to the plaintiffs were not reasonably foreseeable. The record does not support that conclusion. Whether a risk is foreseeable under particular circumstances has traditionally and soundly been left to the trier of fact to resolve, even where the facts are essentially undisputed. The court finds that there are triable issues of fact as to the foreseeability of this catastrophic event, warranting denial of the Port Authority's motion.

A landowner or landlord, who holds its land open to the public, is under a legal duty to exercise reasonable care under the circumstances to maintain the premises in a reasonably safe condition. The duty includes taking minimal security precautions against reasonably foreseeable criminal acts by third parties. This legal duty does not require the landlord to become an insurer of its tenants' and invitees' safety. Rather, it simply imposes a minimum level of care on landlords who "know or have reason to know that there is a likelihood that third parties may endanger the safety of those lawfully on the premises."

Foreseeability includes what the landlord actually knew, as well as what it reasonably should have known. "Foreseeability in this context has generally been equated with the degree to which a landlord has been apprised of the incidence of criminality within a particular building under his or her proprietorship." Moreover, the type of safety measures a landlord is reasonably required to provide is "almost always a question of fact for the jury."

In *Nallan*, the court of appeals stated that a landlord must anticipate the risk of harmful acts of third persons. It followed the description of a landowner's duty of care in the Restatement (Second) of Torts, which provides that a landlord must exercise reasonable care to discover that such harmful acts are being done or are likely to be done, give an adequate warning, or otherwise protect the visitors against it. Thus, foreseeability was cast in terms of past experience that is, that there is a likelihood of conduct by third parties which is likely to endanger the safety of visitors.

In *Jacqueline S. by Ludovina S. v. City of New York*, the court of appeals clarified that to establish a landlord's liability for the foreseeable danger from criminal activity, the operative proof did *not* have to be limited to crimes actually occurring in the specific building where the attack took place. It found that there was no requirement in either *Nallan*, or *Miller v. State of New York*, that to establish foreseeability the criminal activity occur at the exact location where plaintiff was injured, or that it be of the same type of criminal conduct to which plaintiff was subjected.

In *Jacqueline S.*, the plaintiff, a resident in one of several apartment buildings in a public housing complex, was abducted and raped by an assailant in her apartment building. The plaintiff submitted proof of drug-related crimes in her building, and that drug addicts and vagrants gained access and hung around the corridors, stairways, and roof. She also submitted proof that the police had responded to numerous reports of rapes and robberies in the complex, and that the landlord was aware that the lobby doors and the doors to utility rooms on the roofs were not equipped with locks. The court held that this proof was enough to raise a triable issue as to foreseeability, even though there was no evidence that violent crimes had occurred previously in the building where the plaintiff was raped, because there was evidence of crime in the complex, and given the landlord's conceded failure "to supply even the most rudimentary security, e.g., locks for the entrances, it was error to grant summary judgment on the question of foreseeability."

Therefore, contrary to the Port Authority's apparent argument, a landlord does not need to have had a past experience with the exact criminal activity, in the same place, and of the same type, before liability can be imposed for failing to take reasonable precautions to discover, warn, or protect. The inquiry focuses on what risks were reasonably to be perceived. Whether knowledge of prior activities are sufficient to make injuries foreseeable "must depend on the location, nature and extent of those previous criminal activities and their similarity, proximity or other relationship to the crime in question." Where ambient crime has infiltrated a landlord's premises, or where the landlord is otherwise on notice of a serious risk of such infiltration, the landlord's duty to protect arises.

The Port Authority's claim that this bombing was unforeseeable as a matter of law strains credulity. The Port Authority's duty is defined by what risks or dangers were and should reasonably have been anticipated by the Port Authority from having a high profile building, with a public parking garage under it, which permitted "unvetted" vehicles to enter and exit without encountering any barriers or surveillance. The Port Authority clearly perceived a risk since it created the OSP, and sought a report from it, and other outside consultants, regarding the risk of a terrorist attack on the WTC, and seeking recommendations for security measures to protect against the risk.

The Port Authority's argument that ambient crime in the neighborhood, is not enough, as a matter of law, to establish foreseeability, amounts to a contention that landlords can close their eyes to plainly perceived risks, and ignores plaintiffs' proof, which goes beyond simply ambient crime. Plaintiffs have presented proof, including the Port Authority's own OSP report, the reports from its outside security consultants, reports of bomb threats in the WTC itself, and in and around buildings in the downtown area from several years before, and a bomb threat communicated by the FBI only a month before the bombing, which tends to establish, or at the least creates a triable issue, that the Port Authority had foreseen the risk, or that the risk was foreseeable. This evidence, at the least, put the Port Authority on notice of the risk of the infiltration of criminal activity in the WTC.

The predicted scenario, eerily accurate, in the Port Authority's security reports, of a vehicle bomb in the garage, and the evidence of bomb threats in the complex, are sufficiently similar in nature to the bombing to raise a triable issue as to foreseeability. The fact that an explosive-laden vehicle had not previously been placed in the WTC garage does not, as the Port Authority appears to be arguing, make this event unforeseeable as a matter of law. The court is aware, as defendant strenuously argues, that there are no cases in which a landlord was subjected to liability for an unprecedented terrorist bombing in its building, particularly where the ambient crime was not necessarily in the immediate vicinity; however, the evidence of the Port Authority's actual notice of the risk of infiltration of this kind of terrorist activity cannot be ignored.

Landlords have been denied summary judgment in other cases on the issue of foreseeability even where there was no evidence of similar crimes in the building. For example, in *Kahane v. Marriott Hotel Corp.*, the First Department held that there was a triable issue as to whether the defendant hotel should have reasonably foreseen the risk of harm to the decedent, such that it would have had a duty to provide more than minimal security. Decedent, a controversial speaker, was scheduled to speak at an affair at the hotel. On the day of the affair, the hotel received a call from a person who refused to identify himself, but who asked if the decedent would be speaking that night, and if metal detectors would be in place. The hotel's employee who answered the call notified the group sponsoring the affair, and the hotel's security and catering departments, of the call. The court found that this evidence was enough to deny summary judgment on the issue of foreseeability.

In *Gross v. Empire State Bldg. Assocs.*, the court found that violent criminal activity in the Empire State Building's stores and abutting sidewalks, combined with bomb threats to the building, which threats constituted criminal activity, raised a factual issue as to the foreseeability of a shooting on the observation deck. In that case, on February 23, 1997, a Palestinian, in this country on a visa, went to the observation deck and indiscriminately shot at tourists, killing one and injuring five others, before killing himself. The plaintiffs argued that the landlords were negligent, in not installing metal detectors and maintaining a program of inspection of bags. The court found that the criminal activity noted above put the defendants on notice, warranting denial of defendants' summary judgment motion.

In addition, in *Schaeffer v. Vera Wang Bridal House, Ltd.*, the court found that, while there was no evidence of prior crime in the bridal shop, evidence of the landlord's awareness of similar and of other types of crimes in the vicinity was enough to raise a factual issue for trial. Plaintiffs in that case were shopping in the defendant's bridal shop, located in the Hotel Carlyle, when robbers, posing as shoppers, were let into the shop by defendant's employee, drew their guns and attempted to steal one of the plaintiff's rings. Both of the plaintiffs were shot and seriously injured, and brought claims against the bridal shop for failure to provide adequate security. They presented proof of a number of crimes in the areas surrounding the shop and the Hotel, including evidence of a series of highly publicized robberies on the Upper East Side over a three-year period, of which the shop employees were aware. The court concluded that a reasonable jury could find on this evidence that the shop had reason to know that, even though there was no robbery on its premises in the past, there was a likelihood that its customers could be endangered by the criminal acts of others.

Similarly, in cases involving crimes in jewelry stores in the diamond district in Manhattan, the courts have found the risk of criminal activity foreseeable without proof of a prior crime in the building, or even any particular proof of similar crime in the neighborhood. In *Ratanee Jewelry, Inc. v. Art Jewelry Ctr., Inc.*, the court found that, based on the facts that the building tenants were all in the jewelry business, and the building was located in the diamond district, criminal intrusions were plainly foreseeable, requiring adequate security measures. Also, in *Rudel v. National Jewelry Exch. Co.*, the Court held that there was a triable issue on foreseeability, and whether the landlord's duty was breached, based only on the fact that the building was in the diamond district, and that there was only one unarmed security guard on the ground floor, without other security precautions.

Here, the OSP report, and the reports of the Port Authority's outside security consultants, recognized that domestic terrorism was rising, the WTC was an attractive terrorist target, car bombs were becoming the terrorists' method of choice, and the underground parking garage was highly vulnerable to a terrorist attack. Specifically, the Terrorist Planning Section, the predecessor to the OSP, in a report in 1984, warned that the WTC should be considered a prime target for domestic terrorism, and that the public parking lots were highly susceptible to car bombings. OSP's preliminary report states that the staff considered several attack scenarios, including a "[b]omb-laden truck attack." It determined that a strategically placed van or truck could cause significant structural damage and many casualties. The Schnabolk report, in 1985, informed the Port Authority that bombing attempts were probable, and warned that the WTC was "highly vulnerable through the parking lot."

The OSP's final report recited that it was aware that two thirds of domestic terror incidents in 1983–84 occurred in the New York–New Jersey metropolitan area. It warned that the car bomb was a weapon of choice for terrorists, and that the parking garage was a definite security risk. It specifically found that the underground parking garage presented "an enormous opportunity, at present, for terrorists to park an explosive-filled vehicle that could affect vulnerable areas." It clearly warned that the garage was vulnerable because access was "unimpeded" for someone to plant a "car bomb into the World Trade Center parking lot," which would affect all the important buildings systems, which were all located around the parking areas. It predicted that a time bomb-laden vehicle could be driven into the garage, parked in the public parking area, the driver could exit into the WTC, and, at a predetermined time, the bomb would be exploded.

The Port Authority recognized that the threat of terrorism had increased after the end of the Gulf War in 1991. Securacom, one of the Port Authority's outside consultants, warned the Port Authority of the increased threat following the Gulf War, and that the WTC was a likely terrorist target. Securacom specifically warned that "bombs and the threat of their use continues to be the favored weapon of international terrorists," and advised the Port Authority that there was a potential that a vehicle bomb could be driven into the parking garage undetected.

In addition to these reports, plaintiffs produced evidence that, just a month before the bombing, the FBI warned the Port Authority that a Middle Eastern group had threatened to blow up a major office building in New York. These predictions in security reports created at the Port Authority's request, apparently in recognition of some terrorist security risk, and the Port Authority's recognition of a continuing risk, create a triable issue as to whether the bombing was foreseeable.

The cases cited by the Port Authority are distinguishable on the facts. Notably, the Port Authority has not cited any cases in which the court has held that a landlord may disregard its own knowledge about the likelihood of criminal activity and the warnings of its own security experts. *Todorovich v. Columbia Univ.*, relied upon by the Port Authority, in which the tenants were attacked in the building vestibule, is distinguishable, in that the court specifically found that the defendant's building had an enviable security record, based on a report from the police department, and that the landlord had no actual notice of prior incidents in which ambient crime had infiltrated the building. Also, in *Anzalone v. Pan-Am Equities*, in which a tenant was assaulted outside her apartment, the court found that, with proof of the functioning outer door lock on the vestibule to the building, a functioning intercom, and no proof of ambient criminality in the building or neighborhood, the landlord had discharged its duty. Here, there is proof that the Port Authority was on notice of a serious risk of infiltration of terrorist activity in the parking garage, and the reasonableness or unreasonableness of the security measures it had taken is not being challenged by the Port Authority on this motion.

Therefore, summary judgment on the issue of foreseeability would be inappropriate on this record.

CASE COMMENT

This case, in my mind, represents both a chilling reflection of the past and a sign of things to come. In terms of recent history, it is difficult to read the description of the World Trade Towers, knowing that those buildings—and thousands of innocent lives—are now gone. As to prophetic future events, I am convinced that the threat of terrorism is likely to be with us for years. The impact of such, unfortunately, is likely to be as grave or more, than what was experienced on September 11.

As to the legal analysis, this case represents a seminal example of the liability exposures relating to terrorism. In its excellent factual and legal analysis, the court denied the Port Authority's motion for summary judgment. The factual presentation relied heavily on reports tendered by security and terrorism experts and on a warning issued by the FBI one month before the 1993 bombing of the World Trade Towers. Indeed, some of the expert reports included detailed predictions of the exact (or near exact) methods that were used by the terrorists. Ironically, it was the fact that Port Authority engaged these experts and instituted a special unit within Port Authority security to deal with the terrorist threat that negated its subsequent argument that the crime was not foreseeable.

From a legal perspective, the court used case precedent instructively, citing cases that clearly illustrate the legal principles involved. This analysis was generally achieved using cases dealing with "normal" crime. In these cases, crimes such as murders, robberies, batteries, and rapes were committed by criminals. Of course, terrorism, from a legal perspective, is also considered a crime, as are its underlying consequences, including murder, batteries, and the criminal destruction of property. Using this legal analysis, the court correctly determined that the Port Authority did not have immunity, and that the terrorist bombing was foreseeable.

Going forward, this case is likely to be cited for years to come. The legal and factual arguments presented are grounded in well-developed jurisprudence. It is difficult to argue against the analysis and conclusions derived from this case. The problem, however, is the legal principles designed to remedy "normal crime" may not be applicable in cases involving terrorism, especially in those events that result in mass causalities and extensive property damage. While the Terrorism Risk Insurance Act provides some remedy to this dilemma, it does not resolve the implications of terrorism in relation to liability exposure. While this Act will be addressed in Chapter 13, at this point, it suffices to say that the Act does not remedy this basic consequence. As will be more fully presented in the concluding chapter, in my opinion, what is needed is a paradigm shift in judicial and legislative reasoning as to the legal consequences and implications of terrorism.

10 A.D. 3d 223, 781 N.Y.S. 2d 324

Supreme Court, Appellate Division, First Department, New York

WALL STREET GARAGE PARKING CORP., PLAINTIFF-RESPONDENT v. NEW YORK STOCK EXCHANGE, INC., DEFENDANT-APPELLANT.

Aug. 5, 2004

Background

Owner and operator of parking garage located near stock exchange brought action against New York Stock Exchange (NYSE), seeking to enjoin exchange from blocking access to garage and stopping and inspecting vehicles exiting from garage. The Supreme Court, New York County, granted preliminary injunction, and NYSE appealed.

Holding

The Supreme Court, Appellate Division, held that owner was not likely to prevail on its public nuisance claim.

Reversed

At issue on this appeal is whether defendant New York Stock Exchange (NYSE) created a public nuisance by restricting vehicular access to a security zone around the Stock Exchange devised by closing seven traffic intersections in the aftermath of the terrorist attacks of September 11, 2001, thereby entitling plaintiff, a business entity in the area, to preliminary injunctive relief. We find the motion court erred in granting plaintiff a preliminary injunction because enjoining defendant Stock Exchange from inspecting vehicles entering the security zone surrounding NYSE premises changes, rather than preserves, the status quo and because plaintiff has not otherwise satisfied the prerequisites for obtaining preliminary injunctive relief.

Even prior to the events of 9/11, concern that the NYSE, the largest stock exchange in the United States, might be vulnerable to an explosive device hidden in a vehicle prompted the New York City Police Department (NYPD) to close New Street between Wall Street and Exchange Place and the intersection of Wall Street and Broadway to vehicular traffic in

May 1996. A bomb hoax in September 1998 resulted in the closure of the sidewalks surrounding the premises occupied by the NYSE to all pedestrian traffic from 6:00 p.m. to 8:00 a.m. daily. In March 2001, the Stock Exchange began participating in the NYPD Paid Detail Program, in which off-duty police officers, in uniform and acting with full power and authority of regular on-duty police officers, provide security at the expense of a participating entity rather than the New York City taxpayers.

The center of the NYSE's economic activity is its trading floor, which extends across buildings located at 11 Wall Street and at 18, 20, and 30 Broad Street. After the terrorist attacks of September 11, 2001, the area was patrolled by members of the NYPD, including police officers participating in the Paid Detail Program as well as those on regular duty, and including members of NYPD's heavily armed "Hercules Teams," by NYSE's own security personnel and by personnel provided by T & M Protection Resources, Inc. The police department blocked access to NYSE's premises from the seven intersections that surround the trading floor, placing barriers on Wall Street at Broadway and at William Street, on Exchange Place at Broadway and at William Street, on Nassau Street at Pine Street, on Broad Street at Beaver Street and on New Street at Beaver Street. The barriers were later replaced by trucks loaded with sand.

Plaintiff parking garage, which was formerly located within the security zone, claims that its business is being adversely impacted by security measures implemented by defendant NYSE in response to the events of September 11, 2001. Plaintiff garage is located on Exchange Place near the intersection with William Street. As an accommodation to plaintiff, the original security zone was modified and the truck barrier on Exchange Place at William Street was moved west towards Broad Street to permit vehicular access to and from the garage from William Street and Exchange Place. Garage patrons were then able to avoid entering the security zone, thus obviating the need for a search. However, on or about February 21, 2004, the William Street access point was once again blocked when the City began road construction on said street, and plaintiff's customers were again required to enter the security area to gain access to the garage.

The impact on plaintiff's business was substantial. Plaintiff asserts that from an average of 150 to 160 vehicles a day prior to 9/11, patronage dropped to 68 cars a day thereafter, further declining to 65 a day by February 2004. With the commencement of road construction, usage dropped to a mere 38 vehicles daily by the beginning of March, causing plaintiff to commence this action seeking damages as well as preliminary and permanent injunctive relief. Plaintiff sought to prohibit defendant NYSE "from obstructing, blocking or closing in any way ingress or egress to or from Exchange Place or the flow of vehicular traffic thereon, at or near where plaintiff conducts its business, and from stopping, arresting and searching vehicles exiting plaintiff's parking garage on Exchange Place between Broad Street and William Street."

Defendant NYSE took issue with the allegation that its security force had completely taken over the control of security posts located at the blocked intersections. The affidavit of NYSE's Senior Vice President of Security, James Esposito, states that "NYPD officers" are "directly involved in the security zone." Photographs of the area submitted by defendant depict NYPD officers stationed at pedestrian checkpoints with NYSE security personnel, as well as the deployment of the "Hercules Team and other NYPD personnel and vehicles within the security zone." Defendant opposed the application for preliminary relief on the ground that the garage is located outside the secured area and that the unrestricted access to plaintiff's premises available from William Street was subject only to temporary curtailment by street construction by the City at the intersection.

By order entered March 12, 2004, Supreme Court granted plaintiff's Motion for a Preliminary Injunction, enjoining NYSE from blocking access to Exchange Place and from stopping and inspecting vehicles exiting the garage. Expressing doubt as to the authority of the City to delegate responsibility for security to a private entity, the court concluded that subjecting garage customers to search and blocking public streets constitute a public nuisance in violation of New York City Administrative Code Section 19-107. In balancing the equities, the court reasoned that the nuisance represents a sufficient threat both to "plaintiff's civil rights as a private citizen" and to public order to warrant injunctive relief.

At the time plaintiff commenced this petition for a preliminary injunction, the status quo was represented by established security measures, including a series of vehicular and pedestrian checkpoints, had already been in place for some 2½ years. Questions concerning supervision and control notwithstanding, the security measures are not alleged to have undergone any substantial change so as to warrant judicial restoration of established procedures. Rather, the precipitous decline in plaintiff's business is attributed to the total closure of the intersection of William Street and Exchange Place due to construction work by the City. With the completion of the road construction at the intersection, which plaintiff does not materially dispute, the status quo ante has been restored, rendering academic plaintiff's application for preliminary relief.

To be entitled to a preliminary injunction, the proponent is required to demonstrate a probability of ultimate success on the merits, irreparable injury in the event that injunctive relief is denied, and a balancing of the equities in its favor. However, because a public nuisance is inherently a condition for which the law provides a remedy, the proponent of the injunction is relieved from the general requirement to show that it lacks an adequate remedy at law.

It is unlikely, however, that plaintiff will be able to establish its right to recover on the ground that it sustained injury as the result of a public nuisance, the single theory advanced in the complaint. As stated in

532 Madison Ave. Gourmet Foods v. Finlandia Ctr., "a public nuisance exists for conduct that amounts to a substantial interference with the exercise of a common right of the public, thereby offending public morals, interfering with the use by the public of a public place or endangering or injuring the property, health, safety or comfort of a considerable number of persons. A public nuisance is a violation against the State and is subject to abatement or prosecution by the proper governmental authority".

Where, as here, a claim for recovery is predicated on a public nuisance, the claimant must show that it has "suffered a special injury beyond that of the community." As a general rule, "one who suffers damage or injury, beyond that of the general inconvenience to the public at large, may recover for such nuisance in damages or obtain injunction to prevent its continuance."

Plaintiffs claimed economic injury is only partly attributable to the security procedures implemented in the area surrounding the NYSE. The further decline in its business commencing in February 2004 was precipitated by the City's road construction, a condition that has since abated. Furthermore, as Supreme Court noted in its order, "many businesses have suffered as a result of post-September 11, 2001 security measures." The security zone surrounding the New York Stock Exchange covers several square blocks containing large buildings, many of which house businesses that can claim some measure of harm as a consequence of the security measures imposed. Plaintiff, which operates a business located outside the security zone, has not demonstrated a special injury beyond the disruption experienced by the community as a whole. Any impediment to plaintiff's right to operate its garage will not support recovery of damages on a public nuisance theory where the same circumstances have impeded the similar rights of a large number of other businesses located in the area.

On balance, the equities favor defendant NYSE. Plaintiff does not dispute the need for heightened security in the area. Defendant took steps to accommodate plaintiff by moving a checkpoint so as to place the access ramp to the garage outside the secured area. Plaintiff concedes that, as a result, many of its customers were unaffected by the security measures. The abatement of any public nuisance created by alleged improprieties in defendant's security procedures is a governmental prerogative, and the substantial police presence in the vicinity suggests that defendant's security operations are subject to some degree of official scrutiny.

Since plaintiff is unable to establish its right to recover on the ground that it has sustained special damages as the result of a public nuisance, its application for injunctive relief cannot stand because plaintiff is unable to persuasively argue that it has sustained irreparable injury. Its action against the NYSE is predicated on economic loss, compensable by monetary damages. Plaintiff has documented the decline in its patronage as the result of the security measures undertaken by defendant and does not contend that it is impossible to calculate the extent of that loss. Thus, plaintiff cannot demonstrate that it lacks an adequate remedy at law so as to warrant injunctive relief. Moreover, it is clear that plaintiff's loss of business was predominantly caused by the City's construction work, a temporary condition that no longer exists. Therefore, there is no need to enjoin any conduct by defendant NYSE to avoid speculative future damages consequent to a continuing harm.

Accordingly, the order of the Supreme Court, New York County, entered March 12, 2004, which granted plaintiff's Motion for Preliminary Relief and enjoined defendant from maintaining security blockades and conducting vehicle searches in the immediate vicinity of the New York Stock Exchange, should be reversed, on the law and the facts, without costs, and the motion denied.

799 N.Y.S. 2d 165

Supreme Court, New York County, New York

WALL STREET GARAGE PARKING CORP., PLAINTIFF v. NEW YORK STOCK EXCHANGE, INC., DEFENDANT.

Nov. 3, 2004

Background

Owner and operator of parking garage located near stock exchange brought action against New York Stock Exchange (NYSE), seeking economic damages relating to blocking access to garage and stopping and inspecting vehicles exiting from garage. The Supreme Court, New York County, granted preliminary injunction in favor of the plaintiff, finding that NYSE could not legally maintain security checkpoints and vehicle searches. NYSE appealed. The appellate division, reversed.

Holding

The defendant NYSE's Motion to Dismiss both the injunction and the damage claim are granted.

The instant applications mark the second phase of litigation commenced by plaintiff in response to defendant's alleged blockage of access to Exchange Place in lower Manhattan. Plaintiff owns and operates a parking garage located at 45 Wall Street, with entrance and exit ramps located on Exchange Place between William Street and Broad Street. The defendant is the New York Stock Exchange, Inc. (NYSE), operating offices located at 11 Wall Street, 18 Broad Street, 20 Broad Street, and 30 Broad Street.

In the aftermath of September 11, 2001, the NYPD, through the closure of numerous streets, effectuated a multi-block "secure zone" surrounding the NYSE in an attempt to prevent potential attacks on the renowned financial institution. The initial patrolling of the NYSE "secure zone" was handled entirely by a combination of NYPD officers, NYPD Paid Detail officers, and members of the NYPD elite Hercules Teams. However, at some point, and it remains unclear to this court as to when the actual transition took place, the NYSE security team began maintaining the perimeters of the secure zone, and conducting searches of persons and vehicles.

Plaintiff's garage, located at the perimeter of the NYSE secure zone had, prior to the events of September 11, 2001, enjoyed a lucrative parking business, housing on average, 150 to 160 vehicles daily. Following the attacks on lower Manhattan and the subsequent security changes, plaintiff sustained significant business losses, claiming that by 2003, only 68 vehicles on average parked in the garage daily.

On March 12, 2004 this court granted a preliminary injunction in favor of plaintiff, finding that failing evidence of proper authority, the NYSE could not legally maintain the security checkpoints and conduct vehicle searches at the intersections bordering the NYSE secure zone. Defendants appealed, and in the interim, the subject road construction was completed.

On August 5, 2004, the Appellate Division, First Department reversed this court's decision, finding that notwithstanding the questions concerning supervision and control, "the security measures are not alleged to have undergone any substantial change so as to warrant judicial restoration of established procedures. Rather, the precipitous decline in plaintiff's business is attributed to the total closure of the intersection of William Street and Exchange Place due to construction work by the City." The appellate division further concluded that as the offending construction had been completed, the status quo ante had been restored, rendering plaintiff's application for a preliminary injunction academic.

Plaintiff's complaint, comprised of two causes of action, claims a right to preliminary and permanent injunctive relief due to a lack of legal remedy (the first cause of action), and damages (the second cause of action). Both of plaintiff's asserted causes of action are predicated upon the contentions that the "secure zone" as maintained by the NYSE constitutes a public nuisance and that the operation of a private police force that controls and conducts searches on public thoroughfares is illegal.

Defendants contend that dismissal of this action is warranted primarily because the construction project that was the catalyst for this action is now complete, rendering the issue of public access to plaintiff's garage moot. Defendants further argue that dismissal of this action is required because (1) plaintiff failed to join necessary parties to this action; (2) plaintiff can neither prove damages nor their claim of public nuisance; and (3) none of the alleged damages were proximately caused by the NYSE. Defendants additionally argue that even if plaintiff could establish a claim of public nuisance, plaintiff's claims are barred by laches through acquiescence to the NYSE "secure zone" and delay of the instant litigation by over two years.

It is undisputed that access to plaintiff's garage has been severely limited since September 11, 2001. However, what defendants fail to acknowledge, is that notwithstanding the fact that the NYPD may have initially created the "secure zone" surrounding the NYSE, it was defendant who was independently maintaining the "secure zone," restricting access, and conducting searches of vehicles at the time of the City's construction project. Moreover, it appears to this court, that the NYSE's actions were done without any formal City approval for either closure or access restrictions to the streets in question, and without any formal agreement transferring authority from the NYPD to the NYSE. It is therefore quite plausible that the City's construction project at the intersection of William Street and

Exchange Place, though certainly responsible for compounding access issues, was not the sole cause of plaintiff's distress.

Plaintiff's business is located immediately adjacent to one portion of the NYSE "secure zone" perimeter. In the days and months following September 11, 2001, plaintiff believed that for security reasons, the NYPD saw fit to order that the streets surrounding the NYSE be closed to public traffic. In February 2004, two events transpired that resulted in litigation: (1) the City of New York commenced construction and blocked the only remaining public access to plaintiff's garage and (2) plaintiff learned that the actions of the NYSE and not the NYPD were behind the continued restrictions and closures of the surrounding streets.

Defendants argue that regardless of who was or was not named in the action, both the NYPD and the City of New York are implicated via plaintiff's assertion that the NYSE lacked the authority to close, patrol, and/or provide security services to the area surrounding the NYSE. Again, this court disagrees with defendant's argument. When initially faced with the prospect of litigation, plaintiff, much like any other litigant in a tort action, had a choice as to whom to sue. Plaintiff could have chosen to sue the City, which was immediately blocking access to the garage. Plaintiff could have also chosen to sue, and did choose, the NYSE, which had also engaged in blocking access to the garage. However, plaintiff was not under any obligation to sue the City or the NYPD, as neither the City nor the NYPD were necessary to accord complete relief between the parties. More importantly, even were this court to conclude that both the City and the NYPD were necessary parties to this action, it could have, and likely would have, remedied the situation pursuant to the powers given to it.

However, while this court recognizes that plaintiff's business has suffered significant losses at the hands of a private entity, in affording plaintiff the utmost latitude, this court concludes that plaintiff simply is not able to succeed on its asserted claims.

A successful claim of public nuisance requires a plaintiff, by clear and convincing evidence, to establish (1) that a public nuisance exists; (2) that defendant's conduct or omissions created, contributed to, or maintained the public nuisance; and (3) that the harm plaintiff suffered as a result of the public nuisance, constitutes a "special injury" in that the harm suffered by plaintiff is different and beyond that suffered by the community at large.

Plaintiff has no difficulty whatsoever in satisfying the first necessary element, as it is well established by both statute and case law, that the unlawful obstruction of a public street without express authority is tantamount to a public nuisance. Nor does this court believe that plaintiff would have any difficulty establishing the second prong of the test, as it is probable that further discovery would reveal information supporting plaintiff's contention that the NYSE was responsible for at least maintaining the subject street closures.

However, as the appellate division noted in their decision, plaintiff, which operates a business located outside the security zone, has not demonstrated a special injury beyond the disruption experienced by the community as a whole. Any impediment to plaintiff's right to operate its garage will not support recovery of damages on a public nuisance theory where the same circumstances have impeded the similar rights of a large number of other businesses located in the area.

Thus, while it may be that further discovery will yield evidence benefiting plaintiff with respect to its other claims, it is this court's opinion that no amount of discovery that plaintiff may glean from the defendant will be able to establish that plaintiff suffered an injury exceeding that suffered by the community at large. As plaintiff is not able to establish through the aforementioned established test, whether defendant's action or inaction constitutes a public nuisance, reluctantly, this court must dismiss the action.

Accordingly, it is ORDERED that defendant's motion to lift the mandatory stay of discovery is denied as moot; and it is further ORDERED that defendant's Motion to Dismiss is granted.

CASE COMMENT

These cases illustrate a couple of key issues. First, the public nuisance claim was not deemed appropriate by the court. This is partly based on the perceived need for the security methods around the stock exchange. It was also related to the inability for the plaintiff to show that his business was more adversely affected than any other in the area. In addition, since the construction project was completed, the injunction was rendered moot. Second, the security methods used around the stock exchange are similar to public-private arrangements used in various cities in the country. As articulated in the previous chapter, the ongoing terrorist threat is likely to make the use of private police to augment public police forces increasingly commonplace. This trend is sure to raise a number of legal issues and has far-reaching implications.

782 N.Y.S. 2d 522

Supreme Court, New York County, New York

CIPRIANI FIFTH AVENUE, LLC, PLAINTIFF v. RCPI LANDMARK PROPERTIES, LLC AND ROCKEFELLER CENTER TOWER CONDOMINIUM, DEFENDANTS.

May 3, 2004

Background

Lessee, who operated an upscale restaurant in commercial building, sued landlord and property manager, alleging breach of lease relating to proposed security measures, including use of metal detectors that would be applicable solely to lessee's employees and guests. Lessee moved for preliminary injunction.

Holding

The Supreme Court, New York County, held that lessee was not entitled to injunction.

Motion denied

The Rainbow Room, which consists of facilities that include, among other things, first-class restaurants, bars and catering rooms, is located within the condominiums on the uppermost floors of 30 Rockefeller Plaza, the tallest building in the Rockefeller Center complex. The Rainbow Room with its location at the top of the Building is part of the Rockefeller Center complex, a New York City landmark whose construction under the auspices of oil tycoon John D. Rockefeller, Sr., was undertaken and completed in 1934 in the midst of the Great Depression.

For the last six years, under a twenty year lease dated May 15, 1998 with RCPI Trust, plaintiff Cipriani Fifth Avenue, LLC, a company owned by the Cipriani family of Venice, has operated the Rainbow Room. Defendant RCPI Landmark Properties, LLC is the owner of the condominium units in which the Rainbow Room is located. RCPI Trust's duties under the Lease include without limitation all necessary repairs (both structural and nonstructural) to the Building Systems, the public portions of the Building and the structural elements of the Building, both exterior and interior "in conformance with standards applicable to first-class office buildings of comparable age and quality in midtown Manhattan."

Cipriani commenced this action against defendant for breach of Lease, seeking declaratory and injunctive relief. It moves to preliminarily enjoin defendant from carrying out alleged violations of its obligations under the Lease, to wit, from implementing plans to install or use metal detectors as part of a security procedure applicable solely and exclusively to Cipriani's employees and guests; subjecting its guests to unreasonable delays in accessing elevators and/or searching their person and property; closing the 50th Street entrance to the Building; and applying either additional security measures or the rules and regulations applicable to all the Building's Tenants in a manner that discriminates against guests and employees of the Rainbow Room. It is Cipriani's application for preliminary injunctive relief with respect to the security measures that the court determines here.

Cipriani contends that the destruction of its business and damage to its reputation that would result from the implementation of the proposed security measures would not be compensable by money damages. Cipriani founds its contention that it will suffer irreparable harm if interim extraordinary relief is not granted. In its complaint, Cipriani alleges that after commencement of the Lease, it invested substantial sums of money in the Rainbow Room to comply with the Lease provisions governing "Initial Installation" and "Operation and Maintenance Covenants" that required that the "business ... conducted at, through and from the Premises be reputable in every respect" and "be dignified and in conformity with the highest standards of practice of restaurants conducting a similar business in Rockefeller Center or the Fifth Avenue area adjacent thereto."

Specifically, the general manager states that Cipriani pays nearly five million dollars in annual rent and has invested more than six million dollars in improvements to the Rainbow Room in order to maintain its tradition as a world renowned and first class venue. For the first time at a September 2003 meeting with plaintiff's principals, defendant advised in addition to "intrusive and time consuming searches of handbags and other personal property currently being conducted exclusively for employees and guests of the Rainbow," it planned to install walk-through metal detectors at the entrance of the elevator bank servicing the Rainbow Room, through which only guests and employees of the Rainbow Room and no other tenants would be required to walk.

The manager asserts he has already received complaints from party planners, hosts of parties, and their guests about searches of persons and their belongings. He explains that approximately 83 percent of the Rainbow Room's business comes from large parties and events, resulting in the arrival of hundreds of guests during early evening hours. Many of the women wear jewelry and the men are attired in tuxedos with metal buttons and cufflinks. Some guests carry briefcases and most carry cell phones. The manager asserts that metal detectors set to alarm in the presence of a metal firearm, would be triggered in the presence of formal wear, requiring people to empty their pockets or be otherwise searched. Long lines and extensive delays would develop, and guests would have to wait for an hour or more just to enter the elevators. Several party planners, who account for the majority of large events booked at the Rainbow Room, have advised him that if metal detectors were installed, they would no longer be able to recommend the Rainbow Room as a site for large events.

In an affidavit submitted on this motion, one such corporate event planner describes the installation of metal detectors as a "disaster" for the Rainbow Room, whose facilities she would no longer be able to recommend to her clients. Her experience with metal detectors while attending events at United Nations was a "nightmare," due to the huge traffic jams created when large numbers of people arrive at the same time. In her view the presence of metal detectors is antithetical to the ambiance of an upscale, black tie or dressy corporate or social event. Citing her more than ten years of experience in the party planning business, she opined that her clients would not choose the Rainbow Room for their events if they had to pass through metal detectors, which would severely damage the business and reputation of the Rainbow Room.

Defendant counters that Cipriani's contention that its reputation and business will be damaged is entirely speculative. It suggests that in the current environment, patrons welcome security checks to ensure their safety. Defendant also contends that any losses from the installation can be quantified and are compensable in money damages.

In an action that involved another landlord-tenant dispute over alterations, the Appellate Division, First Department, upheld a trial court's determination that the tenant would suffer irreparable harm by the landlord's placement of "panic bars [on] certain doors which prevented [the tenant] from passing between its leased and subleased premises." The harm that Cipriani has demonstrated based upon the representation of a major party planner is no more compensable than the harm to 401 Hotel, LP, resulting from the installation of panic bars. Such an impediment to Cipriani's use of the Rainbow Room, featuring large formal gatherings, represents a diminution in value that would be impossible to measure. Defendant suggests no mechanism for calculating damages, and this court finds that calculation would be not merely difficult, but inestimable. This court notes that while under the lease Cipriani pays a percentage rent that is based on its annual gross sales, an economist would be left to speculate about the proportion of any diminution in gross sales attributable to the number of guests turned away or turned off in the advent of magnetometers. Nor would the granting of an injunction have the effect of awarding Cipriani the ultimate relief it seeks.

An assessment of the state of the balance between this harm and the injury that granting the injunction would inflict upon the defendant shows a rather level scale. Cipriani points out that there has been no incident of violence in the Rainbow Room or anywhere else in the building that would justify the sudden need for metal detectors. It disagrees that metal detectors are necessary to combat terrorism, and points out the remoteness of a person hiding a metal weapon inside formal evening wear. It requests that defendant share its security plans so that both parties may jointly consult an expert to review the options and develop a more suitable plan.

On this question of equities, Cipriani alleges incidentally that defendant contravened the Lease not only as to its security plans, but also with respect to its failures to repair the roof above plaintiff's facilities, resulting in water falling into plaintiff's premises during inclement weather. It posits that defendant's recalcitrance on the repairs as well as plans for security are only ploys to gain leverage in defendant's negotiations with Cipriani on defendant's plans to use a portion of the Rainbow Room to create public access to an observatory on the roof of the building as a tourist attraction and source of additional revenue.

Not surprisingly, the defendant urges that it would suffer inestimable harm were the court to place a restraint on its plans for security. While resulting in only minor inconveniences to Rainbow Room customers, the security measures would confer the benefits of additional safeguards on all occupants and visitors to the Building and reflect heightened security concerns that are completely reasonable in "this post-9/11 world." Any losses that Cipriani might suffer by threats to its business and reputation, which defendant insists are unfounded, are "dwarfed by the potential damages that could be suffered by the Landlord and the public at large" should necessary and desirable security measures not be implemented and enforced "at the very heart of Rockefeller Center."

Defendant also cites the increased threat of litigation. It cites an article in which the authors advise building owners "to provide appropriate security protection against terrorism and other acts of violence that threaten the safety of New York's building stock and tenants." The article cautions that inadequate security measures would invite criminal premises liability lawsuits. That case arose out of the tragic incident on February 23, 1997, at the Empire State Building where a deranged man armed with a semi-automatic pistol went to the 86th Floor observation deck and without warning, indiscriminately shot one tourist to death and seriously injured six others before committing suicide with the same weapon. The trial court denied the owner's summary judgment motion to dismiss, finding that though there was only a minimal showing of criminal activity within the building prior to the incident, evidence of violence in adjoining stores and sidewalks and bomb threats to the building made the question of the adequacy of security provisions in effect, which did not include metal detectors, one of fact for the jury.

In evaluating the parties' positions, it is significant that the Appellate Division, First Department, recently reversed that lower court decision and ordered the action summarily dismissed. The appellate court held in *Gross*, that in 1997, Empire State Building owners could not have reasonably foreseen the events in question, and therefore owed no duty to visitors to employ x-ray machines, metal detectors and scanners.

While acknowledging the proliferation of metal detectors and other security measures that the public now encounters in the aftermath of the attacks on September 11, 2001, the appellate court reiterated the principle that owners are not insurers of the safety of those who use their premises. It described a building owner's common law duty "to take only 'minimal precautions' to protect tenants and visitors from foreseeable harm, including foreseeable criminal acts" as "firmly established."

Another case where metal detectors proved no safe harbor or prophylactic against either violent acts or lawsuits is *Djurkovic*. *Djurkovic* involved a nightclub with a reputation and clientele quite different from that of the Rainbow Room. In *Djurkovic*, metal detectors operated by state-licensed security guards who conducted pat downs at the entrance of the club did not prevent a box cutter–wielding assailant from injuring another patron. The court observed that "[a]dmittedly, the detectors were not set at a level sensitive enough to detect small objects, such as keys, and so it would appear, box cutters." Nevertheless, the court held, as a matter of law, that even though the anticipated presence of large crowds of young people consuming alcohol at a "hip hop" club in early morning hours made the particular criminal act foreseeable, plaintiff failed to establish any breach in the owner's duty to take reasonable security measures to minimize the danger of such a criminal attack.

As for plaintiff's theory that defendant's security proposal is a mere pretext to advance its plan to open an observatory, the court does find the timing of such a proposal, given the challenge to security such public access would generate, to be at odds with defendant's concerns about security expressed in the action at bar. The court is incredulous that the defendant would undermine its "jewel in the crown" tenant in a quest for greater profits, without resolving security challenges it says public access poses even without the additional traffic an observatory would produce. Certainly, all concerned would be loath to see any repeat of the horrible event in 1997 that occurred in the observatory of another landmark, the Empire State Building.

The court views the facts of *Djurkovic* as weighing on the plaintiff's side of the equity scale. Its facts support plaintiff's view that imposition of metal detectors and frisking upon guests, who throughout the Rainbow Room's stellar history, are known for exhibiting only maturity, elegance, and grace, is not only inappropriate, and ill advised, but also rather ineffective security. Nonetheless, the terrible burden of post-911 history counters that weight and justifies owners, in the exercise of their discretion and judgment, undertaking extraordinary precautions. The sad reality is that metal detectors and bag checks have become a "pervasive aspect of everyday life."

Turning to the third prong, evidence demonstrating a likelihood of success need not be conclusive and a prima facie showing of a right to relief is sufficient as actual proof should be left for further court proceedings.

Cipriani argues that it will ultimately prevail on its breach of Lease claim. It cites Article 28 of the Lease, which provides, in pertinent part:

Landlord reserves the right, from time to time, to adopt additional Rules and Regulations and to amend the Rules and Regulations then in effect. Nothing contained in this Lease shall impose upon Landlord any obligation to enforce the Rules and Regulations or terms, covenants or conditions in any other lease against any other Building tenant, and Landlord shall not be liable to Tenant for violation of the Rules and Regulations by any other tenant, its employees, agents, visitors or licensees, except that *Landlord shall not enforce any Rule or Regulation against Tenant in a discriminatory fashion* (emphasis added).

Cipriani contends that installation of metal detectors solely for the Rainbow Room constitutes discrimination against Cipriani, particularly since at least one building tenant and its guests have not complied with the identification and registration measures already in place for office workers and their guests, who routinely bypass electronic turnstiles with which the elevators that service the Rainbow Room are already equipped. Defendant argues that Cipriani has not made any of the showings required to merit an award of preliminary injunctive relief. Defendant urges that plaintiff will not prevail on the merits as Lease Section 7.3 expressly permits the Landlord to alter the building's security systems in its discretion. It reads, in pertinent part:

> Interruption Due to Repairs. Landlord reserves the right to make all changes, alterations, additions, improvements, repairs or replacements to the Building and the Center, including the Building Systems which provide services to Tenant, as Landlord deems necessary or desirable, provided that in no event shall the level of any of the Building service decrease in any material respect the level required of Landlord in this Lease as a result thereof, nor shall there be a denial of Tenant's access to the Premises.

Under the Lease, "Building Systems" is defined as "the mechanical, electrical, plumbing, sanitary, sprinkler, heating, ventilation and air conditioning, security, life-safety, elevator and other service systems or facilities of the Building up to (but to including) the point of localized distribution to the Premises (excluding any systems or facilities exclusively serving the Premises)."

Defendant also argues that Lease Section 7.1 with respect to the landlord's right and responsibilities as to operation, maintenance, and "necessary repairs" includes the public portions of the building of which the elevator banks and turnstiles are a part.

Though defendant is correct that plaintiff cites no specific provision of the Rules and Regulations that relate to security, the Rules and Regulations that are appended to and incorporated by reference in the Lease of each of the building's tenants consists of nineteen paragraphs, which pertain to various and sundry matters, such as mail delivery, vermin extermination, and pertinent to the action at bar, access to the building. Paragraph 2 of the Rules and Regulations pertains here, which provides:

> Landlord may refuse admission to the Business outside of Business Hours to any person not having a pass issued by Landlord or not properly identified, and may require all persons admitted to or leaving the Building outside of Business Hours to register (other than customers of Tenant during its business hours). Any person whose presence in the Building at any time shall, in the judgment of Landlord, be prejudicial to the safety, character, reputation and interest of the Building or of its tenants may be denied access to the Building or may be ejected therefrom. In case of invasion, riot, public excitement or other commotion, Landlord may prohibit all access to the Building during the continuance of the same, by closing doors or otherwise, for the safety of the tenants or protection of property in the Building. Landlord shall, in no way, be liable to Tenant for damages or loss arising from the admission, exclusion or ejection of any person to or from the Premises or the Building under the provisions of this rule. Landlord may require any person leaving the Building with any package or other object to exhibit a pass from Tenant from whose Premises the package or object is being removed, but the establishment or enforcement of such requirement shall not impose any responsibility on the Landlord for the protection of Tenant against the removal of property from the Premises of Tenant.

Countering plaintiff's reliance on the Rules and Regulations, defendant argues that under Section 28 of the Lease, to the extent any Rule and Regulation conflicts or is inconsistent with the Lease, the Lease controls. It contends that irrespective of any Rule or Regulation, the Lease reserves the right to RCPI to install metal detectors at the entrances to the elevator banks.

Nor does defendant agree that its measures discriminate against Cipriani and its guests. It argues that in fact, the security measures in place for Cipriani are less onerous than those for other tenants. The guests of other building tenants are required to register with the security office, present government issued identification and obtain a temporary access pass permitting that guest to pass through security turnstiles, while Cipriani's guests need only inform the security guard at the elevator bank servicing the Rainbow Room that they are customers of the Rainbow Room to move directly via express elevator to the venue.

Plaintiff has failed to offer prima facie evidence that defendant has breached its rights under the Lease sufficient to establish a likelihood of success on the merits of its claims. "It is by no means clear from the contract terms that defendant has in fact violated the parties' agreement, and where contractual language 'leaves the rights of the parties open to doubt and uncertainty,' injunctive relief is inappropriate."

Under the Lease, defendant explicitly reserved the right to make changes, alterations, and/or additions to the security system in the public portion of the premises, where the elevator banks servicing the Rainbow are located. Metal detectors would certainly fall within the "security" systems that defendant has the right to alter. Whether the installation of metal detectors would constitute a "denial of Tenant's access to the Premises" under the lease is an issue for determination in this action and is subject to interpretation of the contractual language.

Nor has Cipriani made a prima facie showing that defendant has or intends to apply the Rules and Regulations with respect to access in a fashion that discriminates against Cipriani. All parties agree that given the occupancy capacity of the Rainbow Room, a registration or "reservation" requirement for Rainbow Room guests is impracticable, so that in fact, defendant has continued to apply the Rules and Regulations, as written, to accommodate Cipriani's enterprise.

Plaintiff's failure to surmount its threshold burden of demonstrating a likelihood of success on the merits of its claims is dispositive on this motion, and the court must therefore deny its Motion for Injunctive Relief.

Accordingly, it is ORDERED that the plaintiff's application for a preliminary injunction is hereby DENIED.

CASE COMMENT

This case represents an interesting conflict between security methods and the viability of a business. The business owner essentially argues that the proposed security methods, especially the installation of metal detectors, would have an extremely adverse impact on his business. The landlord argues that the security methods were necessary given the realities of "post 9/11 America." They further contend the lease provision gives them the right to institute security hardware. It is clear that the security methods instituted by the landlord were at least partly motivated by liability exposures. The court seemed sympathetic to the security concerns raised by the landlord. Ultimately, the court held against the plaintiff based on the lease provisions, which gave the landlord great discretion to make appropriate changes to the building, including security improvements.

4 A.D. 3d 45, 773 N.Y.S. 2d 354

Supreme Court, Appellate Division, First Department, New York

PETER GROSS, ET AL., PLAINTIFFS-RESPONDENTS v. EMPIRE STATE BUILDING ASSOCIATES, ET AL., DEFENDANTS-APPELLANTS

March 2, 2004

Background

Tourists sued landlords that owned historic building, seeking to recover damages resulting from incident in which armed gunman indiscriminately shot at large group of people touring the building which resulted in the death of one tourist and serious injury to six others. The Supreme Court, New York County, denied landlords' Motion for Summary Judgment. Landlords appealed.

Holdings

The Supreme Court, Appellate Division, held that:

1. Landlords were properly found to have taken significant precautions to protect tourists from harm by third parties, and
2. Landlords could not have reasonably foreseen that armed gunman would enter building and indiscriminately shoot at large group of people touring the building, given that there had never been a shooting in 65 years of the building's history and there had only been two muggings or assaults during two years that preceded shooting.

Order reversed; complaint dismissed.

We live in an uncertain and sometimes unpredictable world seemingly filled with daily reports of random acts of violence, including bombings, shootings, and mayhem on our public streets, in work sites, post offices, fast food restaurants, federal office buildings, schools, subways and commuter trains and, of course, the World Trade Center.

Particularly in the aftermath of the attacks on September 11, 2001, we encounter metal detectors, bag checks, and numerous other security measures at airports, sports stadiums, government buildings, and countless other venues. Security has become a pervasive aspect of everyday life.

Nevertheless, landlords—in this case the landlords of the Empire State Building—have a firmly established common-law duty to take only "minimal precautions" to protect tenants and visitors from foreseeable harm, including foreseeable criminal acts. As recognized by the IAS court, landlords are not insurers of the safety of those who use their premises and, even with a history of crime committed on the premises, cannot be held to a duty to take protective measures unless it is shown that they know or, from past experience, have reason to know that there is a likelihood of conduct, criminal or otherwise, likely to endanger the safety of those using their premises. "The question of the scope of an alleged tortfeasor's duty is, in the first instance, a legal issue for the court to resolve."

The IAS court properly found that defendants clearly have shown that significant precautions were undertaken by them in light of undisputed evidence that defendants, among numerous other measures, had installed a million dollar closed circuit television surveillance system in the public areas of the Empire State Building, posted signs that all persons entering the building were subject to a search of packages and bags, employed a large security force and conducted random bag checks. It also found, again correctly, that as of Sunday afternoon, February 23, 1997, the day of this incident, there had been only a minimal amount of actual violent criminal activity within the Empire State Building, particularly the observation decks which attract 10,000 visitors each day and another 25,000 on weekends. That afternoon, a deranged man in his late 60s, armed with a semi-automatic Beretta pistol he purchased in Florida, went to the 86th floor observation deck of the building and, suddenly and without warning, indiscriminately shot at the large crowd of people, killing Christoffer Burmeister, a Swiss tourist, and seriously injuring six others before committing suicide with the same pistol.

Nonetheless, despite evidence that there had never been a shooting in the 65-year history of the building and only two muggings or assaults from January 1995 to 1997, the court found that violent criminal activity, essentially robberies, in the building's ground level retail stores and on the abutting sidewalks, combined with 20 bomb threats to the building, raise a factual issue as to foreseeability. We disagree.

Obviously, with the benefit of 20/20 hindsight, everything is foreseeable. However, without reciting a litany of cases on either side of the issue, it simply cannot be said that in 1997, when, as defendants aptly note, metal detectors were much less prevalent than today, the Empire State Building and its landlords could reasonably have foreseen the events of February 23, 1997, and be held to the duty urged by plaintiffs, namely the use of x-ray machines, metal detectors and scanners together with armed security guards and the inspection of all bags and packages. Nor is there any evidence that the assailant appeared in any way out of the ordinary or acted suspiciously right up to the moment he pulled out the pistol and began shooting.

Accordingly, the order of the Supreme Court, New York County, which denied defendants' Motion for Summary Judgment dismissing the complaint, should be reversed, on the law. The defendants' Motion for Summary Judgment granted and the complaint dismissed.

All concur.

CASE COMMENT

In this case, the court again expressed a deep regard for the need for security measures in post–9/11 America. The court noted the prevalence of crime generally, and the need to institute proper security measures. In this case, however, the court noted the security methods used by the Empire State Building. In assessing these security methods, the court refused to find that the building failed to institute appropriate security methods. In making this decision, the court reversed the lower court's view that the crime was foreseeable. Further, there was no showing that any particular additional security methods would have prevented the shootings. Consequently, this case was dismissed in favor of the building (the defendant).

346 F. Supp. 2d 430

United States District Court, S.D. New York

ABDALLAH HIGAZY, PLAINTIFF v. MILLENNIUM HOTEL AND RESORTS, CDL (NEW YORK) L.L.C., THE HILTON HOTELS CORPORATION, RONALD FERRY, STUART YULE, AND FBI AGENT MICHAEL TEMPLETON, DEFENDANTS.

Sept. 30, 2004

Background

Arrestee detained in connection with terrorist attacks sued federal agent, hotel, and hotel's owner, operator, chief security officer, and security guard, asserting claims for alleged violations of his constitutional rights, false arrest and false imprisonment, malicious prosecution, intentional infliction of emotional distress, negligence, and negligent hiring, retention, training, and supervision. All defendants except security guard moved for summary judgment.

Holdings

The district court held that:

1. Hotel defendants were not vicariously liable for alleged intentional torts of security guard and chief security officer;
2. Hotel defendants were not liable for negligent hiring, training, retention, or supervision of security guard;
3. Factual issues precluded summary judgment for chief security officer on claim for false arrest and false imprisonment; and
4. Chief security officer was not liable for malicious prosecution.

Motions granted in part and denied in part.

On December 17, 2001, the FBI arrested Abdallah Higazy, the plaintiff in this action, as a material witness suspected by the Government of having involvement in or knowledge of the September 11, 2001, attacks on the World Trade Center. These suspicions were founded in large measure on a statement to the FBI by a hotel security guard that a radio bearing a resemblance to a walkie-talkie, along with an Egyptian passport and a Koran, were found locked in a safe in a hotel room adjacent to the site of the attacks. The room had been occupied by Higazy, who had vacated the hotel, along with its other guests, on September 11, 2001. Higazy was ordered detained without bail on December 18, 2001, a status that was renewed ten days later. On January 11, 2002, the Government filed criminal charges against Higazy accusing him of falsely denying ownership or possession or knowledge of the radio. Four days later, the device's true owner—a pilot—came forward. The criminal complaint was promptly dismissed, Higazy was released from his month-long custody, and the security guard was indicted for his false report.

Each of the defendants except for Ferry now moves for summary judgment. Specifically, there are two summary judgment motions before the court—one from Agent Templeton, and the other from Millennium, Hilton, CDL and Yule (collectively, the "Hotel defendants" or the "Hotel"). For the reasons that follow, we grant Templeton's motion and the Hotel defendants' motion with the exception of defendant Yule's motion, which we grant in part and deny in part.

The Retrieval of a Communications Device from the Millennium

The Millennium Hotel is located across the street from the former site of the World Trade Center, and was evacuated and cordoned off shortly after the September 11, 2001, attacks, separating many Hotel guests from their personal belongings. Plaintiff was one of those guests. In either late September or early October, Yule and the other Hotel defendants instituted a plan for retrieving and inventorying guest property, which assigned the responsibility of opening locked room safes to security officer Ronald Ferry, a defendant in this action, and the responsibility of inventorying property found in the safes to another hotel employee, Christiana Franco. As part of the process, Ferry and Franco were to place all property recovered from each room and room safe on the floor in the room ending in "01" on each of the hotel's fifty-five floors. On or about October 11, 2001, Ferry retrieved a radio during the sweep and told Yule that it was found in hotel room 5101, inaccurately referred to in the Hotel defendants' papers as 5501.

Ferry also told Yule that a passport, a yellow metal medallion and copy of the Koran were found with the radio in the room's safe. Yule went up to the room, and, according to an FBI report taken from Yule on January 2, 2002, when Ferry first presented the radio and passport to him, he did not find the objects suspicious and instructed Ferry to "store the device with the rest of the guest's belongings." But in late November, another hotel employee who was conducting a second inventory of guest property in a makeshift storage locker again brought the radio to Yule's attention. Together with the passport, Yule found the "circumstances to be more sinister" and therefore notified the FBI that he had found "something of interest they should see." In the month and a half that lapsed between Ferry's notification to Yule and Yule's call to the FBI, Yule and Ferry did not have a conversation about the radio.

In late November or early December of 2001, following Yule's telephone call, Special Agents Vincent Sullivan and Christopher Bruno of the FBI went to the Millennium Hotel. Yule showed the agents an Egyptian passport and a radio that resembled a walkie-talkie, both of which, Yule explained, were recovered from a guest room when inventorying possessions of guests who were staying in the Hotel on the morning of September 11, 2001. The FBI later determined that the radio was an air-band trans-receiver capable of air-to-air and air-to-ground communication.

Higazy Is Detained as a Material Witness (12/17/01)

On December 17, 2001, plaintiff returned on his own initiative to the Hotel with an appointment to retrieve his belongings. The FBI, having previously been notified that Higazy would be visiting the hotel at this time, dispatched Special Agents Sullivan and Bruno as well as Special Agent Adam Suits to the Millennium. During a three-hour interview with the agents, Higazy emphatically denied ownership of the radio. However, Higazy did eventually divulge his past service as a first lieutenant in the Egyptian Air Force and how, through this service, he acquired some familiarity with radio communications devices.

At the same time as Higazy's interview, the FBI questioned defendant Ferry two times. Each time, Ferry said that he found the radio in Higazy's safe on top of a passport. Apparently armed with Ferry's reiterated claim, the agents re-questioned Higazy about the radio. Higazy again denied ownership. At the conclusion of the interview, the FBI detained Higazy as a material witness.

That same day, shortly after Higazy's arrest, another FBI agent and a detective with the New York City Police Department began questioning Higazy. At first, Higazy indicated an interest in cooperating and speaking with the agents, waiving his right to an attorney by signing an advice of rights form. However, Higazy changed his mind and asked for an attorney after declining to sign a form stating that he did not want the Egyptian Consulate notified of his detention. The day's questioning evidently concluded upon this request.

Higazy's Polygraph Examination (12/27/01)

During the December 17, 2001, hearing, Mr. Dunn conveyed to the court his client's interest in taking a polygraph examination. After the hearing, AUSA Daniel Himmelfarb informed Mr. Dunn that the "Government was not really interested in doing a polygraph ... but they only were relenting to the Judge's invitation to do it." In this regard, as explained to Mr. Dunn, the Government would not place much weight on the polygraph results because if Higazy were a member of Al-Qaeda he could pass it. Further, Assistant USA Himmelfarb expressed to Mr. Dunn that the polygraph would not dissuade the Government in their belief that the radio was found in Higazy's safe. Himmelfarb and Mr. Dunn discussed the procedures for the polygraph, which included excluding Mr. Dunn from the examination room, but allowing Higazy to speak with Mr. Dunn if he needed to, and limiting the examination questioning.

The polygraph examination was scheduled for December 27, 2001, at the United States Attorney's Office in New York. Dunn and Higazy had the opportunity to confer prior to the examination. Before commencing the questioning, Agent Templeton explained to Higazy his rights, and Higazy executed two consent forms. Higazy first signed an Advice of Rights form in which he was advised of his right to remain silent and speak with an attorney at any point during the examination. He also signed a "Consent to Interview with Polygraph" form.

Before placing the polygraph machine's components on Higazy, Agent Templeton informed him that the following questions would be asked: Are you an Egyptian citizen? Are you a U.S. citizen? Do you have a scholarship? Did you have anything to do with September 11, 2001? Once the machine components were attached, Agent Templeton proceeded through this same set of questions twice. Based on the results, Agent Templeton found that Higazy's answers to the questions relating to Higazy's involvement in the attacks were deceptive.

At the end of the second series of questions, Higazy requested that Agent Templeton stop because he could not breathe and because he felt pain in his arm. Templeton removed the polygraph's components from Higazy and left the room to get him water. Upon Templeton's return, Higazy asked, "Has this ever happened to anyone before?" Templeton answered that "it never happened to anyone who told the truth." At this point, Higazy provided Templeton what would prove to be a series of false confessions, the sequence and motivation of which is not entirely agreed upon by Higazy and Templeton on this motion. According to Higazy, he was asked if he stole the radio, to which he responded that the radio was his and was found across the street in a downtown Manhattan electronics store near the Hotel and the World Trade Center site. Both Higazy and Templeton agree that Higazy then recanted this story by disavowing ownership or possession of the radio. Agent Templeton next banged on the table and told Higazy to tell him the truth. Higazy then claimed he found the radio at the base of the Brooklyn Bridge, but once again recanted this story and said the radio was not his. And once again, Templeton banged on the table and demanded the truth.

Finally, Higazy explained to Templeton that he stole the radio from the Egyptian Air Force and used it to eavesdrop on telephone conversations. Higazy did not recant this version. Agent Templeton next prepared a written statement for Higazy to sign that included this explanation.

Higazy did not sign the statement, but instead requested for the first time during the session to see his attorney. Agent Templeton immediately retrieved Mr. Dunn, who met with Higazy and, according to Higazy's handwritten affidavit, said: "You were lying to me?" Higazy replied: "No, but

I thin [*sic*] it's the best option in front of me." Dunn advised Higazy not to sign the statement. Dunn left the room stating Higazy would not sign the statement because it varied from Higazy's prior statements of having no connection to the radio.

No further questioning was conducted that day and Higazy was returned to the facility where he was being held. An independent reviewer of Higazy's polygraph results found deception in his answers.

The Criminal Complaint Against Higazy (1/11/02)

The government re-interviewed Ferry, and, on January 11, 2002, Himmelfarb approved a one-count, five-page criminal complaint sworn out by Agent Bruno. The complaint alleged in pertinent part that: a "hotel security officer" at the Millennium informed the FBI that a radio capable of air-to-air and air-to-ground communication was found in a safe (situated on top of an Egyptian passport and an Arabic book) in hotel room 5101, a room occupied by Higazy on September 11, 2001; Higazy, during his December 17, 2001, interview with the FBI, stated that he had served in the Egyptian Air Corps and had some expertise in communications devices; Higazy, when shown the radio, denied that it was his, that he had ever before seen it, or that it could have been found in his room; during a re-interview with the FBI, Higazy revealed that one of his duties in the Egyptian service was to repair radios used by pilots to communicate with people on the ground, but that he had no knowledge of this particular radio. The complaint charged Higazy with making false statements to the Government in the course of a criminal investigation in violation of 18 U.S.C. Section 1001(a).

Magistrate Judge Maas of this court found probable cause for the complaint. The complaint made no reference to the polygraph examination or the confessions Higazy made at the conclusion of the examination. However, during the arraignment Himmelfarb argued that one of four reasons Higazy should be denied bail was because on each occasion he had been questioned about the radio, Higazy had lied: "[On December 27, 2001], he was questioned about the radio. At first he denied ownership of the radio and later admitted ownership of the radio but told three different versions of how he had come into possession of the radio. So this is not somebody who can be deemed trustworthy." After a considered review of this and other relevant evidence and factors, Judge Maas ordered Higazy to be held without bail.

The Government's Request to Dismiss Its Criminal Complaint

On January 14, 2002, Joseph Verde, a chef for Millennium who, in the post-attack recovery phase, was placed in charge of returning abandoned items to former guests, was approached by an airline pilot who had been staying on the hotel's 50th floor. He had gone to the Millennium to reclaim his abandoned property and noticed that his radio was missing from the collection of items returned to him. Verde immediately contacted Special Agent Bruno at the FBI to relay this development. The FBI verified to its satisfaction that the radio was in fact the pilot's, and not Higazy's, and that the pilot had not had any interaction with Higazy. During a re-interview by the FBI at this time, Ferry, the hotel security officer who first claimed to have discovered the radio in the safe in Higazy's room, revised his account and stated that the radio was found on a table in Higazy's room and not in the safe.

Although it is unclear how the radio was transferred from the 50th floor to the 51st floor of the Millennium, the Government requested the dismissal of the complaint against Mr. Higazy and his immediate release. These applications were granted.

Defendant Ronald Ferry's Criminal Proceedings

After Higazy was cleared of the charges against him, the Government filed an information against Ronald Ferry accusing him of lying to Government agents in the course of their investigation of the radio. On May 30, 2002, Ferry pled guilty to this charge and was sentenced to three years probation plus six months of intermittent confinement on weekends at a community corrections center, halfway house, or similar residential facility. A pre-sentence letter submitted to the court on Ferry's behalf by his counsel made no claim or suggestion that Ferry acted at the request or direction of any of the hotel defendants. While it was reported at the time that the United States Attorney's investigation was continuing, no additional indictments or complaints were filed against any other employee of the hotel, such as defendant Yule.

The facts surrounding the hiring of Mr. Ferry at Millennium are not disputed. On January 6, 1996, he completed a job application and interviewed with Millennium's Human Resources Department and his future department head, defendant Yule. An employment verification form was sent to Ferry's then-current employer, Burns Security. That form was completed to Millennium's satisfaction and contained no negative comments on Ferry's work history. Prior to working at Burns Security, Ferry had resigned from the Newark Police Department, and abused drugs and alcohol before and throughout his tenure with Millennium.

The Employer Entities' Alleged Vicarious Liability

Millennium, CDL, and Hilton—Ferry's and Yule's employers—maintain that they cannot be held vicariously liable for Ferry and Yule's actions because those actions were not undertaken within the scope of their employment.

Ferry's alleged intentional torts—false imprisonment, malicious prosecution, and intentional infliction of emotional distress—cannot be attributed to the Employer Entities under a theory of respondeat superior. Ferry has indicated that his acts were undertaken in a misguided sense of patriotism, which is a personal matter and not one that can be understood as redounding to or furthering the interests of his employer. Even if Ferry's testimony about his motives is discounted entirely, Higazy's vicarious liability claim cannot survive. The Employer Entities have argued that Higazy's actions in no way served to advance his employers' interests, and Higazy in response has failed to even speculate, let alone point to colorable evidence suggesting that Ferry was acting to further his employers' interests. That Ferry chose to commit a tort in the course of recovering abandoned guest property does not mean the tort was committed in furtherance of that task. In the absence of any evidence suggesting how Ferry's actions served his employers' interests, it is appropriate to enter summary judgment in the Employer Entities favor on Higazy's vicarious liability claim.

The Employer Entities' Direct Tort Liability

Higazy claims that Millennium, Hilton, and CDL (the Employer Entities) are directly liable for their negligent hiring, retention, training, and supervision of Ferry and Yule, and that these parties are also directly liable to Higazy for their negligence as founded on a duty of care owed to him as a hotel guest. The Employer Entities move for summary judgment on these claims.

1. Negligent Hiring/Retention/Training/Supervision

Prior to working at Millennium, Ferry was employed by a company called Burns Security for nearly three years. Before that, he was a police officer with the Newark Police Department for nearly nine years. Higazy does not claim the Employer Entities knew at any time before or during his employment with Millennium that Ferry had abused drugs and alcohol, nor has he shown that Ferry was ever subjected to disciplinary action at Millennium during the course of employment.

Higazy has presented no facts from which one could reasonably conclude that the Employer Entities knew or should have known of Ferry's substance abuse problems. The sole basis for asserting that they should have known of these habits is that several years prior to his employment at the hotel, he left the Newark Police Force for personal reasons. According to Higazy, Ferry's departure from a major police force and his subsequent application for employment as a hotel security guard and the attendant salary cut should have alerted the Employer Entities to a potential problem. Higazy further contends that a reasonable investigation into Ferry's background would have revealed his drug abuse.

No reasonable jury could conclude that the Employer Entities had an obligation to investigate Ferry's background simply because he left a stressful position he held for nine years to take on a similar but less profitable job, or that such an investigation would have disclosed his drug abuse.

Moreover, the Employer Entities did conduct a verification of Ferry's work history prior to hiring, and nothing in the course of that effort revealed anything improper. Ferry is rated as uniformly "good" in the "Verification of Employment" form provided by Burns Security. Additionally, the Employer Entities obtained a letter from the Newark Police Department prior to hiring Ferry verifying his employment with the force and indicating that he resigned for personal reasons (as opposed to being fired for cause or general unfitness). Even if there was suspicion as to the "personal reasons" for resignation, nothing in Ferry's personnel record from the Newark Police Department (obtained not in advance of hiring Ferry but instead for purposes of discovery in this action) indicates drug or alcohol abuse. The file only shows that Ferry served on the Newark Police force for almost nine years, and that he resigned for personal reasons.

Other than Millennium's failure to discover Ferry's drug problem, Higazy presents no evidence sufficient to create a triable issue as to whether the Millennium was negligent in its hiring, training, retention or supervision of Ferry. Millennium's first indication that Ferry might have a propensity to lie to his superiors or to law enforcement appears to be the very incident of which Higazy complains. This is an insufficient basis for recovering on a claim of negligent hiring, retention, training, and supervision. Summary judgment on the claim is therefore granted.

2. Negligence

Higazy also claims the Employer Entities were negligent. Specifically, he claims that the Employer Entities, as custodians of his property, had a duty to safeguard such property in such a manner as not to permit unreasonable commingling and confusion of ownership. Higazy claims that the failure to discharge this duty of care created an opportunity for Ferry to falsely claim the radio was found in his safe. We reject this argument.

Although a hotel may owe a duty to a guest to safeguard his property, Higazy does not allege loss or damage to his property, nor may he assert a breach of a duty owed to another guest. To the extent a hotel owes a broader duty to prevent confusion of ownership after an emergency evacuation, Higazy cannot establish proximate causation, which shields a defendant in a negligence suit from liability for unforeseeable injuries. Ferry's behavior was well beyond the ordinary or foreseeable under the circumstances and thus severed any link between the Employer Entities' inattention and

Higazy's injuries. The application for summary judgment against Higazy's negligence claim is therefore granted.

Yule's Tort Liability

The complaint asserts three common-law causes of action against Stuart Yule, the Millennium's head of security, and Ferry's supervisor: false arrest and false imprisonment; malicious prosecution; and intentional infliction of emotional distress. To evaluate the viability of those causes of action, it is necessary to first review the evidentiary record with respect to Yule's involvement in Ferry's false statements to the FBI, noting, as appropriate, disputed and undisputed facts. Also, we note at the outset that the only directly exculpatory testimony against Yule (which Yule in fact disputes) comes from Ferry.

Some time in mid-October 2001, Ferry and Franco, as part of a program to collect and catalog guest property, found a radio scanner among other property in the hotel room occupied by Higazy on September 11, 2001. Upon this discovery, Yule was called to the room to look at the radio and other items that had been found in the room and safe. According to Yule, he examined the objects, determined that no further action was necessary and told Ferry and Franco to store them together with the belongings found in the room.

Ferry gave an account of the initial discovery of the radio, which contradicts Yule's version and also implicates Yule in his misdeeds, in an interview to the FBI on January 16, 2002, after the pilot had come forward to claim his radio. According to Ferry, Christiana Franco, and another hotel employee, Pedro, were in the room when Yule came up to view the radio. Yule then told Ferry to lie to the FBI about where the radio had been found in order to strengthen the case against Higazy, as they had found a "terrorist." Ferry alleges that Yule reminded him on more than one occasion thereafter to maintain that the radio was found in the safe. Apparently, Ferry has not repeated this story.

It is not until after Thanksgiving, following a second report to Yule about the radio, this time by a member of a new inventory team who came across the objects again sometime in late November, that Yule spoke with the FBI and mentioned the items as something of interest they might like to see. Some time thereafter the FBI, while returning other property to the hotel, examined the items and determined to obtain a search warrant for them.

Arrangements were made to call the FBI when Higazy came to the Millennium Hotel to pick up his belongings. He did so on December 17, 2001. The FBI came to the hotel and questioned him in the hotel. After Higazy denied that the radio was his or that it could possibly have been found in his safe, the agents left the room where they were questioning Higazy and asked Yule exactly where the radio had been found. Yule replied that the security guard who found the radio was nearby and contacted Ferry.

Ferry told the agents on two separate occasions (most likely in Yule's presence) that evening that he found the radio in the safe.

The contemporaneous FBI reports and the statements by the FBI during the investigation following the dismissal of the case against Higazy and during depositions in this case consistently support Yule's testimony that he never told the FBI that the radio had been found in the safe.

Ferry told a different story about his interaction with Yule on the location of the radio in his deposition testimony on February 11, 2004. In this account, Ferry and Yule had a conversation in Yule's office sometime before Higazy returned to the hotel but after Ferry had already told the FBI that the radio had been found in the safe. Yule told Ferry that Franco told him she found the radio on the desk, contrary to Ferry's previous advice that he had found the radio in the safe. Ferry admitted that Franco was telling the truth, but Yule replied, "But I believe you." At this point, Ferry explained the importance of "stretching the truth" to strengthen a case, and Yule, according to Ferry, replied, "Only we cops understand that."

Plaintiff also cites to several other comments attributed to Yule to buttress his claims. First, speaking with the FBI after the interview of Higazy, Yule expressed the importance of the fact that the radio was found by Ferry in the safe. Second, plaintiff cites to Verde's testimony concerning Yule's reaction to his calling the FBI without waiting for Yule to tell the FBI about the pilot who came to the hotel looking for his radio. Yule described this conversation differently. Third, there is Yule's comment to Agent Bruno after it became clear that the radio had not been found in Higazy's safe about how they could "spin" this, suggesting that maybe it could be blamed on the safe company.

This approach has applicability here at least with respect to the first story that Ferry told about Yule's proposal allegedly made when the radio was initially found, on or about October 11, 2001. According to Ferry, Yule suggested that they lie to the FBI and claim that the radio had been found in a safe to strengthen the case since they had found a "terrorist." There are at least three reasons why this story is simply incredible.

First, it is totally inconsistent with the undisputed record of Yule's subsequent actions, namely, that he did not report the finding of the radio to the FBI until after Thanksgiving and according to the FBI never told them that it was found in the safe. Second, there is the fact that Ferry never repeated, and indeed changed, his story, as well as the broader issues of Ferry's credibility. Third, it strains credibility that the head of Hotel Security would announce in front of three lower level hotel employees his intent to commit a crime.

Nonetheless, we will proceed (despite our admitted skepticism) on the premise that there is a genuine issue of fact raised by Ferry's second version of Yule's complicity in his repeated lies to the FBI, and assume for the required legal analysis of the common law claims that Ferry and Yule reached an agreement following Ferry's initial statement to the FBI that he had found the radio in the safe. That agreement essentially was that Yule would not contradict Ferry's statement that the radio was found in the safe, which he either knew or suspected, was false.

Malicious Prosecution

Regarding initiation of the proceeding, the Hotel defendants argue that Yule only provided law enforcement with misinformation as to where the radio was found but that law enforcement made its own decision to arrest and detain Higazy. It is well established that merely "reporting a crime to law enforcement and giving testimony" does not constitute "initiation" of a criminal proceeding. As the Second Circuit recently held, "more is required" than simply imparting even false information on authorities. Specifically, "the complainant must have played an active role in the prosecution, such as giving advice and encouragement or importuning the authorities to act."

As the evidentiary review at the outset of this section establishes, Yule did not himself inform the FBI that the radio was found in the safe. Viewing the facts in the light most favorable to Higazy, Yule supported Ferry's decision to lie to the investigators and declined to correct the resulting false impression. However, Yule did not advise, encourage, or importune the authorities to arrest and detain Higazy. Yule is therefore entitled to summary judgment on Higazy's claim of malicious prosecution.

CASE COMMENT

This case presents a clear example of an overzealous security officer, who based on his belief that an individual was involved in the terrorist acts of 9/11, provided false information that led to a federal investigation and this federal lawsuit. The facts enumerated by the court describe a series of circumstances that would lead one to believe that the evidence recovered may have been used in the terrorist attacks. The court upheld each of the summary judgment decisions, except the cause of action against the security supervisor, Yule, in the false arrest and false imprisonment claim. The moral of this case is that security personnel must be professional in their work. Even when faced with a terrible crime, they must remain profession and honest. In this case, the failure to do so resulted in a waste of investigatory resources and attention, the legal costs of defending a lawsuit with substantial potential liability, the exposure of an innocent man to criminal prosecution, the criminal conviction of the security officer, and the potential civil exposure of the security supervisor. These ramifications were not worth the overzealous acts of unprofessional security personnel.

13

Terrorism Statutes and Indicators

STATUTES

Terrorism Risk Insurance Act of 2002 (P.L. 107-297 formerly H.R. 3210)

Because of the financial impact of the terrorist attacks of 9/11, many sought to provide a means to stabilize or even encourage investments throughout the country, particularly in large urban cities such as New York. The risk of loss from terrorism posed a huge disincentive for capital investment, particularly developers and businesses in areas deemed targets of terrorism. Indeed, the threat of terrorism posed such an uncertain risk that insurance companies were hard pressed to insure developers and businesses. If insurance coverage was not provided, why would a prudent investor or corporation risk capital that could be damaged or destroyed in a terrorist attack?

From the perspective of the insurance industry, it is very difficult to accurately price coverage for acts of terrorism. The unknown frequency of such acts, coupled with the potential for severe losses, makes coverage very risky to insurers or very costly to be insured. As evidence of this dilemma, the insurance industry took a huge financial hit from 9/11, reportedly losing more than $30 billion dollars before starting to exclude claims from these terrorist acts.[1]

As means to limit the exposure to terrorism related losses, and to encourage investment, the Terrorism Insurance Act of 2002 was signed into law. This legislation was designed to ensure the continued financial capacity of insurers to provide coverage for risks from terrorism. The congressional findings related to the act provide specific rationale for this act. It provides that:[2]

> (1) the ability of businesses and individuals to obtain property and casualty insurance at reasonable and predictable prices, in order to spread the risk of both routine and catastrophic loss, is critical to economic growth,

urban development, and the construction and maintenance of public and private housing, as well as to the promotion of United States exports and foreign trade in an increasingly interconnected world;

(2) property and casualty insurance firms are important financial institutions, the products of which allow mutualization of risk and the efficient use of financial resources and enhance the ability of the economy to maintain stability, while responding to a variety of economic, political, environmental, and other risks with a minimum of disruption;

(3) the ability of the insurance industry to cover the unprecedented financial risks presented by potential acts of terrorism in the United States can be a major factor in the recovery from terrorist attacks, while maintaining the stability of the economy;

(4) widespread financial market uncertainties have arisen following the terrorist attacks of September 11, 2001, including the absence of information from which financial institutions can make statistically valid estimates of the probability and cost of future terrorist events, and therefore the size, funding, and allocation of the risk of loss caused by such acts of terrorism;

(5) a decision by property and casualty insurers to deal with such uncertainties, either by terminating property and casualty coverage for losses arising from terrorist events, or by radically escalating premium coverage to compensate for risks of loss that are not readily predictable, could seriously hamper ongoing and planned construction, property acquisition, and other business projects, generate a dramatic increase in rents, and otherwise suppress economic activity; and

(6) the United States Government should provide temporary financial compensation to insured parties, contributing to the stabilization of the United States economy in a time of national crisis, while the financial services industry develops the systems, mechanisms, products, and programs necessary to create a viable financial services market for private terrorism risk insurance.

As with the concept of terrorism discussed above, the act provided for a specific definition of terrorism:

Any act that is certified by the Secretary, in concurrence with the Secretary of State, and the Attorney General of the United States:[3]

(i) to be an act of terrorism;
(ii) to be a violent act or an act that is dangerous to:
  (I) human life;
  (II) property; or
  (III) infrastructure;

(iii) to have resulted in damage within the United States, or outside of the United States in the case of:
   (I) an air carrier or vessel described in paragraph (5)(B); or
   (II) the premises of a United States mission;
   and
(iv) to have been committed by an individual or individuals acting on behalf of any foreign person or foreign interest, as part of an effort to coerce the civilian population of the United States or to influence the policy or affect the conduct of the United States government by coercion.

There are important limitations of this act. The most relevant exclusions include; that the terrorist act must have been committed by an individual(s) acting on behalf of a foreign person or interest, or if the terrorist act was committed as part of a war declared by Congress, or if the terrorist act does not result in property and insurance losses in excess of $5 million dollars. In this latter sense, the definition of an insured loss is: "any loss resulting from an act of terrorism (including an act of war, in the case of workers' compensation) that is covered by primary or excess property and casualty insurance issued by an insurer of such loss."[4]

These losses insure property and casualty coverage, which includes all commercial lines of insurance plus excess, workers' compensation, and surety policies. Losses that are not insured include crop, private mortgage, financial guarantee, health or life, flood, or reinsurance.[5] In addition, other provisions cap the amount of insured payments made in any year, provide for mandatory participation and insurance premium surcharges, dispute resolution procedures and certain risk factors associated with urban environments. Finally, the government retains the ability to subrogate any losses paid under this act, and to attach or lien assets of terrorist organizations associated with a particular terrorist act.[6]

Arguably the key aspect of the act is to provide for the nullification of any insurance contract exclusion that would preclude coverage for terrorist acts. Since this exclusion is rather common in the insurance industry, this act serves to make any such provision null and void. In return for this sweeping contractual change, insurers are required to offer terrorism coverage, with the government, through this act, acting as a "re-insurer."[7] Under the act, the insured would be free to reject the coverage or simply free to be uninsured against terrorist acts. If coverage is engaged, the federal government would be responsible for 90 percent of the losses for the insurer above the retention amount, while the insurer would pay the remaining 10 percent of the loss.[8] In this way, the government absorbs the bulk of the insured losses resulting from foreign inspired terrorism (subject to the above mentioned limitations).

From the perspective of the insured, the incentive to purchase terrorism insurance relates to the duty of care to third parties described throughout this book. Particularly from the *World Trade Center Litigation* case mentioned previously, it can be extrapolated that liability exposure will exist from terrorism. Consequently, this act provides for such coverage, and at the same time, provides financial protections to insurance companies to insure the risk, with the federal government acting as a secondary (re-insurer) in the event of a terrorist act. Based on a survey conducted by Marsh Inc., the act appeared to be working, as nearly half of large and midsize companies had terrorism insurance at the end of 2004, up from 27 percent the previous year.[9]

This act was amended in December 2005 pursuant to P.L. 109-144. The key aspect of this amendment is to extend terrorism insurance coverage through the year 2007. In addition, the amended act provides for exclusions for commercial automobile insurance, burglary and theft insurance, surety insurance, professional liability insurance, and farm owners multi-peril insurance.[10] More important, however, the amended act provides for a "program trigger" that prohibits payment of federal compensation monies unless the aggregate industry insured losses resulting from acts of terrorism exceed $50 million for program year 4 (2006), and $100 million for program year 5 (2007). This trigger provision substantially raises the liability exposure to insurance companies. The perceived need for this provision may partly stem from the concern that the U.S. government's financial exposure is too great, particularly when one considers the budget deficits facing the country.[11] Finally, the amended act also changes the "insurance marketplace aggregate retention amount" which was also increased for program years 4 and 5.[12]

Significantly, this act provides no protection against domestic terrorism. As evidenced by the Oklahoma City bombing, this may be a significant limitation of this legislation. There are a number of issues tied to this assertion. First, I see no reason why terrorism is or will remain a matter of foreign action. There are a host of reasons why terrorist acts may stem from purely American roots. While the nuances of this assertion is beyond the scope of this book, suffice it to say that criminal gangs, and extremist groups on both sides of the political spectrum are likely to commit terrorist acts. Indeed, in Chapter 14, I predict that terrorist violence from these groups is likely in the near future. Second, the distinction between a foreign versus domestic terrorist act may be factually difficult to assess. In this sense, the definition of an "terrorist act" focuses on acts "on behalf of any foreign person or foreign interest." This may not be easy to discern. For example, if an American citizen commits an act of terrorism because of his fundamental belief that Islam should rule the world, is this act committed on behalf of any foreign person or foreign interest? Further, if an American citizen is a member of radical gang, whose tenets include the destruction of the United States government, is this act committed on behalf of any foreign person or foreign interest?

Consequently, this limitation may prove to be very costly in financial terms—and difficult to assess in operational or legal terms. For these reasons, it is my opinion that this act will fall short—far short—in its goal to limit the liability exposure of terrorism. Indeed, the amended legislation's "program trigger" is an indication that the government is even backing away from its stated desire to protect against foreign inspired terrorism. In sum, while this legislation is useful, it does little to provide liability protection against terrorism. Much, if not most, future terrorist acts are likely to be assessed in terms of the case law presented earlier. Especially for high profile (trophy) buildings this will not provide adequate liability protection. In my mind, additional protections and incentives are necessary.

Support Anti-terrorism by Fostering Effective Technologies (Commonly Known As the "Safety Act," P.L. 107-296)

This legislation is designed to facilitate and promote the development and deployment of anti-terrorism technologies. The purpose of these technologies is to detect, deter, mitigate, or assist in the recovery from a catastrophic act of terrorism.[13] Underlying this purpose is the desire to create certain liability limitations. In essence, the legislation is designed to foster the development and deployment of anti-terrorism technologies by providing a specific liability limit, which is, in turn, secured through insurance coverage.

The liability limitations achieved through this act is as follows:[14]

1. Exclusive jurisdiction in federal court for suits against sellers of "qualified anti-terrorism technologies"
2. A limitation on the liability of qualified sellers to an amount of liability insurance coverage specified for each individual technology
3. A prohibition on joint and several liability for non-economic damages, so that sellers can only be liable for that percentage of non-economic damages proportionate to their responsibility of the resulting harm
4. A complete bar on punitive damages and prejudgment interest
5. A reduction of plaintiffs' recovery by amounts that plaintiffs received from "collateral sources," such as insurance or government benefits
6. A rebuttal presumption that the seller is entitled to the "government contractor defense"

In addition to these liability limitations provided directly to the seller of "qualified anti-terrorism technologies," the legislation also protects contractors, subcontractors, suppliers, vendors, and customers of the seller from liability caused by an act of terrorism. The scope of this protection even goes to the contractors, subcontractors, suppliers, vendors, and customers of the *customer*. Even third-party claims are limited to the amount of insurance coverage enumerated in the act.[15] Consequently, the protective coverage of this act is broad.

The SAFETY Act applies to a broad range of technologies, including "any qualifying product, equipment, service (including support services), device, or technology that the Secretary of Homeland Security, as an exercise of discretion and judgment, determines to merit designation under the statutory criteria."[16] The criteria to qualify as a seller of "qualified anti-terrorism technologies" are also very broad, and include the following:[17]

1. Prior U.S. government use or demonstrated substantial utility and effectiveness
2. Availability of the technology for immediate deployment in public and private settings
3. Existence of extraordinary large or extraordinarily unquantifiable potential for third-party liability risk exposure to the seller or other provider of such anti-terrorism technology
4. Substantial likelihood that such anti-terrorism technology will not be deployed unless protections under the system of risk management provided under the act are extended
5. Magnitude of risk exposure to the public if such anti-terrorism technology is not deployed
6. Evaluation of all scientific studies that can be feasibly conducted in order to assess the capability of the technology to substantially reduce risks of harm
7. Anti-terrorism technology that would be effective in facilitating the defense against acts of terrorism, including technologies that prevent, defeat or respond to such acts
8. Any other factor that may be considered relevant to determination of the Secretary (of Homeland Security) or of the homeland security of the United States

All of these criteria are not required to be fulfilled. Instead, the legislation provides a good deal of discretion to the decision maker (typically the Undersecretary of Homeland Security). If approved, the seller is given the designation of a seller of "qualified anti-terrorism technology," thereby incorporating the liability protections outlined above.

The incentives to obtain this designation are obvious. Once the "qualified anti-terrorism technology" designation is obtained, the seller and all parties related to the use and distribution of the goods or service is protected by the act. This broad liability protection is incurred for harm caused by an "act of terrorism." This term is defined very broadly, to include any act that is[18]

1. Unlawful;
2. Causes harm to a person, property, or entity, in the United States; or in the case of a domestic United States air carrier or a United States flag vessel, in or outside of the United States; and
3. Uses or attempts to use instrumentalities, weapons or other methods designed or intended to cause mass destruction, injury or other loss to citizens or institutions of the United States.

As this definition implies, the scope of coverage under the act includes any unlawful act resulting in harm to U.S. citizens and interests, regardless of where the act occurred. It is hard to envision language that would encompass a broader category of potential exposures. The only real limitation to the scope of coverage is that the "unlawful" act must be deemed as a terrorist act. While the legislation does not define the term "terrorism," the rules—and the name of the legislation—imply that the liability protections are triggered by an act of terrorism.

In my mind, as compared to provisions of the Terrorism Insurance Act, this legislation provides much more protection against liability stemming from an act of terrorism. Nonetheless, both legislative initiatives help to limit the liability exposures related to terrorism. As illustrated by the cases in the last chapter, lawmakers know that "traditional" jurisprudence will create substantial potential exposure to businesses and property owners. While the "jury is still out" on how effective legislation will be in limiting liability exposure, it is unlikely that any legislation will be enough to deal with the problems created by terrroristic threats. Of course, the most effective liability device is to prevent the act from occurring. In this light, the section below addresses specific anti-terrorism indicators and preventive methods.

DISCUSSION QUESTIONS

What are the strengths and weaknesses of these acts? Specify each act in your answer. What other legislation or court based law is needed, if any? In answering this question, please state the reasons behind your assertion. If no additional legislation is enacted, what implications are likely to result in a tort based assessment of liability exposure? Explain your answer in detail.

TERRORISM INDICATORS

This aspect of this book will address specific security methods and indicators related to terrorism. In reviewing these factors, please keep in mind that this section requires a holistic approach to security. In this way, the security methods discussed in previous chapters must be considered as part of this section. For example, the investigative and interrogation practices mentioned previously are applicable here. In addition, and more importantly, the threat and risk assessment factors are critical in this discussion. These factors and practices are particularly important when one considers the threat and potential impact of terrorism.

The threat of terrorism involves many variables. The nature and degree of risk posed by a potential attack depends on a number of factors, including the goals of the attackers and their means of inciting terror. There are numerous terrorist organizations with agendas ranging from various political ideologies to animal rights, environmental, and reproductive issues. With so many diverse groups and causes in play, the number and variety of potential targets present an enormous challenge.

It is beyond the scope of this book to address likely goals and targets of specific terrorist groups. It is important to understand, however, that the risk posed to any company or environment is related to the nature of the particular threat posed by particular terrorist groups. In addition, while local police play a major role in gathering information about likely terrorist attacks, it is important that the general public (including, of course, employees of companies and organizations) maintain great vigilance.[19] Evidence of the value of vigilance can be illustrated in Israel, where ordinary citizens foil more than 80 percent of attempted terrorist attacks.[20]

Suggested Anti-terrorism Measures

Security related to terrorism must encompass varied measures, with the key focus being on vulnerabilities.[21] As described throughout this book, security measures, of course, are not just effective for terrorism prevention. They are also useful—and suggested—for crime prevention. In this sense, consider this quote from James Poland, who asserts that "the concept of deterring acts of terrorism is based on the old police formula of preventing crime: desire + opportunity = crime."[22] This being said, the following security measures can be performed at little or no cost to the company—and the surrounding environment:[23]

- Maintain situational awareness of world events and ongoing threats.
- Encourage personnel to be alert and to immediately report any suspicious activity or possible threat.
- Know the location of the closest police station, hospitals, schools, etc.
- Encourage personnel to avoid routines, vary times and routes, pre-plan for crisis situations, and keep a low profile—especially during periods of high threat.
- Encourage personnel to take notice and report suspicious packages, devices, unattended briefcases, or other unusual materials immediately. Instruct them not to handle or attempt to remove any such object.
- Encourage personnel to keep their family members and supervisors apprised of their whereabouts.
- Maintain a list of employee cell phones, identifying information, addresses, emergency contacts, etc.
- Encourage personnel to know emergency exists and stairwells, and practice these exit drills.
- Ensure all levels of personnel are notified via briefs, e-mail and voice communications, and signage of any changes in threat conditions and protective measures.

- Post emergency telephone numbers for police, fire, and rescue. Encourage personnel to memorize important phone numbers.
- Take any threatening or malicious telephone call, facsimile, or bomb threat seriously. If such a threat is received, obtain and record as much information as possible to assist in the identification of the source. Record the time of the threat, the exact words, any distinguishing features of the caller, and any background noise or other information related to the threat. Develop bomb threat information forms to assist in codifying this information.
- Rearrange exterior vehicle barriers, traffic cones, and road blocks to alter traffic patterns near facilities.
- Institute or increase vehicle, foot, and roving security patrols varying in size, timing, and routes.
- Implement random security shift changes, and vary patrol procedures.
- Increase the number and visibility of security personnel, whenever possible.
- Arrange for law enforcement vehicles to be parked randomly near entrances and exits.
- If practical, prohibit vehicles from parking within 30 feet of any building or facility.
- Conduct routine sweeps of common or adjacent areas, being attentive to trash, newspaper dispensers, mail boxes, planters, etc. If possible, consider removing any item that can be used to conceal bombs. In any case, keep environment clean and orderly.
- Review contingency plans and if not already in place, develop and implement procedures for receiving and acting on
    - threat information procedures;
    - alert notification procedures;
    - terrorist incident response procedures;
    - evacuation procedures;
    - bomb threat procedures;
    - hostage and barricade procedures;
    - chemical, biological, radiological and nuclear procedures; and
    - media relations and notification procedures.
- When the aforementioned plans and procedures have been implemented, conduct internal training exercises and invite emergency responders (fire, rescue, medical, and police agencies) to participate in joint exercises.
- Coordinate and establish partnerships with local authorities to develop intelligence and information sharing relationships.
- Place personnel on standby for contingency planning.
- Limit the number of access points and strictly enforce access control procedures.
- Implement stringent identification procedures to include conducting "hands-on" checks of security badges for all personnel, if badges are required.

- Remind personnel to properly display badges, if applicable, and enforce visibility.
- Require two forms of photo identification for all visitors.
- Escort all visitors entering and departing.
- X-ray all packages, if possible, prior to entry, and inspect all handbags and briefcases.
- Validate vendor lists of all routine vendor deliveries and repair services.
- Approach all illegally parked vehicles in and around facilities, question drivers and direct them to move immediately, if owner cannot be identified, have vehicle towed.
- Review security camera footage daily (or often) to detect for possible indicators of operational surveillance.
- Consider installing telephone ID, record phone calls, if necessary.
- Increase perimeter lighting.
- Deploy visible security cameras and motion sensors.
- Remove vegetation in and around perimeters, and maintain regular landscaping services.
- Institute a robust vehicle inspection program, to include checking undercarriage of vehicles, under the hood, and in the trunk. Provide vehicle inspection training to security personnel.
- Deploy explosive detection devices and explosive detection canine teams.
- Initiate mail and package screening procedure system.
- Install special locking devices on manhole covers in and around facilities.
- Implement a counter-surveillance detection program, including these factors:
    - Unusual or prolonged interest in security measures or personnel
    - Inspection or observation of entry points, and access controls or perimeter barriers, such as fences and walls
    - Unusual behavior by individuals who stare or quickly look away from security personnel
    - Observation of security reaction drills or procedures
    - Increase in the number of telephone or e-mail threats
    - Increase in the frequency and nature of suspected surveillance incidents
    - Evidence of foot surveillance of two or three individuals who appear to be working together
    - Evidence of mobile surveillance using cars, trucks, motorcycles, scooters, boats, or small aircraft
    - Prolonged static surveillance using operatives disguised as panhandlers, shoe shiners, news agents, street sweepers, and food or flower vendors who were not previously seen in the area

- Abandoned devices that could contain explosives, such as vehicles, suitcases, bags, and the like
- Discreet use of cameras, video recorders, or note taking at key facilities including "trophy" buildings and symbolic targets
- Use of multiple sets of clothing and identification or the use of sketching materials

Suicide Bomb Attack Indicators

Terrorism necessarily requires an understanding of the threat posed by suicide bombers. This threat can be manifested in explosive-laden vehicles or explosives hidden on the bodies of individuals. The indicators mentioned above can be characterized as pre-incident factors. One or more of these factors may have occurred prior to a direct attack by a suicide bomber.

Data on suicide bombers in Israel suggest such individuals are usually young men, with 64 percent younger than 23, and 34 percent between the ages of 23 and 28. Fully 84 percent are single at the time of their deadly act.[24] These individual characteristics should be considered in light of the indicators listed below.

Certain indicators may represent the presence of an immediate threat. Each of these indicators, however, may not be determinative of an imminent threat. Indeed, as with any other security-based profile, the individual who exhibits one or more of these indicators may be completely innocent.[25] Nonetheless, these indicators have been shown to be valuable insights into potential suicide bombers, including the following:[26]

1. Wearing inappropriate attire, such as out of season clothing and loose or bulky clothing that are inconsistent with current weather conditions
2. Protruding budges or exposed wires under clothing
3. Chemical smell or odor emanating from individual
4. Intently focused eyes; individual appears to be unusually vigilant
5. Sweating, mumbling, or praying
6. Unusually calm and detached behaviors
7. Pale face suggesting a recently shaved beard
8. Carrying heavy luggage, bag, or backpack
9. Holding hands tight to body
10. Attempting to gain position near crowds or VIP targets
11. Wearing public safety uniform (police, fire, medical, military) or a disguise to elude detection, such as pregnancy or religious attire
12. Driving vehicle modified to handle heavier loads, increase fuel capacity, vehicle speeds, or storage areas

13. Discovery of batteries, wiring, timers or other power supply or switching components in the passenger compartment of a vehicle
14. Presence of stolen or unauthorized vehicles, or vehicle left unattended for extended periods of time. These vehicles may be parked near buildings, in garage parking, or near a potential target

These and other situational factors must be considered in any anti-terrorist plan. They also should be filtered through the considered judgment and interpretation of security personnel. Of course, to the extent practical, people should be made aware of these factors. Indeed, it is well advised to train employees, particularly security personnel, to be cognizant of these factors. Going beyond awareness, relevant policies and procedures in how to react to these indicators are crucial to an effective anti-terrorism response. Obviously, this is easier said than done. However, short of direct intelligence or mind-reading abilities, these are the best security practices available to date. Above all, it is important to maintain vigilance—and look for ways to prevent terrorist acts and its associated liabilities. I fear that this will be a difficult task, indeed.

NOTES

1. Schroeder, Michael (2005). Insurers Fight to Save Terrorism Safety Net. *The Wall Street Journal,* August 25.
2. See H. R. 3210.
3. Ibid.
4. Ibid.
5. Ibid.
6. Ibid.
7. Player, Thomas A., and Anthony C. Roehl (2004). Terrorism Risk Insurance—The U.S. Way. *Intersec,* Vol. 14, January.
8. Player op cit. at 14; and H.R. 3210-7 & 8.
9. Schroeder op cit. at 3A. See also Freeman, Joe (2004). The Impact of Terrorism. *Security Technology and Design.* September.
10. See P. L. 109-144 formerly S. 467.
11. Schroeder op cit. at 3A.
12. Leikin, Howard (2005). *Interim Guidance Concerning the Terrorism Risk Insurance Extension Act of 2005.* Department of the Treasury, December 29.
13. Regulations Implementing the Support Anti-terrorism by Fostering Effective Technologies Act of 2002 in 6 CFR Part 25 at 59685.
14. Ibid at 59690.
15. Ibid at 59700–701.
16. Ibid at 59692.
17. Ibid at Part 25 Section 25.3(b).
18. Ibid at Part 25 Section 25.9.

19. Chapman, Robert et al. (2004). Local Law Enforcement Responds to Terrorism: Lessons in Prevention and Preparedness. *Office of Community Oriented Programs,* U.S. Department of Justice.
20. Tucker op cit. at 4–5.
21. Pillar, Paul R. (2001). Is the Terrorist Threat Misunderstood? *Security Management,* May.
22. Poland, James M. (2005). *Understanding Terrorism: Groups, Strategies, and Responses.* Upper Saddle River, NJ: Pearson/Prentice Hall at 235.
23. The suggestions contained in this section were derived from various sources, and were compiled and collated by the author.
24. These statistics from the seminar attended by the author in Chicago on March 8, 2006, entitled *Coping with Suicide Terrorism in a Civilian Environment: Aspects of Forensic and Post-blast Investigations,* jointly hosted by the Chicago Police Department and the Israeli Consulate. Data provided by Chief Superintendent Avner Barsofsky of the Israeli National Police.
25. For example of issues related to behavioral profiling, see Behaving Like a Terrorist, *Security Management,* March 2006.
26. The suggestions contained in this section were derived from various sources, and were compiled and collated by the author.

14

Conclusions and Future Issues

This book was written to explain both the legal exposures related to crime and the security methods designed to prevent crime. The examples of case law and suggested security methods presented here are meant to illustrate several important points. First, security law cases are very fact-specific. The cases discussed in this book demonstrate the logic and standards used by courts to assess liability. I believe that reading court opinions is essential to understanding security liability. As the reader considers the unique facts of each case, he or she has the opportunity to see how the court approaches the various issues and thus begins to learn how to assess security liability as a court would.

Second, the security methods presented are designed to provide a road map for ways to limit, or even negate, security liability. These suggested methods are by no means all encompassing. Instead, they should be viewed as a set of principles for the implementation of viable and appropriate security. Just as with security cases, each environment is unique. Each environment has certain characteristics that beget specific security methods. Such characteristics include a myriad of factors such as, structural and physical features, the terrain, the nature of the business or industry, the culture of the firm, the characteristics of the community surrounding the firm and the location of the firm, coupled with the existing policies and procedures of the organization. These factors, and others, must be considered in light of the security methods presented. In this way, the suggested security methods should be critically examined in light of the particular characteristics of the environment.

Based on this analysis, the reader should apply the legal standards and principles discerned from case law along with the security methods and principles reflected in the suggested best practices. Since security exposures and security liability are both a security *and* legal consideration, it is necessary to blend security and legal principles into a cogent, critical analysis. Hopefully, this book served to accomplish this difficult, but necessary, goal.

To my knowledge, this attempt has not been accomplished by any previous book. Only time and discernment will tell if this dual goal was accomplished. I encourage feedback from readers on this note.

Beyond this considerable intellectual desire, another aspect of this book is to look ahead into an uncertain security environment. Much of this uncertainty relates to the level of threat posed by terrorism. Some may argue that the threat of terrorism is overstated. This argument is, at least partly, based on the lack of direct action on American soil since the tragic events of 9/11. In this thinking, the threat of terrorism is a guise, often based on a political agenda. On the other hand, others view terrorism as a real and significant threat. One such person, James M. Poland, argues that "terrorism is becoming the defining issue of the twenty-first century."[1] I happen to agree with this thinking. However, these divergent viewpoints beg obvious questions: who is right, and what implications does terrorism pose?

As to the former question, time will only tell who is right. Is terrorism overrated? Was 9/11 a "lucky and isolated act," as is often implied in the political discourse. Conversely, are we being lulled to sleep again, such as what we fell into after the initial World Trade Center bombing and after the Oklahoma City bombing? Is terrorism really a pervasive threat, or were these attacks just isolated and unrelated events? Do ideologies and mind-sets sufficient to support a sustained terrorist movement actually exist? Are widely accepted ideologies even necessary to make terrorism a real threat?

These are provocative and debatable questions. To me, however, there is no genuine question as to whether terrorism is a real threat. I answer this question in the affirmative. Indeed, I strongly assert, as did Poland, that terrorism is the defining issue of the twenty-first century. Unfortunately in this country, terrorism appears to be more of a political issue than a legitimate reality. Stated another way, terrorism has become the "defining political issue" in American society. Liberals tend to view the issue much differently than conservatives. Gone are the days following 9/11 where the country was united around a common cause—and a common foe. My concern is that the common cause now appears to be the rhetoric of your particular political party. My fear is that the common foe is the other political party.

Those who study terrorism will recognize that divisiveness is, in fact, a clearly defined goal of terrorism. Indeed, terrorism cannot succeed without causing divisions, either between respective political camps or between "the people" and their government. Either such division is dangerous. I see many trends that portend these divisions as real and growing. I hope and pray that I am wrong. If I am not wrong, then this country is going to face difficult times ahead.

Let me articulate a few trends that are likely to appear on the horizon. Since the rationale underlying these factors are complex—and somewhat controversial—an exhaustive explanation of the "why" behind each factor seems beyond the scope of this book. In addition, being sensitive to the tenets of this book, a detailed "justification" related to each factor may be unnessary. Insead, I present these factors as did Kaplan, who also sees many secutity and crime challenges in the years ahead. In this way, these factors are presented to describe the need for the security laws and methods contained in this book. This being said, I believe:

- The threat of terrorism is not limited to A1 Qaeda, or even to Islamic fundamentalism. Indeed, as this book is being drafted the most active terrorist groups in the U.S. are single interest groups concerned with environmental "protection" (Earth Liberation Front-E.L.F.) and animal "rights" (Animal Liberation Front-A.L.F.). Other terrorist action will stem from racial, ethnic, and religious extremists. This threat, I believe, will manifest itself in widespread direct action.
- There will be a general increase—probably significant—in extremism from both the left and right wings of the American political system. These extremists will act out in response to "direct action" (violent acts) of the other. In addition, in response to such extremism, vigilante groups will likely grow in response to the generalized violence from both political extremes.
- Criminal gangs will grow increasingly violent, using more lethal weapons, with some even "graduating" to terrorist groups. The transition of the Blank Panthers to the El Rukns in Chicago is a fore runner of this development. The Hispanic gang "MS-13" is a classic contemporary example of this assertion.
- The rule of law will be increasingly questioned, even disregarded. The "legal system" will be much more widely viewed as corrupt, irrelevant, or subservient to the higher law or the higher purpose of ideological, religious, political and racial extremists. Significantly, this mindset is critical for the development of terrorist movements, as the violence contained in a terrorist campaign must be rationalized as being superior to the existing legal system.

If these occur, the challenges needed to confront and contain the violence will present a massive potential market for security firms. Just as the new asymmetric form of warfare is changing the way the military confronts and combats terrorism, so too police agencies must reinvent the way of policing. This transformation will leave a void, or at least, a gap, in how public safety services are delivered to communities. Security firms are uniquely prepared to bridge this gap. I believe that security firms will deliver needed order maintenance and related services to communities all over this country. In this sense, F. Thomas Braglia, the former president of the Illinois Association of Chiefs of Police, noted that in the current climate what was once considered a "professional relationship" between the public and private sectors has now because a "professional necessity."[2] I believe this professional necessity presents the largest increase in the potential market of security firms since the 1850s, when security personnel "policed" the American "Wild West." This opportunity, however, is a double-edged sword, replete with pitfalls for the unwary.

As this book makes clear, security exposures and security liability have played a major role in the development of the security industry. The typical security provision has focused on client properties and interests. Of course, this usually entails protecting a particular private environment. If terrorism becomes more common, I believe that the private security industry will continue to expand, in both size and scope, as more security personnel are used to protect critical infrastructures and public places.

Making a fluid and thoughtful transition from private "protected facilities" to serving communities in the public realm will bring the activities and operations of security personnel into plain view. Just as public police officers sometimes fail in the public eye, so will private police officers overreact and/or act in an inappropriate manner. This is inevitable. The cases presented in this book illustrate this does and will occur. What is not inevitable or certain is how the security industry or its component firms will respond in the countless discretionary decisions that will occur in this expanding marketplace. If security providers act with professionalism, any deficiency can be overcome. Conversely, if security providers go into this new marketplace without developing the standards and principles to support this desire for professionalism, then the inevitable deficiencies will appear glaring or even reckless.

Going beyond the market opportunities, the desire for professionalism within private policing must center on an even more basic purpose: the safety of the individuals and communities we serve, and the stability of our way of life. It is important to remember that the threat of terrorism is designed not only to kill people and damage property, but also to destroy the very fabric of society. Those in the security industry, especially those protecting public environments, trophy buildings, and critical infrastructure, will be on the front lines of this asymmetric conflict. Advancing standards and principles of professionalism is our best defense. Hopefully this book will act as a guide toward professionalism.

One critical outcome of professionalism is the desire to prevent crime, or at least, address the impact of crime. Strategies designed to address the impact of crime can and must be implemented. Certain policy initiatives, both from policing and from other areas of government, may negate any increases in crime—or deal with the effects of terrorism. However, our ability to successfully combat terrorism is still uncertain. I believe that the government cannot implement the necessary remedies to deal with crime *and* terrorism—including its attendant fears, without significant help from the private sector. For this reason, the role of private security and security methods is likely to increase along with rising fear. This will be in response to the threat of crime and terrorism, particularly if the "reality" of this threat continues to rise. In any event, the movement toward privatized public safety services has been forwarded—albeit slowly and silently—across this country. No less than the public safety, and even viability, of this country are at stake.

While some may still view the threat of terrorism as an unsettled question, I believe it is reasonable to conclude that terrorism will be a fact of life for years to come. If this is true, then the police agencies that deal with the carnage of terrorist attacks will themselves become prime targets of the violence. Studies of terrorism inevitably point to this conclusion.[3] Indeed, we have seen this assertion borne out in the horrendous violence inflicted on Iraqi police and civil defense forces.

The potential impact of terrorism on the operations of police departments could be enormous and will likely include many police fatalities. The hard realities of security forces, who are both first-line responders and potential targets, are bound to give rise to an environment that is extraordinarily complex in operational, psychological, and human terms.

A second likely ramification of terrorism is that it will foster the demise of community policing. This policing model has dominated policing for the past decade or two. While this statement may be subject to criticism from academic and political circles, the fact is that the federal funding used to support community policing programs are now largely exhausted. Without additional monies to support this policing model, it will slowly be de-emphasized into extinction. Significantly, the federal monies currently available are now earmarked for anti-terrorism and homeland security measures. The old adage seems appropriate: *follow the money*. If the money for community policing is gone, and the money is now centered on terrorism, then police agencies will re-direct their mission to account for the funding sources. Simply put, police agencies in the future will focus on the first responder mission, with community policing as we now know it, coming to an end. However, because of their responsiveness to the client (i.e., citizen), and the nature of the service provision, private police may prove to be an excellent provider of community policing services.

With the future focus of police on terrorism and violent crime—including street gangs that are likely to "graduate" to terrorism,[4] the need for alternative service providers becomes paramount. Alternative service providers will be the para-professionals of police departments. These include private police, civilian employees of police agencies, and auxiliary (volunteer) officers. While it is likely that all three types of alternative service providers will co-exist in some form, the most likely and beneficial option is private police. Due to the economic and operational aspects of private police, this model is likely to predominate.

In short, we are on the cusp of a new policing model, one that will heavily rely on services from the private security industry. These services range from alarm response, crime scene and hospital security, mall security, concert and event security, traffic and parking control and enforcement, and "street corner" security and patrols. These service-oriented functions will also be supplemented by any number of technological initiatives, such as cameras in public environments used for crime deterrence, identification, and enforcement. Indeed, look for a dramatic increase in the number and functionality of cameras used by police. In addition, various access control devices, software programs, and identification technologies will be widely used by police agencies—as have become common in the security industry for decades. Overall, the functions and the hardware used by police agencies and private security firms will become more and more interrelated. In the end, these innovations will occur because of two core factors: *fear* and *money*. Just as money will drive the police away from community policing and toward a new model of policing—that I term public safety policing, so will fear motivate—or create—changes in the way public safety services are delivered. The difficulties inherent in this circumstance are echoed by Judith Lewis, former captain with the L.A. County Sheriff's Department, who made this pointed statement:[5]

> The expectations of law enforcement as first responders for homeland security have put an almost unachievable burden on local law enforcement. Local law enforcement is not designed organizationally to support the cooperation needed, and its officers don't have the training and technology to do the job.... Currently, traditional law enforcement is being left behind.

Achieving public safety will require a delicate balance between individual rights and security provisions.[6] This will not be easy. As can be inferred from the cases in this book, providing security within "protected facilities," is a difficult balance to achieve. Every firm must weigh the need to efficiently do business against the need to secure the business, its employees, customers, and visitors. Usually this breaks down to conveniences and sales on one hand versus safety and security on the other.

In the event that security personnel extend the scope of their duties into public areas, the fluidity of the street and the unpredictable nature of the committed terrorist, creates a very delicate balance, indeed. Of course, criminals and terrorists do not accept laws and rules, whereas government—and private security personnel—must adhere to the rule of law.[7] In this sense, we must be both sensitive to our clients, and at the same time, committed to our mission. Given the difficulties inherent in this balance, one can be assured that mistakes will be made. Notwithstanding this reality, the mission must go on. We cannot fail. Our "clients" and our country are counting on us.

While this book is published at a time of relative peace and security, I contend this circumstance will not be sustainable. There is ample evidence of this assertion. It is beyond the scope of this book, however, to make this case. Instead, this book focuses on the intersection of the law and security methods. These predictions, however, are critical. If terrorism and group and gang violence become widespread, the delicate balance between security provisions and legal standards will become ever so more difficult to achieve. Whether or not this becomes a reality, this book may prove to be a useful guide—even in a relatively "calm" environment.

Simply stated, our political and legal systems will need to address the liability exposure related to terrorism. Laws such as the Terrorism Risk Insurance Act and the SAFETY Act will be of some help. However, as evidenced by the *World Trade Center Litigation*, the common-law notion of foreseeability will serve to generate a great deal of liability stemming from terrorism. Of course, this liability does not even assess the profound human, organizational, and operational impact of terrorism. To those businesses that struggle with these implications, this statement by David H. Nozensky, corporate security for the FPL Group, Inc., may be of some insight:[8] It is still true that you can "secure yourself out of business," but ... the boardroom now understands that security represents the ultimate bottom line—survival.

Finally, I will end this book with an old Chinese adage that goes something like this: *may you live in interesting times*. This saying was not considered a blessing but rather was meant as a warning, or a vengeful admonition. I believe we live in interesting times—replete with many challenges. The challenges facing this country are many. Security is, or will be, one of the most significant challenges that lie ahead. More pointedly, the real challenge is larger than security. The ultimate challenge will be how, or if, we are able to balance security needs with individual rights. For those who intellectually or operationally struggle with this balance, my prayers and respect are with you.

NOTES

1. Poland, James M. (2005). *Understanding Terrorism: Groups, Strategies, and Responses.* Upper Saddle River, NJ: Pearson/Prentice Hall.
2. Braglia, Thomas (2004). Public-Private Law Enforcement: A Win-Win Partnership. *Command*, Winter.
3. See examples of the number of police personnel killed in terrorist attacks in Dobson, Christopher and Ronald Payne (1982). *The Terrorists: Their Weapons, Leaders, and Tactics.* New York: Facts on File, Inc.
4. For an excellent piece on the potential for terrorism from streets gangs, see Aidi, Hisham (2005) Jihad's in the Hood: Race, Urban Islam, and the War on Terror, *Violence, and Terrorism*, 05/06 edited by Thomas J. Badey, Dubuque, IA: McGraw-Hill/Dushkin.
5. Quote cited in Stephens, Gene (2005). Policing the Future: Law Enforcement's New Challenges. *The Futurist.* Vol. 39, March/April at 2.
6. This assertion has been examined by a number of authors, including Pastor, James F. (2003). *The Privatization of Police in America: An Analysis and Case Study.* Jefferson, NC: McFarland and Company, Inc.; and Simon, Steven (2004). The New Terrorism: Securing the Nation Against a Messianic Foe, *The New Era of Terrorism: Selected Readings.* Gus Martin (ed.), Thousand Oaks, CA: Sage Publications.
7. Laqueur, Walter (2004). The Terrorism to Come. *Policy Review*, No. 126, taken from www.policyreview.org/aug04/laqueur_print.html on November 1, 2004.
8. Horowitz, Sherry L. (2003). The New Centurions: Terrorism and Other Global Forces are Reshaping Corporate Security, Creating Challenges and Opportunities for Those Who Oversee It. *Security Management*, January.

Index

T